A BIRDW
GUIDE TO INDIA

Krys Kazmierczak and Raj Singh

Illustrations by John C. Anderton and Carl d'Silva

Maps by Krys Kazmierczak

BIRD WATCHERS' GUIDES

Prion Ltd.
Sandy

ACKNOWLEDGEMENTS

S. Asad Akhtar, Vijay Awasre, Maan Barua, Philip Bawden, Seb Buckton, S. Chandrasekaran, Srikumar Chattopadhyay, Tony Forster, Venkat Iyengar, Alan Lewis, Iwein Mauro, Dhananjai Mohan, A. K. Nagar and Shri V. D. Sharma kindly provided much useful information. Per Alström, Ramana & Vidya Athreya, Dr. S. Balachandran, Dr. Anwaruddin Choudhury, Roy Frost, Smaran Ghosal, Bikram Grewal, Peter Harris, Tim Inskipp, Ragupathy Kannan, Nigel Lindsey, Tim Loseby, Rishad Naoroji, Otto Pfister, Aasheesh Pittie, Nigel Redman, Andrew Robertson, Craig Robson, Steve Rooke, Malcolm Roxby, N. C. Sarmah, Ajai Saxena, Pratap Singh, Ravi Singh, Harkirat Singh Sangha, R. G. Soni, Dr. S. Subramanya, Per Undeland and Dr. Harin Vadodaria were unstinting in checking through various drafts and supplying additional material. In this regard Des Allen, Philip Benstead, Raf Drijvers, Jon Hornbuckle and Vibhu Prakash deserve especial thanks. Brian Gee was most helpful and generously allowed us to draw freely from his South India trip report.

Drs. Paul Bates and Ishwar Prakash very kindly assisted with improving the mammals checklist. David Fisher and Chris Harbard provided much advice and encouragement during the long incubation of the project. Rob Hume and David Fisher admirably accomplished the unenviable task of editing the book. Without Paul Holt's input (and red pen) the book would have been much the poorer. Healeys Printers must be congratulated for taking on the task of laying out and printing this book, armed only with some floppy disks and a great deal of determination – thanks especially to Mike Gaydon. Over the years we have enjoyed birding with many people, especially Des Allen, John Anderton, Paul Holt and Dare Šere. We thank them all for the pleasure of their company and everything we have learnt from them.

Samir Acharya, Aitanna, Ashley Banwell, P. L. Barua, Col. R. Tommy Chacko, Krishna Bahadur Chanda, Chhanuka, A. N. Das, Fay Enright, E. Flanders, Gudrun Findeisen, Gayatri Gogoi, Vinod Goswami, Enamul Hoque, Farouk Husain, Akbar Hussain, Carol Inskipp, Björn Johansson, Bholu Abrar Khan, Daisy and Priya Lynrah, Shabir Malik, R. Mallapa, A.V. Manoj, Prachi Mehta, Krister Mild, Peter Morris, Shantanu Mukherjee, Nair, Pardhan, Ber van Perlo, H. P. Phukan, Mridu Praban Phukon, J. N. Prasad, Sundar Raj, R. Rao, S. B. Ravindra, Shanta, Toby Sinclair, Diane Singh, Hashmat Singh, P. S. Sivaprasad, Sudarsanam Sridhar, Hashim Tyabji, Col. John Wakefield and June Warjri all helped in a variety of ways. Many others have contributed both directly and indirectly. We are most grateful to them all even though it is not possible to single every one out by name.

The authors would especially like to thank their families without whose patience and support this book would not have been possible.

CONTENTS

Map of India

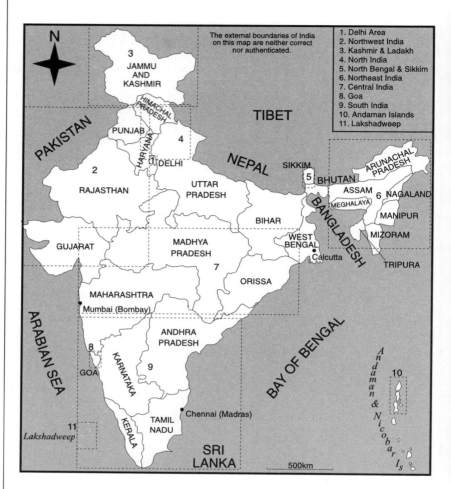

INTRODUCTION

India is a country with an unrivalled range of cultures, landscapes and birds to match. From the Himalaya with the highest mountains in the world and the trans-Himalayan regions of the Tibetan Plateau in the north, to the jungles and beaches of the south; from the great Thar Desert in the west to the wettest places on earth in the northeast – India is truly a land of contrasts which never fails to surprise and fascinate the visitor.

The country's avifauna is largely Oriental with a good admixture of Palearctic elements. With approximately 1220 species recorded, India hosts some 12$\frac{1}{2}$% of the world's birds and nearly half of those of the Oriental Region. The birdwatcher will find plenty to search for and study and will discover that more than just one or two trips are needed to do the indigenous birdlife justice.

In this book we attempt to describe a cross-section of sites covering all of the country's regions and main habitats. We include most of the better-known birding sites and some less well known ones. The choice is to some extent a personal one but is also dictated by factors such as access, availability of accommodation, and travel restrictions. All of the many excellent birdwatching areas could never be covered in a single work and we apologise to anyone whose favourite site is omitted. In a country whose protected areas are fast approaching 600 the potential for the keen naturalist is enormous. On the other hand one does not need to go far out of one's way to find birds. Even in an unfamiliar town one can usually find somewhere to do a few hours' birding by heading for the local park, tank (reservoir), river, or the scrubby wastelands found on the outskirts of most urban areas.

Approximately 150 of the species found in India are endemic to the Indian Subcontinent, or nearly so. Many are relatively poorly known and some have only been seen by a handful of ornithologists, so any observations on distribution, habitat or behaviour could be valuable. Some birds are restricted to border regions and adjoining areas of neighbouring countries that are inaccessible for one reason or another. There is much that can be added to our knowledge of the birds of the Indian Subcontinent by the visiting birder. For more details on individual species see the Selective Bird List in the appendix.

The book is primarily written with the visiting Western birder in mind, but we hope it may prove to be of use to the Indian birdwatcher venturing away from his usual haunts.

Inevitably in a book of this kind some information becomes out-of-date quickly. National Park rules change, new hotels spring up, others close, new roads are built while old ones fall into disuse, bird populations wax and wane. While the authors have made every effort to make this work accurate and up-to-date we would be grateful for any feedback, information, trip reports, updates and corrections with a view to a possible future second edition. Please send any relevant reports or information to the authors at 35 Elmthorpe Road, Wolvercote, Oxford, OX2 8PA, UK.

A trip to India is always an adventure. The most important things to bring with you are an open mind, a sense of humour and a flexible attitude. Armed with those your birding and cultural experiences will always be successful and enjoyable.

PRE-TOUR INFORMATION

Visas   Visa requirements and validity change quite often. Before applying it is best to check with the Indian Consulate in your country about the latest regulations. At the time of writing all foreign nationals, except those of Nepal and Bhutan, required a visa for entry into India. Tourist visas are issued for a period of six months and are valid from **the date of issue**. It is always best to specify that you require a multiple-entry visa, in case you decide to visit a neighbouring country such as Bhutan, Nepal or Sri Lanka and then return to India. There is normally no extra charge for this.

If you apply in person at the Indian consulate in your country of residence, your visa will normally be issued the same day. If you do go in person, check beforehand to make sure that the consulate is not closed on account of a national holiday on the day you intend to go. It may take considerably longer (e.g. up to three months) if you apply by post. It is advisable to obtain your visa in your normal country of residence, otherwise it involves the extra time and cost to you of the local Indian consulate contacting the Indian consulate in your country of residence for 'clearance'. The cost of a visa varies and often depends on your nationality and the current state of relations between India and your country.

Addresses of some of the Indian embassies and consulates are:
Australia: 3-5 Moonah Place, Yarralumla, ACT 2600. ☎06-273-3999
Canada: 10 Springfield Road, Ottawa, K1M 1C9. ☎613-744-3751
Denmark: Vangehusvej 15, 2100 Copenhagen. ☎1-3118-2888
Germany: a) Adenauerallee 262-264, 53113 Bonn, ☎ 0228-5405132
          b) Mittelweg 49, 60318 Frankfurt am Main. ☎069-15300546.
Nepal: Lainchaur, GPO Box 292, Kathmandu. ☎071-41-1940
Netherlands: Buitenrustweg 2, 252 KD Den Haag. ☎070-346-9771
New Zealand: 180 Molesworth Street, Princess Towers, Wellington.
    ☎04-473-6390
Pakistan: a) G-5 Diplomatic Enclave, Islamabad. ☎051-81-4371
          b) India House, 3 Fatima Jinnah Road, Karachi. ☎021-52-2275
Sri Lanka: 36-38 Galle Road, Colombo 3. ☎01-421-605
Sweden: Adolf Fredriks Kyrkog. 12, Box 1340, 111 83 Stockholm.
    ☎08-4113213
Switzerland: Effingerstrasse 45, 3008 Bern. ☎031-3823111
UK: a) India House, Aldwych, London, WC2B 4NA. ☎0171-836-8484
    b) 20 Augusta Street, Hockley, Birmingham, B18 6JL.
       ☎0121-212-2782
USA: 2107 Massachusetts Ave NW, Washington DC 20008. ☎202-939-7000

Visa extensions   If your stay is likely to take you beyond 180 days from the date of issue of your visa, then you should apply in good time for a visa extension at the Office of the Superintendent of Police in one of the state capitals, or at one of the main Foreigners' Registration Offices:
Calcutta: 237 Acharya J.C.Bose Road ☎033-2473301
Chennai (Madras): Shashtri Bhavan Annexe, 26 Haddows Road
    ☎044-8278210
Darjeeling: Laden La Road ☎0354-2261
Mumbai (Bombay): Special Branch II, Annexe 2, Office of the
    Commissioner of Police (Greater Mumbai), Dadabhoy Naoroji Road
    ☎022-2620446
New Delhi: 1st Floor, Hans Bhavan, Tilak Bridge. ☎011-3319489
Visas can usually be extended for a single month, but in recent practice extensions have not always been given. It may be necessary to leave the country and apply for a new visa if you wish to return to India.

Restricted Areas and Permits

There are parts of India, particularly in sensitive border areas, where foreign nationals are not allowed without a Restricted Area Permit (RAP). The ease with which this can be obtained depends on which places you want to visit. Some RAPs are given on the spot, while others take several months to issue, if they are granted at all. There are special exemptions for groups for certain areas where individual travel is difficult. In the following we have listed current regulations, but these are subject to change. Always check with the Indian consulate on the latest situation before you travel.

Andaman & Nicobar Islands:

Most of the islands are off limits to foreigners, but the administration is gradually increasing the number of places that may be visited and there are plenty of opportunities for exploring the birdlife of the Andamans. The Nicobars are still effectively out of reach to all but Indian nationals. Permits for a period of up to 30 days are issued on arrival at Port Blair airport. More recently the authorities have also begun issuing permits to those arriving at Port Blair by sea, but it may be more prudent to obtain a permit for the Andamans at the same time as applying for your visa from an Indian Mission abroad (apply at least six to 12 weeks in advance). Alternatively, in India permits can be granted by the Foreigners' Regional Registration Offices at Delhi, Mumbai (Bombay) or Calcutta; Chief Immigration Officer Chennai (Madras); Immigration Officers at the Immigration Checkpoints at the International Airports in Delhi, Mumbai (Bombay), Calcutta or Chennai (Madras) (this may take a few hours or up to three or four working days). The permit allows you overnight stays on the following islands: South Andaman, Middle Andaman, Little Andaman, Bharatang, North Passage, Havelock, Long and Neil. You are not allowed to visit tribal reserves and on North Andaman the only place foreigners are permitted to stay is Diglipur. You may also make day visits to Cinque, Ross, Narcondam, Viper, Interview, Brother and Sister, as well as all the islands of the Mahatma Gandhi Marine National Park with the exception of Boat, Hobday, Malay, Pluto, Tarmugli and Twin. Regulations may change, so check on arrival.

Lakshadweep (Laccadive Islands):

At present foreigners, unless on a package cruise with permission included, are only allowed to visit the islands of Bangaram and Suheli. Permits are issued by:

New Delhi: Liaison Officer, Lakshadweep, 202 Kasturba Gandhi Marg. ☎38-6807

Administrator, Union Territory of Lakshadweep, Indira Gandhi Road, Willingdon Island, Kochi (Cochin) 682 003, Kerala. ☎69-131

The Northeast:

It is difficult to get RAPs for much of northeastern India and in practice the only way to visit such areas is with an organised tour. To some degree the area is opening up and it is no longer necessary to obtain permits for Darjeeling, the northern part of West Bengal, Assam, Meghalaya and Tripura. You should, however, check with the Indian Consulate on the current situation when planning your trip, as well as locally to determine any areas that are best avoided.

A RAP is required before you can visit Arunachal Pradesh (e.g.

Namdapha National Park). This is fairly readily granted to groups of four or more tourists on a trip organised by a recognised Indian travel agent or tour operator. The state government has set a fixed rate of US $150 per person per day all-inclusive. This naturally makes a visit too costly for the majority of birders. For those willing to make their own arrangements the government demands a fee of $55 per person per day with nothing included. A minimum group of four is still stipulated and you must specify your exact itinerary. Applications need to be made to the Ministry of Home Affairs, Foreigners' Wing, Lok Nayak Bhavan, Khan Market, New Delhi 110 003 or through the Indian Mission in your native country at least six to eight weeks beforehand. In practice it can take several months for permission to come through, if at all, and the only certain way is to book through a travel agent unless you are very lucky or have the right connections.

Indian nationals require an Inner Line Permit and there is no daily fee to be paid. Applications should be sent to the Secretary (Political), Government of Arunachal Pradesh, Itanagar 791 111, Arunachal Pradesh at least two months in advance. The application should include details of the proposed visit and information about the applicant such as Date of Birth, Age, Local Address and Permanent Address. Alternatively, one can apply to the Resident Commissioner, Government of Arunachal Pradesh, Arunachal Bhavan, Chanakyapuri, Kautilya Marg, New Delhi 110 021, ☎ 011-3013915 or 3012153, who is also authorised to issue an Inner Line Permit after consultation with the Secretary Political in Itanagar.

Similar arrangements apply for five-day visits to Imphal and Logtak Lake in Manipur. For other areas in Manipur, Mizoram and Nagaland application must be made many months or years in advance to the Home Ministry in Delhi or via Indian Consulates abroad and there usually has to be a good reason for the visit.

Sikkim:

Tourism to Sikkim has been encouraged in recent years and a 15-day permit to visit southern Sikkim is relatively easy to obtain. You must list the places you are going to visit on the application form. It is better to list more rather than fewer. You can always leave a place out during your trip, but you may encounter problems if you decide to go somewhere not specifically mentioned on your permit. Before applying check which places are currently open to foreign visitors. At the time of writing these were Gangtok (the capital), Rumtek, Phodang, Pemayangtse, Tashiding, Yuksam, Khecheopalri Lake and Naya Bazar and the main routes joining them.
A separate permit is required to trek in the Dzongri/Kanchenjunga region north of Yuksam. This is only given to groups of between four and twenty persons on organised treks, which must be booked through a foreign specialist tour operator or one of the local trekking agents in Gangtok. Time spent on a trek counts as part of the 15 days.

Permits can be obtained within a day or so on production of your passport, a visa photo and photocopies of the main page of your passport and the one with the Indian visa stamped on it at any of the Foreigners' Registration Offices (see above); Immigration Offices at Delhi, Mumbai (Bombay), Calcutta and Chennai (Madras) airports; Deputy Secretary, Home Department, Govt. of West Bengal, Calcutta; Assistant Resident Commissioner, Govt. of Sikkim, 4C Poonam Bldg, 5/2 Russell Street, Calcutta (☎033-297516); Resident Commissioner, Govt of Sikkim, New Sikkim House, 14 Panchsheel Marg, Chanakyapuri, New Delhi (☎011-3015346); Sikkim Tourist Office, SNT Bus Compound, Hill Cart

Road, Siliguri, West Bengal (☎0353-432646). It is better to obtain a permit in India rather than applying for one with your visa as consulates will generally only give seven-day permits for Gangtok, Rumtek and Phodang. If you want to keep your options open, it is fairly easy to obtain a Sikkim permit in Darjeeling (see section in Site Information). There is also a Foreigners' Registration Office on the platform of New Jalpaiguri station (near Siliguri/Bagdogra) if you are travelling by train to Sikkim and Darjeeling.

Exceptionally, 15-day permit extensions can be obtained from the Home Office, Govt of Sikkim, Tashiding Secretariat in the same building as the tourist office in Gangtok. Here foreign tourists in groups of four or more can also obtain a day permit to visit Changu (Tsomgo) Lake near the Tibetan border and a five-day (four-night) permit for Yumthang in north Sikkim.

General information can be obtained from Govt. of India Tourist Offices:
Australia: Level 1, 17 Castlereagh Street, Sydney, NSW 2000.
  ☎02-232-1600
Germany: Kaiserstrasse 77, 60329 Frankfurt am Main. ☎069-235423
Netherlands: Rokin 9-15, 1012 KK Amsterdam. ☎020-208891
Sweden: Sveavägen 9-11, 11157 Stockholm. ☎08-215081
UK: 7 Cork Street, London, W1X 2AB. ☎0171-734-6613
USA: 30 Rockefeller Plaza, 15 North Mezzanine, New York, NY 10112.
  ☎212-586-4901

Travel insurance

Comprehensive travel insurance is strongly recommended and should include full health cover and repatriation in case of a serious medical emergency.

Time

All of India is within one time zone (Indian Standard Time – IST) $5\frac{1}{2}$ hours ahead of Greenwich Mean Time. The Indian concept of time differs from that of Westerners and you should not always expect a high degree of punctuality. The pace of life is generally much slower. Road and traffic conditions are such that average travelling speeds are generally below 30km/h, even less in the mountains. The traveller who can relax and adjust to this rhythm will benefit more from the experience.

Currency and Exchange

The unit of currency is the Indian Rupee, which is subdivided into 100 Paise. In summer 1998 one pound sterling was approximately equivalent to Rs71 and one US dollar equivalent to Rs43.

Money can be exchanged on arrival at the airport, in banks and at better hotels. The latter are more convenient but give a slightly lower rate. Outside major cities it is best to exchange money at the State Bank of India or another nationalised bank. Currency exchange at banks can be very time consuming, especially in the smaller cities, so you may wish to change enough each time to avoid repeating the painful process too often.

Pounds sterling and US dollars are widely recognised in India, but you may have trouble exchanging other currencies outside the bigger cities. For safety take the larger part of your money in the form of travellers' cheques as these are insured in case of loss or theft. It is advisable to bring only the better-known brands such as Thomas Cook or American Express as those of lesser-known companies may not be accepted in some banks. Take some cash in case there is a problem exchanging your brand. Credit cards are becoming more widely known and can often be used to pay bills at the more expensive hotels and sometimes for flight tickets, but this cannot be relied upon. It can be useful to have a small supply of US dollars in various denominations to cover unforeseen eventualities.

You are not allowed to take Indian Rupees in and out of the country. There is no restriction on the amount of foreign currency you are allowed to bring into India, but amounts exceeding US$10,000 in travellers' cheques and $2,500 in cash per person must be declared on arrival to facilitate re-export.

When changing money, ask for and keep your official Foreign Exchange Certificate. This will allow you to re-exchange unspent Rupees on your departure from India and is generally required by airlines, some hotels and by officialdom when extending a visa or suchlike. Rupees may be accepted if backed up by an FEC. Since the liberalisation of the Indian economy the black market in foreign currency has dwindled and the small amount to be gained by using this illegal exchange method does not outweigh the considerable risks involved. Do not accept damaged banknotes in your change, as these are regarded as invalid, and even the banks sometimes refuse to change them. Notes worn to a hole in the centre are unacceptable. The banks themselves staple notes together in bundles and the resulting holes on the side of the notes are no problem.

Customs

The traveller may bring in duty free one bottle (0.95 litres) of spirits and 200 cigarettes. Personal effects such as binoculars, telescope, camera with a reasonable amount of film, personal stereo and video camera are allowed on condition that they are re-exported. If carrying an unusually large amount of equipment, it may be wise to fill in a Tourist Baggage Re-export Form on arrival to avoid complications on departure from India. Customs often check all luggage.

Documents

Always carry your passport with you. This is normally required when changing money or checking into a hotel. A valid certificate of inoculation against yellow fever is necessary if coming from an infected area. No other health certificates are required. An international driving licence is required if you intend hiring a motorbike and can be useful additional identification if, for example, a deposit is required for hiring a bicycle.

Vaccinations

As birdwatching is likely to take you off the beaten track it is highly advisable to take all possible precautions against diseases that you might contact while travelling in India. Currently recommended vaccinations are against Tetanus, Typhoid, Polio and Hepatitis A. Vaccination against Rabies may also be worth considering. Smallpox has been eradicated and immunisation is not necessary. Vaccination against Cholera is no longer required, recommended or even available in most countries. Malaria is a serious problem in some regions and you should take a suitable course of prophylactics. If you are going to be in India for several months, enquire about the current situation regarding Meningitis and Japanese Encephalitis B that may be prevalent in some rural areas especially during the monsoon. Well before your intended date of departure you should check with your doctor to decide on a suitable course of vaccinations, or preferably consult one of the specialised Travel Clinics such as:

Berkeley Travel Clinic, 32 Berkeley Street, London, W1X 5FA.
☎0171-629-6233

Trailfinders' Immunisation Centre, 194 Kensington High Street, London, W8 7RG ☎0171-938-3999

See also the section on Health below.

Photography

India offers many opportunities for the photographer. Film is often available locally but is not particularly good value and may be past its shelf life. It is better to bring enough rolls and spare batteries to cover your needs for the trip. Although light conditions for bird photography are good in some open habitats, faster film speeds up to ISO 800 or 1600 would be useful in many situations. Officials may insist that airport x-ray machines are safe for films, but have your films hand searched in preference. Developing quality is often good but not always.

Do not take photographs at airports, military installations, bridges, railway stations and other places of a sensitive nature. Beware also of using binoculars and cameras in such areas. Many sanctuaries and cultural sites charge a modest camera fee in addition to the entrance charge. Video camera fees can be extremely high.

Airport Departure Tax

The Indian government levies an airport tax on departing international flights. Most airlines now add this to the ticket price, but in some cases you may have to pay on departure. Check with the airline to make sure you have enough rupees left. It is illegal to take Indian Rupees out of the country, but any excess can be re-exchanged into hard currency on production of a Foreign Exchange Certificate at the airport banks after checking in but before going through passport control.

TRAVEL INFORMATION

Travelling to India

By air
Most travellers arrive in India by air. The main airports of entry are Delhi and Mumbai (Bombay) although some international flights arrive at Calcutta and Chennai (Madras). Goa has become a destination for package tours and if you want to combine a family holiday with sunshine, beaches and a reasonable quality of hotel with some exotic birding this could be the option for you. Most major airlines have flights to India, but it is worth shopping around, particularly in London where 'bucket shops' give a sizeable discount on regular fares. A direct flight from London to Delhi takes approximately 9 hours without stopovers. Always check up on the number and length of stopovers on any flight or you may find you have long delays between flights (23 hours in Moscow, for example) and the cost of a night in the airport hotel (the only one you are allowed to use as a transit passenger) is more than you saved by buying a cheaper ticket. Some cheaper airlines are not members of IATA and you could find yourself stranded if something goes wrong, so check when booking. It is very important to reconfirm your return flight at least 72 hours in advance, otherwise you may be removed from the passenger list. This can sometimes be done by phone, but check with the airline office on arrival. If flying from Nepal to India, the flight to Patna is far less expensive than that to Delhi.

By land
It is usually possible to cross into India by land from Bangladesh, Bhutan, Nepal and Pakistan, although subject to the vagaries of the current political situation. Make enquiries locally before you set off as to whether your chosen route is open. **Visas for India are not available at the border checkposts.**

From Bangladesh to India there are normally only two routes open to foreigners. The one from Dhaka to Calcutta involves a nine-hour bus ride to Benapole followed by a 10-minute rickshaw ride to the border. From the Indian side of the border it is about 10km by rickshaw to the town of Bangaon from where a bus to Calcutta takes 2 hours. The crossing from Bangladesh on the direct route to Darjeeling involves a 7km walk along a disused railway line and you may need an exit permit.

From Bhutan Westerners can cross into India at Phuntsholing and Darrang but it is normally a condition of the Bhutanese visa that you fly into Bhutan with Druk Air.

From Nepal there are several possibilities including direct buses from Kathmandu to Delhi if you can stand 36 hours of torture. It may be better to make your own way to Birganj and cross into India there. Coming from Pokhara or Chitwan in Nepal you can cross into India at Bhairawa. If heading for the Darjeeling area, then you can conveniently bird your way eastwards across Nepal and cross into India at Kakarbhitta.

From Pakistan there are, in theory, daily trains between Lahore and Amritsar (61km), but they can take up to 5 hours to clear customs. It is quicker to take a taxi or minibus from the railway station to the border crossing at Wagah, walk across the border (open 09.00 to 15.00) and then one of the two daily buses or a taxi to Amritsar.

Travelling within India

By car
For those who can afford it travel by hire car is convenient as you can stop when and where you like. A hire car comes complete with driver. Self-drive hire cars are not available except in Goa. It would be more expensive to insure a foreigner to drive than to pay for a driver. Make sure the driver

speaks English and specify if you only want one driver without an assistant. Having a driver has advantages. He can keep an eye on the car and your belongings while you go off birding. He knows the roads and driving conditions and can ask the way or act as interpreter. When agreeing terms, make sure it is clear who is paying for fuel and the driver's overnight and meal allowances. It is best to agree on an amount for this rather than pay for the driver's meals as you go along – expensive tastes can develop when someone else is paying. The car is usually an old-fashioned but tough Ambassador (modelled on the old British Morris Oxford) or a Maruti-Suzuki minibus. They can take three passengers with luggage comfortably but become cramped with more than that. Make sure you try out the vehicle you intend to hire before agreeing terms. The vehicle must have a permit covering all of the states that you wish to visit, or else this can be a problem at state borderlines.

By bicycle   It is possible to cycle around India. You can take your own bike, with all the spares you might need for the duration of your trip, as there are none available in India; or you can buy a local bike which is cheap and solid but can be repaired on any street corner of most towns. A disadvantage is that they do not have gears. In some places, like Bharatpur, you can hire bikes by the day, but check them over first, as they are often rather the worse for wear.

By motorbike   There are not many places where you can hire a motorbike. Port Blair, on the Andamans, and Goa are exceptions. You need an international driving licence. If you are going to be in India for a longer period, it might be worth thinking about buying a motorbike and selling it again at the end of your stay.

By train   This is comfortable although second class carriages can be dirty and overcrowded. Travelling first class or air-conditioned class by rail requires advance booking of tickets and advance reservations, best done as far in advance as possible, as some routes can be fully booked for days or weeks ahead. If possible, book your train out of a town as soon as you arrive. Many trains give a convenient overnight journey. Booking a berth can save time and the cost of an overnight hotel. With computerised booking the procedure is less painful and time-consuming than it used to be, although queues can be extremely long. At some main stations a separate ticket window for foreign tourists saves a bit of queuing.

If you use trains frequently, an Indrail Pass, which allows unlimited rail travel for 7, 15, 21, 30, 60 or 90 days, can make sense. The pass does not guarantee a seat. For that you need a reservation. If time is limited and you can plan your itinerary before you leave home, it may be worth making train reservations from abroad. Indrail passes can be bought at some railway stations in India or at General Sales Agents abroad. In the UK the General Sales Agent is S.D. Enterprises Ltd., 103 Wembley Park Drive, Middlesex, HA9 8HG ☎0181-903-3411, Fax 0181-903-0392. If you buy an Indrail pass from them, they make advance reservations for no extra charge. They also issue half-day, one-day, two-day and four-day passes that are not available in India. Govt. of India Tourist Offices in other countries should be able to put you in touch with the local General Sales Agent.

By bus   Buses are often more convenient and the only way of reaching some destinations. They are generally more frequent than trains and often quicker although less comfortable. It is usually possible (and advisable) to book longer routes a day or two in advance. For journeys of a few hours it is usually a case of catching the next bus going in your direction. Whenever possible, get on a bus at its starting point as you then have a chance of getting a reasonable seat. Seats at the back should be avoided if you want to remain in possession of all your fillings. The price is usually somewhere between that of first and second class train fares for the same route.

Taxis and rickshaws

In and around towns, especially to get to a site outside or on the edge of town in the early morning, the use of taxis or auto-rickshaws is unavoidable. Finding a local bus to the exact obscure place you want to go to at five o'clock in the morning is usually impossible. For returning to base it is often possible to hop on a bus going to the centre of town.

Taxis are the most expensive but most comfortable option. Always try to get the driver to use the meter. With rises in approved fares taking place more quickly than meters can be calibrated there may be a surcharge on the meter reading, in which case there should be an official fare chart in the taxi, which you can demand to see. If the meter 'does not work', agree a price before you set off. Do not accept the first price demanded, as this may be three times the usual rate. It helps to know how far away your destination is!

Auto-rickshaws are small motor-cycle driven contraptions known as autos, three-wheelers or scooters – cheap and convenient if there are only one or two of you (three at a pinch without luggage). Use the meter or bargain as for a taxi. In some places there are man-powered **cycle-rickshaws**, slower and not always cheaper than an auto-rickshaw but less polluting. **Tempos** are like overgrown auto-rickshaws that run along fixed routes. You can hop on and off wherever you like and fares are not much more than for local buses.

Hitching

Although hitchhiking is not particularly common in India you may find yourself in remote areas without any good option. Waving a passing vehicle down will often work but do not just stick your thumb out.

STAYING IN INDIA

Accommodation

There is an enormous range of accommodation varying from former Maharajah's palaces turned into luxury hotels to simple lodges where the room contains only a bed and a sheet. Many protected areas are well off the beaten track and to explore these you may have to rough it on the floor with a sleeping bag and mat. If you intend trekking, these would be needed in any case.

Most places described have at least some reasonable accommodation at the site or nearby. Further details are given in the site descriptions where we try to suggest hotels in three price brackets – upper, middle and budget. Tariffs change so rapidly that we only attempt to give approximate price categories as follows:

A: more than Rs 1500

B: Rs 1000–1500

C: Rs 500–1000

D: Rs 200–500

E: less than Rs 200

State governments tax hotel bills by from 5% to 40%, depending on the state and the hotel category. If more than one price is given for a hotel, this reflects rooms of different standards. For example a hotel may have 'standard doubles' at Rs250, 'deluxe air-conditioned doubles' at Rs550, but also dormitory beds at Rs50, so the classification would read (C/D/E). The price is not always an indication of quality. Hotels in metropolises offer far less value for money than those in the provinces, though some at popular National Parks cash in on the tourist boom by charging inflated rates.

Rooms in the upper and middle bracket hotels normally have a private bathroom, though the toilet may be of the Asian 'hole in the ground' style. In budget lodges you may have to ask for a 'room with attached bath'. Always check that the room is acceptable before you agree to take it. Your own cotton sheet sleeping bag or sheets are recommended if you plan to stay in budget hotels.

Food

Indian food is more popular than any other ethnic cuisine in the UK so British birdwatchers should have no trouble adapting to local eating habits. Indian food largely consists of meat and vegetables cooked in a spicy sauce known as a curry. There are a number of curry sauce styles such as Madras, Vindaloo, Jalfrezi and Dopiaza of varying strengths. If you are not used to hot spicy food, ask for the mildest dishes. The main dish is usually accompanied by a second vegetable dish, a lentil sauce (dhal), pickles, chutney and rice or one of a variety of freshly baked or roasted breads, of which the most popular are chapati, puri and nan.

There is considerable regional variation. In northern India the main meal is eaten fairly late in the evening. In the south the main repast is normally at midday and consists of rice, accompanied by a brown sauce known as sambar and a white coconut chutney sauce, and sometimes also vegetables (sabzi). It may be served on a banana leaf that you wash with water beforehand. In simpler restaurants this may be all that is available at this time of day, but traditionally you can eat as much as you like. At other times there are snacks such as Masala Dosa, Puri and Uttapam accompanied by sambar and chutney.

Throughout the country the better hotels and restaurants serve a wide selection of Indian, Western and Chinese food. In these one can generally assume that food is safe to eat. In less salubrious establishments avoid meat, fish, salad and ice cream which are the main causes of stomach upsets. A vegetarian lifestyle has much to recommend it in a country where most of the population does not eat meat. 'Cook it, peel it or forget it' if you wish to avoid tummy bugs.

Indian people have a sweet tooth and there are many deserts (sweets) often made from caramelised milk. The high concentration of sugar kills bacteria making them relatively safe to eat.

You may be out for much of the day and may want to return to the hotel for late morning breakfast or brunch, in which case check the timings, or arrange for a packed lunch and/or breakfast. Otherwise, fruit and biscuits can be bought in the markets. In winter mandarin-type oranges are widely available and a good source of fluid.

Drink

Always carry drinking water. Do not drink water served at table at any other than the very best establishments. Bottled 'mineral' water is widely available at restaurants, grocery stores and pharmacies: stick to this and bottled soft drinks. Tea and coffee are generally okay as they are boiled. Cold milk may be unpasteurised. A refreshing drink is fresh lime soda (not lime water) plain or with sugar. Make sure that ice is not added, as it is usually not safe. Indian lager beer is generally available in most of the better hotels and restaurants although prohibition is in force in some states. Other alcoholic drinks are best avoided, though you might occasionally sample a local speciality.

In southern India green coconuts (tender coconuts) sold at the roadside give safe, refreshing drinking fluid. If buying bottled drinks from a roadside vendor, check that the cap is not rusty: an indication that the cap has been 'recycled' and the bottle may have been refilled with a drink using unsafe water. 'Freshly' pressed cane-sugar and fruit drinks are not always safe.

Make sure that drinking water has been boiled. The answer to the question 'Has the water been boiled?' is likely to be 'Yes!', even if the person has not understood the question. Filtering does not remove all the bugs. If in doubt, use water purification tablets bought from chemists and camping suppliers in Western countries. Micropur is a general-purpose tablet that is silver-based with no unpleasant taste. Chlorine-based tablets (Puritabs or Steritabs) are more widely available. If you suspect water may be less pure, use iodine-based tablets (e.g. Potable Aqua), the only ones effective against some pathogens such as Giardia and Amoebae, but try not to use these too often. Always follow the manufacturer's instructions.

Language

There are 18 languages officially recognised in India plus hundreds of minor tongues and dialects. Hindi has been encouraged as a national language, but English is a widespread lingua franca and the first language for many educated people. In most urban settings and official dealings English will get you through. A few words of Hindi might help, particularly numbers that are similar in many Indian languages.

hello	*namaste* or *Ram Ram*
yes	*haa(n)*
no	*nahi(n)*
okay	*thiik hai*
today	*aj*
tomorrow/yesterday	*kal*
right now	*abhi*
day	*din*
week	*haftaa*
month	*maheenaa*

big	*baraa*		
small	*chhotaa*		
hot	*garam*		
cold	*thandaa*		
very good	*bahut achchaa*		

water	*paani*
tea	*chai*
coffee	*kaafi*
milk	*dudh*
sugar	*chini*

food	*khaana*
vegetables	*sabzi*
potato	*aloo*
cauliflower	*gobi*
lentils	*daal*
peas	*matar*
egg	*aanda*
omelette	*aamlet*
fruit	*phal*
banana	*kelaa*
apple	*seb*
orange	*santaraa*
enough	*bas*
bill	*bill* or *hisab*

room	*kamraa*
road	*raastaa*
straight on	*siidhaa*
left/right	*baaien/daahinaa*
Where is . . .?	*kaha(n) hai?*
My name is . . .	*meraa naam . . . hai.*
How many Rupees?	*kitna rupaya?*
What is this?	*yeh kyaa hai?*

1	*ek*	15	*pandraa*	29	*untiis*
2	*do*	16	*solaa*	30	*tiis*
3	*tiin*	17	*sataraa*	40	*chaaliis*
4	*chaar*	18	*atharaa*	50	*pachaas*
5	*paanch*	19	*unniis*	60	*saath*
6	*chhe*	20	*biis*	70	*sattar*
7	*saat*	21	*ikkiis*	80	*assii*
8	*aath*	22	*baaiis*	90	*nabbe*
9	*nau*	23	*teiis*	100	*(ek) sau*
10	*das*	24	*chaubiis*	200	*do sau*
11	*gyaaraa*	25	*pachchiis*	1000	*(ek) hazaar*
12	*baaraa*	26	*chhabbiis*	100,000	*lakh*
13	*teraa*	27	*sattaaiis*	10M	*crore*
14	*chaudaa*	28	*atthaaiis*		

The word *achchaa* meaning 'okay' or 'good' is frequently used to indicate understanding but does not necessarily imply agreement.

Opening Times

There is much variation but offices are generally open Monday to Friday from 09.30 to 17.00 while banks are open from 10.00 to 14.00. Shops open Monday to Saturday 09.30 to 18.00, Post Offices weekdays 10.00 to 17.00 and on Saturday morning when some banks and offices may also open. Most shops and offices close on Sundays and Bank Holidays. Booking offices at railway stations have peculiar opening times that vary widely from place to place. Many offices close at lunchtime.

Holidays

There are many festivals and public holidays, both regional and national. Most are religious and follow the Indian lunar calendar with no fixed date. The exceptions are Republic Day on 26 January, Independence Day on 15 August, Mahatma Gandhi's Birthday on 2 October and Christmas Day on 25 December. For details of moveable dates contact your local Indian National Tourist Office (see Pre-tour Information for addresses). It is a good idea to obtain these so you can plan your itinerary and official business around them.

Postal Services

The Indian postal service is fairly reliable for letters. Airmail to and from India usually arrives within two weeks. Stamps can be bought at better hotels, which saves time queuing at the post office.

If you want to have letters sent to you, then have them addressed:
    John <u>BIRDER</u>
    Poste Restante
    GPO (name of city)
    INDIA

When you check for your letters at the post office, you may need to show identification. Normally the clerk will give you the whole stack of letters beginning with the same letter as your name. Ask also to check the letters under the same letter as your first name as they may be filed there by mistake.

Sending parcels from India involves a complicated ritual. Books can be sent by bookpost which is cheaper but involves wrapping the parcel so that it can be inspected by customs, i.e. the string undone and the parcel unwrapped or the ends left open so that books can be seen. Most reputable bookshops do this for you. Ask for the parcel to be sent registered and get a receipt. Do not expect books to arrive in pristine condition.

Telecommunications

Telephone services have improved immensely, but the internal system is not keeping pace with demand. It is easier to telephone another continent than across the road. Many people do not have a private telephone so 'phone booths have sprung up all over the place, often operated as a sideline by shop owners. Look for signs saying STD/ISD or PCO. Although we give local dialling codes it is not always customary and you have to tell the telephone-booth operator the name of the town you want. It is often best to let him do the dialling, as he will be more familiar with the plethora of engaged tones and messages. Try to get a telephone with an electronic meter to monitor the cost of your call. The international access code from India is 00. Better hotels often have direct dialling facilities from rooms but charge much higher rates. If the hotel has a fax machine, you can have messages sent to and from it.

Electricity

Mains electricity supplies are 230–240 Volts at 50 cycles. Sockets are of a round three-pin variety. Some European round-pin plugs fit these loosely, but take a travel adapter if you have anything that needs plugging into the mains. Electricity blackouts are common and hotels usually supply candles. Better class hotels have generators. In some Rest Houses there may be no electricity supply.

AA-size batteries are widely available but often of poor quality. Better quality batteries are obtainable in some cities, but if there are specialist batteries you need, bring your own. Before an internal plane journey all electrical equipment must be emptied of batteries which (along with penknives) must not be kept in your hand luggage.

Baksheesh/Tips

Hotel porters expect a tip and waiters expect 5–10% of the bill. It is not necessary to tip taxi drivers with whom you have agreed a price for a single journey, but if you keep the same car for a day or more, it is appropriate. If you go trekking and use a guide and porters, reward them at the end of the trek. In some situations the judicious use of baksheesh may expedite matters, perhaps producing that berth on the train that was unavailable moments before.

Giving money to beggars is a personal matter but not officially encouraged. In India beggars can be extraordinarily tenacious and keeping loose change can resolve the situation. Unfortunately, some tourists misguidedly give away pens and sweets, so children now consider pestering tourists for pens (Gimme one pen!) and sweets (Mithai!) normal. If you really want to help children, consider contacting the local school to find out their needs and perhaps even make a long-term commitment.

Safety

It is generally safe to travel in India although petty theft is common in the bigger cities and on public transport where items may be pilfered from unattended baggage, or more seriously, whole bags may be stolen while the owner is asleep. A good method of preventing total theft is to attach your bag to the luggage rack using a strong cycle-lock. All side pockets should be individually padlocked. Theft from hotel rooms can occur (usually in the cheaper establishments) so keep luggage locked and use your own padlock on the room door rather than one supplied by the lodge. Make sure your travel insurance gives adequate cover for valuables and equipment.

In better class hotels deposit valuables in the hotel safe, but do not forget to claim them before your departure. Otherwise keep valuables on your person and out of sight in a money belt. Keep smaller amounts of money for the day in a separate small purse or wallet. This avoids exposing large wads of money in public. Expensive cameras and optical equipment are best kept out of sight when not in use. Binoculars attract requests for a look, but bear in mind the risk of transmitting eye infection.

Bring a photocopy of the main pages of your passport and visa together with extra passport photographs in case your passport is lost.

CLIMATE AND CLOTHING

Climate   India's huge size and varied topography means the climate varies from place to place quite markedly. Broadly speaking India has a hot tropical climate and, with the exception of the Himalayan region, one can divide the year into three periods: the hot, the wet and the cool. During the hot and dry 'summer' from the end of March to the end of May/beginning of June temperatures reach the 40°sC during the middle of the day. The onset of the southwest monsoon usually begins in South India at the end of May and works its way to Delhi by late June/early July. During the monsoon it can rain every day – heavily, lightly or not at all. It can be hot and humid although temperatures are not usually as high as in the 'summer'. Travel at this time of year can be difficult in out of the way areas of the peninsula, and many national parks are closed. For the birdwatcher and photographer this time of year can be rewarding as many species are breeding. The southwest monsoon usually lasts until September retreating from the northwest to the southeast. It is followed by the short northeast monsoon which normally only affects the east coast of South India and the northeastern States. From October to February is the cool season when daytime temperatures in the south can be in the mid-20°sC and 30°sC. At this time of year it can be quite cold in the north, with nighttime temperatures in Delhi regularly below 10°C. The cool season is usually relatively dry.

    The broad range of the Himalaya has its own peculiarities of climate. Generally speaking, rainfall increases from west to east so that Northeast India has some of the wettest places on earth, whereas the Vale of Kashmir has a climate in some ways not dissimilar to Northern Europe. Ladakh, at high altitude in the rain shadow of the Himalaya, has very little precipitation, but temperatures in January fall to 40°C below zero. Only from June to September do daytime temperatures rise into the 20°sC.

Clothing   Due to the varied climate, clothing required depends on where and when you go. Three or four weeks in Delhi and Rajasthan from March to May only requires light summer clothing, plus a warm sweater or jacket for early morning jeep rides. At the other extreme a winter visit to the Himalayan region dictates very warm clothing and a four-season sleeping bag.

    Indian sensibilities may be offended by the sight of too much bare skin and whereas a pair of longish shorts and a T-shirt are suitable and comfortable for a man, women should keep shoulders and legs covered as far as possible and not wear clothing that is too tight or otherwise immodest. In any case, it is best to wear long-sleeved shirts and long trousers as protection against biting insects, particularly at and after dusk. A sun hat, sunglasses and sun cream should always be carried in your daypack. Outside the dry season a folding umbrella is more suitable than a poncho except in the mountains. A good pair of boots or walking shoes is recommended as the terrain can be rough and thorns can penetrate the soles of heavy hiking boots, let alone training shoes.

    For high altitude trekking you need an outer breathable waterproof jacket, an inner fleece or down jacket, thermal underwear, woollen hat and gloves. A layering of clothes is best so that you can add or remove layers depending on the temperature; e.g. one thick and one thin pullover can either be worn separately or together, as the situation requires.

HEALTH

For recommended vaccinations see Pre-tour Information. Travel to India, as with all tropical countries, presents the Westerner with particular health hazards but with a little care most can be avoided. The most common problems are stomach bugs due to insanitary preparation of food and especial care must be taken regarding food hygiene – see Staying in India. Most **stomach upsets** are fairly mild, last less than 24 hours and are best treated by resting, eating little, avoiding fruit and dairy products and drinking plenty of fluid with a little sugar and added salt. Drugs such as Imodium do not cure the cause of diarrhoea but simply alleviate the symptoms. They should only be used when absolutely necessary – on long journeys or in other circumstances where access to a lavatory may be difficult. If symptoms are particularly severe with stool containing blood and mucus, or last for more than three days, seek the advice of a doctor. If you are in a situation where no doctor is within reach, a course of antibiotics may be appropriate – Ciprofloxacin 500mg or Norfloxacin 400mg twice a day for three days. **Giardiasis (Giardia)** can also cause diarrhoea with frequent foul-smelling wind. The symptoms appear one or two weeks after infection and may disappear and return for a few days at a time. The cure is a single dose of Flagyl (metronidazole) or Fasigyn (tinidazole).

Malaria is prevalent in India especially during the monsoon and it is essential to take precautions including the currently recommended prophylactic drugs (consult your doctor for the latest advice). Start taking tablets a week before your trip and continue the course of treatment for six weeks after leaving the malarial zone. It is unlikely, but possible, to catch malaria in spite of taking the treatment. Avoid getting bitten by mosquitoes. These are particularly active between dusk and dawn when you should cover exposed skin by wearing light-coloured long-sleeved shirts of a dense weave, long-trousers and mosquito-repellent. Sleep under a mosquito net or use a mosquito coil or tablet. The same precautions are helpful against the risk of infection with **Dengue Fever** for which there is no prophylactic. If affected by fever, shivering or severe headaches together with joint and muscle pains, seek medical advice.

Disinfect **cuts** and **scratches** but dress with a plaster only if there is serious danger of dirt entering the wound. Healing takes place much faster if the skin is exposed to the sun and air.

AIDS is spreading fast in India, mainly through heterosexual transmission. Practice safe sex. If you need an injection, make sure a sterile needle is used.

AMS (Acute Mountain Sickness) is a serious threat at high altitudes. It can affect anyone without regard to age or fitness, normally at altitudes above 3500m though fatal cases have been known as low as 3000m. If going on a trek in the high Himalaya, or travelling in Ladakh, make sure that you spend some time acclimatising by spending two or three nights at each altitude above 2000m for every 1000m climbed. Drink more than you would normally to compensate for the moisture lost through your breath in the dry air. Avoid alcohol and sedatives in spite of possible sleeplessness. The low levels of oxygen mean that most people will experience some breathlessness but the other main symptoms of AMS are severe headache, dizziness, confusion, loss of appetite, a dry cough, nausea and vomiting. Mild symptoms will usually subside after a couple of days' acclimatisation but anyone suffering acutely should immediately descend to a lower altitude. Even a few hundred metres can help.

Jet-lag, sun and **heat** can cause problems. Acclimatise by taking it relatively easy for the first few days. Wear loose cotton clothes, drink plenty of liquid and take care to eat sufficient salt with your food. **Sunburn** can occur surprisingly fast in the tropics. Wear a wide-brimmed hat, keep arms, legs and feet covered and/or use a high factor sun cream. Apply a zinc sun block to the nose, lips and forehead and anywhere else you burn quickly. Use sunglasses. Spending too much time out in the sun can also cause **heat stroke**, particularly during the middle of the day when you should seek out the shade. Victims are likely to feel unwell with a throbbing headache, be unable to sweat, have a high body temperature with flushed skin and become confused and aggressive. They should be taken to a hospital or doctor immediately. An itchy rash called **prickly heat** is not uncommon in newly arrived visitors. Keeping cool, wearing loose clothes, using talcum powder and bathing regularly can help.

Fungal infections can cause an itchy skin rash, particularly between the toes and fingers, around the groin or on the scalp. Wear loose clothes of natural fibres and use plastic or rubber thongs (shoes) in the bathroom and shower. Infections are best treated with a fungicide such as Tinaderm and by regular washing with medicated soap and exposure to as much air and sun as possible. Clothes and towels should be washed thoroughly and frequently.

Intestinal worms are common and can be caught by ingesting unhygienically prepared food or walking barefoot. Possible symptoms include an itching around the anus, particularly at night, and diarrhoea. De-worming tablets are available at pharmacies.

Leeches can be a problem, mainly in rainforests during and after the rainy season. They are not known to transmit diseases but are a nuisance as the ensuing bleeding may be difficult to stop. Coating feet and legs or boots with an insect repellent containing Deet provides protection for up to several hours. Remove leeches by applying a squirt of insect repellent, salt or a lighted match.

The change of climate often makes visitors prone to catching **colds** and **coughs**. Cold remedies are readily available at pharmacies, but the strongest cough lozenges are usually Strepsils, so you may prefer to bring your own.

Although there are doctors and hospitals in most towns throughout India standards of hygiene often leave much to be desired. Most hotels can put you in touch with a good English-speaking doctor. Fees are usually reasonable though luxury hotels are likely to work together with doctors whose fees reflect their high-class treatment. If you have a serious problem and are in a place that does not have the standard of health care you require, the best solution may be to get on a plane to the nearest place that does. The large metropolises have good clinics and your country's embassy or consulate may be able to recommend one.

Common remedies are inexpensive and available over the counter at pharmacies in most towns, but care is not always taken regarding storage and expiry date. If you need a specific medicine, take adequate supplies with you in case it is not available locally. If you wear spectacles, take a spare pair with you. New prescription glasses can be made up the same day in Delhi and some other big cities.

A small travel medical kit should include the following:

Antacid Tablets – for acid indigestion

Antibiotics – in case of a serious infection while travelling off the beaten track. Take a copy of the prescription with you.

Aspirin or Paracetamol – pain-killer and fever depressant

Calamine Lotion or Antihistamine Cream – to reduce itching from insect bites

Diarolytes – for rehydration

Dequacaine – for severe sore throats and coughs

Imodium or Lomotil – to control diarrhoea

Insect repellent containing DEET or 'Mosiguard'

Plaster and Bandages – for dressing wounds

Scissors

Sterile-packed Syringes – in case you need injections in less hygienic circumstances. Ask for a note from your doctor to explain why you have them.

Sun Block

Sun Cream

Tweezers

Water Purification Tablets

If you have any medicines left over at the end of your trip, you may wish to donate them to a local clinic.

For a more thorough treatment of health issues relevant to the tropics consult one of the following:

Staying Healthy in Asia, Africa and Latin America by Dirk Schroeder, Moon Publications. 1994.

Travellers' Health by Dr. Richard Dawood, OUP. 1992.

The Preservation of Personal Health in Warm Climates produced by MASTA (Medical Advisory Service for Travellers Abroad) at the London School of Hygiene and Tropical Medicine, Keppel Street, London, WC1E 7HT. ☎0171-636-3924

The American Center for Disease Control Internet Web Site at www.cdc.gov.

BOOKS AND MAPS

Books and maps published in India are usually far cheaper there than abroad, but they tend to become unavailable fairly quickly. The visiting birder should not rely on being able to buy any important reference work on arrival.

Field Guides

No single field guide to date covers all 1220 Indian birds. Identification should be facilitated by three new guides in preparation, *viz.* Ripley, Rasmussen and Anderton's *Birds of South Asia: A Field Guide,* Grimmett, Inskipp & Inskipp *et al's Birds of the Indian Subcontinent,* and Kazmierczak & van Perlo's *Field Guide to the Birds of the Indian Subcontinent.* In the meantime for a complete treatment of all the birds of the Subcontinent Ali and Ripley's *Handbook of the Birds of India and Pakistan* in 10 Volumes is the standard work. Even in the single volume compact edition this is not conveniently portable. A serviceable compromise is the *Pictorial Guide to the Birds of the Indian Subcontinent* by Salim Ali and S. Dillon Ripley with illustrations by John Henry Dick. This basically consists of the plates to the 2nd edition of the Handbook with an extremely limited text giving details of size, habitat and distribution. It suffers from inaccuracies and omissions, and for some groups of birds such as warblers and pipits it would be best not to rely on this book alone.

For the beginner the most useful books are Salim Ali's *Book of Indian Birds* in the recently revised 12th edition and Martin Woodcock's *Collins Handguide to the Birds of the Indian Sub-Continent.* Both are fairly well illustrated but only cover the commoner birds. *Birds of India, Bangladesh, Nepal, Pakistan and Shri Lanka* by Bikram Grewal describes some 500 species, most of them illustrated with excellent though small photographs.

Salim Ali wrote a number of regional works which are interesting when birding the areas in question: *The Birds of Sikkim* was more or less incorporated into the later *Field Guide to the Birds of the Eastern Himalayas* making the latter more useful when visiting Northeast India; *The Birds of Kerala* has been out of print for some time but is useful for South India if you can get hold of a copy; if visiting any of the mountains or hill ranges, then his *Indian Hill Birds* is relevant.

Many birds in India occur in neighbouring countries. Field guides to those countries can be useful. The identification section from Carol and Tim Inskipp's *Birds of Nepal* is one of the most useful for sorting out more difficult groups although it does not cover all the species in India. The Flemings' *Birds of Nepal,* more useful for text than illustrations, covers most birds in the Himalaya. T. J. Roberts' two volume *Birds of Pakistan* is a good source of reference to the avifauna of northwest India. When travelling in the latter area, it can be useful to have the *Field Guide to the Birds of the Middle East* by Porter, Christensen and Schiermacker-Hansen. In the eastern parts of the country (including the Andaman & Nicobar Islands) have a copy of either Boonsong & Round's *A Guide to the Birds of Thailand* or *A Field Guide to the Birds of South-East Asia* by King, Woodcock and Dickinson. While the latter covers a wider range of species, the former is more up-to-date and better illustrated. In South India G. M. Henry's *Birds of Ceylon* and the forthcoming Sri Lankan field guide by John Harrison and Tim Worfolk may be helpful. In using these books bear in mind that some species described occur as distinct races and may be visibly different from sub-species in India.

For those with a more specialist interest in a particular group, or family, of birds there are specific books available, especially in the excellent series published by Helm and Pica which include separate works on Seabirds; Wildfowl; Shorebirds; Finches and Sparrows; Crows and Jays; Kingfishers,

Bee-eaters and Rollers; Swallows and Martins; Tits, Nuthatches and
Treecreepers; Buntings and Sparrows; Woodpeckers; Swifts, Nightjars, and
other volumes to follow. These can, however, be quite expensive and a little
too bulky to be carried comfortably in the field. A smaller, useful book,
published with the Asian Waterfowl Survey participants in mind, is the
Field Guide to Asian Waterbirds by Bharat Bhushan *et al.*

For Indian mammals *The Book of Indian Animals* by S. H. Prater is
generally regarded as the standard work. *A Field Guide to the Mammals of the
Indian Subcontinent* by K. K. Gurung and Raj Singh is handier for those who
just want to identify commoner larger mammals but does not contain all
species likely to be encountered. Those interested in reptiles need J. C.
Daniels' *Book of Indian Reptiles* and R. Whittaker's *Common Indian Snakes*.
Butterflies are covered to some extent in *Common Butterflies of India* by T.
Gay *et al.* published by WWF – India and more thoroughly in M. A.
Wynter-Blyth's *Butterflies of the Indian Region,* now out of print and hard to
come by. The excellent *Butterflies of Sikkim Himalaya and their Natural History*
covers 400 species and is the best guide in the northern part of the country.
There are many other books dealing with India and Indian Wildlife. For a
more detailed listing see the bibliography at the end of the book.

Audio Guides   There are a number of bird recordings in private collections and lodged
with the National Sound Archive (formerly BLOWS) in London and the
Library of Natural Sounds in New York (see Useful Addresses), but little
has been published. P. S. Sivaprasad's *An Audio Guide to the Birds of South
India* was thus a welcome addition to the published written material. The
cassette has a selection of good sound recordings of 66 species found in
India. Many are fairly common and widely distributed throughout the
country but there are also recordings of birds which are endemic to the
South. Deepal Warakagoda's *The Bird Sounds of Sri Lanka* and Steve Smith's
Bird Recordings from Sri Lanka include a number of species found in
southern India. For north India and the Himalaya *Birdsongs of Nepal* and
Birdsongs of the Himalayas by Scott Connop are extremely valuable covering
many unusual as well as commoner species. The set of two cassettes
compiled by Terry White under the title *A Field Guide to the Bird Songs of
South-East Asia* includes recordings of many species that also occur in India.

Trip Reports   Visiting birders often write trip reports that they may circulate to friends
and other interested parties. These are often extremely useful as they have
up-to-date information on travel, accommodation and bird sightings in the
areas visited. Many can be obtained for a fee to cover photocopying, post
and packing from the FBRIS, DBTRS or the Information Officer of the OBC
(see Useful Addresses).

Travel Guides   A general travel guide with detailed information on hotels, transport and
so on is almost indispensable. The best are the India volumes in the Lonely
Planet Travel Survival Kit and Rough Guide series, and the *India Handbook*
by Robert and Roma Bradnock, not necessarily in that order of preference.
The one you choose may depend on which has the most up-to-date edition.
For those who would like to explore some of the many lesser-known Indian
sanctuaries there is a fairly extensive catalogue of protected areas in S. S.
Negi's *Handbook of National Parks, Sanctuaries and Biosphere Reserves in India*
which may be available through a good bookshop in India.

Bookshops   In Delhi there are a few good bookshops around Connaught Place.
E. D. Galgotia & Sons at 17B Connaught Place and Amrit Book Co. at

21N Connaught Circus, among others, have a fairly good selection of natural history books. There are quite a number of good bookshops in Calcutta, which is also the headquarters of the Zoological Survey of India. The sales office for their own, often specialised, publications is on the 13th Floor, Nizam Palace, 2nd M.S.O. Building, 234/4 Acharya J.C.Bose Road, Calcutta – 700 020. The Bombay Natural History Society sells its own publications (see Useful Addresses). Most reputable bookshops in India will pack and ship books home for you at a reasonable rate, if you do not want to carry them yourself.

Maps   The Lascelles, Bartholemew and Nelles maps covering the Indian Subcontinent in one sheet at a scale of 1:4,000,000, are fairly good general maps but are not really detailed enough for birdwatchers' needs. Birdwatchers will find the Nelles series of maps or the Lonely Planet *India Travel Atlas* suitable for most purposes. The former cover India in five sheets at 1:1,500,000 and are sold as separate maps. They are not always available in India. The Lonely Planet production covers the whole country in a single book at 1:1,250,000 and shows slightly more detail than the Nelles maps but is more bulky. The 'Road Guide' series produced by T. T. Maps & Publications Ltd., Chennai (Madras), covers most of India and often indicates roads not shown on the Nelles maps.

If engaged in a more detailed study, you might buy one of the 1:250,000 or 1:50,000 topographic maps produced by the Survey of India. Those covering border and coastal areas are not for sale to the public. The Survey of India Map Office in Delhi is on Janpath, above the Bankura Cafe behind the market opposite the Govt of India Tourist Office. They also have useful maps of the major Indian cities as well as State Maps at 1:1 Million. It is illegal to take any map of scale larger than 1:250,000 out of India. Some topographic maps, often older versions, are available at the Royal Geographical Society, 1 Kensington Gore, London, SW7 2AR. The US Army Corps of Engineers produced a series of 1:250,000 topo sheets, available for study at the British Library and some bigger university libraries. Most National Park, Wildlife Sanctuary and Forest Department offices have topographic maps covering the area under their administration. These may be viewed on request but are not for sale. At some protected areas small brochures with rough maps and a bird checklist may be available.

More detailed trekking maps of Himachal Pradesh and other Himalayan regions are sometimes available locally, but this cannot be guaranteed.

The general travel guides have good maps of most sizeable towns. Other maps vary in availability, accuracy and quality.

Stanfords, 12-14 Long Acre, Covent Garden, London, WC2E 9LP ☎ 0171-836-1321 have a good selection of maps and travel guides and provide a mail order service. Try also The National Map Centre, 22-24 Caxton Street, London, SW1H 0QU ☎ 0171-222-2466, Fax 0171-222-2619 or Books from India, 45 Museum Street, London, WC1A 1LR ☎ 0171-405-7226, Fax 0171-831-4517. One of a number of good mapsellers in the US is Map Link, 30 So. LaPatera Lane, Santa Barbara, CA 93117 ☎805-965-4402.

Please note that no maps are entirely reliable.

WHEN TO GO

Birdwatching in India can be rewarding at any time of year, although there is regional variation in the best time to visit. Most visiting birders will maximise the number of species seen by timing their trip to coincide with wintering Palearctic migrants between **mid-October and mid-March**. Many Himalayan species can be found at lower altitudes during this period that coincides with the cool and dry season.

By the end of **March** most Palearctic migrants have left and altitudinal migrants move up to higher elevations. The hot dry weather through **April** and **May** in most of the peninsula and plains sees waterbodies drying out and makes observation of resident waterfowl and wildlife easier as they concentrate at remaining pools and reservoirs. The extreme heat during mid-day means that birding is largely restricted to the early morning and late afternoon.

May and **June** are best for high altitude birding in the Himalaya when many species are breeding and the conditions are good for trekking. Summer visitors arrive in north India and the Himalaya making this the ideal time to see the various cuckoos, for example, which are silent and elusive at other times.

Most rainfall is brought by the southwest monsoon that can begin in the extreme northeast of the country as early as **mid-March.** It usually hits the extreme southeast at the end of **May** and works its way in a broad front across the country to the northwest to reach Delhi in **late June**. By the time it reaches western Rajasthan at the beginning of July it has often spent much of its force precipitating little or no rainfall in desert regions. Its advent triggers breeding activity in resident waterbirds making this the ideal time to observe heronries. The heavy rains, however, make unmetalled roads impassable so many protected areas remain closed until the clear-up is completed between **October** and **mid-November**. Ladakh lies in the rain shadow of the Himalaya and **July to September** can be good months to explore this region.

The post-monsoon season is excellent for trekking in the Himalaya with visibility generally extremely clear and conditions underfoot good from late **October** until the snows in early **December**.

More information on the best time to visit particular regions and individual sites is given under the regional summaries and in the *Strategy* sections of the site descriptions.

PROTECTED AREAS AND THE FOREST DEPARTMENT

Many of India's best habitats and birding areas have legal protection as National Parks or Sanctuaries. It would take more than one lifetime to bird all of these thoroughly. Most larger preserves are divided into three zones. The core zone is kept free of all interference so that nature and wildlife remain undisturbed. Exceptions are sometimes made for scientific research. This has in many cases meant that villagers and tribal people have been relocated away from the core zone, difficult to carry out while retaining the goodwill of people involved. Surrounding the core is a buffer zone where local people are allowed limited access in order to harvest forest produce and gather fallen timber for fuel, though actual felling is normally prohibited. The tourist zone is maintained with the intention of educating and instructing people about nature. There is often a Visitor Centre with accommodation, a canteen, an exhibition and facilities for lectures and slide shows. In some parks it is possible to explore on foot, but in many access is only allowed at certain times of day in a vehicle accompanied by a Forest Guard. Birding may be better in areas outside park boundaries where there are no restrictions. Details are given with each site description under the heading of *Strategy*.

Most protected areas come under the jurisdiction of the Forest Department. Where sanctuaries have a well-developed tourist infrastructure it is not always necessary to deal directly with the Forest Department, other than paying fees at the entrance gate. However, to visit reserves off the beaten track you often have to obtain permission and make arrangements with the relevant office in advance. Trying to do this by post is a waste of time. The chances of getting a reply are very slim. A letter ahead of a personal visit will help smooth the way, but a visit is the only way to get results unless you make arrangements through a reputable travel agent or tour operator. Even then there is no guarantee of success as the responsible officials may be 'out station' and their subordinates unable or unwilling to give you permits. Inevitably the bureaucratic hassle can be time-consuming and frustrating, particularly if the office is in a town some distance from the place you want to visit. A little patience, forward planning and willingness to accept alternative arrangements are required. At times everything seems hopeless, at others doors open magically and things work out better than you had ever expected.

Generally, when visiting the Forest Department try to see the DFO (Divisional Forest Officer) in charge. The designation is often loosely applied to high-ranking officials within the Forest Administration. They are usually well educated, speak good English and have a genuine interest in wildlife. Particularly if you have a specific project, they can be extremely helpful. Another title commonly used is Conservator of Forests, abbreviated to CF. The positions range from Principal Chief Conservator of Forests (PCCF), responsible for the whole state, down through CCF, Deputy CF and Assistant CF. The Forest Department is divided into sections, but the birder normally has to deal with the Wildlife Wing headed by the Chief Wildlife Warden. Thus a DFO may also have the title of Wildlife Warden.

Apart from Parks and Sanctuaries, the Forest Department is responsible for Reserved Forests. In these they may have Forest Rest Houses, largely intended for the use of officials. They are often in prime birding habitat and it is usually possible to get permission to stay there. The quality of accommodation varies from comfortable to extremely basic, or even rough and dilapidated. Find out whether you need your own bedding, food and other provisions. There is usually a *chowkidar*, or caretaker, who may double as a cook. In some cases porters can be arranged to carry everything up to the Rest House, if it is not accessible by road. You may have to supply them with food and this should be clarified in advance. Do not forget basic items like chilli, salt, cooking oil, sugar, candles, matches and so on.

One drawback of Forest Department accommodation is that you may need to vacate at short notice if a VIP suddenly arrives. It is not usually advisable to just turn up at a Forest Rest House as you will not be allowed to stay without the necessary permit. At a pinch they might find floor space for your sleeping bag. If you are stuck, ask to see the Range Officer or Beat Officer who may be able to help. The Forest Department Office is an important institution and most taxi drivers and rickshaw wallahs know where it is. Ask for the Forest Office (often pronounced *farrest affice)* rather than trying to give an address.

White-headed
Starling

INTRODUCTION TO SITE INFORMATION

For convenience we divide the country into 11 regions. Avifaunally there is a degree of overlap although each region has its specialities. We concentrate on species of most interest to the Western visitor. In a country where a site like the 29km^2 Bharatpur has a birdlist longer than that of many a country this has proved difficult. A complete listing of birds at each site would make the book too unwieldy so most commoner and widespread species are omitted. We give more detail for sites such as Bharatpur, Corbett, Delhi and Goa, more likely to be visited on a first trip to Asia.

The letters S or W, in brackets following a bird's name, indicate that the species is only found in summer or winter respectively. P indicates a passage migrant. R stands for rare, U for uncommon and B for breeding. Species endemic to the Indian Subcontinent are marked*. Species endemic to India (including the Andamans & Nicobars) are marked**. It has not always been possible to obtain accurate information on local status and abundance of species and in many cases we give an informed estimate.

English names follow Inskipp, Lindsey & Duckworth *An Annotated Checklist of the Birds of the Oriental Region* et al (Oriental Bird Club. 1996) since this will be the basis for at least two of the forthcoming field guides. We have, however, retained the older systematic order used by Ali & Ripley. Where the new names differ significantly we list common alternatives in the appendix.

Indian place names are subject to a variety of spellings. Many towns have different local and English names, often rendered in imaginative transliterations. We generally give preference to the names used in the Nelles maps. Major alternative transliterations are given in brackets at the first mention of the place in the text.

We sometimes give times of trains and buses as general guidelines only. Schedules often change and enquiries should be made locally to check timings.

ABBREVIATIONS

The following abbreviations are commonly used in the text:

ACF	Assistant Conservator of Forests
aka	also known as
BNHS	Bombay Natural History Society
BS	Bird Sanctuary
DCF	Deputy Conservator of Forests
DFO	Divisional Forest Officer
FRH	Forest Rest House
IB	Inspection Bungalow
ISBT	Interstate Bus Terminal
NH	National Highway
NP	National Park
Rd	Road
OBC	Oriental Bird Club
WLS	Wildlife Sanctuary
TDC	Tourism Development Corporation, e.g. Indian (ITDC) or Rajasthan (RTDC)

DELHI AREA

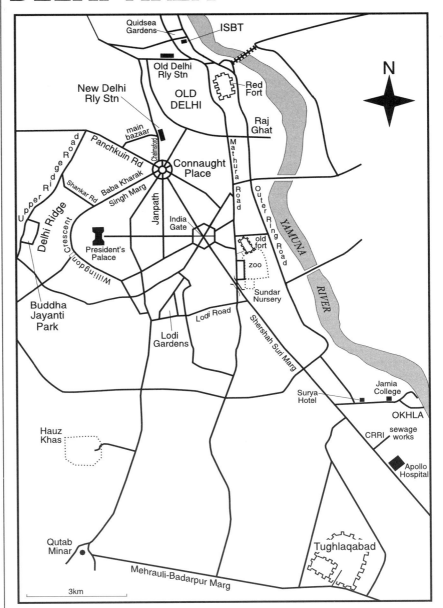

Map of Delhi

Most first time visitors to India will arrive in Delhi and may not realise the wealth of birdlife in various corners of the capital. The birder on business or just passing through may only have a few hours to spare to do some birdwatching yet the sites in and around the metropolis can be worth far longer. Delhi, with its bird list of more than 430 species, rivals any other area in India and with effort it is possible to see more than 150 species in a day. The capital is well watched and well documented, and there is a richness of habitats in various parts of the city. One of the most important is the River Yamuna along the eastern edge of the city. Good birding can be had almost anywhere along its banks. The parks and gardens have a good selection of species and some historical sites have become overgrown and provide suitable conditions for many birds.

For those with more time it is worth getting a copy of the Delhi Guide Map (Scale 1:25,000), published by the Survey of India or the new city map published by Eicher. These show most areas of green and scrub that provide good birding. The Delhi-based birder may join the local environmental organisation known as Kalpavriksh and buy a copy of *What's that bird? – A guide to birdwatching, with special reference to Delhi* which includes a complete checklist for the area. The recently formed Delhi Bird Club holds regular outings and can help with further information on specific sites. Interesting bird records should also be sent to them (see Useful Addresses).

Location

Delhi is in northern India and well situated for visiting the northern and western parts of the country. Bharatpur, India's premier bird sanctuary, is only half a day away and the Taj Mahal, the world's most famous man-made wonder, is almost on the way there. Delhi is not at the geographical centre of India but is very much the hub in terms of communication, with rail and air connections to nearly all important towns of the subcontinent.

Delhi's airport, on the southern side of the city, is split into international and domestic sections some distance from each other. If taking a taxi from the city to the airport, you should specify which terminal you want. The most economical way to and from the airport is the bus run by EATS (the ex-servicemen's airport transport service). They have a ticket counter in each terminal lobby and just off Connaught Place on Radial Rd 8 (which runs into Janpath), in the centre of Delhi. The bus starts and terminates opposite this office. EATS buses drop off at most larger hotels on the way into town on request. A pre-paid taxi desk in the lobby simplifies dealing with taxis at the airport after clearing customs. You book your destination and pay the fare according to an official list at the counter. You are then given a ticket that you take outside to the taxi rank and give to the driver as payment at the end of the journey. This avoids having to haggle with the driver, though a small tip would be appropriate.

If arriving at the international terminal, exchange money at one of the banks while waiting for luggage to come through on the carousel. The exchange is far simpler and quicker than in the city where there is a shortage of banks with foreign exchange facilities.

The city is more or less divided into Old Delhi, the more crowded bustling city of narrow streets to the north of Connaught Place, and the city of New Delhi with wide boulevards and parks and open spaces to its south. Connaught Place is generally regarded as the centre of the metropolis.

Most important long-distance trains leave from New Delhi station, but some depart from Old Delhi station. Check which when booking. The main booking office is in New Delhi station, confusingly on the edge of Old Delhi, just north of Connaught Place. Delhi is one of the few places you can make advance reservations for trains leaving from other stations, (e.g. Bharatpur to Sawai Madhopur or Chennai/Madras to Calcutta). Taking advantage of this is a good idea if you can plan ahead, as trains on some important routes are often fully booked for days or weeks ahead. The booking office is on Chelmsford Rd between New Delhi station and Connaught Place.

Most long-distance buses leave from the Interstate Bus Terminus (ISBT), near the Kashmiri Gate in North Delhi, but check if booking through a travel agent.

Accommodation

Delhi suffers from a chronic shortage of hotels and those without a hotel reservation should try to arrive early in the day. There is a reservations desk at the airport for middle- and higher-class hotels that can be helpful. Most cheaper accommodation is in Pahar Ganj, the main bazaar, conveniently situated opposite New Delhi Railway Station. There are hotels around Connaught Place, a convenient base for transport to sites around the city. The cheaper ones are mainly around Janpath, on the south side of Connaught Place.

The Pahar Ganj area has cheap places to eat. The Hotel Metropolis Restaurant is more up-market but has one of the most varied and extensive menus in Delhi. One of the best places for Western-style food, including a safe eat-as-much-as-you-like salad buffet, is Nirula's on Connaught Place, where a number of other restaurants are located.

For more detailed information on accommodation and food refer to one of the general travel guides.

Strategy Early morning visits to most sites are best. This means taking a taxi or auto-rickshaw, as finding the right bus in the early hours can be difficult. Auto-rickshaws are not expensive if shared. Get the driver to use the meter, or negotiate a price before you start. It is often possible to make one's way back to the centre by bus, although these are often full anywhere other than at their starting point.

First time visitors to Asia can have a gentle introduction to common birds in the Lodi Gardens close to the town centre. The Buddha Jayanti Park is not quite as near but holds a wider variety of birds. Adjoining this is the Delhi Ridge – scrub and acacia forest with interesting birdlife. The grounds of the Old Fort (Purana Qila) and Zoo are only a 10-minute auto-rickshaw ride from Connaught Place and harbour a good selection of species. The birders' favourite section of the Yamuna (Jumna) River at Okhla is some distance away at the southeastern end of the city. The complex of the Tughlaqabad abandoned city and fort, which has excellent birds, is also south of the city. The latter two sites merit at least half a day each and will be the main target for more experienced birders with limited time in Delhi.

Lodi Gardens

The Lodi Gardens are close to the centre of Delhi, 4km due south of Connaught Place, and most easily accessible by taxi or auto-rickshaw although buses 521 and 522 are available from Connaught Place. A visit can be a good introduction to the commoner garden birds of India such as Rose-ringed Parakeet, Asian Koel, White-throated Kingfisher, Common Hoopoe, Brown-headed* and Coppersmith Barbets, Black-rumped Flameback, Common Myna, House Crow, Red-vented Bulbul, Jungle Babbler*, Oriental Magpie Robin and Purple Sunbird. Yellow-footed Green Pigeon and Indian Grey Hornbill* are also possibilities. The Gardens are open from 05.00 to 21.00 in summer (1/4–30/9) and from 06.00 to 20.00 in winter (1/10–31/3). Nearby at 172B Lodi Estate is the HQ of WWF-India with an interesting bookshop.

Buddha Jayanti Park

Buddha Jayanti Park has a good mixture of ornamental and native trees with scrubby areas, and hence provides food and shelter for a good cross-section of common birds. The park is adjacent to the wilderness of the southern Delhi Ridge so a number of birds from that area use the park. The park is separated from the Ridge by a new wire fence and access is not normally possible from this side.

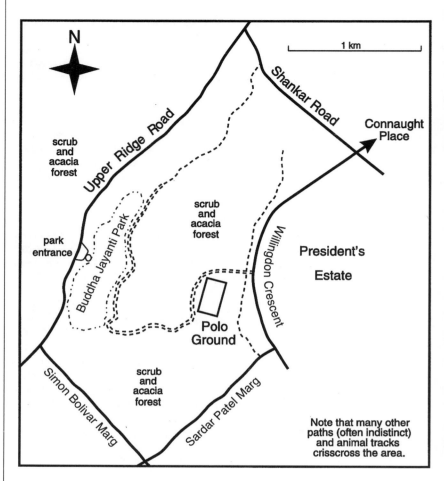

Map of
Delhi Ridge &
Buddha Jayanti
Gardens

Location

The entrance to the park is on the western side of Delhi about 6km by road from Connaught Place and, as usual in Delhi, most easily reached by taxi or auto-rickshaw. Bus no. 820 goes from Connaught Place to a large roundabout where you get off and turn left onto Upper Ridge Rd. The entrance to the Park is 2–3km down this road on the left. Walk or try to get a bus to stop and take you. Entrance is free and the park is open from dawn to dusk. The park can be good for a couple of hours, birdwatching at any time, but avoid Sundays and holidays when it is more crowded. There is a restaurant in the park.

Birds

Most commoner garden species are found here as well as Plum-headed Parakeet*, Brown-headed* and Coppersmith Barbets, Yellow-crowned Woodpecker, Bay-backed and Long-tailed Shrikes, Rufous Treepie, Common Woodshrike, Small Minivet, Jungle Babbler*, White-browed Fantail, Ashy Prinia*, Lesser Whitethroat (W), Common Chiffchaff of the race *tristis* (W), Hume's and Greenish Warblers (W), Bluethroat (W), Indian Silverbill and Common Rosefinch (W).

Delhi Ridge

The low ridge running through Delhi from southwest to northeast is the northernmost extremity of the Aravalli range of hills. There are several sections apparent in Delhi of which two are reasonably good for birdwatching. The Northern Ridge near Delhi University is largely turned into gardens, while the Southern Ridge is mainly acacia forest and thick thorny scrub. Unfortunately, this is being encroached upon, but is still worth visiting for species not always easy to find elsewhere in the Delhi area.

Location

The main part of the Southern Ridge is bounded by Shankar Rd to the north, Willingdon Crescent to the east, Simon Bolivar Marg to the southwest and the Upper Ridge Rd on the western edge. It used to be possible to cross over onto the Ridge from Buddha Jayanti Park but a new barbed wire fence has made this impracticable, so it is best to access from Willingdon Crescent just behind and to the west of Rashtrapati Bhavan (the Presidential Palace).

Strategy

An early morning visit is best. Evenings should be avoided for safety reasons. Get the taxi or auto-rickshaw driver to drop you off at the Polo Club on Willingdon Crescent. Follow the dirt roads, tracks and bridleways through the ridge. Work your way in a northerly direction to eventually emerge on the Shankar Rd from where you can go to the Buddha Jayanti Park by turning left and left again onto Upper Ridge Rd, or catch a bus or taxi back to town. Be careful on bridleways and wider trails that are used for horse riding.

Birds

Some 200 birds have been recorded from Delhi Ridge so there is plenty of scope for valuable observations. Particular species to look for are: Grey Francolin, Indian Peafowl*, Small and Barred (U) Buttonquails, Sirkeer Malkoha* (U), Yellow-crowned Woodpecker, Bay-backed Shrike, Small Minivet, Yellow-eyed Babbler, Grey-breasted and Rufous-fronted* Prinias (U), Orphean, Tickell's Leaf (U), Hume's and Greenish Warblers (W), Long-billed Pipit and White-capped Bunting (W). Brooks's Leaf Warbler is much sought-after and sometimes found in winter in the acacias where it prefers the canopy. Marshall's Iora** has become very rare in recent years. A Green Avadavat** reported from here is thought to have been an escape.

Overhead, especially during the middle of the day in winter, rarer raptors may be seen among the commoner Egyptian, White-backed and Long-billed Vultures. Oriental Honey-buzzard, Long-legged and White-eyed Buzzards, and Steppe (W), Greater Spotted (W) and Short-toed Snake Eagles are all regular in Delhi and many other birds of prey feature on the Delhi list.

Old Fort and Delhi Zoo

The Old Fort, or Purana Qila, is what is left of a 16th century walled city, and overgrown areas within the complex hold a good variety of birds. The Delhi zoo is adjacent and its 87ha of parkland, pools and mature trees attract many wild birds. These two sites have many commoner Indian species and there is a good chance of a rarity.

The zoo is important for its breeding colonies of waterbirds, the largest in the area, with Painted Storks breeding between August and March. Cormorants, egrets, storks and herons, when not breeding, feed by the Yamuna River and return to roost at night. The collection of animals and birds in the zoo can be instructive although conditions are far from ideal.

Location   Access to fort and zoo is from the same entrance road on the Mathura Rd, about 4–5km southeast of Connaught Place. If taking a taxi or auto-rickshaw, ask for Purana Qila or Delhi Zoo (zoo is pronounced 'jew'). The zoo is open daily except Fridays and National Holidays. There is a small entrance fee and admission times are 09.00 to 17.00 in summer (1 April–15 October) and 09.30 to 16.00 in winter (16 October–31 March). Entrance to the fort is free and it is open from dawn to dusk.

Strategy   Half a day is enough to cover both zoo and fort, and either can usefully fill a couple of free hours in the city. The boating pool near the entrance to the fort has a marshy section worth looking at. Adjoining the zoo is the Sundar Nursery, a good spot for birds. Its entrance is off the Mathura road about 1km south of the zoo entrance. Birdwatching is allowed if you ask permission, but the nursery is closed at weekends and on public holidays. There is good birding at the River Yamuna within walking distance east of the fort but it is across the extremely busy ring road, so it is better to take an autorickshaw.

Birds   The zoo has nesting Indian and Little Cormorants, Indian Pond Heron, Cattle, Intermediate and Little Egrets, Black-crowned Night Heron, Painted Stork, and Black-headed Ibis. Wild Great White Pelicans are seen occasionally and have bred with the captive birds. The boating pool has ducks in spring and autumn, as well as Little Grebe, Purple Heron, White-breasted Waterhen, Common Moorhen, and Coot.
     Birds in both the fort and zoo include Yellow-footed Green Pigeon, Laughing Dove, Alexandrine Parakeet, Greater Coucal, Spotted Owlet, Green Bee-eater, Indian Grey Hornbill*, Brown-headed Barbet*, House Swift, Dusky Crag Martin, Yellow-eyed, Common, Large Grey* and Jungle* Babblers, Red-breasted Flycatcher (W), Hume's Warbler (W), Bluethroat (W), Black Redstart (W), Brown Rock-chat*, Indian Robin*, wagtails, Spanish Sparrow (W), Red Avadavat, Indian Silverbill and Scaly-breasted Munia. Flocks of Scaly-breasted Munias sometimes have individuals with greenish underparts: escaped cage-birds colour-dyed by the locals which should not be confused with the very rare Green Munia**, unlikely in Delhi. Brown Crake, Smoky Warbler (RW) and Streaked Weaver (U) have been seen. Overhead, as the day warms up, numerous Black Kites and White-backed Vultures are often joined by other raptors. In winter look for Black-shouldered and Brahminy Kites, Long-billed Vulture, Steppe Eagles, and the Black-eared race of Black Kite (sometimes treated as a separate species).

Okhla

     The River Yamuna flows southward along the eastern side of Delhi and offers excellent birding in winter and during migration when there are large numbers of waterbirds. Several areas are accessible and Okhla is arguably the best for birds, though suffering increased development. The locally distributed Striated Babbler, White-tailed Bushchat and Streaked Weaver are resident specialities here. Other stretches of the Yamuna such as those east of Delhi Zoo, at Wazirabad in the north, near the Nizamuddin Bridge (Mother Dairy) and between Raj Ghat and the railway bridge near the Inter-State Bus Terminus (ISBT) offer opportunities for good birdwatching.

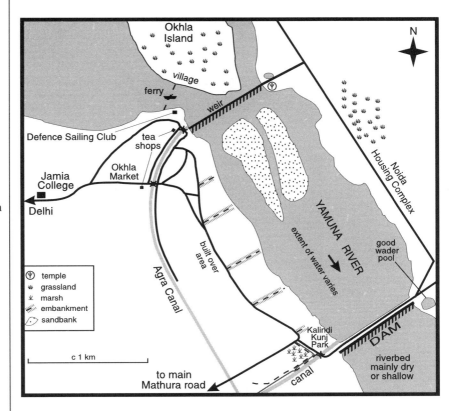

Map of Okhla

Location

Okhla is 10km southeast of Connaught Place. There are three or four sections, each meriting half a day's birding: Okhla Island; the river and fields south and west of the dam; the area east of the river; the river between the dam and Okhla Market. The number 400 bus from the eastern side of New Delhi Station terminates at Okhla Market. From there it is a short walk to the river and the Defence Sailing Club for the ferry to Okhla Island. If the taxi or auto-rickshaw driver does not know where it is, ask for the Surya Hotel, carry on past this along the main road and continue about 800m past the Jamia College. Alternatively, to explore near the dam ask for Kalindi Kunj Park – south along the main Mathura road without turning off to the Surya Hotel and next left after the Indraprastha Apollo Hospital. It may be difficult to catch a taxi or auto-rickshaw back to Delhi, so consider keeping your vehicle all morning.

Shops and tea stalls at Okhla Market sell snacks and drinks, but it is better to bring drinks with you. Bus numbers 400 and 402 are fairly frequent back to the centre of Delhi. It is also possible to get a train from New Delhi station to Okhla railway station, a 20-minute walk away.

Strategy

A morning visit is best as heat haze later can impair visibility. Birding is excellent and relatively undisturbed on Okhla island north of the weir. The locals ferry you over for a fee haggled in advance. Arrange to be picked up later. Find the boats behind the Defence Sailing Club, north of the weir. Check trees near the Sailing Club for Indian Grey Hornbill*. Common Babblers are often present. A full morning can be usefully spent exploring tracks on the island for grassland birds including Black Francolin, Striated Babbler, Yellow-bellied and Graceful Prinias, and Striated Grassbird (U).

White-tailed Stonechat is fairly common but must be distinguished from the similar Common (Asian) Stonechat. Streaked Weaver is the rarest of three weaver species that occur at Okhla and may need searching for. Look for Yellow Weaver: in summer 1993 a pair bred at Okhla, well outside its usual range. There are several places with a view of the river and banks further upstream. A telescope is useful for scanning the storks, herons, ducks and waders. White-crowned Penduline Tit, a recent split from Penduline Tit, has been seen in winter. There are huts on the island but no shops.

Depending on water level, it is sometimes possible to cross the weir to sand banks and fields on the eastern side. If this is flooded, cross by the main dam further south. Explore around the small temple and grasslands behind it for a similar range of species and open country birds such as Rufous-tailed Shrike (W) and Oriental Skylark. The rare and localised Bristled Grassbird* probably breeds in reeds near the temple in August and has also been seen in the winter.

If you have time, walk south along the western bank of the Yamuna and out along the embankments to survey the huge rafts of duck in winter. Scan for Spot-billed and Comb Ducks as well as Ruddy Shelduck (W), and Ferruginous and Red-crested Pochards (W). If you are lucky, you might come across a rarity such as Falcated Duck or Marbled Teal. There are high numbers of Black Kites, and White-rumped and Egyptian Vultures, and Eurasian Marsh Harriers worry the ducks and waders. Since the area is quite open there is potential for many of the 44 other birds of prey on the Delhi list. Of these Red-necked Falcon is occasionally seen at dusk. You may see all three species of cormorant, Oriental Darter, herons, egrets, and Painted, Open-billed, Woolly-necked and Black-necked Storks. Watch for Brown-headed Gull (W) and River Tern along the river. Black-bellied Terns are less common, though this is as likely a place as any to see this increasingly rare species, and even Indian Skimmer. The water level and the amount and whereabouts of exposed mud, fields and sandbanks varies with the seasons.

If coming by car, drive as far as the large dam next to Kalindi Kunj park and then bird the river and adjacent fields south and west of it. The river south of the dam is shallower or dry with pools that are good for waders: expect River and White-tailed (W) Lapwings, Black-tailed Godwit (W), Marsh Sandpiper (W), Little and Temminck's Stints (W) among others. Greater Painted-snipe and Grey-headed Lapwing (W) are more difficult. Another excellent area is reached by turning right 50m short of the Dam as you approach from the Kalindi Kunj side and drive south along the river for exactly 2.9km, where a small track takes you to the riverbank. Particularly good during migration in May and June when Curlew Sandpiper, Dunlin, Pied Avocet, Little and Temminck's Stints may be expected. At this time flocks of up to 100 Small Pratincoles can be seen over the river. The whole area is good for Black Ibis (often on electricity pylons), Large Grey Babbler*, larks, pipits, and wagtails. Any patches of reeds and marsh can be searched for grassland specialities, though these may be easier on Okhla Island. Watercock, and Little and Black Bitterns are uncommon and best looked for flying low over the reedbeds at dawn and dusk.

If you do not mind the emanations, check out the Okhla Sewage Works behind the Central Roads Research Institute (CRRI) on the eastern side of Mathura Road north of the Apollo Hospital.

Birds   Among other species at Okhla and various places in Delhi on the river, shore, sandbanks and fields of the Yamuna are Great White and Dalmatian Pelicans (U), Lesser Adjutant (R), Glossy Ibis (U), Eurasian Spoonbill, Greater Flamingo (RW), Bar-headed Goose (W), many species of duck, raptors including Booted and Greater Spotted Eagles (W), Eurasian Marsh Harrier (W) and Peregrine Falcon, Baillon's (W), Ruddy-breasted and Brown Crakes (U), Pheasant-tailed Jacana, waders including Avocet (W), Great Thick-knee, White-tailed Plover (W), River Lapwing, and Little and Temminck's Stints (W), Pallas's Gull (UW), Whiskered, White-winged (Black) (UW) and Caspian (U) Terns, Sand Lark, Oriental Skylark, Streak-throated and Wire-tailed Swallows, Brahminy and Asian Pied Starlings, Bank Myna*, Striated Grassbird, Zitting Cisticola, Blyth's Reed (P), Paddyfield (P) and Clamorous Reed Warblers, Bluethroat (W), Pied Bushchat, Blue Rock Thrush (UW), pipits including Richard's (W), Rosy (W) and Paddyfield, four species of wagtail including Large Pied*, Red Avadavat, Black-throated Weaver and Indian Silverbill.

Cinnamon and Yellow Bitterns, Common and Demoiselle Cranes, Slender-billed, Little and Common Gulls, Little Tern and Variable Wheatear are just some of the rarer birds that have turned up at Okhla.

Tughlaqabad

The old third city of Delhi was constructed in the 14th century and abandoned shortly afterwards. 'Cursed' by the saint Nizam-ud-din to be inhabited only by shepherds, the area within its disintegrating wall and fort has largely remained a wilderness. Tughlaqabad has habitat for birds of scrub and semi-arid areas. A half-day visit can produce interesting endemics such as Yellow-wattled Lapwing* and Rufous-fronted Prinia*, and there is a chance of difficult species including Jungle Bush Quail*, White-bellied Minivet, Blyth's Pipit (W), and Sulphur-bellied and Brooks's Leaf Warblers (W).

Map of Tughlaqabad

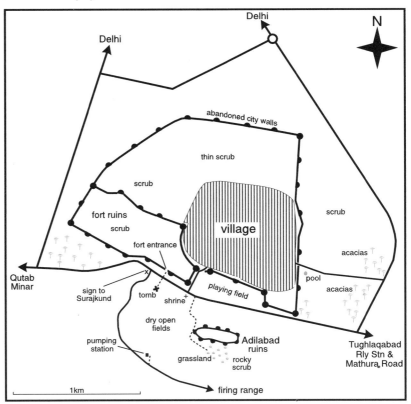

Delhi Area

Location

Tughlaqabad is on the edge of Delhi, approximately 15km, rather more south than west, from Connaught Place. Quite a large complex measuring some 2½km across it is best reached by taxi. Ask for Tughlaqabad Fort (Fort = Qila pronounced 'key-la'). Alternatively, catch a local train from New Delhi station to Tughlaqabad and an auto-rickshaw to the fort, or bus number RL 42 from Connaught Place.

Strategy

The entrance to the fort is from the road along the south side of Tughlaqabad, but a morning visit is best begun from the road east of the city walls so the sun is behind you. There is a network of small paths and tracks through the scrub, and access is unrestricted. Search the acacia woodland for Orphean and Brooks's Leaf Warblers (W). Check the foot of the fort walls for Sulphur-bellied Warbler (W) and scan cavities in the walls for Eurasian Eagle Owl. The local race, *bengalensis*, is sometimes split under the name Rock Eagle Owl*. There are several places where it is possible to cross through the walls to the ruins and scrub inside.

Fields south of the main road opposite the entrance hold pipits and larks including the uncommon and shy Singing Bushlark, which has been seen near the ruins of the Adilabad Fort. Eurasian Eagle Owl is sometimes active during the daytime at the back of Adilabad. Yellow-wattled Lapwing*, and Long-billed, Blyth's and Tawny Pipits (W) can be seen here and anywhere in open dry areas in and around Tughlaqabad. White-bellied Minivet (W?), a much sought-after species, is occasional in the acacias and scrub with scattered trees. Stay away from the army camp and firing range.

Birds

Other Tughlaqabad species: Pallid Harrier (RW), Grey Francolin, Jungle Bush Quail*, Barred Buttonquail, Eurasian Thick-knee, Sirkeer Malkoha* (U), Eurasian Wryneck (W), Spotted Owlet, Indian Bushlark*, Crested Lark, Ashy-crowned Sparrow Lark*, Small Minivet, Marshall's Iora** (U), Yellow-eyed, Common and Large Grey* Babblers, Red-breasted Flycatcher (W), Plain and Ashy* Prinias, Booted and Hume's Warblers (W), Brown Rock-chat*, Variable Wheatear (UW), Blue Rock Thrush (W), Orange-headed Ground Thrush (UP), Blyth's, Richard's (U), Tawny and Long-billed Pipits (W), Chestnut-shouldered Petronia, Red Avadavat, Indian Silverbill and White-capped Bunting (UW). Striated Scops Owl has been seen.

Other Sites

Other parks in Delhi can be worth a short visit: **Quidsea** and **Roshnara** in North (Old) Delhi and some architectural monuments such as the **Red Fort** (Lal Qila) and **Humayun's Tomb** with ornamental gardens have commoner garden species. The **Deer Park** at Hauz Khas opposite the IIT (Indian Institute of Technology) is a good spot in southwest New Delhi. Broken country around the **Qutub Minar** complex, a famous tourist spot at the southern edge of New Delhi, is recommended. Try behind the Minar in the direction of the Jawaharlal Nehru University and the area enclosed by DDA behind the statue of Lord Mahavir – Shantisthal. If you have transport, take the NH1 out of Delhi north to **Stormwater Drain No. 8**. There is good birding following the drain westwards along its bunds with over 160 species recorded. The **Bhindawas Bird Sanctuary,** an excellent wetland said by some to rival Bharatpur, is in Haryana about 2 hours drive west of Delhi via Bahadurgarh and Jhajjar. It can be difficult to find so ensure that your taxi driver knows where it is before you set off. Alternatively, it can be combined with a visit to Sultanpur Jheel. From Sultanpur continue to Farrukh Nagar where you turn right to Jhajjar. From Jhajjar take the road to Chuchakwas. At Chuchakwas take the road next to the temple; Bhindawas is 7km from there. Total driving time is 2-3 hours from Central Delhi. The road is mostly unmarked so ask directions at every stage. **Badkhal Lake,** east of Faridabad and 32km south of Delhi, harbours a wide range of waterbirds and is worth a stop if you are driving to Agra or Bharatpur and time permits.

Sultanpur Jheel

A small area of wetland, acacia woodland and open dry area attracts wintering waterfowl as well as migrants. Haryana State's only wildlife sanctuary, it has been protected as a National Park. Although less than one square mile in area Sultanpur has an impressive list of 240 species and rarities turn up regularly. It is one of the best places around Delhi for Indian Courser.

Map of
Sultanpur Jheel

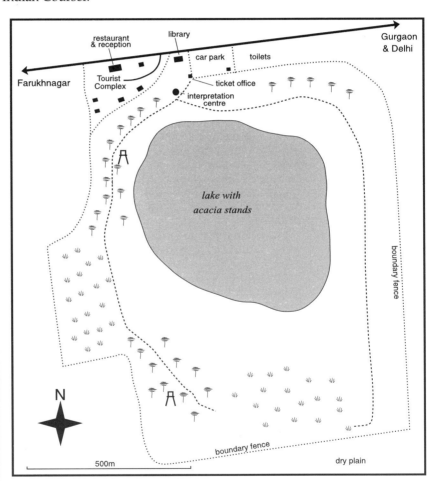

Location

Only 47km southwest of Delhi, Sultanpur can be visited for a day or half-day. The journey takes $1^1/_2$–2 hours, depending on traffic. If taking a taxi, make sure that it has a permit for Haryana State. Delhi municipal taxis are not allowed into Haryana without a permit. Hotels can help in arranging a car and driver.

A day trip by public transport would only leave the mid-day hours for birding. It is necessary to first go to Gurgaon, for which buses leave fairly frequently from the Inter-State Bus Terminus in North Delhi. These usually stop on the highway at Dhaula Kuan in South Delhi, which may be a more convenient place to board. Some buses stop at the Pahar Ganj Police Station (near New Delhi railway station). Buses from the Gurgaon bus stand to Sultanpur are not so frequent, but tempos (see section on travel) also ply the route. Sultanpur can be conveniently visited en route between Delhi and Bharatpur if travelling by car. The Sanctuary is 4km from Sultanpur Railway Station, but most trains from Delhi do not stop there. There is a small entrance fee to the park which is open daily all year round from 06.00 to dusk.

Accommodation

An overnight stay at Sultanpur is recommended if you have time. There is a hotel, restaurant and cottages run by *Haryana Tourism* (C/D). This is the only accommodation near the sanctuary and should be booked several days in advance at the Haryana Tourist Office, Chanderlok Building, 36 Janpath, New Delhi – 110 001 ☎3324911. If you just turn up a room cannot be guaranteed.

Strategy

The best time to visit Sultanpur is October to February/March as it has few species in summer. Avoid weekends and holidays as it is a popular tourist spot, although people do not normally disturb the birds and it is possible to get away from crowds. If making an afternoon trip, stay on until dusk when cranes fly in to roost from the fields where they feed during the day. They disperse before dawn. The *jheel* (lake) can be viewed from the embankments. A telescope is useful for scanning ducks and waders for rarer species such as Falcated Teal or Grey-headed Lapwing. Check the acacias for species such as Common Hawk-cuckoo, Spotted Owlet, Yellow-crowned Woodpecker, and warblers including Brooks's Leaf (W).

The level of the *jheel* varies according to the rain and the season. If the water is low, dry land south of the lake can be good for larks with Bimaculated, Greater Short-toed and Hume's Short-toed Larks sometimes in large flocks in winter. Six species of pipit including Blyth's are more or less regular. Indian Courser* and Yellow-wattled Lapwing* are two more dry land species for which it may be necessary to search the areas outside the sanctuary south and east of the boundary fence. The grassy area west of the sanctuary can turn up Eurasian Thick-knee, and Grey and Black Francolins.

During the daytime many waterbirds, including the cranes, often feed in a marshy area to the right of the road about 5km towards Farukhnagar.

Birds

The species at Sultanpur vary from year to year and depend on the rainfall during the summer monsoon, but a visit in winter should also produce many of the following: Great White and Dalmatian Pelicans, herons, egrets, Painted Stork, Asian Openbill, Woolly-necked and Black-necked Storks, Black-headed and Red-naped (R) Ibises, Spoonbill, Greater Flamingo, Bar-headed Goose, ducks including Ruddy Shelduck, Spot-billed Duck (B), Cotton Teal, and Comb Duck (U), Oriental Honey, Long-legged and White-eyed Buzzards, Imperial, Greater Spotted and Steppe Eagles, Pallid, Montagu's and Eurasian Marsh Harriers, Osprey, Merlin (R), Common, Sarus (B) and Demoiselle Cranes, Purple Swamphen, waders including Painted Snipe, Pied Avocet, Small Pratincole, White-tailed and Eurasian (U) Lapwing, Marsh Sandpiper, Common Snipe, Little and Temminck's Stints, Gull-billed Tern, Painted* and Chestnut-bellied

Sandgrouse (U), Rufous Turtle Dove (R), Plum-headed Parakeet* (U), Black-rumped Flameback, Indian Bushlark*, Oriental Skylark, Crested and Ashy-crowned Sparrow* Larks, Great Grey, Bay-backed, Long-tailed and Isabelline Shrikes, Rosy Starling (P), Large Grey Babbler*, Zitting Cisticola, Plain Prinia, Booted (U), Hume's and Greenish Warblers, Bluethroat, Black Redstart, Pied Bushchat, Variable, Isabelline and Desert Wheatears, Tree, Rosy (U), Paddyfield, Tawny and Long-billed Pipits, Baya and Black-throated Weavers, and Crested Bunting (U).

Other Wildlife   Nilgai (Blue Bull) are the most obvious mammals. You might see Small Indian Mongoose, Jackal, Indian Fox, Black-naped Hare or a Jungle Cat. The Indian Mud (or Flapshell) Turtle can sometimes be seen on the *jheel*.

Large Grey Babblers

NORTHWEST INDIA

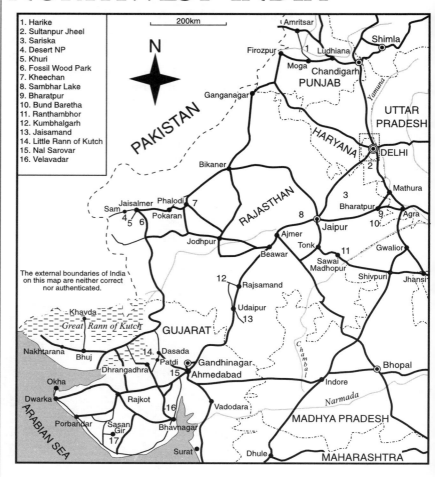

1. Harike
2. Sultanpur Jheel
3. Sariska
4. Desert NP
5. Khuri
6. Fossil Wood Park
7. Kheechan
8. Sambhar Lake
9. Bharatpur
10. Bund Baretha
11. Ranthambhor
12. Kumbhalgarh
13. Jaisamand
14. Little Rann of Kutch
15. Nal Sarovar
16. Velavadar

The external boundaries of India on this map are neither correct nor authenticated.

Map of
Northwest India

Northwest India includes the states of Rajasthan, Punjab, Haryana and Gujarat and extends from Delhi in the east to the border with Pakistan in the west. Some of the country's finest birding sites are found here. The best known is Keoladeo Ghana NP at Bharatpur in Rajasthan, with a wealth of birds that alone justifies a trip to India. A few days during the prime season will produce more than 200 species.

Many important habitats are wetlands that attract wintering waterbirds from the Palearctic as well as resident species. October to February is the best time for winter and passage migrants, happily also the dry season.

The region is relatively flat but with the deserts of the Thar in the west separated from the moister region to the east by the ancient Aravalli Range with its highest point at Mount Abu (1722m). The specialities of the Thar can be found around Jaisalmer and the Desert National Park. In the north the Punjab is predominantly agricultural, but Harike at the confluence of the Beas and Sutlej rivers has excellent birding with species such as Yellow-eyed Pigeon, White-crowned Penduline Tit and Sind Sparrow not normally found further east. The low-lying plains and salt flats of Gujarat and the Rann of Kutch are sadly underwatched and offer rich pickings to the birder willing to stray off the beaten track. Spectacular flocks of Common and Demoiselle Cranes winter here, while the lark enthusiast can find a dozen or more species to exercise his identification skills.

Bharatpur

Bharatpur (or more correctly the Keoladeo Ghana National Park as Bharatpur is the nearby town) is deservedly India's most famous bird sanctuary and the one site you must visit on a first trip to northern India. It is surely one of only a handful of places in the world where it is possible see 150 species in a single morning's birding. Bharatpur is geared up to birdwatching, birds are relatively approachable, and local people are used to the peculiarities of birders. The Sanctuary is of a manageable size (29km^2) so the whole park can be covered on foot and bicycle, and there is no danger from large mammals as at some National Parks. Bharatpur's bird list is more than 400 and five days or so in winter could produce about half that number. If you spend a month and include a few day excursions into surrounding areas, you might reach 300. The checklist on sale at the entrance has not been updated for a number of years.

The Sanctuary began as the wildfowling preserve of the Maharajah of Bharatpur, inspired after duck shoots in Britain in the last century. A suitable area of marshes already existed. The Maharajah improved and extended this for shooting by dikes, canals and trails. The stone table of duck-shooting records near the Keoladeo Temple bears witness to the huge numbers of waterfowl shot early this century, including 4,273 birds 'bagged' by Lord Linlithgow, the Viceroy, and his party on a single day in 1938. Dr. Salim Ali, the father of Indian ornithology, recognised the importance of the preserve for birds and worked for the creation of a sanctuary at the Kheoladeo Ghana. There has been no shooting since 1971.

The diversity of birds at Bharatpur is partly explained by the mixture of shallow marshy lakes (*jheels*), patches of mature woodland, scrub and dry open grassy areas. During the rainy season islands in the *jheels* are home to large breeding colonies of waterbirds.

The biggest tragedy of recent years has been the decline and probable imminent extinction of a small western population of Siberian Crane, for which Bharatpur was the wintering site. In the winter of 1997/1998 just three wild birds returned to the Keoladeo *jheels*. Efforts are still being made by the International Crane Foundation to save the species with the help of introductions, but prospects are not good.

Location

Bharatpur lies 180km due south of Delhi and together with the latter and the towns of Agra and Jaipur, forms part of the 'Golden Triangle' tourist circuit. The sanctuary is just off NH11 between Jaipur (178km) and Agra (56km). The usual itinerary is to visit the Taj Mahal at Agra, easily reached by rail from Delhi, and then continue by bus or taxi to Bharatpur with a stop at the ruined city of Fatehpur Sikri en route.

Buses from Agra to Bharatpur take about 2 hours and usually stop outside the Saras Tourist Bungalow, before the town centre and not far from the park entrance. Bharatpur (Junction) is on the main railway line from New Delhi to Mumbai (Bombay) as well as on the Agra–Jaipur line. Most trains stop at Bharatpur, but check when booking. The most convenient one from Delhi is the Frontier Mail departing New Delhi station at 08.10 and reaching Bharatpur at 10.50. From the station a cycle-rickshaw to the Sanctuary takes about 25 minutes. Auto-rickshaws are quicker but not always available. It is not possible to reserve seats at Bharatpur itself for an onward or return rail journey. This can only be done in advance from a bigger centre such as Delhi; otherwise you buy your ticket half an hour before departure and see the ticket collector on the train.

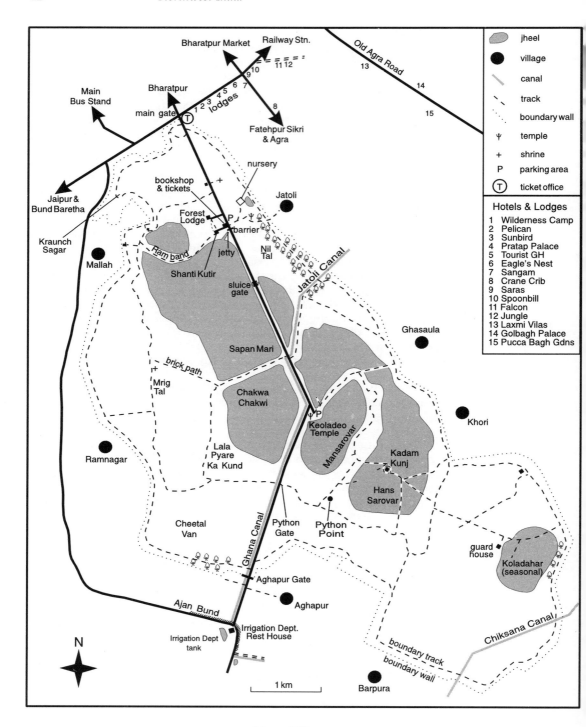

Map of Bharatpur

Buses to Delhi, Agra and Jaipur are fairly frequent from the bus stand 2km from the Park. For those wishing to continue to Ranthambhor NP it is better to take the train to Sawai Madhopur Junction (on the line to Mumbai/Bombay) rather than the bus. This journey takes 2–4 hours depending on the train.

The nearest airport to Bharatpur is at Agra, though from Delhi it would be quicker and cheaper to take a taxi from there. Indeed, if time is of the essence, you might wish to take a taxi to Bharatpur directly on landing at Delhi airport, which is also to the south of the capital.

Accommodation   The only two places to stay within the sanctuary are rather overpriced for the comfort and service offered, and both tend to be fully booked in the main season. The *Forest Lodge* (A+), run by the Ashoka Group, is for those who prefer more comfort. Reservations can be difficult and best arranged through a reputable Indian travel agent. The address is Forest Lodge, Keoladeo National Park, Bharatpur 321 001, Rajasthan ☎05664-22760 or 22722, Fax 22864. A buffet lunch and dinner are available but are not cheap. There are five double rooms at *Shanti Kutir* (B), the *FRH* run by the Forest Department. These are primarily intended for visiting officials but may be rented out if available. Reservation is through the Deputy Chief Wildlife Warden, Keoladeo NP, Bharatpur 321 001, Rajasthan ☎05644-22777. At Shanti Kutir meals have to be ordered in advance. There is a small canteen next to the Keoladeo Temple in the centre of the Park where drinks and biscuits are usually available during the daytime, every day except Tuesdays. It may be best to take water and a packed lunch or fruit with you. Staying at accommodation within the Park has the advantage that you do not have to wait for the ticket office and gate to open in the morning to start birding.

Many private lodges have sprung up along the main road to the park. The *Wilderness Camp* (C/D) charges the price of a room with all facilities to enjoy the 'exciting experience' of a night in a small tent. The *Pelican* (B/C/D/E) ☎05664-24221 is a small friendly place with clean rooms and a varied menu and plenty of experience of catering for birdwatchers as it is run by the owner of the *Tourist Lodge* (D/E), the original birders' and backpackers' favourite lodge near the market in Bharatpur (just off the map). The latter is recommended for a longer stay on a tight budget if you do not mind cycling the few extra kilometres each day. The *Sunbird* (B/C/D) is similar to the Pelican and recommended. It has a small library and is owned by a birder. The *Pratap Palace* (B/C/D) ☎05664-25144 is more upmarket with good clean rooms, the ordinary ones being better value. The *Tourist Guest House* (D/E) is passable if you need to economise and can't get one of the cheaper rooms at the Pelican. They also have a small dormitory. The *Eagle's Nest* (B/C) has a pleasant garden though the rooms are nothing special and a little overpriced. The rooms at the *Sangam* (C/D) are okay, but the location is a bit noisy, next to the main crossroads. The *Crane Crib* (C/D/E) ☎05664-24224 is quieter, being set back from the road. They offer a free pick up if you phone from the station. The mid-range *Saras Tourist Bungalow* (B/C/D/E) run by the Rajasthan Tourism is uninspiring but reasonable value with air-conditioned and ordinary rooms as well as a dormitory. A friendly and helpful retired army officer runs the *Spoonbill* (D/E) next door. Even if you are not staying here you might want to try the restaurant. The *Falcon Guest House* (C/D) ☎05664-23815 is good, has a bird logbook, and is one of the best bets in this category. The *Jungle Lodge* next door is similarly priced.

If you prefer to spend a bit more to experience the relative luxury of staying in the former royal residence of the Maharaja's uncle, try the *Laxmi Vilas Palace Hotel* (A/B) a little further away. From the park entrance gate take the road past the Saras Tourist Bungalow without turning off towards the Falcon. Turn right at the T-junction at the bottom of the road. The Laxmi Vilas is on the right after about 500m. In the same category the *Golbagh Palace* (A/B) may be worth considering. It is 500m past the Laxmi Vilas on the left inside the Moti Mahal Palace Complex. A small guesthouse is soon to be opened at the *Pucca Bagh Gardens*, on the right about 1km past the Laxmi Vilas Palace Hotel. It is set in orchards where the fruiting trees attract a lot of birds. There is a canal nearby with many ducks and waders and a dry area which supports Yellow-wattled Lapwings*. The basic lodges near the station are too far away to be worth considering.

Strategy   A stay of at least four or five days is recommended, perhaps even a week or two. On a first visit to India, Bharatpur should form the core of your itinerary.

The National Park is open from sunrise to sunset all year. Entrance fees must be paid at the main gate and tickets retained as these are checked at the barrier near Shanti Kutir. There are additional charges for bicycles, cars and cameras. There is a small interpretation centre next to this ticket office. If you stay within the sanctuary, you pay entrance fees on subsequent days at the ticket office next to the bookshop near Shanti Kutir.

The most interesting season is late October to early March when huge numbers of Palearctic migrants join resident birds. The hot season, from the end of March until the monsoon, is relatively quiet though wildlife tends to concentrate around dwindling pools making observation easier. The monsoon rains in July attract huge numbers of waterbirds that nest in the marshes until November. The heronry with breeding cormorants, Oriental Darters, egrets, Painted Storks, Asian Openbills, Black-headed Ibis and Eurasian Spoonbills can be visited by boat if the water level is sufficiently high, normally from mid-October to March. Tickets can be obtained at the Shanti Kutir ticket office. The boat jetty is nearby.

An excellent network of tracks covers the reserve. Many run along acacia-lined bunds between *jheels* and can be explored on foot or by bicycles hired at the lodges or from the main ticket office. Prices vary according to demand, condition of the bicycle and your bargaining ability. Be careful to stay on main tracks with the bicycle, otherwise the chances of a thorn in the tyre become high and you may spend most of the time pushing. Do not leave it unattended because someone may deflate your tyres as a joke.

A number of licensed cycle-rickshaws ply their trade within the sanctuary charging an official hourly rate to carry a theoretical maximum of two passengers. These can be fun, at least for your first outing or until you get your bearings. It has the added advantage of supporting the local economy. Most rickshaw-wallahs are friendly and know the larger birds as well as regular roosting sites for some specialities, particularly owls, along the main road and point them out to you. The rickshaws are restricted to the metalled road through the centre of the park, though one or two drivers offer guided hikes. If you do not want to be saddled with a bicycle, consider a cycle-rickshaw down to the temple and arrange to be picked up there at the end of the day.

There are two Electra Vans (electric buses) for hire. These can be taken round some dirt roads, but are often out of commission or booked by groups. Rates depend on the number of passengers (maximum 14). Private vehicles are only allowed as far as the Forest Lodge and Shanti Kutir.

Several 'naturalist guides' work freelance at Bharatpur, with up-to-date knowledge of breeding sites, roosting owls, nightjars and where to find other specialities. They can be contacted via the lodges, or look for customers near the ticket office, where official guiding fees are posted. They may help you 'clean up' some trickier species at the end of your stay.

If you have time, a day or half-day trip to Bund Baretha for specialities such as Great Thick-knee, Indian Skimmer, and Brown Crake should be taken. For details see below.

Birds   The following text applies to a winter visit. First explorations normally concentrate on wetlands along the main road from the barrier to the Keoladeo Temple. This is the busiest part of the sanctuary, particularly at weekends when it is popular with tourists who rarely stray further afield. The road takes you between shallow *jheels* with several points where you can divert right and left to look for waterbirds. It is possible to loop around individual *jheels* – see the map. Tree-lined dikes, or bunds, serving as pathways bound the *jheels*. Islets with clumps of acacias are used by waterbirds for nesting and as roosts throughout the year. Perhaps the best loop to begin with is the one around Mansarovar that begins by the Keoladeo temple. A few hours can be spent here. For a wider variety of habitats the best loop is probably Sapan Mari to Lala Pyare Ka Kund and the Python Gate. This will produce a good variety of water birds and dry land species including the possibility of specialities such as Brooks's Leaf and Smoky (U/R) Warblers.

The most sought-after species is the Siberian Crane, a beautiful but endangered bird almost as well known throughout India as the national symbol, the Indian Peafowl*. The cranes arrive between October and December and depart during late February or early March. One can only hope for a miracle to prevent the extinction of the tiny remnant population. Someone will tell you if they have come back and where they are. A favourite area used to be Mansarovar with best views from the road south of the temple. The Sarus Crane is a resident whose declining population also gives cause for concern. The birds usually keep in pairs or family groups dotted around the reserve though may prefer fields outside if water levels are high. About 150 Common Cranes usually winter at Bharatpur but spend much time outside the reserve. Demoiselle Cranes are rather scarce. Among the obvious waterfowl are Grey and Purple Herons alongside the ubiquitous Indian Pond Heron, or Paddybird. Little, Intermediate and Great Egrets can be found next to each other for comparison. The declining Oriental Darter is still easy to find on the *jheels*. In winter flocks of Great White Pelican may fly in to the open water; Dalmatian occurs annually and Spot-billed as a vagrant.

Bharatpur occasionally has Greater Flamingos, but rarely for long, and there are a couple of records of Lessers. Painted Storks can be found, often with Eurasian Spoonbills and Black-headed Ibis, in open shallows, resting in trees or on a grassy bank. Woolly-necked Storks are less numerous but breed. Asian Openbills are uncommon outside the breeding season when they are more regular at Bund Baretha. Glossy Ibis prefer slightly less open habitat. The magnificent Black-necked Stork is tragically declining but can still be found at Bharatpur. Its huge size means it is unlikely to be overlooked. The remaining storks are rare.

Black-crowned Night Herons are plentiful at their daytime roost in the bushes on the other side of the Ghana Canal from the temple. Black Bittern is uncommon and secretive, but there is often one in the bushes along the canal on the eastern side of the road at Sapan Mari. These two areas are also good for Yellow and Cinnamon Bitterns (U), Greater Painted-snipe and Ruddy-breasted Crake.

More than 20 species of duck have been seen at Bharatpur, with commoner winter visitors such as Ruddy Shelduck, Northern Pintail, Common Teal, Eurasian Wigeon, Garganey, Tufted Duck and Northern Shoveler alongside resident Lesser Whistling-duck and Spot-billed Duck. Cotton Pygmy-geese are easy to see, usually on the Ghana Canal next to the main road. As a rule Comb Duck are fewer, mostly near the temple or behind Shanti Kutir. Scrutiny of the open *jheels* may reveal scarcer visitors such as Red-crested and Ferruginous Pochard, or a rarity such as a Falcated or Marbled Duck. In most winters Greylag and Bar-headed Geese are present in impressive numbers. Scan thoroughly for a vagrant Greater or Lesser White-fronted Goose.

Gallinules are plentiful with White-breasted Waterhen in every ditch and bush, while Purple Swamphens gather, often in hundreds, in favourable areas of marshy grass and water hyacinth. Both Pheasant-tailed and Bronze-winged Jacanas should not take long to locate alongside the commoner Palearctic waders and also Marsh Sandpiper, Temminck's Stint, White-tailed and Red-wattled Lapwings. Grey-headed Lapwing is rare and not reported every year. Resident kingfishers are Pied, Common and White-throated, but Black-capped (normally coastal in India) occasionally turns up. Stork-billed Kingfisher is very unusual. The reserve is not as good for *Laridae* as one might expect, though you see the occasional tern, usually Whiskered, River or Black-bellied. Acacias and bushes on the bunds are good for Brown-capped Pygmy Woodpecker*, Red-throated Flycatcher, Bluethroat, and Blyth's Reed, Clamorous Reed and Dusky Warblers.

Bharatpur attracts many birds of prey including the magnificent Pallas's Fish Eagle. Eurasian Marsh Harriers regularly quarter the swamp. This is the place to hone your eagle identification skills, with Steppe, Imperial and Greater Spotted frequent, and occasional White-tailed, Bonelli's, Crested Serpent, or even Booted Eagles. At least one pair of Lesser Spotted Eagles apparently breeds. The open dry country at the southern end of the reserve around Koladahar is likely to produce Short-toed Snake Eagle and the other harriers: even Pied, unusual this far west, has turned up. Oriental Honey-buzzard prefers wooded parts of the sanctuary and sometimes breeds, while Shikra is likely to be seen in the trees along the main road. White-rumped Vulture breeds commonly in areas of scrub with scattered tall trees with Red-headed in smaller numbers. Long-billed Vulture is a less common visitor and Egyptian is more frequent outside the reserve. Eurasian Griffon is scarcer still and there are a few records of Himalayan Griffon each winter. Falcons can be difficult to locate and it may be worth asking around for known roosting sites. Peregrine and Laggar are regular in drier open areas, but the exquisite Red-necked Falcon is rare.

The Nursery is a favourite area for interesting passerines. This and the temple (remove shoes) are good for Indian Grey Hornbill*, Black-hooded Oriole, White-browed Fantail, Grey-headed Canary Flycatcher, Greenish Warbler, and Siberian Rubythroat, as well as the roosting sites of Large-tailed, Indian and Grey Nightjars. This part of the reserve is favoured by thrushes, Tickell's* and Orange-headed being common, with Scaly, Eyebrowed and Dark-throated less so. Check the pool behind the nursery for crakes and otters. White-bellied Drongo* can sometimes be found around here or in the wooded area along the main road as you head towards the main gate from the Forest Lodge. The latter is also a good place for Yellow-footed Green Pigeon early in the moring.

The track south from the Nursery to the Jatoli Canal passes through mature Kadam woodland where the spectacular Dusky Eagle Owl nests, their booming *Wo Wo wo wo-wo-wo-o-o-o* is often heard at dusk. Mottled Wood Owl* used to breed, but has been driven out by the more aggressive Duskies. They can sometimes be seen around the Aghapur Gate southwest of the reserve. The commonest nightbird is the Spotted Owlet. You often hear their chattering calls before dawn and after dusk when they perch on telegraph posts and it should not take long to find one at a roost. Brown Hawk Owl is not as regular as it was and roosting sites vary. For many years there has been a roost of Collared Scops Owl (split by some as Indian Scops Owl) in trees around the car park next to the Keoladeo Temple. Brown Fish Owl and Eurasian Eagle Owl are very rare.

Taking the first path to the right after coming in through the main entrance accesses Kraunch Sagar, at the extreme northwestern corner of the sanctuary. It is largely scrub and acacia woodland, often flooded in parts. The avifauna is typical of such woodlands with many commoner Indian species to be found including Black-rumped Flameback, shrikes, orioles, minivets, Lesser Whitethroat, Orphean Warbler (U), White-browed Fantail, Black Redstart and Olive-backed Pipit. Further south where the woodland becomes more open towards Mrig Tal look out for White-eyed Buzzard, Eurasian Thick-knee, Common Hawk Cuckoo, Sirkeer Malkoha*, Eurasian Wryneck, Yellow-crowned Woodpecker, Bay-backed Shrike, Large Grey Babbler*, and Pied Bushchat. The narrow, acacia-lined red-brick path that leads from here to Sapan Mari is where the elusive Spotted Creeper is most often sighted, though it could turn up anywhere. There have been few sightings in recent years.

Much of the southern part of Kheoladeo Ghana is a mosaic of savannah grassland with scrub, acacia woodland and intermediate habitats. Search drier, more open areas for Chestnut-bellied Sandgrouse, Red Collared Dove, Rufous-tailed Lark*, Rufous-tailed Shrike, Baya, Black-breasted* (U) and Streaked (R) Weavers, Black-headed and Red-headed Buntings and, if you are very lucky, an Indian Courser* or a Sociable Plover. The lake at Koladahar in the southern extreme of the sanctuary dries up early in the season. Here and 2km to the west can be good for Indian Courser* (U), Oriental Skylark, Crested Lark, Ashy-crowned Sparrow Lark*, Singing (U) and Indian* Bushlarks, Greater and Hume's (U) Short-toed Larks, and pipits including Long-billed, Richard's, Paddyfield, Tawny and Blyth's.

Warbler fans will find Lesser Whitethroat, *tristis* Chiffchaff and Hume's fairly widespread throughout the sanctuary. Tickell's Leaf and Smoky Warblers are specialities best looked for in the emergent vegetation along the Sapan Mari trail or near Python Point. Brooks's Leaf Warbler prefers acacias and bushes around Koladahar and Python Point. The Sapan Mari trail and the Koladahar area are perhaps the best sites for *rama* Booted Warbler.

The sanctuary environs are given over to agriculture interspersed with 'wasteland', scrub and irrigation tanks. Those staying longer may explore these for Oriental Skylark, Crested Lark, Ashy-crowned Sparrow Lark*, pipits, wagtails, Desert and Variable Wheatears, and other open country birds.

The subcontinental endemic Yellow-wattled Lapwing* is a bird of drier habitats, mostly outside the park. Walk along the boundary path and scan dry fields on the other side of the wall, notably 300m west of the main gate. Try the sports field on the right of the road a little north of the Saras Tourist Bungalow on the way to the market. Failing that explore open areas of short grass, barren ground and scrub in the general area to the south by bicycle.

The following gives an idea of the rich variety of birds one might see in winter, unless otherwise indicated (P = passage, S = summer). The list does not repeat the species mentioned in the body of the text above; species that are common and widespread are not included; those that are uncommon are marked (U) and those that are rare or vagrant are marked (R): Black-necked (R), Great Crested (U) and Little Grebes, Great, Indian and Little Cormorants, White and Black Storks (R), Black Ibis (U), Common Shelduck (U), Smew (R), Gadwall, Common Pochard, Brahminy Kite, Long-legged and Common Buzzards (R), Golden and Tawny Eagles (R), Osprey, Eurasian Hobby (U), Black (R) and Grey Francolins, Jungle Bush* and Common Quails, Barred Buttonquail, Water Rail, Baillon's and Spotted (R) Crakes, Watercock (RP), Pied Avocet, Northern and River Lapwings (U), Grey, Pacific Golden, Common Ringed (R), Little Ringed, Kentish (U) and Lesser Sand (R) Plovers, Eurasian Curlew, Black-tailed Godwit, Spotted and Common Redshanks, Common Greenshank, Green, Wood, Terek (R) and Common Sandpipers, Ruddy Turnstone (R), Pintail, Common and Jack (U) Snipes, Red Knot (R), Little Stint, Dunlin, Curlew and Broad-billed (R) Sandpipers, Ruff, Red-necked Phalarope (R), Pallas's and Brown-headed Gulls (U), Gull-billed, Caspian (R), Common (U), Black (R), White-winged (Black) (R) and Little (U) Terns, Oriental Turtle (U), Eurasian Collared and Laughing Doves, Pied and Grey-bellied* Cuckoos (S), Short-eared Owl (R), Savanna Nightjar (US), Alpine (R), House and Asian Palm Swifts, Blue-cheeked (RP), Blue-tailed (RP) and Green Bee-eaters, Indian Pitta* (S), Dusky Crag (U), Plain and Sand Martins, Barn, Wire-tailed, Streak-throated and Red-rumped Swallows, Brown Shrike (R), Eurasian Golden Oriole, Greater Racket-tailed and Spangled Drongos (R), Brahminy, Rosy (P), Common and Asian Pied Starlings, Bank Myna*, Rufous Treepie, Large Cuckooshrike (U), Scarlet and White-bellied (R) Minivets, White-eared Bulbul, Yellow-eyed, Common, Large Grey* and Jungle* Babblers, Asian Brown (R), Blue-throated (R), Tickell's Blue (U) and Verditer (U) Flycatchers, Asian Paradise-flycatcher (U), Zitting Cisticola (U), Plain and Ashy* Prinias, Cetti's Bush, Grasshopper, Paddyfield, Moustached and Desert Warblers (R), Sulphur-bellied and Golden-spectacled Warblers (U-R), Brown Rock-chat* (U), Grey Bushchat (R), Isabelline Wheatear (R), Blue Rock Thrush (R), Tree, Richard's, Rosy, Long-billed and Water (R) Pipits, Yellow, Citrine, Grey, White and White-browed* Wagtails, Purple Sunbird, Oriental White-Eye, Spanish Sparrow (U), Chestnut-shouldered Petronia, Red Avadavat, Indian Silverbill*, White-rumped, Scaly-breasted and Black-headed (U) Munias, Common Rosefinch (UP), and Grey-necked (R), White-capped (U), Reed (R) and Crested (R) Buntings.

Other Wildlife | The Kheoladeo Ghana NP has a fairly impressive list of mammals, but being walled off and surrounded by a fairly high human population there is not much influx from outside and populations of most are not high. During a few days you would see plenty of the park's ungulates: Nilgai and Sambar on the marshes, Chital and Blackbuck in drier areas. The Five-striped Palm Squirrel is ubiquitous, as in much of northern India, and both Common and Small Indian Mongoose are likely along the bunds between *jheels*. The Smooth Indian Otter is the only otter on the reserve. It may turn up on any marsh, but one of the best places is the pool behind the nursery. Jackals are fairly common and can usually be heard, if not always seen, at dusk along the main road north of the barrier. You are likely to encounter Wild Boar and Black-naped Hare, often around the Forest Lodge. Striped Hyaena, Small Indian Civet, Common Palm Civet (Toddy Cat), Jungle Cat and the extremely rare and exquisite Fishing Cat inhabit the Sanctuary in small numbers, but the best chance of seeing one is at dawn and dusk, when it is worth keeping a lookout from your balcony if you are staying within the Sanctuary. The Indian Porcupine is not uncommon and is sometimes seen crossing the road near the barrier at dusk. If you ask around, someone might be able to show you an active lair.

Bharatpur is famous for Indian Rock Pythons: a good place is the area around Python Point. They live underground in hollows often shared with Porcupines and can be found sunning themselves at midday or curled up beneath a bush. Another area where they can be seen is a little south of where the Jatoli Canal meets the boundary wall. If you have trouble finding one, consider investing in the services of a naturalist-guide for a few hours.

Bund Baretha

The only easy way to reach Bund Baretha WLS is by hiring a taxi, or preferably a jeep, for a half or full day excursion from Bharatpur. Most lodges will be happy to arrange this. The journey takes about 1½ hours. The prime attraction at the reservoir is Indian Skimmer, but there has been a lot of disturbance by fishermen so Skimmers are not always present. There are, however, other species more regular here than at Bharatpur.

The best initial viewpoint is from the dam at the northern end of the lake. There are several islands and sandbanks, the number and size depending on the water level. Scan the further islands, preferably with a telescope, for Skimmers which like to loaf there. Asian Openbill and Great Thick-knee are usually on the nearer islands and margins of the lake along with commoner waders. Great Crested Grebe (W), Comb Duck, and Osprey (W) may be visible from here, but you might have to search further up the lake or view from the Kishen Mahal, the Maharaja's palace, (4km from the dam by a fairly rough road passable by any reasonably solid vehicle, including the standard Indian Ambassador taxis). While at the dam end of the lake, check the park for Sulphur-bellied Warbler (W), Orange-headed and Tickell's Thrushes (W). Trees along the dam may produce Tickell's Leaf and Hume's Warblers (W). The small pools and canalised stream usually hold Brown Crake and sometimes Ruddy-breasted Crake and Greater Painted-snipe, best at dawn or dusk but also possible during the day. Keep an eye on the rocky ridge overlooking the western side of the lake for Dusky Crag Martin and the rarer Crag Martin (W). Raptors use thermals over the rock during mid-day. The rough track on this side of the lake is likely to turn up House Swift, Bengal Bushlark, Black Redstart (W), Brown Rock-chat* and Blue Rock Thrush (W). The latter species may also

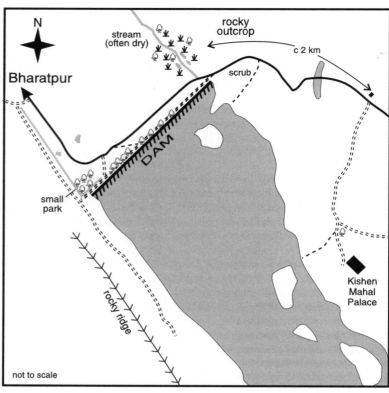

Map of
Bund Baretha

be seen on the rocky outcrop at the other end of the dam and is regular
along the road up to the Palace.

The vicinity of the palace is good for Jungle Bush Quail*, Plum-headed
Parakeet*, Tree Pipit (W), White-capped Bunting (W), and Sulphur-bellied
Warbler (W), though numbers of the latter decline by mid-February. A short
walk back down the track from the palace could produce Marshall's
Iora** (U) and White-browed Fantail. Take the track to the lake for a better
view of the Skimmers. Look for Booted Warbler (W) in the scrub below the
palace. There are plans to turn the palace into a hotel which would be a
convenient place to stay.

Other species around Bund Baretha are Eurasian Spoonbill, Booted
Eagle, Eurasian Griffon, Eurasian Thick-knee, Pintail Snipe, Whiskered (W),
Gull-billed (W) and River Terns, Chestnut-bellied Sandgrouse (U), Singing
Bushlark, Ashy-crowned Sparrow Lark*, Rufous-tailed Lark*, Oriental
Skylark, Asian Palm Swift, Citrine (W) and White-browed* Wagtails and
Red-headed Bunting (UW).

A leisurely return to Bharatpur gives time to stop at likely looking spots
for Booted and Brooks's Leaf Warblers (W), Desert Wheatear (W), Tawny,
Blyth's and Long-billed Pipits (W), Spanish Sparrow (W), and Baya, Black-
breasted* and Streaked Weavers.

Other Sites   Those travelling by car between Bharatpur and Delhi may stop at **Sonkh**,
about 15km from Bharatpur on the road to Mathura, to see the Black Ibis in
fields around here. Past Mathura is an area of small lakes and pools by the
roadside between **Chaumuha** and **Kosi**, good for waterbirds as well as
Sarus Cranes.

Most first time visitors to India visit the **Taj Mahal at Agra**, an unforgettable experience. The fastest and most comfortable train from Delhi to Agra is the Shatabdi Express that leaves New Delhi station at 06.15 and reaches Agra Cantt station just 2 hours later. There are plenty of taxis and rickshaws at the station. The town has a good selection of hotels in all categories. Most of the cheaper ones favoured by backpackers are in the Taj Ganj Bazar just south of the Taj. The birder for whom Shah Jahan's magnificent marble monument to his wife Mumtaz Mahal is not enough may find added attractions by the River Yamuna seen from the terrace behind the Taj. Here Pied Kingfishers hover over the river, River Lapwings dart along the muddy shores and a Pallas's Gull (W) or Black-bellied Tern is possible. The gardens often have Spotted Owlet, House Swift, Brown-headed Barbet* and Indian Grey Hornbill*. You may also visit the massive Fort about a mile away on the banks of the Yamuna.

The deep water reservoir of **Sur Sarovar (Keetam Lake)**, an excellent site for diving ducks, and Great White and Dalmatian Pelicans (W), is reached in about 30 minutes drive from Agra by taking NH2 towards Delhi and turning off to the right after about 20km (10km after Sikandra). The lake is reached by following this road for another 7km. Around its margins Brown Crake and Greater Painted-snipe are found and there is good scrub habitat nearby. The site is particularly valuable during droughts when other waterbodies dry up.

Fatehpur Sikri is a convenient stop en route from Agra to Bharatpur. Spend an hour or two exploring the abandoned red sandstone city inhabited by Brown Rock-chat* and Dusky Crag Martin. Buses from the Idgah Bus Stand in Agra take less than an hour. Fatehpur Sikri also has a railway station on the line from Agra to Kota and Sawai Madhopur (for Ranthambhor NP), but not on the direct line to Bharatpur. Trains leave Agra Fort station and stop at Bund Baretha station, but there is no local transport to the birding site there. If you need to leave your luggage somewhere at Fatehpur Sikri while you explore, you can do so at the Maurya Rest House not far from the bus station.

Ranthambhor

The National Park of Ranthambhor, a former maharaja's hunting preserve, offers good birding and an exceptional chance of seeing Tigers as they are relatively diurnal here. It is easily incorporated into a tour of northwest India, more or less en route from Bharatpur to Jaisalmer and the Thar Desert.

The habitat is mainly tropical dry deciduous and dry thorn forest in an area of 1334km^2. The park is centred on five lakes that attract waterbirds and mammals in the dry winter months. The scenery with steep cliffs and great expanses of jungle dotted with ruins is worth the journey in itself. In surrounding areas of semi-desert and cultivation specialities include Painted Spurfowl**, Painted Sandgrouse* and the *bengalensis* race of Eurasian Eagle Owl which is sometimes split as Rock Eagle Owl*.

Location   Ranthambhor is in Rajasthan near Sawai Madhopur Junction (SMJ), well served by the main Delhi (350km) to Mumbai/Bombay (1000km) railway. The Tourist Office at SMJ has a useful list of bus and train times to most important destinations. The Golden Temple Mail is a convenient train that leaves New Delhi Station at 08.00, stops at Bharatpur at 10.45 and arrives at SMJ at 13.15. There are several direct trains from Bharatpur (170km – 3 hours). Jaipur, with the nearest airport, is about 130km away and takes about 4^1/$_2$ hours by bus but the superfast train makes the journey in less than 2 hours.

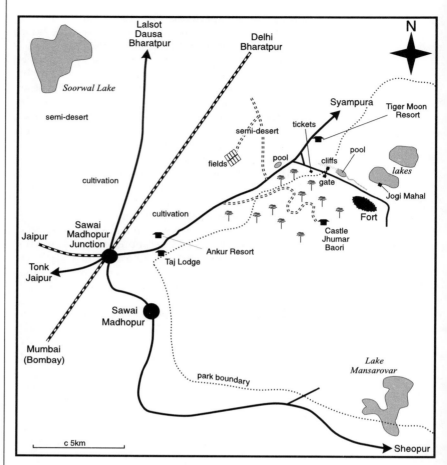

Map of
Ranthambhor

The first park entrance is about 10km northeast of SMJ and from there it is another 3km or so to the main gate at the foot of Ranthambhor Fort. Two buses a day from the railway station to the Fort leave at 07.30 and 14.30 and depart for the return journey at 10.00 and 17.00, but the timetable is somewhat elastic. Jeeps ply the route to and from the fort at more frequent though irregular intervals and can be flagged down along the road.

Accommodation

The most convenient budget accommodation is at SMJ, where there are several hotels (D/E) in the bazaar area just north of the station, e.g. *Ankur Guest House* where the son is interested in birds and may be able to show you one or two specialities. If travelling by rail and only staying for a short time, you can use the railway retiring rooms at the station. There are a number of mid-range hotels along the road towards the park. The nearest are 2km from the station: the rather overpriced *Cave Tented Camp* (B/C), the more comfortable *Ankur Resort* (C) ☎07462-20792 and the *Anurag Resort* (C) ☎07462-20451 which also has dorm beds.

The Rajasthan government-run *Castle Jhumar Baori* (B/C) is pleasant and nicely situated on a hill southwest of Ranthambhor Fort in open acacia forest, where tigers and leopards are occasionally seen, but is inconvenient without your own transport. For those who like luxury there are the *Sawai Madhopur Lodge* (aka *Taj Lodge*) ☎07462-20541 and the *Tiger Moon Resort* (reservations ☎022-6406399) with prices at around $100 per person. There is no accommodation inside the Sanctuary. The *Jogi Mahal*, formerly a popular place to stay right by one of the lakes, is now reserved for Forest Department officials only.

Map of Sawai Madhopur Junction

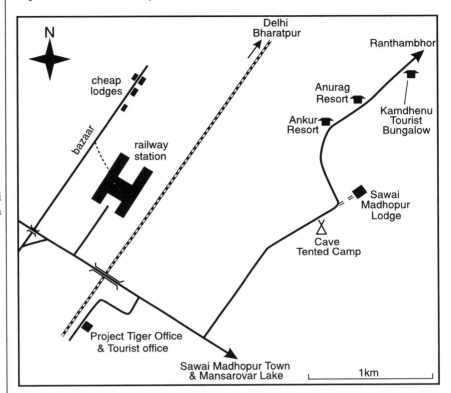

Strategy

One of the most popular National Parks in India, it is best avoided at weekends and public holidays as accommodation and jeeps can be very scarce. The park is closed from the end of June to 1 October.

Access to the park is by jeep (Gypsy) and open-topped lorry-bus (Canter) only, and due to heavy pressure from visitors, it has become necessary to regulate the number of vehicles inside the park. The system does not always work as it should. In theory seats are booked at the Tourist Office and Project Tiger Office at SMJ, which are together about 500m south of the railway station. If you follow the railway lines underneath an overpass, you soon come to the office on your left. Alternatively, cross the road bridge over the railway lines then turn immediately to the right. Booking for the afternoon trip of the same day is from 10.00 to 12.00, and for the morning trip of the following day from 18.00 to 20.00. Advance booking can be made between 10.00 and 17.00 but not during the (moveable) lunch hour. In theory bookings can be made at the RTDC hotels (Kamdhenu and Jhumar Baori), but this does not always work. A maximum of 10 Gypsies and three Canters are allowed in the Park, allocated to four routes at random. This sounds a lot, but in practice vehicles soon spread out. Since booking arrangements change regularly check immediately on arrival. Currently the first five Gypsies can be booked in advance while seats on the remainder are available on the day, on a first come first served basis. The Gypsies charge a fixed rate per trip independent of mileage, including picking up and dropping off at your hotel, and take up to five people.

Drivers are generally co-operative, if informed at the start, of your interest in birds. The Canters are accompanied by a Forest Department guide and have seats for 22 persons. The entrance, camera and guide fees are not included in the fee for the Gypsy and are payable at the ticket office at the park entrance. If you have not had time to get to the Project Tiger Office, you might get a seat in a vehicle here if there is space. Safari times are from 06.30 to 10.00 and 14.30 to 17.00 (one hour later in summer).

Birding is surprisingly good from the Gypsies, but difficult from Canters, since most tourists are only interested in larger mammals. At least one trip should be made into the reserve as this is the best way to see a good number of mammals as well as forest birds and waterbirds that frequent the lakes. The latter are good for species such as Black Stork (W), Brown Crake and Great Thick-knee not usually found at Bharatpur, as well as commoner Indian waterfowl. Riding in a jeep is one of the best ways to see quails, which seem less shy of people in vehicles. Barred Buttonquail is quite common, Jungle Bush Quail*, Yellow-legged Buttonquail and Common Quail less so.

There is plenty of good birding in and around Ranthambhor outside the park. The public is allowed on foot on the park road as far as the Fort and this can be an excellent birdwatching walk in the dry season, even during the heat of the day, as many birds are attracted to the water in the stream by the road and the relative cool of the vegetation. This is one of the best places for Painted Spurfowl*, usually spotted in the undergrowth not far from the road. The cliffs should be scanned for Eurasian (Rock) Eagle Owl at dawn and dusk. The fairly easy climb of 200m up the steps to the Fort itself is recommended for the view and for birds such as Brown Rock-chat*. The Fort is so huge that a whole day could be spent exploring it. In the middle of the day watch the sky for raptors.

A half day should be spent investigating the semi-desert and cultivation northwest of the main road from SMJ to Ranthambhor (see map). Indian Courser* and Yellow-wattled Lapwing* are two specialities that can be found here. Check small gullies with scrub for Painted Sandgrouse*. At dusk they come to the pool near the junction with the road leading up to the Fort to drink (see map). The acacia woodland on the opposite side of the road is worth exploring for White-bellied Drongo* and the scarce White-naped Woodpecker*.

Another good site 15km north of SMJ is a dam and reservoir known as **Soorwal Bunder**, surrounded by semi-desert and cultivation. This is difficult to get to without a four-wheel drive, as the dirt roads are sometimes washed away, but a jeep can be hired for half a day at the tourist office or through your hotel. The lake often holds Indian Skimmer, and in winter pelicans and other waterbirds. The dry margins of the lake are good for larks including Greater Short-toed (W), Rufous-tailed* and Ashy-crowned Sparrow Lark*. In winter Rufous-tailed Shrike can be found with its commoner congeners – try the area below the dam.

Mansarowar is another large lake about 21km southeast of SMJ on the northern side of the road to Sheopuri and Gwalior. It tends to have different birds from those at Soorwal including Little Heron, Red-crested Pochard (W) and Comb Duck with the chance of a Greater Flamingo or the near-threatened Black Ibis. The lake is most easily reached by car, but you should be able to persuade the Sheopuri bus to drop you off here.

Birds | The Park itself has a fairly long list of birds. Some of the more interesting species on jeep rides inside the Sanctuary are: Oriental Darter, cormorants, egrets and herons, Painted, Woolly-necked and Black-necked (U) Storks,

Black-headed Ibis, Eurasian Spoonbill, Cotton Pygmy-goose, Oriental Honey-buzzard, Northern Goshawk (RW), Besra (RW), Bonelli's, Steppe (W), Greater (W) and Lesser Spotted (W) Eagles, Red-headed Vulture, Black, Short-toed Snake and Crested Serpent Eagles, Osprey (W), Painted* (R) and Grey Francolins, Indian Peafowl*, Pheasant-tailed and Bronze-winged Jacanas, Greater Painted-snipe, Great Thick-knee and other waders, River and Black-bellied (R) Terns, Yellow-footed Green Pigeon, Red Collared Dove, Alexandrine (U) and Plum-headed* Parakeets, Pied (S) and Common Hawk Cuckoos, Sirkeer Malkoha* (U), Brown Fish (U), Dusky Eagle (U) and Collared Scops Owls, Stork-billed Kingfisher (U), Indian Grey Hornbill*, Eurasian Wryneck (UW), Black-rumped Flameback, Indian Pitta* (US), Wire-tailed Swallow, Southern Grey, Bay-backed and Long-tailed Shrikes, Common Woodshrike, Large and Black-headed Cuckooshrikes (U), Marshall's Iora**, Tawny-bellied and Large Grey Babblers*, Tickell's Blue Flycatcher, White-browed Fantail, Asian Paradise-flycatcher (S), Plain and Ashy* Prinias, Hume's Warbler (W), Bluethroat (W), Black Redstart (W), Blue Rock Thrush (W), Fire-capped Tit (RW), Chestnut-bellied Nuthatch, Spotted Creeper (R), Olive-backed Pipit (W), Baya and Streaked (U) Weavers, Indian Silverbill, Scaly-breasted Munia, and White-capped and Crested Buntings (W). Long-billed Vultures nest on the cliffs below the Fort. Falcated Duck has been seen.

The semi-desert west of the Park is good for harriers including Hen, Montagu's and Pallid (W), Indian Courser*, Chestnut-bellied Sandgrouse, Indian Bushlark*, Ashy-crowned Sparrow Lark*, Bimaculated Lark (W), Oriental Skylark, Southern Grey Shrike, Isabelline, Desert and Variable Wheatears (W), and Tawny, Blyth's and Long-billed Pipits (W).

The acacia woodland around Jhoomar Baori holds Plum-headed Parakeet*, Green Bee-eater, Black-rumped Flameback, Yellow-crowned Woodpecker, Bank Myna*, Large and Black-headed Cuckooshrikes, Small Minivet, Common Iora, White-browed Fantail, Lesser Whitethroat (W), Black Redstart (W) and Spotted Creeper (R).

The fields, pools and scrub around SMJ can be explored for some of the commoner lowland species as well as Barred Buttonquail, Marsh Sandpiper (W), Red Collared Dove, Wire-tailed Swallow, Rosy Starling (W), Spanish Sparrow (W), and Chestnut-shouldered Petronia.

At Soorwal Lake: Great White and Dalmatian Pelicans (W), Oriental Darter, herons, egrets, Greater Flamingo, Eurasian Spoonbill, Bar-headed Goose (W), ducks (W), Eurasian Sparrowhawk (W), waders including Pied Avocet (W), Great Thick-knee, White-tailed (W) and River Lapwings, Little and Temminck's Stints (W), Whiskered, Black-bellied and River Terns, Ashy-crowned Sparrow Lark*, Rufous-tailed*, Crested and Greater Short-toed (W) Larks, Plain Martin, Rufous-tailed Shrike (W), Desert and Variable Wheatears (W), Richard's and Tawny Pipits (W) and White-browed Wagtail*.

At Lake Mansarovar: Asian Openbill, Painted and Woolly-necked Storks, Greater Flamingo, Cotton Pygmy-goose and many species as at Soorwal.

Other species recorded include Black-crowned Night Heron, Great Bittern (RW), Ruddy Shelduck (W), Spot-billed Duck, White-rumped and Egyptian Vultures, Eurasian Curlew (W), Black-tailed Godwit (W), Spotted Redshank (W), Ruff (W), Collared Scops Owl, Spotted Owlet, Savanna Nightjar, Singing Bushlark (U), Hume's Short-toed Lark (W), Eurasian (W) and Dusky Crag Martins, Brahminy Starling, Marshall's Iora**, White-eared Bulbul, Yellow-eyed and Common Babblers, Ultramarine and Verditer Flycatchers (W), Grey-breasted, Rufous-fronted* and Jungle* Prinias, Desert

Warbler (W), *tristis* Common Chiffchaff (W), Sulphur-bellied, Brooks's Leaf and Greenish Warblers (W), Grey (W) and Stoliczka's* (R) Bushchats, *maura* Common Stonechat (W), Orange-headed Thrush (W), Tree (W) and Paddyfield Pipits, Yellow and Citrine Wagtails (W), Red Avadavat, and Red-headed and Grey-necked Buntings (W).

Other Wildlife

Ranthambhor was a success story of Project Tiger, with estimated numbers rising from just 14 in 1972 to 40 in the 1986 census. Unfortunately, poaching increased in the early 1990s and the tiger population suffered, but it had recovered to an estimated 27 individuals by 1997. If you want to see a tiger, be prepared to spend several days here and make repeated trips into the reserve, although you may be lucky and see one at the first attempt. It is hoped that problems with poachers can be resolved and that the tiger can once again live in peace in this beautiful wilderness area.

Most trips into the Park should produce commoner large animals such as Spotted Deer, Sambar, Nilgai, Wild Boar, Grey Langur, and Marsh Crocodile. Leopards, often known as Panthers in India, are probably more numerous than Tigers but just as difficult to see. The chances of encountering Chinkara, Jackal or a mongoose are somewhat better. Sloth Bear, Striped Hyaena, Indian Pangolin and some of the smaller wild cats also occur but are difficult to find.

Other Sites

There is a small population of Indian Bustard* in the grasslands of the **Sorsan Closed Area.** Take a train from Sawai Madhopur to Kota and then a taxi for the remaining 60km to Sorsan. It is possible to stay overnight with the local chief.

From Sawai Madhopur the sanctuary of **Shivpuri** (Sheopuri – 160km), good for White-bellied Minivet, is accessible in about 5 hours by taking a bus to Pali, then a ferry across the **Chambal River**, followed by a connecting bus. A boat trip on the latter river, itself a sanctuary, is said to be good for Indian Skimmer.

An alternative to Ranthambhor is the Tiger Reserve and National Park of **Sariska**, less frequently visited by birders though it has a similar avifauna and is nearer to Delhi. It is a good area for the rather scarce and localised Painted Francolin*. The nearest town and railhead is 35km away at Alwar between Delhi (170km) and Jaipur (146km). There are buses and taxis from Alwar to Sariska. Accommodation is available at the *Hotel Sariska Palace* (A) ☎0146-524247 and the RTDC *Hotel Tiger Den* (C/D) ☎0146-41342, as well as a *FRH* (E).

Jaipur Area

The Pink City of Jaipur, an important tourist destination on the classic 'Golden Triangle', is worth a visit in itself as well as being a convenient stop on the way from Bharatpur or Ranthambhor to the Thar Desert. There are a few interesting birding possibilities in the area.

Location

Jaipur is in Rajasthan on the NH8 southwest of Delhi, with buses and trains both taking about 5 hours. The train journey from Bharatpur is now faster than the 4 hours needed by bus. Trains from Sawai Madhopur Junction (Ranthambhor) take 2 hours, while the fast *Intercity* to Jodhpur takes 5 hours.

Accommodation

Because of its touristic significance there is a vast range of hotels in Jaipur.

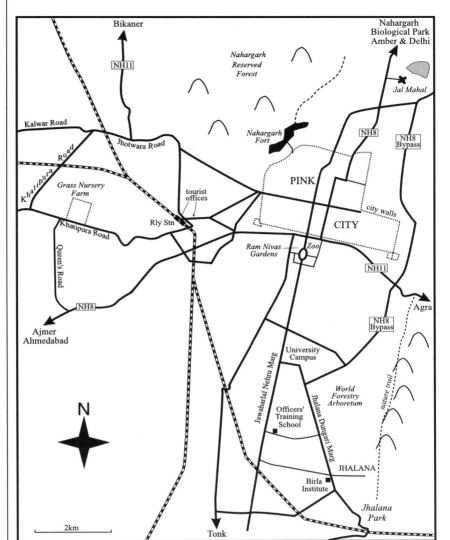

Map of Jaipur

Strategy

If you just have a couple of hours, try the **Ram Niwas Gardens** and **Zoo** which are less than 1km south of the City Palace, or the fairly large open maidan and tank at the **Jal Mahal** on the right on the way to the well-known Amber Fort.

The scarce and endangered endemic White-naped Tit** breeds around the **Nahargarh (Tiger) Fort** on a ridge to the north overlooking Jaipur. Take an auto-rickshaw to the bottom of the 2km long path that winds up to the fort. A particularly good spot for this species is a little further away at the **Nahargarh Biological Park** near Ramsagar, a small lake near Odhi: take the main road (NH8) towards Delhi. About 6km beyond Amber a dirt road leads off to the left. Follow this exploring any likely looking areas of acacia scrub.

The 60-acre **Grass Nursery Farm**, on the Khatipura Road about 6km west of Jaipur railway station, is good for the scarce and local Spotted Creeper, which breeds regularly in the Khejri (*Prosopis*) grove at the southern end of the nursery. Shikra and Indian Grey Hornbill* also breed here. The **World**

Forestry Arboretum near Jhalana is worth a visit for breeding Indian Pitta* and Asian Paradise-flycatcher. The site is 15km from Jaipur Railway Station – beyond the Officers' Training School turn left towards the badly scarred hills. The nearby Jhalana Park and Forest Dept Nursery are at the end of the Jhalana Dungari Marg (Quarry Rd). From there you can follow the 6km long nature trail to the top of the hill.

Sambhar Salt Lake

Sambhar Lake in Rajasthan is the largest salt-water lake in India and probably the most important wintering area for flamingos in the Subcontinent outside the Rann of Kutch. Both Greater and Lesser are found, fluctuating between 2,000 and 23,000. The lake's location near Jaipur means that it can be integrated into a birding tour of Rajasthan.

Sambhar was relatively unknown and rarely visited until its recent designation as a Wetland of International Importance. In years of normal rainfall the lake starts drying up by February. It is fed by ephemeral rivers and monsoon rains so the water level and number and variety of birds vary considerably from year to year. At its most extensive it covers an area of 190km^2 reaching a maximum depth of 3m during the monsoon. The lake, together with the brackish water marshes around it, hosts an abundance of waterbirds on passage and in winter with nearly 50 species recorded.

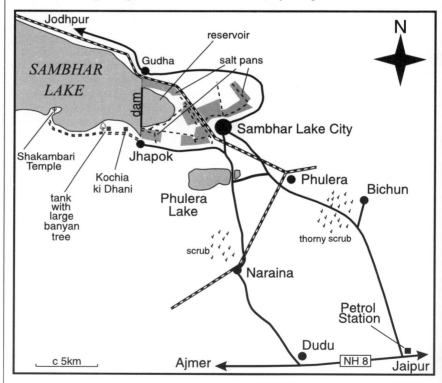

Map of Sambhar Salt Lake

Location   The lake lies west of Sambhar Lake City, 90km west of Jaipur by road. State buses take about 3 hours. From Sambhar you need a jeep to get to the lake. The locals are unaware of the importance of the lake for birds and may not know where to take you. Ask for Shakambari Temple, a major landmark 20km away, reached by driving along the dry bed of the lake or around its southern margins depending on the water level.

It is quicker and more convenient, though costlier, to hire a jeep in Jaipur. This would enable you to also bird the lakes at Phulera and Deedwana, as well as the drier areas en route to Sambhar. For assistance locally contact Mr. H. S. Sangha, B-27 Gautam Marg, Hanuman Nagar, Jaipur 302021 ☎0141-351583. He organises personalised bird trips to Sambhar by Suzuki jeep for up to three persons, as well as to other destinations in the region.

Accommodation

There are very basic lodges at Sambhar Lake City. The 17th century *Rupangarh (Rupnagar) Fort*, which has been recently converted into a heritage hotel (A), is located about 20km southwest of the lake near Kishangarh.

Strategy

The best season is late October to early March. A full day is needed for a visit to Sambhar from Jaipur. Leave early and carry enough food and drink with you. The open scrub between Naraina and Phulera Lake is good for Yellow-wattled Lapwing*. A stop at the latter lake could produce a few species not likely to be seen at Sambhar such as Painted Stork and Oriental Pratincole.

The open thorny scrub between Bichun and Sambhar Lake supports plenty of larks including Crested, Greater Short-toed (W), Bimaculated (W), Oriental Skylark, Ashy-crowned Sparrow Lark* and Indian Bushlark* as well as White-bellied Minivet (U) and Common Babbler. Desert and Variable Wheatears (W) are quite common.

Between Sambhar town and the main lake is a small freshwater tank at Kochia ki Dhani and another near the main lake, recognised by the huge banyan tree on its bund. Stop for a few minutes to scan the area and see where the flamingos are feeding. This depends on the water and salinity levels of the lake. Often they can be found near the southern shore and there is no need to go any further in search of them. Sometimes they are also seen on the main reservoir of the salt works east of the dam. A walk along the latter may afford better views of the birds.

Birds

Other notable birds to look for at the lakes are Great White Pelican (W), Bar-headed and Greylag Geese (W), Red-crested Pochard (W), Common and Demoiselle Cranes (W), Eurasian Marsh Harrier (W), Pied Avocet (W), Great Thick-knee, Eurasian Curlew (W), Black-tailed Godwit (W), Little Stint (W), Brown-headed Gull (W), and Whiskered Tern. Indian Courser*, Chestnut-bellied Sandgrouse, Tawny Pipit (W) and Lesser Whitethroat (W) also inhabit the area.

Other Sites

The **Sonkhaliya Closed Area** is one of the best places in India to see the endangered Indian Bustard* as well as Indian Courser* and Rufous-fronted Prinia*. Since the rare Stoliczka's Bushchat* and White-naped Tit** are also found here a visit may be very attractive for those who do not have time to go to Jaisalmer and the Desert National Park. It is a small reserve of some 17km^2 consisting mainly of agricultural fields, scrub and thorn forest about 30km southeast of Ajmer on the road between Nasirabad and Kekri. The threatened Lesser Florican* is found in the crop fields during the monsoon breeding season. Common (W), Demoiselle (W) and Sarus Cranes also occur. A small lake in which monsoon water accumulates is attractive for waterbirds. Arrangements to visit must be made with the DFO in Ajmer, 138km (3 hours by bus) southwest of Jaipur on the way to Jodhpur and Jaisalmer. The Forest Department Office is at Meer Shah Ali Colony about 2km from the bus stand along the road to Jaipur. There are hotels in Ajmer but the nearby, peaceful pilgrimage centre of **Pushkar** (11km to the northwest) is a more pleasant place to stay and being right on the edge of the desert offers some good birding. Specialities include Painted Francolin*, Rock Bush Quail**, Laggar Falcon, and Desert and Variable Wheatears (W). Avoid the Camel Fair in October/November that attracts huge crowds from all over the world making accommodation hard to find. From Ajmer it is a short bus ride to Pushkar. Another interesting place to stay is the village of Juniya, about 30km from Sonkhaliya towards Tonk and Ranthambhor, where there is a resort (A) consisting of individual cottages in an orchard overlooking a lake. They can organise safari trips into the surrounding area.

Thar Desert

The great expanse of Rajasthan's Thar Desert lies in the extreme west of India and stretches into Pakistan. This fascinating landscape is one of the last strongholds of the Indian Bustard* and hosts wintering MacQueen's Bustards (recently split from Houbara), whose numbers are plummeting due to excessive hunting elsewhere. The Thar is the most important site for Stoliczka's Bushchat*, a little-known endemic with a very restricted range. Other local specialities such as Cream-coloured Courser, Spotted and Black-bellied Sandgrouse, Greater Hoopoe Lark, Plain Leaf Warbler, and Trumpeter Finch are mainly winter visitors. These, together with 20 raptor species, make the prospect of a visit here very enticing.

The 'desert' is more correctly semi-desert. About half is sand dunes, the remainder sparsely vegetated with low bushes, grasses and occasional pockets of trees, populated by semi-nomadic tribesmen with their herds of sheep and goats. The Thar only became a desert some four or five thousand years ago. Over the centuries an equilibrium has become established with the vegetation kept in check by the animals and the number of animals being kept within limits by the lack of water. This equilibrium is now under threat from increasing human pressures including the building of the mammoth Indira Gandhi Canal (Rajasthan Canal). Over 3,000km^2 of the Thar have been given protection within the Desert National Park (DNP). The desert citadel of Jaisalmer, is a convenient base from which to explore the area.

Map of Jaisalmer

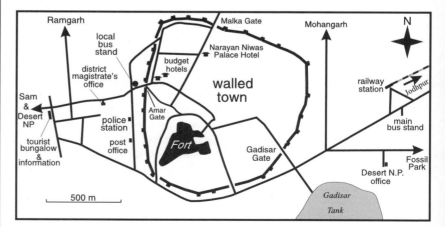

Location

Jaisalmer, the gateway to the Thar, is 290km west of Jodhpur where the nearest airport is located. Many travellers prefer to save time by using the overnight train leaving Jodhpur at 22.30 and arriving in Jaisalmer at 06.00 the following day. The daytime service leaves at 08.20 and takes 10 hours.

You can enjoy the scenery and perhaps spot your first bustard from the train. Plenty of raptors including Long-legged Buzzard (W), Tawny Eagle and Laggar Falcon can be seen perched on the telegraph poles.

The journey by road is much quicker. A very convenient bus service operates between the Tourist Bungalows in Jodhpur and Jaisalmer, leaving at 06.00 and arriving 5 hours later. The deluxe services from the main bus station are inexpensive and take 6-7 hours. You might consider travelling via Phalodi for a visit to Kheechan en route (see *Other Sites*).

From Jaisalmer there are direct buses to Mount Abu (12 hours), Barmer (3 hours), Udaipur (12 hours) and Ahmedabad (12 hours). For transport in and around town it can be useful to hire a bicycle. Otherwise, it is not difficult to find an auto-rickshaw. To visit the DNP hire a jeep as there is only one bus a day as far as Sam. Ask around, compare prices and bargain.

Accommodation   Jaisalmer is a popular tourist destination and there is a wide range of hotels. There are budget hotels inside the Amar Sagar Gate on the western edge of the walled city. The *Swastika* (E) and *Renuka* (E) are probably the friendliest. The *Moomal Tourist Bungalow* (C/D/E) ☎02992-52392 is a popular reliable choice on the western side of town beyond the walled city. The more upmarket hotels in Jaisalmer are not very good value and are often full with tour groups. The *Narayan Niwas Palace* (A) ☎02992-52753 is the most expensive. The comfortable *Gorbandh Palace* (A) ☎02992-53111 is 2km west of town on the road to Sam.

It is not permitted to overnight within the DNP itself, but there is a *Tourist Bungalow* (D/E) at Sam that can be booked at the Moomal Tourist Bungalow in Jaisalmer.

Strategy   Four or five days are the recommended minimum for a visit to the Thar, not including the time it takes to get there and back. The best season is winter, ideally late November to late January, as some wintering species leave soon after that. Daytime temperatures reach the comfortable 20°sC. It is quite cold at night so warm clothing is necessary, particularly if you use a jeep in the early morning. Rain is extremely unlikely in winter. Try not to arrive at the weekend when all the relevant offices are shut.

The first day can be spent around the town and arranging necessary permits for your visit to the DNP. Since an overnight stay in the park would save time and energy travelling, enquire whether or not this has become possible. You would need to take food, drink and a sleeping bag with you. The alternative is to stay a night or two at the Tourist Bungalow at Sam or a couple of early starts from your hotel in Jaisalmer. Two or three full days in the DNP are recommended if you want to find all the specialities. A day or half-day should be spent on a trip to the Fossil Wood Park (*Other Sites*) at Akal, 17km south of Jaisalmer.

A popular attraction is the organised camel trek through the desert. This can last from an hour to as long as several days. This may not seem of great interest to the dedicated birder, as it is almost impossible to keep a camel still enough to use binoculars for longer than a few seconds. However, as a means of transporting your gear at a slightly fast walking pace, the possibility becomes more interesting. A few years ago it was possible to see much the same bird species you would expect to see at the DNP by doing a four or five day camel trek. The trick is to walk ahead of the camel and start off along the agreed route in the morning while the camel driver breaks camp. When you tire of walking, climb onto the camel and let him do the walking for you. Make sure you do not end up in the middle of a crowd of other camel trekkers for the whole tour, as the camel drivers generally prefer to stick together. Now that camel treks are much more popular and stick to well worn routes it may be more difficult to organise a suitable itinerary, but, especially if permits for the DNP prove to be unobtainable, it might be a viable alternative. Do not be pressurised into taking a camel trek unless you are completely happy with the arrangements and know exactly where you will stay overnight.

Permits   It is less easy to obtain permits since foreigners were caught trying to cross the border illegally into Pakistan. The best way is to entrust the proceedings to a reliable local travel agent who will supply a jeep and guide for your trip into the DNP. If you make arrangements in the early morning of a normal working weekday, you should be able to obtain permits for the following day. A recommended travel agent is Rajasthan Tours ☎02992-2561 with an office just inside the Amar Gate near the Mandir Palace (Hotel). They will need your passport.

Dealing with the bureaucracy yourself is less costly but more time consuming, maybe taking two or more days, but with luck, persistence and good humour you might get the permit the day you apply. It could save time if you check the current situation at the tourist office in the Tourist Bungalow immediately on your arrival. Since the DNP lies in a sensitive border area you first need a Restricted Area Permit (RAP) from the office of the District Magistrate, between the walled town and the Tourist Bungalow (see map). Here you obtain a form to be filled out and taken to the Superintendent of Police for his signature. You then return to the District Magistrate for the RAP. The RAP is needed before you can go to the other side of town to the DNP office to obtain an entrance permit. The fee, as is usual in India, depends on the number of people, vehicles, cameras, videos, etc. you are taking into the park. If you are unsuccessful with the do-it-yourself approach, you can still try a travel agent. Either way you will probably have to have a forest guard accompany you on your trips and possibly also a police escort. Jeep hire can be arranged through Rajasthan Tours or the Tourist Bungalow.

Jaisalmer

Jaisalmer is worth the journey in itself, retaining its *1001 Arabian Nights* atmosphere. The best birding before and after red tape is the Gadisar Tank and areas of open scrub beyond it southeast of the town. The tank with its small temple is a popular tourist spot so any rickshaw driver will find it. The water level varies with the season and monsoon, but the reservoir usually harbours commoner waterfowl and waders with a chance of something rarer: Baikal Teal and Western Reef Egret (!) have been seen here. Other species to look for are Tawny, Imperial (W), Bonelli's and Short-toed Snake Eagles, Cream-coloured Courser (W), House Swift, Plain Martin, Southern Grey, Rufous-tailed (W) and Long-tailed Shrikes, Desert Lesser Whitethroat (W), Desert Warbler (W), Brown Rock-chat*, and Isabelline, Rufous-tailed, Desert and Variable Wheatears (W). A full morning at the tank may produce some sandgrouse.

Desert National Park

Concern for the Indian Bustard* and the need to preserve the desert habitat led to the designation of the DNP. A number of sections have been fenced off. This has resulted in an almost luxuriant growth of grasses with little 'desert' within the fence and Indian Bustards* often outside.

The DNP begins just past Sam Sand Dunes about 40km west of Jaisalmer.

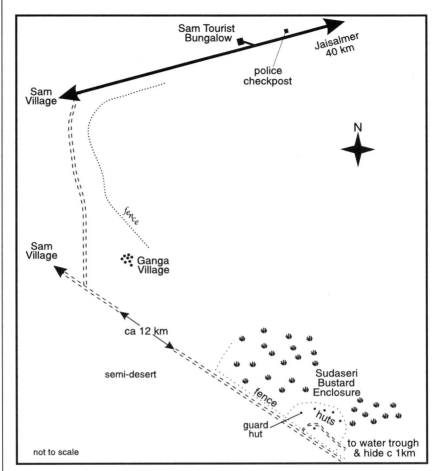

Map of Desert
National Park

At a police checkpost here you have to show your permits. The main road
from Jaisalmer is tarmac. Just past km-marker 43 at the end of a long fence
turn left onto a dirt track for about 17km to the Bustard Enclosure at
Sudaseri (Sudasary). The track is quite easy to follow though there may be
small sand-drifts. Look for Stoliczka's Bushchat* in dry open areas with
scattered bushes as well as fallow fields. Although often on the ground
they occasionally fly up to a low bush in typical bushchat fashion. It should
not be difficult to discover the commoner desert inhabitants such as Long-
legged Buzzard (W), Tawny Eagle, Pallid Harrier (W), Laggar Falcon,
Cream-coloured Courser (W), Chestnut-bellied Sandgrouse, Black-crowned
Sparrow Lark, Greater Short-toed and Bimaculated Larks (W), Rufous-
tailed Shrike (W), White-eared Bulbul, Graceful Prinia, Desert Warbler (W),
and Isabelline, Rufous-tailed, Desert and Variable Wheatears (W). You need
a little more luck or effort for Lesser Spotted, Imperial (W), Bonelli's and
Short-toed Eagles, Black-bellied (W) and Spotted (RW) Sandgrouse, Short-
eared Owl (RW), Greater Hoopoe Lark (R), Plain Leaf Warbler (RW) and
Trumpeter Finch (W).

Keep an eye open for both MacQueen's and Indian* Bustards. While the
latter is resident, the former is a winter visitor mainly from the end of
November to mid-January. If you have not seen any Indian Bustard* by the
time you reach Sudaseri, enquire about their whereabouts with the forest
guards there.

Much of the jeep track runs parallel to a water pipe. Pools of water which form wherever this leaks are worth watching for the birds they attract. Even if you are travelling by jeep it is a good idea to bird some of the route on foot. Arrange for the driver to go ahead a certain distance or catch you up after a time but it is advisable not to stray too far off the main track.

There is a small water trough and hide about 1km southeast of Sudaseri. This can be rewarding or a complete waste of time. It is probably only worth trying if you have two or three full days in the Park. A sighting of Green Avadavat** at Sudaseri in July 1993 was unusual for this region.

The most likely mammals are Chinkara, Desert Gerbil, Desert Fox and the desert form of Wild Cat. The Desert Hare found here is a subspecies of Indian or Black-naped Hare without the black nape. A good variety of reptiles have been recorded including Desert Monitor, Spiny-tailed Lizard, Sand Gecko, Fat-tailed Gecko, Common Krait, John's Earth Boa, Condanarous Sandsnake and Saw-scaled Viper.

En route to the DNP from Jaisalmer a small tank about 800m south of the road can be seen from km-marker 23 looking southwest. You should recognise the stone pavilion and small grove of trees around it. This can be a good early morning site for sandgrouse coming in to drink if there is water in the tank.

Other Sites   Southeast of Jaisalmer on the road to Barmer fossilised remains of 180 million-year-old trees are on view in the **Wood Fossil Park,** a walled area where a cage to prevent damage from overenthusiastic visitors protects each fossil. The surrounding area is quite good for birds and probably the best site in India to find wintering Plain Leaf Warbler. Look for it in acacias near the entrance, over the wall behind the park and in acacias along the road back towards Jaisalmer.

It is about 14km from Jaisalmer to the Park entrance (small fee) on the right of the road, and then 3km along a dirt road to the fossils – easiest by taxi, autorickshaw or bicycle. You could catch a Barmer bound bus and get dropped at the entrance, but it might be difficult to get one to stop for you when you want to return, though you could try hitching a lift.

Other interesting birds around the Fossil Park are: Tawny and Short-toed Snake Eagles, Chestnut-bellied Sandgrouse, Desert Lark, Black-crowned Sparrow Lark, Bay-backed and Rufous-tailed (W) Shrikes, Common Raven, Desert Lesser Whitethroat (W), Desert and Orphean Warblers (W), Rufous-tailed, Desert and Variable Wheatears (W), Tawny Pipit (W), and House Bunting. Eurasian (Rock) Eagle Owl, White-bellied Minivet and Booted Warbler (W) have been seen between Jaisalmer and the Park.

The small picturesque desert village of **Khuri**, 40km southwest of Jaisalmer, is an attractive alternative to the DNP at Sudaseri/Sam as there are direct buses taking 2 hours to Khuri. Being in a sensitive border region it is necessary to obtain permits from the District Magistrate (less hassle than those for the DNP). There are two or three slightly overpriced guesthouses (C/D). *Mama's Guest House*, run by the Singh family, organises camel treks and may be able to help with finding the Indian Bustard*.

The area around **Miajalar**, 30km southwest of Khuri, is good for Indian* and MacQueen's (W) Bustards and the resident rodent population attracts birds of prey. It might be possible to arrange an overnight here at the forest chowki.

The birder is likely to pass through **Jodhpur** en route to Jaisalmer and the Thar Desert. Given a few hours spare time you can leave your luggage at the station cloakroom and go to the Mandore Gardens at the northern edge of town. City Buses (mini-buses) run from near the railway station past the *Ghoomar Tourist Bungalow* (C/D/E) to the terminus outside the main gate of the Gardens. The Gardens have commoner garden birds. The good arid areas of acacia and euphorbia scrub to the north of the park are reached by following the main canal through the Gardens. This used to be a regular site for the very rare and localised endemic White-naped Tit** which frequented the acacias, but there are no recent records. A few good birds are still found, including both Chestnut-bellied and Painted* Sandgrouse, Dusky Crag Martin, White-bellied Minivet (U), Booted Warbler (W), Variable Wheatear (W), Brown Rock-chat*, Blue Rock Thrush (W), Tawny and Long-billed Pipits (W), and House Bunting.

Vishnoi (Bishnoi) people, who put a high value on all forms of life, inhabit the whole area around Jodhpur. The protection they afford to wild animals leads to a healthy population of Blackbuck, Chinkara (Indian Gazelle) and Nilgai. The **Gudha Vishnoi Closed Area** with good numbers of Blackbuck and a tank supporting the usual selection of waterbirds is only 25km from Jodhpur, while another good site for waterbirds is **Sardar Samand Lake** an hour's drive from Jodhpur.

For those not on a tight budget who wish to explore desert and semi-desert around Jodhpur some hotels, such as the Chandelaogarh (B) ☎0291-545873, 9 Chami Maidan, Paota "C" Rd, Jodhpur 342006, offer wildlife safaris by jeep or camel. The Chandelaogarh is a newly restored 200 year-old castle at the village of **Chandelao** 40km along the Ajmer road. Nearby lakes attract waterbirds.

One of the most spectacular avian sights of Asia can be seen at the small village of **Kheechan** (Kichan), a short detour from the route between Jodhpur and Jaisalmer, or en route if you are returning from Jaisalmer to Delhi via Bikaner. Every morning and evening between October and March, thousands of wild Demoiselle Cranes fly in to rub shoulders within a 60m x 60m fenced-off compound to feed on grain put out for them. The 'Bird's Feeding Home' has operated for many years and is run by a local voluntary organisation. The cranes feed between six and nine in the morning and again from four to six in the afternoon. The rest of the day they are in surrounding fields and by the village tanks, not too difficult to find. To find out more about the cranes, ask for Nauchi, the local teacher, who speaks English.

To get to Kheechan, you need to go to Phalodi (Pholodi), the largest town on the railway line between Jaisalmer and Jodhpur. Kheechan is just 8km east of here and the auto-rickshaw wallah will know exactly where to take you if you mention the local word *pakshi* for bird, or *kuruj* for crane. There are one or two very basic lodges at Phalodi of which the *Sharma* (E) opposite the railway station is reasonably clean. For a more comfortable stay the *Datha Ka Ravala* (C) is a new guest house at Shaitan Singh Nagar village on the main road from Phalodi about 10km north of Kheechan. Jeep and Camel safaris can be organised. Direct buses to Jodhpur leave from the bus stand not far from Phalodi railway station every hour or so and take 3 hours. Private jeep buses from the railway station do not leave before they are overfull but are a bit quicker.

A couple of village tanks at Kheechan together with nearby semi-desert scrub repay investigation. Among the birds are Black Stork (W), Laggar Falcon, Chestnut-bellied Sandgrouse, Eurasian (Rock) Eagle Owl, Greater Short-toed Lark (W) and Brown Rock-chat*.

If you have transport, stop at the **Spiny-tailed Lizard Exclosures** near the temple of **Ramdevra (Ram Deo Ra)**, en route back to Delhi via Bikaner to observe the concentration of birds of prey. Coming from Jaisalmer follow NH15 bypassing Pokaran and Ramdevra after a further 10km. Just past Ramdevra take the main road off the National Highway to the northeast towards Sirdon (Sihar), Bap and Bikaner. The three wire-fenced exclosures of 400 hectares each are about 100m to the right of the main road about 5–7km from Ramdevra and 20km before Sirdon. The healthy population of 40cm long reptiles basks in the winter sunshine, attracting raptors in search of an easy meal. Continuing on this road about 65km before Bikaner is the **Diyatra Closed Area**, another site for the Indian Bustard*. 32km before Bikaner is the 10km^2 **Gajner Wildlife Preserve**, an important wintering area for Black-bellied Sandgrouse. A part of the preserve belongs to the Gajner Palace, an upmarket hotel. There is a high entrance fee to the grounds and lake where the sandgrouse drink (telescope useful). Two-thirds of the sanctuary are, however, under the Forest Department with entrance free from the village of Golari. It should be possible to locate sandgrouse there. The area around **Lohawat**, about 30km from Phalodi on the road to Jodhpur, is good for raptors as well as having a very large population of Chinkara.

Harike

A very rich wetland off the regular birder's route is the Harike Bird Sanctuary, a shallow man-made lake on the River Sutlej below its confluence with the River Beas. Because of its huge concentrations of wintering waterfowl it is a Ramsar site. This site attracts some species not normally found elsewhere in India.

The endangered Indian Skimmer is regular and large flocks of Yellow-eyed Pigeon winter here. The localised Sind Sparrow and Sykes's Nightjar are most reliable at Harike, and the very rare Bristled Grassbird* has recently been found to breed. Rufous-vented Prinia* is a vulnerable species for which this is an important site, while White-crowned Penduline Tit, and Cetti's Bush and Moustached Warblers are sought-after winter visitors.

The variety of habitats supports a diverse avifauna with more than 140 species breeding. Its location in the intensively cultivated plains of northwestern India makes Harike an extremely important staging site for migrants to and from the Western Himalaya, Central Asia and Siberia, with passage lasting for 10 months of the year. The number of species recorded from Harike of some highly migratory groups demonstrates this: 23 ducks and geese, 31 raptors, 50 waders, 19 *Laridae,* 10 flycatchers, nine leaf warblers, 10 pipits and nine buntings. Further observation is bound to add to the 365 species recorded. Visitors are encouraged to add Harike to the usual northwest Indian birding itinerary to help demonstrate its importance for wildlife to the local populace and authorities.

Location   Harike is in the Punjab of northwest India, not far from the border with Pakistan, and can be visited directly from Delhi, on the way to Kashmir, or as part of an itinerary involving the Thar Desert to the south. The nearest big towns are Amritsar, the religious capital of the Sikhs, 60km to the north, and the textile centre of Ludhiana 100km to the east. The airport at Amritsar has Indian Airlines flights to Delhi and Srinagar in Kashmir.

Probably the best way to get to Harike is by rail and road. The fastest train, the Shatabdi Express, currently leaves New Delhi Station at 16.30 and takes about 4 hours to reach Ludhiana and another two to Amritsar. From Ludhiana you can take a bus to the town of Moga (1–2 hours) 40km to the southeast of Harike on the road to Firozpur. From Moga the regular

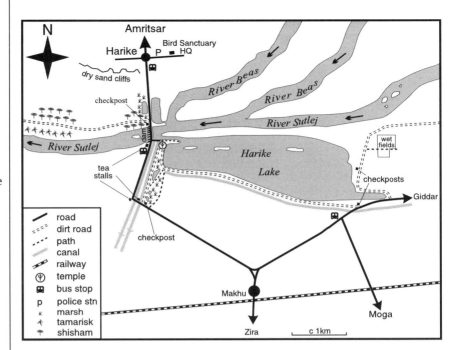

Map of Harike

Amritsar bound buses pass through Harike. The journey takes 1–1½ hours and the first bus of the morning leaves at 05.30. Get off the bus at the Nanaksar-Ishar Dham Gurdwara (Sikh Temple) at the southern end of the dam on the Sutlej River. Taxis are easily available in Moga, Ludhiana and Amritsar but hard to find in Harike. Some people might find it more convenient to take one of the overnight trains from Delhi to Amritsar and a southbound bus from there. Check locally, but the last buses usually leave Harike again at about 17.00.

Accommodation

The nearest good accommodation is in hotels at Moga and Amritsar. At Moga there are several reasonable lodges including Punjab Tourism's *Kaner Tourist Complex* (C/D) (01636-24348, near Bhugipura By-pass, on the main road to Ludhiana. Other possibilities are the slightly more expensive but less congenial *Hotel Samrat* (C/D) (01636-24343 on G.T. Rd, the more central but uninspiring *Hotel Dev* (C/D), opposite the Civil Hospital, Main Bazaar, or the basic *Hotel Pride* (D/E) at Shahid Bhagat Singh Market on G.T. Rd. At the village of Harike itself you may be allowed to stay in the double room at the Bird Sanctuary Information Centre though food is only available from the tea stalls on the main road. You could also contact Mr. Madho Singh at the Nanaksar-Ishar Dham Gurdwara (01682-52213, who might be able to arrange accommodation at the temple.

Strategy

A visit to Harike can be productive at any time, though is best for winter visitors from November to February. Two or three days could be enough, but a longer visit would give time to explore more thoroughly. September to November and March to May are good for migrants. The region has little rainfall with most from the end of June to September. Warm clothes are necessary in winter when nighttime temperatures fall to zero. Permits are not required.

Birds

Wintering Yellow-eyed Pigeon roost in trees behind the temple until about 08.00. Up to 2000 have been counted at Harike. You should find the subcontinental near-endemic Sind Sparrow in the shisham and acacia. Check the lake for Indian Cormorant, Ferruginous Pochard (W) and Greater Spotted Eagle. Continue south looking for Cinnamon, Yellow (S) and Black Bitterns, and Cetti's Bush and Moustached Warblers (W) in the marshy scrub and reeds lining the canals. Rufous-vented Prinia* skulks here but is easily located by its distinctive up and down warbling around dawn and dusk.

Retrace your steps and cross the dam, checking sandbars downstream for gulls and terns. Heuglin's, Yellow-legged and Pallas's Gulls, Caspian and Black-bellied Terns are regular, Slender-billed Gull, Common and Sandwich Terns occasional. This is the best spot to see the increasingly rare Pallas's Fish Eagle while Wallcreepers frequent the dam in winter. Do not take a camera out on the dam and make sure that police on guard understand that you are birdwatching and that your binoculars (*durbin* in the local Punjabi language) and telescope are not cameras.

In winter a small shisham wood north of the Sutlej and west of the main road is good for White-crowned Penduline Tit and Brooks's Leaf Warbler as well as Slaty-blue Flycatcher, White-throated Fantail, Grey-hooded Warbler, Scaly and Dark-throated Thrushes, Bar-tailed Treecreeper, and Olive-backed Pipit. During migration the trees teem with passerines: Red-breasted Flycatchers, Sulphur-bellied, Greenish and Western Crowned Warblers, Spanish Sparrows, and Common Rosefinches; also regular are Ultramarine Flycatcher, Grey-headed Canary Flycatcher, Asian Paradise-flycatcher and White-capped Bunting. Just north of the wood is a small pond surrounded by reeds, bullrush and bushes, the preferred habitat of the very shy Bristled Grassbird*. A pair was located here in August 1997, but it is not known whether it is present at other times of the year.

Continue west along the sandy banks of the Sutlej through tamarisk and encroaching cultivation. About 4–5km from the dam the middle density tamarisk scrub is preferred by the localised Sykes's Nightjar that roosts at the base of the low tamarisk bushes in the daytime between February and June. Sand and Crested Larks, Paddyfield, Tawny and Long-billed Pipits are common; Booted Warbler has recently bred; Rufous-tailed Shrike, Desert Warbler, and Desert Wheatear occur in winter and on passage. Keep watch overhead for migrating raptors crossing the river. Great Thick-knee occurs on the sandbanks; Small Pratincoles and River Terns are common. The area near the dry sand cliffs southwest of Harike village is good for Variable Wheatear (W) and Rufous-fronted Prinia*.

If you have a vehicle, drive down to the checkpost where the main road crosses the canal to check the marshy areas there and then to the eastern end of the lake. Just north of where the road turns south towards Moga is a good spot for Cinnamon and Black Bitterns, crakes, and Cetti's Bush and Moustached Warblers (W).

Continuing east from the junction along the paved road, turn left onto a dirt road just past the end of the lake. Before you reach the Sutlej River, fields on your right are normally wet and in winter White-tailed Lapwing, Jack Snipe and Rosy Pipit are common, while Greater Painted-snipe, Richard's and Red-throated Pipits are regular. During the monsoon Watercocks can be found in the flooded rice fields. This part of the river holds wintering and migrating ducks, waders, gulls and terns. Pacific Golden, Common Ringed and Lesser Sand Plovers, Terek and Broad-billed Sandpipers, and White-winged (Black) Tern are regular. Rarities include Collared Pratincole, Asian Dowitcher and Long-toed Stint.

During peak periods more than 20,000 ducks have been counted at Harike. Ruddy Shelduck, Northern Pintail, Common Teal, Gadwall, Eurasian Wigeon, Northern Shoveler, Common and Red-crested Pochard are among the most numerous. Most winters turn up the occasional rarity such as Common Shelduck, Falcated Duck, Greater Scaup or Smew.

Keep an eye out for raptors. Long-legged (WP) and White-eyed Buzzards, Bonelli's (W), Booted (WP), Steppe (WP), Imperial (W), Greater (W) and Lesser Spotted Eagles, Hen, Pallid and Eurasian Marsh Harriers (WP), Short-toed Snake Eagle (P), Merlin (W), Peregrine (WP), and Red-necked Falcons (U) are regular, but Brahminy Kite (R), and Pied (R) and Montagu's (P) Harriers have also been seen.

Other notable species: Black-necked Grebe (W), Oriental Darter, Black-necked Stork, Comb Duck, Oriental Pratincole (S), Sirkeer Malkoha* (R), Eurasian and Dusky Eagle Owls, Blue-cheeked Bee-eater (common August – November), Singing (S) and Bengal Bushlarks, Striated Babbler, Striated Grassbird, White-tailed Stonechat, Black-headed Munia and Red-headed Bunting (P).

White-headed Duck, European Golden Plover, Long-billed Dowitcher, Pectoral and Buff-breasted Sandpipers, Little and Mew Gulls, Black Tern, Eurasian Linnet and Corn Bunting are among the national rarities discovered at Harike.

Other Sites

The artificial wetland created by the **Pong Dam** some 110km east-northeast of Amritsar is excellent for wintering waterfowl and waders, though water levels and the exact whereabouts of birds are rather variable. Red-necked and Black-necked Grebes appear to be regular in winter.

Jaisamand

One of the rarest of India's endemic species is the White-naped Tit** with a very restricted and peculiarly disjunct range. Its main distribution is in Western India in northern Gujarat and central and southern Rajasthan. There are a handful of records from the part of its range in South India. The species has suffered a worrying decline and few birders have seen it in recent years. The small 52km² Wildlife Sanctuary of Jaisamand is one of the best places to see it and is worth a visit if you are planning a Western India itinerary.

Location

The Sanctuary and Lake of Jaisamand are 50km southeast of Udaipur in southern Rajasthan, easily reached by taxi or a state bus which leave hourly from the bus stand from 05.30. The Lake is a popular picnic spot. For long the second largest artificial lake in Asia, it was formed by damming the River Gomti in the 17th century. The entrance to the Wildlife Sanctuary is just after the 50km marker on the left of the main road, about 2km before you reach the lake. Look for an obvious gate painted in the yellow and green of the Forest Department across the entrance to a dirt road. The sanctuary is the former hunting preserve of the Maharanas of Udaipur and the locals still know it as the Game Sanctuary.

The airport at Udaipur is served by flights from Mumbai (Bombay), Delhi, Jaipur and Jodhpur and Aurangabad. Metre gauge trains from Delhi to Udaipur come via Jaipur and Ajmer taking 15-20 hours. There are also trains to Ahmedabad (9 hours).

Accommodation

Udaipur is on the tourist circuit of Rajasthan and has a good selection of hotels. These range from the luxurious *Lake Palace Hotel* (A+)

Map of Jaisamand

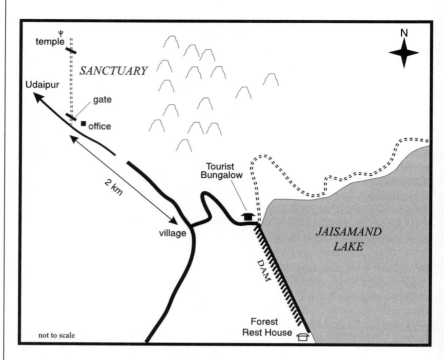

☎0294-527961, Fax 527974, on an island in Lake Pichola to a number of budget hotels. Those around Jagdish Temple are best value. If you want something different but inexpensive, try the paying guest scheme where you stay with an Indian family. Contact the Udaipur Tourist Office at the *Kajri Tourist Bungalow* about 1km north of the bus station. There is a *FRH* and a *Tourist Bungalow* right by the lake at Jaisamand, but check availability in Udaipur. A new hotel (A+) on Baba Magra Island in Jaisamand Lake is reached by a 15-minute boat ride.

Strategy

Early morning or late afternoon is best. From the sanctuary entrance follow the dirt road a little west of north through thin dry acacia woodland before bearing west below the old hunting gallery of the Maharanas. Explore paths off the main track. This acacia and thorny scrub woodland is typical habitat for White-naped Tit**. Though Ali & Ripley's Handbook states 'The occurrence of this species and *P. major* is mutually exclusive.' this is not the case here, but it is a moot point whether the spread of the Great Tit is a factor in the White-naped's decline.

The lake is relatively poor for birds at the western end, but worth a quick look. A rough road runs along its northern shore from the Dam for about 20km to the eastern end that is shallower and holds more birds.

Birds

The birdlife of Jaisamand is typical of its dry thorn forest habitat: Grey Francolin, Spotted and Laughing Doves, Rose-ringed and Plum-headed Parakeet*, Greater Coucal, Coppersmith Barbet, Dusky Crag Martin, Wire-tailed Swallow, Long-tailed Shrike, Rufous Treepie, Common Woodshrike, Small Minivet, Common Iora, Red-vented Bulbul, Jungle Babbler*, Red-breasted Flycatcher (W), Chiffchaff (W), Brown Rock-chat*, Indian Robin*, Purple Sunbird, Chestnut-shouldered Petronia and Indian Silverbill.

Other Wildlife

Among the mammals recorded are Grey Langur, Chinkara, Wild Boar,

Leopard, Jackal, Striped Hyaena, Black-naped Hare, and a few Spotted
Deer. The lake is well stocked with fish, good for the Marsh Crocodiles
which live there.

Other Sites   There is fairly good birding in **Udaipur**, particularly around the wooded
southern shore of Lake Pichola. A spare hour or two can be spent in the
Sajjan Niwas Gardens, which contain the zoo and offices of the Deputy
Chief Wildlife Warden.

Kumbhalgarh

Kumbhalgarh is associated with the magnificent fort of the Mewar rulers
in southern Rajasthan. Built in the 15th century by the Maharana Kumbha,
the fort is in the vast rocky Aravalli Hills at an altitude of 1080m. The
former game reserve west of the fort is a Wildlife Sanctuary, 578km^2 of
mixed deciduous forest and scrub. You can expect a good selection of
species including Sulphur-bellied Warbler, which is quite common in
winter. Green Avadavat** has become a major rarity for which this is one of
the few sites with recent records. White-naped Tit**, another endangered
species only seen by a few Western birders, is occasionally found. Grey
Junglefowl** are fairly common in the reserve which is at the northern limit
of the species' range.

Map of
Kumbhalgarh

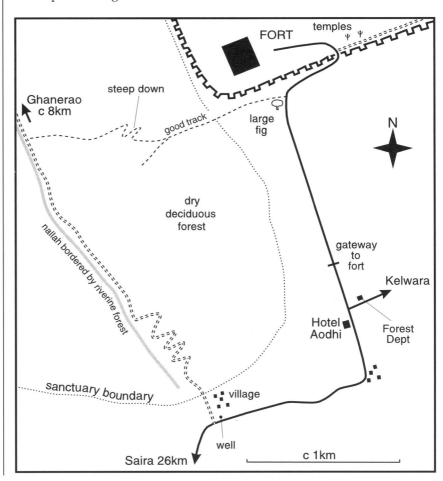

Location

Kumbhalgarh Fort is about 80km north of Udaipur, most easily reached by private transport with a journey time of 2 hours. The nearest small town is Kelwara (7km) reached by public and private buses from Udaipur in about 3 hours. From there the bus to Saira passes within 2km of the Fort.

Accommodation

The expensive *Hotel Aodhi* (A/B) ☎02954-4222, is conveniently located below the fort with comfortable rooms in a pleasant setting, best booked through the H.R.H. Hotel Group in Udaipur ☎0294-28239. If on a limited budget stay in Kelwara at the *Hotel Ratnadeep* (C/D)☎02954-4217. Within the sanctuary a *FRH* overlooks a small lake at Thandi Beri. This, along with rest houses at Roopan Mata (near Bijaipur) and Sumer, can be booked through the Deputy Chief Wildlife Warden's office at the Zoo in Udaipur ☎0294-28413. The Wildlife Sanctuary can be accessed on its north side from Ghanerao where there are more basic lodges, less convenient for the Fort.

Strategy

Kumbhalgarh has good birding in and around the fort all year. Recent sightings of Green Avadavat** have been from here and the road to Saira. Walk along the road checking fields of cane, mustard, wheat and millet. Sulphur-bellied Warblers occur along the approach road to the fort and around its base in winter. Unlike most *Phylloscopus* warblers they tend to forage on the ground and over the rocks and walls.

Look for White-naped Tit** in any patches of acacia. The outer walls of the fort have a circumference of 36km and it is possible to follow around them for a good part of the way.

To go inside the Wildlife Sanctuary proper requires permission from the Forest Department at the office near the junction of the main road with the approach road to the fort. If you stay at the Aodhi, they obtain this for you and supply a guide. A good path into the Wildlife Sanctuary leads left from just past a large banyan tree where the approach road to the fort bends right at the foot of the walls. The jeep track into the sanctuary begins near a small village along the road to Saira – see map. This follows a seasonal river where Red Spurfowl* and Grey Junglefowl** can be found.

Birds

Other species at Kumbhalgarh are Changeable Hawk Eagle, Short-toed Snake Eagle, Grey Francolin, Jungle Bush Quail*, Indian Peafowl*, Yellow-footed Green Pigeon, Alexandrine and Plum-headed* Parakeets, Jungle and Spotted Owlets, House Swift, Brown-headed Barbet*, Yellow-crowned and Brown-capped* Woodpeckers, Indian Pitta* (S), Dusky Crag Martin, Eurasian Golden Oriole, White-bellied Drongo*, Tawny-bellied* and Yellow-eyed Babblers, Tickell's Blue Flycatcher, White-browed and White-throated Fantails, Grey-breasted, Rufous-fronted*, Plain and Ashy* Prinias, Hume's Warbler (W), Brown Rock-chat*, Pied Bushchat, Blue Rock Thrush (W), Black-lored Tit*, Thick-billed Flowerpecker, Chestnut-shouldered Petronia, Baya Weaver, Indian Silverbill, Common Rosefinch (W), and White-capped (W) and Crested Buntings.

Other Wildlife

The commonest mammals are Grey Langur, Sambar, Nilgai, Striped Hyaena, Jungle Cat and Wild Boar. The Chowsingha (Four-horned Antelope), an endemic mammal at home in the hilly terrain, is unusual in having two pairs of horns. The Wolf is faring badly in many parts of the country, but there is a fairly good population at Kumbhalgarh. If you are lucky, you may catch sight of a Sloth Bear, but as always with this most dangerous of animals, it is best given a wide berth. A few Leopard, Chinkara, Ratel, Jackal and Indian Fox also inhabit the area.

Nal Sarovar

The lake of Nal Sarovar (Nalsarovar) lies in the shallow depression of a former estuary that once separated the Kathiawar Peninsula from the rest of the Subcontinent. The lake being shallow and marshy, particularly on its southern shores, is extremely attractive to waterbirds. From November to February enormous numbers of waterfowl flock here and the site is particularly important for wintering cranes. Both flamingos can be found and all three Indian pelicans frequent the lake, though Spot-billed is scarce.

Two small rivers feed the lake, but the majority of its water comes from the monsoon, and consequently its extent and depth vary enormously. At its maximum in late September the lake can cover 130km² and reach a depth of 3m. As the dry season progresses it retreats leaving swampy and muddy areas along its margins. These attract waders, while herons, flamingos and pelicans work the shallows. There are 360 islands in the lake, some important for breeding birds. The variety of birds using Nal Sarovar depends on the salinity of the water that increases markedly as the lake recedes. In years when the monsoon fails the lake sometimes dries out.

In 1969 121km² of the lake were declared a Bird Sanctuary, and have since been proposed as a Ramsar site. A core zone of 100ha should be free of human interference, but the Padhar people subsist by farming, fishing and, to some extent, by trapping birds.

Map of Nal Sarovar

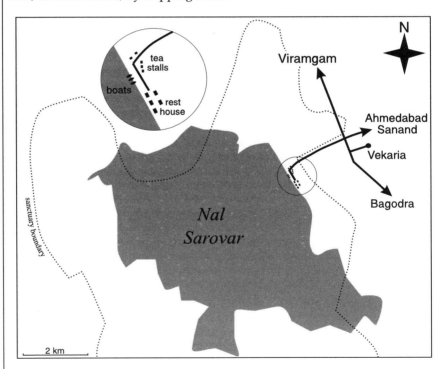

Location   Nal Sarovar is 64km southwest of Ahmedabad, the main city of the western Indian state of Gujarat. This makes it popular for day trips from the city. The lake is reached by car in 1¹/₂–2 hours via Sanand (Sanant). There are two direct buses a day leaving Ahmedabad at 07.00 and 15.00. Alternatively take one of the frequent buses to Sanand from where buses leave for Nal Sarovar at 12.15, 13.45 and 18.45. The last bus back to Sanand leaves at 18.00.

Ahmedabad has an airport with daily flights to Delhi and Mumbai (Bombay). The train journey to the former takes about 17 hours while the Mumbai run takes 9-15 hours depending on the train.

From Ahmedabad a birding itinerary could continue further into Gujarat initially either heading south to Velavadar and the Gir Forest Lion Sanctuary or west to the Little Rann of Kutch and the Marine National Park.

Accommodation

There are hotels of every conceivable category in Ahmedabad. Sanand, which is considerably nearer, only has basic lodges. The only accommodation at the lake is in a two room *Rest House* run by the Forest Department. Unfortunately, this must be booked in Gandhinagar, the administrative capital of the state, 30km northeast of Ahmedabad. The office is behind the town hall and the address is: Office of the Deputy Conservator of Forests, Nursery, G–4, Sector 17, Gandhinagar, Gujarat ☎02712-21260/21217.

Strategy

Before planning a trip to Nal Sarovar check whether there is water in the lake. Even with good rainfall the lake can be almost dry by early summer. Avoid weekends and public holidays. Peak months for wintering birds are December to February, but a visit is worthwhile at any time outside the rainy season, which normally lasts from the end of June to mid-September. The best time is early morning which means an early start if you are staying in Ahmedabad. Mid-day temperatures reach 30°C even in the cooler winter months, and there is not much shade. Bird activity picks up again late afternoon.

The lake is best explored by boat from the Rest House and tea stalls where the road reaches the lake. Hard bargaining is the order of the day; make sure that the person who punts your boat is clear about the length of time you have rented it for. The broader flat-bottomed boats are more stable, and a tripod and scope can be used if it is not too windy. The boatmen know the names and whereabouts of larger birds such as cranes, flamingos and pelicans. The locals delight in scaring flamingos and cranes resulting in constant disturbance. Try to counter this and make sure your boatman does not come too close or try to make them panic. If you can get to the larger islands, you can explore on foot. On some there are observation towers, though officially you need permission from the Forest Department to use them. Ask at the office of the Sanctuary Superintendent near the Rest House or at the Range Office in Vekaria.

Birds

Common and Demoiselle Cranes in their thousands are found in winter. The Sarus Crane is resident. Flamingos gather in mixed flocks with Lesser predominating. Of the pelicans Great White is by far the commonest, but both Dalmatian and Spot-billed occur. Storks include White, Woolly-necked, Black-necked and rather uncommonly Black. The ducks are commoner wintering species, but both Cotton Pygmy-goose and Comb Duck are resident, the latter difficult to find. A good variety of waders winter, with the occasional rarity such as Crab-plover. River and Black-bellied Terns should be looked for, though the latter seems increasingly scarce. Eurasian Marsh Harrier (W) is fairly common, and there is a good chance of Greater Spotted Eagle and other *Aquilas*.

Surrounding cultivated fields, scrub and wasteland can be productive with Laggar Falcon, Indian Courser*, Yellow-wattled Lapwing*, Rufous-tailed Shrike (W), Rosy Starling (W) and Bluethroat (W) among the attractions.

Other species include: Little Grebe, Indian and Little Cormorants, Purple Heron, egrets, Black-crowned Night Heron, Painted Stork, Asian Openbill, Black-headed, Black and Glossy Ibises, Eurasian Spoonbill, Greylag Goose (W), Lesser Whistling-duck, Ruddy Shelduck (W), Spot-billed Duck, Purple Swamphen, Pheasant-tailed and Bronze-winged Jacanas, Pied Avocet, Eurasian Thick-knee, Small Pratincole, White-tailed Lapwing (W), Kentish Plover, Black-tailed Godwit (W), Marsh, Green, Wood and Common Sandpipers (W), Little and Temminck's Stints (W), Ruff (W), Brown-headed Gull (W), Whiskered and Caspian Terns (W), Red Collared Dove, Sand Martin, Red-rumped Swallow, Southern Grey, Bay-backed, Rufous-tailed (W) and Long-tailed Shrikes, Bank Myna*, White-eared Bulbul, Common and Large Grey* Babblers, Zitting Cisticola, Graceful, Plain and Ashy* Prinias, Paddyfield Warbler (W), Lesser Whitethroat (W), Bluethroat (W), Black Redstart (W), Pied Bushchat (W), Tree (W) and Paddyfield Pipits, Yellow (W), Citrine (W) and White-browed* Wagtails, and Baya Weaver.

Other Sites **Sukhbhadar**, **Moti Moladi**, **Sayala**, **Muli** and **Thoriani** are smaller lakes that are good for birds. The latter two still tend to have water in them when the others have dried up.

Little Rann of Kutch

In western India in the state of Gujarat is a rather unusual region, the Rann of Kutch. Few birders make it this far. Yet, in spite of being at first sight a vast expanse of saltflat wilderness, the Rann is astonishingly rich in birds, particularly during winter when it is home to millions of waterfowl alongside desert birds such as bustards, sandgrouse and larks. There can't be many places where one can see eight or 10 species of the latter in a single day.

Part of the extreme west of India juts out into the sea. This region of Gujarat is the Kathiawar Peninsula, separated from land to the north by the Gulf of Kutch (or Kachchh). A large proportion of this low-lying peninsula becomes a vast swamp during the rainy season, drying out to a desert-like expanse of dry silt punctuated by lagoons and small 'islands' of vegetated ground known as *bets* (pronounced 'baits'). This is the Rann of Kutch. The larger part of it, the Great Rann, extends along the border with Pakistan and is a Restricted Area. The southeastern portion is the Little Rann, more accessible for tourists and only a few hours' drive from the city of Ahmedabad.

Those with a keen interest in mammals visit the Little Rann as the last refuge of the Khur, the Indian subspecies of Asiatic Wild Ass. The Khur maintain a fairly stable population, now they are protected within the Indian Wild Ass Sanctuary, which covers 4950km² of the Rann, one of the largest protected areas in India.

Location The Little Rann lies 100km west of Ahmedabad and Gandhinagar, the chief cities of Gujarat. The nearest airport is at Ahmedabad which is also connected by rail to most major destinations. Most visitors access the Little Rann from the small towns of Zainabad or Dhrangadhra, both reached by bus from Ahmedabad with a change at Viramgam. There are direct buses from Zainabad to Rajkot to the south. If you have booked accommodation at Camp Zainabad, they can arrange for transport from Ahmedabad (2 hours). The local railways are mainly used for transporting salt rather than people.

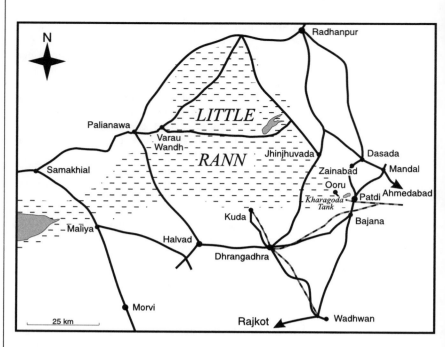

Map of Little
Rann of Kutch

Accommodation

    The visitor to the Little Rann will probably come via Ahmedabad, a good
place to halt and make arrangements, as the best base for exploring the
Rann is provided by Desert Coursers. Their head office is at 1 Kinner Apts,
opposite Vijay Park, near Municipal Market, Ahmedabad 380 009 ☎079-
448699. Desert Coursers run *Camp Zainabad* on the eastern edge of the Little
Rann about 10km west of Dasada. It is best to make a prior reservation
with the Ahmedabad office, but it is possible to turn up at Zainabad where
accommodation is in cosy two-bedded thatched huts complete with private
facilities. There are rates to suit most pockets with reductions for students.
The 'Luxury Arrangement' includes food, accommodation, permits and
guided tours by jeep. Camel and jeep safaris lasting up to several days can
also be arranged. The address is Desert Coursers, Camp Zainabad, Via
Dasada, Gujarat 382 751 ☎02757-33322. Zainabad has a bird list totalling
over 360 species. It is open from 1 October to April.

    There is basic accommodation in one or two cheap lodges at Patdi
(Patadi) where the *Gaby Girnar Lodge* and *Joshi Lodge* have been recom-
mended for lodging and food respectively. At Dhrangadhra there is a basic
FRH under the jurisdiction of the Superintendent, Wild Ass Sanctuary,
Halvad Rd, Dhrangadhra 363 310, Gujarat, ☎23716, from whom you need
permission if you wish to enter the Sanctuary. If you are staying at Camp
Zainabad, this is arranged for you. There is a basic *FRH* at Adesar.

    If you bring your own jeep (sometimes available at Dhrangadhra), you
could camp in the Rann, provided you bring tents. Do, however, beware
of scorpions.

    Tourism assistance locally is provided by Mr. Devji Dhamecha, 'Dev
Krupa', Gin Plot, Dhrangadhra 363310 ☎23160.

Strategy

    The major problem is that the terrain is extremely treacherous due to the
disorienting lack of landmarks and ever-present danger of sinking through
dry surface mud into soft ooze beneath. For the unwary it is very easy to
get lost and/or stuck. A local guide and a camel or four-wheel drive vehicle

are indispensable. Exploring the Rann is only practicable during the dry winter season with the best months for wintering birds being from November to February, though the area is interesting for migrants during October/November and March. A minimum of three or four days is recommended. Explorations by jeep should concentrate not only on the open expanses of the Rann itself but also give time to explore some of the *bets* on foot. Examine the wetlands with huge gatherings of cranes, flamingos, pelicans, herons, ducks and waders. One of the most important habitats is the interzonal vegetation at the edge of the Rann, where acacias, toothbrush trees and caper bushes have often given way to plantations of mesquite and cotton separated by hedges, but there is still enough habitat to shelter a variety of interesting passerines. Stoliczka's Bushchat* has been seen at the edge of a cotton field here.

Birds   Large numbers of Demoiselles and even more Common Cranes winter in the Rann. Sarus Crane is a breeding resident. Great White is the most numerous pelican, but Dalmatian and Spot-billed are also present. Both flamingos mix freely in winter with Lesser remaining to breed in the Little Rann. Painted, Openbill, Woolly-necked, White (W), Black (UW) and Black-necked (U) Storks are found. Most common wintering duck are here together with resident Lesser Whistling-duck, and Spot-billed and Comb Ducks (U). Marbled Teal has been seen. Waders are well represented with Collared (UW), Oriental (U) and Small Pratincoles, White-tailed (UW), Sociable (RW) and Yellow-wattled* Lapwings of particular note. Indian Skimmer is scarce. The village sewage ponds at Patdi are a paradise for the commoner wintering waders as they are exceedingly approachable, and rarities, such as Long-billed Plover, occasionally turn up.

On the vast plains and mudflats numerous raptors include Long-legged, Common (UW) and White-eyed Buzzards, Bonelli's (U), Imperial (UW), Tawny, Steppe (W), Greater Spotted, Lesser Spotted (U), Booted (UW) and Short-toed Snake Eagles, six species of vulture, Pallid and Montagu's Harriers (W), Merlin (R), and Red-necked Falcon. The flats have Cream-coloured (W) and Indian* Coursers, and Chestnut-bellied and Spotted (W) Sandgrouse. Look for MacQueen's Bustard, an extremely shy visitor, from the beginning of October to the beginning of March, in open areas, the *bets* and the edges of cotton fields and mesquite. Lesser Florican* is scarce, though Gujarat is its chief stronghold with birds nesting in the grasslands during the monsoon, usually beginning in July. The males become more obvious then due to spectacular display jumps which may be seen for two or three months.

The Rann is good for larks with 13 species on the Camp Zainabad list: Singing and Indian* Bushlarks (U), Ashy-crowned* and Black-crowned (R) Sparrow Larks, Rufous-tailed*, Greater Hoopoe (U), Greater Short-toed, Sand (R), Bimaculated (UW), Crested and Sykes's** Larks (U) and Oriental Skylark. Lesser Short-toed Lark should be looked for in winter and a complete description and, if possible, photographs taken. The only records from India do not rule out Asian Short-toed Lark. Larks are found in fields around the edges as well as on the open Rann itself. At night they shelter in wheel ruts and imprints of the Khurs' hooves.

Other birds of the area include: Rain, Jungle Bush* and Rock Bush** Quails, Small (U), Yellow-legged (U) and Barred Buttonquails, Pied Cuckoo (S), Sirkeer Malkoha* (U), Blue-cheeked Bee-eater (S), European Roller (P), Eagle and Short-eared (UW) Owls, Grey (U), Sykes's (U), Indian and Savanna (U) Nightjars, Wryneck (UW), Plain (U), Crag (UW) and Dusky Crag (U) Martins, Wire-tailed Swallow, Southern Grey, Bay-backed and Rufous-tailed (W) Shrikes, Rosy Starling (W), Common Raven (U), Large Grey Babbler*, Red-breasted (W) and Asian Paradise (R) Flycatchers, Grey-breasted (U), Rufous-fronted* (U), Ashy*, Graceful and Jungle* (U) Prinias, Blyth's Reed, Booted, Orphean, Desert (U) and Sulphur-bellied Warblers (W), Greater (P) and Lesser Whitethroat (W), Rufous-tailed Scrub Robin (UP), Bluethroat (W), Brown Rock-chat* (U), Pied Bushchat, Isabelline, Desert and Variable Wheatears (W), Blue-headed Rock Thrush (RP), Tawny and Long-billed (U) Pipits (W), Chestnut-shouldered Petronia, Baya and Streaked (U) Weavers, and Black-headed (UW), Grey-necked (UW) and House (U) Buntings. Ortolan Bunting, a rarity on the subcontinent, has also been seen here. A Hume's Wheatear photographed here in 1996 was only the second record for India.

Other Wildlife

The most sought-after mammal of the Rann is the handsome Khur. They tend to keep in herds and spend the day on the open mudflats and are fairly easy to find. Somewhat unusually for such a large animal they are more approachable on foot and are put to flight more quickly by a vehicle. They can reach speeds of 80 kph.

Other inhabitants of the Rann include Nilgai, Chinkara, Jackal, both Indian and Red Foxes, Striped Hyaena, Wolf, Jungle Cat, Desert Cat, Common Indian Mongoose, Small Indian Mongoose, Indian Hare and Desert Gerbil. Spiny-tailed Lizards are common.

Other Sites

The **Great Rann of Kutch** has huge nesting colonies of Greater Flamingos. Unfortunately, their breeding is irregular and dependent on the water level being exactly right. They nest between September and April or not at all. This is a Restricted Area for which permission is rarely granted, and reaching the site entails travelling through miles of mud, so trying to find the right place at the right time becomes a nightmare.

An excellent site in the **Banni Grasslands** of the northern Kutch is **Chhari Dhand,** about 15km northeast of Nakhtarana (55km west of Bhuj). A dhand is a depression and in years when this fills with water the area is crawling with birds. Raptors are particularly numerous with Steppe (W) and Imperial Eagles, Cinereous Vulture, Eurasian Griffon, and Laggar and Saker regular. Both Tawny and Bonelli's Eagles breed, while Red-necked Falcon is a particular speciality. Merlin and Red Kite have been recorded – rare in India. The lake hosts many waterbirds including pelicans and flamingos. Following a good monsoon the Eurasian Marsh Harrier roost may number 100. Unfortunately, in dry years which average three out of five, the Dhand is just a dustbowl. In winter Grey Hypocolius are fairly easy to see in scrub jungle near **Fulay** (Phulai) on the way to Chhari Dhand from Nakhtarana via Motivirani. They are partial to berries of *Salvadora persica,* known as the Toothbrush Tree. Nearby, at **Mata No Madh,** is a small temple grove where the rare and localised White-naped Tit** is regular and the Hypocolius are also sometimes seen. **Please note that permits to visit the Great Rann and the area around Chhari Dhand must be obtained from the office of the Deputy Commissioner in Bhuj.**

Those proceeding north from the Kutch to Jaisalmer and the Thar Desert should take the main road from **Bhuj** to **Barmer** which is excellent for raptors, particularly in the border area between Gujarat and Rajasthan. In winter look for Saker as well as Red-capped Shahin (*babylonicus* race of Peregrine Falcon, sometimes split as a race of Barbary Falcon). It is also occasionally seen around **Khavda**.

The town of **Rajkot** south of the Little Rann is a good place to find the rather sporadically distributed Sykes's Lark**. The best site is the Aji Dam (no.5), a lake where the species appears in good numbers on the dry surrounds throughout the year. To find the dam, take a bus to the zoo and walk through to the other side. Demoiselle and Common Cranes roost and many other waterbirds are present.

Beyt Dwarka (Okha Island), in the mouth of the Gulf of Kutch at the western tip of the Saurashtra Peninsula, is excellent for Crab-plover. There are a few basic lodges in Okha, a small port on the mainland 30km north of Dwarka. Both buses and trains connect the port with Dwarka and Rajkot. A ferry plies from the port to the island every few minutes. Crab-plovers can be found in good numbers on the northeastern side of the island which is also good for migrants. On the mainland the salt pans north of the port are good for Greater and Lesser Flamingo, the fish drying area attracts gulls, and many waders can be found in wetlands around the town. Saunders's Tern and Great Knot have been seen in April. If you would like to explore the area and visit the islands of the nearby **Marine National Park,** you must seek permission and assistance from the Park Director in Jamnagar. While in Jamnagar the **Khijadiya Wildlife Sanctuary** just 6km to the east is worth exploring for thousands of wintering Common and Demoiselle Cranes as well as other waterbirds including both flamingos, ducks, waders and Indian Skimmer.

The proposed **Lala Bustard Sanctuary** in the Abdasa *taluka* of the Kutch district has a small population of Indian Bustard*. The adjacent grasslands at Bara, Bilta, Tera, Prajau, Sindrodi and Vanku have small numbers of Lesser Florican* (S) and MacQueen's Bustard (W), as well as mammals such as Chinkara and Wolf. Pingleshwar, 15km from Lala, is important for Olive Ridley Turtles.

Velavadar

This national park of 34km² was created to protect Blackbuck. A huge harrier roost forms in winter, and Stoliczka's Bushchat* can be seen. Velavadar is one of the best sites for Lesser Florican* during August to September. The most important habitat is the savannah grasslands, but there is a large area of mesquite and dry deciduous scrub. Velavadar is an essential refuge for one of the few remaining populations of wolves in India.

Map of Velavadar

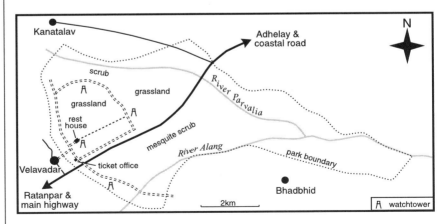

Location

Velavadar lies inland from the Gulf of Khambhat (Cambay) on the Arabian Sea, about 30km north of Bhavnagar (but 64km by road). The usual route is from the main highway between Bhavnagar and

Ahmedabad, where the NP is signposted at around km-marker 155. From here Velavadar is 22km east, although the route is not well signposted and at times appears to double back on itself. The road runs through the middle of the park with grasslands on its northern side and scrub to the south. It is possible to continue towards Adhelay to meet the main north-south coastal road to return to Bhavnagar – a route not shown on all maps.

There are three buses to Velavadar from Bhavnagar each afternoon with a journey time of 2–2¹/₂ hours. The last leaves at 17.00. When stating your destination specify Velavadar-Bhal as there is more than one Velavadar in the area. Buses return in the morning at 06.30, 09.00 and 09.30.

Accommodation

There is a simple *Lodge* (E) run by the Forest Department at Velavadar. Food is available if booked in advance with the ACF, Forest Department, Bhavnagar Division, Multi-storey Building (next to the bus stand), Bhavnagar, Gujarat. In the dry season water can be in short supply so it should be used sparingly. There are plenty of hotels in Bhavnagar.

Strategy

The park is closed from the end of June until September or October. The harriers arrive in October with peak numbers in January; most have left by mid- to late February.

Pay modest entrance and guiding fees at the park gates and walk or drive around the dirt roads through the grasslands, although some may be impassable after heavy rain. One or two watch-towers and the lodge itself give good views over the long grass. During the monsoon breeding season three or four male Lesser Florican* can be seen displaying from the lodge. In front of the building Blackbuck often come to drink, particularly in the early morning.

The dirt track past the lodge can be followed in a circle. Stoliczka's Bushchat* occurs in open scrub, particularly on the northern side of this loop. This localised endemic can also be found by following the road towards Adhelay then turning right onto the main coastal road towards Bhavnagar. Continue past the first set of salt pans and search for the Bushchat* in the scrub on the left.

An overnight stay is recommended to see the harrier roost at dusk, longer if you wish to look for wolves.

Birds

A peak count of 2000 harriers was made in January 1993, the dominant species being Montagu's. Pallid and Eurasian Marsh Harriers are less numerous and Hen Harriers relatively scarce. Among other raptors are Black-shouldered Kite, Shikra and Short-toed Snake Eagle. The grasslands have good numbers of Common Crane in winter, as well as Ashy-crowned Sparrow Lark*, Rufous-tailed* and Crested Larks, Southern Grey and Rufous-tailed (W) Shrikes, and Desert and Variable Wheatears (W). Eurasian (Rock*) Eagle Owl sometimes hunts here during daylight.

The mesquite scrub can be explored for commoner species. The River Alang runs through the southern edge of the reserve about 5km from the lodge and may be worth exploring for waders. Cranes often roost on the mud-banks in winter.

Other Wildlife

Velavadar has the highest concentration of Blackbuck in India with around 2000 individuals. They are impossible to miss! The Wolves are much more difficult to see. They are smaller and leaner than their northern relatives, very shy and largely nocturnal/crepuscular. There are about

12 to 15 in the Park and many have their lairs along the Alang River. Other mammals in the reserve are: Nilgai, Jackal, Bengal Fox, Black-naped Hare, Indian Desert Gerbil, Jungle Cat, Small and Common Indian Mongoose.

Painted Sandgrouse

Other Sites   Lagoons, ponds and salt pans between **Bhavnagar** and the New Port (6km) form an excellent wetland complex, good for flamingos, waders, gulls, and terns. **Victoria Park** on the edge of Bhavnagar has good mixed woodland and scrub. The lakes at **Bhor Talao** in Bhavnagar and **Khodiyar Temple** between the town and Vallabhipur may be worth a visit.

The **Gir National Park** in southern Gujarat is the last refuge of Asiatic Lion and can also be good for birding. Some 300 species have been recorded, but there are few not likely to be seen elsewhere. Black Ibis, Woolly-necked Stork, Changeable Hawk, Bonelli's and Crested Serpent Eagles, Rock Bush Quail**, Painted Sandgrouse*, Crested Tree Swift, Greater Racket-tailed Drongo, Black-headed Cuckooshrike and Asian Paradise-flycatcher are present. The accommodation and entrance to the park is at Sasan Gir (200km southwest of Bhavnagar by road), reached by bus or train. Here the choice is between the Taj Group's *Gir Lodge* (A), the privately owned *Maneland Lodge* (A) and the government run *Sinh Sadan Forest Lodge* (C/D/E). The nearest big town is Junagadh 60km to the northwest. The park is closed from mid-May to mid-October. Some good birding can be had by following along the river which runs behind the lodges at Sasan Gir.

NORTH INDIA

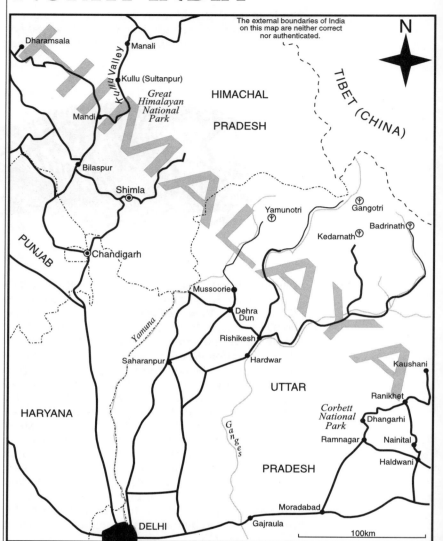

The external boundaries of India on this map are neither correct nor authenticated.

Map of North India

The Western Himalaya, with its foothills and the terai north and northeast of Delhi, offers some excellent birding. The major sites are within Uttar Pradesh and Himachal Pradesh states and reached fairly easily from Delhi. For a first time visitor Corbett NP and Nainital are recommended. There are many other areas worth exploring and any of the towns and hill stations in this area form a good base.

This region can be visited at any time of the year, but Corbett and other protected areas in the terai are closed during the monsoon from mid-June to late October with clearing up continuing to mid-November. Ideally two visits would be necessary to do the region justice: one for the Palearctic and altitudinal migrants in winter, when access in the Himalaya is limited by snow down to 2000–2500m; another for the breeding birds and high-altitude specialities in May/early June. At any time you need warm clothes unless you are only planning a trip to the terai in summer.

Corbett and Ramnagar

India's oldest tiger reserve is excellent for birds and other wildlife. Set up in 1933, it was later renamed after Jim Corbett, India's best-known Tiger hunter. He was one of the first to realise that the country's wildlife was diminishing and became a staunch convert to conservation. He helped obtain protection for an area of forest centred on the Ramganga River in the foothills of the Himalaya.

Corbett NP encompasses a wide range of habitats between 400 and 1200 m above sea level. The most important is the forest which consists primarily of Sal *Shorea robusta,* the commonest tree in the sub-Himalayan *Bhabar* zone. Sal is a tall, broad-leaved tree which sheds its leaves in March, and Corbett is renowned for almost pure stands of this, one of India's finest hardwoods. Haldu *Adina cordifolia,* Kamala *Mallotus philippensis* and the Easter Tree *Hollarhena antidysentrica* are important components of the forest which help support a diversity of birds.

The Ramganga River with its reservoir and tributaries are the life-blood of the preserve. The reservoir supports storks and other wading birds while the river is important for crocodiles, cormorants, kingfishers and several raptors.

The flat, open grasslands known as *chaurs* are also important at Corbett. These are often the result of abandoned man-made forest clearings with a rich growth of medium to tall grasses. *Chaurs* are a favourite grazing ground for deer and elephants which often congregate in large numbers. They also have specialised grassland birds such as Bright-headed Cisticola and Red Avadavat.

At Corbett the avifauna of the lower Himalaya meets that of the Indian plains and well over 400 species have been seen within the sanctuary. Birding on foot is restricted to the rest house compounds, nearby watchtowers, and areas outside the park. Lower bird densities than at places like Bharatpur can make birding disappointing at first, but a few days in the prime season can, with a little effort, produce 200 species

Map of Corbett National Park

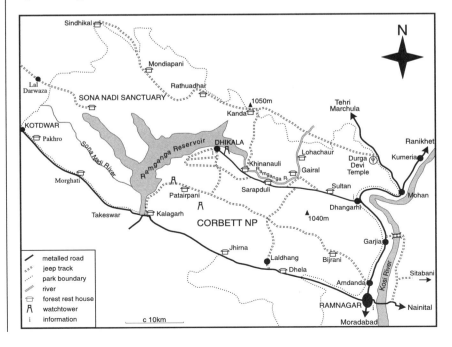

including such gems as Lesser Fish Eagle, Ibisbill and White-tailed Rubythroat. The spectacular scenery and a possible encounter with one of the big cats in the wild make a visit to this Tiger Reserve very rewarding.

Location

Corbett lies in the Siwalik Hills in Uttar Pradesh 280km by road northeast of Delhi via Moradabad. The nearest town is Ramnagar 19km south of the main park entrance at Dhangarhi (Dhangadhi). Unless you arrive with an organised group it is necessary to stop at the Corbett Reception Centre (open daily 08.00–13.00 & 15.00–17.00) in Ramnagar to make arrangements and obtain permits. There are only two public entrances to the park – at Amdanda and Dhangarhi. Visitors need to have secured overnight accommodation to enter at the latter. The Amdanda gate is mainly used for day visits.

There is a railway station at Ramnagar about 1½km south of the town, but trains are slow. The overnight train (2nd class only) leaves at 23.00 from Old Delhi station arriving at Ramnagar at 06.10. The return train leaves at 21.30.

Buses are much more frequent and leave from the ISBT near Kashmiri Gate in Delhi taking 6-8 hours to Ramnagar. Try to get a direct express bus or take one of the fast buses to Moradabad and change there. Buses back to Delhi leave from the corner of the road next to the Bharat Restaurant in Ramnagar. If there is a long wait for a direct bus, take one as far as Moradabad from where there are many more buses to Delhi. There is often such a crowd at Ramnagar that people pay porters to fight their way on and reserve a seat.

For several people travelling together it may be worthwhile taking a taxi from Delhi. This gives greater freedom enabling other stops to be made en route (e.g. the **Ganges River Crossing** near Gajraula 90km east of Delhi, a regular site for Sand Lark, Pallas's Gull and Gangetic Dolphin).

A journey to Corbett can be combined with a trip to one of the hill stations in the nearby Himalaya. The most popular is Nainital 85km by road east of Ramnagar. A number of private operators run buses taking 3½ hours. These are best booked in advance in Ramnagar. Alternatively catch a local bus to Haldwani and change to another bus or share-taxi from there. With your own transport, stop at the Corbett Museum, the legendary naturalist's former home in Kaladhungi, about half way between Ramnagar and Nainital.

There is one bus a day from Ramnagar to the Dhikala Tourist Complex within the park at 15.30. It takes about 2 hours to cover the 51km and returns at 09.00 the next morning. Timings may change so check at Ramnagar. The Dhangari Gate entrance closes at 16.30.

Accommodation

Accommodation within the park is in *Forest Rest Houses* scattered around the sanctuary. Of these, the main tourist area and the only place that can be reached by public transport is Dhikala (altitude 380m), in the Patli Dun, where the valley of the River Ramganga broadens out, (*dun* being a flat valley in the Himalayan foothills). Facilities are moderate but there is a restaurant as well as a library and information centre. Dhikala is the only Rest House inside the park where there is electricity, albeit erratic, although generator sets are available at Sarapduli (Sarpduli) and Bijrani. There is accommodation with catering facilities but no public transport at Bijrani. If you plan to stay at one of the other rest houses, you must have transport (preferably a jeep) and take your own food. It is possible but difficult to arrange jeep hire in Ramnagar. Ask at the Reception Centre, the Tourist

Bungalow or the Bharat Restaurant (see map of Ramnagar). If you want to be absolutely sure of a jeep, and it is within your budget, arrange one in Delhi. Accommodation within the park is often full for a day or two ahead, but there is good birdwatching around Ramnagar, so a stay here is not wasted. You are normally only allowed two or three nights at each rest house, but sometimes it is possible to extend an extra night or two if places are available. Park rates are overpriced for the quality offered. Accommodation is in dormitory beds (E) and other double or triple rooms (A/B). In addition there are camera fees and a single entrance fee valid for three days. Students are eligible for reductions. In theory it is possible to reserve accommodation in advance by writing to the Field Director, Project Tiger, Corbett National Park, Ramnagar (District Nainital) – 244 715, Uttar Pradesh, enclosing a Bank Draft in Indian Rupees for the full amount payable but this does not always work.

There are expensive resort-type establishments outside the park, mainly along the road along the eastern side of Corbett. These offer good facilities at an all-in price including meals. The selection includes the *Shergaon Huts* (A) about 6km north of Ramnagar, the *Claridges Corbett Hideaway* (A+) at Garjia and the *Tiger Tops* (A++) 1km north of Shergaon. Probably the best value of these resorts is the *Quality Inn* (A), Kumeria Reserve Forest, P.O. Mohan, District Almora, Uttar Pradesh – 244 715 ☎05946-85520, Fax 85230. It is at Kumeria to the northeast of Corbett 29km north of Ramnagar. The main advantage here is that it is in good forest outside the National Park with no restrictions on movement on foot in the jungle. All of these resorts organise guided elephant rides and jeep trips into the park (through the Amdanda gate only), sometimes at extra cost, and most can be booked as package tours from Delhi.

Nearly all of the budget accommodation is in Ramnagar where there are basic hotels like the *Govind* (E without bathroom), the *Everest* (E) and the *Banwari* (D/E). The best value is the Uttar Pradesh government-run *Tourist Rest House* (D/E) ☎853225 near the Corbett Reception Centre. They have standard and 'deluxe' rooms as well as cheaper dormitory beds. The food in the restaurant is good. There is a cheap and basic *Tourist Guest Home* just north of the village of Mohan which is handy for exploring the forest north of the reserve. The *FRH* at Mohan can be booked with the DFO, Ramnagar Forest Division, Ramnagar (Nainital District) ☎244715.

Strategy   The best time for Corbett is between late November and February when there are altitudinal and long-distance migrants. Day-time temperatures are pleasant, but nights are cold and a heavy mist often hampers early morning birding. By March much of the grass of the *chaurs* has been burnt to help new growth – a good time for seeing mammals. By mid-April it becomes rather hot, although birding is good in early morning and late afternoon. The park is less visited during early summer although this is the best time for summer visitors such as Indian Pitta*, various cuckoos, Rosy Minivet, Blue-throated Blue Flycatcher, Asian Paradise-flycatcher, Pale-footed Bush Warbler, and Orange-headed Thrush some of which can be quite common. Mammals tend to be easier at this time when they concentrate at watering places. Corbett is closed from 15 June to 15 November. A visit of several days is recommended in order to cover areas inside the park, around Ramnagar, as well as those to the northeast of Corbett.

For those on a flying visit with their own transport day trips can only be made through the Amdanda Gate. Permits must be obtained at the Reception Centre in Ramnagar first, as visitors are regulated on a first come first served basis.

Map of Ramnagar

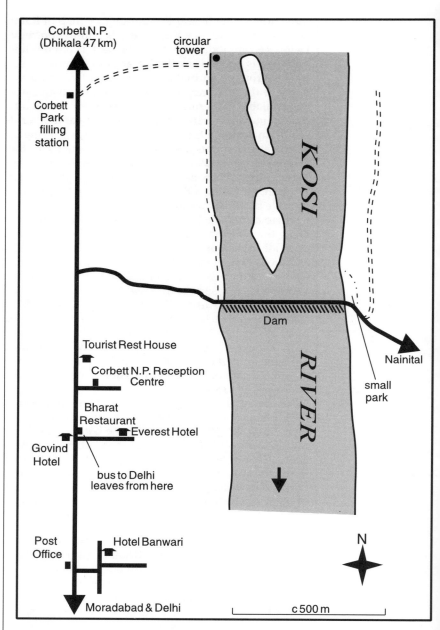

A day can be spent at Ramnagar searching along the Kosi River itself from the dam northwards for Ibisbill and Wallcreeper. The Ibisbill can usually be found in winter by walking down a road opposite the 'Corbett Park Filling Station' at the northern end of Ramnagar to a tower by the river and scanning the islands and river banks. If not, work your way upstream checking carefully among the stones and boulders where the birds are surprisingly well camouflaged. Long-billed Plover has been reported from the river north of Ramnagar. A dirt road runs through reasonable habitat parallel to the river on its eastern side (see map) for about 12km to a bridge just north of Garjia where the river can be re-crossed. From here work back to Ramnagar or catch a bus back. Birds include Crested Serpent Eagle, Crested Kingfisher, Blue-bearded Bee-eater, Indian Grey Hornbill*, Grey-capped Pygmy Woodpecker, Spangled Drongo, and White-capped and Crested Buntings. Check bushes for Jungle Prinia* and White-tailed Rubythroat. Flocks of swifts are frequent over Ramnagar before dusk and Jungle Myna can be found in the town itself.

If you have spare time, catch one of the frequent Ranikhet buses to the park entrance at Dhangari, an excellent area where Sirkeer Malkoha*, Streak-throated Woodpecker and White-tailed Rubythroat have been seen, then connect with the daily bus to Dhikala in the afternoon. The Dhangarhi Gate area can repay more than one visit.

Staying inside the park at Dhikala you may only explore the immediate vicinity of the compound on foot. Dhikala is on the edge of a *chaur* on the south bank of the Ramganga River at the eastern end of a reservoir. The bushes and trees of the compound may have White-tailed Rubythroat (W), Dark-throated Thrush (W), or *Phylloscopus* warblers such as Dusky (W), Tickell's Leaf (W) or Lemon-rumped (W). Grey-crowned Prinia* (R) has been seen here.

Grassland specialists immediately around Dhikala include Hen Harrier (W), Black Francolin, Bright-headed Cisticola, Chestnut-capped Babbler, and Red Avadavat. Savanna Nightjars are quite common and become vocal from late February.

The reservoir should be investigated for storks, egrets and waders. A scan with a telescope will usually reveal an Osprey (W) or Pallas's Fish Eagle on a dead tree in the water. River Lapwings are common and Pallas's Gulls not too difficult. Stork-billed Kingfisher and Great Thick-knee are reasonably regular.

The watchtower, 800m east of the Dhikala compound, overlooks the river and a pool at the edge of the forest. This can be excellent for forest species, often easier than in the middle of the jungle. If the walk to here and along the track by the river beyond are permitted, it can be productive. With your own vehicle you can drive slowly through the sal forest east of Dhikala. Remember that, particularly during winter, birds tend to forage in large mixed-species flocks. Concentrating on these can turn up an astonishing variety.

Early morning and late afternoon elephant rides are available at Dhikala and Bijrani. These should be booked beforehand as seats are limited. This is an excellent way of seeing larger mammals with tiger sightings regular, but their value for birds is limited.

With your own vehicle, spend half a day exploring the grasslands and reservoir west of Dhikala. Stop at a quiet spot on the forest edge south of the grasslands to watch the dirt road and hope for some skulkers to pop out of the grass and bushes. Driving slowly through the forest east of Dhikala is bound to produce Kalij Pheasant and Red Junglefowl and if you are lucky you might find a fish owl roosting in large trees by a pool. Brown Fish Owls are much commoner than Tawny and care should be taken separating the two.

On your way to or from Dhikala make detours to the viewpoints over the Ramganga at High Bank and Sarapduli. These can be good for Grey-headed Fish Eagle and Crested Kingfisher as well as Mugger and Gharial Crocodiles. If you spend time by the river, you might spot a group of Common Otter.

An excellent route if you have a jeep is the road up to Kanda which crosses the river near Khinanauli. This steep dirt road goes through fine forest to a Rest House at an altitude of just over 1000m. This is a part of

Corbett not much visited by birders. Several species that are not seen at lower altitudes such as Pin-tailed Green Pigeon, Orange-bellied Leafbird, Blue-winged Minla and Chestnut-bellied Rock Thrush can be found here. After crossing the river the road climbs steeply for 1–2km and then flattens out for about 200m. This flat stretch is excellent for the rare Great Slaty Woodpecker in the early morning and just before dusk with up to 15 or 20 individuals here.

If you do not have transport, it might be possible to hitch a lift with someone else for the day; a jeep can sometimes be hired at Dhikala.

A couple of days at one or two of the Forest Rest Houses away from Dhikala enable other areas of the park to be explored and yield some different species. Lohachaur and Kanda are particularly recommended.

Two good areas outside the National Park are just northeast of Corbett around Mohan and Kumeria. You can base yourself here for a couple of days (e.g. at the Quality Inn) or make day trips by car or bus from Ramnagar. Particularly good are the first few kilometres of road from Mohan towards Tehri, which runs northwest along a river marking the park boundary. The area around and to the north of Kumeria as well as the Kosi River are also outstanding. There are excellent species such as Little, Slaty-backed and Spotted Forktails, Long-billed Thrush, Common Green and Red-billed Blue Magpies, and Brown Dipper which cannot be found easily in the reserve. Do, however, be aware of the dangers of birding on foot, as Tigers are not uncommon.

A recent development is the promotion of two excellent birding areas at Jhirna and Sitabani Temple (northeast of Ramnagar). Both have Forest Rest Houses booked through the Forest Department at the office in Ramnagar. The main advantage is that they are outside the park and walking is permitted though you need to hire a vehicle to take you there.

For those with time and entrepreneurial spirit the Sona Nadi Sanctuary, recently incorporated to form the northwestern half of the Tiger Reserve, offers opportunities. There are several rest houses which can be booked at the new reception centre at Kotdwar at the western corner of the reserve and there is talk of making this part of the park accessible on foot.

Biannual birdwatching camps are planned which should give access to sections of Corbett less frequently visited. If interested in these, contact Kalpavriksh in Delhi (see Useful Addresses) or the Deputy Director, Corbett National Park, Ramnagar, U.P.

Birds   Additional species along the River Kosi at Ramnagar are various waders, Small Pratincole, Great Thick-knee, River Lapwing, Ashy-crowned Sparrow Lark*, Plain Martin, Plumbeous and White-capped Water-Redstarts, five species of wagtail, and Crested Bunting. India's first Horned Grebe was seen here in 1993.

Other birds around here include: 7 species of vulture including Cinereous (R), Lammergeier and Himalayan Griffon, Alexandrine, Slaty-headed and Plum-headed* Parakeets, Jungle Owlet, Brown-headed* and Lineated Barbets, Streak-throated and Yellow-crowned Woodpeckers, White-bellied Drongo*, Gold-fronted Leafbird, Himalayan Bulbul, Ultramarine (RW) and Slaty-blue (W) Flycatchers, Grey-headed Canary Flycatcher (W), Grey-breasted and Plain Prinias, Hume's Warbler (W), Siberian Rubythroat (W), Pied and Grey Bushchats, Chestnut-bellied Nuthatch, Olive-backed (W) and Paddyfield Pipits, Thick-billed Flowerpecker, Indian Silverbill, Scaly-breasted Munia and White-capped Bunting (W).

The reservoir and river near Dhikala: Oriental Darter, Black-crowned Night Heron, Woolly-necked, Black (W) and Black-necked Storks, Ruddy Shelduck (W), Common Merganser (W), Brahminy Kite, White-tailed Eagle (RW), Grey-headed and Lesser Fish Eagles, Oriental Hobby (R), Great Thick-Knee, Crested Kingfisher and Rosy Pipit (W).

The lowland sal forests often seem fairly quiet but provide a home for many species including Collared Falconet, Emerald Dove, Alexandrine, Red-breasted (R), Plum-headed* and Slaty-headed Parakeets, Asian Barred and Jungle Owlets, Brown Hawk Owl, Large-tailed and Indian (U) Nightjars, White-rumped Needletail* (over clearings), Crested Treeswift, Oriental Pied and Great Hornbills, Blue-throated Barbet, Speckled Piculet, Fulvous-breasted, Rufous, Scaly-bellied and Grey-headed Woodpeckers, Lesser and Greater Yellownapes, Himalayan and Greater Flamebacks, Indian Pitta* (S), Maroon (U) and Black-headed Orioles, Ashy (U), White-bellied*, Bronzed, Lesser Racket-tailed (U), Greater Racket-tailed (R) and Spangled Drongos, Bar-winged Flycatcher-shrike, Large and Black-winged (U) Cuckooshrikes, Scarlet Minivet, Black-crested Bulbul, Black-chinned Babbler, White-crested Laughingthrush, Rufous-tailed (R) and Verditer Flycatchers, Yellow-bellied and White-throated Fantails, Asian Paradise-flycatcher (S), Chestnut-headed Tesia (U), Aberrant and Grey-sided Bush (W), Blyth's Leaf (W), Golden-spectacled and Grey-hooded Warblers, Velvet-fronted Nuthatch, Pale-billed Flowerpecker and Crimson Sunbird.

The immediate vicinity of the compound at Dhikala: Himalayan Swiftlet, Alpine Swift, Eurasian Wryneck (W), woodpeckers, Ashy Woodswallow, Dark-throated Thrush (W), Tickell's Blue and Grey-headed Canary Flycatchers, Blyth's Reed, Dusky, Tickell's Leaf, Hume's, Lemon-rumped and Greenish Warblers (W), Blue Rock Thrush (W), Blue Whistling Thrush and Bar-tailed Treecreeper as well as many forest species passing through. Large-tailed Nightjar and Brown Hawk Owl can often be heard at night inside the compound itself.

The *chaur* at Dhikala: Eurasian Marsh and Pallid Harriers (W), Oriental Skylark, Yellow-eyed Babbler, Ashy Prinia, Common Stonechat, Paddyfield Pipit, Black-throated and Baya Weavers, and Crested and Chestnut-eared (W) Buntings. At dusk flocks of swifts often form over the grasslands. These may include White-rumped Needletail*, Fork-tailed Swift and Crested Treeswift.

A trip to the higher reaches of the park such as Kanda may produce Lammergeier, Himalayan Griffon, Great Barbet, Maroon Oriole, Long-tailed Minivet, Brown-eared and Black Bulbuls, White-browed Scimitar-Babbler (R), Scaly-breasted Wren Babbler, White-throated and Streaked Laughingthrushes, Silver-eared Mesia, Black-lored and Black-throated Tits.

The forest around Mohan and Kumeria: Great Barbet, Grey Treepie, Bar-winged Flycatcher-Shrike, Orange-bellied and Gold-fronted Leafbird, Black Bulbul, Rusty-cheeked Scimitar Babbler, White-throated Laughingthrush, Red-billed Leiothrix, Rufous-gorgeted, Little Pied and Slaty-blue Fly-catchers (W), Rufous-bellied Niltava (W) and Grey-winged Blackbird (W).

The area is good for raptors with 50 species reported from Corbett including: Oriental Honey-buzzard, White-eyed, Common (UW) and Long-legged Buzzards (W), Eurasian Griffon, Egyptian, White-rumped, Long-billed and Red-headed Vultures, Short-toed Snake, Black (R), Lesser Spotted, Greater Spotted, Steppe, Imperial (UW), Bonelli's (R) and Booted (U) Eagles, Rufous-bellied (R), Changeable and Mountain (U) Hawk Eagles, Eurasian Sparrowhawk, Northern Goshawk, Eurasian Hobby (U), and Red-necked (U), Laggar (R) and Peregrine Falcons. Spot-bellied Eagle Owl is sometimes seen near Dhangari.

Crested Kingfisher

Other Wildlife

Corbett is excellent for larger mammals. Spotted Deer, Sambar and Wild Boar are fairly common. Hog Deer frequent the grasslands. Barking Deer are likely to be seen singly in the forest. The wild Elephants at Corbett spend most of the year in higher parts of the reserve, coming to the Ramganga Valley from February to June. The best chance for Tiger and Leopard is an organised elephant ride. The mahouts know the habits and movements of the big cats and approach is often possible where a jeep cannot follow. As with any such shy, rare animals, getting a good look is a matter of luck. Sometimes they are even seen from the bus on the way to Dhikala, so keep your eyes open.

Rhesus Macaques and Grey Langur are quite common, and there is a good chance of Common Indian Mongoose. Jackal are less frequent than in some national parks and smaller mammals such as Yellow-throated Marten, Jungle and Leopard Cats, and Small Indian, Common and Masked Palm Civets, although not uncommon, are difficult. Indian Porcupine is sometimes seen at night near the garbage dump at Dhikala. Dhole (Wild Dog) is rare. Of smaller mammals Black-naped Hare is most likely. Sloth Bears are uncommon and mostly keep to the Bijrani-Malani area and the ridge which runs parallel and south of the main road through the park. Asiatic Black Bear is rare and usually only seen in winter in the higher northern parts of the park. The Goral, a kind of goat-antelope, is occasionally seen on the road up to Kanda. Common Otters hunt in packs along the quieter reaches of the Ramganga and there are lookout points (signposted) off the main road between Dhangarhi and Dhikala where, with a bit of luck one can see Mugger and Gharial Crocodiles on sand banks. The river is well-known for its Mahseer fish (sometimes called 'the Indian salmon').

Nainital

A first birding trip to north India is not complete without a taste of the western Himalayan avifauna. The pleasant hill station of Nainital in the Kumaon Hills is ideal, surrounded by forests with many montane specialities. Nainital is easily accessible and fairly close to Corbett National Park so a visit to the two can be combined.

Nainital lies at 1940m and surrounding peaks reach over 2600m. Many interesting birds are found in the town's gardens and parks as well as in forests on adjacent hillsides. If you would like to see Black-headed Jay, Red-billed Blue Magpie and Chestnut-crowned Laughingthrush within walking distance of your hotel, Nainital is an excellent choice. You can visit the Mongoli Valley and forests around Sat Tal at slightly lower elevations, where in winter good numbers of altitudinal and northern migrants appear. Orange-flanked Bush Robins are common, while at times it is hard to believe that there can be so many Red-breasted and Slaty-headed Parakeets. Add the occasional Spotted Forktail, Chestnut-headed Tesia or a Black-throated Accentor and you have an irresistible mix of species.

The Himalayan Quail**, formerly found in this region, is feared extinct since it has not been seen since 1876. Birders should nevertheless bear in mind the possibility on steep grassy hillsides between 1650m and 2000m.

Map of Nainital

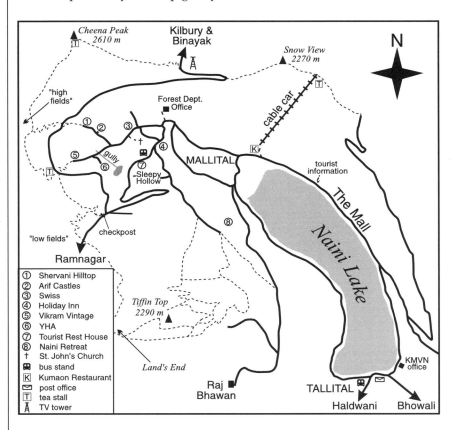

Location

Nainital surrounds the lake of the same name in the Kumaon region of Uttar Pradesh northeast of Delhi. The part of the town at the southern end is known as Tallital, the northern end is Mallital. The Mall which runs down the eastern side of the lake connects the two. Cycle rickshaws ply the length of the Mall for a small fixed charge while motorised vehicles have to pay a toll.

In a straight line, Nainital is little more than 30km east of Corbett NP, though the road distance to Ramnagar is somewhat greater. Buses take about 2½ hours for the journey. U.P. State Roadways buses leave the bus stand at Tallital and private buses leave from Mallital. The 320km road journey from Delhi to Nainital is covered by private bus in about 9 hours, both daytime and overnight. Most run from the ISBT in Delhi to the Mallital bus stand. For an overnight bus book through a travel agent at least the day before. There are overnight trains in each direction, though the journey after delays is likely to be considerably longer. The Ranikhet Express leaves from Old Delhi station at 23.00 and arrives at 06.05 at Kathgodam, the nearest railhead 35km south of Nainital. The new Superfast Express leaves from New Delhi station at 06.00 arriving at Kathgodam at midday. From Kathgodam there are buses and share-taxis (flat fare per passenger) to Nainital.

Accommodation

Most birders visit Nainital in winter when numerous migrants from the north join resident birds. However, there is no reason not to visit during spring or autumn, although the peak tourist seasons of May–June and late September – early November see hotel prices rocket. Although many hotels are closed, prices in the winter months are more reasonable, and there is room for bargaining. Check whether the room tariff includes charges for extra blankets and heating. The following classifications are based on winter prices. Generally it is more convenient to stay at Mallital as the better birding is at this end of town. Here two of the best hotels are the *Vikram Vintage Inn* (A) ☎05942-36177 and *Naini Retreat* (A) 05942-26105. The *Shervani Hill Top* (C) ☎05942-36304 is comfortable if a little chaotic, while the *Swiss* (C) ☎05942-36013 has character but tends to be cold. These hotels are up the hill from Mallital and run a courtesy service to town. If you phone, they send a vehicle to pick you up. There are a number of cheaper lodges around Mallital bazaar.

Budget accommodation is in dormitories run by the Kumaon Mandal Vikas Nigam (KMVN) in *Rest Houses* in Tallital and a few hundred metres from the Mallital Bus Stand in Sukhatal, as well as the *YHA* in Mallital. The former ☎05942-35400 has good value mid- and low-price rooms. These can be booked in advance at the office of the KMVN, Chandralok Building, 36 Janpath in Delhi. Altogether there are more than 100 hotels to choose from in Nainital.

Apart from hotel restaurants there are many places to eat in Nainital though some close in the winter. Among the better ones are the Kwality, Capri and Embassy at the northern end of the Mall.

Strategy

Spend at least four days here including day trips to the Mongoli Valley and Sat Tal. A longer stay improves chances of less common species. Winters are cold, though temperatures generally stay above zero. Snow is possible from December to February, pushing many birds into the town where temperatures are higher than on the mountains. Many of the best birds occur when the weather is bad.

Initial explorations should concentrate on parks, gardens and scrub on the northern and western sides of town. Blue Whistling Thrushes are ubiquitous. Roving flocks of Green-backed, Spot-winged, Black-lored* and Black-throated Tits may be accompanied by a White-tailed Nuthatch or a Bar-tailed Treecreeper. Blue-capped and Blue-fronted Redstarts perch on prominent posts while Streaked Laughingthrushes lurk in patches of ground cover.

The gully down the hill opposite the Arvind Restaurant on the road joining the Swiss Hotel to the Vikram Vintage Inn is not a delight to the senses but attracts good birds. Chestnut Thrush, Grey-winged and White-collared Blackbirds, Orange-flanked Bush Robin, and White-capped

Water-Redstart are likely, though numbers of thrushes at Nainital vary considerably. Rarer species such as Spectacled Finch* pop in to bathe. Scan any other gullies, especially early in the morning when Spotted Forktail is possible. Further explorations of gardens may yield Great Barbet, Scaly Thrush or Asian Barred Owlet, the latter most vociferous just before dawn.

Next should be a trip up to Snow View Ridge. The easy way is by cable car (ropeway) from the valley station, reached by a path right of the Kumaon Restaurant at the northern end of the Mall. This carries you to 2260m. Explore the ridge in both directions and look at rubbish tips behind or opposite the houses west of the ropeway station. This may lead to your first White-throated or Chestnut-crowned Laughingthrushes, and you might surprise a Common Hill Partridge. Follow up jay-like calls as the Black-headed species is often found in trees on the ridge and keep an eye open for both Long-tailed and Plain-backed (U) Thrushes. A number of paths wind steeply back down to the town; while another continues west along the ridge to meet the road which carries on past the TV tower to a bend where a broad track leads to the highest summit on the 2610m Cheena (China or Naina) Peak. It may be better to keep this excursion for a clear morning as clouds often roll in from mid-day dampening bird activity and obscuring the spectacular view of the main Himalayan range. The ridge can be excellent for raptors with Himalayan Griffon and Lammergeier almost guaranteed and the forests offer the best chances of Himalayan and Rufous-bellied Woodpeckers. The climb up via the TV tower is gentler, but steeper trails wind up from the roads leading past the Vikram Vintage Inn and the Shervani Hilltop Hotel respectively. If you go this way, check the area known as the 'high fields' (see map) for Dark-throated Thrush, Rufous-breasted and Black-throated Accentors as well as Plain Mountain Finch.

Just after the trail from the Vikram Vintage Inn crosses the main road a level path leads to the left. This can be good for Altai Accentor and Red-billed Blue Magpie. If you come across a flock of Collared Grosbeaks (U), check carefully for Black-and-Yellows (R) which can associate with them in winter. This trail winds down and eventually meets the main road again at Khupratal by some terraced cultivation, sometimes known as the 'low fields'. Explore these for Brownish-flanked Bush Warbler (R), Golden Bush Robin (U) and White-capped Bunting as well as accentors. Rufous-backed Redstart is probably a vagrant. Upland Pipit is regularly heard and occasionally seen on steep grassy slopes.

Other places to look at in the town are the area known as Sleepy Hollow and the little wilderness around St. John's Church. Walks up to Tiffin Top and Land's End southwest of the lake can also be rewarding as this area is usually less frequented by tourists.

Birds Birds likely in and around Nainital include (largely in winter): Common Buzzard, Golden (R) and Steppe Eagles, Eurasian Griffon (R), Red-headed and White-rumped Vultures, Lammergeier, Peregrine Falcon, Eurasian Hobby (S), Kalij, Koklass (U) and Cheer (R) Pheasants, Woodcock (U), Oriental Turtle Dove, Blossom-headed and Slaty-headed Parakeets, Alpine and House Swifts, Speckled Piculet, Greater Yellownape, Scaly-bellied, Grey-headed, Brown-fronted and Grey-capped Pygmy Woodpeckers, Grey-backed Shrike, Maroon Oriole, Eurasian Jay, Spotted Nutcracker (R), Large-billed Crow, Long-tailed Minivet, Himalayan and Mountain Bulbuls, Rusty-cheeked Scimitar Babbler, Black-chinned Babbler*, Striated Laughingthrush, White-browed and Green Shrike Babblers, Rufous Sibia, Rusty-tailed Flycatcher (S), Grey-headed Canary Flycatcher, Aberrant Bush, Smoky, Buff-barred, Lemon-rumped, Ashy-throated Leaf and Grey-hooded Warblers,

Goldcrest, Siberian Rubythroat, Golden Bush Robin (U), Plumbeous Water-Redstart, Grey Bushchat, Chestnut-bellied Rock Thrush, Blue Rock Thrush, Long-billed (U) and Mistle (R) Thrushes, Yellow-browed Tit, Chestnut-bellied Nuthatch, Wallcreeper, Olive-backed Pipit, Grey Wagtail, Oriental White-Eye, Russet Sparrow, Spot-winged Grosbeak (R), European Goldfinch, Yellow-breasted Greenfinch, Fire-fronted Serin, Dark-breasted, Pink-browed and Vinaceous (R) Rosefinches, Brown Bullfinch (R) and Rock Bunting.

Mongoli Valley

This is an area of excellent open woodland, streamside vegetation and fields easily visited in a day trip from Nainital. The entrance to the valley is at Bajún, a few houses and tea stalls near the top of a ridge 12km from Nainital on the road to Kaladunghi and Ramnagar (Corbett NP). Buses ply this route every 40 minutes or so with the first leaving from the private bus stand near the Holiday Inn in Mallital at 07.00. Ask to be set down at Bajún. The journey takes 40 minutes.

Map of
Mongoli Valley

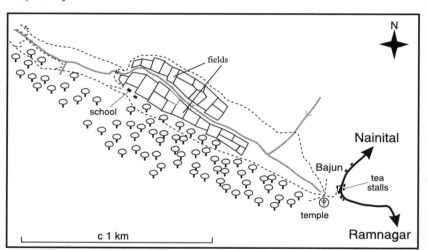

When you get off the bus, take the broad path up to the right as you face away from Nainital. This curves over a ridge with a shrine on your left. Take your time as birds funnel along this small pass. Scarlet Finch, a rarity here, has been seen. Continue down through thin forest along the left flank of the valley. The peculiar aspect of many trees here is due to the fact that they are lopped to provide animal fodder. The whole forest is good for woodpeckers with Brown-fronted the commonest. With luck you could encounter Greater Yellownape, Scaly-bellied and Grey-headed, as well as the delightful little Speckled Piculet.

The track slopes gently down, passing the first fields and houses below. Lammergeier nest on cliffs across the valley. After 1–1¹/₂km you pass a small school on the right. At the next major steep gully scramble down one of the indistinct paths to a stream lined with good undergrowth or carry on another few hundred metres to an easier path which leads down to houses and a bathing pool in the stream not visible from the main trail. Working along the stream can produce Small and Rufous-bellied Niltavas, Chestnut-headed Tesia, Golden-spectacled, Grey-sided, Brownish-flanked and Aberrant Bush Warblers, Spotted and Slaty-backed Forktails and Long-billed Thrush.

On the other side of the stream a broader path leads back to the fields below the school. Keep an eye open for Rufous-breasted and Black-throated Accentors. Slaty-headed Parakeet, Himalayan Greenfinch and Fire-fronted Serin should be around and you might see an Asian Barred Owlet hunting in daylight. Bushes along the stream are excellent for warblers, with Chestnut-crowned Bush, Tickell's Leaf and Ashy-throated among others.

You can return to Bajún by following the path along the other side of the valley, but be careful not to take the side valley that comes down from the left by mistake.

Birds   Many species listed above for Nainital can be seen more easily in the Mongoli Valley in winter. In addition look out for the following: Crested Goshawk (U), Long-legged Buzzard (R), Mountain Hawk Eagle (U), Crested Serpent Eagle, Black Francolin, Blue-bearded Bee-eater (R), Blue-throated Barbet, Eurasian Crag and Nepal House Martins, Bronzed Drongo, Grey Treepie, Bar-winged Flycatcher-shrike, Black-crested and Ashy Bulbuls, White-crested Laughingthrush, Red-billed Leiothrix, Blue-winged Minla, Whiskered Yuhina, Red-throated, Rufous-gorgeted, Slaty-blue and Verditer (S) Flycatchers, Yellow-bellied and White-throated Fantails, Hill Prinia, Fire-breasted Flowerpecker, Green-tailed and Black-throated Sunbirds and Common Rosefinch.

Sat Tal

Sat Tal is popular for tourist trips from Nainital. The seven lakes are set in well wooded hills which provide good mid-altitude habitat (1300–1450m). There are no regular buses to Sat Tal so hire a taxi for the day, get it to drop you off and pick you up again later, or use the first bus to Bhimtal, which leaves from Tallital bus stand at 08.00. Get off the bus 6km past Bhowali, where there is a junction with a tea stall on the left and a yellow sign on the right inscribed 'Tourist Bungalow Sat Tal 7km'. From here is a good birding walk along the road to the main lake with the Tourist Rest House. Be careful to return to the junction in good time to catch the last bus to Nainital which is supposed to leave Bhimtal at 17.00. The alternative is to walk or hitch a further 6km back to Bhowali.

The area has a diversity of species and you might stay here for a night or two. The Rest House (D/E) is not luxurious but pleasantly situated in the lakeside forest and can be booked at the KMVN office on the Mall in Nainital (near the Tallital bus stand) or at their Rest House at Sukhatal. In this case arrange a taxi to drop you there and pick you up again at the end of your stay. If you have a tent, there is a campsite near the dam on the main lake. Food is available at the Rest House and tea stalls by the lake.

In winter the road from the junction to Sat Tal is not very busy as it ends at the lake and there are few tourists. About 1km from the junction is a factory belonging to Eureka Forbes. The fenced off fields are good for both ruby-throats and Rufous-breasted Accentor as well as the less common Black-throated. View quietly from the main road and you should see some come to feed at the field margins along with Russet Sparrows and White-capped Bunt-ings. The same species can be found in nearby cultivated fields and hedges.

The road continues through fields and scrub good for Rusty-cheeked Scimitar Babbler, Slaty-blue Flycatcher, Tickell's Leaf Warbler, and Common and Pink-browed Rosefinches. After a kilometre or two is a small pass with a tea stall. Here you can either continue birding along the road with side excursions into the mixed forest or take the track left through a pine forest to a Christian Ashram from where another path leads steeply down to the main lake. Work carefully through mixed flocks as they may have Speckled

Map of Sat Tal

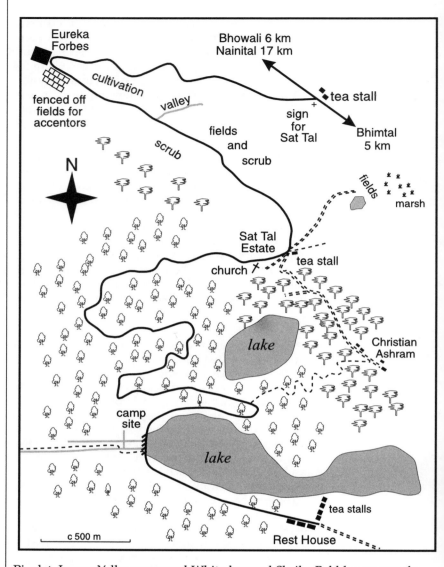

Piculet, Lesser Yellownape and White-browed Shrike Babbler among the commoner tits and warblers. Other birds are Nepal House Martin, White-crested and Rufous-chinned Laughingthrushes, and Rufous-gorgeted and Snowy-browed Flycatchers.

A good track leads west from the dam at the end of the main lake. The wet area between the water channels below the dam should be approached carefully as it sometimes holds Long-billed Thrush. The path is worth following. Look for Greater Yellownape, Scaly-breasted Wren Babbler, Chestnut-headed Tesia, Golden Bush Robin, Spotted Forktail, Scaly Thrush and Vinaceous Rosefinch (R).

As can be seen, Sat Tal shares many species with Nainital and Mongoli though a lot of birds may be pushed down here in hard weather. Other species recorded but not mentioned from the previous two sites are: Black Eagle, Collared Owlet, Fulvous-breasted Woodpecker (U), Greater Flameback, Black-chinned Yuhina (R), Rosy Pipit, White-browed Wagtail* and Chestnut-eared Bunting (U).

Other Sites

Beyond Cheena Peak is some superb forest with a FRH at **Kilbury** (2190m–12km) and at **Binayak** (2225m–22km). These can be booked through the Forest Department in Nainital. You can get a taxi to take you there or trek through the forest. If you need a guide or porter, contact the tourist office. It is also possible to trek from Nainital down to Corbett NP.

The KMVN has a good network of Rest Houses throughout the Kumaon region. For those who would like to spend more time birding and hiking here these provide excellent bases. The ones at **Binsar** and **Kausani** are recommended.

Further north the **Uttarakhand** region of Uttar Pradesh offers superb opportunities for trekking in the western Himalaya. The Nanda Devi Sanctuary is generally off limits, but a trek into the **Kedarnath Sanctuary** (or to one of the other holy temples such as at Yamunotri, Gangotri and Badrinath) with its enormous altitudinal range (1160-7070m) gives an opportunity to get to grips with species such as Golden Eagle, Himalayan Snowcock (U), Snow, Hill and Rufous-throated Partridges, Koklass Pheasant, Spotted Laughingthrush, Spotted Bush Warbler, Gould's Shortwing (R), Grandala (R), Little Forktail, White-throated Tit*, Upland Pipit, White-browed and Red-fronted Rosefinches, Scarlet Finch (U), and Crested Bunting (in cultivated fields).

The famous town of **Dehra Dun** (Dehra Doon, 700m) is one of the nearest Himalayan hill stations to Delhi (5–7 hours by train or bus). There are plenty of hotels to choose from. The best birding site is the FRI (Forest Research Institute), 5km west of the town centre by auto-rickshaw or one of the six-seater 'Vikrams' (tempos) which ply the route from the Clock Tower at the centre of town to the main gate. In theory one should obtain permission to bird here but in practice there is no restriction. The best birding is in the forested northern and eastern parts of the 4^{1}/$_2$km^2 grounds. The campus bird list stands at around 260 and includes Red-breasted (W), Alexandrine and Slaty-headed (W) Parakeets, Indian Cuckoo (S), Great (W), Lineated and Blue-throated Barbets, Streak-throated Woodpecker (U), Collared Scops and Brown Hawk Owls, Black-headed and Maroon (UW) Orioles, Spot-winged Starling (S), Puff-throated Babbler, Scaly-breasted Wren Babbler (W), Rufous-chinned Laughingthrush (U), Sooty, Orange-gorgeted (W), Blue-throated (S), Slaty-blue (W), Verditer (P) and Asian Paradise (S) Flycatchers, Grey-sided Bush Warbler (RW), Rufous-bellied Niltava (W), Hume's, Lemon-rumped, Golden-spectacled and Grey-hooded Warblers (W), Bluethroat (UW), White-tailed Rubythroat (W), Grey Bushchat (W), Orange-headed (S) and Dark-throated (W) Thrushes, Himalayan Treecreeper (W), Thick-billed and Fire-breasted (W) Flowerpeckers, Yellow-breasted Greenfinch (W) and White-capped Bunting.

The **Asan Baraj** lake at Dhalipur village 40km west of Dehra Dun has a selection of waterfowl in winter including local rarities such as Black-necked Grebe, as well as resident Pallas's Fish Eagles.

Mussoorie, another hill station at considerably higher altitude (2000m), is 34km further north and easily reached by bus from Dehra Dun. This is a good base for exploring altitudes up to nearly 3000m and the corresponding west Himalayan avifauna.

The nearest access gate to the **Rajaji NP** in the Shiwalik Hills is at Ramgarh, about 14km from Dehra Dun. The avifauna is similar to that of Corbett NP (see above) though less diverse. There are 10 Forest Rest Houses in the park and bookings can be made with the Rajaji NP office at 5/1 Ansari Marg, Dehra Dun ☎0135-23794.

Great Himalayan National Park and the Kullu Valley

At the heart of the western Himalaya lies the Kullu (Kulu) Valley along the upper Beas River with many tributaries flowing from the surrounding mountains. The forests were once extremely rich in wildlife but have suffered deforestation and encroachment. Nevertheless, they still have scarce and localised birds such as Western Tragopan*, Koklass Pheasant and White-throated Tit*. The magnificent birds and spectacular mountain scenery induce surprisingly few birders to visit this delightful part of India perhaps because nearly all of the species can be found elsewhere in Kashmir, Uttar Pradesh and Nepal. Thus much remains to be discovered.

Map of Kullu Valley

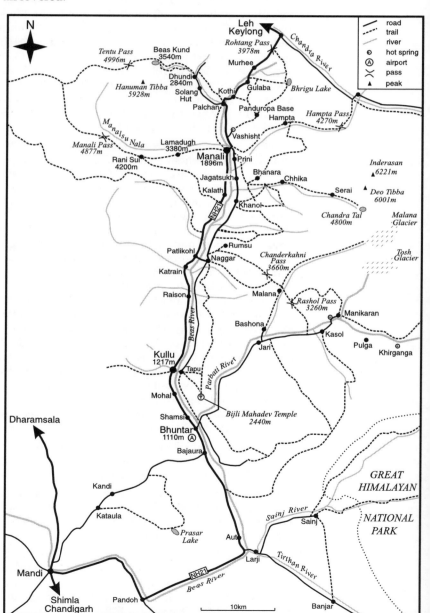

The Kullu Valley is a popular alternative summer retreat to Kashmir, but most tourists do not stray far from the main road. Birders will find many opportunities for quieter birding treks in the area, but the best preserved habitat is in the Great Himalayan National Park (GHNP). This protected area of some 620km^2 covers an altitudinal range from 1700m right up to 5800m in the catchment area of the rivers Jiwa, Sainj and Tirthan, tributaries of the Beas. The forest communities range from mixed deciduous in the lower regions, through mid-altitude pine and spruce, to oak and rhododendron on the higher slopes. Near the tree-line at around 3500m dwarf birch is the habitat for White-throated Tit*, while the alpine meadows, rocky slopes and snowfields above support such diverse birds as the exquisitely blue Grandala and the majestic Lammergeier.

Location The town of Kullu (Kulu, aka Sultanpur, altitude 1217m) is in the state of Himachal Pradesh, 510km due north of Delhi. The nearest airport is 10km south at Bhuntar with private airlines operating daily flights to Delhi in the tourist season. The 17 hour journey by private bus from Delhi is via Chandigarh (270km, 12 hours), the nearest railhead. Kullu has bus connections with Dharamsala and Shimla. For most buses Kullu is not the terminus as they continue to Manali (2050m), the main tourist and trekking centre 40km to the north. For long distance routes it is necessary to book your seat out of Kullu at least a day in advance. Many buses ply the two hour route between Kullu and Manali.

The HQ of the GHNP is at the office of the Forest Department (Wildlife) in Shamsi, 8km south of Kullu, just north of Bhuntar. The park itself is southeast of Kullu. There are two points of access both reached by road via Aut, 29km south of Kullu, and Larji (Largi) 4km further southeast: Sainj is a village on the river of the same name east of Larji, while Banjar is on the Tirthan southeast of Larji. They can be reached by bus (several daily) or taxi from Kullu in 2–3 hours.

The Kullu valley can be incorporated into an overland itinerary from Delhi to Ladakh. Regular buses run from Manali to Leh, the Ladakhi capital, from June to late September. The season varies according to weather and snow conditions with the road sometimes not passable until July and occasionally open into mid-October. The route crosses the 5328m Taglang La, the second highest motorable pass in the world, so be prepared for the possibility of altitude sickness. The journey takes at least two days with an overnight stop in tents en route and may be prolonged by several days if the weather is bad.

Accommodation There are a number of hotels in Kullu including the budget *Hotel Bijleshwar View* behind the Tourist Office, the mid-range HPTDC *Hotel Sarvari* with a pleasant garden a little west of the main NH21 at the south end of town, and the top-end *Hotel Shobla* in the town centre near the river. Prices vary according to the season, current demand and your bargaining skills.

If you only plan to visit the GHNP, you can spend the night nearer the park HQ. There are basic lodges north of the airport gate at Bhuntar. The *Hotel Airport End* opposite the gate is better.

Accommodation within the park is in *Forest Rest Houses* and very basic huts. You need your own sleeping bags, mats and provisions. The highest huts are above 3000m, very cold even in summer. The park authorities help to organise porters, guides and a cook for whom you must also provide food. Shopping is probably best done in Kullu.

Strategy Permission to trek and accommodation within the park must be arranged with the GHNP director. His subordinates may not have the authority to grant permission in his absence. It is prudent to send a letter in advance to advise of your plans, but do not expect a reply. Letters should be addressed to The Director, Great Himalayan National Park, Forest Dept. (Wildlife), Shamsi, District Kullu, Himachal Pradesh. A visit in person to the office is necessary in any case. If, for some reason, it is not possible to organise a trip into the park, there are many possibilities for trekking in and around the Kullu Valley – see *Other Sites* below.

The best time for birding in the Kullu Valley is spring after the snow has melted and before the monsoon. The optimum period is relatively short between May and mid-June. This is the best time for finding the pheasants which become more vocal in the breeding season. Earlier in the year you will contend with snow down to 2500m (exceptionally 2000m) in mid-winter, though gradually receding to about 3500m by mid-May. The snows often push high-altitude species down the valleys making them easier to find, though it can be very heavy going underfoot. Monsoon rains make life difficult, usually to mid-September. The ensuing dry period with excellent visibility normally lasts until November making this another good trekking season.

It is possible to hike up all three river valleys of the GHNP, using rest houses and huts overnight (see map), but the Sainj Valley trek has most to commend it. A thorough exploration requires one or two weeks. The rarer pheasants such as the Western Tragopan occur in ringal bamboo and dense shrubbery and are hard to see. More time spent between 2000m and the treeline allows better chances of finding this threatened species. Koklass Pheasant is fairly common in the oak and conifer forests, but Cheer Pheasant are fewer, preferring patches of mature grass on precipitous south-facing slopes.

Map of Great Himalayan National Park

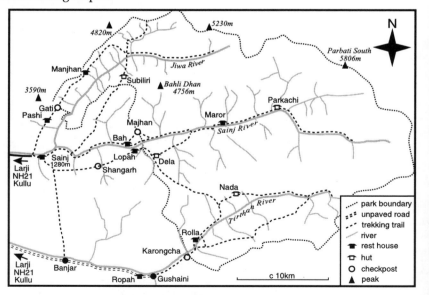

Birds   Other notable species recorded from the park and its environs: Booted, Golden and Black Eagles, Himalayan Griffon, Hen Harrier (UW), Eurasian Hobby, Snow Partridge (R), Himalayan Snowcock, Chukar, Black Francolin, Hill Partridge, Himalayan Monal, Kalij Pheasant, Solitary Snipe, Eurasian Woodcock, Wedge-tailed Green Pigeon, Snow Pigeon, Speckled Wood Pigeon, Oriental Turtle Dove (S), Slaty-headed Parakeet, Pied, Indian, Eurasian, Oriental and Large Hawk Cuckoos (S), Mountain Scops Owl (U),

Tawny Owl, Collared Owlet, Grey Nightjar, Himalayan Swiftlet, White-throated Needletail, Fork-tailed Swift (S), Great Barbet, Speckled Piculet, Scaly-bellied, Himalayan and Brown-fronted Woodpeckers, Yellow-billed Blue Magpie, Grey Treepie, Spotted Nutcracker, Yellow-billed and Red-billed Choughs, Common Raven, Long-tailed Minivet, Himalayan Bulbul, Rusty-cheeked Scimitar Babbler, Scaly-breasted Wren Babbler (U), Black-chinned Babbler*, White-throated, Striated, Variegated* (U) and Chestnut-crowned Laughingthrushes, White-browed and Green Shrike Babblers, Chestnut-tailed Minla, Whiskered Yuhina, White-browed Fulvetta, Dark-sided (S), Asian Brown (S), Rusty-tailed (S), Rufous-gorgeted, Little Pied (R), Ultramarine (S), Slaty-blue (S), Blue-throated (S) and Verditer (S) Flycatchers, Rufous-bellied Niltava (S), Yellow-bellied and White-throated (S) Fantails, Chestnut-headed Tesia, Brownish-flanked and Grey-sided Bush Warblers, Striated Prinia, *tristis* Common Chiffchaff (WP), Tickell's Leaf (S), Buff-barred, Lemon-rumped, Ashy-throated, Greenish (S), Western Crowned (S), Blyth's Leaf (S), Golden-spectacled and Grey-hooded Warblers, White-browed Shortwing (R), Orange-flanked and Golden (U) Bush Robins, Blue-capped and Blue-fronted Redstarts, Little and Spotted Forktails, Grey Bushchat, Chestnut-bellied and Blue Rock (S) Thrushes, Plain-backed, Scaly, Long-billed (U) and Chestnut Thrushes, White-collared and Grey-winged Blackbirds, Brown Dipper, Altai (W) and Rufous-breasted Accentors, Spot-winged, Rufous-naped, Rufous-vented (R), Grey-crested, Black-lored*, Yellow-browed, Fire-capped (S) and Black-throated Tits, White-cheeked and White-tailed Nuthatches, Wallcreeper, Eurasian and Bar-tailed Treecreepers, Olive-backed, Rosy (S) and Upland Pipits, Fire-breasted Flowerpecker, Crimson Sunbird (S), Russet Sparrow, Black-and-yellow, Collared, White-winged and Spot-winged Grosbeaks, Yellow-breasted Greenfinch, Spectacled Finch* (U), Fire-fronted Serin, Plain Mountain Finch, Dark-breasted and Pink-browed Rosefinches, Red Crossbill, Brown, Red-headed and Orange* (R) Bullfinches and Rock Bunting. Note that a number of these are altitudinal migrants and will only be found in the lower reaches of the park and on the approach roads in winter and at higher elevations in summer.

Other Sites   Walks in the immediate area around **Kullu** produce Plum-headed Parakeet*, House Swift, Great Barbet, Yellow-billed Blue Magpie, Whiskered Yuhina, Asian Paradise-flycatcher (S), Striated Prinia, Grey Bushchat, Blue-capped Rock Thrush, Eurasian Treecreeper and Russet Sparrow. Walk or take a taxi to Puin (1600m) and then bird up to the **Bijli Mahadev Temple** (2440m) a popular pilgrimage spot at the end of a long ridge with views down the Beas Valley. Birds: Himalayan Griffon, Black Francolin, Slaty-headed Parakeet, Asian Barred Owlet, Scaly-bellied Woodpecker, Long-tailed Minivet, Hume's and Western Crowned Warblers, Spot-winged Tit, White-cheeked Nuthatch, Yellow-breasted Greenfinch, and White-capped and Rock Buntings. A good wooded area can be explored by taking a taxi to **Dohra Nala** (1400m) on the western side of the valley and birding the path up from there for Wedge-tailed Green Pigeon, Indian Cuckoo (S), Black-chinned Babbler, White-throated, Variegated and Lineated Laughingthrushes, Dark-sided Flycatcher, Spotted Forktail, Grey-winged Blackbird and Fire-breasted Flowerpecker.

Manali (1896m), 40km north of Kullu, with plenty of hotels, is the best place for organising treks around the Kullu Valley. Some good birding on a day trek can be had by walking up into the **Manali Wildlife Sanctuary** on the western side of the valley above Manali via the Hadimba Temple and up to Lamadugh (3380m) towards Manali Pass (4880m). You may encounter birds such as Lammergeier, Cheer Pheasant (U), Himalayan Swiftlet, Yellow-billed Blue Magpie, Ultramarine Flycatcher (S), Brownish-flanked Bush Warbler (S), Indian Blue Robin (S) and Bar-tailed Treecreeper.

Operators in Manali provide camping equipment, porters and guides. The owner of Arohi Travels (☎01901-2139) on the Mall is reliable, interested in natural history and arranges subsidised nature awareness camps for schoolchildren. The treks vary depending on weather and snow conditions. We give two of many possibilities. For others see the map. Enquire locally as to what is possible.

A short 3-4 day trek to the northwest begins in Manali overnighting at Solang (2480m) with a second campsite above Dhundi (2840m) enabling exploration up to **Beas Kund** (Lake – 3540m), the source of the river Beas. Return by the same route or descend to the main road and catch a bus back from Palchan. Birds on this trek in May include Snow Pigeon, Himalayan Woodpecker, Red-billed Chough, Himalayan Bulbul, Dark-sided Flycatcher, Lemon-rumped and Western Crowned Warblers, Orange-flanked Bush Robin, Blue-fronted Redstart, Tickell's Thrush, Brown Dipper, Rufous-breasted Accentor, Spot-winged and Rufous-naped Tits, Olive-backed and Rosy Pipits, Black-and-yellow Grosbeak, and Pink-browed Rosefinch. Look for White-throated Tit* in birches near the treeline here and anywhere in the upper Kullu Valley. Western Tragopan* occurs in better wooded parts but is scarce.

The **Panduropa Trek** is best begun by taking a jeep with your equipment and porters up the Rohtang Pass Rd and setting up camp at Gulaba Camp Site (2940m). Do this early enough to spend the rest of the day exploring above Gulaba towards the Bhrigu Lake. The following day head south via Kothi (2460m) to Panduropa Base Camp (2820m). It is worth spending two nights here so a whole day can be devoted to the Panduropa slopes above looking for Himalayan Monal, White-throated Tit* and Grandala (U above tree-line). The climb reaches 3930m. The following day you can descend to the bottom of the valley via Kothi and Palchan or Vashisht. Most species mentioned above can be seen on this trek as well as Besra, Booted Eagle, Eurasian Hobby, Oriental and Lesser Cuckoos (S), Spotted Nutcracker, Chestnut-tailed Minla, Rusty-tailed and Slaty-blue Flycatchers (S), Aberrant Bush Warbler, Large-billed Leaf Warbler (S), White-collared Blackbird, Scaly and Chestnut Thrushes, Grey-crested and Fire-capped (S) Tits and Plain Mountain Finch.

If you are not keen on trekking and camping, you can see alpine and subalpine species by exploring around the top of the **Rohtang Pass** (3978m). Snow Partridge, Himalayan Snowcock and Solitary Snipe (on marshy pools) are worth searching for but are few and far between. It is best to hire a jeep from Manali, as organised tours leave little time to look around. In summer when the pass is open it might be possible to get a bus to the pass and a bus or lift back to Manali.

The state capital of Himachal Pradesh, the old British summer capital of **Shimla (Simla)**, situated at an altitude of 2200, is a good base for western Himalayan montane forest birding. It is not in the Kullu Valley but 8 hours south of Kullu by bus. There are fairly good road and rail connections with Delhi and plenty of hotels. Bird the Glen Forest on the western edge of the town and the Shimla Water Catchment Sanctuary 12km east of Shimla, south of the NH22 (ask for Wildflower Hall), for many of the same birds of similar altitudes in the GHNP. Many other birding walks and day hikes are possible.

The **Chail Wildlife Sanctuary,** near the small town of Chail about 45km south of Shimla by road, has a good population of Cheer Pheasant.

KASHMIR & LADAKH

Kashmir and Ladakh lie at the northern extreme of the Indian Subcontinent and in terms of birding, as well as culture, offer a stark contrast to the rest of the country and each other. Together they form part of the Indian state known as Jammu and Kashmir but are separated by the Great Himalayan Chain. Their position means that, particularly in winter and during migration, birds from the northern Palearctic turn up as vagrants, and there are a number of sightings of species not recorded elsewhere in India. Spring and summer, however, see peak avian activity with a number of local breeding specialities.

Map of Kashmir & Ladakh

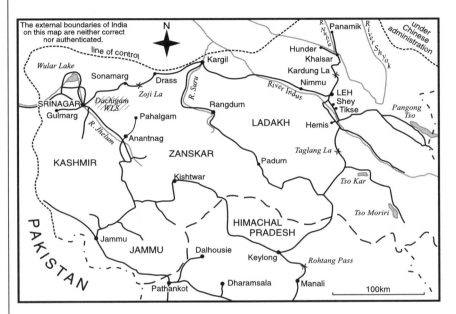

Kashmir

The Vale of Kashmir 1600 m above sea level experiences its fair share of rain. This turns the valley into a green and fertile land, considered by many to be among the most beautiful places on Earth. Over the years it has received some attention from ornithologists and several protected areas have been established. Tytler's Leaf Warbler*, Fire-capped Tit and Orange Bullfinch* are three specialities almost impossible to guarantee anywhere else.

Kashmiri peoples of Moslem persuasion inhabit the Vale and their culture and religion are evident throughout. This was once one of India's most popular tourist areas with masses of holidaymakers escaping the summer heat of the plains and relaxing on the picturesque houseboats of Dal Lake, or trekking in the Lidder Valley. In winter Gulmarg used to be a popular ski resort but political violence reduced tourists to a trickle. The situation now appears to be stabilising. While it is possible to visit the area in any case, one should enquire with the authorities and recently returned travellers to find out whether it is safe to travel.

Kashmir is temperate with an almost European seasonality. The most pleasant months are May to September with daytime temperatures in the upper 20°sC. The winters are fiercely cold from November to March, even down in the Vale, with snow in the higher regions into May and June. Birding at this time of year, though difficult, can be very rewarding. Some trekking is possible as early as April, but snow may prevent access to the upper parts of the routes until June. The main trekking season is June until October when it begins to get cold at night. Kashmir does not experience monsoons, rainfall being fairly even through the year.

Fire-capped tit

Srinagar

Srinagar is the capital of Kashmir at the southern end of the picturesque Dal lake in a valley between the main range of the Himalaya and the Pir Panjal mountains. It is the point of entry to the region by air and a base for exploring a number of sites.

Map of Srinagar

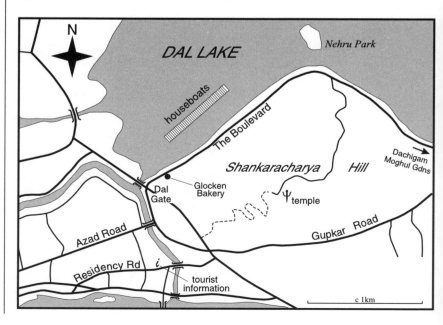

Location Srinagar is served by daily Indian Airlines flights from Delhi and Jammu. Flights from Amritsar and Leh are less frequent. All routes to and from Srinagar are usually heavily booked: make reservations well in advance. The overland route is via Jammu with a direct bus from Delhi taking 24 hours but often up to 12 hours late. It can be more convenient to get a train to Jammu and then a bus from there. Buses meet the overnight *Shalimar Express* from Delhi and reach Srinagar 10–12 hours later. Share taxis go from the railway station at Jammu and are faster but more expensive. For the route to Leh see that section.

Accommodation The troubles in Kashmir have meant that practically all the hotels closed down. The only hotel remaining half open was the expensive but poorly maintained *Centaur* at the eastern end of the lake. In peaceful times there is a wide choice of accommodation. *Houseboats* on Dal Lake, however, are among the main tourist attractions and many operated throughout. On arrival in Srinagar it is best to catch an auto-rickshaw to Dal Gate and take one of the Shikaras (boats) to look at the houseboats. Do not be pressurised into taking one until you look at a few. Prices are extremely negotiable and normally include meals. Make sure that everything included in the price is spelt out, e.g. teas, coffees and transport to and from the shore.

Dal Lake is several stretches of open water interconnected by a series of waterways. The houseboats on Nagin Lake are quieter as it is further away from town, but those opposite the Boulevard near Dal Gate are more convenient, especially for early morning starts. The Glocken (German) Bakery, down a side-street east of Dal Gate, is a good source of supplies.

Strategy The area immediately around Dal Lake can be explored on foot or by bicycle hired by the day from a store near Dal Gate. A boat trip on the lake is a must and can turn up interesting species. During migration large numbers of waterfowl visit the lake. Shankaracharya Hill is a nature reserve and a walk up the main road from the eastern end of the Boulevard can be productive. The Moghul Gardens can be reached by bike and hold a few interesting birds. Until the situation improves the only way to cover the rest of the Valley is by day trips by bus or taxi from Srinagar, although the hotel at Tangmarg remained open most of the time, and would be a good base for exploring the mountains around Gulmarg to the west. There are several taxi stands in Srinagar, including one at the bottom of the road up to Shankaracharya Hill and one near Dal Gate. They have 'set fares' for most destinations posted outside, but there is room for bargaining.

Birds Large numbers of waterfowl join the residents of Dal Lake during migration. Black-crowned Night Heron and Pied Kingfisher are resident. In summer Clamorous Reed Warblers are common and a few Little Bittern inhabit the reed beds while Whiskered Terns hunt over the water. Unfortunately, birds have declined on the lake due to pollution and disturbance.

The much sought-after endemic Orange Bullfinch* has a restricted range, and Shankaracharya Hill is probably one of the easiest places to find it in winter. Here and in the parks and gardens around the lake look for Chukar, Eurasian Wryneck (S), Brown-fronted Woodpecker, Eurasian Golden Oriole (S), Long-tailed Minivet (S), Himalayan and Black Bulbuls, Streaked and Variegated* (W) Laughingthrushes, Asian Paradise-flycatcher (S), Brownish-flanked Bush Warbler, Mountain Chiffchaff (P), Tickell's Leaf (P), Hume's (P), Lemon-rumped (P) and Western Crowned (S) Warblers, Indian Blue Robin (S), Orange-flanked Bush Robin (W), Blue-capped Redstart (U),

Spotted Forktail, Grey Bushchat, Blue-capped and Blue Rock Thrushes (S),
Tickell's Thrush (S), Grey-winged Blackbird (W), Chestnut Thrush (U),
Black-throated Accentor (W), Green-backed, Spot-winged and Rufous-
vented Tits and White-capped Bunting (S).

**Map of
Around Srinagar**

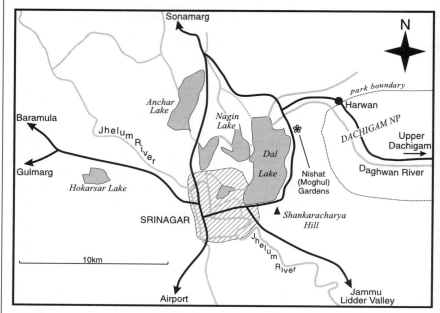

Dachigam

Dachigam was a game reserve, turned into a National Park to protect the
endangered Hangul, or Kashmir Stag, as well as the drinking water
catchment for Srinagar. It has an area of some 140km² and covers a wide
altitudinal range from the edge of the Kashmir Valley up to about 4200m in
Upper Dachigam. The park encompasses the valley of the River Daghwan
and surrounding peaks.

**Map of Dachigam
National Park**

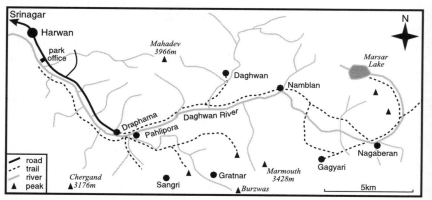

Location

The entrance to Dachigam is a five minute walk past the village of
Harwan a little over 20km by road northeast of Srinagar. It is possible to
get a bus to Harwan (one hour) or a taxi to the entrance. A tarmac road
runs for several kilometres into the park, then a trail follows the course of
the river. Upper Dachigam remains snow covered for much of the year
with trekking possible from June to October.

Accommodation

There are *Forest Rest Houses* in the park which may become available if the situation in Kashmir normalises. Until then trekking in Dachigam is only possible with special permission; a tent and food supplies must be carried. Lower Dachigam can be explored on a day trip from Srinagar.

Strategy

To visit Dachigam, permission must be obtained from the office of the Chief Wildlife Warden in the same building as the tourist office in Srinagar. It is necessary to take a Park Ranger as a guide. The rangers are sharp-eyed and useful as they know the habits of the wildlife in the park. Birding is good along the main trail through the valley bottom which should only be departed from in the company of a ranger. Take food and drink as none is available in the park.

Birds

The park list numbers more than 150 birds many of which breed. Among the more notable are Besra, Northern Goshawk, Himalayan Griffon, Lammergeier, Himalayan Monal, Koklass Pheasant, Solitary Snipe, Collared Owlet, Tawny Owl, Scaly-bellied and Himalayan Woodpeckers, Yellow-billed Blue Magpie, Kashmir*, Slaty-blue and Ultramarine Flycatchers (S), Yellow-bellied Fantail, several species of *Phylloscopus* warbler including Tytler's Leaf* (S), White-tailed Rubythroat, Rufous-backed Redstart (W), Plumbeous and White-capped Water Redstarts, Brown Dipper, White-throated Tit*, Bar-tailed Treecreeper, Wallcreeper, Russet Sparrow, Black-and-yellow Grosbeak, Spectacled Finch*, Fire-fronted Serin and Yellow-breasted Greenfinch, as well as most of the others found on Shankaracharya Hill including Orange Bullfinch*.

Other Wildlife

The Hangul is a race of Red Deer, though some consider it a full species. While formerly more widespread, Dachigam contains most of the world's remaining wild population. In summer they go higher, returning to Lower Dachigam in September for the rut. In winter they congregate in herds of up to 50 animals and are then easiest to see.

The Himalayan Black Bear is more common in the Park than the Brown Bear and should be treated with the greatest respect as they may attack humans. Keep still and allow the animal to move away, which it usually does. If absolutely necessary, you can sometimes frighten a bear off with loud noises and wild gesticulation. At all times follow the instructions of your guide. Leopards are occasionally seen and prey on the Hangul. Grey Langur, Fox, Jackal and Yellow-throated Marten are more common. Musk Deer and Serow are uncommon in Upper Dachigam where Snow Leopard has also been seen.

Other Sites

West of Srinagar the two lakes of **Haigam Rakh** and **Hokarsar Rakh** with their large reed-beds are particularly important for winter waterfowl and breeding Little Bittern. Their avifauna is similar although Haigam, being larger and further from the town, harbours greater numbers of birds. Duck shooting is allowed in winter, but there is a proposal to declare Hokarsar a Sanctuary. Both are on the road to Baramulla with Hokarsar within cycling range (10km) of Srinagar. Haigam is about 30km away near the southern end of Lake Wular, the nearest town being Sopore. A bus or taxi would be needed.

The commonest wintering duck are Northern Pintail, Common Teal, Mallard, Gadwall, Eurasian Wigeon, Northern Shoveler and Common Pochard with smaller numbers of Ferruginous and Red-crested Pochard. A number of species stop on migration when up to 4000 Garganey have been recorded. In summer Little Bitterns are common together with smaller numbers of Black-crowned Night Herons. Other birds include Pallas's Fish Eagle, Water Rail, Baillon's and Ruddy Crakes, Pheasant-tailed Jacana, Greater Painted-snipe, Whiskered Tern (B), Tawny Owl, Stork-billed Kingfisher, European Bee-eater, European Roller, Bluethroat (P), *rama* Booted, Paddyfield and Blunt-winged (B) Warblers, Clamorous Reed Warbler (B) and Mountain Chiffchaff, as well as numbers of other species that occur around Srinagar. Slaty-headed Parakeets roost in the trees at the edge of Haigam Rakh.

The once popular ski resort of **Gulmarg** at an altitude of 2700m on the western rim of the Kashmir Valley offers the opportunity to get to grips with higher altitude species. 52km from Srinagar, it is reached by bus or taxi in about 2–3 hours. During times of unrest buses only run as far as Tangmarg at the foot of the mountain. The name means Meadow of Flowers and in spring it is a flower-carpeted expanse with pine forests round about. If the weather is fine, Nanga Parbat (8125m), one of the highest mountains in the western Himalaya, can be seen.

In normal times there are a number of hotels in Gulmarg. One basic hotel still operates in Tangmarg, but it would be advisable to check the situation in advance before moving here.

Gulmarg can be good for trekking, or for one or more day trips. Either catch a bus to Tangmarg (2 hours) and bird up the road as far as time allows, or try to get a lift and bird back down along the road (13km) or the shorter steeper trail. If coming by car, go up to Gulmarg and do the 11km 'Outer Circular Walk' or walk across to Khilanmarg (6km) and back. If Gulmarg itself is above the snow-line, it may be better to bird back down the road to Tangmarg and get your vehicle to pick you up there. Birds include Golden Eagle, Himalayan Griffon, Lammergeier, Tawny Owl, Himalayan and Scaly-bellied Woodpeckers, Spotted Nutcracker, Rufous-tailed, Ultramarine and Slaty-blue Flycatchers (S), Western Crowned Warbler (S), Indian Blue Robin (S), Blue Whistling Thrush, Alpine Accentor, Spot-winged and Rufous-naped Tits, White-cheeked Nuthatch, Bar-tailed Treecreeper, Russet Sparrow, Black-and-yellow Grosbeak and Spectacled Finch*.

Explore the foothills and fields on the way back to Srinagar for species such as Striated Prinia, Rufous-backed Redstart (W), Tickell's Thrush (S), Altai and Black-throated Accentors (W), Spanish Sparrow (W) and Hodgson's Mountain Finch (W).

Lidder Valley Trek

This popular short, easy trekking route has a number of species such as Tytler's Leaf Warbler* (S), Fire-capped Tit (S) and White-throated Tit* more easily seen here than elsewhere in Kashmir. Overa Wildlife Sanctuary is an area of mountains above the valley where eight species of leaf warbler including Hume's, Orange-barred, Tickell's Leaf and Tytler's Leaf breed. The monkeys seen occasionally throughout the trek are Rhesus Macaques with much heavier coats than in most of India.

Location

The trekking route begins at Pahalgam which suffered badly due to the loss of its tourist trade. Pahalgam is 90km from Srinagar and reached in 2–3 hours by car, or somewhat longer by bus. A wide road goes as far as Aru and a path continues along the valley to Lidderwat then branches off towards the Kolahoi Glacier. The trek as far as Lidderwat may be possible as early as April when Fire-capped Tits return, but in some years snow makes conditions difficult or impossible until June. Make enquiries in Srinagar before you set off.

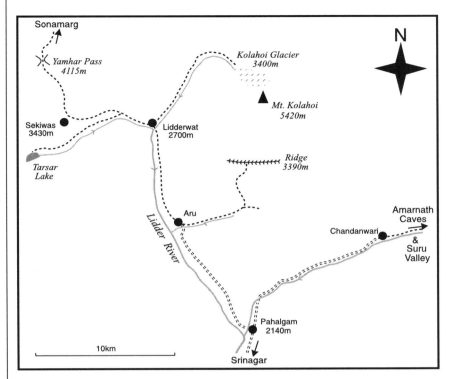

Map of Lidder
Valley Trek

Accommodation

The hotels and lodges along the route may re-open as normality returns. It may be preferable to organise the trek from Srinagar using tents and bringing food – ask your houseboat owner. Ponies and porters are usually available in Pahalgam.

Strategy

1st Day: Pahalgam to Aru

The route follows an easy gradient dirt road along the right bank of the Lidder River for a distance of some 12km. Plumbeous and White-capped River Redstarts, Blue Whistling Thrush, and Brown Dipper are quite common on the river. In the forests and clearings look for Himalayan Griffon, Rufous Turtle Dove, Scaly-bellied and Himalayan Woodpeckers, Long-tailed Minivet, Streaked Laughingthrush, Kashmir*, Rufous-tailed and Ultramarine Flycatchers (S), Western Crowned Warbler (S), Grey Bushchat, Blue-headed Rock Thrush, Green-backed, Spot-winged and Rufous-naped Tits, Bar-tailed Treecreeper, Russet Sparrow, Yellow-breasted Greenfinch, and Rock Bunting. Check bushes for Slaty Blue Flycatcher (S), Tickell's Leaf and Tytler's Leaf Warblers (S) and Orange Bullfinch*. Fire-capped Tits (S) are not common but can be found anywhere from here up to Lidderwat particularly where the forest is mixed with deciduous trees.

(Extra Day)

If time is available, use Aru as a base camp and make a day-trek up the side-valley to the east. Follow the main trail around to the left through forest interspersed with alpine meadows to a ridge at about 3390m. As this is a south facing slope the snow melts earlier here and this can be an alternative to the Lidderwat – Kolahoi section in early summer. Among the species here are Eurasian Hobby, Snow Pigeon, Pallas's and Western

Crowned Warblers, Black-throated and Mistle Thrushes, Rosy Pipit, Plain Mountain Finch and Spectacled Finch*.

2nd Day: Aru to Lidderwat

The trail becomes a steep path up into the conifer forest and then undulates through patches of forest and open grassy meadows to reach Lidderwat after 12km. Most of the trail is fairly high above the river on the eastern side of the valley. Birds found on this section are Eurasian Sparrowhawk, Lammergeier, Eurasian Hobby, Snow Pigeon, Sooty Flycatcher (S), Large-billed Warbler (S), Indian Blue Robin (S), Orange-flanked Bush Robin, Blue-fronted and White-bellied Redstarts, Kashmir and White-cheeked Nuthatches, Plain Mountain Finch, and Black-and-yellow Grosbeak.

3rd & 4th Days: Lidderwat area

Using Lidderwat as a base, trek up towards the Kolahoi Glacier exploring pine forest, patches of birches, open areas and bushes. Look for Snow Pigeon, Lesser Cuckoo (S), Spotted Nutcracker, Yellow-billed Chough, Tickell's Leaf Warbler (S), White-tailed Rubythroat (S), White-bellied Redstart (S), Blue Rock Thrush, White-throated Tit*, and Red-fronted Rosefinch.

5th Day: Lidderwat to Pahalgam

The return to Pahalgam can be done in one day. If the Yamhar Pass (4120m) is not snowed up, it is possible to trek for another three days north via Sekiwas from Lidderwat to reach the main road near Kulan. From there buses go to Srinagar or Sonamarg.

With more time, there are many other treks possible in Kashmir. For more details see the Lonely Planet Guides to the *Indian Himalaya* and *Trekking in the Indian Himalaya*.

Other Sites   **Wular Lake** 34km northwest of Srinagar is one of the largest freshwater lakes in Asia and a Ramsar site, mainly important for waterfowl on migration as it freezes in winter.

Sonamarg at 2740m is the last town in Kashmir on the road towards Ladakh and can be used as a base for trekking. Otherwise it is a little far for a comfortable day trip from Srinagar.

Kishtwar National Park about 60km from Kishtwar in southern Kashmir consists mainly of coniferous forests, scrub and alpine meadows at 1700 to 4800m in the catchment area of the Chenab River. Permission to visit must be obtained from the Regional Wildlife Warden for North Jammu, Nr. Jammu Ashok Hotel, Manda (Ramnagar), Jammu.

Ladakh

Ladakh lies in the rain shadow of the Himalaya more than 3000m above sea level. The low precipitation results in a barren moon-like landscape traversed by green ribbons of river valley surrounded by spectacular snow-clad mountains. The Ladakhis are a friendly Tibeto-Mongoloid people who, for the most part, follow the Buddhist religion. Refugees from Tibet, who find the climate and culture similar to that of their home country, have swelled the population. The avifauna is more Palearctic than Oriental and includes interesting Tibetan elements. The number and diversity of birds is not as great as in some parts of India, but 300 species have been recorded, including many not found elsewhere in the country. The fascinating people and landscapes are themselves reason enough to venture here.

As a result of the extreme altitude average temperatures in Ladakh are very low and it is only from June to September that daytime temperatures reach the 20°sC. This is naturally when most visitors arrive. Temperatures in mid-winter drop as low as –40°C. At this time of year high altitude species may be easier to see as the cold and snow bring them lower.

In summer there are regular buses from Srinagar in Kashmir and Manali in Himachal Pradesh. However, for much of the year the only way to reach Ladakh is by air, as the high passes can only be crossed from early June to September/October. Buses and flights are often subject to cancellations and delays of days at a time due to weather conditions. This should be borne in mind if you have an important connection to make.

It is important to spend 3–4 days acclimatising to the high altitude on arrival in Ladakh and avoid strenuous activity at the beginning of your stay. If you arrive from Kashmir or Himachal, you may be partially acclimatised, but coming directly from Delhi you may feel uncomfortable for a few days. If you feel the effects of the altitude badly and your symptoms do not subside after 36 hours, get help from the medical clinic which is manned 24 hours a day ☎560.

Permits

This is a restricted border region so visitors are not allowed more than one mile north of the Srinagar to Leh road. The Nubra Valley, Pangong Tso (Tso = Lake), Tso Kar and Tso Moriri close to the Chinese border, have been opened to tourists in groups of four or more people. These are worth exploring and have not been much visited by birders. To visit these and Hemis NP, you need a 'letter of introduction' from a local travel agent then a permit from the office of the District Magistrate (Deputy Commissioner) near the Polo Ground in Leh. The office is open 10.00 to 16.00 every day except Sundays and public holidays. If you are not part of a group of four, ask other travellers if they are interested, or enquire at local travel agents in case they can make up numbers. Check to see if it is still necessary to travel together once you have the permit. Applications submitted with a passport photo through a travel agent are usually processed within a day and allow visits of up to a week. See *Other Sites* below.

Leh

The capital of Ladakh is the point of entry by air and a convenient base for exploring. Many specialities can be found within walking distance.

Location

Leh can be reached by regular Indian Airlines flights from Delhi, Jammu, Chandigarh and Srinagar although it can be difficult to get a flight at short notice. It is best to book your return at the same time as the outbound flight as planes are often full. The return can be changed at a later date if seats are available. The flight from Srinagar takes 30 minutes and from Delhi about 1¹/₄ hours. Leh airport is a few kilometres south of the town. The airport bus does not always run, but taxi drivers are reliable and charge a standard fare to the hotel of your choice. You can stop off at the tourist information office on the way into town.

The bus from Srinagar takes two days including overnight at Kargil. Buses leave the Tourist Reception Centre in Srinagar at 08.00. If you intend breaking the journey in Kargil in order to bird Suru Valley, do so on your return journey, as many people take the bus to Leh and fly back. This means that buses to Leh are more crowded and it can be difficult getting a

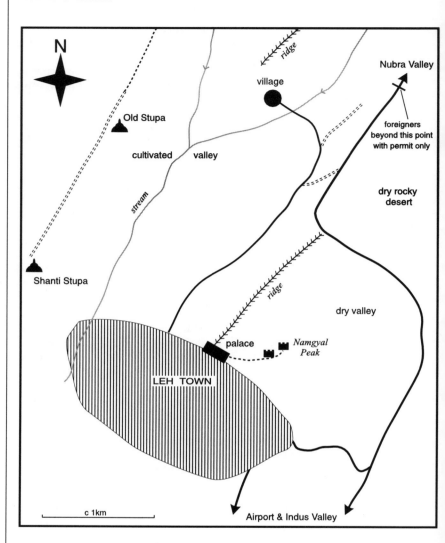

Map of Leh

N

Nubra Valley

ridge

village

Old Stupa

cultivated   valley

foreigners
beyond this point
with permit only

stream

dry rocky
desert

Shanti Stupa

ridge

dry valley

palace   *Namgyal Peak*

LEH TOWN

c 1km

Airport & Indus Valley

seat if you board in Kargil. In some years the overland route may open as
early as mid May, but more often it is passable from June to October.

From Manali in the Kullu Valley of Himachal Pradesh the bus also takes
two days with an overnight stop in Sarchu. This route is open from July to
September depending on the weather. Since the main pass is over 5300m
high most people suffer from headaches and sickness due to the altitude
and motion of the bus. It may be better to fly into Leh and return by bus
after having acclimatised.

For those with financial resources the overland journey by share taxi or
jeep can be more attractive.

Accommodation   During the summer there are plenty of hotels and lodges to suit all tastes
and pockets, though rooms may be in short supply in the July/August
peak season. During the off season only two or three hotels remain open,
but it is fairly easy to find private accommodation by asking locally. Most
restaurants close during this time of year and finding somewhere good to
eat can require a bit of hunting around. If making day trips out from Leh in

the off season, you have to take something to eat and drink with you. A sleeping bag can be useful even if you are not planning to go trekking. Sun cream and a hat are indispensable.

Strategy   There are few 'birding sites' in Ladakh and anywhere can turn up good birds. The first day or two at this altitude can be used for gentle exploration of Leh and its surroundings. Check patches of trees and bushes for passerines. Look along the stream that runs through the western part of the town. Explore the fields in the cultivated valley to the northwest. The area where cultivation ends and barren slopes begin can be productive for finches and larks. Early morning bird activity is greater on the western side of the valley as this catches the first rays of the rising sun.

Birds   In and around the town you can see Black-billed Magpie (common in Ladakh but not found elsewhere in India), Red-billed Chough, Robin and Brown Accentors and Fire-fronted Serin. Along the stream in winter look for Solitary Snipe and White-throated Dipper. The valley and rocky desert edges to the northwest hold large flocks of Horned Lark, Mongolian Finch and Tibetan Snowfinch in winter although the latter can be extremely flighty. Chukar and Hill Pigeon are resident whereas Eurasian Crag Martin, Common Swift, Oriental Skylark and Desert Wheatear are mainly summer visitors. Look for the less common Snow Pigeon – alone or in flocks of Hill Pigeon. Check trees and bushes for Hume's Lesser Whitethroat (S), Mountain Chiffchaff (S), Bluethroat (S), White-winged Redstart, Twite (W), Fire-fronted Serin, and Common (S), Red-mantled (S), Streaked and Great Rosefinches. Sulphur-bellied Warblers (S) prefer the stony hillsides with scattered bushes.

Raptors are not common but can turn up anywhere: Northern Goshawk (W), Eurasian Sparrowhawk (W), Long-legged Buzzard (WP), (Steppe) Common Buzzard, Golden Eagle, Himalayan Griffon, Lammergeier, Saker Falcon (WP), Merlin (WP), Common Kestrel (SP) and Eurasian Hobby (S).

Indus Valley near Leh

The River Indus flows through Ladakh through a broad, relatively fertile valley and at times through deep narrow gorges. The river nearest to Leh is well populated, but most settlements are strung out along the river, usually in association with the spectacular gompas (Buddhist monasteries). The habitat consists of cultivated fields, patches of bushes and trees as well as plantations of willows and poplars. Further away the mountains become more barren and rocky, suitable habitat for larks and finches. Many of Ladakh's birds are within a kilometre or so of the river and its tributaries. In summer Ibisbills nest on banks and islands in the river and are occasionally there in winter.

Location   For most of its course in Ladakh the Indus flows northwesterly. It passes 10km south of Leh at a lower altitude which means there are times in winter when Leh is covered in snow but the fields by the river remain snow free and attract many birds. The area between the town and the river has settlements, the airport and military barracks best avoided. The most interesting section of river is between Spitok, 10km south of Leh and Hemis 45km southeast. There are fairly regular bus services to all places in this area, much less frequent in winter. Enquire about timings at the bus stand the day before your trip.

Map of Indus Valley
(note orientation)

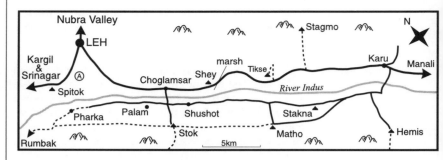

Accommodation

During summer basic accommodation is found at Tikse, Stok and Hemis, but this is normally closed at other times of the year. Most tea stalls and restaurants are closed in the off season so bring your own food and drink.

Strategy

In summer the Indus Valley can be explored from Tikse, Stok or Hemis. In winter you are restricted to day trips from Leh. The main autumn bird passage is from mid-August to early October while spring migrants pass through in April and May.

Catch an early morning bus or taxi to Shey (16km) or Tikse (20km) and walk back to Spitok or only as far as Choglamsar where there are tea stalls at the main junction and frequent mini-buses back to Leh. Explore the fields, riverside trees and bushes; the marsh and streams between the river and Shey turn up interesting species. Investigate the barren areas away from the river, but do not venture too far as foreigners are not allowed more than 1.6km north of the main road. It can be worth spending a couple or more days doing this combined with visits to the gompas. If intending to return by bus, find out when the last one goes before you leave Leh.

A visit to the gorge at Stok in summer can produce Yellow-billed Chough, Sulphur-bellied Warbler and Wallcreeper.

White-winged
Redstart

Birds   Ibisbills breed on the river in summer – try the area around Tikse. In winter the marsh and streams at Shey hold Solitary Snipe. Great Bittern has overwintered here. White-winged Redstart and Streaked Rosefinch are abundant in the valley in winter but less so in summer. Other birds to look out for are Ruddy Shelduck (B), Common Merganser (B), Northern Goshawk (WP), Long-legged Buzzard (WP), Booted Eagle (P), Eurasian Marsh, Hen, Montagu's and Pallid Harriers (P), Steppe Eagle (RP), Pallas's Fish Eagle (RP), Merlin (W), Pallas's Gull (P), Common Tern (B), Baillon's and Spotted Crakes (P), Long-eared and Short-eared Owls (P), Common (S) and Fork-tailed Swifts (P), European and Blue-cheeked Bee-eaters (P), Hume's Short-toed (S) and Horned (W) Larks, Oriental Skylark (S), Grey-backed Shrike (S), Common Raven, Hume's Lesser Whitethroat (S), Mountain Chiffchaff (S), White-browed Tit Warbler (W), Bluethroat (SP), Desert Wheatear (S), Dark-throated Thrush (WP), Brown Dipper, Alpine (W), Robin, Brown and Black-throated Accentors (WP), Tibetan Snowfinch (W), Twite, Plain Mountain Finch, Mongolian Finch, Common Rosefinch (S), Great Rosefinch (W), and Pine Bunting (W). Black-crowned Night Heron, Black Stork, Rosy Pipit, Little Forktail, Dusky and Song Thrushes, Spanish Sparrow, Yellowhammer and Reed Bunting have also been recorded from the Indus Valley.

Other Sites   The **Rumbak Valley** is formed by a small river that flows into the Indus from the south 16km west of Leh. To reach it, cross the Indus at Choglamsar-Stok bridge and head west. The upper reaches of the Valley beyond Rumbak towards the Ganda La are good for Himalayan Snowcock, Golden Eagle, Lammergeier, Grandala and Wallcreeper.

Suru Valley

Kargil is the second largest town in Ladakh, at 2650m in the Valley of the River Suru. Since the town is the overnight stop on the main route between Leh and Srinagar this area can be conveniently visited en route. A road goes up through the upper Suru Valley over the Pensi La at 4400m and down to Padum, the capital of the Zanskar Region. The road is rough and only open between June and October. In summer it is possible to trek the route in a minimum of seven days, but you must take provisions and equipment and only a limited amount of the latter may be available in Kargil. The avifauna is to some extent similar to that of the Indus Valley but is less studied.

Birds   This region has hardly been visited outside April to October so all records apply to this period: Ruddy Shelduck, Common Merganser (Rangdum area), Golden Eagle, Lammergeier, Himalayan Griffon, Eurasian Hobby, Himalayan Snowcock (mountainsides above the valley around Rangdum and Juldo), Ibisbill (on the river between Kargil and Parkachik), Lesser Sand Plover (breeds in the Rangdum area), Solitary Snipe (R), Common Tern, Snow, Rock and Hill Pigeons, Oriental Turtle Dove, (Tibetan) Little Owl, Common and Alpine (R) Swifts, Wryneck (between Kargil and Panikhar), Eurasian Crag Martin, Hume's Short-toed Lark (dry areas on the valley bottom), Horned Lark (on scree slopes), Oriental Skylark, Rosy Pipit (around Rangdum), Citrine Wagtail (common breeder), Golden Oriole (plantations between Kargil and Sanku), Red-billed and Yellow-billed Choughs, White-throated Dipper (on tributaries of the Suru), Brown Dipper, Robin Accentor (common around Rangdum), Rufous-breasted, Brown (R) and Black-throated (R) Accentors, Hume's Lesser Whitethroat (common in

Map of Suru Valley

scrub between Kargil and Panikhar), Mountain Chiffchaff, Tickell's Leaf (U), Sulphur-bellied (stony hillsides and scree slopes), Hume's (P?) and Greenish Warblers, White-browed Tit Warbler (R), White-tailed Ruby-throat (R), Bluethroat (common Kargil to Panikhar), Little Forktail (R), Pied (cultivated areas around Kargil), Variable (rare around Kargil) and Desert (R) Wheatears, Blue Rock Thrush, Fire-capped Tit (U), Wallcreeper, Rosy Pipit, Spanish Sparrow, Tibetan Snowfinch (around Rangdum), Fire-fronted Serin, Plain and Brandt's Mountain Finches (latter less common than but often associated with the former), Common, Great (near Rangdum) and Red-fronted Rosefinches (Rangdum area) and Rock Bunting.

Other Wildlife   The area supports interesting high altitude mammals including Wolf, Brown Bear, Himalayan Marmot, Ibex, Urial and Bharal (Blue Sheep), as well as the almost mythical and rarely seen Snow Leopard.

Other Sites   The **Hemis National Park** above Hemis Gompa covers 600km^2 and offers possibilities for high-altitude trekking in summer. Search for Tibetan and Himalayan Snowcocks beside Lammergeier and Golden Eagle. There are Blue Sheep and Nayan (Great Tibetan Sheep, a race of Argali), as well as the chance of a Wolf. The best area is on the Nimaling Plateau between Hankar and Konmaru La.

There are several remote lakes (lake = tso) in eastern Ladakh recently opened to foreign tourists with permission (see above). Here breeding species include Bar-headed Goose, Ruddy Shelduck, Brown-headed Gull and Lesser Sand Plover. Tibetan Sandgrouse come to drink from streams that feed the alkaline lakes. A very few of the highly endangered Black-necked Cranes breed in remote regions of Ladakh and sometimes feed in the salt marshes here. If you come across any, do not disturb them. The high-altitude plains are home to Himalayan Marmot and Kiang (Tibetan Wild Ass), both fairly common in some areas. Generally you need to organise a jeep with a driver/guide and bring your own tents and provisions.

The easiest lake to visit is **Tso Kar** (Tsokar, Kartso), about 100km southeast of Leh. It is reached by a five hour plus drive along the Leh-Manali road crossing the 5328m Taglang La (look out for Tibetan Snowcock) to the road head at Pongunagu. Blanford's Snowfinch bred at Tso Kar in June 1993. Also in the Rupshu (Rupsu, Rupchu) Valley is **Tso Moriri** (Tsomorari), 50km further southeast. The lake is known for breeding Bar-headed Geese, but other species can be found on and around its margins. There is a PWD Rest House at Karzog on the western side of the lake, but this must be booked in Leh. The whole Rupshu Valley with elevations ranging from 3000m to more than 5000m is excellent for the region's specialities. May can be good as the birds are often at lower elevations at the beginning of the month before moving to higher breeding grounds. The nearest of the lakes to Leh is **Pangong Tso** (Bangong Co), just 80km to the east on the Chinese border, but it is more difficult to get to and only a small part of the lake is accessible.

The **Nubra (Green) Valley** in north Ladakh is likely to be interesting. Travel involves crossing the Kardung La, at 5602m the highest motorable pass in the world. This area and Pangong Tso are probably as near as you can get to the region where the only two known specimens of Sillem's Mountain Finch were collected in 1929 at an altitude of 5125m, 40km east-southeast of the Karakorum Pass, an area under Chinese administration. Only identified as a separate species in 1992 it has never been seen since its discovery. It would be a coup to find it again. There are two valleys here. Permits only allow you as far as Panamik in the northern and Hunder in the southern valley. There are irregular buses (not daily) from Leh to the Nubra Valley and basic lodges in Diskit, Khalsar, Hunder, Sumur, and Panamik. Take tinned food, vegetables, chocolate and other rations from Leh to enliven the rather limited food available locally.

NORTH BENGAL AND SIKKIM

The Himalayan region of northern West Bengal has received the attention of visiting birders in recent years though few venture further north into Sikkim. With Darjeeling and Lava more accessible, superb birds such as Satyr Tragopan, Fire-tailed Myzornis, Yellow-throated Fulvetta and Blue-fronted Robin have found their way onto birders' trip lists. The best time is partly dependent on the rainy season which usually lasts from mid/late May to September. April and early May are ideal months as resident birds are in full song and the rich red rhododendron flowers are attractive to the avian population as well as the human eye. Late October to early December is a good time to visit the mountains, as relatively clear skies bring good conditions and excellent views of the awe-inspiring backdrop provided by Everest and Kanchenjunga to the north. Visibility in the mountains may be hampered by thick mists and cloud during the earlier part of the year, while snowfall can make treks to Sandakphu difficult or impossible

Map of North
Bengal and Sikkim

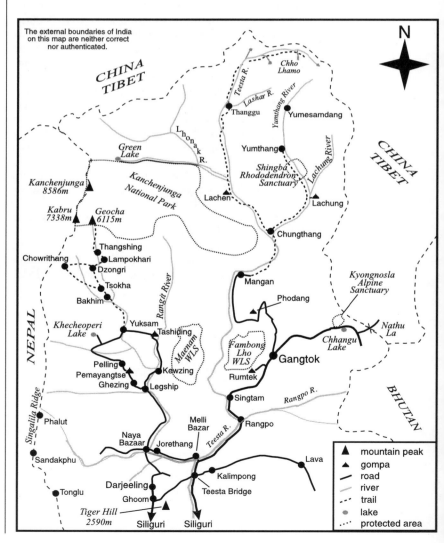

between late December and March but has the advantage of forcing some altitudinal migrants down to lower elevations.

Access to Darjeeling and Lava is unrestricted. A permit, easily obtainable in Darjeeling, is needed to visit Sikkim.

Darjeeling and Tiger Hill

Few people have not heard of Darjeeling (Darjiling), at least in connection with the fine tea from the surrounding plantations. The town became an important hill station during the Raj and today is still popular with those who want to escape the summer heat of the plains. At an altitude of 2130m it is an excellent first base for the birdwatcher who wants to discover the avifauna of the eastern Himalaya. The nearby Tiger Hill is an excellent viewpoint for watching the sun come up over Kanchenjunga, the world's third highest mountain, and is home to Yellow-billed Blue Magpie, Red-tailed Minla, Maroon-backed Accentor, Red-headed Bullfinch and many other colourful species. With luck you may find the superb Satyr Tragopan or one of the Himalaya's rarest warblers – the Broad-billed Warbler.

Darjeeling is an obvious stepping-stone on the way to Lava or the magical land of Sikkim and the best place from which to organise a trek to Sandakphu, a good birdwatching area on the high-altitude Singalila ridge that forms the border with Nepal.

Location   Darjeeling is in the northern part of West Bengal, where a tongue of India separates the two Himalayan kingdoms of Nepal and Bhutan. The nearest airport with regular flights from Calcutta, Delhi and Guwahati is 90km away in the plains at Bagdogra, 11km from the town of Siliguri. From the airport a direct bus that connects with incoming flights takes 3^1/$_2$ hours to Darjeeling. A share-taxi may be slightly quicker.

The classic route to Darjeeling is by the famous toy train. The journey can be rather slow (8–9 hours) and cramped, but it is an experience not to be missed. In principle, the train runs daily, but sometimes services are cancelled due to maintenance on the track, particularly in the rainy season. The train leaves Siliguri at 09.00 with an additional departure at 07.15 during the main tourist season. If you do not feel like spending the whole day on the train, take it as far as Kurseong (5 hours) and then a bus from there (1 hour). Siliguri is served by mainline train services from Calcutta and Delhi. There are three stations here to confuse the unwary; the main one is at New Jalpaiguri where you connect with the toy train. It should be possible to book your ticket through to Darjeeling from your starting point if the toy train is running. Numerous buses, share-taxis and jeeps ply the route from Siliguri to Darjeeling.

Tiger Hill is 11km from Darjeeling above the small town and monastery of Ghoom (8km) which you pass through as you approach from the plains. The number one tourist attraction in Darjeeling is a trip to Tiger Hill to watch the sunrise over Kanchenjunga, and any hotel can arrange an early morning jeep for you. During the daytime jeeps run a shuttle-bus service between the two towns.

The easiest way to continue on to Kalimpong is by share-jeep (2 hours) from the main Bazaar in Darjeeling. Buses are much slower and not much cheaper. From Kalimpong you can visit Lava and then continue on to Sikkim.

If you want to go to Nepal, book a ticket with an agent in Darjeeling. This involves a change of buses at Siliguri. To do it yourself, get a bus or

Map of Darjeeling

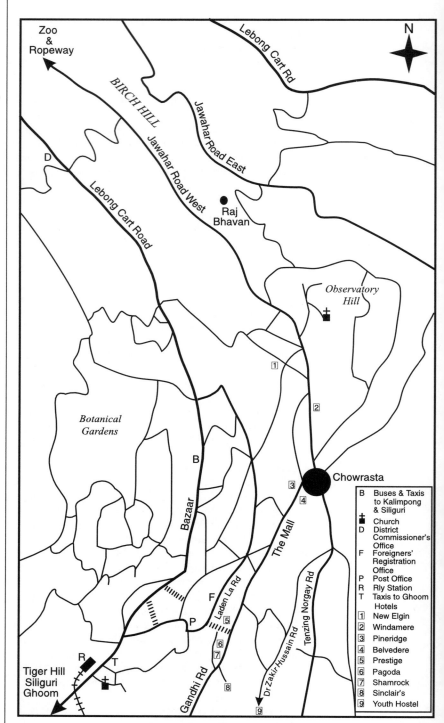

Zoo & Ropeway

Lebong Cart Rd

BIRCH HILL

Jawahar Road East

Jawahar Road West

D

Lebong Cart Road

Raj Bhavan

Observatory Hill

1

2

Botanical Gardens

B

3

4

Chowrasta

Bazaar

The Mall

Laden La Rd

Tenzing Norgay Rd

F

P

5

6

7

Dr Zakir Hussain Rd

R

T

Tiger Hill
Siliguri
Ghoom

Gandhi Rd

8

9

B	Buses & Taxis to Kalimpong & Siliguri
✝	Church
D	District Commissioner's Office
F	Foreigners' Registration Office
P	Post Office
R	Rly Station
T	Taxis to Ghoom Hotels
1	New Elgin
2	Windamere
3	Pineridge
4	Belvedere
5	Prestige
6	Pagoda
7	Shamrock
8	Sinclair's
9	Youth Hostel

share-taxi to Siliguri, a bus or jeep from Siliguri to Panitanki on the Indian side of the border and then a cycle-rickshaw across the border to Kakarbhitta on the Nepali side. From there either bird the sites in eastern Nepal or continue on to Kathmandu. There is no Nepali consulate in

Darjeeling, the nearest being in Calcutta, but you can obtain a visa valid for 30 days at the border for $US25 in cash. You can extend the visa in Kathmandu. From the other direction, make sure you have a valid visa for India as it is not normally possible to obtain one at the border.

Accommodation   Darjeeling is popular in summer with a selection of places to stay. As at most hill stations prices are inflated by up to 100% during the main season when accommodation can be difficult to find. It is better to book a room in advance or arrive early in the day. The following categorisations are based on high season prices (mid-March to mid-July and mid-September to mid-November). During the off-season rates are open to negotiation as demand is relatively low, though some hotels close during the slack period.

Arguably the best hotel in Darjeeling is the delightfully nostalgic *Windamere* (A+ including all meals) ☎0354-54041, Fax 54043 on Observatory Hill. The *Hotel Sinclairs* (A including breakfast and dinner) ☎/Fax 0354-54355 on Gandhi Rd has recently been renovated so all rooms have central heating and hot water. The popular *New Elgin* (A including all meals) ☎0354-54114, Fax 54267 on H.M.Lama Rd, just off Robertson Rd, was renovated in 1994 and is also quite a good choice in this category. The new *Sterling Resorts* (A) ☎ 0354-2691, Fax 54696 at Ghoom is handy for birding Tiger Hill in the early morning.

In the mid-price category the best choice is the *Bellevue Hotel* (B/C) ☎ 0354-54075, Fax 54330 by the plaza (Chowrasta) at the top end of The Mall (Nehru Rd). It is run by a friendly and helpful Tibetan family, has comfortable rooms, heating and good views. Just above it is the so-called *Main Bellevue Hotel* ☎ 0354-54178 run by a branch of the same family. It is quieter and more economical than its namesake. The *Pineridge Hotel* (B/C) ☎0354-54074 opposite the Bellevue has large doubles and triples with bathrooms and hot water.

For those on a tight budget there are cheapies on and around Laden La Rd, just above the post office. In this area the *Hotels Prestige, Shamrock* and *Pagoda* (all D/E) offer good value. The *Youth Hostel* (E) ☎0345-2290 on Dr. Zakir Hussain Rd at the top of the ridge used to be a popular choice but has become dilapidated in recent years. It still has a reputation as being friendly and helpful, particularly as regards information about trekking in the area, and offers the cheapest dorm beds in town.

Darjeeling suffers from regular power shortages and a torch can be useful. You may prefer a hotel that has a generator. Make enquiries when booking. Check whether there are charges for extra blankets and heating.

Many of the hotels have restaurants. There are inexpensive eating establishments along Laden La Rd, but beware of the early closing times. You generally need to be at a restaurant by 19.00 to be sure of eating. For a touch of the Raj try Glenary's on The Mall.

Strategy   The best seasons are April/early May and mid-October to early December, though any time of year can be productive. Be equipped with warm clothing, particularly during the winter months when it can be very cold at night. The best birding is in the early morning and you should be prepared for the possibility of rain and mist later in the day even if the weather looks perfect when you set off. Weather conditions change very rapidly in the mountains.

A first birding excursion might be to the zoo about 2km from Chowrasta along Jawahar Rd West. The zoo has some interesting birds including Satyr Tragopan and Brown Wood Owl in its collection, but the conditions are depressing and it's better to get on to the woods on the slope behind the zoo. It can be worth checking this out from behind the cages in the zoo before exploring the nature trail through a gate behind the bear enclosure on the opposite side of the zoo from the main entrance. It is sometimes fairly quiet, but good birds have been recorded including Pygmy Wren Babbler, Red-billed Leiothrix, Red-tailed Minla, Rufous-winged Fulvetta, Large Niltava (US), White-tailed Robin (U) and Scaly Thrush. The zoo is open daily from 08.00 to 16.00. If the zoo is closed, or you have time, carry on along Jawahar Rd as it bears right past the Ropeway to come to a fairly quiet road through reasonable habitat along the north-facing slope of Birch Hill. Continue on this track and work your way back up the hill to the centre of town.

Closer to the town centre and hotels, the Botanical Gardens (below the bus stand and bazaar) are easily reached on foot and hold a number of species typical of the Darjeeling area. Morning is the best time.

Birds   Further species from Darjeeling: Himalayan Griffon, Great Barbet, Long-tailed Minivet, Streaked Laughingthrush (U), Silver-eared Mesia (U), Black-eared Shrike Babbler, Rusty-fronted Barwing (US), Red-tailed Minla, Whiskered Yuhina, Rufous-winged Fulvetta, Rufous Sibia, Little Pied, Verditer and Grey-headed Flycatchers (S), Rufous-bellied Niltava, White-throated Fantail (S), Brownish-flanked and Russet Bush Warblers, Hill Prinia, Smoky (UP), Buff-barred (W), Lemon-rumped, Ashy-throated, Grey-hooded and Chestnut-crowned Warblers, Blue-fronted Redstart, Grey Bushchat, Chestnut-bellied Rock Thrush, Blue Whistling Thrush, Grey-winged Blackbird (U), Green-backed and Black-throated Tits, White-tailed Nuthatch, Olive-backed Pipit (W), Mrs Gould's (U), Green-tailed and Fire-tailed (W) Sunbirds, Yellow-breasted Greenfinch and Little Bunting (W).

Tiger Hill

This site merits more than one visit, especially if you do not have time to do the Sandakphu Trek or visit Lava and Sikkim. At 2590m the highest point in the vicinity of Darjeeling is frequented by myriad tourists every morning before dawn for the sunrise over the Himalayan peaks. From here Kanchenjunga (8598m) is the most impressive of the snow-covered summits, but on a clear day Mt. Everest (8848m) is also visible.

Having enjoyed the spectacle, everyone except the intrepid birder piles back into the waiting vehicles to return for breakfast. Check the bamboo below the summit by following an indistinct trail down behind the small tea shop. This is good habitat for Slender-billed Scimitar Babbler, Black-throated Parrotbill, Yellowish-bellied Bush Warbler and White-browed Shortwing though they are more often heard than seen. A little further down the road a short path to the right leads through bamboo and oak to a small temple. This can be good if there are no people around. Birds and Orange-bellied Squirrels feed on rice put out by devotees. You are likely to see Chestnut-crowned Laughingthrush and Dark-breasted Rosefinch (W) here. Scaly Laughingthrush and Dark-rumped Rosefinch (W) are less common but possible. Scarce birds such as Rufous-throated Wren Babbler*, Gould's Shortwing and Blue-fronted Robin have been found in the denser bamboo and rhododendron/oak jungle but require a lot of time to tease out.

The main birding trail starts near the big archway 1km below the summit. It is best to go anticlockwise, starting along the track to the right as you face uphill. This leads down through bamboo and degraded forest

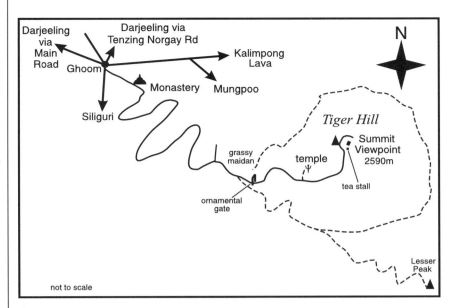

Map of Tiger Hill

before rising to the summit of a lower peak clothed in bamboo. Time exploring this trail and woodcutters paths leading off it is likely to be rewarded with birds such as Yellow-billed Blue Magpie, Golden-breasted and White-browed Fulvettas, Chestnut-tailed and Blue-winged Minlas, Stripe-throated Yuhina, Chestnut-bellied Rock Thrush, Scaly Thrush (S) and Maroon-backed Accentor (W). A number of warblers are likely to be encountered with Buff-barred, Lemon-rumped, Ashy-throated, Grey-hooded, and Golden-spectacled ('upper species' – see Selective Bird List) probably the most common. The endangered Broad-billed Warbler is more often seen in spring. Raptors are not common though Oriental Honey Buzzard, Common Buzzard, Mountain Hawk Eagle, Himalayan Griffon, Black and Booted Eagles, Peregrine Falcon and Eurasian Hobby could appear. Rufous-throated Wren Babbler* has been recorded (responds to pishing) but is easier at Lava.

Arrange a jeep to pick you up later or wander back down to Ghoom (4km) from where it is fairly easy to get a jeep-bus or walk back to Darjeeling (8km). If you walk back, the Tenzing Norgay Rd is quieter and better birding; Brownish-flanked Bush Warbler and Yellow-breasted Greenfinch are regular. Russet Bush Warbler, perhaps previously overlooked due to the fact that its *zeerit, zeerit* . . . song was erroneously attributed to Brown Bush Warbler, is present here and in other areas of scrub around Darjeeling including near the zoo. The scarce but exquisite Scarlet Finch has been seen here.

Apart from Tiger Hill, little forest remains in the vicinity of Darjeeling. One area worth exploring if you have transport is the Mungpoo (Mangpu) road, which connects Rambi Bazar (on the Teesta River) with Ghoom; turn right off the Ghoom-Kalimpong road shortly after leaving Ghoom (Jore Bungalow). Some degraded forest and steep gullies before reaching Mungpoo hold many of the area's typical birds. Notable, though uncommon, species include Bay Woodpecker, Pygmy and Rufous-throated Wren Babblers, Cutia, Yellow-throated Fulvetta and Black-chinned Yuhina.

Birds   Other species to look out for are Hill Partridge (U), Kalij Pheasant, Large Hawk Cuckoo (S), Oriental and Lesser Cuckoos (S), Spot-bellied Eagle

Owl (R), Collared Owlet, Himalayan Swiftlet, Fork-tailed (U) and House
Swifts, White-throated Needletail (R), Darjeeling Woodpecker (U), Streak-
breasted Scimitar Babbler (U), Scaly-breasted Wren Babbler (U), Rufous-
capped Babbler, Fulvous and Grey-headed Parrotbills (R), Blue-winged
Laughingthrush (U), Black-headed Shrike Babbler (R), Hoary-throated
Barwing (U), Snowy-browed (S), Sapphire (RS) and Rufous-gorgeted
Flycatchers, Rufous-bellied Niltava, Yellow-bellied Fantail, Chestnut-
headed Tesia, Aberrant and Grey-sided Bush Warblers, Blyth's Leaf
Warbler, Goldcrest (UW), Indian Blue Robin (S), Orange-flanked (W),
Golden (UW) and White-browed (UW) Bush Robins, White-tailed
Robin (S), White-collared Blackbird (U), Plain-backed (W), Long-billed (R)
and Dark-throated (W) Thrushes, Rufous-breasted Accentor (W), Yellow-
browed Tit, Olive-backed and Rosy (W) Pipits, Plain Mountain Finch (W),
Gold-naped Finch and Red-headed Bullfinch.

Sikkim Permit   If you did not obtain a permit for Sikkim when you got your visa,
arrange one in Darjeeling. The permit procedure usually takes 1–3 hours.
You need your passport and a photograph. First visit the Office of the
Deputy Commissioner (aka District Magistrate) on Hill Cart Rd (Lebong
Cart Rd) to fill in a form. Take this to the Foreigners' Registration Office on
Laden La Rd ☎0354-2261 to get it endorsed then return to the DC's office
for your permit. The offices are open Monday to Friday 11.00 to 13.00 and
14.00 to 16.00. See also section on Sikkim.

Other Sites   The main road from Siliguri to Darjeeling passes though good terai and
bhabar sal forest in the **Mahananda WLS** and **Sukna Reserved Forest** but
foreigners need written permission from the office of the Chief Wildlife
Warden in Calcutta to bird anywhere other than along the road. The HQ
and FRH are 8km from Siliguri. Good, though mostly uncommon birds
include Black Baza, Collared Falconet, Pin-tailed Green Pigeon, Barred
Cuckoo Dove, Blue-bearded Bee-eater, Dollarbird, Long-tailed Broadbill,
Golden-crested Myna, White-tailed Robin (W) and Yellow-vented
Warbler (W).

Sandakphu (Singalila) Trek

This fairly easy trek takes you along the Singalila Ridge providing
excellent birding in bamboo, oak and rhododendron forest between 2000
and 3600m. Major prizes are Blood Pheasant, Satyr Tragopan, Fire-tailed
Myzornis, and Fulvous and Brown Parrotbills, with a host of other
wonderful birds and spectacular scenery as you approach the point where
Nepal, Sikkim and India meet. There are magnificent views of
Kanchenjunga and the main Himalayan range.

Part of the area is the Singalila National Park, but permission is not
necessary for the trek. Trekking facilities are improving with new lodges
and trekking huts. For those with less time and energy it is possible to
reach Sandakphu (3640m) by jeep enabling birding at various points en
route.

Location   The Singalila Ridge, in the extreme northwest of West Bengal, runs north
to south forming the border between Nepal and India. The trek begins at
Manebhanjhang (2130m) reached by bus or jeep from Darjeeling (30km) in
about 1¹/₂–2 hours. Most birders trek to Sandakphu and back, some 35km
each way, but it is possible to make a circular tour by continuing to Rimbik,
21km east of Sandakphu, directly or via Phalut, the northernmost place

Map of Sandakphu
(Singalila Trek)

before the Sikkimese border. From Rimbik buses back to Darjeeling take about 5 hours.

Parts of the trekking route passes through Nepalese territory. There are no customs or immigration formalities, but it is not permitted to use this route to cross into Nepal. Similarly foreigners are forbidden to continue into Sikkim via any of the places on this trek and attempting to do so may incur severe penalties.

Accommodation

A number of basic and inexpensive (E) lodges and trekkers' huts have been constructed since most old ones were burnt down in the 1980s. You can usually find accommodation in villages on the trekking route. It can, however, be difficult to find a bed in the main season if there are a lot of trekking groups on the trail. To be sure of your accommodation, book it through a trekking agent in Darjeeling, such as the friendly and helpful Trek-Mate ☎0354-54074 at the Pineridge Hotel on the Mall (Nehru Rd) or Clubside Motors ☎0354-54646 on Robertson Rd. Although a sleeping bag and sleeping mat are not essential, they give extra flexibility should beds or bedding be in short supply, or of a standard you are not comfortable with.

It is always best to enquire in Darjeeling about conditions on the trek before setting off. Normally it is possible to trek between October and mid-December, the time of least rain and best visibility, but a late monsoon may rule out the early part of the season and by December it is getting very cold. Snowfall in winter varies and it is sometimes possible to do part of the trek at this time of year. If not, there are shorter treks, from Rimbik for example, which can be good for birds. The main route is usually clear by the time the rhododendrons bloom in April-May. This is a good time as many species are in song, but it is a good idea to carry a light waterproof, poncho or umbrella. The monsoon usually arrives in late May/June but many species are breeding at this time. It is advisable to first spend two or three days at Darjeeling acclimatising to the altitude if you have just come from the plains.

It is possible to do the trek in four or five days, but with this type of forest birding it is worth more time to give a better chance of seeing scarcer species. Bird activity is very low during mist and low cloud when visibility is poor, allow extra time for poor weather. Stop an extra day at any of the lodges to explore areas away from the main trail: Kalipokhari and Sandakphu are recommended. You can sometimes find a local to act as a guide if you ask at the villages, but this cannot be relied upon. Trekking agencies in Darjeeling can provide a guide and/or porter, as well as supplying extra trekking equipment.

A water bottle is essential and biscuits, chocolate, the excellent Kalimpong cheese, coffee, tinned fish, peanuts and raisins brought from Darjeeling can be a welcome supplement to the basic fare. Make sure you take your passport with you, rather than leaving it at your hotel in Darjeeling for safekeeping, as you may need it to register with the police in Sukiapokhari and Manebhanjang.

Day 1: Manebhanjang (2130m) to Megma (2900m) or Tonglu (3070m): 11–13km.

The morning bus (07.00) or jeep from Darjeeling via Sukiapokhari to Manebhanjang takes 1½–2 hours. The main jeep track to Sandakphu begins as a rough paved road 1km north of the town on your left. It zigzags steeply up for the first couple of kilometres before easing slightly for 8km up to Megma at 2900m. The habitat for the first 5km or so is fairly poor so try the short cuts beginning with the trail in Manebhanjang itself where the main road makes a sharp bend to the right. Walking time without birding is about 4 hours. If you prefer, stay overnight at Megma at the *Hotel Indica* or climb on up a further 2km to Tonglu (3070m) where there is a *Trekkers' Hut*.

The habitat along the first section is largely deforested but it improves as you continue and enter broad-leaved evergreen forest. There is good birding along the jeep track for 2–3km before Megma with Satyr Tragopan (U), White-throated Needletail (U), Slender-billed Scimitar Babbler, Rufous-throated Wren Babbler* (U), Brown Parrotbill (U), Spotted Laughingthrush and Dark-rumped Rosefinch among the highlights. Other species on the first day's trek include Hill Partridge, Kalij Pheasant, Yellow-billed Blue Magpie, Black-throated Parrotbill, Black-faced Laughingthrush, Black-headed Shrike Babbler (U), Red-tailed Minla, Rufous-winged Fulvetta, Rufous-gorgeted and Verditer (S) Flycatchers, Brownish-flanked and Grey-sided Bush Warblers (S), Hill Prinia, Rufous-fronted Tit, Fire-tailed Sunbird, Streaked Spiderhunter (US), Gold-naped Finch and Little Bunting (WP).

Day 2: Megma (2900m) to Kalipokhari (3110m): 13km

From Megma there is a choice of routes as far as Gairibans (Gairibas, 2620m). The main trekking path keeps left following the ridge via Tunling and Jaubari (*Teacher's Lodge*). Much of this route is deforested so the preferred choice is along the jeep track to the right through oak and rhododendron woods. After the climb to Tonglu (3070m) the track levels out as far as the beginning of the Singalila National Park marked by a signboard and building. Take the right-hand jeep track which descends slowly through the forest to Gairibans where there is a *Trekkers' Hut* and lodge. From here up to Kalipokhari is a 4km steady climb along the jeep track. Accommodation at Kalipokhari is at the *KB Hotel* at the beginning of the village. Walking time without birding is 5½ hours.

Birds: Mountain Hawk Eagle (U), Hill Partridge, Satyr Tragopan (U), Barred Cuckoo Dove (U), White-throated Needletail, Spotted Nutcracker, Yellow-billed Blue Magpie, Slender-billed Scimitar Babbler (U), Fulvous Parrotbill (U), Spotted (U), Black-faced and Chestnut-crowned Laughingthrushes, Black-headed (U) and Green Shrike Babblers, Hoary-throated Barwing, Red-tailed and Chestnut-tailed Minlas, Rufous-winged Fulvetta, Grey-sided Bush, Buff-barred, Ashy-throated, Greenish and Broad-billed (U) Warblers, Golden Bush Robin, White-collared Blackbird, Rufous-fronted Tit, Olive-backed and Rosy Pipits, and Green-tailed and Fire-tailed Sunbirds.

Those with more time might spend an extra day at the excellent lodge in Gairibans. Some birders report that this is one of the nicest areas in India! The best trail is along a jeepable track (not the main jeep track) from the lodge continuing for many kilometres uphill.

Birds in late May include many of the above as well as Kalij Pheasant, Hodgson's Hawk Cuckoo, Darjeeling and Crimson-breasted Woodpeckers, Streak-breasted Scimitar Babbler, Black-throated Parrotbill, Scaly Laughingthrush, Black-eared Shrike Babbler, Golden-breasted Fulvetta, Dark-sided and Ferruginous Flycatchers, Chestnut-headed Tesia, Large-billed and Blyth's Leaf Warblers, Golden-spectacled Warbler ('upper species' – see Selective Bird List), White-browed Shortwing, White-tailed Robin, Indian Blue Robin, Yellow-browed Tit, Scarlet Finch and Brown Bullfinch.

Day 3: Kalipokhari

A day or two based here can be productive. The best birding area is along the abandoned jeep track about an hour below the village. This can

Map of Kalipokhari

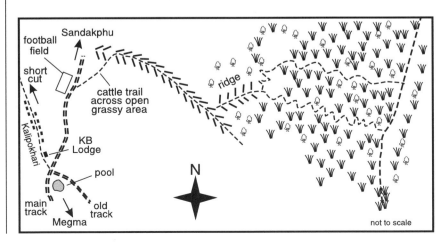

be a little difficult to find: follow the main track north to the football field on your left. Cross the open grassy area right of the track and follow the main cattle trail onto a ridge and then descend into the oak and rhododendron forest. This track becomes rather steep and indistinct through bamboo but emerges onto the old jeep track. If you lose it, just keep heading down. Conversely to find your way back work your way up to the ridge. Bird along the track for as long as you have time. To the right it becomes almost impassable, but the going is quite good and level in the opposite direction, though a little overgrown at times.

Look for Satyr Tragopan on the track early in the morning. The oak and rhododendron hold Rufous-bellied and Crimson-breasted Woodpeckers, Spotted Laughingthrush, Fire-tailed Myzornis (U), Hoary-throated Barwing, Slaty-blue Flycatcher, Chestnut-headed and Broad-billed (U) Warblers and Rufous-fronted Tit. The large tracts of bamboo are favoured by elusive species such as Slender-billed Scimitar Babbler, and Great, Brown and Fulvous Parrotbills. Golden-breasted Fulvetta, Yellowish-bellied Bush Warbler, Golden Bush Robin and Gold-naped Finch are more likely in bushes along the track while the dense streamside vegetation is the haunt of White-browed Shortwing and White-tailed Robin. Other birds here include Rufous-capped Babbler, Green Shrike Babbler, Dark-sided and Ferruginous (US) Flycatchers, Little and Spotted Forktails (U), Plain-backed Thrush, Rosy Pipit and Fire-tailed Sunbird.

Fire-tailed Myzornis

JCA © 96

Day 4: Kalipokhari (3110) to Sandakphu (3640): 8km

Keeping right in order to follow the jeep track rather than the trekking short cuts, the trail winds through forest for about 6km before reaching a tea-shop at Bhikebhanjang. From here it is a steep hike up the final 3km to Sandakphu at 3640m where there is a choice of accommodation in the shape of two *PWD Bungalows* and a *Trekkers' Hut*; 2¹/₂ hours pure walking time.

Birds: Northern Goshawk (U), Eurasian Hobby, Blood Pheasant (U),
Fire-tailed Myzornis (U), Yellowish-bellied Bush Warbler, Large-billed Leaf
Warbler (US), White-browed Bush Robin, Maroon-backed Accentor (U),
Rufous-fronted Tit, Fire-tailed Sunbird, White-winged Grosbeak and
White-browed Rosefinch.

Map of Sandakphu

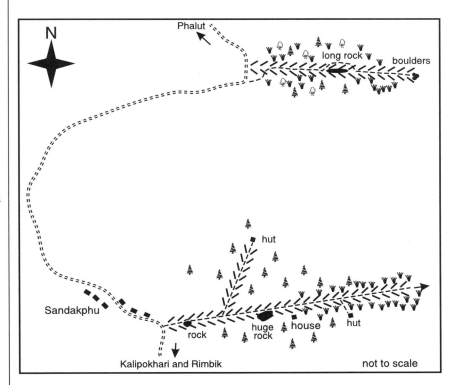

Day 5: Sandakphu

Sandakphu is surrounded by silver fir, birch and rhododendron forests
covering slopes below the Singalila Ridge. If you have time, spend two
days here. Explore north of the settlement on the main track and along
cattle and woodcutters tracks leading off it. There are two particularly
good ridge trails leading down into a basin east of the main Singalila ridge.
One begins at the southern end of Sandakphu and the other at a left hand
bend about 2km north of the village. Blood Pheasants are best seen early
morning or late afternoon feeding in clearings in bamboo or by working
your way slowly through the forest between the ridges. The bamboo is
also where to look for Fulvous and Great Parrotbills (U).

Other birds: Rufous-bellied Woodpecker, Hume's Short-toed Lark (RS),
Slender-billed Scimitar Babbler (U), Spotted and Black-faced
Laughingthrushes, Fire-tailed Myzornis (U), Yellowish-bellied Bush
Warbler, Buff-barred and Greenish Warblers (S), Rufous-breasted (S),
White-browed and Golden Bush Robins, Plain-backed, Scaly and Long-
billed (U) Thrushes, Altai (UWP), Rufous-breasted and Maroon-backed (U)
Accentors, Rosy Pipit, Fire-tailed Sunbird, White-winged Grosbeak (U),
Tibetan Siskin, Dark-breasted, Pink-browed (S), Beautiful (U), White-
browed (U) and Dark-rumped Rosefinches, Red Crossbill, Gold-naped
Finch, and Red-headed and Brown Bullfinches.

Day 6: Sandakphu (3640m) to Rimbik (2290m): 18km

Retrace your route as far as Bhikebhanjhang then take the left fork. The going is fairly easy downhill through good forest for almost the entire length of this trail, but take provisions as there are none along the way. At Rimbik there are a couple of good private lodges, the *Sherpa* and the *Shiva Pradhan* where you can rest and recuperate or undertake day treks in the area before catching the bus back to Darjeeling (5 hours). Long-billed Thrush has been seen on the stream through Rimbik itself. It is also possible to trek from Rimbik via Lodoma, Jhepi and Kaijali down to Bijanbari (760m), a walking time of 5½ hours, and catch a bus back from there.

Birds: Mountain Hawk Eagle (U), Steppe and Black Eagles (U), Amur Falcon (UP), Hill Partridge, Kalij Pheasant, Rufous-bellied and Darjeeling Woodpeckers, Streak-breasted, Rusty-cheeked and Slender-billed (U) Scimitar Babblers, Rufous-capped Babbler, Black-faced and Chestnut-crowned Laughingthrushes, Red-billed Leiothrix, Green Shrike Babbler, Hoary-throated Barwing, Red-tailed Minla, Slaty-backed (US) and Ferruginous Flycatchers, Yellow-bellied Fantail, Buff-barred, Ashy-throated, Large-billed Leaf (US), Lemon-rumped and Chestnut-crowned Warblers, Golden and White-browed Bush Robins, Spotted Forktail, Plain-backed and Long-tailed (U) Thrushes, White-collared and Grey-winged (U) Blackbirds, Rufous-fronted and Grey-crested Tits, Olive-backed Pipit, Altai and Rufous-breasted Accentors, and Dark-rumped Rosefinch (U).

Those with time can extend the trek by continuing from Sandakphu via lodges and Trekkers' Huts at Molley (below Sabarkum, 3540m, 16km), Phalut (3600m, 9km), Gorkhey (7km), Rammam (2560m, 12km) and via Siri Khola round to Rimbik.

If you have transport, explore the good forest between Dhodrey and Manebhanjang for Scaly Laughingthrush, Golden-breasted Fulvetta and Rufous-breasted Bush Robin on the way back from Rimbik to Darjeeling.

Among other species are Common 'Japanese' (W) and Long-legged Buzzards, Himalayan Griffon, Peregrine Falcon (U), Oriental Turtle Dove, Large Hawk, Common, Indian, Oriental and Lesser Cuckoos (S), Collared and Asian Barred Owlets, Himalayan Swiftlet, Fork-tailed Swift, Golden-throated Barbet (U), Wryneck (P), Nepal and Asian House Martins (R), Large-billed Crow, Long-tailed and Short-billed (S) Minivets, Mountain and Black Bulbuls (U), Pygmy and Scaly-breasted Wren Babblers, Striated and White-throated Laughingthrushes, Blue-winged and Chestnut-tailed Minlas, White-browed Fulvetta, Rufous Sibia, Whiskered, Stripe-throated and Rufous-vented Yuhinas, Little Pied Flycatcher, Rufous-bellied Niltava, Yellow-bellied Fantail, Chestnut-headed Tesia, Brownish-flanked, Aberrant and Russet Bush Warblers, Tickell's Leaf (S), Blyth's Leaf, Golden-spectacled and Grey-hooded Warblers, Indian Blue Robin (S), Orange-flanked Bush Robin, Blue-capped, White-throated (U), Hodgson's (U) and Blue-fronted Redstarts, Blue-fronted Robin (R), Plumbeous and White-capped River-Redstarts, Grey Bushchat, Chestnut-bellied Rock Thrush, Blue Whistling Thrush, Dark-throated Thrush, Green-backed, Coal, Rufous-vented, Grey-crested and Yellow-browed Tits, White-tailed Nuthatch, Eurasian, Brown-throated and Rusty-flanked Treecreepers, Upland Pipit (R), Grey Wagtail, Mrs Gould's Sunbird, Plain Mountain Finch, Yellow-breasted Greenfinch, Collared Grosbeak (U), Common (U) and Spot-winged (R) Rosefinches and Scarlet Finch (R). Keep an eye open for the rare Rusty-bellied Shortwing of which there is an old 1912 record from Tonglu, as well as one or two more recent possible sightings.

Other Wildlife

Those used to Rhesus Macaques in other parts of India may dismiss roadside parties of monkeys as belonging to that species, but they lack the red colour on the rump and are in fact Assamese Macaques, a distinct species. The Indian Muntjac (Barking Deer) is the only other large mammal regularly encountered on the trek, but there is a chance of Yellow-throated Marten or the delightfully agile Red Panda. Although Clouded Leopard inhabits the region, the likelihood of coming across one is slight. You are more likely to see smaller inhabitants of the forest such as the Orange-bellied Himalayan Squirrel or perhaps a Himalayan Weasel.

Lava

Some of India's least-known and most sought-after birds can be found around the village of Lava (Labha) in the hills of North Bengal near Bhutan's western border. Here the mature evergreen forest between 1600 and 2400m harbours such rarities as Satyr Tragopan, Ashy Wood Pigeon, Rufous-throated* and Spotted Wren Babblers, Yellow-throated Fulvetta, Red-faced Liocichla, Cutia, Rusty-bellied Shortwing, Blue-fronted Robin and Long-billed Thrush. The area has been opened up in recent years and it is no longer necessary to obtain a special permit to visit.

Map of Lava

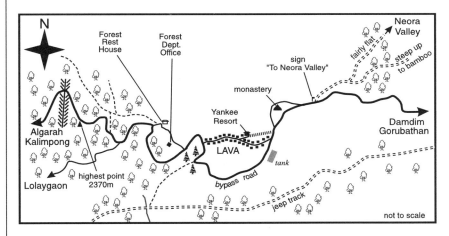

Location

The village of Lava lies on a ridge 32km east of Kalimpong – one hour plus by bus or taxi via Algarah. Buses, as well as the more frequent and comfortable share-jeeps, leave for Kalimpong from the Bazaar bus stand in Darjeeling (2–3 hours). Kalimpong has direct buses to Gangtok, the capital of Sikkim. The journey takes 4 hours and it is best to book a seat a day or two in advance. The nearest railhead is in the plains at New Jalpaiguri, near Siliguri, but it is possible to book berths for some trains at the Railway Booking Office near the Mayal Lyang Lodge in Kalimpong. There are several buses including an early morning one from Kalimpong to Siliguri and Bagdogra Airport (3 hours) run by Mintri Transport (the Indian Airlines agent), ☎03552-55241, whose office is on Main Rd.

Accommodation

There are now several lodges in Lava. The *Yankee Resort* (D), in the centre of the village, is the one usually frequented by birders. Address: P.O. Lava Bazar, Via. Kalimpong-734301, Dist. Darjeeling ☎03552-52340. Mr S. K. Lama, the manager, is friendly and helpful, and cooks good food. There are several other restaurants in the village and a few shops selling cookies, chocolates, mineral water, soft drinks etc. If you prefer to stay at the *FRH* you need written permission from the DFO in Kalimpong and you have to bring your own food.

If you need to stay in Kalimpong the *Himalayan Hotel* (A/B) ☎03552-55248, Fax 55368, has character, history and Brown Hawk Owls in the garden. It is about 1km south of the bus stand on Upper Cart Rd on the right past the post office and *Hotel Silver Oaks* (A) ☎03552-55296 (a more modern alternative). In the mid-range the best bet is the *Park Hotel* (B/C) ☎03552-55304 on Rinkingpong Rd – go past the Hotel Silver Oaks, turn left then right. There are also cheap and friendly lodges such as the *Sherpa* (D), *Deki* (D/E) and *Gompu's* (D/E) around the bus stand and main road.

Strategy   You need quite a few days here to see most of the specialities, especially as most are great skulkers and rather scarce. Birding can be rather slow, as densities are not very high, though the list of birds recorded from Lava is long. Separate winter and spring/early summer visits are best for optimum results. Winter is best for migrants from the north as well as those species which leave high Himalayan breeding grounds for lower altitudes. April to June sees most of the local specialities in song and is a good time for cuckoos with Large Hawk, Indian, Oriental, Lesser, Grey-bellied* (U at lower altitudes), Plaintive and Asian Emerald (U at lower altitudes) all possible. As in Darjeeling mist and rain can be a problem, so be prepared.

The Paktham Forest extends 6–7km west of Lava with the road to Kalimpong passing through it. Many good birds can be seen along the road, the traffic not being too heavy. It is a good idea to be here at dawn as there is a better chance that skulkers such as White-browed Shortwing, Rufous-breasted Bush Robin (W) and Long-billed Thrush may venture onto the roadside verges and gullies.

The roadside shrubbery is home to Rufous-capped Babbler, Grey-sided (U), Blue-winged (U), Scaly (U), Black-faced (UW) and Chestnut-crowned Laughingthrushes, Rufous-winged Fulvetta, Golden and White-browed Bush Robins (W) and Gold-naped Finch (mainly W). Yellow-throated Fulvetta is not uncommon and is worth searching for as it is an endangered species with a rather restricted range. The ravine just after the highest point on the road and before the 4km-marker (coming from the village towards Kalimpong) is particularly good for it. This is also one of the best spots for the little known Blue-fronted Robin, though it has also been seen in the bushes a kilometre further along the road and in a spinach patch in Lava village itself. The gully can hold White-browed Shortwing, White-tailed Robin (S), Large Niltava, Sapphire Flycatcher (S) and Rufous-throated Wren Babbler*. The area between kms 4 and 6 has a lot of scrub and undergrowth, a favourite area with the last-named species, at least in spring when it can be tape-lured.

A number of scarce Himalayan pigeons occur. They can be somewhat erratic in their movements but look out for Wedge-tailed Green Pigeon, and Ashy and Speckled Wood Pigeons alongside commoner Oriental Turtle and Barred Cuckoo Doves. A fruiting tree can repay watching from a distance and perhaps more than one visit. Warbler fans will be interested in the Grey-cheeked, a rather scarce species not infrequent here in early spring (also seen in winter) alongside commoner species encountered at Darjeeling. The very fortunate may encounter Cutias climbing about like colourful overgrown nuthatches on the mossy branches of trees by the road.

The road descends towards Algarah through degraded forest, only worth exploring for one or two species such as Spangled Drongo and Yellow-bellied Flowerpecker if you have plenty of time.

Above the main Kalimpong road is a good track for several kilometres before it begins to peter out. It is best accessed by a path up to the right between the FRH and the main road in the direction of Kalimpong. Turn left at the top of the ridge and bird along the trail. Many of the same species are likely to be seen along here as from the main road including Fire-tailed Myzornis (U), Black-headed (U), White-browed and Black-eared Shrike Babblers, Ferruginous and Pygmy Blue Flycatchers, Maroon-backed Accentor (W), Tibetan Siskin (W), Crimson-browed and Scarlet Finches (U), and Brown Bullfinch. If you are lucky, you might find a Brown Wood Owl during the daytime, but a night-time sortie between January and March is best for calling birds.

A good jeep track below Lava is reached by taking a path down off the first hairpin bend on the main road where it bypasses the village. Follow this for about 15–20 minutes until it reaches the jeep track and then follow it east. Rufous-throated Partridge (U), White-browed Piculet, Grey-chinned Minivet, Rufous-throated and Spotted Wren Babblers (U), Grey-sided and Blue-winged Laughinghthrushes, Red-faced Liocichla (U), Yellow-throated Fulvetta, White-gorgeted Flycatcher (U), Grey-bellied and Slaty-bellied (US) Tesias, Russet Bush Warbler (U in plantations), Grey-cheeked Warbler (S), White-tailed Robin (U), Dark-sided Thrush (R), Tibetan Siskin (W), and Gold-naped and Scarlet (U) Finches are among the best birds on this route.

Another good trail begins on the left of the Damdim road past the monastery. This is the broad trail (signposted) that leads to **Neora Valley NP** on the border with Bhutan. Previous permission to visit the park must be obtained from the Forest Dept in Kalimpong (although it is not clear where the park begins). If you have the time and energy, arrange a trek to this little known sanctuary. (Ask in Kalimpong at the Sherpa Lodge or at Kalimtrek at the Himalayan Stores in the main market.) It may be possible to stay at a basic Rest House in the park. Otherwise you have to settle for day hikes along this track unless you take a sleeping bag and bivouac sack with you. Another possibility is to hire a jeep. You may have to go some way down the trail before you get into Satyr Tragopan territory, but before that you can encounter many of the above-mentioned species as well as Black Eagle, Bay Woodpecker, Golden-breasted Fulvetta (W), Plain-backed Thrush (W), White-collared Blackbird, Rufous-breasted Accentor (W), and Crimson-browed Finch (UW). In spring Broad-billed Warbler is fairly common, mainly in bamboo, which is also good habitat for Yellowish-bellied Bush Warbler and the extremely skulking Blue-fronted Robin (may be difficult to find before it starts singing in April).

The western outskirts of Lava village are good for thrushes at dawn and dusk. There are several other places worth exploring near Lava including taking the road towards **Lolaygaon** (Lolegaon, aka Kaffer), where there is also an FRH, and working the area below the village on its northern side.

Birds

Rusty-bellied Shortwing is an enigmatic and little-recorded species listed as globally threatened by BirdLife International. When some birders recorded its song in April 1996 it proved not to be as scarce as thought, particularly in June when up to nine individuals responded to a tape. The best area seems to be along the trail to the Neora Valley, though they were found along other main trails including the road to Algarah and the jeep track below Lava. Spotted Wren Babbler is another particularly scarce bird found at Lava in spring, mainly on the jeep track below the village but also along the trail to the Neora Valley.

Particular attention should be paid to the Golden-spectacled Warblers at Lava. There may be two different species (separable by voice) here: an 'upper species' above 2000–2100m and a 'lower species' below this altitude.

Almost all the species found at Darjeeling and Tiger Hill occur around Lava with many being more common here. In addition to those listed in that section and above you might see Steppe Eagle (P), Mountain Scops Owl, Fork-tailed Swift (S), Great Hornbill (U), Golden-throated Barbet, Greater and Lesser Yellownapes, Crimson-breasted Woodpecker, Long-tailed Broadbill (U in the lower forests), Grey-backed Shrike (W), Maroon Oriole, Hill Myna (U in the lower forests), Grey Treepie, Black-winged Cuckooshrike (S), Short-billed Minivet (S), Orange-bellied Leafbird (S), Striated, Himalayan (U) and Mountain Bulbuls, Rusty-cheeked and Coral-billed (R) Scimitar Babblers, Long-billed Wren Babbler (R), Golden Babbler (U), White-throated Laughingthrush, Fire-tailed Myzornis (RW), Rufous-vented Yuhina (W), Nepal Fulvetta, Dark-sided, Red-throated (W) and White-gorgeted (U) Flycatchers, Tickell's Leaf (P), Yellow-browed (P), Large-billed Leaf (P?), Greenish (WP), Chestnut-crowned, White-spectacled (RS) and Black-faced Warblers, Lesser Shortwing (U), Spotted Forktail (U), Chestnut, Eyebrowed and Dusky Thrushes (RW), Grey-winged Blackbird, Yellow-cheeked Tit (S), Eurasian (W), Brown-throated and Rusty-flanked (W) Treecreepers, Fire-breasted Flowerpecker, Black-throated Sunbird (S), Streaked Spiderhunter (US), Common Rosefinch (P) and Red Crossbill (UW).

Sikkim

The legendary land of Sikkim was an independent kingdom until 1975 when India annexed it. Sandwiched between Nepal to the west, Bhutan to the east and Tibet to the north, Sikkim is extremely mountainous. Kanchenjunga, India's highest mountain at 8586m, forms part of the Singalila Ridge on the border between Sikkim and Nepal. The population is largely Nepali and Lepcha. Hinduism is the majority religion but a significant part is still played by Buddhism, and the Buddhist gompas (monasteries) are a focus of many settlements in the region.

Sikkim's avifauna is typically eastern Himalayan with Palearctic species predominating in the largely inaccessible regions in the far north. In spite of travel being mostly restricted to southern Sikkim, one can cover a number of interesting sites and there is potential for discoveries in a region which has had relatively little attention from birdwatchers.

Sikkim can be visited throughout the year. Winter can be very cold and warm clothing is necessary, but this is a good time for Himalayan altitudinal migrants wintering in south Sikkim. It is essential to carry protection against rain at any time of the year, but the main wet season is from May to September.

N.B. In order to visit Sikkim you must have a permit (see Pre-tour Information).

Map of Gangtok (note orientation)

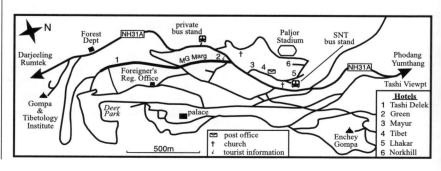

Gangtok

The logical first stop on a Sikkimese itinerary is Gangtok, the capital. Not generally considered a birding destination, there are good birds at one or two places around town and it can be used as a base to explore further afield. You have to stop in Gangtok to arrange permits to visit Fambong Lho, Changu (Tsomgo) Lake or the Yumthang region (see below), or to go trekking.

Location

Gangtok (meaning 'hilltop') is spread along a ridge overlooking the Rora River in southeastern Sikkim and can only be reached by road. The nearest airport is 120km away to the south at Bagdogra near Siliguri in West Bengal (4^1/$_2$–5 hours by bus). The most convenient railhead is New Jalpaiguri 8km from Siliguri. Most birders come from Darjeeling (5 hours by bus) or Kalimpong (4 hours by bus). Both SNT (Sikkim Nationalised Transport) and private buses link all of these destinations with Gangtok. Share-jeeps are quicker but more expensive. The SNT bus stand is near the Paljor Stadium in north Gangtok, while share-jeeps leave from the private bus stand on NH31A. At the former you can make advance bookings for out-of-state destinations from 06.00 to 13.00 and 14.00 to 15.30. For places within Sikkim only current booking is possible – from 06.30 to 08.00 and 11.30 to 16.00.

The Office (Secretariat) of the Sikkim Forest Department, ☎03592-23191 is on the main NH31A at Deorali on the southern edge of Gangtok. The Tibetology Institute is ten minutes walk south of here. The office for trekking permits is in the same building as the tourist office at the northern end of MG Marg.

Small Maruti-van taxis are reasonably priced for getting around town and can be hired for longer tours. There is a convenient taxi stand near the tourist office. It is also possible to hire a car and driver for a two week tour of Sikkim from Darjeeling.

Accommodation

The best hotels in Gangtok are the *Tashi Delek* (A++) ☎03592-22991, Fax 22362, on MG Marg and the *Norkhill* (A++) ☎03592-23186, Fax 23187, near the Paljor Stadium. In the mid-price category the *Hotel Tibet* (A/B) ☎03592-22523, Fax 22707, on Paljor Stadium Rd and the nearby *Hotel Mayur* (B/C) ☎03592-22825 are recommended. Among the budget options are the *Green Hotel* (C/D) on MG Marg and the *Hotel Lhakhar* (C/D/E) opposite the SNT bus stand.

Strategy

Government offices are usually open weekdays from 10.00 to 16.00 and it is a good idea to arrive early to be sure of enough time to sort everything out. If you intend to visit Pemayangtse or Yuksom, you might want to reserve accommodation at the tourist office. For spare hours between bureaucratic red tape you can birdwatch in the forest around the Tibetology Institute, in the Deer Park near the Tashiling Secretariat and at the Tashi Viewpoint 10km to the north.

Birds

The Tibetology Institute is perched on a hilltop (1700m) surrounded by woodland. There is disturbance here and much of the undergrowth is damaged, but there are still good birds including Golden-throated Barbet (U), Speckled Piculet (U), Grey-crowned Pygmy Woodpecker, Spangled Drongo, Jungle Myna, Common Green Magpie, Himalayan Bulbul, Rusty-cheeked Scimitar Babbler, Puff-throated, and Black-chinned Babblers, Silver-eared Mesia, Red-billed Leiothrix, White-browed and

Black-eared Shrike Babblers, Blue-winged and Red-tailed Minlas, White-bellied Yuhina, Nepal Fulvetta, Rufous-gorgeted and Sapphire (U) Flycatchers (W), Small Niltava (S), Chestnut-headed Tesia (W), Hill Prinia, Buff-barred (W), Lemon-rumped (W), Golden-spectacled (W), Grey-hooded and Chestnut-crowned (W) Warblers, Orange-flanked Bush Robin (W), Blue-fronted Redstart (W), Chestnut-bellied Rock Thrush, Grey-winged Blackbird (W), Green-backed Tit, Chestnut-bellied Nuthatch and Olive-backed Pipit (W).

Other birds from the Gangtok area: Oriental Hobby (U), Slaty-headed Parakeet, Himalayan Swiftlet, White-throated Needletail, Fork-tailed (SP) and House Swifts, Nepal House Martin, Short-billed Minivet (W), Whiskered Yuhina (W), Rufous Sibia, Verditer Flycatcher (S), Brownish-flanked Bush Warbler (W), Rufous-breasted Accentor (W), Fire-breasted Flowerpecker, Green-tailed Sunbird (W) and Little Spiderhunter (U).

Other Sites   If you travel to Gangtok with your own transport, you might like to do some birding en route, perhaps making an overnight stop at **Rangpo**. Check the Rivers Teesta and Rongni for Small Pratincole, Crested Kingfisher and wintering Ibisbill. Blyth's Kingfisher has been seen along the river between Singtam and Rangpo, but you would probably need to bird the quieter west bank. Other notable birds: Kalij Pheasant, River Lapwing, Pin-tailed Green Pigeon, Pale-headed Woodpecker (U in bamboo), Hill Myna, Rufous-bellied Niltava (W) and Wallcreeper (W).

The **Rumtek Gompa** (1550m), though visible from Gangtok, is 24km by road to the southwest. You can visit the area in a day by hiring a taxi or taking a share-jeep from Lall Market, but check on the last time to return (usually between 15.00 and 16.00 according to season). If you prefer, stay overnight at the basic *Sangay Hotel* (E) or *Hotel Kunga Delek* (D/E), or the more comfortable *Martam Resort* (A) 5km before Rumtek. Bird around the monastery and along the dirt road towards Song. Birds include Maroon Oriole, Blue-winged Laughingthrush, Sapphire Flycatcher (UW), Yellow-bellied Warbler (U), Rufous-breasted Bush Robin (UW) and Hodgson's Redstart (W).

The **Fambong Lho WLS** is about 25km northwest of Gangtok and covers some 52km² of moist mixed deciduous and coniferous forests at altitudes from 1520 to 2750m. Rumtek Gompa is at its southeastern edge. The sanctuary is normally open from October to April. A permit must be obtained from the DFO in Gangtok (see above). A Forest Department guide must accompany you and there are modest charges. There are two small Rest Houses (Log Huts) within the sanctuary. The one at Golitar (1660m) is about an hour's hike from the road. A good path leads up from here through mossy oak and bamboo forest for 5km to a watchtower on a hilltop at Tinjurey (2100m). You need a sleeping bag and mat and all your own provisions. The Forest Department can arrange porters to carry equipment up to the huts. The alternative is to stay in Gangtok and visit Fambong Lho on day trips.

Fambong Lho has a lot of potential as a birding site. The following are some of the birds recorded on a short visit at the beginning of March: Eurasian Woodcock, Collared Owlet, Himalayan Swiftlet, Bay Woodpecker, Nepal House Martin, Common Green Magpie, Streak-breasted Scimitar, Pygmy Wren and Rufous-capped Babblers, Striated and Chestnut-crowned Laughingthrushes, Chestnut-tailed Minla, Black-eared Shrike Babbler, Whiskered and Rufous-vented Yuhinas, Rufous-winged Fulvetta, Large Niltava, Grey-headed Canary Flycatcher, Ashy-throated and Chestnut-crowned Warblers, Orange-flanked Bush Robin, Blue-fronted Redstart, Long-tailed and Dark-throated Thrushes, Yellow-cheeked Tit, White-tailed Nuthatch, Rusty-flanked Treecreeper, Olive-backed Pipit, Green-tailed Sunbird, Dark-rumped Rosefinch, and Red-headed Bullfinch. Other species known to occur include Black Eagle, Hill Partridge, Satyr Tragopan, Kalij Pheasant, Brown Wood Owl, Silver-breasted Broadbill, Maroon Oriole, Yellow-billed Blue Magpie, Orange-bellied Leafbird and Red-tailed Minla. Mammals of note include the Red Panda and Himalayan Black Bear.

The **Phodang Gompa** is 38km from Gangtok and is as far north as one is allowed in Sikkim without additional permits and being part of a group of four people. There are four buses a day from the SNT bus stand in Gangtok to Phodang Village (2¹/₂ hours) where there are a couple of basic lodges such as the friendly *Yak & Yeti* (E) and the *Northway* (E). The monastery is 1km above the main road and the turn off to it is 1km before the village. Bird around here and the Labrang Gompa about 2km further on. Mountain Hawk Eagle, White-browed Piculet, Hooded Pitta, Cutia, Black-eared Shrike Babbler, White-naped Yuhina, Large Niltava, Pale Blue Flycatcher, Spotted Forktail, Fire-capped Tit, and Dark-rumped Rosefinch are among the more noteworthy species that have been seen here.

It is seriously worth considering **Changu Lake** (3800m) near the Tibetan Border northeast of Gangtok (36km). Day permits are issued for the lake and most easily obtained through a local travel agent. The **Kyongnosla Alpine Sanctuary** (3200–4100m) is 31km from Gangtok on the road to Changu Lake on the old silk route over the Natu La to Lhasa in Tibet. The sanctuary stretches from the '15-Mile' police checkpost to the Changu Lake Ridge and encompasses 31km² on the northern side of the road. Blood Pheasant (the state bird of Sikkim), Himalayan Monal, Satyr Tragopan, Solitary Snipe, and various laughingthrushes and rosefinches occur. There are two small Rest Houses (Log Huts). Indian nationals may camp and trek here. Enquire with the Forest Department in Gangtok as to possibilities for foreigners.

The **Yumthang** region in north Sikkim has been opened to tourists in groups of four or more with up to five days (four nights) allowed. This should be organised through a local travel agent. If you do not have your own group, you can join an organised tour. The 43km² **Shingba Rhododendron Sanctuary** is in the Lachung (Yumthang) Valley, 137km north of Sikkim, between Lachung and Yumthang (3500m). The altitude ranges from 3050m at the lower end of the valley bottom to 4570m in the mountains flanking it. Birds include Snow Partridge, Blood Pheasant, Himalayan Monal, Satyr Tragopan, and Ibisbill. There are four Rest and Log Houses bookable though the Forest Department in Gangtok.

Pemayangtse

There is excellent birding around Pemayangtse Gompa. The monastery, the second oldest in Sikkim, is fascinating in its own right, but the location on a hill (2085m) with awe-inspiring views of the main Himalayan chain and the 8586m high Kanchenjunga provides an added attraction. Below the monastery the mossy oak forest harbours a rich diversity of birds as well as plenty of orchids.

Location

Pemayangtse is just 3km south of the town of Pelling and 9km north of the busy market town of Gezing in southwestern Sikkim. Buses leave from the SNT bus stand in Gangtok for Gezing (112km) at 07.00 taking 4¹/₂ hours via Singtam, Rablonga, Kewzing and Legship. Buses leave Gezing for

Pelling at 13.00 and 14.00. If you are staying at Pemayangtse itself, ask the bus driver to drop you off at the turn off 2km before Pelling, from where it is a steep few hundred metres up to the monastery. Share-jeeps are more frequent and also ply the route between Gezing and Jorethang (2–3 hours) where you can change for Darjeeling (2 hours). The daily bus to Siliguri leaves Gezing at 07.00.

Accommodation

The *Hotel Mount Pandim* (B/C) adjacent to the monastery in a delightfully tranquil setting has good views and birding on the doorstep. The nearby *Trekkers' Hut* (E) has dorm beds. Both are run by Sikkim Tourism and the latter in particular must be reserved in Gangtok.

Pelling also has good places to stay: the popular *Hotel Garuda* (C/D/E) ☎03593-50614, right on the main cross-roads; the friendly *Hotel Pradhan* (D/E) ☎03593-50615 in Upper Pelling; and the mid-bracket *Sikkim Tourist Centre* (A/B) ☎03593-50855 near the cross-roads in Upper Pelling.

Strategy

It takes 45 minutes to walk from Pelling to Pemayangtse, signposted from the main road to Gezing near a large white stupa. A good birding path circles the hill below the monastery.

A good walk up through forest begins from the football field (helipad) in Pelling. Ask for the way up to Sangachoeling Gompa (the oldest in Sikkim). The trail continues past the gompa for another 4 hours or so to the Queen's Stone (Rani Dhunga).

A good day's birding hike can be undertaken to the Tashiding Gompa (5 hours walking time one way). Make sure your permit specifies Tashiding. If not, get it endorsed beforehand in Gangtok, though in practice there will probably be no-one to stop you along this walking trail.

It can repay spending several days exploring the area thoroughly including the lower forested slopes on both sides of the ridge and down as far as Gezing (1530m). For those who enjoy trekking it is possible to do a circular route from Pemayangtse/Pelling stopping overnight at Khecheopheri Lake (4 hours), Yuksom (3 hours) and Tashiding (6 hours) – see *Other Sites* below. You do not need a trekking permit for this.

Birds

Nearly all the species mentioned under Gangtok and Fambong Lho can be seen in the Pemayangtse area. In addition the following have been recorded: Besra (U), Mountain Hawk Eagle, Black Eagle, Himalayan Griffon, Kalij Pheasant, Barred Cuckoo Dove, Oriental Turtle Dove, Oriental and Banded Bay Cuckoos (S), Asian Barred Owlet, Brown Wood Owl, Yellow-rumped Honeyguide (R), Greater Yellownape, Grey-headed, Darjeeling and Crimson-breasted Woodpeckers, Grey-backed Shrike (W), Grey Treepie, Black-winged Cuckooshrike, Long-tailed Minivet, Orange-bellied Leafbird, Striated Bulbul, Slender-billed Scimitar Babbler (W), Grey-throated Babbler, White-throated, Greater Necklaced, White-crested, Grey-sided (U), Rufous-necked (U) and Black-faced Laughingthrushes, Fire-tailed Myzornis (U), Cutia, Rusty-fronted and Hoary-throated Barwings, Dark-sided (W), Ferruginous (S), Snowy-browed, Little Pied, Slaty-blue (W) and Pygmy Blue (UW) Flycatchers, Rufous-bellied Niltava, Yellow-bellied and White-throated Fantails, Grey-bellied Tesia, Grey-sided Bush (W), Tickell's Leaf (W), Blyth's Leaf and Yellow-vented (U) Warblers, Lesser and White-browed Shortwings (U), Golden (W), White-browed (UW) and Rufous-breasted (UW) Bush Robins, White-tailed Robin (U), Plain-backed (W), Scaly (W) and Tickell's* Thrushes, White-collared Blackbird (UW), Maroon-backed Accentor (UW), Yellow-browed and Black-throated Tits, Brown-throated Treecreeper, Yellow-bellied Flowerpecker (U), Mrs. Gould's and

Black-throated Sunbirds, Yellow-breasted Greenfinch, Dark-breasted Rosefinch (W), Gold-naped Finch (W) and Little Bunting (W).

Other Sites   The small **Khecheoperi Lake** (1980m) in southwest Sikkim is about 28km from Pemayangtse and north of the main road to Yuksom. The name Khecheoperi (wishing lake) is subject to various transliterations but usually pronounced 'ketchuperi'. When one sees the lake set in a natural crater-like basin, it is not difficult to understand how it came to be regarded as sacred. The lake often hosts migrant ducks and the occasional rarity such as Black-necked Grebe, Baer's Pochard or Greater Scaup. Perhaps of more interest are the forests clothing the slopes of the crater which probably owe their continued existence to religious sentiment. Here are excellent birds including Speckled Wood Pigeon, Emerald Cuckoo (S), Blue-winged and Scaly Laughingthrushes, White-naped Yuhina and many of those at Pemayangtse.

If you have transport, or hire a taxi in Pelling, you can visit Khecheoperi as a day trip from Pemayangtse or Yuksom. Otherwise, only very basic accommodation is available in a *Trekkers' Hut* or the slightly better *Pilgrims' Hut.* You could try the monastery or ask at the chai stalls in the car park. The bus journey from Pelling takes about 2 hours, departing at 15.00 and returning early morning at 07.00. This means two nights are required for a full day's birding. A good birding trail loops through the forest around the lake though the path is often indistinct.

The small village of **Yuksom** (Yaksum, 1780m) lies at the end of the road from Pemayangtse. From here the only way further north is on foot. The *Pemthang Lodge* (D/E) and *Hotel Demazong* (D) are opposite each other and both owned by friendly people. The two *Forest Rest Houses* (E) are for the more budget conscious and have to be booked through the Forest Department in Gangtok. There is one SNT bus and one share-jeep a day between Gezing and Yuksom.

Yuksom is the starting point for treks north into the Dzongri region and the Kanchenjunga NP. This is a good way to see some higher altitude birds as the treks go up to over 4500m. Among the birds recorded from a trek to Dzongri and Thangshing are Blood Pheasant, Brown Parrotbill, Fire-tailed Myzornis, Cutia, Sapphire Flycatcher, White-browed Bush Robin, Grandala, Robin and Rufous-breasted Accentors, White-winged and Collared (U) Grosbeaks, Spot-winged Rosefinch and Scarlet Finch. Treks require groups of at least four persons organised through a recognised travel agent. The latter will arrange the required permits and a Police Liaison Officer to accompany the group, as well as porters, yaks, food and accommodation (tents and huts) on the trek. There are several tour operators in Gangtok offering treks of up to 12 days ranging in price from $35 to $50 per person per day. Make sure you agree on everything included in the price and if tents are involved, check their condition. The best time is from late October to early December and the end of April until June.

If you do not have the time and energy for a full trek, a day or two around Yuksom is still worthwhile. There is little information on the birds, but Mountain Hawk Eagle, Darjeeling and Crimson-breasted Woodpeckers, Maroon Oriole, Short-billed and Grey-chinned Minivets, Himalayan and Striated Bulbuls, Striated and Scaly Laughingthrushes, Red-tailed Minla, White-naped Yuhina, Plain-backed and Long-tailed Thrushes, Grey-winged Blackbird, Yellow-browed, Black-throated and Rufous-fronted Tits, White-tailed Nuthatch, Brown-throated Treecreeper, and Mrs Gould's, Green-tailed, Black-throated and Fire-tailed Sunbirds were recorded on a March day trip from Pemayangtse.

NORTHEAST INDIA

The relatively little-visited northeast of the Indian Subcontinent supports some of the rarest, least-known and most sought-after birds of the Oriental Region. If you want to see White-winged Duck, Bengal Florican, Dark-rumped Swift or Marsh Babbler*, the Northeast is for you. The tremendous bird diversity of the region is due to the enormous range of altitudes and habitats and because the eastern Himalaya and the Valley of the Brahmaputra receive very high precipitation. Indeed Cherrapunjee and Mawsynram in Meghalaya have world record levels of rainfall. It can rain at any time of the year, but equally every day of your stay may be bathed in sunshine. The monsoon in eastern Assam from mid-March can make roads impassable until November. In western Assam the monsoon does not usually set in until mid-April.

Map of
Northeast India

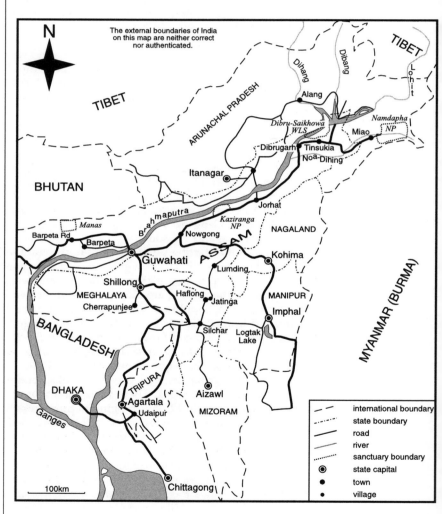

In 1995 the government lifted restrictions on visiting Assam, Meghalaya and Tripura and a permit is no longer necessary. The states of Arunachal Pradesh, Nagaland, Manipur and Mizoram are still considered to be sensitive border areas and can only be visited with a Restricted Area Permit (RAP) from the home office in Delhi (see also Pre-tour Info.). In practice it is normally only possible to visit these areas as part of a package tour organised through a recognised Indian travel agent. One or two specialist bird tour companies offer trips to the Northeast and these are worth considering in spite of the high price which is partly due to the daily tariff imposed by the government. This is almost the only way to get to see such rarities as White-bellied Heron, Snowy-throated Babbler**, Rufous-vented Laughingthrush, Rufous-backed Sibia and Beautiful Nuthatch to name but a few.

Guwahati

Guwahati (Gauhati) is the capital of Assam and the communications hub for the Northeast Hill States of Arunachal Pradesh, Manipur, Meghalaya, Mizoram, Nagaland and Tripura. If you visit the region, Guwahati is the best place to start and you will probably have to stop here to deal with bureaucracy at the beginning of your trip. Luckily there are interesting birdwatching sites to enliven a stay, including one of the best places in the world to see Greater Adjutant at close range.

Location

The city of Guwahati lies on the south bank of the mighty Brahmaputra River in western Assam 1450km east of Delhi and 520km northeast of Calcutta. There are regular daily flights by Indian Airlines and private operators from both cities, with services more frequent from the latter. The town centre is 25km east of the airport on NH37 and is reached by the airport bus which connects with Indian Airline flights or by (share) taxi. The overland route to Guwahati is considerably longer and is best undertaken by rail. The Rajdhani Express is by far the quickest train from Delhi taking 28 hours but only runs three times a week. From Howrah in Calcutta the daily Kamrup Express takes 24 hours.

Guwahati appears very well connected to the remainder of the Northeast by air, as new private airlines operate unprofitable routes in the region in exchange for being allowed to provide services on more lucrative runs. In practice this leads to a lot of cancellations, so flights become a little unreliable. Railway journeys are notoriously slow and subject to long delays, though this may improve when the programme of gauge conversion is completed. In many cases buses remain the best option with private operators running more comfortable buses than Assam State Transport. The longer routes usually have overnight services. Away from the main east-west arterial NH37 transport and connections are often very slow; allow plenty of time.

Accommodation

Hotels at Paltan Bazar are just south of Guwahati railway station, conveniently central. The best of these is the *Nandan* (B) while the nearby *Trimurti International* (D) is reasonable for those wanting something more basic. They are both on G.S. (Guwahati-Shillong) Rd along with a few other lodges. The *Tourist Lodge* (D) run by Assam Tourism is in the same building as their tourist office on Station Rd north of the main station. The *Bellevue* (B) has a nice setting overlooking the Brahmaputra and has a few birds in the garden. You might be able to 'scope a Greater Adjutant on the opposite bank of the river from your window. The *Brahmaputra Ashok* (A/B) is one of the best hotels in Guwahati and also has a riverside location.

Strategy

It is wise to check on the current political situation in the Northeast in case there are any areas to be avoided. Assam Tourism should be able to advise and might be able to reserve your accommodation ahead at

Kaziranga. If you intend to go to less well-known Assamese sanctuaries, such as Dibru-Saikhowa, you must obtain permits from the Office of the Chief Conservator of Forests (Wildlife), R.G. Baruah Rd, Guwahati, Assam 781024 ☎0361-566064, on the right about 1km before the zoo. **Gauhati Zoo** is in reasonable habitat and can be worth a couple of spare hours if you have time to kill. It can be reached from town by bus nos.1 and 2 and is open daily except Fridays from 08.00 to 16.00 (1 October to 31 March) and 07.00 to 16.30 (1 April to 30 September).

Greater Adjutants frequent a small plot of land belonging to Assam State Transport opposite the Rhino Sports Club at **Ulubari Bazar**. This is a few hundred metres along the road to South Sarania from the Ulubari Chariali cross-roads on G.S. Rd about 1km from Paltan Bazar. Birds can be seen throughout the day as they feed on refuse from the market.

Map of
Ulubari Bazar

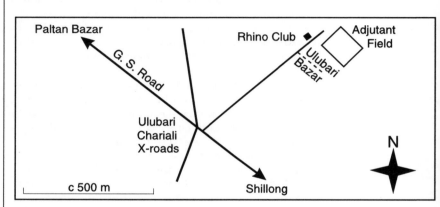

Deepor Beel is an extensive wetland within the municipal limits of Guwahati 13km southwest of the town centre. The northern side is easily accessible as NH37, the main road to the airport, passes along it. Take a taxi or one of the buses to Goalpara and get off at the Siotia Steels works near km-marker 141. View the lake and marsh from a dirt road on the western side of the steelworks leading to a brickworks. Unfortunately, the more interesting part of the lake, which is a bird sanctuary, is on the southern side and difficult to reach. You need a local guide here. If you contact the Office of the DFO, Kamrup East Division, near the DC's Court, Pan Bazar, Guwahati 1 ☎ 0361-543143, they can arrange for a forest guard to accompany you. The local fishermen need little financial persuasion to boat you round the *beel*.

The lake is one of the largest in lower Assam reaching a depth of about 4m during the monsoon but falling to about 1m in the dry season. Many waterbirds winter here including Ferruginous Pochard and Grey-headed Lapwing. Among more interesting residents are Greater and Lesser Adjutant, Watercock, Cinnamon Bittern, Fulvous Whistling-duck (small numbers among the commoner Lesser Whistling-duck), and Greater Painted-snipe. An uncommon winter visitor, the Solitary Snipe, and the extremely rare and endangered Goliath Heron have been reported from here. The surrounding agricultural fields support some interesting birds including Bengal Bushlark, Ashy Woodswallow, Striated Grassbird, Bluethroat (W), Rosy, Richard's and Blyth's (U) Pipits (W), and Black-faced Bunting (W). Among the raptors recorded are Brahminy Kite, Pallas's Fish Eagle, White-backed and Long-billed Vultures, Himalayan Griffon, Marsh

Map of Deepor Beel

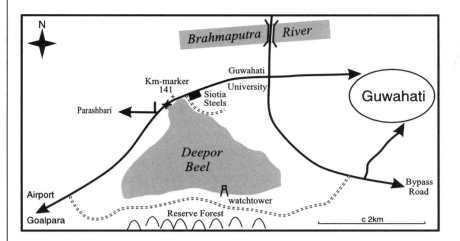

and Pied Harriers, and Spotted, Steppe, Booted and Black Eagles.

Pobitora is a small 16km² Wildlife Sanctuary just 48km east of Guwahati. A rare sighting of the highly endangered Rufous-vented Prinia of the eastern population, regarded by some as a separate species, Swamp Prinia *Prinia (burnesii) cinerascens,* has been reported from the grasslands here. Accommodation at the Forest IB must be booked with the DFO in Nowgong.

Manas

One of the most fascinating and beautiful sanctuaries in India is Manas in western Assam. The name is taken from a river which has its source high in the Himalaya of eastern Bhutan and enters the plain of the Brahmaputra at the Indian border. The two countries have co-operated to create sanctuaries on both sides of the border, giving protection to some 3,500km² of wild and beautiful jungles. On the Indian side the terai is largely grassland providing excellent habitat for specialised birds such as Swamp Francolin* and Bengal Florican. On the northern side of the reserve where the elevation reaches 150m there are dry and moist deciduous forests with scattered pockets of rainforest. Some of the best birding, however, is in dense tropical forests on the Bhutanese side of the border. Here the wilderness is relatively little disturbed and the mountains rise to over 4000m within 60km. Day treks into the jungles will not get you to those heights, but there are excellent birds to be seen in the foothills. Great Hornbills are fairly common and other delights such as Collared Falconet, Speckled Piculet, and Rufous-vented Laughingthrush are further incentives.

The jungles of Manas support the most diverse mammalian fauna of the subcontinent including 20 species on the Red Data List. Any visit would be amply rewarded by sightings of Golden Langur, a species that had only been legend until its discovery by science in 1953, yet the sanctuary supports almost 100 other mammal species.

Manas was only reopened to visitors in October 1995 and anyone contemplating a visit is advised to make enquiries locally first to check on the current situation. Although the Rhino population has been tragically decimated by poachers and insurgents the sanctuary still holds an abundance of other birds and animals to make a trip memorable.

Location   Access to Manas is from the town of Barpeta Rd (not Barpeta), which has

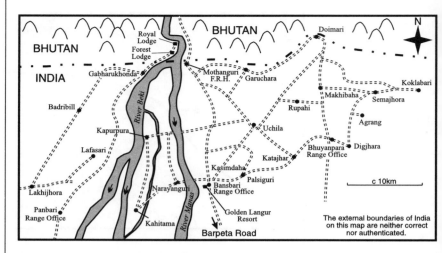

Map of Manas

fairly good bus and train connections with Guwahati, the Assamese capital, 132km east where the nearest airport is located. Since the town lies on the main east-west route connecting the Northeast with the rest of India, it is feasible to stop on your way from Darjeeling or Calcutta. Mothanguri, with the main FRH in the sanctuary, is about 40km due north of Barpeta Rd along a fair weather road. There is no regular bus service so a (jeep) taxi must be hired in Barpeta Rd if you do not have a vehicle. Forest Dept jeeps are not always available so keeping the hired jeep for the duration is useful. Otherwise arrange for the vehicle to pick you up again at the end of your stay.

Accommodation

The best quality accommodation is at the *Golden Langur Resort* at Bansbari south of the main entrance to the park, but the future of this private development is somewhat in doubt. Information and bookings at Blue Hill Travels, Blue Hill Complex, (behind the Hotel Nandan), Paltan Bazaar, Guwahati 781 008. They can arrange permits and trips into the sanctuary for you. Assam Tourism also has a lodge nearby.

Logistically and scenically the best place to stay is at the *Upper FRH* (E) at Mothanguri. This is simple but clean, and bed-linen is provided. Although there is a basic shop selling eggs, rice and biscuits a few hundred metres along the road inside Bhutan it is best to bring all your own supplies, especially fruit and vegetables, from Barpeta Rd. There are good cooks at the rest house to prepare meals. The *Lower Rest House* (E) is less comfortable. A small rest house run by Bhutan Forest Dept is located on the Bhutanese side of the border near Mothanguri not far from where the King of Bhutan has his Royal Lodge, but a Bhutanese visa would probably be necessary to stay there. A camp site is available if you have a tent.

There is a *Tourist Bungalow* and basic lodges including the friendly *Hotel Joli* (E) near the railway station in Barpeta Rd if you need to overnight there.

Strategy

The sanctuary closes during the monsoon from May (sometimes earlier) to October. The best season is from December to March. To arrange permits and accommodation, you must visit the office of the Field Director, Manas Project Tiger, P.O. Barpeta Rd, Assam 781 315, ☎03666-32253. It may help to write in advance. Without a permit you will be turned away at the main gate. The main road into the park and the area around Mothanguri are best avoided on weekends and holidays when day-trippers are in abundance.

To walk within the park, you should have permission and be accompanied by a forest guard. Elephant rides of 2-3 hours offer outstanding value. Half-day boat rides down the river from Mothanguri to Kapurpura can be an excellent way of seeing mammals, but you need to arrange a vehicle to bring you back. The boatmen need two days to work their way back against the current.

The forests on the Bhutanese side are more luxuriant and harbour a greater diversity of birds. One good trail leads up into Bhutan along the east bank of the river from Mothanguri where a small punted ferry crosses to the western side of the Manas. Strictly-speaking forays into Bhutan may not be permitted, but if you are discreet, you may find that they are possible. A visit to see the Royal Lodge, the best area for Golden Langur, is normally allowed. Keep to the trails as it is easy to lose one's bearings in the more remote areas. The track southwest from the Royal Lodge of the King of Bhutan is very good for birds.

Birds

Manas has the largest population of Bengal Florican in the world. The best area is probably in the grasslands just to the north and northeast of the park entrance at Bansbari. They are most easily seen when displaying in late March and April. Look for Swamp Francolin* in the same area. Other notable grassland birds include Pied Harrier (has bred), Black Francolin, Rain and Blue-breasted Quails (U), Barred Buttonquail, Lesser Coucal, Grass Owl (R), Bengal Bushlark, Chestnut-capped and Striated Babblers, Pale-footed Bush Warbler (UW), Zitting and Bright-headed Cisticolas, Rufous-rumped (U) and Striated Grassbirds, Blunt-winged Warbler (U), White-tailed Rubythroat, *maura* Common Stonechat, Black-headed Munia and Finn's Weaver* (U).

Along the river you can find Little Heron, Ruddy Shelduck (W), Common Merganser (W), Osprey (W), Great Thick-knee, Small Pratincole, River Lapwing, River and Black-bellied Terns, and Crested and Pied Kingfishers. Ibisbill winters along the stony riverbed but can take time to find.

Among more interesting forest birds are Collared Falconet, Pin-tailed, Wedge-tailed, Thick-billed and Orange-breasted Green Pigeons, Ashy Wood Pigeon (R), Pale-capped Pigeon (U), Barred Cuckoo Dove, Mountain Scops Owl, Spot-bellied Eagle Owl (R), Brown and Tawny (U) Fish Owls, Red-headed Trogon, Chestnut-headed and Blue-bearded Bee-eaters, Wreathed, Oriental Pied and Great Hornbills, Speckled Piculet, Long-tailed Broadbill, Blue-naped (U), Indian* (S), Hooded (U) and Blue (R) Pittas, Himalayan Flameback, Maroon Oriole, Spot-winged Starling (W), Rosy Minivet (U), Scaly Laughingthrush (U), Dark-sided (UW), Ferruginous (U), Snowy-browed, Little Pied, Pale-chinned, Pygmy Blue (UW), Pale Blue (U) and Blue-throated (U) Flycatchers, Tickell's Leaf (WP), Large-billed Leaf (UW), Blyth's Leaf (W), Yellow-vented (W), Chestnut-crowned (W) and Broad-billed (R) Warblers, White-rumped Shama, Orange-headed Thrush, Grey-winged Blackbird (UW), Sultan, Yellow-cheeked and Black-throated Tits, Thick-billed and Yellow-vented Flowerpeckers, and Ruby-cheeked, Mrs. Gould's, Green-tailed and Black-throated Sunbirds. It is worth searching here for the rather scarce and localised Rufous-vented Laughingthrush, an altitudinal migrant.

The Manas checklist collated by the authors numbers some 380 species and there are no doubt numerous others to be added to this. Many are the same as can be found at Kaziranga (which see) but among those perhaps more likely to be seen at Manas are: Cinnamon and Black Bitterns (U), Black-necked Stork, Red-crested Pochard (W), Black Baza (U), Crested

Goshawk, Rufous-bellied Eagle (U), Pallas's and Lesser Fish Eagles, Oriental Hobby (U), Greater Painted-snipe, Slaty-headed Parakeet, Vernal Hanging Parrot, Chestnut-winged Cuckoo (S), Grey and Savanna Nightjars, Crested Treeswift, Ruddy Kingfisher, Eurasian Wryneck (W), Streak-throated and Grey-headed Woodpeckers, Wire-tailed Swallow (S), Nepal House Martin, Black-naped Oriole, Crow-billed (U), Orange-bellied Leafbird, Himalayan, Ashy and Black Bulbuls, Grey-throated and Yellow-eyed Babblers, White-throated, Striated Laughingthrush, Rusty-fronted Barwing, Red-tailed Minla, Rufous Sibia, Rufous-bellied Niltava, Ashy Prinia*, Buff-barred (W), Ashy-throated (W) and Grey-hooded Warblers, Black-backed, Slaty-backed and Spotted Forktails, Dark-throated Thrush (W), Brown Dipper, White-tailed Nuthatch, Wallcreeper (W), Streaked Spiderhunter, and Chestnut (RW) and Crested Buntings.

Other Wildlife

One of the main attractions is the Golden Langur. It is more common in forests on the Bhutanese side where several troops of these delightful blond creatures inhabit the foothills. One troop is usually found in trees around the King of Bhutan's Lodge near the boat landing.

Manas is significant for two other extremely rare mammals: Hispid Hare and Pygmy Hog for both of which the sanctuary is the single most important site. Both inhabit thatch-scrub and grassland and were thought extinct until rediscovered in 1971. The Pygmy Hog is a small hairy version of the Wild Boar, with a more attenuated snout and rounded rear. The Hispid Hare, or Assamese Rabbit, is darker brown than the Black-naped Hare, and is covered in coarse bristly hair. The best chance of spotting them is as they cross the track through the grasslands between Bansbari and Mothanguri at dusk.

Most larger mammals are shier than at Kaziranga, but visitors are rarely dissatisfied. The best bet is on the elephant rides from Mothanguri in the mornings and afternoons. The elephant grass is very high and obscures the animals on jeep drives, making viewing best after areas of grass have been burnt off in February. The Wild Buffalo of Manas, being of pure strain, are particularly important because in many other areas interbreeding with domestic stock has diluted wild herds. A boat trip downstream is a good way to see these creatures as they retreat to the river during the heat of the day and also gives the opportunity of seeing a rare Ganges Dolphin. The Gaur (Indian Bison) occur in herds but are much more retiring. Rhino have been reduced to as few as 10 or 15 individuals. The Tiger has also suffered and the 1997 estimate of 89 may be optimistic but there is a reasonable chance of seeing one on an elephant ride. Wild Elephant can usually be found, while Hog Deer, Sambar, Muntjac and Swamp Deer are sometimes seen. Manas is on the eastern edge of the Chital's range so numbers are few. Capped Langur are fairly common in Assamese jungles where the shy Hoolock Gibbons also occur. Rhesus Macaques are sometimes seen on islands downstream from Mothanguri. Assamese Macaque is rare.

Manas's list of mammals is too long to print but includes Binturong, Sloth Bear, Chinese Pangolin, Golden (Bhutan), Marbled, Fishing and Leopard Cats, Common and Clouded Leopards, Yellow-throated Marten, Yellow-bellied Weasel, Slow Loris, Black Giant Squirrel, Large Indian, Small Indian, Common Palm and Masked Palm Civets, Eurasian Otter and Small Indian Mongoose.

Other Sites

The intrepid birder with time available may explore one or two sites in the extreme northeast of West Bengal, just over the border from Assam. The

Buxa Tiger Reserve is contiguous with Manas Tiger Reserve, separated by the Sankosh River which forms the state boundary. There are excellent blocks of primary lowland forest and teak plantations near the rest house at Jainti, but of more interest is a stay at the Buxa Fort Rest House (870m) enabling exploration of the forests on slopes up to the Bhutan border at 1900m. Rufous-necked Hornbill, Long-billed Wren Babbler, Greater Rufous-headed Parrotbill, Coral-billed Scimitar Babbler, Cutia, White-naped Yuhina and Beautiful Nuthatch are but some of the scarce prize birds to be found here, though you would need a long stay to find them all. Arrangements to visit must first be made with the Field Director, Buxa Tiger Reserve, Alipur Duar, the nearest main town to the south. There is a tea stall at Buxa Fort which may be persuaded to cook food for a small number of people, but it might be best to bring your own provisions.

Jaldapara WLS can make an interesting stop if travelling by road between Darjeeling and Buxa, though more for the mammals seen on elephant rides than for the birds. The accommodation and entrance to the park are near the town of Madari Hat.

Long-billed Wren
Babbler

Kaziranga and Panbari

Famous as a last refuge of the Indian Rhinoceros this superb 430km² tract of low-lying grasslands sprinkled with shallow *beels* and patches of open woodland has much to offer. It is probably the best place to see the endangered Bengal Florican and Swamp Francolin*. Greater Adjutant can be found alongside Lesser Adjutant, while the graceful Black-necked Stork retains a foothold here though declining elsewhere. There are good populations of Pallas's and Grey-headed Fish Eagles, as well as Pied Harrier. The sought-after Spot-winged Starling occurs in large flocks in winter but is usually gone by March. The adjacent forests at Panbari and the Mikir Hills hold many specialities and in winter harbour Himalayan species. Well over 300 species have been recorded in the park and its immediate environs and there are plenty of fascinating mammals. Unlike Manas, Kaziranga has never suffered from problems with insurgents.

Location

Kaziranga National Park lies in the heart of Assam. It is bounded to the north by the Brahmaputra and to the south by NH37, the state's main artery linking Guwahati with eastern Assam. The main tourist centre is at

Map of Kaziranga

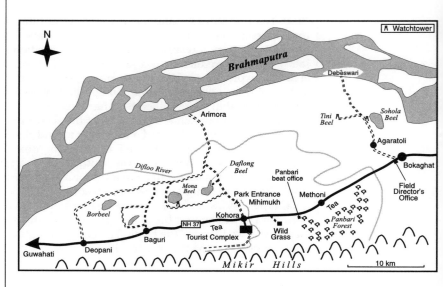

Kohora, 218km from Guwahati, the nearest airport. This is served by
regular flights from Delhi, Calcutta and Bagdogra as well as being the hub
for flights to other destinations in the Northeast. The nearest railway
station is inconveniently situated at Furkating, 75km east of Kohora. A train
is probably only worth considering if you are coming from, say, Jatinga to
the south. From Furkating get a bus or taxi for the 9km to Golaghat from
where there are buses to Kaziranga.

The usual approach to Kaziranga is by road. All buses between
Guwahati and the east use this route. Private buses (6 hours) are more
comfortable and faster than those of Assam State Transport. Ask to be set
down at Kohora unless you intend to stay at the Wild Grass Hotel which is
5km further east. To leave Kaziranga, flag down a bus on the main road.
Alternatively try to get one of the Assam Tourism tour buses overnighting
here to take you for the appropriate fare – ask at your lodge.

The National Park is divided into three ranges: Eastern, Central and
Western. Access and transport is by jeep which should be booked as early
as possible. The State Tourism Dept jeeps available through Aranya and
Bonani Lodges are less expensive than private jeeps and are often booked
out. Jeeps are only allowed into the Park from 07.30 to noon and from 14.30
to dusk. For the Central Range you need an entry pass and forest guard
from the Information (Education and Interpretation) Centre which opens at
07.30 and 14.30. A guide is optional. For the Western Range go to the Range
Office and entrance at Baguri (12km from Kohora) at the same times. The
Eastern Range is less well-frequented by visitors and access may be
allowed earlier if you come with a guide and ask at the Range Office at
Agaratola (25km).

Panbari Reserve Forest (10km east of Kohora) is on the southern side of
NH37 and may be explored on foot. You must obtain permission from the
Range Office at Kohora and arrange a jeep to take you to Panbari Beat
Office from where a forest guard will escort you. It is usually fairly easy to
wave down a bus to take you back to Kohora.

The elephant rides at Kaziranga are popular and it is best to book at least
two or three through your lodge as early as possible to avoid
disappointment. Booking is possible at the Information Centre the previous
evening, but this can involve much queuing. Rides last one hour at 06.00

and at 07.00 from the main park entrance at Mihimukh, 2km north of Kohora. Reporting time is half an hour beforehand. Make sure your transport to the appropriate 'riding point' is arranged through your lodge. There are no afternoon rides.

Accommodation   With the increasing popularity of Kaziranga and the opening up of Assam, tourist facilities are likely to become overburdened. Avoid public holidays and weekends and make reservations in advance if you can. If you arrive without a reservation, you should get a room, but you may have to move lodges.

Most lodges are at Kohora, run by Assam Tourism whose main office is on Station Rd near Guwahati railway station. It may be possible to book accommodation through them, but they may need at least 15 days. It is better to book through a good travel agent in Delhi or Calcutta. The *Aranya* (C) is the best of these lodges with the better restaurant. Order main meals beforehand to avoid a long wait. The *Bonani* is slightly cheaper but nearly as comfortable; food is more limited and ordered in advance. The *Bonoshree* (D) is more basic while the Kunjaban has cheap dormitory beds. To economise on food, try the Rhinorica Restaurant on the main road.

The best accommodation at Kaziranga is provided by the *Wild Grass Resort* (B) ☎037765-437, 5¹/₂km east of Kohora. For those willing to pay, Wild Grass will take much of the hassle out of your trip by organising permits, jeep and elephant rides for you. The son of the owner is very knowledgeable about Northeast Indian birds. Reservations address: Wild Grass, Barua Bhavan, 107 M.C. Rd, Uzan Bazar, Guwahati 781001, Assam ☎0361-546827, Fax541186.

Map of Kohora
(note orientation)

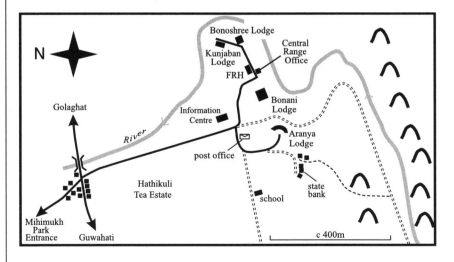

Strategy   The park is closed for the rainy season when dirt roads are impassable. The exact dates vary – normally from the first week of May to the beginning of November – so to be sure, go between the end of November and the first week of April. Much grassland is burnt during late February and early March and the period immediately afterwards is good for mammal viewing. A stay of 4–5 days is recommended and you can easily fill a week or more.

Bengal Florican is not easy to find. The best opportunity is afforded by elephant rides at Mihimukh, but you may need more than one. Try to organise some other birders to share an elephant with you and tell the mahout that you are looking for Florican. Ask him to stop when you want to look at something. The two or three-seater elephants are better, as you face forwards rather than sideways. Elephant rides can turn up other grassland species such as Swamp Francolin*, Chestnut-capped Babbler, all four weavers on the Indian list (Finn's* is scarce) and possibly even rarities such as Slender-billed Babbler. It is, however, hard to resist the temptation to spend most of the time looking at Rhino and wild Water Buffalo.

A good area for the Florican is in the grasslands at Debeswari in the Eastern Range. An early start is necessary; it takes 2 hours to reach this end of the park without stops en route. The Eastern Range has good woodland where woodpeckers such as Streak-throated, and Himalayan Flameback can be seen alongside Chestnut-headed and Blue-bearded Bee-eaters. Swamp Francolin* is likely on the dirt roads here early in the day and is fairly common throughout the park though not easy to see. The *beel* at Sohola supports plenty of waterfowl, and this is one of the best sites for Greater Adjutant. Pallas's Fish Eagle is much in evidence while Grey-headed prefers riverine habitat. Most sightings of another major rarity, the White-bellied Heron, are from this part of the Sanctuary. Try to get permission for a full day here and do not forget provisions for the driver and guard.

The Central and Western Ranges are easier to explore by jeep and have broadly similar habitat. In the Central Range you can go on foot if accompanied by an armed guard for 1¹/₂km past the entrance. Do this while the jeep follows on behind. After that you are only allowed to get out at certain points, usually watchtowers.

One or two half-day trips should be made to Panbari Reserved Forest. The woodland is somewhat degraded but still holds good birds. Asian Fairy Bluebird and Black-crested Bulbul are common, as are Abbott's and Puff-throated Babblers, the latter two more skulking, haunting the undergrowth along with Pale-chinned Flycatcher. Both Oriental and Great Hornbills are frequent, but you need to be lucky to see Wreathed. Banded Bay and Drongo Cuckoos are relatively easy to see when they begin calling in late March. Grey Peacock Pheasant, Pale-capped Pigeon, Silver-breasted Broadbill, Golden-crested Myna, White-hooded Babbler, Lesser Shortwing (W) and Black-breasted Thrush (W) are among rarer species to look for. The forest guard will guide you through the maze of tracks on a loop that brings you via a tea plantation onto the main highway a couple of kilometres down the main road.

A couple of hours can be spent exploring fields between the main road at Kohora and the park entrance at Mihimukh. This area is good for wagtails, larks and pipits including Blyth's (W). Scan the grassland for scarcer species among the more obvious Striated Grassbirds.

If you have just an hour or two to spare, the scrub and cultivation along the south side of the Hathikuli Tea Estate, reached by the path past the school at Kohora, can yield interesting birds such as Blue-tailed Bee-eater, Ashy Woodswallow, Common Green Magpie, Thick-billed Warbler (W), and Greater Necklaced and Rufous-necked Laughingthrushes. Alternatively just bird around Aranya Lodge. You might see White-vented Myna among the commoner Jungle Mynas or discover a Yellow-vented or a Scarlet-backed Flowerpecker in the Loranthus clumps (mistletoe) on trees in the garden.

If you stay at the Wild Grass Resort, the nearby tea plantation can yield similar species; even White-cheeked Partridge and Blue-naped Pitta have been seen here.

If you have had enough of jeeps, permits, guides and guards take a packed lunch and follow the dirt road behind the Tourist Complex at Kohora, which eventually bears round to the southwest along the river and up into the Mikir Hills of Karbi Anglong. Look for Pale-headed Woodpecker among the stands of bamboo and maybe spot the delightful Blue-throated Flycatcher as it sits quietly in the shadows. Towards the end of the day look for Brown Crakes in the shallow lower reaches of the river.

Birds   Other species in the park: Spot-billed and Great White (UW) Pelicans, Oriental Darter, Asian Openbill, Woolly-necked and Black (W) Storks, Bar-headed Goose (W), Ruddy Shelduck (W), Spot-billed Duck, Falcated Duck (RW), Ferruginous Pochard (W), Cotton Pygmy-goose, Brahminy Kite, Changeable Hawk, Booted (U), Rufous-bellied, Steppe (W), Greater Spotted (W) and White-tailed (RW) Eagles, Red-headed and Cinereous (W) Vultures, Himalayan Griffon (UW), Osprey (W), Oriental Hobby (WP), Red-necked Falcon (R), Kalij Pheasant, Red Junglefowl, Yellow-legged Buttonquail (U), Watercock, Purple Swamphen, Great Thick-knee, Small Pratincole (U), Grey-headed Lapwing (W), River and Black-bellied Terns, Red Collared Dove, Alexandrine and Red-breasted Parakeets, Green-billed Malkoha, Lesser Coucal, Collared Scops Owl, Tawny Fish Owl (U), Jungle and Asian Barred Owlets, Brown Hawk Owl, Large-tailed Nightjar, Himalayan Swiftlet, Stork-billed Kingfisher, Blue-tailed Bee-eater, Dollarbird, Great, Lineated, Blue-throated and Blue-eared Barbets, Greater Flameback, Fulvous-breasted Woodpecker, Grey-capped Pygmy Woodpecker, Bengal Bushlark, Sand Lark, Pale, Sand and Plain Martins, Grey-backed Shrike, Ashy Woodswallow, Chestnut-tailed Starling, Large Woodshrike, Large and Black-winged Cuckooshrikes, Scarlet, Short-billed (W) and Long-tailed (W) Minivets, Golden-fronted Leafbird, Striated Babbler, Black-breasted Parrotbill* (R), Brownish-flanked, Grey-sided and Chinese (R) Bush Warblers (W), Zitting and Bright-headed Cisticolas, Bristled Grassbird* (R), Thick-billed, Blyth's Reed and Paddyfield Warblers (W), Tickell's Leaf, Smoky, Dusky, Yellow-browed and Greenish Warblers (W), Bluethroat (W), Siberian and White-tailed Rubythroats (W), Black and Daurian Redstarts (W), *maura* Common Stonechat, Jerdon's Bushchat (R), Velvet-fronted Nuthatch, Richard's (W), Paddyfield and Rosy (W) Pipits, Yellow and Citrine Wagtails (W), Red Avadavat, Black-headed Munia, Yellow-breasted, and Black-faced and Little Buntings (W).

A number of other species are more likely to be seen at Panbari: Grey Peacock Pheasant, Wedge-tailed (U), Pompadour and Yellow-footed Green Pigeons, Green and Mountain Imperial Pigeons, Emerald Dove, Indian, Grey-bellied* and Plaintive Cuckoos (S), Red-headed Trogon, Speckled and White-browed Piculets (U), Rufous Woodpecker, Greater and Lesser Yellownapes, Maroon Oriole (U), Bronzed, Lesser Racket-tailed, Spangled and Greater Racket-tailed Drongos, Hill Myna, Bar-winged Flycatcher-shrike, White-throated Bulbul (W), White-browed Scimitar Babbler, Golden Babbler (R), Greater Necklaced, Lesser Necklaced and White-crested Laughingthrushes, Brown-cheeked and Nepal Fulvettas, Little Pied (U), Slaty-blue, Slaty-backed (U), Pygmy Blue (U) and Verditer Flycatchers (W), Small Niltava (W), Black-naped Monarch, Grey-bellied, Slaty-bellied and Chestnut-headed Tesias (UW), Dark-necked (U) and Mountain Tailorbirds, White-spectacled, Grey-cheeked (U), Chestnut-crowned (U), Yellow-bellied (U), Large-billed Leaf (U), Blyth's Leaf and Yellow-vented Warblers (W), White-rumped Shama, White-tailed Robin (UW), Sultan Tit, Olive-backed Pipit (W), Thick-billed (U), Ruby-cheeked, Black-throated and Crimson Sunbirds, and Little Spiderhunter.

Other Wildlife   Kaziranga is superb for mammals. You can hardly fail to see Rhino and wild Water Buffalo on any trip into the park. There are more than a thousand of each within the Reserve and almost as many wild Elephants, though these are seen less frequently. Both Swamp and Hog Deer are plentiful though the latter can be adept at hiding in the grass. Wild Boar are fewer in number but still seen frequently, while the 70 or so Tigers are as elusive as anywhere. The best way to see animals is from an Elephant. Some time at a watchtower overlooking one of the larger waterbodies might be rewarded by a pack of Smooth Indian Otters, while a period on the banks of the Brahmaputra could result in a glimpse of the rare Ganges River Dolphin, also sometimes seen in the first river after entering the park at Mihimukh.

Another local speciality is the Hoolock Gibbon. To find these, go to the Panbari Forest where they are more likely to spot you first and set the woods resounding with their whooping calls while keeping a safe distance and plenty of foliage between themselves and you. Capped Langurs are easier to see and you might even catch sight of a Yellow-throated Marten.

Other Sites   There is good grassland and woodland at **Burapahar** west of Kaziranga. Being outside the National Park you can walk, but you need permission from the Range Office at Gorakati. The **Nameri Wildlife Sanctuary** is 2 hours northeast of Tezpur and contiguous with the Pakhui Wildlife Sanctuary of Arunachal Pradesh. Though not guaranteed, this is one of the best places to see White-winged Duck. Ibisbill is regular in winter on the Bhorelli River here, Long-billed Plover perhaps less so. Other specialities: Collared Falconet, Rufous-necked and Wreathed Hornbills, Ruddy Kingfisher (U), and Black-breasted Thrush (W). There is tented accommodation at the Eco Camp bookable through the Assam (Bhorelli) Anglers' Association, c/o Tezpur Station Club Ltd., Tezpur 784001, Assam ☎03712-2004, 30478, Fax21583 or Assam (Bhorelli) Anglers' Association, c/o Rip Burman, H.M. Das Rd, Rehabari, Guwahati 781008, Assam ☎/Fax 0361-545847. Transport and accommodation can also be arranged through Wild Grass at Kaziranga. The **Sonai Rupa Sanctuary** was a good site, but is currently being used as an army firing range.

Dibru-Saikhowa

The flood plains of the Brahmaputra in Northeast India have a number of rare specialised grassland and swamp forest birds such as the threatened Marsh Babbler*, Jerdon's Babbler, Black-throated Parrotbill, Rufous-vented (Swamp) Prinia, and Jerdon's Bushchat. The Dibru-Saikhowa Wildlife Sanctuary is the best place to see these and was set up in 1986 in an attempt to protect their fast disappearing habitats. The 340km^2 Reserve encompasses a patchwork of seasonally flooded forests, beels and grassy pockets between the braided arms of the rivers Dibru and Brahmaputra. Lack of funding means that the sanctuary is not adequately protected. Illegal logging and overgrazing are major problems.

Other interesting residents and altitudinal migrants such as Pale-capped Pigeon, White-tailed Rubythroat and Black-breasted Thrush may be seen alongside a good assortment of wintering warblers. Over 300 species have been recorded and visiting birdwatchers are likely to find more.

Prior permission to visit and stay at the Sanctuary must be obtained in Guwahati from the Chief Conservator of Forests (Wildlife), R.G. Baruah Rd, Guwahati 781024, Assam ☎566064. Send a letter first and follow it up by calling in personally.

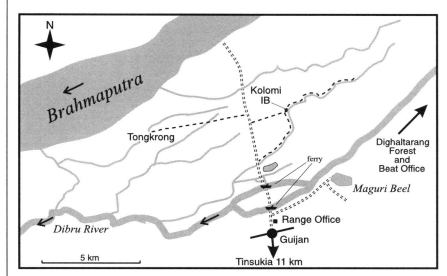

Map of
Dibru-Saikhowa

Location
The Sanctuary comes under the jurisdiction of the DFO (Wildlife) at Tinsukia, 490km east of Guwahati. Bring your permit from the CCF Guwahati and call at the DFO's office on the north side of town to confirm arrangements for your stay. The 12-hour overnight journey by private bus is less comfortable but much quicker than the rail connection. The airport at Dibrugarh (48km) is served by regular flights from Calcutta and Guwahati, but these are sometimes cancelled at short notice.

The Park HQ, the Forest Range Office, is at the village of Guijan (Guizan) just outside the southern boundary of the Sanctuary, 11km north of Tinsukia. Coming from the latter continue through the village straight across the cross-roads onto an unmetalled road. The Range Office is a few hundred metres on the right. A mini-bus service runs at fairly frequent intervals from the Paradise Cinema Hall, half a kilometre from Tinsukia Railway Station, to Guijan during the daytime. Taxis, jeeps and auto-rickshaws are available for hire in Tinsukia.

Within the reserve movement is on foot or by boat (ask at the Range Office). Much of the park is flooded from late April to October.

Accommodation
There is an *IB* with one large double bedroom and attached bathroom at Guijan Range Office where basic meals can be provided. The rather dilapidated *IB* at Kolomi, 6km inside the Sanctuary is more convenient for good habitat, but only provides shelter. Well water is available but should be treated with purifying tablets. The Range Office can arrange a guide and porters who will cook. There is another basic *IB* at Hathiguli at the eastern end of Dibru-Saikhowa, but nearby grassland habitat at Surkey (Churke) was badly overgrazed in 1996. More comfortable accommodation is available in Tinsukia where the best hotels are the *Urmila* (B/C) and *Jyoti* (C/D), both on the road towards Guijan.

Strategy
The dry season is normally from November to mid/late March. The rainy season reduces time for birding but makes access by boat to parts of the sanctuary easier. This is the breeding season for some grassland species which may make them easier to see. Several days or more are recommended.

To enter the Sanctuary, a forest guard must accompany you from the

Guijan Range office. From the office continue ½km north to where the road terminates at Guijan Ghat on the south bank of the river Dibru, the southern boundary of the Wildlife Sanctuary. Here you cross by ferry to a large island from where a dirt road leads through a scattered village to another ferry crossing point. The only wheeled transport which continues north from here are villagers' bicycles. You can continue on foot wading through two or three river channels or carry on a little further by boat. The dirt road eventually reaches the south bank of the Brahmaputra after 10km.

Birding is good once you have crossed the second arm of the Dibru. Check open waterbodies and adjacent wet areas for Lesser Adjutant, Black Stork, various waders, pipits, and wagtails. A few Spot-billed Pelicans occur. Pied Harriers hunt low over the meadows, the park generally supporting a selection of raptors. Pale-footed, Brownish-flanked, Chestnut-crowned, Grey-sided and Spotted Bush Warblers favour dense bushes and clumps of grass in winter. Look for Yellow-bellied Prinia, Mountain Tailorbird, and Smoky Warbler here.

Where more trees intermingle with the bushes occasional mixed parties could include Rosy Minivet, Green Magpie, and Chestnut-crowned and Yellow-vented Warblers (W). Roving bands of Rufous-necked Laughingthrushes are not uncommon.

Five km north of Guijan a path leads to the right reaching Kolomi IB after about 1½km. A little further along the main track north another path goes left to Tongkrong Camp where the IB has been destroyed by floods. The forest is interspersed with patches of long grass and the whole area is particularly rich in birds with White-tailed Rubythroat, Black-breasted Thrush, and Ferruginous Flycatchers among the winter visitors. The endangered Pale-capped Pigeon and Spot-winged Starling (UW) can be found in trees around Kolomi. Jerdon's Bushchat is not uncommon in the elephant grass along the river where the highly skulking Marsh Babbler* is also present. Pishing may help. Several species of woodpecker are found at Dibru-Saikhowa including both Greater and Lesser Yellownapes, while a good view of a splendid male Red-headed Trogon, a Sultan Tit or a Ruby-cheeked Sunbird brightens up anyone's day. A network of trails used by Elephants and wild Water Buffalo allows exploration, but steer clear if there are fresh signs of their presence.

The Kolomi IB stands on a bank of the river which gives it its name. To the east is a stretch where Blyth's Kingfisher has reportedly been seen. Its Stork-billed relative is common throughout the sanctuary. You can take a different route back to Guijan by following the river back from Kolomi as far as the main track. Make sure you allow time for wading the rivers in daylight and finding a ferry back across the northern arm of the Dibru River, which is not easy after dark.

There is some good grassland habitat supporting Jerdon's Babbler and the rare *cinerascens* race of Rufous-vented Prinia about 10km upstream on the northern side of the Dibru River opposite Dighaltarang. Amarpur, a remote region to the northeast of the reserve, has thick grassland managed for thatch with good populations of Jerdon's Babbler, Black-breasted Parrotbill, and other grassland species. If you want to look for White-winged Duck, try Sal Beel or Pani Kawri Nallah near Tongkrong. Ask for guidance at the Range Office.

Birds   Other species include most of those listed under Kaziranga/Panbari *Birds*, but also Malayan Night Heron (R), Little, Cinnamon, Yellow and Black Bitterns, Black-necked Stork, Glossy Ibis, Comb Duck, Red-crested Pochard (W), Black Baza (U), Crested Goshawk, Bonelli's Eagle,

Pallas's (U), Grey-headed and Lesser (U) Fish Eagles, Eurasian Griffon (R), Swamp Francolin* (U), Common and Sarus Cranes (R), Bengal Florican, River Lapwing, Lesser Sand Plover (W), Nordmann's Greenshank (RW), Long-toed Stint (W), Pallas's Gull (W), Thick-billed Green Pigeon (U), Chestnut-winged and Lesser Cuckoos (S), Lesser Coucal, Brown Fish Owl, Blue-eared (R) and Ruddy (R) Kingfishers, Blue-bearded Bee-eater (U), Oriental Pied and Great Hornbills (U), Streak-throated and Grey-headed Woodpeckers, Bengal Bushlark, Brahminy Starling, Bank* (R) and White-vented Mynas, Black-crested, Ashy (U) and Black Bulbuls, Puff-throated, Buff-breasted (U), Rufous-fronted, Grey-throated, Chestnut-capped, Sapphire Flycatcher (UW), Large and Rufous-bellied Niltavas, Rufous-rumped (R) and Striated Grassbirds, Black-browed Reed, Golden-spectacled and Grey-hooded Warblers (W), Blue Whistling Thrush, Chestnut-bellied Nuthatch, Rosy Pipit (W), Scarlet-backed and Fire-breasted (RW) Flowerpeckers, and Black-breasted* and Streaked Weavers. Other rare possibilities here: Manipur Bush Quail**, Slender-billed Babbler and Bristled Grassbird*.

Other Wildlife   Dibru-Saikhowa supports a number of mammals though not such spectacular numbers as at Kaziranga. The most obvious animals are wild Water Buffalo. Elephants are quite common, as are macaques of which both Assamese and Rhesus are found here. Tiger and Leopard are the main predators of Sambar, Barking Deer, Hog Deer and Wild Boar. You need luck to see some of the other residents such as Indian Porcupine, Leopard Cat or Smooth Indian Otter. A local speciality is the Feral Horse, common and tame around Surkey in the eastern part of the Sanctuary. Along the Brahmaputra you might see Ganges River Dolphin.

Other Sites   **Maguri Beel** is an excellent wetland outside the Sanctuary boundary 4km east along a dirt road from Guijan. Fulvous Whistling-duck are occasionally seen and there may be rarer species such as Baer's Pochard or Falcated Duck in winter. You can normally persuade one of the fishing boats to take you round the marshy lake for a small payment.
  The small reserve forests of **Bherjan, Padumani** and **Borajan** are rich in birds and have been proposed as primate sanctuaries, the last-named being particularly famous for its primates. They are easily accessible from Tinsukia, only a few kilometres away, and can be worth a visit. You need to take a guide from the forest office.

Namdapha

Arunachal Pradesh in the extreme northeast of India is one of the most biologically diverse parts of the subcontinent. Its avifauna is a unique blend of Himalayan, Sino-Tibetan and Indo-Burmese forms. Although not thoroughly explored, 665 species of bird have been recorded within the state. Fabulous species such as Blyth's Tragopan, Ward's Trogon, Rufous-necked Hornbill , Blue-naped Pitta, Wedge-billed Wren Babbler, Snowy-throated Babbler and Beautiful Nuthatch are found in this remote region. A diverse range of ethnic tribes populates the province. This and its politically sensitive situation mean that the former North-East Frontier Agency (NEFA) had long been closed to foreign nationals. Only recently has the government allowed access to certain parts for groups of tourists. Fortunately, one of these designated areas is one of the finest National Parks in India – Namdapha.
  Spread over an area of 1985km^2 Namdapha is among the larger protected

areas of India. The park is at the eastern end of the province in the Changlang (formerly Tirap) district. Its eastern and southern boundaries are international borders with neighbouring Myanmar. The area is mountainous, criss-crossed by innumerable watercourses forming part of the catchment for the Brahmaputra through the Noa-Dihing (Diyun) river system. The park is named after the Namdapha River, a main tributary of the Noa-Dihing. Managed under Project Tiger since 1983 the sanctuary is reputed to be unique in harbouring all four big Himalayan cats: Tiger, Leopard, the rarely seen Clouded Leopard and the almost mythical Snow Leopard.

Namdapha has a huge altitudinal range: from 200m at the western entrance to the park up to 4578m at Dapha Bum on the park's northern boundary ridge. With an average annual rainfall of 2500–4000mm it supports an unusually varied and spectacular avifauna.

The habitats may be broadly classified into tropical, temperate and alpine types. The multi-layered evergreen timberland clothing the lower slopes is probably the largest remaining dipterocarp forest in India. Some specimens of *Dipterocarpus macrocarpus* reach above the main canopy to heights of 150m. Botanists are still cataloguing the flora including an abundance of tree species, from Cinnamon and Assam Sal to Spruce, Birch and Juniper. Bamboos occur extensively as do various species of cane adding to the impenetrability of the undergrowth. Numerous species of orchid make this a paradise for the enthusiast while many creepers adorn the trees adding their unique attraction to this unspoilt wilderness. Grasslands are limited to pockets along the Noa-Dihing and Namdapha rivers. For the dedicated and keen naturalist Namdapha is a rewarding experience perhaps unequalled anywhere else in the country.

N.B. In order to visit Arunachal Pradesh you must have a Restricted Area Permit (see Pre-tour Information).

Map of Namdapha

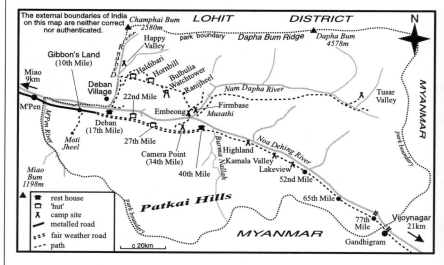

Location

Arunachal Pradesh is one of the remotest parts of India. There are no railway lines in Arunachal Pradesh itself and to get from one part of this mountainous state to another it is usually necessary to travel via the plains of Assam.

The nearest airport to Namdapha is at Dibrugarh (Mohanbari) served by Indian Airlines flights from Calcutta four times a week. There are also flights from Guwahati. At Dibrugarh you can hire a vehicle, preferably a jeep, to continue via Tinsukia, Digboi, Margherita, Jagun and the Arunachal border checkpost at Namchik to the National Park HQ at Miao (86km from Digboi, 9km before the park entrance). The journey by Assam or Arunachal State Transport bus takes 6–7 hours. By train it is best to terminate at Tinsukia and continue by bus or taxi to Miao (110km) unless you are making the recommended visit to Digboi (see *Other Sites* below). There are overnight buses (c.13 hours) from Guwahati to Jagun about 35km before Miao. Plenty of buses and taxis ply between Jagun and Miao. Jagun is the nearest town with reliable telephone services. The luxury day bus between Guwahati and Tinsukia conveniently stops for lunch at the Wild Grass Resort, Kaziranga NP, if you want to visit there.

At Miao you need to contact the Field Director, Namdapha Tiger Reserve, P.O. Miao, Changlang District, Arunachal Pradesh to make further arrangements. Write ahead to inform of your visit. Taxis are available at Miao to take you on the 27km to Deban within the park.

The park is mostly thick primary forest and has just one main access road and a few walkable trails. The dirt road is fairly good until shortly before the Deban Rest House (17th Mile) and continues as a jeep track as far as the 40th Mile PWD Rest House. (The old route that runs right through the park south of the Noa-Dihing was marked with milestones and the locals refer to places along it with the mile number rather than by name.) Rain quickly makes the road impassable beyond 22nd Mile, even for 4-wheel drive vehicles. A little beyond 40th Mile the track is impassable and the locals who trek up to Vijaynagar (Vijoynagar), near the Myanmar border, do so along the banks of the Noa-Dihing (dangerous and often impossible during the monsoon). The Noa-Dihing cannot be crossed during the rainy season, but as the waters subside in October, a small ferryboat is used at Deban and in Nov-Jan it may be possible to wade or use elephants to ford the river in places.

Accommodation

There are good hotels at Tinsukia (see section on Dibru-Saikhowa) and a good *IOC Guest House* at Digboi (*Other Sites*). At Miao there is a simple lodge called the *Tourist Home*, as well as a *Circuit House* and an *IB* under the jurisdiction of the Extra Assistant Commissioner. At Deban, in lower Namdapha (27km from Miao), there is a *Rest House* with five basic rooms and a dormitory with 12 beds . There are simple huts at Haldibari (two rooms), Hornbill (four rooms), Bulbulia (large open-sided watchtower), 27th Mile (two rooms), 34th Mile Camp (two rooms) and two *IBs* at 40th Mile Camp. A sleeping bag and sleeping mat are indispensable and a tent has its advantages, especially if you want to go as far as Embeong.

Strategy

The park is only accessible to altitudes up to 850m, so a winter visit is desirable when altitudinal migrants are at lower elevations. Try to spend as much time as possible in the park. The maximum ten days currently allowed are scarcely enough for the keen birder who wants to see the specialities, many of which are uncommon and shy. It can rain at any time though November to mid-January is driest. By late March the rains may make the main river impassable and the monsoon makes birding difficult on to September. Namdapha is a popular destination with the people of Assam so it might be best to avoid public holidays.

Miao is a small town at 260m surrounded by green hills. A night here with birding around the Circuit House and by the river is not wasted but may be better spent inside the park. In winter Ibisbill can be found along the river here and on the way to Deban. Little Heron, Black Stork,

Blue-bearded Bee-eater, Lineated Barbet, Sand Lark and Striated Grassbird are more likely to be seen here than in the sanctuary itself while commoner forest species are also present.

On the way to Deban explore the area known as Gibbon's Land, just at the beginning of the park proper. Just past the checkpost a 4km long track goes off to the right to Moti Jheel. Slender-billed Scimitar-Babbler, Snowy-throated Babbler** (U – one of the rarer Indian endemics), Rufous-necked Laughingthrush, Pale Blue Flycatcher, and Large-billed Leaf Warbler have been seen here along with Mountain Hawk Eagle, Eurasian Hobby, Lesser Coucal, Bengal Bushlark, Grey-bellied Tesia and White-tailed Robin. Small Pratincole and Ibisbill frequent the river beyond the checkpost.

The Deban Rest House is picturesquely situated above the confluence of the Deban and Noa-Dihing rivers and is surrounded by forest rich in woodpeckers, babblers and thrushes. The grounds of the Rest House itself have turned up surprises such as Blyth's Kingfisher and Black-breasted Thrush. Scour the river for wintering Ibisbill (more regular further downstream), Crested Kingfisher, White-bellied Heron (a rare, globally threatened resident – sometimes seen flying downstream at dusk) and the increasingly rare Lesser Fish Eagle (U). You might get your first opportunity to sort out the Greater and Lesser Necklaced Laughing-thrushes, or see your first Sultan Tit, Asian Barred Owlet, Grey-headed Parrotbill or Long-tailed Sibia. Pied Falconet is one of the rarest Indian raptors and this is probably one of the best sites. The skulking Spotted Wren Babbler was only recorded for the first time in 1994 but is present near Deban and through much of the lower part of the reserve.

If the river is in full flood, birding is restricted to the main jeep track which continues east through excellent forest. It is muddy going but worth the journey just to see some of the excellent birds along this road: White-cheeked Partridge, Pale-headed Woodpecker, Blue-naped Pitta, Collared Treepie (U), Large Scimitar Babbler, Wedge-billed Wren Babbler (U), Snowy-throated Babbler**, Greater and Lesser Rufous-headed Parrotbills, Chestnut-backed Laughingthrush (U), White-naped Yuhina, Rufous-throated Fulvetta, Green Cochoa (R), and Dark-sided Thrush are among the most mouth-watering that have been seen along here.

In the dry season cross the river for an easy trek staying at the various forest huts. Short easy stages leave time for birding and exploring the area around each overnight stop.

Day 1: Deban (390m) to Haldibari Camp (425m) – 6km.
Day 2: Haldibari (425m) to Hornbill (520m)) – 5 km.
Day 3: Hornbill (520m) to Bulbulia (640m)) – 3 km.
Day 4: Based at Bulbulia. Day trek up to Ranijheel (800m) and beyond –
4km plus each way.
Day 5: Return to Deban.

Add extra days at Haldibari and Hornbill, or if you have camping equipment, continue on to the campsites at Ranijheel (4km), Firm Base (5km) and/or Embeong (3km). Sometimes the Noa-Dihing can be crossed here; you could then complete a circular tour via Chiria Camp (6km), Camera Point (10km), 27 Miles (11km) and Deban (16km).

Visiting the higher reaches of the sanctuary is impossible until trails are cut. The Upper Noa Dihing Valley beyond the eastern boundary of the park on the way to Vijaynagar, requires special permission and the only way in for most of the year is by helicopter. There you might have a chance of seeing scarce species such as Mountain Bamboo Partridge, Blyth's

Tragopan, Long-billed, Long-tailed, Bar-winged and Wedge-billed Wren Babblers, Grey-sided Laughingthrush and Brown-throated Fulvetta.

Birds   A winter visit is assumed. The following specialities appear to be fairly widespread though not necessarily common or easy to see: Grey Peacock Pheasant, Wreathed Hornbill, Blue-naped Pitta, Collared Treepie, Large Scimitar Babbler, Streaked and Eyebrowed Wren Babblers, Rufous-vented Laughingthrush, White-hooded Babbler, Rufous-throated Fulvetta, Rufous-backed and Beautiful Sibias, Green Cochoa, Black-breasted Thrush. Others seem to be more localised with Great Slaty Woodpecker found mainly between Deban and Haldibari; Brown Hornbill around Haldibari; Rufous-necked Hornbill and Slender-billed Scimitar Babbler near Hornbill; Beautiful Nuthatch beyond Hornbill/Bulbulia; White-bellied Heron, Red-faced Liocichla, Black-headed Shrike Babbler, White-tailed Flycatcher and Rusty-bellied Shortwing near Embeong.

About 2–3km past Bulbulia there is a good stand of bamboo for specialists such as Pale-headed Woodpecker, Red-billed Scimitar Babbler, Snowy-throated Babbler**, and Lesser and Greater Rufous-headed Parrotbills. White-winged Duck has been seen on the pool at Ranijheel.

Other species include: Crested Goshawk, Rufous-bellied Eagle (U), White-tailed Eagle (U-R), Oriental Hobby (U), White-cheeked Partridge, Kalij Pheasant, Pallas's Gull, Pompadour, Pin-tailed and Thick-billed Green Pigeons (U), Green (U) and Mountain Imperial Pigeons, Barred Cuckoo Dove (U), Emerald Dove, Plaintive, Indian and Drongo Cuckoos (S), Green-billed Malkoha, Mountain and Collared Scops Owls, Collared Owlet, Brown Hawk Owl (U), Himalayan Swiftlet, Silver-backed Needletail, Red-headed Trogon, Blue-bearded Bee-eater, Great Hornbill, Blue-throated Barbet, Speckled and White-browed Piculets (U), Greater and Lesser Yellownapes, Bay, Rufous and Fulvous-breasted Woodpeckers, Silver-breasted and Long-tailed Broadbills, Plain Martin, Maroon Oriole, Spangled, Greater and Lesser Racket-tailed Drongos, Hill Myna, Green Magpie, Bar-winged Flycatcher-shrike, Large and Black-winged Cuckooshrikes, Orange-bellied Leafbird, Black-crested (U), White-throated, Ashy and Black Bulbuls, Buff-breasted, Rufous-fronted and Golden Babblers, Pygmy Wren Babbler, Grey-headed Parrotbill (U), White-crested, Greater Necklaced, Lesser Necklaced and Blue-winged (U) Laughingthrushes, White-browed and Black-eared Shrike-Babblers (U), Silver-eared Mesia, Red-tailed and Blue-winged Minlas, Rusty-fronted Barwing, Whiskered, Striated, White-bellied and Black-chinned Yuhinas, Rufous-winged and Nepal Fulvettas, *albicilla* Red-breasted Flycatcher, Rufous-gorgeted, Little Pied (U), Ultramarine (U), Slaty-blue (U), Hill Blue (R), Pygmy Blue (U), Snowy-browed and Sapphire Flycatchers, Large, Small and Rufous-bellied Niltavas, Slaty-bellied, Grey-bellied and Chestnut-headed (U) Tesias, Mountain Tailorbird, Yellow-browed, Lemon-rumped, Blyth's Leaf, Yellow-vented, Ashy-throated, White-spectacled, Grey-hooded, Golden-spectacled, Grey-cheeked, Chestnut-headed, Rufous-faced, Yellow-bellied and Broad-billed (R) Warblers, White-browed Shortwing (U), White-crowned, Little (U) and Slaty-backed Forktails, White-tailed and Blue-fronted (R) Robins, Siberian, Scaly, Plain-backed and Dark-sided Thrushes (U), Brown Dipper (U), Sultan Tit, Chestnut-bellied and Velvet-fronted (U) Nuthatches, Yellow-bellied Flowerpecker (U), Black-throated Sunbird, and Little and Streaked Spiderhunters.

Other Wildlife   Namdapha is blessed with a rich mammalian fauna though mostly secretive or nocturnal. Of the primates the most easily seen are usually

Capped Langurs. The spectacular Hoolock Gibbons are very noisy but shy though a few days should produce at least one good sighting. The Yellow-throated Marten appears to be fairly common and there are good chances of spotting this during the daytime. Muntjac is also likely.

A number of squirrel species inhabit the reserve and because of their diurnal habits the Orange-bellied Himalayan, Malayan Giant, Hoary-bellied and Himalayan Striped are likely. The flying squirrels, though not uncommon, are largely nocturnal: an object flying through the air and landing with a crash into a nearby tree may alert you to their presence. The Namdapha Flying Squirrel was first described from Deban in 1981. It differs from other large flying squirrels in having the entire underparts white except for a faint orange-rufous tinge on the wing-membrane. There are four other flying squirrels (Red Giant, Spotted Giant, Hairy-footed and Particoloured) in the park and identifying them in the field is not easy. A night-time recce with a torch might also turn up one of the civet species such as the Common Palm, Large and Small Indian.

Big cats inhabit Namdapha but the nearest you are likely to get is seeing the pug-marks or droppings. The smaller Marbled, Leopard, Golden and Fishing Cats could cross your path if you are very lucky. Look for signs of bear and elephant and try to avoid coming too close. Other mammals you might see are Hog Deer, Wild Boar, Slow Loris, Indian Porcupine, and Gaur. Altogether more than 90 species have been recorded at Namdapha.

Other Sites

The town of **Digboi** in eastern Assam is a convenient last night's stopover en route to Namdapha. It is, however, well worth spending two or more days here to explore the nature reserve being set up by the IOC (Indian Oil Corporation) to protect the lowland forests in and around the oldest operating oilfield in the world. These still harbour an excellent array of birds including Oriental Hobby (near the guesthouse), White-cheeked Partridge, Grey Peacock Pheasant, Wreathed Hornbill, Blue-naped Pitta (U), Collared Treepie (for which this is an excellent site), Streaked and Spotted Wren Babblers, Chestnut-backed and Rufous-necked Laughing-thrushes, White-hooded Babbler, Pygmy Blue Flycatcher (W), White-spectacled and Grey-cheeked Warblers (W) and Black-breasted Thrush (W). White-winged Duck has been seen but is evidently quite rare. Elephants and Hoolock Gibbon are not uncommon and if you are lucky you may even see a Leopard or Hog-badger. Accommodation is available at the IOC Guesthouses (B/C). Contact Mr. P.L. Barua, Dy. Gen. Manager (Human Resources), IOC (Assam Oil Divn.), Digboi 786171, Assam ☎037539-2768, Fax2470; email <plbarua@iocl_aod.iocdel.ernet.in> or Shri S.R. Koneru, Chief Admin Manager, IOC (AOD), ☎2715; email <Sarkar@iocl_aod.iocdel.ernet.in>. It is best if you have your own transport but the IOC may be able to help arrange a taxi to get around the reserve.

If you can afford the time and money to explore more of Arunachal Pradesh, consider some of the other places open to tourists: Itanagar, Ziro, Along, Pasighat, Tipi (Orchid Research Centre) and Bhalukpong, but check on the latest situation. The rules are the same as explained under the section on permits above. Of particular interest are the **Tale WLS** (20km from Ziro) with its subtropical and temperate forests harbouring species such as Purple Cochoa (U/R) and Rufous-throated Wren Babbler*, **D'Ering Memorial WLS** (30km from Pasighat) whose grasslands are home to Bengal Florican and Swamp Francolin*, and the tropical semi-evergreen and subtropical forests of **Pakhui WLS** adjoining Tipi. Adjoining Pakhui the **Eagle's Nest WLS** offers premium birding along an old road (hardly used) through very good forests ranging from tropical to temperate (600m-2700m).

Shillong and Cherrapunjee

The southern mountainous part of Assam was declared a separate state, Meghalaya (abode of the clouds), in 1972. The most accessible place is its capital, Shillong, a popular hill station and education centre. The visitor to 'the Scotland of the east' is at first struck by the terrible deforestation on the Shillong plateau, but a few pockets of good habitat harbour such wonderful specialities as Long-tailed Wren Babbler and Grey Sibia. Add the possibility of Dark-rumped Swift, one of the world's rarest and least-known *Apus* species, at nearby Cherrapunjee, and a visit to Meghalaya becomes an attractive proposition. According to local custom small patches of forest, known as *khlaw bley*, are left untouched as sacred groves. These are attractive for birds, but when exploring be careful not to remove anything or damage any trees.

Map of Shillong

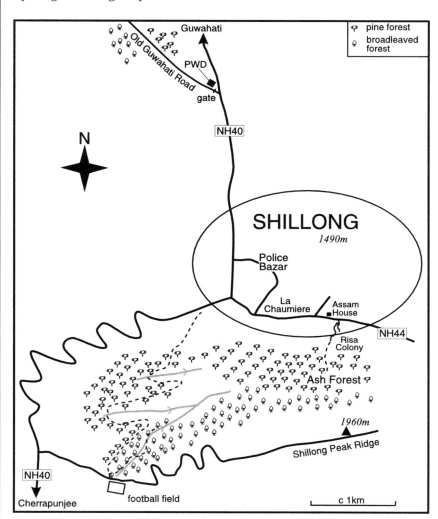

Location

Shillong lies at 1500m in the Khasi Hills, 103km south of Guwahati. It has an airport, but there are no regular flights. Private and state-run buses run hourly from Guwahati taking 3$^{1}/_{2}$ hours. Share-taxis can be found at the south side of Guwahati station. These take up to five passengers but do not leave until they are full or the passengers agree to pay the difference.

On a map of the northeast, it appears logical to continue on to Haflong and Jatinga from Shillong. This is possible but probably entails an overnight stop at Garampani (Hot Springs). Most local people prefer to travel via Guwahati.

Accommodation

The hotels in Shillong are good value in comparison with other state capitals. Most are in the centre of town around Police Bazaar. The most expensive is the Tourism Department's *Pinewood Hotel* (B) – poorly maintained though the food is okay. The *Centre Point Hotel* (B/C) ☎0364-225210, Fax224647 is built to four-star specifications and has an excellent restaurant. The *Polo Tower* (C) has satisfactory rooms, but the restaurant has less to recommend it. The *Alpine Continental* (C) is fairly good value for this price bracket. Budget birders are well catered for with about 15 lodges of which the *Neo* (E) and *Seven Sisters* (E) are among the best. If it is within your budget, one of the nicest places to stay is at Sikandra (B), a small comfortable guest house run by June Warjri close to the Loreto Convent at 23 Upper La Chaumiere, Shillong 793001 ☎0364-226216. Dinner and breakfast are available on request.

Strategy

Climatically, the best time is the November to February dry season. However, the Dark-rumped Swift is only known at its breeding cliffs near Cherrapunji from late February to the end of April so a visit at this time is essential if you want to see this rarest of swifts. Cherrapunjee holds the world record for the most rainfall in a single month (9,300 mm) as well as the most in a year (26,461 mm), while nearby Mawsynram has the world's highest average annual rainfall (11,873 mm), most between April and October.

The number of bird species in Shillong itself seems to be restricted so you need to get out to the birding areas. The best to visit first is the **Old Guwahati-Shillong Rd.** The lower end is submerged beneath the Umiam reservoir leaving a relatively traffic-free road through reasonable habitat. The forest appears to enjoy some protection as a water catchment, but the birds are mercilessly shot, catapulted and trapped, so you can't blame them for being shy. A red-and-white barrier marks the beginning of the old road where it forks left at the PWD office on the NH40 to Guwahati, 5km north of the centre of Shillong. The road winds down through good mixed deciduous forest for 9km to Umiam Lake (1025m). It is best early in the morning when activity is at its peak. You should see Grey Sibia, a species that is restricted to the hills from Meghalaya through the Patkai Range, Nagaland, Manipur and Mizoram. The tree tops are full of birds with Crested Finchbills and Ashy Bulbuls alongside their more familiar relatives. Stripe-breasted Woodpeckers are fairly common, while Maroon Orioles give away their presence by their cat-like, wailing calls. Check gullies for Spotted Forktail, Grey-winged Blackbird, and Eyebrowed Thrush. Rufescent Prinia inhabit the grassy patches near the road, while Grey-breasted and Striated are nearer the lake.

Shillong Peak is the highest point in Meghalaya and dominates the skyline south of the town. Much is still clothed in forest although the pine woods are generally poor for birds. The broad-leaved wet evergreen forest on the higher slopes and along the river courses support more species. The ridge has been taken over by the air force, though the peak viewpoint itself is accessible. A good plan is to get a taxi to drop you off at a large football field about 1km after the peak road turns off from the main Cherrapunjee NH40. A good ravine begins opposite the football field and you can take a morning or more to follow the stream back to Shillong through rather dense undergrowth. Another path contours the southern slope of the valley higher up, mainly through pine woods. Birds include Grey Peacock Pheasant, Crested Finchbill, Red-billed Scimitar Babbler, Tawny-breasted Wren Babbler* (U), Rusty-fronted Barwing, Grey Sibia, Little Pied Flycatcher, Chestnut-headed Tesia, Buff-barred (W), Lemon-rumped (W), Ashy-throated Leaf (W) and Chestnut-crowned Warblers, White-browed and Lesser Shortwings, Yellow-cheeked Tit (*spilonotus*), Buff-bellied Flowerpecker, and Mrs. Gould's Sunbird. The peak can also be accessed from Shillong by the road up to Risa Colony and the path up to the so-called Ash Forest – see map. Rampant bird liming has had a very damaging impact on terrestrial species that prefer damp ravines in the area and the likes of wren babblers may be difficult or impossible to find.

The small town of **Cherrapunjee** (Cherra) is on a plateau alongside steep cliffs that overlook the plains of Bangladesh. The 56km trip from Shillong takes about 2 hours by taxi, rather longer by bus. At the right time of year it should be easy to find the Dark-rumped Swift, aka Khasi Hills Swift. This is the only known breeding area for this species and their movements outside the breeding period are largely undocumented. Their whereabouts may depend on the weather, but normally they prefer the vicinity of the water-falls. The first place to look is the cliffs directly opposite the town. If they are not here, check the Nohkallikai waterfalls about 4km to the west. Another site is the Nohsngithiang Falls at Mawsmai on the other side of Cherra. There is a famous limestone cave nearby where a sacred grove is good for forest species. The place to stay is the *Circuit House*, primarily intended for visiting officials, so permission must be obtained from the Sub-divisional Officer, Cherrapunjee. The Cement Factory has a guest house where they may allow you to stay. The *Orchid Rest* at Mawsmai might reopen.

Spend a day taking a vehicle to **Mawsynram** (56km southwest of Shillong) and beyond and exploring patches of good-looking habitat. The sacred grove at **Mawphlang** (25km), a short diversion from the Mawsynram road, harbours good birds including Golden Babbler, Chestnut-crowned Laughingthrush, White-browed Shrike Babbler, Rufous-winged Fulvetta, Grey Sibia, Large Niltava, Buff-barred (W), Ashy-throated (W) and Chestnut-crowned Warblers, Orange-flanked and Golden Bush Robins (W), Spotted Forktail and Green-tailed Sunbird. This is where the Indian Subcontinent's only Buff-throated Warbler was collected in 1953. The scrub on the sides of the valley beyond is the only accessible site known to the authors for Rusty-capped Fulvetta.

Birds   Other birds found in the general area include Black and Crested Serpent Eagles, Oriental Turtle and Emerald Doves, Red-headed Trogon, Great, Golden-throated and Blue-throated Barbets, White-browed Piculet, Bay Woodpecker, Long-tailed Broadbill, Crag Martin, Brown, Grey-backed and Long-tailed Shrikes, Black-naped Oriole, Bar-winged Flycatcher-Shrike, Large Cuckooshrike, Scarlet and Short-billed Minivets, Black-crested, White-throated, Mountain, Flavescent and Black Bulbuls, Puff-throated Babbler, White-browed and Streak-breasted Scimitar Babblers, Grey-throated Babbler, Silver-eared Mesia, Red-billed Leiothrix, Blue-winged Minla, Whiskered Yuhina, Nepal Fulvetta, Orange-gorgeted Flycatcher, Grey-bellied and Chestnut-headed Tesias, Mountain Tailorbird, Large-billed Leaf (W), White-spectacled, Golden-spectacled and Grey-hooded Warblers, Grey Bushchat, Plumbeous and White-capped River Redstarts, Blue Whistling Thrush, Green-backed Tit, Chestnut-bellied and Velvet-fronted Nuthatches, Olive-backed Pipit, Russet Sparrow and Little Bunting (W).

Other Sites   The relatively unexplored **Nokrek** and **Balpakaram National Parks** in the Garo Hills of western Meghalaya are said to be good for forest raptors such as Jerdon's and Black Bazas, Crested Goshawk, and Rufous-bellied Eagle. The main town is Tura (320km from Shillong via Guwahati by road) at the foot of Nokrek Peak (1457m) and a good base for exploring the hill forest there. The Balpakram plateau is 167km away on the border with Bangladesh and has a *Tourist Lodge* run by Meghalaya Tourism. The only record of Chestnut-fronted Shrike Babbler from the Indian Subcontinent is a specimen from the Garo Hills.

Jatinga

The small village of Jatinga in the North Cachar Hills is famous throughout India because of the so-called Bird Mystery which is played out here every autumn. The village lies on a saddle in the mountains of the Barail Range, and when conditions are right birds are attracted to bright lights placed on the ridge. It has to be a dark, moonless foggy night sometime between the end of August and late October; the wind must be from the southwest and there should preferably be a light drizzle. The locals regard such occasions as a heaven sent bounty and 'harvest' the unfortunate disoriented birds by hitting them with long bamboo poles. Interestingly, most of the birds involved appear to be the young of lowland diurnal residents such as Indian Pond Heron, Cattle Egret and Cotton Pygmy-goose, perhaps involved in post-breeding dispersal or short-distance migration. Surprisingly, the most common birds attracted to the lights at Jatinga are said to be Oriental Dwarf and Ruddy Kingfishers, Indian* and Hooded Pittas, Pompadour Green Pigeon and Koel. Even White-winged Duck has been seen to come in out of the mist.

The other attraction of Jatinga is the 1750m **Ham Pu Ped Peak**, the higher reaches of which are still clothed in reasonably good forest in spite of continuing logging, woodcutting and *jhooming* in the area. Birding here is not easy for the terrain is very steep and rugged, but for those willing to put in the required amount of effort there are Coral-billed Scimitar-Babbler, Spotted and Eyebrowed Wren Babblers, White-tailed Flycatcher, Beautiful Nuthatch and many others to be found.

Location   Jatinga is 9km south of Haflong, a small hill resort in southern Assam. They are both at about 700m in a mountain range linking the Khasi and Jaintia Hills to those of Nagaland.

From Guwahati, Jatinga is perhaps best reached by an overnight bus (350km, 9 hours), or by train with a change to the picturesque metre-gauge line at Lumding. The latter is much slower but slightly more comfortable. You could also fly to Silchar from Guwahati or Calcutta and take one of the two or three daily buses that connect to Haflong in about 3½ hours.

Jatinga is a 20-minute auto-rickshaw ride from Haflong. Arrange for the driver to pick you up again at the required time, or wait for a suitable conveyance at the police checkpost in Jatinga. Vehicles can be few and far between after dark.

Accommodation   Not many tourists venture to this out-of-the-way region so accommodation is limited. In Haflong the *Tourist Lodge* has been taken over by the army. The *Rahamaniya* (E) and *Eastern Hotel* (E) are probably the best of several basic lodges along the main road. The *Hotel Elite* (D) next to the cinema is better and has the best restaurant. The government *Circuit House* (E) is more comfortable but less convenient. Permission to stay must be obtained from the Deputy Commissioner, Haflong.

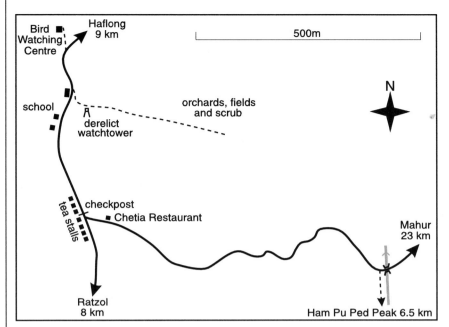

Map of Jatinga

In Jatinga it is possible to stay at the *'Bird Watching Centre'*. The one double room is basic but with clean bed linen and has added entomological interest. There is an outside toilet but no running water, which has to be brought in buckets. A stay has to be arranged through the DFO in Haflong (auto-rickshaw to the DFO office) ☎2356.

Simple food is available from tea-stalls near the Jatinga checkpost. The Chetia Restaurant seems the best of these.

Strategy

In 1996 the North Cachar District was a 'disturbed area' so it was necessary to register personally with the Superintendent of Police (☎2325 and 2384) in Haflong on arrival and keep him informed of one's movements. Check to see if this is still required.

To experience the Jatinga Bird Phenomenon, you will have to select a period of several moonless days between the end of August and late October and hope that weather conditions will be favourable. For general birding, the drier months of November to March are better as the mountain can be treacherous when wet.

The main trail to the peak begins by a bridge (altitude 670m) about 600m from the Jatinga checkpost on the road to Mahur. The track crosses the river several times (stepping stones and/or wading) during the first 2km before climbing very steeply to where good forest begins above 1000m. The ridge is reached at 1670m while the peak itself is at 1750m. It is essential to take a local guide for the climb: an experienced mountaineer and birder once got lost and the police and Fifth Assam Rifles spent a day combing the area searching for him. The locals say that spirits on the mountain confuse the unwary, particularly near the top where several ridges intersect and paths become indistinct and peter out. Even they sometimes get lost only to emerge from the jungle several days later many miles away. A guide should be arranged by contacting Mr. E. W.Suchiang, the *Gaon burha* (village headman). Anyone can guide you to him or take a message. An early start is recommended as the most interesting birds are in the forest below the ridge at low densities. If you are fit, you should manage to cover the 1000m climb in 3–4 hours.

The secondary growth, bamboo and orange groves below the village support many species. A good path leads down into the valley past the derelict watchtower.

The Barail range has a wide range of species and you need more than just a few days to see most of the specialities. An old PWD road is easier to bird up from the village of Ratzol, 8km southwest of Jatinga. Explore the road that carries on to Harangajao. The FRH there is bookable through the DFO in Haflong if you want to birdwatch in the **Barail Reserve Forest** nearby.

Birds

There have been a few attempts to study the bird phenomenon at Jatinga and the following have been recorded: Grey, Purple and Malayan Night Herons, Cinnamon, Yellow, Black and Great Bitterns, Lesser Whistling-duck, Blue-breasted Quail, Kalij Pheasant, Yellow-legged and Barred Buttonquails, Banded Crake, Common and Purple Moorhens, White-breasted Waterhen, Watercock, Slaty-breasted Rail, Pheasant-tailed Jacana, Eurasian Curlew, Eurasian Woodcock, Spotted and Emerald Doves, Chestnut-winged, Indian, Violet and Common Hawk Cuckoos, Common Swift, White-throated Kingfisher, Brown Shrike, Bronzed and Greater Racket-tailed Drongos, Ashy Woodswallow, Black-crested Bulbul, Asian Paradise-flycatcher, Black-naped Monarch and Blue Rock Thrush.

Birding the lower part of the trail to the peak you may come across Red-headed Trogon, Great Barbet, Lesser and Greater Yellownapes, Long-tailed Broadbill, Blue Whistling Thrush, Slaty-backed and Spotted Forktails, Spangled Drongo, White-browed Scimitar Babbler, White-crested, Lesser and Greater Necklaced Laughingthrushes, Nepal Fulvetta, Rufous-gorgeted Flycatcher, Golden-spectacled Warbler, White-capped Water-Redstart, Fire-breasted Flowerpecker and Black-throated Sunbird.

The forests on the higher slopes support Wedge-tailed Green and Mountain Imperial Pigeons, Bay Woodpecker, Maroon Oriole, Crested Finchbill, Striated Bulbul, Coral-billed and Red-billed Scimitar Babblers, Long-billed, Streaked, Eyebrowed, Pygmy and Spotted Wren Babblers, Golden Babbler, Black-throated and Grey-headed Parrotbills, White-browed and Black-eared Shrike Babblers, Rusty-fronted Barwing, Striated, White-naped and Black-chinned Yuhinas, Yellow-throated and Rufous-winged Fulvettas, Rufous-backed Sibia, White-gorgeted and White-tailed (R) Flycatchers, Grey-bellied, Slaty-bellied and Chestnut-headed Tesias, Mountain Tailorbird, White-browed Shortwing, White-tailed Robin (U) and Beautiful Nuthatch (U).

Below the village you can find Mountain Bamboo Partridge (U), White-browed Piculet, Pale-headed Woodpecker, Plaintive Cuckoo, Grey-backed and Long-tailed Shrikes, Grey Treepie, Black-headed Cuckooshrike, Puff-throated and Buff-breasted Babblers, Yellow-bellied Warbler, Siberian Rubythroat (W), Olive-backed Pipit (W) and White-rumped Munia.

The general area also holds Oriental Honey-buzzard, Crested Serpent Eagle, Grey Peacock Pheasant (U), Red Junglefowl, Oriental Turtle and Emerald Doves, Red-breasted Parakeet, Vernal Hanging Parrot, Brown Hornbill, Golden- and Blue-throated Barbets, Speckled Piculet, Collared and Asian Barred Owlets, Himalayan Swiftlet, Brown Needletail, Asian House Martin, Striated Swallow, Bronzed, Lesser and Greater Racket-tailed Drongos, Green Magpie, Bar-winged Flycatcher-shrike, Scarlet and Grey-chinned Minivets, Golden-fronted, Orange-bellied and Blue-winged

Leafbirds, Black-crested, Flavescent, Ashy, Mountain and Black Bulbuls, Streak-breasted Scimitar Babbler, Rufous-capped and Grey-throated Babblers, Striped Tit Babbler, Rufous-chinned and Chestnut-crowned Laughingthrushes, Silver-eared Mesia, Blue-winged Minla, Whiskered and White-bellied Yuhinas, Grey Sibia, Snowy-browed, Slaty-blue, Little Pied, Sapphire, Blue-throated and Pygmy Blue Flycatchers, Yellow-bellied and White-throated Fantails, Black-naped Monarch, Rufescent and Grey-breasted Prinias, Buff-barred (W), Yellow-browed (W), Lemon-rumped (W), Greenish, Blyth's, Yellow-vented, Grey-hooded, Golden-spectacled, Grey-cheeked (U), Chestnut-crowned and Rufous-faced (U) Warblers, White-rumped Shama, Little Forktail, Chestnut-bellied and Blue Rock (W) Thrushes, Orange-headed, Scaly and Long-billed Thrushes, Sultan Tit, Green-tailed Sunbird, Little and Streaked Spiderhunters and Scarlet Finch (U).

CENTRAL INDIA

The central states of Maharashtra, Madhya Pradesh and Orissa are less well-known for their birdlife than other parts of India. Although few species cannot be found elsewhere, the forests of Madhya Pradesh are among the most extensive in the country and arguably the most important remaining habitat for the country's sadly declining Tigers; the threatened endemic Green Avadavat** is largely restricted to this area; and the region boasts excellent protected areas including Chilka Lake, one of Asia's richest wetlands.

Much of central India is taken up by the Deccan plateau, separated from the coastal regions by the Western and Eastern Ghats. The climate is typically monsoonal with most rain falling between June and October when many sanctuaries are closed. During the winter skies are generally clear and daytime temperatures comfortable though a warm sweater or jacket is needed in the early morning. From late March until the rains break temperatures soar into the 40s centigrade. Most visitors prefer the winter season when migrants from the north augment resident birds.

Map of
Central India
1. Bandhavgarh
2. Pachmarhi
3. Kanha
4. Simlipal
5. Melghat
6. Chilka Lake

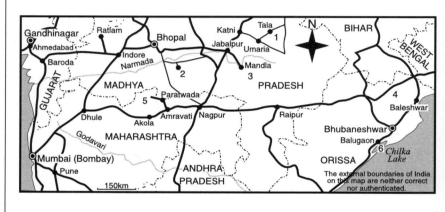

Mumbai (Bombay)

India's financial and economic powerhouse on the west coast is not one of the country's prime birding destinations, but as it is the 'Gateway to India', the travelling birdwatcher may find him or herself with some spare time in Mumbai. There are several places where a few hours can be usefully spent away from the hustle and bustle of the city. The Sanjay Gandhi NP is right on Mumbai's doorstep at Borivli, and Elephanta Island is only an hour away by boat.

Location

Mumbai has grown on offshore islands towards the northern end of the Malabar coast. The islands have gradually joined into one (Salsette) and the city lies at its southern tip with suburbs sprawling north. It is the busiest airline destination in India, served by most major international carriers and with domestic routes to most important cities within the country. Bus and train connections are profuse.

As in most of India's cities the easiest way of getting around is by taxi or auto-rickshaw, though the latter are not allowed into the city south of Bandra. If coming back from Borivli, say, you can take an auto-rickshaw along the National Highway as far as Bandra where the rickshaw-wallah can drop you off at the taxi rank.

Instructions are included on how to reach the sites by public transport for those on a more limited budget. Buses and suburban trains are, however, hopelessly overcrowded and almost impossible to get onto

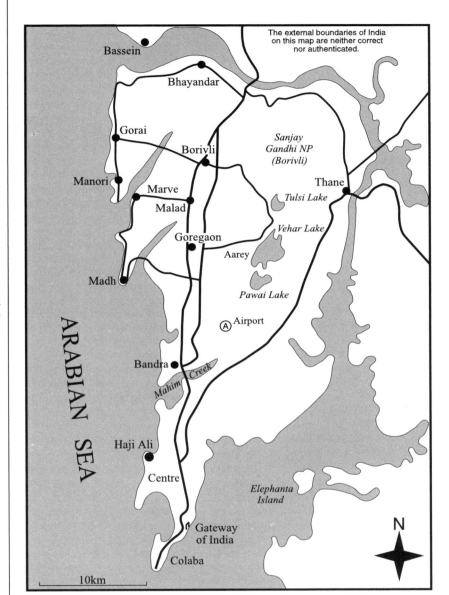

Map of Mumbai
(Bombay)

anywhere except at the starting point. The trains are usually manageable in the early hours of the morning, become like sardine cans later on, and require the skills of a marine to storm during rush hour. Mumbai's pickpockets are notorious and it is extremely difficult keeping belongings safe on the city public transport system.

Accommodation   Unfortunately, with Mumbai being India's most expensive city, there are no great hotel bargains. The chronic shortage of rooms means that it is best to have an advance reservation or arrive early in the morning to be sure of finding a room. Most travellers stay in the Colaba area at the southern end of the island. Here there is a complete range from the best hotel in Mumbai, the *Taj Mahal* (A++) ☎022-2023366, Fax2872711, through mid-range places like the *Diplomat* (A/B) ☎022-2021661, *Garden* (A/B) ☎022-2841476 or

Regent (A/B)☎022-2020363, to the rock-bottom cheapies like the *Carlton Hotel* (C/D) or the popular *Red Shield Hostel* (D/E), which even has dormitory beds. Colaba is less convenient for the birding sites in the north of the city, but is handy if you have official business or want to visit the BNHS headquarters (see Useful Addresses), and the departure point for boats to Elephanta is nearby.

Marine Drive is further north and has a range of hotels, though the selection is not as great as at Colaba. If you are only staying one or two nights and flying in and out of Mumbai, it may be preferable to stay in a hotel near the airport, although most are in the middle to upper price bracket. For something less expensive try the *Aircraft International* (C) ☎022-6121419. If you arrive late at night without a reservation, ask around at the airport: there are usually hotel agents near the exit who know where there are vacant rooms.

Strategy   If you only have a few hours to spare, a taxi to Sanjay Gandhi NP is probably the best bet. You can go to the main entrance to the park at Borivli, or perhaps better to the Aarey Milk Colony and explore the scrub outside the park. Most of the area around the airport has been built over or belongs to the airports authority and is off-limits. If you have longer, try one or two half-day visits to Borivli, as well as a trip to Elephanta Island or one of the other sites described below.

Borivli (Sanjay Gandhi NP)

Surprisingly, about 40km² of the metropolitan area of Mumbai is a forest forming part of the 103km² Sanjay Gandhi NP, usually still known as Borivli. It is the most popular sanctuary in India with three million visitors annually, but they nearly all concentrate in a small tourist zone near the main entrance, known as Krishnagiri Upavan, and the Kanheri Caves, so you can get away from the crowds.

The park was partly set up to protect a forested area of the Sahyadri Hills as a water catchment for Mumbai. The terrain of Borivli ranges from sea-level to Jambulmal, the park's highest peak at 490m, with a mixture of dry and moist deciduous woodland as well as bamboo, scrub and small patches of rainforest. Some 280 species have been recorded from Borivli and a few hours can turn up the likes of Red Spurfowl*, Asian Paradise-flycatcher, Greater Racket-tailed Drongo and Malabar Trogon*.

Location   Borivli is about 30km north of the main hotel area at Colaba, a road journey of up to 2 hours if traffic is heavy. The fast suburban train goes from platform 3 or 4 of Churchgate Station every few minutes from 04.30 to 22.30 and takes about 45 minutes to Borivli Station. The main gate of the park is a 10-minute walk from the east side of the station turning left out of the main entrance. After about 100m turn (first) right and continue 600m crossing the Western Express Highway to the park entrance on the other side.

To visit the southern end of the park around the lakes Tulsi and Vehar, you need a permit from the office of the DCF, Sanjay Gandhi NP, Mumbai 400 066 ☎6057362 (near the Safari Park about 1km inside the Borivli entrance). Access is from Goregaon Suburban Railway Station, the stop before Borivli for the fast trains. Exit on the east side of the station. Take a taxi or auto-rickshaw as the buses (no.343) are not very frequent. Ask for Film City or the Aarey Milk Colony. Just before Film City you pass through a check-post, then after a kilometre or two there is a right turn into Film

Map of Borivli

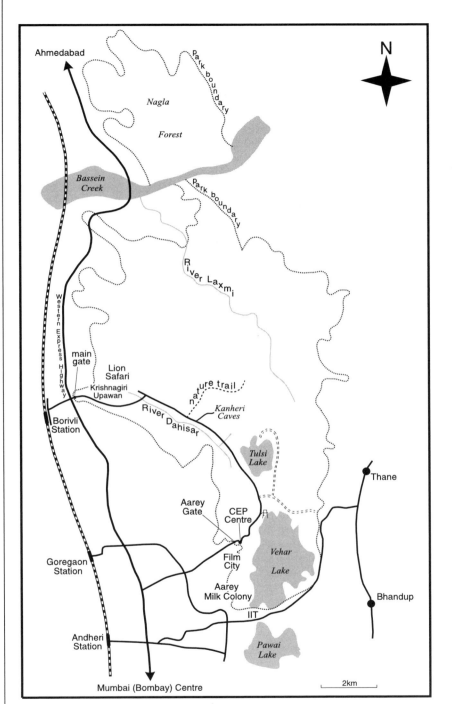

City itself. Do not take this turn, but carry straight on for 200m to the Forest Department checkpost, the entrance to the park. (If unsure, ask for the Aarey Gate Forest Office. Bus 343 terminates at Santosh Nagar or Film City.) The metalled road continues past the northern end of Vehar Lake bearing north and eventually coming to the Kanheri Caves and the main entrance to the park at Borivli.

For the southern end of the lake (good for ducks and waders – permit not necessary), take a taxi or bus from Andheri Station (south of Goregaon and Borivli) to the Indian Institute of Technology (IIT). First have a look at Pavai lake on the southern side of the road, then go straight through the campus on the northern side of the road to Vehar Lake. A hill on the edge of the campus has good views over the lake for those with a telescope.

Accommodation

There are several *Rest Houses* belonging to the Forest Department within the park. These can be booked at the office of the DCF as above. Unfortunately, the Rest Houses are often full and cannot be booked at short notice, making a stay in the city the only alternative. There are a number of stalls selling food and drinks in the tourist zone of the park.

Strategy

The park is open all year, though heavy rain in the monsoon can make birding difficult. December to February are the optimum months. Admission at the Borivli entrance is from 07.30 to 18.30. It is best to be here when the park gates open before the crowds arrive. You can walk or take an auto-rickshaw (haggle) for the 5km to the Kanheri Caves and explore around there. On Sundays and holidays, when visitor pressure is greatest, there are buses. You can also take your own vehicle as far as Kanheri for an additional fee, but only from the Borivli entrance. On your way back you can pop in to the DCF's office (09.00 to 16.00) to get a permit. With this you can spend a day exploring the core zone away from the tourists, following the trails in from Kanheri.

From the Aarey Gate at the southern end of the park you can follow the road for about 1–2km to Vehar Lake. Take the path to the right, just before a bridge on a sharp left-hand bend, that leads to a tower overlooking the lake. This is good for looking into the reeds with Paddyfield and Blyth's Reed Warblers (W), as well as over the lake. Birding is good along this road as cars are not allowed. A new Conservation Education Project Centre has been built by the BNHS near the Aarey Checkpost and it is worth asking if there is anyone around who knows about birds.

Birds

In winter it is possible to see 120 species in a day at Borivli. Birds include Purple Heron, Asian Openbill, Black-shouldered and Brahminy Kites, Tawny, Steppe (W), Greater and Lesser Spotted Eagles (UW), Black Eagle, White-bellied Sea Eagle, Pallid and Eurasian Marsh Harriers (W), Crested Serpent Eagle, Peregrine (Shaheen) Falcon, Oriental Hobby (R), Blue-breasted Quail (U), Jungle Bush Quail*, Grey Junglefowl**, Common Peafowl*, Pheasant-tailed and Bronze-winged Jacanas, Gull-billed Tern, Emerald Dove, Plum-headed Parakeet*, Vernal Hanging Parrot (U), Pied Cuckoo (BS), Eurasian (Rock) Eagle Owl, Jungle Owlet, Brown Hawk Owl, Crested Treeswift, Oriental Dwarf Kingfisher (RBS), Indian Grey Hornbill*, Brown-headed* and White-cheeked** Barbets, Rufous, Heart-spotted (U) and Black-backed* (U) Woodpeckers, Lesser Goldenback, Indian Pitta (P), Long-tailed Shrike, Eurasian Golden and Black-headed Orioles, six species of drongo, Ashy Woodswallow, Rosy Starling (W), Black-headed Cuckoo-shrike, Blue-winged Leafbird, Puff-throated Babbler, Indian Scimitar Babbler*, Tickell's Blue Flycatcher, Black-naped Monarch, Ashy Prinia*, Greenish Warbler (W), Orange-headed Thrush, Thick-billed, Tickell's and Plain (U) Flowerpeckers, Purple-rumped, Crimson-backed** (U) and Purple Sunbirds, Chestnut-shouldered Petronia and Red Avadavat.

Other Wildlife

Since the last Tiger was shot in 1928 the only large predator in the sanctuary is the Leopard. This magnificent animal is happily estimated at around 50. Their main prey are Spotted Deer, Sambar and Barking Deer plus Four-horned Antelope and Wild Boar. Grey Langur, Rhesus and Bonnet Macaques are the primates found in the reserve. These are fairly easy to find, but it is much more difficult to see secretive inhabitants such as the Indian Chevrotain, Jungle Cat, Indian Pangolin, Porcupine, and Small Indian Civet. The chances of glimpsing Jackal, Black-naped Hare, and Common and Ruddy Mongoose are better, as they are active during the daytime.

Twenty-nine species of snake have been recorded from Borivli including the 'big four' poisonous species: Common Cobra, Common Krait, and Russell's and Saw-scaled Pit Vipers. Muggers, or Marsh Crocodiles, have been introduced into Tulsi Lake.

Elephanta Island

This popular tourist spot east of Mumbai is easily reached by the launches that ply from the Gateway of India. The island can provide good birding with shore and forest species as well as raptors. Western Reef Egret, Brahminy Kite, White-bellied Sea Eagle, Peregrine (Shahin) Falcon, Whimbrel (W), Eurasian Curlew (W), Terek and Curlew Sandpipers (W), and Black-capped and Stork-billed Kingfishers are likely to be encountered. Laggar Falcon, and Steppe and Booted Eagles have been seen in winter. Watch for seabirds on the crossing; Heuglin's, Pallas's and Brown-headed Gulls (W), and Gull-billed and Sandwich Terns (W) are possible.

The tourists are mainly interested in the famous Elephanta Cave Temples, reached by climbing a long stone stairway from the end of the jetty. For birders there is good forest beyond the caves and it is possible to walk round the island at a leisurely pace in 5 hours.

The launches for Elephanta leave every hour from 09.00 until 14.00 and return 4 hours later. The crossing takes one hour. For sufficient time catch the first boat out and the last one back. A catamaran makes the journey in 45 minutes but is considerably more expensive. There are tea stalls and basic restaurants on the island.

Other Sites   There is a fairly productive coastal walk north of **Manori,** 40km north of the city centre. Take a suburban train from Churchgate to Malad, followed by bus no.272 west to Marve and then the ferry across the creek to the northwest. Follow the coast north to Gorai and bus back to Borivli. Flamingos of both species are occasional while the commoner waders may be joined by a Greater Sand Plover (W), Sanderling (W) or even a Crab-plover (W) if you are extremely fortunate. Gull-billed Terns (W) are frequent, White-bellied Sea Eagles less so. If you prefer accommodation outside the city, try the *Manoribel Hotel* (A/B/C) ☎022-2833918 or the budget *Hotel Dominica* in Manori.

If you do not mind the sewer-like atmosphere **Mahim Creek Sanctuary** (15km north of Colaba) can be worth a visit. You can expect commoner waders, gulls and terns, but there is always a chance of something special. It is best to take a taxi to the Dharavi side of the creek. The nearest suburban railway station is at Bandra.

Another accessible site of some interest for gulls and terns as well as waders at low tide is the area around the mosque of **Haji Ali,** a tourist spot on the west coast 7km north of Colaba (bus nos. 83, 124, 132R and 133R). A somewhat better site is further out some 10km northwest of the airport at **Madh Island,** good for winter waders including Terek Sandpiper, Ruddy Turnstone and Curlew Sandpiper.

Somewhat further afield is the small (4km²) **Karnala Wildlife Sanctuary** 90km east of Mumbai. Take one of the regular buses to Panvel on the main Konkan Goa road and then a local bus or taxi for the remaining 12km. Some 140 species have been recorded in the dry deciduous forest. Residents include Heart-spotted Woodpecker, Greater Racket-tailed Drongo, Black-headed Cuckooshrike, White-browed Bulbul*, Asian Paradise-flycatcher and Malabar Whistling Thrush**. Winter migrants include Red-throated Flycatcher and Blue-capped Rock Thrush, while Ashy Minivet, a straggler to the subcontinent, has been recorded. Mammals include Grey Langur, Muntjac, Chowsingha and Leopard. The wetlands at the nearby Ransai Dam across the Pen-Panvel road may be of interest. There is a limited amount of accommodation in two FRHs.

Bandhavgarh

This central Indian national park consists of 1162km² of forest surrounding the ancient hill-fort of the Maharajahs of Rewa. Bandhavgarh is known for one of the densest populations of Tigers in India and was included in Project Tiger in 1994. Mohan, the legendary White Tiger that fathered a line of offspring found in zoos the world over, was captured near here in 1951.

The forests are dominated by Sal and Bamboo, good for species such as White-naped Woodpecker*, Red Junglefowl, Red* and Painted Spurfowl**. The habitat is enriched by riverine forest, open grasslands and marshy areas where Lesser Adjutants survive in small numbers. The steep cliffs of Bandhavgarh Hill surmounted by the 2000-year old fort provide nesting habitat for Long-billed Vultures, House Swifts and the resident race of Peregrine Falcon known as Shahin. At night Mottled Wood Owl* and Brown Fish Owl hunt for prey. Most northern migrants are present during winter, but April and May see the arrival of interesting species such as cuckoos and Indian Pitta from the south. There are some 250 species on the sanctuary's list.

Location

The National Park lies in the Vindhyan Mountains in Madhya Pradesh State at 450m (rising to 800m at the fort on its rocky crag). The entrance to the park is at the village of Tala, 32km from Umaria, a town on the Katni-Bilaspur section of the main southeastern railway line from Orissa to Delhi. The line from Mumbai (Bombay) to Calcutta passes through Katni, about 60km northwest of Umaria. The Utkal Express is convenient if you come from the north, as it leaves Delhi in the early afternoon and reaches Umaria the following morning. Several buses a day take just over an hour from Umaria to Tala. There may be a jeep at Umaria willing to take you to Tala at a price. Tala can be reached by bus via Satna from the famous temple town of Khajurao, 220km to the north, where the nearest airport is situated.

Accommodation

There is a variety of lodges in and around Tala. The cheapest and most basic is *Tiger Lodge* (E) in Tala itself, all rooms without bath. The *Hotel Baghela* (D), a little further down the road, has rooms with attached bath. The best value is the *White Tiger Forest Lodge* (C). The restaurant here, run by the Madhya Pradesh State TDC, is good and the staff friendly. You may be lucky if you just turn up, but normally it is necessary to book rooms well in advance at one of their offices:

4th Floor, Gangotri T.T. Nagar, Bhopal – 462 003. ☎0755-554340,1,2,3.

74 World Trade Centre, Cuffe Parade, Colaba, Mumbai (Bombay) – 400 005. ☎022-2184860, 2187603.

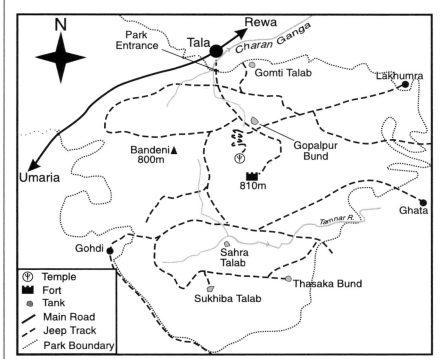

Map of
Bandhavgarh

Chitrakoot Room No.7, 6th Floor, 230A A.J.C. Bose Rd, Calcutta – 700 020. ☎033-2478543, 2475855.

204-205, 2nd Floor, Kanishka Shopping Plaza, 19 Ashoka Rd, New Delhi – 110 001 ☎011-3321187.

Between four and ten days in advance contact their office at the railway station in Jabalpur ☎0761-322111.

Less than four days in advance try phoning the Lodge directly on 07653-65308.

Those willing and able to pay over $100 per day can stay in luxury tented accommodation at the former Maharajah's hunting lodge at the *Bandhavgarh Jungle Camp*. The price includes all meals, lectures, slide shows, and jeep and elephant rides into the park with guides. Reservations, and arrangements to be met at the railway station, have to be made in advance at their office in Delhi: Bandhavgarh Wildlife Camp Ltd., B/21 Greater Kailash Enclave II, New Delhi 110 048 ☎011-6854626.

The *Bandhavgarh Jungle Lodge* (A), not far from the entrance gate to the Park, offers an all-in package but is less well appointed. *Tiger Trails* (B/C) and *Bandhavgarh Jungle Huts* (B/C) are a few kilometres east of Tala. The Forest Department has an office and *Rest House* near the Tala checkpost, but the accommodation here has to be booked with their office in Umaria.

Try to avoid Bandhavgarh during public holidays without a prior reservation.

Strategy

The park and lodges are closed for the monsoon from 1 July to 31 October. In winter the mornings and evenings can be very cold but during the day it becomes warm enough for shirt sleeves. In November and from mid-February to mid-March the weather is pleasant though warm clothes are needed for early morning rides. From mid-March it gets hot with temperatures reaching 40°C in May and June.

Map of Tala

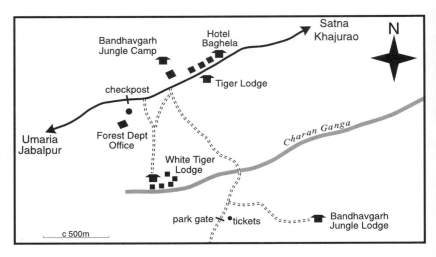

Birding is largely by open-top jeep into the reserve where it is forbidden to explore on foot. The lodges arrange jeep hire at a fixed rate. Each vehicle takes up to five, so you can sometimes economise by sharing, but make sure the others understand you want to stop for birds. Gypsy jeeps are much quieter than older jeeps and Land Rovers, useful when listening out for calls. At the park gate you pay a modest entrance fee and a small fee for the compulsory guide. Ask for a guide that knows the birds: enquire about this at your lodge beforehand. Entry times are from 06.00 to 10.00 and 15.00 to 18.00.

The main track passes along the shady valley of the Charan Ganga river soon after entering the park. Look for Brown Fish Owl and Jungle Owlet. Lesser Adjutant can be found in the open marshy areas. There is an extensive network of tracks throughout the tourist zone of the sanctuary. Red Junglefowl and Painted Spurfowl** can appear at the edges of the tracks. Get the jeep driver to stop at clearings, water-holes and forest edge, and spend time listening with the engine off.

The only place you are allowed to get out of the jeep is at the statue of the reclining Vishnu below the fort. Make the most of this and explore the area which is good for thrushes in winter. There is a resident pair of Peregrine (Shahin) Falcon on the cliffs. This is a good place for Malabar Pied Hornbill* which like the ripe figs of the Banyan trees in the fort. It is possible to visit the fort, which is still owned by the Maharajah, but this privilege is usually reserved for those staying at Bandhavgarh Jungle Camp. The track from the Vishnu statue leads up to the main gate of the fort.

It may be possible to obtain permission to spend the middle of the day in one of the machans or watchtowers inside the park. Badrashila Machan is recommended as it overlooks a small lake.

Some good birds such as Tickell's Thrush* (W) and Black-backed Woodpecker* can be found around the lodges. The White Tiger Lodge seems especially good with Black Ibis, Jungle Owlet, Blue-bearded Bee-eater (R), Crested Bunting and Mottled Wood Owl* recorded. If looking for the latter, try the compound of the Bandhavgarh Jungle Camp or the trees just inside the park gate, or any groves of Mango trees. Otherwise birding outside the park is less good, although you can walk the course of the Charan Ganga eastwards from the back of the White Tiger Lodge, or explore the degraded forests east of Tala.

Elephant rides start from the Park Office at the checkpost on the main road at Tala between 07.30 and 10.30. Charges are per Elephant per hour with each carrying a maximum of four people. Booking is the same morning from 06.30 to 07.30.

Mottled Wood Owl

Birds   Other species at Bandhavgarh include Oriental Darter (U), Woolly-necked Stork (U), White-eyed Buzzard, Changeable Hawk Eagle (U), Bonelli's (U), Steppe (W) and Grey-headed Fish (U) Eagles, Red-headed Vulture (U), Crested Serpent Eagle, Osprey (UW), Eurasian Hobby (UW), Painted Francolin*, Jungle Bush Quail* (U), Barred Buttonquail (U), Sarus Crane (U), Eurasian Thick-knee, Yellow-wattled Lapwing* (U), Chestnut-bellied and Painted* Sandgrouse (U), Oriental Turtle, Red Collared (U) and Emerald (U) Doves, Alexandrine and Plum-headed* Parakeets, Pied, Indian, Grey-bellied* and Drongo Cuckoos (US), Sirkeer Malkoha* (U), Collared Scops Owl, Grey, Indian and Savanna Nightjars (U), Crested Treeswift, Stork-billed Kingfisher (U), Indian Grey Hornbill*, Rufous (US), Streak-throated (U) and Yellow-crowned Woodpeckers, Indian Bushlark* (U), Eurasian (UW) and Dusky Crag Martins, Wire-tailed Swallow (U), Brown (W) and Bay-backed Shrikes, White-bellied* and Greater Racket-tailed Drongos, Chestnut-tailed and Brahminy Starlings, Large Cuckooshrike, Long-tailed Minivet (W), Golden-fronted Leafbird (U), Puff-throated (U), Indian Scimitar* (U), Tawny-bellied* and Yellow-eyed (U) Babblers, Brown-cheeked Fulvetta (U), Asian Brown (UP), Ultramarine (UW),Tickell's Blue and Verditer (UW) Flycatchers, Asian Paradise-flycatcher (S), Black-naped Monarch, Grey-breasted and Jungle*

Prinias, Blyth's Reed, Tickell's Leaf (U), Sulphur-bellied, Dusky (U), Hume's (U), Brooks's Leaf (U) and Greenish Warblers (W), Siberian Rubythroat (UW), Grey Bushchat (W), Blue-capped and Blue Rock Thrushes (UW), Orange-headed and Scaly (RW) Thrushes, Chestnut-bellied Nuthatch, Olive-backed (W), Tree (P), Paddyfield, Tawny (W), Blyth's (UW) and Long-billed (W) Pipits, Citrine (UPW) and White-browed* Wagtails (U), Thick-billed and Pale-billed Flowerpeckers, Chestnut-shouldered Petronia and Common Rosefinch (UW).

Rarities at Bandhavgarh worth looking out for include Lesser Spotted Eagle, Pied Harrier (W), Greater Painted-snipe, Brown Hawk Owl, White-rumped Spinetail*, Rosy Starling (W), Black-winged and Black-headed (S) Cuckooshrikes, White-bellied Minivet, Little Pied Flycatcher (W), Spotted Creeper, Forest Wagtail (W), and White-capped Bunting (W).

For a more complete listing of the Park's birds see Hashim Tyabji's *Bandhavgarh National Park – A Guide*, which should be available from some of the lodges.

Other Wildlife   The chances of seeing a Tiger at Bandhavgarh are relatively good; stay several days, take jeep rides into the Sanctuary morning and evening; and concentrate more on following up alarm calls of deer than just birding. The Tiger's main prey are Chital, which are abundant, but you should also see Grey Langur, Flying Fox, Sambar, Muntjac and Wild Boar.

Rhesus Macaques, Nilgai, Chinkara, Jackal, Jungle Cat, and Ruddy and Common Mongoose are regular and there is a possibility of Leopard, Gaur, Sloth Bear, Black-naped Hare, Indian Fox, Wolf, and Dhole. More difficult are Small Indian Civet, Indian Porcupine, Honey-badger and Four-horned Antelope, whereas scales are the only trace ever found in the reserve of the rare Indian Pangolin. Toddy Cat feeds at night in fruiting trees in the garden of the White Tiger Lodge.

Other Sites   **Kanha NP** is better known than Bandhavgarh, but the avifauna is largely the same. It is one of the best places for seeing Tiger and attracts many visitors. If you have time to cover this part of India more thoroughly, Kanha can be combined fairly easily with Bandhavgarh. Kanha is 260km southwest of Bandhavgarh and reached by car in 7–8 hours. By bus, you have to change at Shajpura and Mandla. It may be more convenient to go the longer route via Jabalpur with an overnight stop. MP Tourism has accommodation at Kanha with booking arrangements as for Bandhavgarh. Private lodges are dotted along the approach road to the main gate at Khatia.

Melghat

In 1973 Melghat was one of the original nine areas selected as reserves for Tiger. Today some 1670km^2 of dry deciduous forests in the hilly northern tracts of Maharashtra are protected. Nearly a quarter has been declared a National Park under the name of Gangamal, where no human interference is allowed. Most of the remainder falls within the Melghat Sanctuary. Teak is by far the most common tree, but with such a large area, and terrain that ranges in altitude from 380m at the Tapti River in the northwest to 1178m in the Gawilgarh Hills on its southern border, a variety of other tree species are found. This explains why, in spite of a lack of wetlands, more than 270 species of bird have been recorded. Melghat's prime attraction is probably Green Avadavat**, one of India's most endangered endemics. A few days here should give a reasonable chance of seeing this as well as interesting species such as Grey Junglefowl**, White-naped Woodpecker* and Sulphur-bellied Warbler (W).

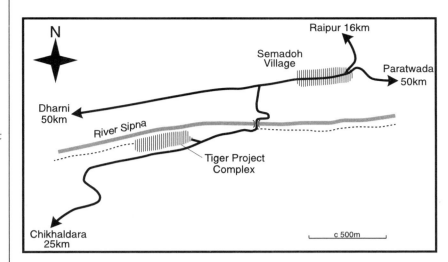

Map of Melghat

Location   Melghat lies in the northern part of Maharashtra on its border with Madhya Pradesh. The Project Tiger Tourist Complex on the banks of the River Sipna is 1km from the village of Semadoh 48km northwest of Paratwada on the State Highway to Dharni (50km) and Burhanpur (123km). By train, the most convenient station is Badnera on the main Mumbai (Bombay) to Nagpur line, from where buses travel the 60km north to the Project Tiger HQ at Paratwada. Several buses a day from Paratwada to Semadoh take about 1½ hours.

Accommodation   Project Tiger has an *Information and Education Centre* at Semadoh with dormitories and inexpensive, basic double-bedded huts with attached Indian-style bathrooms. The food is limited to vegetable, rice, dal and chapati meals ordered at least an hour in advance but liable to arrive an hour or two late. Bring supplementary fruit, biscuits and so on. Mineral water is not available at Semadoh. Rooms have to be booked with the Field Director, Project Tiger, Melghat Sanctuary, Paratwada, Amravati District – 444 805, Maharashtra. The Project Tiger Compound at Paratwada has a resident pair of Mottled Wood Owls*. If you need to stay overnight, there are basic lodges in town, the best being the *Konarak*. The Sanctuary is not as well-visited as Kanha and Bandhavgarh, but it may be best to avoid weekends and holidays unless you make reservations in advance. At Semadoh there are no lodges, but tea stalls at the village cross-roads have basic snack-type food and are a popular stop for buses and trucks. There are *Forest Rest Houses* scattered throughout the Sanctuary, if you want to explore parts other birders do not reach, but these need to be booked in Paratwada.
  An alternative is to stay at Chikhaldara (Chikhalda), a minor hill station on the southern edge of the Sanctuary, with mid-price accommodation in the form of the *Maharashtra State Tourism Hotel* and the *Green Valleys Resort* (C/D). Good food and beer can be had at the Gavildad Restaurant opposite the Green Valleys Resort. There are direct buses to Chikhaldara from Paratwada, Amravati and Akola but not from Semadoh.

Strategy   The best time at Melghat is October to February, when most winter visitors are present. Mid-winter temperatures can be quite low, so take warm clothes. From March to May it gets quite hot, while the rainy season lasts from June to September.

There are good birds around the Tourist Complex at Semadoh with Jungle Owlet, Brown Fish Owl and Indian Grey Hornbill* coming into the compound. Green Avadavat** has been seen in the Lantana scrub here. For walks into the forest you need a Forest Department guide, but there is no objection to birding alone along the roads. There is a museum display and library at the Semadoh Complex, and wildlife films are shown in the evenings.

A good road wends its way for 25km up to Chikhaldara, a climb of about 600m. This can make a good day's birding trek as there is normally very little traffic. Take a few basic essentials, spend the night at Chikhaldara and bird back to Semadoh next day. Green Avadavat** can be found along this road. The Lantana scrub 3–4km before Chikhaldara is a good area for them, at least in late March, though they probably are not as common as the Sanctuary Checklist suggests. Take plenty of water, particularly in summer when one litre per person may not be enough, as there is no habitation between Semadoh and Chikhalda. Half-way along its route the road crosses a river where you can cool your feet while looking out for White-naped Woodpecker*. The road up to Raipur, north from the Semadoh village cross-roads is equally traffic free. Another recommended walk is westwards along the river for 3–4km to an area of bamboo at Katang Bas and Warada, though you need a local guide for this.

Birds

Other species in Melghat include Woolly-necked Stork (U), Crested Goshawk (U), White-eyed Buzzard, Changeable Hawk Eagle, Bonelli's Eagle (U), Red-headed Vulture (U), Pallid Harrier (W), Short-toed Snake Eagle (U), Eurasian Hobby (UW), Painted Francolin* (U), Jungle*, Rock** and Painted** Bush Quails, Red* and Painted** Spurfowls (U), Yellow-wattled Lapwing* (U), Rufous Turtle and Red Collared Doves, Alexandrine and Red-breasted Parakeets, Pied, Indian, Lesser, Banded Bay, Grey-bellied and Drongo Cuckoos (U), Blue-faced and Sirkeer Malkohas*, Collared Scops Owls, Eurasian and Dusky Eagle Owls (U), Brown Hawk Owl, Mottled* and Brown Wood Owls (U), Grey, Indian and Savanna Nightjars, White-rumped Needletail* (U), Alpine Swift, Crested Treeswift, Brown-headed Barbet*, Streak-throated (U), White-bellied and Heart-spotted (U) Woodpeckers, Indian Pitta* (W), Indian Bushlark*, Eurasian (W) and Dusky Crag Martins, Wire-tailed and Streak-throated Swallows, Bay-backed and Rufous-tailed (UW) Shrikes, White-bellied* and Greater Racket-tailed (U) Drongos, Ashy Woodswallow (U), Brahminy, Chestnut-tailed and Rosy (UW) Starlings, Bar-winged Flycatcher-shrike, Large and Black-headed Cuckooshrikes, Scarlet and White-bellied (R) Minivets, White-browed Bulbul* (U), Puff-throated Babbler, Indian Scimitar Babbler*, Tawny-bellied*, Yellow-eyed and Large Grey* (U) Babblers, Brown-cheeked Fulvetta, Ultramarine (UW), Tickell's Blue and Verditer (W) Flycatchers, White-browed and White-throated Fantails, Asian Paradise-flycatcher, Black-naped Monarch, Grey-breasted, Rufous-fronted and Jungle Prinias*, Striated Grassbird (R), Orphean (UW), Tickell's Leaf (UW), Sulphur-bellied (W), Hume's and Greenish Warblers (W), Blue Rock Thrush (UW), Malabar Whistling Thrush** (U), Orange-headed Thrush, Black-lored Tit*, Chestnut-bellied and Velvet-fronted Nuthatches, Spotted Creeper (U), Olive-backed (W) and Paddyfield Pipits, Citrine (W) and White-browed* Wagtails, Thick-billed (U) and Tickell's Flowerpeckers, Purple-rumped Sunbird, Chestnut-shouldered Petronia, Baya and Streaked Weavers (U), Red Avadavat (U), and Black-headed and Red-headed Buntings (W). The first Yellow-rumped Flycatcher for the Subcontinent was recorded here in April 1989, and another bird answering to its description was reported by Forest Department staff in March 1995.

Other Wildlife   Project Tiger has minibuses for early morning and late evening game viewing drives. You can book individual seats. This is the best way to see mammals with reasonable chances of Gaur, Sambar, and Wild Dog. To see Tiger, of which there are some 70 in the Sanctuary, or Leopard, you need luck. There are relatively few deer in the park, but the population of Gaur is one of the largest of any protected area in India. On foot you are unlikely to find more than a few Grey Langur, Rhesus Macaque, Muntjac, Wild Boar and Black-naped Hare.

Pachmarhi

This small town in the Satpura mountains is the premier hill station of Madhya Pradesh State. Surrounded by extensive forests it offers good birding walks without restrictions. One or two specialities such as Malabar Pied Hornbill* and Malabar Whistling Thrush** may be easier to find here than elsewhere.

Map of Pachmarhi

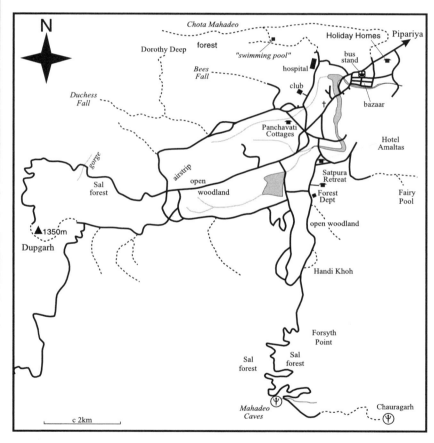

Location   Pachmarhi lies on a plateau, crossed by ravines and gorges, at an altitude of 1050m in the Mahadeo Range of the Satpura Mountains. Approach is generally via Pipariya, on the main Mumbai (Bombay) to Calcutta railway line, about 140km southeast of Bhopal. From Pipariya regular local buses and share-jeeps take 1^1/$_2$–2 hours for the 54km to Pachmarhi. Bhopal has an airport with connections to Mumbai, Delhi, Gwalior and Indore, and can also be reached by an overnight train ride from Delhi. There are three direct buses a day between Bhopal and Pachmarhi.

Accommodation

The best, as well as best value, accommodation at Pachmarhi is in hotels run by Madhya Pradesh Tourism. It is advisable to book in advance, especially during a holiday or at the weekend. For advance booking details see the section on Bandhavgarh. The best hotel is MPT's *Satpura Retreat* (B/C), a former Raj Bungalow with just six rooms. The MPT's *Amaltas* (C/D), another old colonial house, only has four rooms. The MPT *Panchavati Huts* and *Cottages* are in the C/D category, while the rooms at MPT's *Holiday Homes* (D) are cheap and friendly. There are cheaper private hotels around the bus stand and bazaar, generally overpriced but amenable to bargaining. It is best to check a few to see what the rooms are like. The SADA *New Hotel* (E) is better value having rooms with attached bath and a cheap, reasonably good restaurant. The Forest Department has a number of *Rest Houses* in the area for which booking can be made at their office on the road to the Mahadeo Caves.

Strategy

Almost all the beauty spots around Pachmarhi, advertised as tourist attractions, are in good habitat and worth exploring. Early morning is best before tourist activity begins. The hotels or the travel agent at the bus stand can arrange a taxi or jeep for a half-day sightseeing. It is possible to hire a bicycle or scooter – ask at your hotel or in the bazaar. The town is very green with plenty of mature trees, gardens and scrubby areas good for birds. Both Indian Grey* and Malabar Pied* Hornbills are attracted by fruiting trees, the latter in flocks of up to 20 or more. They are usually present from November to the end of March, though individuals have been seen at other times.

A good walk goes along the 10km of road to Dupgarh, the highest peak (1350m) in the area. The route goes through open woodland, sal forest and dry rocky scrub with possibilities for exploring off the road. Malabar Whistling Thrush** can be found in the ravine 3.2km before Dupgarh. The rocky crags have Dusky Crag Martin. The woodland with denser undergrowth towards the end of the road has Tawny-bellied Babbler* and Orange-headed Thrush.

Some good forest is accessed by the trail to Chota Mahadeo which starts behind the Government Hospital and is good for Painted Spurfowl**, White-naped Woodpecker* and Blue-headed Rock Thrush (UW).

The road south to the Mahadeo Caves goes through almost pure stands of Sal, less productive than mixed forest. There are more birds around the caves where Malabar Whistling Thrush** is tame and easy to see. You can finish the morning's birding by negotiating the 1300 steps to the temple at the top of Chauragarh – not many birds but nice views.

There is an area of woodland with undergrowth of Lantana on the left past the Forest Office on the road to the Mahadeo Caves, which is good for Malabar Pied Hornbill*, Puff-throated Babbler, flycatchers, Sulphur-bellied Warbler (W), Orange-headed Thrush and Grey Nightjar.

Half-day jeep visits into the nearby **Satpura NP** can be arranged through the hotels. They take care of obtaining permits from the Forest Department. The park covers 524km^2 with an altitude range of 350–1300m. The ranges of Red and Grey Junglefowl** overlap here.

Birds

There is a checklist of the birds of the area available at the Forest Department Office. This runs to just under 200 species, but an experienced birder would no doubt add new species to the list during a few days here. Some of the more interesting species not mentioned above are: Crested Goshawk, White-eyed Buzzard, Changeable Hawk Eagle, Painted Francolin*, Rain and Jungle Bush* Quails, Red Spurfowl*, Yellow-wattled

Lapwing* (in the plains), Chestnut-bellied Sandgrouse, Oriental and Red
Turtle Doves, Alexandrine and Plum-headed* Parakeets, Pied, Indian and
Grey-bellied* Cuckoos, Collared Scops, Eurasian Eagle and Brown Fish
Owls, Alpine Swift (U), Crested Treeswift, Lesser Yellownape, Rufous and
Yellow-crowned Woodpeckers, Indian Pitta*, Indian Bushlark*, Ashy-
crowned Sparrow Lark*, Rufous-tailed Lark*, Eurasian Crag Martin (W),
Wire-tailed and Streak-throated Swallows, Bay-backed Shrike, White-
bellied*, Spangled and Greater Racket-tailed Drongos, Ashy Woodswallow,
Chestnut-tailed, Brahminy and Rosy Starlings, Bank Myna* (plains), Large
Cuckooshrike, Scarlet Minivet, Golden-fronted Leafbird, Black-crested and
White-browed* Bulbuls, Large Grey Babbler*, Tickell's Blue and Verditer
Flycatchers, White-browed and White-throated Fantails, Asian Paradise-
flycatcher, Black-naped Monarch, Grey-breasted and Ashy* Prinias, Blyth's
Reed, Tickell's Leaf, Hume's, Greenish and Western Crowned
Warblers (W), Blue Rock Thrush (W), Black-lored Tit*, Chestnut-bellied and
Velvet-fronted Nuthatches, Spotted Creeper (R), Olive-backed Pipit (W),
Thick-billed and Pale-billed Flowerpeckers, Purple-rumped Sunbird,
Chestnut-shouldered Petronia, Baya Weaver, Red Avadavat and White-
capped Bunting (W). Green Avadavat** has been reported.

Simlipal

The Simlipal Hills in northern Orissa, once hunting grounds of the
Maharajahs of Mayurbhanj, are now a 2750km² Project Tiger Reserve. In
1980, 846km² of the core zone were declared a National Park; the remainder
retains the status of Sanctuary, where tribal peoples are allowed to follow
their traditional way of life. The forests of Orissa are among the most
extensive of Peninsular India. At Simlipal they are mixed deciduous and
semi-evergreen with Sal the dominant species, but within an altitude range
of 300–1160m a variety of other habitats can be found including bamboo,
grassland, deep ravines and barren, rocky tracts. Numerous streams and
rivers traverse the region and give rise to rapids, spectacular waterfalls and
pools. The birdlife is fairly typical of central India and includes a number
of species endemic to the peninsula, such as Malabar Trogon*, Malabar
Pied Hornbill* and Malabar Whistling Thrush** at the northeastern extreme
of their range, while one or two Himalayan species such as Green-billed
Malkoha and Blue-throated Barbet are near their southern limit. Being less
than a day's journey from both Calcutta and Bhubaneshwar, Orissa's
capital, Simlipal can be easily reached from either.

Location

Access to Simlipal is via Baripada at the northeastern edge of the Park
and Joshipur (Jashipur) to its west. The Park Office at the former has to be
visited first, if you wish to stay at one of the Rest Houses inside the
Reserve. It can be reached by rail from Calcutta (250km to the northeast) or
Bhubaneshwar (260km to the south) as far as Baleshwar (Balasore – 61km
to the southeast), from where there are buses and jeeps available. Joshipur
can be reached by bus from Baripada (105km).

Accommodation

There are *Forest Rest Houses* scattered throughout the park at Chahala,
Nawana, Joranda, Jenabil, Upper Barakamra, and Barehapani. The latter is
most popular because of the 400m high waterfall. The 150m fall at Joranda
is almost as impressive. The Rest Houses are fairly basic and you need your
own provisions, though the *chowkidar* will usually do the cooking.
Reservations often need to be made well in advance with the Field Director,
Simlipal Tiger Reserve, PO Baripada 757 002 ☎06792-52593.

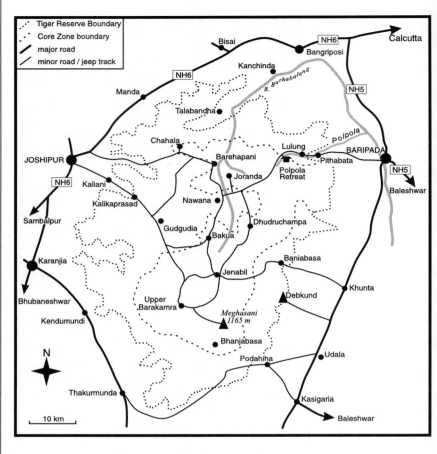

Map of Simlipal

There is a more comfortable *Tourist Complex* at Lulung on the edge of the Sanctuary 15km west of Baripada. This is run by the OTDC – see the section on Lake Chilika for the addresses of their offices. The *Rest Houses* at Gudgudia and Jamuanri can be booked with the Simlipal Forest Development Corporation, PO Karanjia; the *Rest House* at Lulung and the Panthasala at Bangriposi with the tourist office at Baripada ☎06792-52710. The *Tourist Lodge* in Joshipur is cheap and can arrange jeep rides into the Park. There are several small lodges in Baripada.

More expensive but pleasant and interesting accommodation is provided by the *Polpola Retreat*, a comfortable tented camp by a small river near the village of Purnapani just west of Lulung. Full catering is provided and treks into the jungle with native guides are good for birds. Bookings should be made with Pugmarks Nature Resorts Pvt Ltd, 10 Meher Ali Rd, Park Circus, Calcutta – 700 017. ☎ (mobile) 098310-06491, Fax033-2407737; email <pugmarks@usa.net>. There are special rates for students and transport can be arranged from the station at Baleshwar to the camp.

Strategy   If possible, avoid weekends and public holidays as many people come from Calcutta. A stay of at least three days is recommended with the best time from November to April. The park is officially closed from 15 June to 31 October as most of the region's rain (up to 2000 mm) falls during this period and unmetalled roads become impassable. It can take quite a while for them to dry after the rains, with the more important roads to the waterfalls being repaired first. In winter the temperatures in the higher reaches of Simlipal can be quite cool at night but become a fairly pleasant 20°C during the day. At Joshipur temperatures climb to 45°C during May and June.

You need permits before you enter the reserve, unless you stay at Polpola, in which case they will be arranged for you. They can be obtained from the ACF, Joshipur, District Mayurbhanj, Orissa or the Field Director, Simlipal Tiger Reserve, Baripada 757 002, Orissa, though the latter can only issue restricted permits for certain areas.

Most trips into the Reserve are undertaken by jeep. Try to make sure that you get a good one with functioning four-wheel drive as the tracks are often extremely steep.

Birds

The avifauna of Simlipal is not well documented, but species include: Cinnamon and Black Bitterns (U), Glossy Ibis, Woolly-necked Stork, Black Baza (U), Black Eagle (U), Pied Harrier (RW), Collared Falconet (R), Peregrine (Shaheen) Falcon, Red-necked Falcon (U), Red and Painted Spurfowl*, Red Junglefowl, Yellow-wattled Lapwing*, Pale-capped Pigeon (U), Emerald Dove, Alexandrine and Plum-headed* Parakeets, Indian Cuckoo, Green-billed Malkoha, Dusky Eagle Owl, Brown Fish Owl, Jungle Owlet, Brown Hawk Owl, Grey, Large-tailed and Indian Nightjars, Crested Treeswift, Chestnut-headed and Blue-bearded Bee-eaters, Indian Grey*, Malabar Pied* and Great Hornbills, Brown-headed*, Lineated and Blue-throated Barbets, Greater and Lesser Yellownapes, Rufous, Fulvous-breasted, Yellow-fronted and Heart-spotted Woodpeckers, Black-headed and Black-naped Orioles, White-bellied*, Bronzed, Spangled and Greater Racket-tailed Drongos, Chestnut-tailed Starling, Hill Myna, Large and Black-winged Cuckooshrikes, Scarlet and Long-tailed Minivets, Gold-fronted Leafbird, Black-crested Bulbul, Puff-throated Babbler, Verditer Flycatcher (W), Asian Paradise-flycatcher, Black-naped Monarch, Jungle Prinia*, Greenish Warbler (W), White-rumped Shama, White-tailed Stonechat (R), Malabar Whistling Thrush**, Scaly and Tickell's* Thrushes (W), Black-lored Tit*, Chestnut-bellied and Velvet-fronted Nuthatches, Thick-billed Flowerpecker, Crimson Sunbird, Black-headed Munia, Common Rosefinch (W) and Crested Bunting (UP).

Other Wildlife

Simlipal harbours good numbers of mammals, but they can be hard to find. Tigers number around 90–100 with a slightly larger population of Leopards. Elephants number 400–500. Sambar are relatively common, perhaps more so than Chital, Muntjac, and Mouse Deer. Rhesus Macaques and Grey Langur are the resident primates.

You may come across Gaur, Dhole, Wild Boar, Four-horned Antelope, Indian Giant Squirrel, Indian Hare, Sloth Bear, Common Otter, Indian Fox, Jackal, and Common Indian Mongoose. If you stay at the Chahala Rest House, a late afternoon or early morning in the hide overlooking the salt lick and water hole can be rewarding.

At Polpola you can go for late evening walks to look for flying squirrels, Indian Pangolin, Indian Porcupine, Ratel, Hyaena, Common Palm Civet, Leopard, and Jungle and Fishing Cats.

Among the Sanctuary's reptiles are Monitor Lizard, Indian Rock Python, Indian Cobra, King Cobra, and Mugger Crocodile. There is a Crocodile Breeding Centre at Joshipur.

Simlipal is home to 87 species of orchid and those interested in botany are recommended to visit the orchidarium at Gudgudia.

Chilka Lake

This enormous brackish water lagoon is one of the most important wetlands in Asia. According to Asian Waterfowl Censuses, Chilka (Chilika) has the highest diversity of wintering waterbirds of any site in the Orient. This may be explained by the amount of coverage it receives but also by its sheer size, which varies from 800km² to 1100km² (a maximum during the July to September monsoon), as well as the fact that it lies on a major flyway. The shallow water with islands, mud-flats, marshes and sandy sea-shores offers first-class conditions for wintering ducks, waders, gulls and terns. At times Chilka supports important populations of Spot-billed Pelican, Asian Openbill, Greater and Lesser Flamingos, Bar-headed Goose and Red-crested Pochard. The lake has a regular small wintering population of the rare and endangered Asian Dowitcher, a bird not easily found in India, while rarities such as Goliath Heron, Baer's Pochard and Spoon-billed Sandpiper have been recorded. A visit is a must for anyone with a special interest in Indian waterfowl and waders.

The lake is separated from the sea by a narrow sandy ridge interrupted by a channel. There are numerous islands within the lake, the most important being the 32km² Nalabana (Nalban), known as Bird Island. This is a flat expanse of mud, covered in water during the monsoon and emerging during the dry season until it becomes covered in grass by about March. The area around the island absolutely teems with birdlife, and was declared a Bird Sanctuary in 1973. The whole of Chilka was designated a Ramsar Site in 1981 and efforts are made to control the use of the lake which is threatened by increasing human activity and siltation.

Map of Chilka Lake

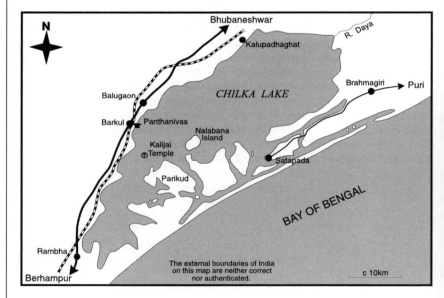

Location

Lake Chilka is in Orissa State on the Indian east coast. It lies on the main road (NH5) and rail routes south from the state capital Bhubaneshwar. The airport at Bhubaneshwar is served by Indian Airlines flights from Calcutta, Delhi, Hyderabad, Chennai (Madras) and Nagpur. From here it is about 94km to Balugaon, on the west side of the lake, the usual point of access for visitors. Most trains to Chennai (Madras) stop at Balugaon, while buses connect the town with Khurda and Berhampur. Mini-buses run from the

Balugaon bus stand to Bhubaneshwar at half-hourly intervals taking about 2 hours.

The eastern side of the lake is less well explored but accessible from Puri (about 50km south of Bhubaneshwar), a pilgrimage place and coastal resort popular with travellers. Hire a taxi or auto-rickshaw for the 48km to where the rather rough road terminates on the island of Satapada (Satpara), joined to the mainland by a new bridge. Buses from the New Bus Stand in Puri take about $2^1/2$ hours.

Accommodation   In Balugaon there are two places to stay – the cheap and basic *Gajendra Lodge* (E) on Chilika Rd and the *Hotel Ashoka* (D) on the main road in the town centre. However, most birders stay at Barkul 5–6km south of Balugaon at the *Panthanivas* (C/D), a hotel run by the Orissa TDC. It has rooms with and without A/C, and a restaurant which is open from 06.30 to 23.00. There are also some small shops, and tea and food stalls near the entrance. Rooms can be in short supply during the tourist season (October to January), so it is best to arrive early in the day or book in advance at one of the following offices:

OTDC, 9 Satyanagar, Bhubaneshwar – 751 007, Orissa ☎0674-54727

Govt. of Orissa Tourist Office, Utkalika, B4 Baba Kharak Singh Marg, New Delhi – 110 001 ☎011-344580

Govt. of Orissa Tourist Office, Utkal Bhawan, 55 Lenin Sarani, Calcutta – 700 013 ☎ 033-243653

At the southernmost tip of the island of Satapada, where the road from Puri ends, Orissa Tourism (as opposed to the OTDC) has opened a new hotel, the *Yatri Niwas*, with good-value double rooms (E). There is a restaurant at the Yatri Niwas and some tea-stalls nearby.

For those who wish to explore a different part of Chilka there is another *Panthanivas* at Rambha on NH5 at the southern end of the lake. This section of the lake does not seem as bird rich, partly because the lake is deeper. Not all trains stop at Rambha and it is easier to get there by bus from Balugaon.

Strategy   The main season for wintering birds is October to March with numbers peaking in December and January, but some birds can be seen all year. The premier birding spot is Nalabana Island where the arrival of birds depends partly on the water level. Nalabana is most easily reached by hired boat from Barkul. This can be arranged at the Panthanivas, where there are 6-seater and 20-seater boats with outboard motors for hire at fixed rates. Alternatively negotiate directly with the private boats at the jetty behind the Panthanivas. Make it plain that you want to spend a longer time there, unlike most tourists who make a quick trip to the island and back, usually via the temple on Kalijai Island. The Hotel Ashoka can arrange a boat, or you can deal directly with fishermen at Balugaon. The journey to Nalabana by motorised boat without stops takes about $1^1/2$ hours. You need several hours there. The boats cannot normally reach dry land as the water is too shallow, but it is easy to wade around the edge of the island. A telescope is useful for searching through the large flocks. Asian Dowitchers are often mixed in with numerous Black-tailed Godwits. It would be worth bringing a sleeping bag and mat and staying overnight in one of the three obvious watchtowers. You would need food and drink as there is nothing on Nalabana. Make sure you are well protected from the sun, as there is no shade other than in the watchtowers, and the smaller boats have no awnings.

Other areas with high concentrations of birds are at Gerasara, the Bhusandpur-Kalpadhaghat-Sorana sector and the region around Parikud Island.

The shores of the lake can be explored quite easily on foot or you can hire a bicycle in Balugaon, or sometimes from the staff at the Panthanivas. At the latter it is possible to hire a kayak but the wind usually comes up in the afternoon and makes the lake quite choppy.

If you have time, you can stay at Satapada and/or Rambha. The former can be reached by boat from Barkul in about 4 hours. Both locations are less convenient for Nalabana as the journey takes 3 hours one way. The last 15km of the road from Puri to Satapada runs along the 'lake shore' with a mosaic of pools, lagoons, grazing grasslands and marshes accessible by paths along the dividing bunds.

Birds

During winter a good selection of waders can be seen along the lake shore around Barkul with Black-winged Stilt, Redshank, Marsh and Wood Sandpipers and Common Snipe among the more frequent species. Whiskered Terns perch on fishermen's poles near the edge of the lake, and it is not too difficult to find White-winged (Black) Tern among them. Brahminy Kites are conspicuous, as are magnificent White-bellied Sea Eagles; both resident here. Chilka is the southernmost breeding area in India for Pallas's Sea Eagle, often seen at Nalabana. Peregrine Falcons arrive in winter. Ducks form huge rafts on the lake and should be examined for scarcer species such as Baer's Pochard, Red-crested Pochard, and Falcated Duck. Nalabana is host to Spot-billed Pelican, Greater and Lesser Flamingos, Bar-headed Goose, Greater Sand Plover, Eurasian Curlew, Black-tailed Godwit, Asian Dowitcher, Little and Temminck's Stints, and Curlew Sandpiper.

Other species at Chilka in winter are Little Cormorant, Little Heron, Painted Stork, Black-headed Ibis, Eurasian Spoonbill, Greylag Goose, Ruddy Shelduck, Spot-billed Duck, Cotton Pygmy-goose, Booted Eagle, Purple Swamphen, Pheasant-tailed and Bronze-winged Jacanas, Greater Painted-snipe, Pied Avocet, Small Pratincole, Yellow-wattled Lapwing*, Kentish Plover, Lesser Sand Plover, Spotted Redshank, Ruddy Turnstone, Dunlin, Terek and Broad-billed Sandpipers, Ruff, Pallas's, Brown-headed and Black-headed Gulls, Caspian, River, Great Crested and Lesser Crested Terns, Blue-tailed Bee-eater, Eurasian Golden Oriole, Brahminy Starling, Yellow-billed Babbler*, Greenish Warbler, Richard's and Paddyfield Pipits, and Citrine Wagtail.

The end of March sees the beginning of the breeding season for Oriental Pratincole, Gull-billed and Little Terns, and Oriental Skylark on Nalabana.

Other Wildlife

The Lake has more than 150 species of fish. Many are commercially valuable and fishing is the way of life for most people around the lake. Irrawady Dolphins are sometimes seen between Satapada and the mouth of the lagoon. Dugong has not been seen in recent years. Indian Fox, Hyaena, Jackal, and civets inhabit the long narrow strip that separates Chilka from the sea. A few Olive Ridley Turtles lay their eggs on the beaches.

Other Sites

Balukhand is a small coastal sanctuary with mangroves and littoral forest about 8km northeast of Puri. There is a FRH which can be booked with the DFO in Puri. The **Nandankanan Zoological Park**, famous for white Tigers, is good for wild birds. It is 25km northwest of Bhubaneshwar and easily visited on a half-day trip from there. The adjoining **Chandaka Wildlife Sanctuary** protects some 230km² of the Eastern Ghat forests.

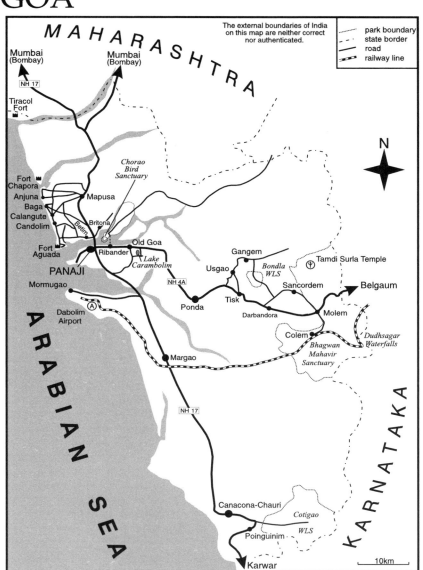

Map of Goa

The former Portuguese colony of Goa is wonderful for a laid back introduction to Indian birding. The advent of low cost package tours and charter flights from Europe makes this destination really attractive, particularly if you only have a week or two to spare. If bringing non-birding family members with you, this is the place to keep them happy with beautiful beaches, sightseeing, boat trips and good sea-food. Goa has excellent wetland, scrub and dry grassland habitats as well as good forest sanctuaries to explore. An experienced party of keen birders can expect to see over 200 species. With a good leader on a specialised tour this can exceed 250, not only common local birds and Palearctic migrants, but also some South Indian specialities such as Malabar Trogon*, Malabar Crested Lark** and Small Sunbird**. Even on the beach you can admire White-bellied Sea Eagles gliding by or enjoy a group of Lesser Sand Plovers working their way along the shore.

Goa is India's smallest state about 100km by 50km. Konkani is the native tongue, but English is fairly widely spoken, more so than Portuguese. The coastal regions are far more densely inhabited than the uplands in the east of the state. These still have extensive forests cloaking the Western Ghats at altitudes up to just over 1000m.

Location

On a map of India, you will find Goa on the west coast 400km south of Mumbai (Bombay). On a package tour, your plane will arrive at Dabolim airport, from where you will be transferred to your resort by bus. If you want to visit other parts of the country, there are flights to Bangalore, Mumbai (Bombay), Cochin, Delhi, Chennai (Madras) and Trivandrum with Indian Airlines and Jet Airways.

The new Konkan coastal railway line has improved connections with the rest of the country, particularly Mumbai to the north and Mangalore to the south. There are also many private overnight buses to Bangalore (14 hours), Mumbai (14–18 hours), Mangalore (11 hours), or Mysore (16 hours). Try to avoid the video buses if you want some sleep. Frank (Damania) Shipping runs a 7hr luxury catamaran service between Mumbai (Bombay Docks) and Goa. Tickets are available from most reputable travel agents in Mumbai and the Frank office at the terminal opposite the Hotel Mandovi in Panaji (**Panjim**, the Goan capital). The service runs five times a week, but check locally for departure times which may vary.

Panaji is a good base for trips, if you are not interested in staying at a beach resort. WWF-India has a divisional office in Goa at Hill Side Apartments, Block B, Flat B-2, Ground Floor, Fontainhas, Panaji, Goa – 403 001 ☎ 0832-226020. If you prefer a smaller resort with a good selection of habitats within walking distance, Baga Beach, 18km northwest of **Panaji**, is the favourite, with excellent birding on your doorstep.

The public bus system is very crowded and it can be difficult reaching some sites for the prime early morning hours. If there are three or four of you, taxi hire is very reasonable. Haggle and agree a price before you set off. The first asking price is likely to be more than double the real one. Taxis consist of older Ambassador cars, comfortable for three passengers, and Maruthi Vans which take four. If you intend using hired cars a lot, consult one of the Tourist Offices in Panaji and/or your hotel about standard rates. It is possible to hire self-drive cars in Goa, but this is not necessarily cheaper than hiring one with a driver, who will be used to traffic conditions and know how to find places, or can ask for directions. Maps of Goa are readily available.

A flexible and relatively inexpensive option is to hire a motorbike or scooter or, for shorter distances, a bicycle. Be careful where you leave the bike so that it is not tampered with. Hotels can arrange a motorbike or tell you where to get one. If you are on your own, consider motorcycle-taxis, which are peculiar to Goa. They are painted yellow. The rates are about one quarter of those for taxis. Bear in mind that roads are poorly maintained, crash helmets rarely provided, road signs often illegible or absent and traffic conditions chaotic.

Accommodation

If booking a package, a room only arrangement gives more flexibility, although you may find that after birding all day you're too tired to go out to find a restaurant in the evening anyway. It may be best to book half-board (breakfast and evening meal) and ask the hotel to make a packed breakfast/lunch when required.

For the independent traveller there is a wide range of hotels throughout Goa. In Panaji budget birders can try the *Republican Hotel*, José Falcão Rd,

at the back of the Secretariat or the *Udipi Boarding and Lodging* not far from
the General Post Office. In the mid-price category the *Panjim Inn* (B/C)
☎0832-226523 is highly recommended for a touch of Old Goan style.
In the top range there is the *Hotel Fidalgo* (A/B) ☎0832-226291 on 18th June
Rd, or the *Hotel Mandovi* (A) ☎0832-224405, Fax 225451, on Dayamond
Bandokar Marg opposite the boat cruise jetty.

There are plenty of restaurants in Goa and it is one of the best places in
India for local sea-food. The restaurant at the *Hotel Venite*, 31 January Rd,
has some of the best food in Panaji. The owner is interested in birds and
wildlife, but the hotel only has four basic rooms.

If you prefer a touch of luxury, try the *Cidade de Goa* (A+) ☎0832-253301,
Fax 223303 at Dona Paula south of Panaji.

See also the section on Baga below.

Strategy   Goa is hot and humid from March to June. Prices are lower from June to
September, when monsoon rains make birding difficult. November to
February is probably the best season for birding when most Palearctic
visitors are present. October and March are good for passage migrants. A
two week stay is good, but a third week would be useful.

The best birding is normally for the first few hours after dawn at about
06.30. Due to the heat midday is a good time to rest and catch up on chores
or sightseeing. Spend the last 3 hours of the day birding again. Protect
yourself against the sun by using sun cream and wearing a hat and
adequate clothing. Do not stay out during the middle of the day,
particularly until you become acclimatised, as sunburn and sunstroke
could ruin your holiday.

Initially concentrate on the vicinity of your resort and cover all the
habitats: gardens, scrub, wooded areas, paddyfields, salt pans, cultivation,
pastures, marshy areas, mangroves, creeks, and coast. All can be found
around Baga and Aguada. If staying at Panaji, there is a good area of pools,
scrub and mangroves east of the town from the main road to Old Goa. At
least one half-day visit should be made to Carambolim Lake. Bondla
Wildlife Sanctuary and Bhagwan Mahavir National Park (Molem) are
worth a journey with an overnight stay or two, even more at the latter if
you want to get into the higher hills.

There is no shortage of boats in Goa, and it is not difficult to persuade
fishermen to take you round the backwaters and mangroves for a suitable
fee. Try to explain you want to look at birds – 'sukanay' or 'pakshi'. You
can join an organised cruise, e.g. the Crocodile Cruise, not for a long bird
list, but for a relaxing day or half day with close views of terns and a good
chance of the scarce Collared Kingfisher.

Baga

Most birders on a package tour stay at Baga. There is an excellent
selection of habitats in and around the village, and there is the added
attraction of a good beach and plenty of hotels and restaurants. Other
birders around may have information on the whereabouts of
specialities.

Location   Baga is a beach-side village 18km northwest of Panjim. Taxi is the easiest
form of transport, but there are buses from Panjim and Mapusa, 10km to
the east. These arrive and depart from the 'main square' at the northern
end of the village where a small river meets the sea, though many
terminate at Calangute 2km south.

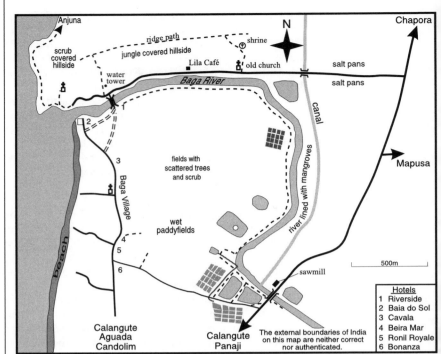

Map of Baga

Accommodation

The modern two star *Baia do Sol* (A) ☎0832-721141 is the best hotel in Baga, but the *Ronil Royale* (A/B) ☎0832-276183 has been enjoyed by first time visitors. Almost next door is the *Beira Mar* (B) ☎0832-276246, Fax263103 with excellent cuisine and good poolside birding for Greater Painted-snipe and Cinnamon Bittern, especially at dusk. The *Riverside* (C) ☎0832-276062 is less well appointed but quieter and overlooks the river. There are cheaper guest houses and private rooms, but Baga can get full during December and January. If you arrive without pre-booked accommodation, you need to get here early in the morning, otherwise it might be best to spend the first night in Panjim.

Strategy

As shown on the map the main areas to explore are: the path from the Riverside Hotel along the southern bank of the river, mostly lined by mangroves; the scrub- and jungle-covered hillside north of the river reached by crossing the narrow covered bridge by the Riverside Hotel; the salt pans southeast of the hotel for waders; the cultivation just east of the village – access generally unrestricted, but avoid damaging crops; the paddyfields, pools and the marshy areas south of here. Many species prefer the trees and gardens around the village and there is the chance of gems like Indian Pitta*. Baga and its surroundings, combined with trips to sites listed below, should give a long bird list at the end of a fortnight, but it is also worth trying to find new sites.

Birds

Birds in the gardens of Baga include Rose-ringed Parakeet, Asian Koel, Greater Coucal, Spotted Owlet, White-cheeked Barbet **, Rufous Treepie, Small Minivet, Common Iora, Blue-winged Leafbird, Red-whiskered Bulbul, Asian Brown Flycatcher (W), Asian Paradise-flycatcher, Common Tailorbird, Oriental Magpie Robin, Black-lored Tit (U), Pale-billed Flowerpecker, and Purple and Purple-rumped Sunbirds.

Contrary to what has been written elsewhere, by far the commonest wintering warbler on the Goan coast is the Green Warbler, currently lumped as the *nitidus* subspecies of Greenish Warbler *Phylloscopus trochiloides*. The nominate race occurs in smaller numbers, but with practice it is possible to separate their calls. The nominate Greenish has a disyllabic *tisswit* whereas the usual call of the Green is a more trisyllabic *tissuwit*.

The open cultivated fields and scrub are good for Pallid Harrier (UW), Red-wattled Lapwing, Pintail Snipe (W), Alexandrine Parakeet (U), Green and Blue-tailed Bee-eaters, Long-tailed and Brown (UW) Shrikes, Clamorous Reed Warbler (W), Tree (W), Paddyfield, Tawny (UW), Blyth's and Red-throated (UW) Pipits, White-browed Wagtail*, and White-rumped, Black-headed (R) and Scaly-breasted Munias. Drier areas should be searched for Yellow-wattled Lapwing*, Ashy-crowned Sparrow Lark* and Malabar** Lark. Check bushes and hedgerows for Red Turtle Dove, Eurasian Wryneck (W), Pied Bushchat and Black-headed Bunting (W). Grey-necked Bunting is sometimes seen.

The river should produce herons including Little, Osprey (W), waders and five species of kingfisher including Pied, Stork-billed and Black-capped (U). Raptors and swifts could include Brahminy Kite, Tawny (U), Greater Spotted (UW) and Booted (W) Eagles, White-bellied Sea Eagle, Laggar (U), Peregrine (W) and Red-necked (R) Falcons, Indian Swiftlet*, and Alpine (R), Fork-tailed (UW), House and Palm Swifts.

The jungle on the other side of the river needs several visits. In addition to the garden species look for Oriental Honey-buzzard, Black Eagle, Indian Peafowl*, Plum-headed Parakeet, Malabar Grey Hornbill**, Speckled Piculet (R), Rufous Woodpecker (U), Black-rumped Goldenback, Eurasian Golden and Black-hooded Orioles, Ashy (W), Bronzed and White-bellied* Drongos, Ashy Woodswallow, Common Woodshrike, Golden-fronted Leafbird, Grey-headed** (U), White-browed* and Yellow-browed* Bulbuls, Puff-throated, Jungle and Tawny-bellied* (U) Babblers, Brown-cheeked Fulvetta, Brown-breasted* (UW) and Tickell's Blue Flycatchers, White-spotted ssp of White-throated Fantail, Asian Paradise-flycatcher, Sulphur-bellied Warbler (RW), Orange-headed Thrush, Thick-billed and Plain Flowerpeckers and Loten's Sunbird*. The scarce and elusive Rock Bush Quail** has also been seen. A number of these are easier to see at Bondla and Molem.

The marshy areas and wet paddyfields hold several egrets and herons as well as wintering waders, among them Small Pratincole (U), Pacific Golden Plover, Greenshank, Marsh, Green, Wood and Common Sandpipers, Pintail Snipe, and Little and Temminck's Stints. Cinnamon Bittern (U), Ruddy-breasted Crake and Greater Painted-snipe should be looked for at dusk when they emerge from cover.

Carambolim Lake

There is an excellent marshy lake at Carambolim, 2km southeast of Old Goa. It abounds with birds and there is a good mixture of scrub, wasteland and trees on its eastern side, paddyfields to the south and a little woodland to the west. The new Konkan railway line along the western edge of the lake destroyed valuable habitat, though the site remains an important wetland.

Location   Old Goa is 10km east of Panaji with frequent buses from the bus stand. If coming from Panaji along the NH4A, carry on straight past the main roundabout with the Gandhi statue in the middle. After about 1¹/₂km cross

Map of
Carambolim Lake

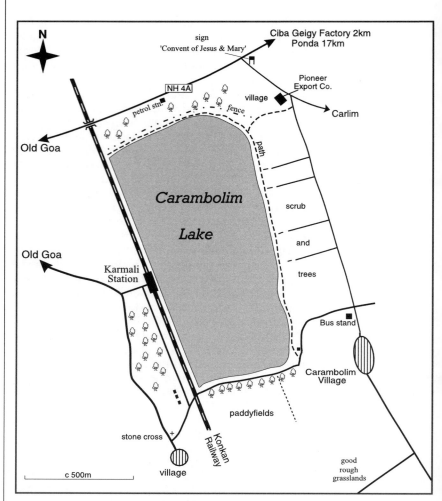

the new railway line and look for the lake through trees on the right. Take the next right turn, then right again at the Pioneer Export Co. and then any of the roads on the right will bring you down to the path that flanks the eastern shore.

Strategy   Start on the eastern side of the lake scanning for ducks, herons, jacanas and gallinules. Check the margins for waders, pipits, and wagtails. Look at the scrub and wasteland for bulbuls, chats, and pipits. Cuckoos, barbets, woodpeckers, and flycatchers frequent the trees, some of them partial to the Mangoes and Cashews. The White-browed Bulbul* is not uncommon but is shy. Scan from the road south of the lake and/or walk along the path through the paddyfields looking for herons, egrets and waders including Small Pratincole (U) and White-tailed Lapwing (UW). Woodland on the other side of the railway line holds interesting species and is worth exploring. There are other good patches of woodland and an excellent area of dry grassland along the road a couple of kilometres south of Carambolim village.

While at Carambolim it is worth looking at pools in the nearby Ciba-Geigy factory. The best time is late afternoon when waterbirds come to roost. Indian Cormorant, Oriental Darter, Asian Openbill, Woolly-necked

Stork and Stork-billed Kingfisher are specialities with Lesser Adjutant frequent. The factory is on NH4A, about 2km east beyond the turn off for Carambolim. Ask at the main gate for permission to enter the compound.

Birds   The lake has Little and Indian (U) Cormorants, Oriental Darter (U), Little Heron (U), Black-crowned Night Heron (U), Asian Openbill (U), Glossy Ibis (R), Lesser Whistling- and Spot-billed Ducks, Red-crested Pochard (U), Ferruginous Pochard (U), Cotton Pygmy-goose, Comb Duck, Eurasian Marsh Harrier (W), Watercock (U), Purple Swamphen, Pheasant-tailed and Bronze-winged Jacanas, Small Pratincole, Whiskered and Gull-billed Terns (W), Pied and Stork-billed (U) Kingfishers among others. Marsh Sandpiper (W), Clamorous Reed Warbler (W), Paddyfield Pipit, and Yellow (W), Citrine (W) and Large Pied* Wagtails can be found around the margins. Marbled Duck is probably the rarest bird ever seen here.

The scrub and fruit trees on the eastern side can produce Asian Koel, Blue-tailed and Chestnut-headed Bee-eaters, Brown-headed* (U) and White-cheeked** Barbets, Black-rumped Flameback, Yellow-crowned Woodpecker, Eurasian Golden and Black-naped Orioles, Chestnut-tailed Starling, Asian Paradise-flycatcher, Blyth's Reed and Booted Warblers (W), Tree Pipit (W), Purple-rumped Sunbird, Chestnut-shouldered Petronia, Baya Weaver and White-rumped Munia as well as some of the commoner Indian birds.

A walk through the paddyfields on the bunds is good for herons and egrets, waders, Paddyfield Warbler (UW) and Citrine Wagtail. In the woodland look for Rufous Woodpecker, Plum-headed Parakeet*, Greater Racket-tailed Drongo, Common Woodshrike, Small Minivet, Asian Brown Flycatcher (UW), Green and Greenish Warblers (W), and Jungle Babbler. The area south of the main village is good for raptors; Brahminy Kite and Greater Spotted (W), Lesser Spotted (U), Booted (W), Tawny (W) and Black (U) Eagles have been seen. The dry fields have both Malabar** and Rufous-tailed* (U) Larks, Common (Asian) Stonechat, Yellow-throated Sparrow. Both Wire-tailed and Streak-throated Swallows can be found in the area. Ashy Woodswallow may fly over.

Bondla

This excellent small sanctuary of some 8km² is at the foot of the Western Ghats. The habitat is largely mixed forest in undulating terrain. The sanctuary is easily accessible and harbours a good number of South Indian endemics such as Malabar Trogon*, Malabar Grey Hornbill** and Malabar Whistling Thrush** (U) which are not usually found near the coast. It is popular with tourists who come to visit the zoo, botanical gardens and safari park. Since most day-trippers arrive late morning and concentrate in the tourist zones, it is possible to bird without much disturbance.

Location   Bondla is 52km east of Panaji. The most flexible option is a taxi via Ponda, Usgao and Gangem. Buses run from Panaji bus stand to the reserve at weekends. During the week get a bus to Ponda or Tisk (on the NH4A to Belgaum) and then a taxi or auto-rickshaw from there. Alternatively the Forest Department mini-bus from Tisk to Bondla runs daily except Thursdays leaving at 11.00 (10.30 on Sundays) and 19.00. The departure times for the return are 08.15 and 17.45.

Map of Bondla

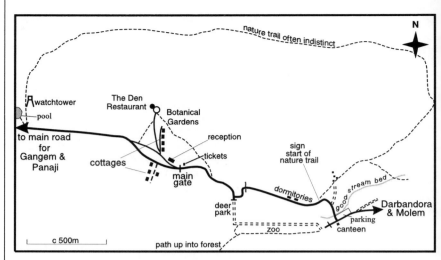

If you have your own transport, the journey from Panaji takes 1½ hours. To carry on to Molem (Bhagwan Mahavir NP), you can drive the short cut through forest along the departmental road (the only road through Bondla) which meets the main road from Darbandora to Sancordem and Molem. This route is quieter and is just over 20km from the canteen at Bondla to the crossroads at Molem.

Accommodation

There are a number of *Cottages* (E) run by the Forest Department at Bondla, most rather basic and some dilapidated with no hot water. These should be booked in advance at the office of the Deputy Conservator of Forests (Wildlife Division), 3rd Floor, Junta House, Panaji (opposite the Hotel Fidalgo), though this may not always be necessary other than for weekends and holidays. At Bondla a canteen is open for snacks and drinks from 08.00 to 17.30, as well as a basic bar and restaurant called 'The Den' from 08.30 to 21.30. Service is slow and it is best to order meals the day before if possible. Bring emergency rations with you.

It may be best to stay at your resort and visit on a day trip, which would necessitate a very early start (05.00) for the essential early morning birding. An alternative is to stay at Ponda 10km away at the *Hotel President* (C/D) ☎08343-312287 which has large clean rooms (some air-conditioned) with attached bathroom, or at Farmagudi, 4km northwest of Ponda on NH4A, in the 3-star *Hotel Atash* (B) ☎08343-313239, Fax313239.

Strategy

The Sanctuary is open every day except Thursdays, accommodation and restaurant remaining open throughout. Some of the best birding is along the approach road from Gangem, around the accommodation itself and the road as far as the canteen. These areas are best worked early before bus-loads of visitors arrive. Drive to the main gate of the sanctuary and bird back down the road asking the driver to catch up at suitable intervals.

There is a Nature Trail (see map), but it is difficult to follow and birding is generally better from the road. Check the stream opposite the canteen and entrance to the zoo for Brown-breasted Flycatcher (W) and the scarce Oriental Dwarf Kingfisher. Another trail leads from the back of the zoo (near the bear enclosure) and can be good for Grey Junglefowl**. The forest road to Darbandora has little or no traffic, though birdwise it is often quiet.

Bondla is one of the best sites for nightbirds, another reason for staying the night here. A good torch and tape should give a chance of Oriental Scops Owl, Spot-bellied Eagle Owl (R), Jungle Owlet, Brown Fish Owl (U), Brown Hawk Owl and Sri Lanka Frogmouth*.

If you can stand the smell, check the nearby Merck meat factory tip for vultures en route: coming from Panaji continue along the NH4A for about 7km past the centre of Ponda to the Khandepar bridge. Turn left after a further 100m at the sign 'Merck Meat Factory 2km'. The tip attracts White-backed, Long-billed and Egyptian (U) Vultures. It is 500m down a track to the right just past Hindustan Foods on the opposite side of the road to Merck. The best time is usually between 10.00 and 11.00 when remains from the factory are dumped.

Birds Other species found at Bondla: Oriental Honey-buzzard, Crested Goshawk (R), Black Eagle, Crested Serpent Eagle, Indian Peafowl*, Pompadour Green Pigeon, Nilgiri Wood Pigeon** (R), Emerald Dove, Vernal Hanging Parrot, Common Hawk Cuckoo, Grey-bellied Cuckoo*, Drongo Cuckoo (RW), Indian Swiftlet*, Crested Treeswift, Chestnut-headed Bee-eater, Brown-headed Barbet* (U), Speckled Piculet (U), Black-rumped Flameback, Brown-capped Pygmy Woodpecker*, Heart-spotted Woodpecker, Indian Pitta* (U), Dusky Crag Martin, Wire-tailed Swallow, Eurasian Golden and Black-hooded Orioles, Ashy (W), White-bellied*, Bronzed, Spangled (U) and Greater Racket-tailed Drongos, Bar-winged Flycatcher-shrike, Large and Common Woodshrikes, Black-headed Cuckooshrike, Small and Scarlet Minivets, Golden-fronted Leafbird, Asian Fairy Bluebird, Black-crested Bulbul, Puff-throated and Dark-fronted* Babblers, Brown-cheeked Fulvetta, White-bellied** and Tickell's Blue Flycatchers, Asian Paradise-flycatcher, Black-naped Monarch, Blyth's Reed Warbler (W), Lesser Whitethroat (W), Hume's, Green, Greenish, Large-billed and Western Crowned Warblers (W), White-rumped Shama, Blue-capped Rock Thrush (W), Malabar Whistling Thrush** (U – near streams), Orange-headed Thrush, Black-lored Tit*, Velvet-fronted Nuthatch, Thick-billed, Pale-billed and Plain Flowerpeckers, Purple-rumped, Small**, Loten's* and Crimson Sunbirds, Chestnut-shouldered Petronia and Common Rosefinch (W).

Other Wildlife Grey Langur, Malabar Giant Squirrel, and Black-naped Hare are fairly common, diurnal and more easily seen than other mammals of the Sanctuary which include Chital, Sambar, Leopard, and Gaur.

Molem

The Bhagwan Mahavir NP and Wildlife Sanctuary is often better known as Molem (Mollem, Molen). There were formerly two sanctuaries now combined to cover 250km² in the Sahyadri Hills on the western side of the Ghats. Bird densities often seem lower than at Bondla but the avifauna is more extensive, given the Park's much greater size. Molem is much further away from the coast so there are fewer tourists. A stay of at least two nights is recommended – longer if you want to get to grips with rarer inhabitants such as Nilgiri Woodpigeon**, Sri Lanka Frogmouth*, Blue-bearded Bee-eater or White-bellied Woodpecker.

Location Molem is a small junction town on the NH4A at the edge of the Park. Since this is the main road to Belgaum and Bangalore many buses from Panaji stop at the checkpost. Buses usually take 2 hours for the 58km journey. It would be possible to visit for a day trip with your own

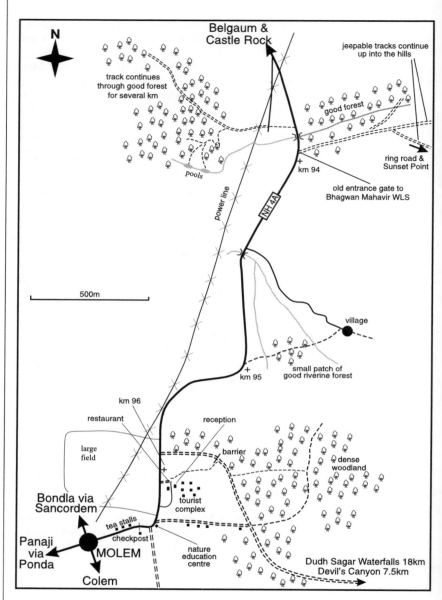

Map of Molem

transport, with a very early start to make it worthwhile; attempting both Bondla and Molem in one day is too much. You can reach Molem by train from Vasco Da Gama or Margao to Colem, 5km south of Molem, and then walk, hitch or catch a bus from there. This may be convenient if you stay at one of the resorts south of Panaji.

Accommodation

There is no accommodation in Molem village, but the so-called *Tourist Complex* (D) ☎0834-600238 is just along the main road towards Belgaum at the edge of the park less than 1km from the crossroads. A room can be booked in advance with the Goa Tourism Development Corporation Ltd, Trionora Apartments, Dr. Alvares Costa Rd, Panaji, Goa – 403 001 ☎0832-226515 or 226728, Fax223926. Reservation is normally only necessary on a weekend or holiday. Rooms are basic but clean, with a small veranda, shower and toilet, the latter often of the traditional seatless Indian style. Some rooms have air-con. The basic restaurant is open from 07.30 to about 23.00. Tea-stalls serve simple Indian food near the check-post in Molem. The two rooms at the *FRH* must be booked in advance with the Forest Department in Panaji (see Bondla section for address).

Strategy   Molem can be visited at any time of the year, although the dirt roads become impassable during the rainy season, and it can take months for them to be cleared again. Even at the weekends most trails are quiet, and during the week you meet few people, if any. There is a small charge for a ticket from the Nature Education Centre (between the checkpost and the Tourist Complex) open from 09.00 to 17.00. Insist on tickets covering the whole of your stay. If the office is closed, this should not stop you birding, but come back for the tickets later.

A jeep or a motorbike can be useful for deeper forays into the reserve. Organise one from your resort or Panaji as they are not always available at Molem. Otherwise, enquire at the Tourist Complex in Molem, or at Colem railway station. Ask at the Information Centre, or preferably the Forest Department in Panaji beforehand, for permission and to see if the roads have been cleared recently. Someone will have to unlock the barrier gate each time for you to drive into the Sanctuary. Make sure they leave it unlocked for you to get out or arrange a time to meet if they are not coming with you.

You do not have to go far to see good birds. Find a trail into the mature forest immediately behind the Tourist Complex. Here the undergrowth is fairly thick and trees achieve a good height.

The dirt road just north of the Complex is closed to traffic without permission and goes through open forest for 7¹/₂km to Devil's Canyon where Blue-eared Kingfisher is a possibility. There is a bathing pool where you can freshen up. Look for the scarce Malabar Trogon* in denser, moister parts of the forest. The road continues for 10–11km to the spectacular Dudh Sagar Waterfalls. The round trip makes a long day's hike if you are fit, experienced and acclimatised. The easier alternative is to visit the Waterfalls by train from Colem (see *Other Sites* below). There is a café of sorts at Dudhsagar station, but take your own provisions.

The old entrance to the Bhagwan Mahavir WLS is 2km north of the Tourist Complex near km-marker 94. There is a good dirt road towards the hills starting here (barrier locked to prevent unauthorised vehicles). If you have permission for a jeep, you can explore the network of roads here by a mixture of driving and walking with the vehicle following on at intervals. The right fork at the first junction after about 1km leads shortly to a ring road, fork right onto this and then take the second (more obvious) track to the right which leads up to Sunset Point in about 3km. Bird along this road for Red Spurfowl*, Grey Junglefowl**, Malabar Pied Hornbill* (U), Dark-fronted* and Rufous** Babblers, Indian Scimitar Babbler*, and Malabar Whistling Thrush** but do not expect to see all of them in one visit.

Cross the bridge on the National Highway just past the Sanctuary entrance and turn onto a path on the left, immediately after the bridge; cross the old abandoned tarmac road onto a jeep track through good forest to the northwest (see map). A side trail leads back to a couple of pools on the river where Blue-eared Kingfisher is sometimes seen.

The day hike from Castle Rock, just over the border in Karnataka, back downhill to Molem via the village of Anvoldem (Anmod) is also recommended.

Birds Molem supports most species mentioned under Bondla but also: Besra (U), Changeable Hawk Eagle, Rufous-bellied Eagle (U), Peregrine Falcon, Plum-headed* and Malabar** Parakeets, Collared Scops Owl, Eurasian Eagle Owl (R), Grey Nightjar (R), White-rumped Needletail*, House and Asian Palm Swifts, Blue-bearded Bee-eater (U), Malabar Grey** and Great (R) Hornbills, White-cheeked** and Crimson-fronted* Barbets, Lesser Yellownape, Common and Greater Flamebacks, Rufous, White-bellied (U) and White-naped* (U) Woodpeckers, Eurasian (W) and Dusky Crag Martins, Streak-throated Swallow (U), Black-naped Oriole (RW), Ashy Woodswallow, Chestnut-tailed Starling, Hill Myna, Large and Black-winged (U) Cuckooshrikes, Grey-headed** (U), White-browed*, Yellow-browed* and Black (U) Bulbuls, Asian Brown, Brown-breasted (U), Rusty-tailed (U) and Ultramarine (R) Flycatchers (W), Sulphur-bellied Warbler (UW), Black Redstart (W), Blue Rock Thrush (W), Tickell's* Thrush (RW), Chestnut-bellied Nuthatch, Olive-backed and Tree Pipits (W), Forest Wagtail (W), Little Spiderhunter, Baya Weaver, White-rumped Munia and Black-headed Bunting (RP?).

Other Wildlife Larger mammals are not obvious at Molem though Chital, Sambar, Barking Deer, Gaur, Leopard, and Sloth Bear are present. You are most likely to see Grey Langur, Bonnet Macaque, Malabar Giant Squirrel and one or two species of mongoose including Stripe-necked. Wild Indian Elephants are very rarely seen in the area. The park list makes mention of Palm Civet, Mouse Deer, Jungle Cat and Wild Dog, but Tiger is not present.

Fort Aguada

Aguada Fort is a prominent landmark at the mouth of the River Mandovi. The beaches to its north are popular resorts, but there is a good area of marsh and mangroves between the main road and a broad creek and canal that flow into the main river a little to the east. The mangroves are fast disappearing, but in some ways this makes birds easier to see. The whole area is good for herons, egrets and waders and up to five species of kingfisher can be seen.

Location Aguada is 16km by road northwest of Panaji and 8km south of Baga. There is a path opposite the Taj Holiday Village that leads into the marshes proper though access can be difficult after rains. Another path runs along a bund between the canal and the creek starting from a white cross by the road near where the two meet. Depending on the state of repair of the embankment and the tide it may be possible to follow this as far as the big bridge where the main road to Panaji crosses the creek and beyond. Access is also possible from this bridge and there is good birding to the north of it.

Birds Along the canal/river footpath you can find Purple and Little Herons, Black-crowned Night Heron, Great White Egret, waders sometimes including Greater Painted-snipe (U), Whimbrel (W), Greater Sand Plover (W), Marsh (W), Terek (W) and Broad-billed (UW) Sandpipers, Pintail and Common Snipes (W), Little and Temminck's Stints (W), Asian Koel, and Pied, Stork-billed and Black-capped Kingfishers.

On the fields, marshes and pools between the mangroves and the road look for herons, egrets, and waders as above, House Swift, kingfishers, Wire-tailed and Red-rumped Swallows, the White-spotted subspecies of White-throated Fantail, and Paddyfield Pipit. Great Bittern, Slaty-breasted Rail and Banded Crake have been reported.

Check the trees and bushes for Koel, Spotted Owlet, Brown-headed

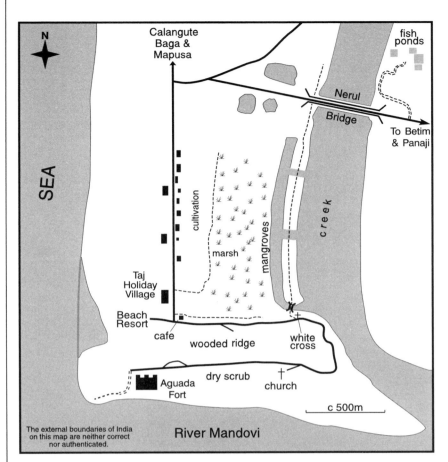

Map of Fort Aguada

Barbet, Lesser Goldenback, Long-tailed Shrike, Eurasian Golden Oriole, Black and Ashy (W) Drongos, Rose-coloured (W) and Chestnut-tailed Starlings, Rufous Treepie, Black-headed Cuckooshrike, Common Iora, Blue-winged Leafbird, White-browed Bulbul*, Tickell's Blue Flycatcher, Grey-headed Canary Flycatcher (W), Asian Paradise-flycatchers, Ashy Prinia*, Blyth's Reed and Green Warblers (W), and Baya Weaver. Look out for White-bellied Sea Eagle overhead. The wooded ridge sometimes has wintering Indian Pitta* best located by calls at dawn and dusk. One has wintered in recent years in bushes reached by the path behind the café on the corner opposite the Taj Holiday Village. The scrub near the fort itself sometimes holds Booted Warblers (W).

Other Sites   The mouth of the **Chapora River** is 5km north of Baga and supports waders including Lesser and Greater Sand Plovers, Terek Sandpiper (U), gulls including Pallas's, Yellow-legged (apparently mainly *barabensis*), Heuglin's (mainly *taimyrensis*) and Slender-billed (U), and terns including Sandwich, Gull-billed, Caspian, River (U), White-cheeked (R), Great and Lesser Crested on its sand- and mud-banks at low tide. The best area is on the northern side of the river mouth at **Morjim (Morji) Beach** where there is a large high tide roost. Get here by taxi via the regular ferry across the river at Siolim (bridge under construction). Crab-plover is a rarity along this coast occasionally seen on the sandbanks. Look for dolphins where the river meets the sea. If you go further upstream, you can explore mangroves.

A small woodland with a damp gully not far from Baga near the village of **Saligao** is a regular site for Brown Wood Owl, best seen at dawn in the trees around the pool. Take the road from Baga towards the NH17 for Panaji. After 6km you reach a cross-roads on the western edge of Saligao. Turn right and then again after less than 1km onto a narrow track between the houses. Take the left fork after about 600m and park at the end. A path leads through to the pool and wood. If you can't find it, ask for the Zor (spring).

Maem (Mayem) Lake 35km northeast of Panaji is a popular tourist destination for day trips. Walk between the lake and irrigation channel starting from the Lake Resort on the Chorao to Bicholim road on the western side of the lake. The track skirts the southern end of the lake leading into some fairly good wooded areas on the eastern shore. The occasional rarity has been recorded from the lake itself.

One speciality of South India is the Malabar Lark** which generally frequents arid, open stony areas with short sparse grass and dry fallow cultivation. If you can't find it elsewhere (e.g. Baga), try the barren areas on top of the hill just east of **Dona Paula** (7km south of Panaji), before and after the entrance gate to the Hotel Cidade de Goa; also good for Yellow-wattled Lapwing* and Indian Nightjar at dusk. The small marsh and scrub behind the hotel has had Cinnamon Bittern and Greater Painted-snipe. To reach this, carry on eastwards along the main road past the hotel gate to a road on the right marked Vainguinim Valley. Follow this down and right into the valley. If you stay at Dona Paula, the nearby Raj Bhawan (Governor's Residence) at the western end of the promontory is situated in gardens and a wooded compound that make for interesting birding when open to the public on Sunday afternoons from 15.30 to 17.30.

A visit to the **Dudhsagar Waterfalls** can be combined with a trip to Molem or undertaken as a day trip. Some travel operators offer coach tours leaving early in the morning to connect with the 09.30 train from Colem, the only way to get to the falls other than by four-wheel drive. Specialities are Changeable Hawk Eagle, Rufous-bellied and Black Eagles, White-rumped Needletail*, Malabar Trogon*, Blue-eared Kingfisher, Dusky Crag Martin, and Grey-headed** (in bamboo and fruiting trees) and Yellow-browed* Bulbuls.

The **Salim Ali BS** is an area of protected mangroves at the southwestern tip of **Chorao Island** a few kilometres northeast of Panaji. Access was along an embankment which has collapsed in places so that it is almost impossible to reach it on foot without wading through mud. It is easier to observe with a telescope from the church on the opposite bank near Britona on the northern side of the Mandovi River or between Panaji and Ribander. Better still get a fisherman to take you through the creeks in a dugout. Lesser Adjutants are often seen, but not always. Look for them flying above the mangroves. The other birds of the sanctuary are seen more easily at any other area of mangroves along the coast and rivers of Goa. Regular ferries run between Ribander (5km east of Panaji) and Chorao Island approximately every half hour from 06.00 to 22.00. The path into the sanctuary runs left as you arrive at the landing stage. A walk along the embankment in the opposite direction can be productive. Depending on the tide good numbers of waders can be seen on the sandbanks in the Mandovi River or on fields north of the embankment. A telescope is useful. Explore the marshy fields and pools of the prawn farm nearby for shorebirds including Marsh and Broad-billed Sandpipers as well as hirundines. A good area for waders is on the north shore of the island past the prawn farm to the north; bear right at the church and take a left turn after about 700m. Follow this road to the tidal mudflats and fishing grounds.

The **Cotigao WLS** lies on the southern edge of Goa State on its border with Karnataka. Being 85km from Panaji it is less visited than Bondla and Molem. The avifauna is similar to that of those two sites though some species such as Green and Mountain Imperial Pigeons, Great Hornbill and Spangled Drongo may be easier to see here. The nearest accommodation is at Chaudi-Canacona (*Hotel Molyma* ☎0834-643028 or 643087) on NH17 about 10km west of the Sanctuary or at Chaudi and Palolem Beaches. You could try booking the *FRH* suite at Panaguinim along with the departmental jeep (often out of order) with the Forest Department in Panaji.

The **Dandeli WLS** is just over the state border in Karnataka and contiguous with Molem but more than three times its size. The nearest town is Dandeli, 2km from the sanctuary. Luxury tented accommodation (A++) is available at the *Kali River Camp* bookable through Jungle Lodges and Resorts Ltd, Shrungar Shopping Centre, 2nd Floor, Mahatma Gandhi Rd, Bangalore 560 001 ☎080-5597025. The *FRH* (E) can be booked through the ACF at Dharwad.

SOUTH INDIA

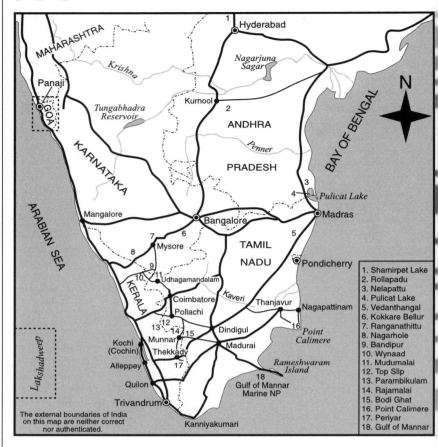

Map of South India

1. Shamirpet Lake
2. Rollapadu
3. Nelapattu
4. Pulicat Lake
5. Vedanthangal
6. Kokkare Bellur
7. Ranganathittu
8. Nagarhole
9. Bandipur
10. Wynaad
11. Mudumalai
12. Top Slip
13. Parambikulam
14. Rajamalai
15. Bodi Ghat
16. Point Calimere
17. Periyar
18. Gulf of Mannar

The external boundaries of India on this map are neither correct nor authenticated.

The southern part of the Indian peninsula has been undeservedly neglected by visiting birders but happily seems to be enjoying something of a revival. The character of the people and the landscapes are quite different from those of the north and the visitor will be pleasantly surprised by the friendly relaxed pace of life. We define South India as the present day Indian states of Andhra Pradesh, Karnataka, Kerala and Tamil Nadu. Geographically it is characterised by the Western Ghats range separating the western seaboard from the relatively dry high tableland of the interior known as the Deccan. Another shorter, less massive range known as the Eastern Ghats extends down the other side of the country through Andhra Pradesh into northern Tamil Nadu.

Of primary interest is the southern part of the Western Ghats and its forests, the centre of distribution for 20 of India's endemic species as well as another 15 shared with Sri Lanka. BirdLife International has recognised the Western Ghats as one of the most important Endemic Bird Areas in Asia. Since most birders will have previously been to northern India we give emphasis to these restricted range species. If you concentrate on searching for those, you should manage to find most South Indian specialities in the process.

Visitors with a limited amount of time wishing to see as many of the endemics as possible should plan a two to three week trip incorporating Mudumalai, Ooty, Top Slip, Munnar and Periyar. If you are short of time, the best option is to fly in to Coimbatore and hire a car and driver to visit these sites in two loops. The more usual itinerary is an international flight to Mumbai (Bombay) connecting on to Bangalore, whence visiting Mysore and Ranganathittu, Nagarhole and the above sites before taking a flight back from Cochin to Mumbai, or vice versa. Wader and waterfowl fans incorporate some sites on the east coast, particularly Pt. Calimere. You could then fly home directly from Chennai (Madras) or on to the Andaman Islands (see the relevant section) with the prospect of a further 11 endemic birds.

The timing of a visit is not crucial as the endemic birds are largely resident, but the southwest monsoon from June to September can make life difficult. Hot on its heels follows the lighter northeast monsoon which usually brings some rain into late November/early December. Since December and January are peak months for migrants this is generally the best season for birdwatchers, though some migrants stay into March. April and May are generally hot and dry, a good time to escape to the cool of the higher hill stations and their singular birdlife.

Whether looking for Nilgiri Pipit** and Painted Bushquail** on the grassy peaks of the Cardamom Hills, admiring the colourful Malabar Trogon* and Nilgiri Laughingthrush** in the evergreen forests or scouring the pools and beaches at Pt. Calimere for possible wintering Crab-plover and Spoon-billed Sandpiper, there is plenty to discover. And one is never more than half a day away from a palm-fringed beach.

Ranganathittu and Mysore

The famous heronry at Ranganathittu (Rangantittoo) on islands in the Kaveri (Cauvery) River near Mysore was declared a Bird Sanctuary in 1940. It is an excellent site at any time of year for astonishingly close views of species such as Eurasian Spoonbill and Black-crowned Night Heron and a chance to compare all three species of cormorant commonly found in the subcontinent. River Tern and Great Thick-knee are resident and Ranganathittu is one of the best places in India to get close to a Mugger (Marsh Crocodile) in the wild. The breeding season for the heronry is from June to October.

Location

The Bird Sanctuary is 16km north of Mysore in Karnataka, 3km off the main road to Bangalore. It can be easily visited from Mysore by taxi or by one of the frequent (every 15 minutes) Bangalore buses from the Central Bus Stand, getting off at Srirangapattna. From here it is 6km by auto-rickshaw. There is a railway station at Srirangapattna, but trains are less frequent. The Sanctuary is open from 08.30 to 18.00 daily all year round.

Accommodation

There is a range of hotels in Mysore from the deluxe *Lalita Mahal Palace* (A+) ☎0821-27650 and the *Quality Inn Southern Star* (A) ☎0821-27217 or the more characterful *Metropole* (A/B) ☎0821-20681 to cheap lodges like the hotels *Maurya* (D/E) and *Mona* (E) near Gandhi Square. For a good, clean reasonably-priced hotel in the mid-range try the *Plaza Palace* (C/D) ☎0821-30875 or one of several on Curzon Park Rd near the Clock Tower.

One of the best mid-budget places to eat is Shilpashri Restaurant off Gandhi Square. Its rooftop restaurant can, however, get quite full.

It is possible to stay in basic lodges at Srirangapattna and the nicely situated *Hotel Mayura River View* in the mid-price bracket. At the sanctuary there are only a couple of drinks stalls.

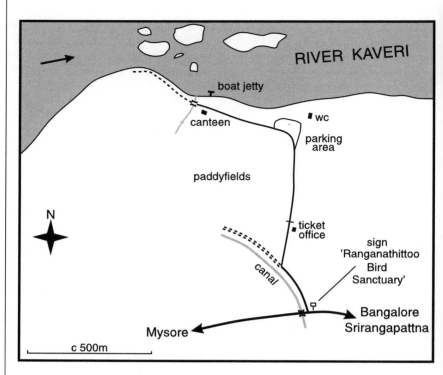

Map of
Ranganathittu

Strategy

A couple of hours or half day can be spent in the sanctuary and along the river nearby. If hiring a car for a day, combine it with early morning in the dry lands north of Mysore, and a visit to Kokkare Bellur afterwards (see *Other Sites* below). The Forest Department has boats for hire at the jetty. Charges are per person if sharing a boat, but you can hire a whole boat, allowing you to decide what to look at. The standard hire period is 20 minutes and includes the services of a guide/oarsman. The experience is not to be missed as the birds are used to boats and you get superb close views.

In July 1994 the Forest Department introduced higher entrance fees to the sanctuary for foreigners. If you consider this unreasonable, view the islands from the river bank by finding a way through cultivation west of the sanctuary. In any case, the cultivation and riverside vegetation adjoining the reserve are worth exploring.

Birds

The main breeding species are Great, Indian and Little Cormorants, Oriental Darter, Purple Heron, Great White, Intermediate, Little and Cattle Egrets, Indian Pond Heron, Black-crowned Night Heron, Asian Openbill, Painted Stork, Black-headed Ibis and Eurasian Spoonbill. Great Stone Plover and River Tern nest and are easy to see all year. From December to April Streak-throated Swallows nest on a 'vertical stone' a little upstream. Streaked and Baya Weavers breed after the monsoon rains.

Other birds include: Little Heron, Woolly-necked Stork, Lesser Whistling-duck, Spot-billed Duck, Oriental Honey-buzzard, Brahminy Kite, Grey-headed Fish Eagle, Pallid and Eurasian Marsh Harriers (W), Crested Serpent Eagle, Osprey (W), Pied Kingfisher, Indian Grey Hornbill*, Tawny-bellied Babbler*, Tickell's Blue Flycatcher, the White-spotted race of White-throated Fantail and White-browed Wagtail*.

Other Wildlife

Muggers have increased from just four in the 1970s to a healthy population of over 30, some of which usually bask on the rocks at Ranganathittu. Otters are occasional but appear to have declined. The large colony of Flying Foxes is impossible to overlook. Bonnet Macaques used to be a threat to breeding birds but are trapped and released in suitable habitat elsewhere.

Other Sites   There is a good area of dry grassland with scattered bushes and trees just north of **Mysore**. It is approximately 8km along the road to the Brindavan Gardens from the Hotel Metropole. A good place to start is just by a small temple or shrine next to a large banyan tree on a low hill by the side of the road (on your left as you come from Mysore). Specialities include White-eyed Buzzard, Tawny and Short-toed Snake Eagles, Eurasian Wryneck (W), Rufous-tailed Lark*, Indian Bushlark*, Large Grey Babbler*, Jungle Prinia* (U), Blyth's and Tree Pipits (W) and Indian Silverbill. Grey-necked Bunting has been seen.

Chamundi Hill (1060m) on the southern outskirts of Mysore is worth a few hours. It is popular with pilgrims so there are buses (no.101) from the city bus stand to the top of the hill from where you can bird down the road or the path (1000 steps). Most pilgrims do the reverse. The hill is covered in dry deciduous woodland and scrub. Look for Blue-faced Malkoha* and Indian Pitta* (W), and also for Indian Grey Hornbill**, Pale-billed Flowerpecker and Purple-rumped Sunbird. Check the tank at the bottom of the hill for Black Ibis.

Kokkare Bellur (Kokre Belur), 'village of herons' in the local Kannada language, is a magical place where Spot-billed Pelicans and Painted Storks nest on trees around the houses from November to June. The village is roughly halfway between Bangalore and Mysore, with the Sanctuary signposted from the main highway just east of km-marker 75 near Somanahalli. From here it is 12km along a rough tarmac road. Head south and take the right fork after about 5km. By express bus from either city, the nearest regular stop is the bus stand on the National Highway in Maddur (4km west of Somanahalli). Then go to the so-called Civil Bus Stand to catch one of the infrequent local buses to Kokkare Bellur. Alternatively, there are relatively expensive auto-rickshaws for hire at the New Bus Stand. This gives you the chance to stop at Tilur Tank, a shallow lake on the left a kilometre or two south of the turn-off from the main road. Make sure the auto-rickshaw takes this route and not the short-cut from Maddur. The tank has excellent wintering ducks and waders along with Glossy and Black Ibises, Bar-headed Goose (W), Spot-billed Duck, and Cotton Pygmy-goose. The general area also holds Blue-tailed Bee-eater, Indian Grey Hornbill*, Rufous-tailed Lark*, Zitting Cisticola, Ashy Prinia* and Blyth's Reed Warbler (W).

Nagarhole (Rajiv Gandhi NP)

Some of the finest forests in South India are found where the states of Karnataka, Kerala and Tamil Nadu meet. Each state has recognised this by designating sanctuaries. Karnataka set up two independently administered National Parks separated by the River Kabini, a broad lake since the construction of a dam in 1974. The National Park north from its shores for 642km² was the hunting preserve of the Maharajahs of Mysore. It is still known by its old name of Nagarhole (Nagarahole – pronounced *Nagarholay*). The 'Snake River' of the old name flows through the centre of the park and forms the Taraka Reservoir where it has been dammed at the eastern boundary.

Nagarhole consists largely of moist mixed deciduous forest in the northern and western parts of the Park, dry thorn forest in the east, and dry deciduous in the southeast. The forests are very rich in bird and other wildlife, though you need a few days to see a reasonable cross-section. In spite of being on the edge of the Western Ghats the terrain is fairly gentle with most of the Park on a plateau at 800m rising to the Masalbetta at 960m.

This is a convenient stop after Mysore with a chance to see species such as Malabar Pied Hornbill* and Green Imperial Pigeon which are more difficult further south. There is a chance of rarities such as Spot-bellied Eagle Owl and White-bellied Woodpecker, hard to find anywhere, as well as other South Indian specialities.

Map of Nagarhole

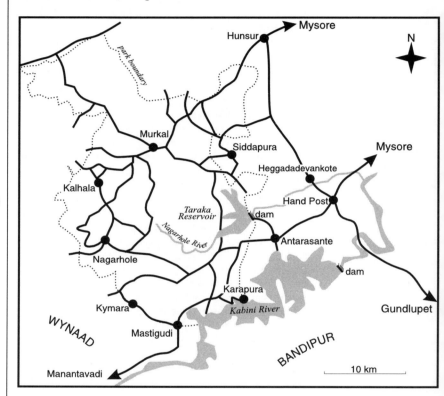

Location and Accommodation   Nagarhole is in southern Karnataka about 80km west of Mysore, famous for its sandalwood products and royal palaces. Tourists can enter the Park around Karapura at the southeastern edge of the Reserve and Nagarhole itself in the western part. There is accommodation at the latter, two dormitories and four suites which have to be booked with the DCF at the Forest Department office in the town of Hunsur ☎52041. It is not possible to make reservations in Mysore or Bangalore. The major problem is that you are not allowed to explore on foot, and the only transport is in departmental minibuses. To make a trip through the jungle they require a minimum of 15 passengers. Birding from a minibus is not very good. There is a daily fee to the Park and food can only be arranged on prior booking, as there is no restaurant. The main road from Mysore (96km) goes via Hunsur and a bus leaves at 09.00 to arrive 3¹/₂ hours later.

The Taj Group's *Gateway Tusker Lodge* (A – 50 rooms) at Murkal (Moorkal) in the northern part of the reserve may be closed for political reasons. Enquire in advance: ☎080-5584545, Fax5584030.

The best arrangement is provided by the *Kabini River Lodge* beautifully situated on the Kabini Reservoir at Karapura, recently voted one of the best wildlife viewing lodges in the world. If you can stretch to $100 per day, less for Indian nationals, this is the place for you. It is the 18th century hunting lodge of the Maharajah of Mysore with new wings in the same style. Meals are usually al fresco, often around a camp fire, and there are evening film and slide shows. The price includes permits, jeep trips and coracle rides. The Lodge is run in conjunction with Karnataka Tourism and booking must be made with Jungle Lodges and Resorts Ltd, Shrungar Shopping Centre, 2nd Floor, Mahatma Gandhi Rd, Bangalore 560 001 ☎080-5597025, Fax5586163 or with their agents in Mysore: Skyway, Hotel Madhu Nivas No.10, First Floor, Gandhi Square, Mysore 570 001 ☎0821-32900, Fax22559, who can also arrange transport.

Strategy

If you have your own transport allow extra time between Mysore and Nagarhole for good birding in areas of scrub and cultivation, together with small *jheels* for waterbirds en route.

Birding in the Park is surprisingly good from the jeeps. The drivers look and stop for birds and animals, and trips are accompanied by trained naturalist-guides, who know the birds and places to find them, not always the case at other similar establishments. It is not possible to get down from the jeeps except along the main road and at certain points in the forest, such as viewing towers, but this kind of birding can be rewarding. Animals and some birds come out to feed on areas kept clear beside tracks, especially just after dawn and just before dusk. These are good places for Red Spurfowl*, Grey Junglefowl** and Indian Peafowl*. Thicker, luxuriant undergrowth adjacent to the viewing lines is best for Blue-faced Malkoha*. The mature Teak forest supports many woodpecker species including Rufous, Streak-throated, White-bellied and Heart-spotted.

The Kabini Lodge compound is excellent for birds. Barn and Brown Hawk Owls are resident and species such as White-cheeked Barbet**, Black-hooded Oriole, Large Cuckooshrike, Scarlet Minivet and Velvet-fronted Nuthatch are in the taller trees especially early in the morning. The wooded area between the lake, the lodge and the fence can produce Indian Pitta* (W) and Puff-throated Babbler, while Alpine Swifts are not uncommon. Birds at the lake could include storks such as Painted, Asian Openbill or Woolly-necked. Ospreys (W) are regular and careful scrutiny should produce a Grey-headed Fishing Eagle. Indian and Little Cormorant usually perch on a tree just in front of the dining area. Spend time around the village of Karapura for the peninsular endemic Malabar Lark** in the drier and fallow fields. The coracle and motorboat rides are good fun and excellent for wildlife drinking at the water's edge. Malabar Pied Hornbill* usually pass along the lakeside forest late in the afternoon.

Birds

Nagarhole has well over 250 species on its bird list; the following is a selection of species not mentioned above: Oriental Darter, Lesser Adjutant (U), Black-headed and Black Ibis, Cotton Pygmy-goose, Brahminy Kite, Changeable Hawk, Booted, Black and White-bellied Sea (U) Eagles, Hen (R) and Pallid (W) Harriers, Merlin (R), Jungle* and Painted Bush** Quails (U), Barred Buttonquail, Demoiselle Crane (UW), Brown Crake (U), Greater Painted-snipe, Eurasian and Great Thick-knees, Small Pratincole, Yellow-wattled Lapwing*, River and Black-bellied (U) Terns , Painted Sandgrouse* (U), Pompadour Green Pigeon, Alexandrine, Plum-headed* and Malabar** Parakeets, Vernal Hanging Parrot, Large (W) and Common Hawk Cuckoos, Pied, Indian, Grey-bellied* and Drongo Cuckoos, Sirkeer

Malabar Pied
Hornbill

Malkoha*, Lesser Coucal (R), Oriental Scops, Eurasian Eagle, Brown Fish, Mottled Wood* (U) and Brown Wood Owls (U), Large-tailed, Indian and Savanna Nightjars, Indian Swiftlet*, Brown-backed and White-rumped* Needletails, Crested Treeswift, Malabar Trogon* (U), Stork-billed Kingfisher, Chestnut-headed, Blue-tailed and Blue-bearded (U) Bee-eaters, Malabar Grey Hornbill**, Crimson-throated Barbet, Black-rumped, Common and Greater Flamebacks, Jerdon's Bushlark*, Ashy-crowned Sparrow Lark*, Dusky Crag Martin, Wire-tailed Swallow, Bay-backed and Brown (W) Shrikes, White-bellied*, Bronzed, Spangled (R) and Greater Racket-tailed Drongo, Ashy Woodswallow, Chestnut-tailed, Brahminy and Rosy (W) Starlings, Hill Myna, Bar-winged Flycatcher-shrike, Large Woodshrike, Black-headed Cuckooshrike, Golden-fronted and Blue-winged Leafbirds, Asian Fairy Bluebird, Yellow-browed Bulbul*, Puff-throated, Tawny-bellied*, Yellow-eyed and Rufous** Babblers, Brown-cheeked Fulvetta, Asian Brown (W), Rusty-tailed (W), Tickell's Blue and Nilgiri** (U) Flycatchers, White-browed Fantail, Asian Paradise-flycatcher, Zitting Cisticola, Grey-breasted, Ashy* and Jungle* Prinias, Clamorous Reed, Blyth's Reed (W), Paddyfield (W), Booted (W), Tickell's Leaf (W), Hume's (W), Greenish (W) and Western Crowned (W) Warblers, White-rumped Shama, Pied Bushchat, Malabar Whistling Thrush** (U), Orange-headed Thrush, Black-lored Tit*, Chestnut-bellied Nuthatch, Olive-backed Pipit (W), Forest (W) and White-browed* Wagtails, Pale-billed Flowerpecker, Purple-rumped Sunbird, Chestnut-shouldered Petronia, Streaked Weaver, Red Avadavat, Indian Silverbill*, Black-headed Munia and Common Rosefinch (W).

Other Wildlife   The relatively open Teak forests of the southern part of the Sanctuary offer quite good visibility so that on most trips Chital, Sambar, Wild Boar, Indian Hare, Malabar Giant Squirrel, Elephant, and Gaur should be seen. Tigers reach a population density of around 15 per 100km^2, but several trips have to be made to have a good chance of seeing this magnificent predator. Your guide is likely to find pug-marks. The chance of Leopard around Karapura is higher as Grey Langur, their favourite prey, are fairly common here. If you see a mongoose look for the dark stripe from neck to shoulder on the Stripe-necked or the black-tipped tail of the Ruddy which distinguishes them from the Common. Other mammals are Muntjac, Indian Chevrotain, Four-horned Antelope, Indian Porcupine, Indian Pangolin, Slender Loris, Sloth Bear, Jackal, Dhole, Jungle and Leopard Cats, and Small Indian and Common Palm Civets.

Other Sites   The **Bhadra WLS** is between Chickmagalur and Shimoga in Karnataka about 180km northwest of Mysore. Less well-known than many South Indian protected areas, its 490km² of dry deciduous forests with plenty of bamboo, evergreen sholas, grasslands and swampy areas support a rich avifauna broadly similar to that of Nagarhole. Accommodation is available at Muthodi, 30km from Chickmagalur. Bookings as for Kabini Lodge above.

Nearby is Nagarhole's twin to the south, **Bandipur NP.** The avifauna is similar to that of Nagarhole, though the terrain is more rugged. Accommodation and offices are located on the main road from Mysore to Ooty, but the park can be reached from Nagarhole by the short cut to Gundlupet. A good new hotel, the *Tusker Lodge* (A) is at the edge of the park. If you plan to visit Mudumalai (following section), it is not necessary to stop at Bandipur.

The other contiguous reserve on Nagarhole's southwest flank is the **Wynaad Sanctuary** which belongs to Kerala. An overnight stop in one of the lodges at the lesser-known hill station of Ganapathivattam (Sultan's Battery) makes an afternoon and morning excursion into interesting habitat possible. Sultan's Battery is on a back route from Nagarhole to Mudumalai, but the road is in bad repair and slow. Take the Mysore road from Sultan's Battery until you come to the village of Naikatty after about 7km. At the end of the village you will see an old milestone inscribed Calicut 65 Mysore. A good track into the forest begins here. Grey-headed Bulbul** is regular in the streamside bamboo. White-rumped Shama is quite common. Indian Blue Robin, the *nigropileus* race of Blackbird, Orange-headed Thrush, Crimson-throated Barbet*, Dark-fronted* and Rufous** Babblers, Little Spiderhunter and Black-throated Munia* (U) are among the other attractions.

Mudumalai and Masinagudi

The sanctuary at Mudumalai in Tamil Nadu together with those of Bandipur and Nagarhole in Karnataka, and Wynaad in Kerala forms one of the largest areas of protected forest in India. The avifauna is similar in all the reserves, but Mudumalai is the most accessible and conveniently situated. The sanctuary is officially the **Dr. J. Jayalalitha WLS**, but is referred to as Mudumalai. Birding within the sanctuary is restricted but there are excellent opportunities around Masinagudi, on the eastern edge of Mudumalai, for South Indian endemics such as Malabar Parakeet**, Grey-headed Bulbul** and Malabar Whistling Thrush**. A stop here is essential to find the otherwise difficult Malabar Lark**, while searching will usually produce the near-threatened White-bellied Minivet and a host of other excellent birds including Sirkeer Malkoha*, Indian Pitta* and Booted Warbler (W).

Most of the sanctuary consists of dry deciduous forest with pockets of teak plantation on a plateau (900m above sea level) at the foot of the Nilgiri Mountains. The southwestern part of Mudumalai receives higher average rainfall resulting in moist evergreen forest. The area around Masinagudi and the eastern end of the park is largely dry thorn forest and scrub, supporting a surprisingly diverse avifauna, though not always at high densities. Several rivers and seasonal watercourses with riverine forest cross the sanctuary.

Map of Mudumalai and Masinagudi

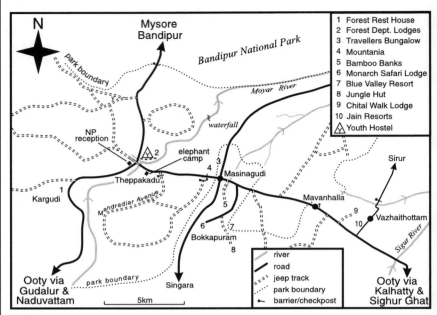

Location

The Forest Department Reception and Accommodation Centre (06.30–1800, ☎0423-56235) is at Theppakadu in the heart of the sanctuary on the main road from Mysore (90km) to Ooty (Udhagamandalam, 66km). The first bus from Mysore leaves about 06.15 while the last bus back leaves from Theppakadu around 20.00, the journey taking about 2½ hours. For most buses Theppakadu is just a stop between Ooty and Bangalore which can make it difficult to get on them as they arrive full.

From Theppakadu the long-distance buses to Ooty use the less hair-raising main road via Gudalur and Naduvattam and take about 2½ hours. A second, shorter route (40km) via Masinagudi and Kalhatty up the very steep and winding Sighur Ghat road is not suitable for most vehicles. Some specially adapted small buses use this starting from the bus-stand at Masinagudi.

Masinagudi, on the edge of the sanctuary, is 7km east of Theppakadu, but there are few buses. All of the private accommodation is on this side of the reserve, inconvenient without transport. One solution would be to spend a night or two at Theppakadu and two or three at Masinagudi. The nearest fuel is at Gudalur.

Accommodation

At Theppakadu the newer and better *Log House* (E) and the older *Sylvan Lodge* (E) with restaurant (book meals in advance) are beside the river Moyar, a few minutes walk from the Reception Centre. There are two small dormitories, the *Minivet* and *Morgan*. The Forest Department has Rest Houses at Kargudi, Abhayaranyam and Masinagudi, but you need your own food there. Another possibility is a night in a watch tower (no food, water or electricity) overlooking a waterhole. This can be excellent if you stay awake to watch for animals but can be disappointing on a quiet night.

To stay in the Forest Department accommodation, it is absolutely necessary to book first with the Wildlife Warden, Mudumalai WLS, 1st Floor, Mahalingam Bldg, Coonoor Rd, Ooty ☎0423-44098. If coming from Mysore, this means an inconvenient trip to Ooty first. The staff at Theppakadu do not know the advance booking situation and have to wait until the evening to find out if there is any accommodation left that night. There is a *Youth Hostel* (E) at Theppakadu, often full with rather noisy groups. There are no shops but a tea stall sells drinks and biscuits at the cross-roads opposite the Reception Centre.

Private lodges are on the eastern edge of the reserve near Masinagudi, the nearest village with a bazaar. The *Mountania* (B/C) ☎0423-56337 with rooms in cottages is 500m from the bus stand back along the road to Theppakadu. The *Belleview* (D/E) ☎0423-56351 is about 1km south of the bus stand and has dorm beds as well as single and double rooms. The basic *Traveller's Bungalow* (E) is opposite the police station.

Some better lodges are further out, particularly near Bokkapuram, 6km southeast of Masinagudi. Most will pick you up from Masinagudi if you phone. The family run *Jungle Hut* (B/C) ☎0423-56240 (advance booking on a better phone line to Bangalore ☎0821-5463848) is probably the best with excellent birds and competitive prices. The camp-fire barbecue dinners are a bonus. From Theppakadu the turn off is on the right about 1km past Masinagudi; follow this road for 5km. The *Monarch Safari Park* (B) ☎0423-56326 has cottages on stilts on a hill – good facilities, but the film set atmosphere is not to everyone's taste. The *Blue Valley Resorts* (B/C) ☎0423-56244, just before the Jungle Hut has been recommended. *Bamboo Banks* (A/B) is best avoided unless you are a hunter.

Jungle Trails (Chital Walk) Lodge (C/D) ☎0423-56256 is marvellous if you want somewhere quiet and are not too worried about mod cons. It is about 8km east of Masinagudi in a nature reserve. There is a good view towards the river where Elephants emerge at dusk and the place is magical if a White-naped Woodpecker* works the small tree in front of you while you drink tea. There are only four rooms, so phone in advance. Meals are provided. The lodge is 1km north along a track from the road towards the Sighur Ghat. There is only a very small 'pugmark' sign at the beginning of the track; if you reach the Jain Resort/Vaizhaithottam (pronounced Valaitotam) junction you have gone past it.

Warning   Be very wary of wild Elephants which are common inside the sanctuary and around Masinagudi. Lone bulls especially can be unpredictable and aggressive. Give them a wide berth and, if possible, take a guide who is used to keeping an eye open for them. They can be surprisingly well hidden. If one blocks your path, you must turn back.

Strategy   Mudumalai is open all year round and is less affected by the southwest monsoon as most of the sanctuary lies in the rain shadow of the Nilgiris. The park may close during the dry season, February to April, if the fire risk is particularly high, but it is still worth staying outside the sanctuary at Masinagudi, where most of the specialities can be found. Daytime temperatures in winter reach into the comfortable low 20°sC, though it can be cold in the early morning in an open-topped jeep. By March mid-day highs attain 35°C so most birding is restricted to the first few hours of the morning and the hours before sunset.

Movement on foot inside the park is not permitted without special permission and a guide, so if you stay at Theppakadu your birding is confined to the vicinity of the compound and the public roads. The Forest

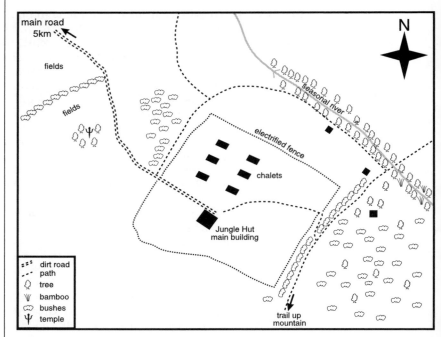

Map of Jungle Hut

Department minibus trips into the reserve are fairly useless for birds, so the only alternatives are departmental jeep and elephant rides. Let the jeep driver and guide know you want to stop for birds. On elephants this is more difficult, but it is great fun and excellent for the park's mammals. Book as early as possible, preferably when you book accommodation with the Wildlife Warden in Ooty, otherwise at the Reception Centre.

The main species at Theppakadu is the Grey-headed Bulbul** which is rather shy and prefers bamboo, of which there is plenty along the Moyar River on the road from the Reception Centre towards Gudalur. It usually keeps low but comes to fruiting trees when it may be found in the canopy. Listen for its buzzy, ringing *dzee* call. Grey Junglefowl** can be quite common along the road in the early morning and a slow drive can be productive just after dawn with Red Spurfowl* a possibility. Malabar Parakeets** are fairly common throughout Mudumalai along with Plum-headed*. Other birds along the river and around Theppakadu are Vernal Hanging Parrot, Indian Swiftlet*, Crested Treeswift, White-cheeked Barbet**, Indian Scimitar Babbler*, Rufous Babbler**, White-browed Wagtail* and Chestnut-shouldered Petronia.

The deciduous forests have a dozen or so resident woodpeckers. The commonest are Streak-throated, Brown-capped Pygmy*, and Black-rumped Flameback, but there is a good chance of Rufous, White-naped*, Common and Greater Goldenbacks, and Lesser Yellownape. You need luck for Speckled Piculet, Heart-spotted and White-bellied but try to see the latter here as it is unlikely around Masinagudi. Yellow-crowned Woodpecker is commoner in the drier areas to the east. The Mandradiar Avenue dirt road loop, a short way beyond the elephant camp on the right hand side of the road from Theppakadu to Masinagudi, offers good deciduous forest birding, but walking is forbidden.

There is scope for exploration around Masinagudi. If you stay at Jungle Hut, you are close to most specialities. You might find Asian Paradise-flycatcher and White-browed Fantail within the compound. Indian Pitta* is not uncommon in winter. It is easier at dawn and dusk when it is vocal, earning it the nickname 'six o'clock bird'. The call is a wolf-whistle like *wheet-whiyou.* Try the bushes outside the southern perimeter fence of the Jungle Hut. The path to the left brings you to a nallah with excellent riverine forest. Even in the dry season there are usually pools of water in the river bed attractive to birds. Work your way along the river to find the very shy Malabar Whistling Thrush**. It may be better to find a spot to sit and wait quietly for one to come along. Brown Fish Owls also live here and if flushed do not usually fly far. Grey-headed Bulbul** might turn up in the bamboo thickets, but there is better bamboo along the river bed north of the road just before the Jungle Hut turn-off. Other species include Emerald Dove, Bronzed and Greater Racket-tailed Drongos, Bar-winged Flycatcher-shrike, Indian Scimitar Babbler*, Brown-breasted (U) and Verditer Flycatchers (W), Indian Blue Robin (W), Orange-headed Thrush and Eurasian Blackbird. The river is a good place during mid-day when many birds are attracted by the cool shade. Spotted Creeper is a local rarity which has been seen during such a break.

Retrace your steps but instead of turning into the Jungle Hut compound continue up the path into the hills, into thick thorn forest and scrub with Grey Junglefowl**, Eurasian Thick-knee, Malabar Parakeet**, Grey-bellied Cuckoo* (U), Sirkeer Malkoha* (U), Indian Swiftlet*, Chestnut-headed Bee-eater, Dusky Crag Martin, Pacific (Hill) Swallow, Bay-backed Shrike and White-bellied Drongo*. Rufous-bellied and Black Eagles are regular; Oriental Hobby is very scarce.

Masinagudi is good for Malabar Lark**, in open wasteland and fallow fields which sometimes also hold Yellow-wattled Lapwing* and Jerdon's Bushlark*. Try fields near the temple before the entrance to Jungle Hut or the fields around the Bethesda Bible church at Mavanhalla Village. Another good spot is a small patch of wasteland in a bend in the road just beyond Vazhaithottam Village. In the early morning Wire-tailed Swallows perch on wires, Yellow-eyed Babblers skulk in the hedges, Booted Warblers (W) feed on the ground. The river is a spot for Stork-billed Kingfisher; cross it and take a path to the right to a grove of banyan trees which, if in fruit, attract many pigeons, barbets, orioles, starlings, mynas and flycatchers. The metalled road continues past the river into drier habitat, good for Yellow-crowned Woodpecker as well as Tawny-bellied and Yellow-billed Babblers*.

Another speciality difficult elsewhere on the South India itinerary is the near-threatened White-bellied Minivet, only found in India and Burma. This is seen in dry open thorn either side of the road between Mavanhalla and the Jain Resort/Vazhaithottam junction, but requires effort to find. They like low acacias and bushes, but also perch on hummocks of grass. Look for Booted Warbler (W) and Jungle Prinia* (similar to the commoner Plain Prinia but larger and with a less distinct supercilium not extending beyond the back of the eye).

If time permits, continue on the main Ooty road towards Sighur Ghat and explore the area where the road crosses the Sighur River shortly before it makes a sharp right-hand bend; good for Grey-headed Bulbul** in the bamboo. White-bellied Minivet and Brown Fish Owl have been seen here. There is good birding all the way up the Sighur Ghat, but it may be easier to do this from Ooty (which see), as birding along the steep road is easier down than up.

A night-time foray in the vicinity of Jungle Hut should produce Jerdon's Nightjar*, a small version of Large-tailed Nightjar with a similar but slower hollow *chonk-chonk-chonk* call. Indian and Savanna Nightjars occur, the latter in more open fields.

Birds

The area is rich in birds though many species are thin on the ground. It is easy to spend a week or two and still be finding new species. Notable residents include: Oriental Honey-buzzard, Tawny (U) and Changeable Hawk Eagles, Grey-headed Fish Eagle (on the forest *jheels* in the sanctuary), Short-toed Snake Eagle, Grey Francolin, Blue-faced Malkoha*, White-rumped Needletail*, Blue-bearded Bee-eater (U), Malabar Grey Hornbill**, Ashy-crowned Sparrow Lark*, Hill Myna, Large and Common Wood-shrikes, Large and Black-headed Cuckooshrikes, Asian Fairy Bluebird, Golden-fronted Leafbird, White-browed Bulbul* (U), Puff-throated Babbler, Brown-cheeked Fulvetta, Tickell's Blue Flycatcher, Black-naped Monarch, Thick-billed (U), Pale-billed and Plain Flowerpeckers, Purple, Purple-rumped and Loten's* Sunbirds, and Black-throated Munia* (R).

Winter visitors: Pied Cuckoo (U), Brown Shrike, Rosy Starling, Rusty-tailed (U) Flycatcher, Thick-billed (U), Blyth's Reed, Greenish (nominate and *nitidus*) and Western Crowned (U) Warblers. Nilgiri Wood Pigeon** is seen exceptionally in very cold weather.

Other Wildlife

The forests of Mudumalai support a wide range of mammals, including Bonnet Macaques frequently beside the road by the river and main bridge at Theppakadu. On a Forest Department ride you should see Spotted Deer, Sambar, Grey Langur, Elephant, Wild Boar, and Malabar Giant Squirrel and with luck a Black-naped Hare, Dhole (Red Dog), Muntjac or Gaur (locally known as Bison), but Tiger and Leopard are harder. If you have a vehicle try night drives along the public roads to look for the big cats; you might also see one of the civets or flying squirrels. Striped Hyaena, Indian Pangolin, Four-horned Antelope and Sloth Bear are rather scarce.

Snakes include King Cobra, Saw-scaled Viper and Indian Python. Indian Monitor Lizards grow to over a metre. Just as spectacular is the 20cm long Draco, which glides from tree to tree on membranes between its front and hind legs, justifying its name of Flying Lizard.

Udhagamandalam (Ooty)

The rolling Nilgiris, or Blue Mountains, among the highest in South India, are home to some restricted range endemic species – Nilgiri Wood Pigeon**, Nilgiri Laughingthrush**, Nilgiri Flycatcher**, and White-bellied Shortwing** inhabiting the evergreen sholas with their rhododendrons, magnolias and orchids. The word shola comes from the Tamil 'solai' referring to any verdant patch. Scientifically speaking it refers to montane elfin forests, interspersed with rolling grassy hills, of the South Indian highlands (2000m and above), but the word is commonly just used for evergreen forest.

Of many hill stations in South India the town of Udhagamandalam (Ootacamund, usually shortened to Ooty) at an altitude of 2,200m is the largest and most important. It was developed as a summer retreat, but although there are many reminders of the Raj, the 'Queen of the Nilgiris' has lost much of her charm and is a sprawling mixture of run-down and modern buildings, hugely overcrowded in the main season. Unfortunately, most forest has disappeared beneath developments, farms and plantations, but the town is convenient for exploring the Nilgiri Hills. This is the only area outside Sri Lanka where the Kashmir Flycatcher* is regularly seen in winter.

Location

Ooty is in northwestern Tamil Nadu not far from its borders with Kerala and Karnataka. It can be reached by bus from Coimbatore (90km, 3 hours), Mysore (156km, 5 hours), Theppakadu/Mudumalai (66km, 2 hours via

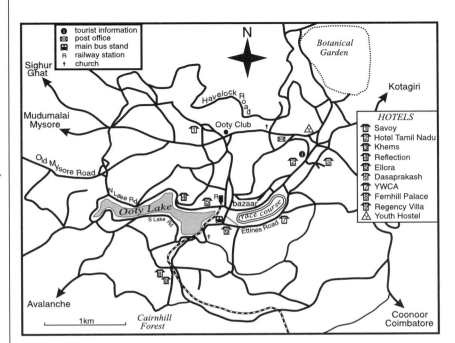

Map of Ooty

Gudalur and Naduvattam) or Masinagudi/Mudumalai (32km, 50mins on
the steep Sighur Ghat road).

Train enthusiasts will want to take the famous Blue Mountains Railway
which winds through spectacular scenery as it covers the 1800m difference
in altitude between Ooty and Mettupalayam (53km north of Coimbatore) in
the plains below. The train departs Mettupalayam at 07.30 stopping at
Coonoor on the way before reaching Ooty around mid-day. It leaves for the
three hour return journey at 14.50. There are extra services between
Coonoor and Mettupalayam where trains connect with main line services.
Try to reserve a seat in the front coach (C1) for the best views; all carriages
can be very crowded. The nearest airport is at Coimbatore with flights four
or five times a week to Calicut, Chennai (Madras) and Mumbai (Bombay).

Ooty is spread out among hills so getting around often means a long
walk or an auto-rickshaw. The main sites are out of town and detailed
below. If you spend a few days here, it might pay to hire a motor-scooter
from U-Rent ☎0423-42128 on Shoreham Palace Rd, but check to see if it
will get up the steep Sighur Ghat road before setting off to explore that site.

If you travel by car, consider the longer back route between Ooty and
Coimbatore via Kotagiri. This road is quiet and passes through the Nilgiri
Biosphere Reserve allowing roadside birding at various points including
temple groves with fig trees, very attractive to the elusive Nilgiri Wood
Pigeons**. Heavy traffic along the main road via Coonoor makes birding
impracticable.

Accommodation

There is a wide range of accommodation. Rooms are in great demand
from April to mid-June with tariffs correspondingly inflated. Most birders
visit outside this period when you can bargain over the price. It can be
quite cold so try to get a room with hot water; the basic lodges usually
supply buckets of hot water if requested. Cheaper accommodation is in
the centre near the main bazaar but is best avoided. Most better options
are less central: the friendly *Reflections Guest House* (D/E) ☎0423-43834

Nilgiri
Laughingthrush

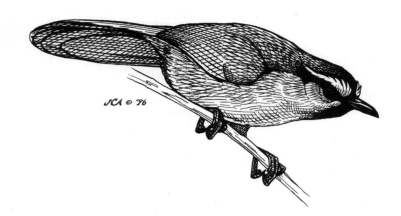

overlooks a lake on North Lake Rd; the *Ellora* (E) ☎0423-44266 is nearby
with a nice garden on the same road; the TTDC *Youth Hostel* (D/E)
☎0423-43665 near the tourist office at Charing Cross has doubles as well as
dorm beds; the *YWCA* (D/E)☎ 0423-42218 on Ettines Rd can get full. In the
mid-range the TTDC *Hotel Tamil Nadu* (C/D) near the tourist office is good
value; the Indian-style *Hotel Dasaprakash* (C/D)☎0423-42434 on Ettines Rd is
passable; the *Hotel Khems* (C/D) ☎0423-44188 on Shoreham Palace Rd is
more upmarket. Most upper bracket hotels are out of town so you need
a car or taxi: The *Fernhill Palace* (A+) ☎0423-43910 is the place to stay,
formerly the summer palace of the Maharajah of Mysore, but check your
room first as they vary in size and comfort. The hotel is in nice gardens
within walking distance of the Cairnhill Forest. The *Regency Villa* (B) next
door was the hunting lodge, and offers better value; the Taj Group's *Savoy
Hotel* (A++) ☎0423-44142, Fax43318, on Sylks Rd, provides old-fashioned
luxury at a price; the *Aruna Comfort Inn* (A+) ☎0423-44308, Fax44229,
on Gorishola Rd, is more modern in a quiet setting with a magnificent view.

Strategy

You can visit Ooty at any time of the year as the main species are
resident, though migrants such as Kashmir Flycatcher* and Tickell's Leaf
Warbler are only present in winter. The rainy season is May to October, but
it can rain in any month. Winter temperatures sink to 5°C necessitating
warm clothes.

The specialities are Painted Bushquail**, Nilgiri Wood Pigeon**, Nilgiri
Laughingthrush** Kashmir Flycatcher* (W), Black-and-orange Flycatcher**,
Nilgiri Flycatcher** and White-bellied Shortwing**. There are several sites
which can be explored in trips of a couple of hours to half-a-day each. You
might spend two to six nights in the area.

Cairnhill Reserved Forest

The Cairnhill Forest (2150m), sometimes known as 'the ravine at Ooty',
is a small area of degraded shola with a stream running through it
surrounded by tea, fir and eucalyptus. It is conveniently near the
southwestern side of Ooty on the main road towards Avalanche
(Avalanchi). If you stay on this side of town, it is within walking distance,
about 1km past the Fernhill Palace Hotel. Otherwise it is best to take an
auto-rickshaw. If coming from town, turn left at the Fernhill junction after
crossing the railway line; turn right towards Avalanche at the next T-
junction and the shola, marked by a signboard, is on the left at the next
sharp right-hand bend.

The noteworthy species can be found within a few hundred metres of the main road. Dawn is best for skulkers such as White-bellied Shortwing**, Indian Blue Robin (W) and Scaly Thrush. Otherwise, these usually keep to denser cover, particularly near the stream, but check the ditch near the road when you arrive. In winter Kashmir (Red-breasted) Flycatcher* is usually around the small clearing by the pool or along the short track to the left before the bridge. Other birds in the shola are Nilgiri Woodpigeon (R), White-cheeked Barbet**, Nilgiri Laughingthrush** (R), Black-and-orange Flycatcher**, Nilgiri Flycatcher**, Eurasian Blackbird, Orange-headed Thrush and Tickell's Leaf Warbler (W). Olive-backed Pipit (W) and Forest Wagtail (W) are commoner in more open plantation. Some species are commoner and easier to find in the better sholas further afield, but the site is worth at least an hour or two. With more time, you can continue along the dirt road to a number of trails in the plantation forests to the west of the main ravine where Grey Junglefowl** is more likely. A night-time visit might produce Brown Wood Owl.

Other birds: Bar-winged Flycatcher-shrike, Black-headed Cuckooshrike, Indian Scimitar Babbler*, Tickell's Blue Flycatcher, the white-spotted form of White-throated Fantail, Velvet-fronted Nuthatch, Plain Flowerpecker (U) and Common Rosefinch (W).

Map of Carnhill Forest

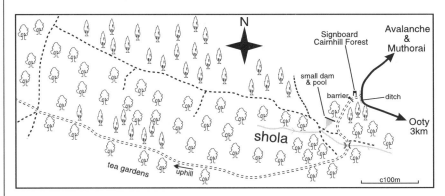

Potato Research Station – Muthorai

This is the best place for Nilgiri Wood Pigeon**, which can be difficult to find. It is not common and birds tend to be nomadic following irregular seasonal fruiting of favoured trees. Here they come to roost in tall trees between the main Avalanche road and the Potato Research Station near the small village of Muthorai 6km from Ooty (3km beyond Cairnhill). Look for a large lay-by on the right at a left-hand bend by a bridge before the sign for Muthorai. The trees are best viewed from the track in front of the Research Station reached by climbing mud steps from the lay-by and turning left at the top. Birds come in to roost here up to 2½ hours before sunset and can be difficult to pick out once they settle so arrive in good time. Although fairly regular there is no guarantee of seeing them.

Explore the track south from the other side of the main road at the lay-by. The imported eucalyptus is generally a disaster for birds but a few hundred metres down on the right is a patch of swampy grass where Paddyfield Warbler has been seen. Bushy areas on the left hold Black-and-orange Flycatcher**, White-bellied Shortwing**, and sometimes Kashmir Flycatcher* (W). Possibilities include Nilgiri Laughingthrush** (U), Western Crowned and Large-billed Leaf Warblers (W), Blue-capped Rock Thrush and other species as at Cairnhill. Dry and ploughed arable fields, further down the Avalanche road and on the way back to town, sometimes hold Malabar Crested Lark**.

Map of Muthorai

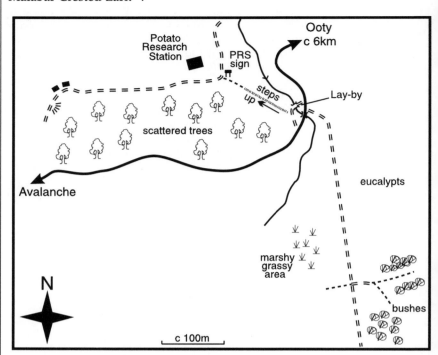

Naduvattam and Nadugani

An excellent shola extends east of Naduvattam village on the road between Ooty and Theppakadu (Mudumalai). Catch an early morning Mysore bus and get off where the shola begins at the 19km post to Gudalur (31 to Ooty). Walk down the road as far as a track to the right about 200m before the large sign saying 'Gudalur 17'. Walk this track to a ridge. A small stream is particularly good for White-bellied Shortwing**. This and other streams can produce Malabar Whistling Thrush**, though not common. Nilgiri Laughingthrush** is the main target here as it is scarce at the two previous sites. The delightful Crimson-backed Sunbird** is fairly common. Other species: Grey Junglefowl**, Woodcock (UW), Indian Scimitar Babbler*, Black-and-orange and Nilgiri Flycatchers**,

Map of Naduvattam

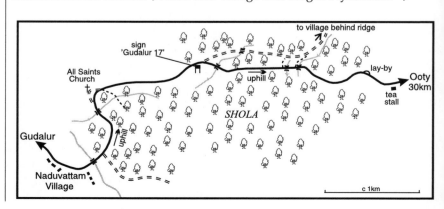

Large-billed Leaf, Greenish and Western Crowned Warblers (W), Indian
Blue Robin (W), Scaly Thrush, Eurasian Blackbird, Black-lored Tit and
Forest Wagtail (W).

Continue down the road into Naduvattam to catch a bus back to Ooty or,
with your own transport, make a full day by carrying on past Naduvattam
to Gudalur and taking the Nilambur road towards the coast. Approximately 5km past Nadugani (11km west of Gudalur) this road passes
through degraded rainforest and semi-abandoned coffee plantations. Try to
find the path next to a watchman's hut on the right of the road between km
markers 32 and 31 (to Nilambur) into the valley. It is possible, though not
as good, to do some birding along the road.

There are superb birds on this western side of the ghats, though they can
all be seen at various other sites. A visit here, though recommended, is not
essential: Pompadour Green Pigeon, Mountain Imperial Pigeon, Nilgiri
Wood Pigeon**, Malabar Parakeet**, Malabar Grey** and Great Hornbills,
Crimson-fronted Barbet*, Malabar Trogon* (U), White-bellied Treepie**,
Grey-headed** (U) and Yellow-browed* Bulbuls, Indian Scimitar Babbler**,
Dark-fronted* and Rufous** Babblers, Wynaad Laughingthrush** (U),
Rufous-tailed (W) and White-bellied Blue** Flycatchers, Malabar Whistling
Thrush**, Crimson-backed Sunbird** and Little Spiderhunter.

Map of Nadugani
(note orientation)

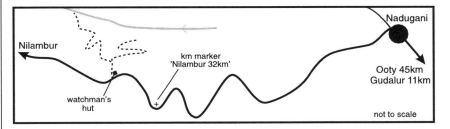

Sighur Ghat (Kalhatty)

The steep slope from Ooty down to the eastern end of Mudumalai is
known as the Sighur (Sigur) Ghat after the Sighur River at the bottom. The
road snakes down the 1000m descent in a series of hairpin bends restricting
traffic and making birding a reasonable proposition; birding off the road is
impossible. The ghat can be visited from Ooty or en route to Masinagudi/
Mudumalai. Take a taxi or a bus for Masinagudi (earliest at 07.00) and get
off at the Kalhatty Checkpost, where there is an obvious barrier across the
road next to a bridge and tea stall. Walk downhill from here.

The prime attraction is the Painted Bushquail**, not uncommon in
suitable habitat throughout the Western Ghats but difficult to see well. The
best chance is beside the road or as they cross it. Watch the road as far
ahead as possible and walk round the hairpins quietly. The birds are most
frequent in the middle section of the ghat below the Kalhatty Checkpost, in
thorny scrub and long grass with luxuriant vegetation in gullies.

If you have time, try the whole section of road from the Kalhatty Estate
Village at the top end of the ghat (11km from Ooty), to the bottom where
the road crosses the Sighur River, a distance of about 10km. (For the area
west of here see Mudumalai.) Raptors including Common Buzzard (W),
and Bonelli's and Black Eagles are often seen. Indian Swiftlet** and Pacific
(Hill) Swallow are frequent at the upper end of the ghat while Indian
Pitta (W), White-browed Bulbul*, Indian Scimitar, and Tawny-bellied
Babblers* are commoner on the lower slopes. Catching a bus or hitching a

lift back to Ooty can be tricky, as vehicles do not like to stop on the hill. Make your way back to the Kalhatty Checkpost or carry on past the Sighur River bridge for another 1¹/₂km to the Jain Resort/Vazhaithottam junction (see map) where the buses usually stop.

Other species: Grey Junglefowl** (U), Malabar Parakeet**, Blue-faced Malkoha* (U), White-cheeked Barbet**, Yellow-browed Bulbul* (U), Indian Blue Robin (W), Blue-headed Rock Thrush (W), Verditer Flycatcher (W). Watch the slopes on the opposite side of the valley for larger mammals such as Gaur and Elephant.

Map of Sighur Ghat (note orientation)

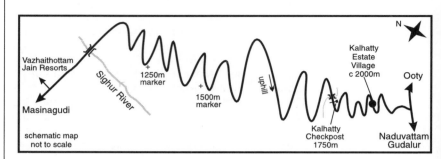

Other Sites

In the **Botanical Gardens** on the northern edge of town you are unlikely to find anything you will not see elsewhere, but they do turn up good birds.

If you do not want to go to Naduvattam, you can find similar species at a good shola stretching for 3–4km along the Mysore Rd 14km from Ooty. Early morning is best. Half way along the shola a side road to the left leads to Mukurti Lake and the 2554m **Mukurti Peak** in the grasshills of the Nilgiri Tahr WLS. This makes an excellent trek with an overnight stop at one of the IBs. To arrange this contact the DFO, Forest Department North Division Office, Mt Stewart Hills in Ooty ☎0423-44083 or the Nilgiri Wildlife Association ☎0423-43968 next door.

There is another extensive shola and grasshills at **Avalanche** (often pronounced and spelt Avalanchi, altitude 2100m) 29km from Ooty. There is a comfortable *FRH* at the edge of the shola. Food can be provided, but check when booking. Few people visit making for quiet birding with good chances of Nilgiri Wood Pigeon** as well as other specialities. White-bellied Shortwings** inhabit the streamside next to the FRH. There is only one bus per day and if this does not turn up for your return journey, the nearest main road is a 5km hike away. Book this Rest House with the DFO, Forest Department South Division Office in Ooty.

If you have missed the Nilgiri Wood Pigeon**, or one or other of the Nilgiri endemics, try the sholas around **Coonoor** (1800m), a hill station 12km southeast of Ooty, on the main road (frequent buses) and railway line (one train a day) south to Coimbatore. Hotels vary from the *Shree Venkateswara* (D/E), on the main Ooty road near the Bus Stand, to the *YWCA Guest House* (D/E quiet with a nice garden) and the Taj Group's *Garden Retreat* (A) ☎04264-20021 in Upper Coonoor. Take a bus (first of the day at 07.00) or taxi the 11km to a popular viewpoint known as Dolphin's Nose and bird back along the road through several sholas among tea plantations. You can take a side track down to another tourist lookout at Lamb's Rock. Similar possibilities exist around **Kotagiri** (1950m), a much smaller and quieter hill resort 28km east of Ooty (regular buses from Ooty, Coonoor and Mettupalayam).

Top Slip (Anaimalai)

The Western Ghats are subdivided into smaller ranges: the Anaimalais, or Elephant Hills, of Tamil Nadu form the next range south of the Nilgiris, separated by the lowlands of the Palghat (Palakkad) Gap. Originally these hills were covered by one of the largest tracts of rainforest in South India until the British discovered that teak and rosewood occurred here and began systematic logging and planting of these valuable timbers. Cleared land was ideal for coffee and tea. Some rainforest remained intact and in 1976 an area of 958km^2 was proclaimed the Anaimalai WLS. Nowadays it encompasses 1250km^2 and its official title is the Indira Gandhi WLS.

The tourist zone is at Top Slip (740m) on the edge of the **Karian Shola**, an outstanding patch of rainforest of approximately 9km^2, which harbours a good number of South Indian endemic birds. Part of the sanctuary forms the Karian Shola NP. Although many of the birds can also be seen at Periyar, some such as Sri Lanka Frogmouth*, Wynaad Laughingthrush**, and Black-throated Munia* are more easily found at Top Slip. For the mammal enthusiast a visit to Anaimalai is a must to see one of the world's rarest primates, the endangered Lion-tailed Macaque.

Map of Top Slip

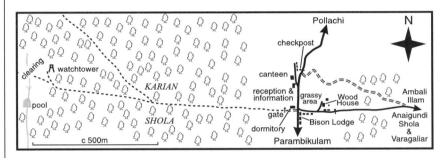

Location

The Anaimalais are in Tamil Nadu at the northern end of the Cardamom Hills. The National Park is contiguous with the Eravikulam NP and Parambikulam Sanctuary of Kerala State. Access is by road via Pollachi (35km, 1hour), which must be visited first to arrange accommodation with the Forest Department. From the Pollachi bus stand there are two buses a day to Top Slip at 10.00 and 17.30. There are more frequent buses to Anaimalai and the Sethumadai Checkpost, but it is difficult hitching to Top Slip from there. Return buses leave for Pollachi from Top Slip at 08.00 and 13.30. Taxis are available at Pollachi if you find buses inconvenient, but haggle over the price or ask when booking accommodation.

From Pollachi there are frequent buses to Coimbatore (40km, 1–1^1/2 hours) for Ooty/Udhagamandalam (another 90km and 4 hours), and Munnar (115km, 4–5 hours with a possible change at Udumalpet).

Movement within the park is entirely on foot unless you have your own vehicle, in which case you need the permission of the forest range officer, Sungam Range (Top Slip area). He can provide a guide and keys for barriers.

Accommodation

In the Top Slip area there are three 'lodges' and a dormitory. *Wood House* is a slightly better standard than the extremely basic *Bison*. The *Ambuli Illam* is about 2km from Top Slip in a quiet setting with good birding in surrounding bamboo and deciduous jungle but it is a 20 minute walk from Karian Shola. None of these is much more than basic and if you prefer comfort stay in one of the better class hotels such as the *City Tower*

(☎0422-230681, Fax 230103) or the *Surya International* (☎0422-217751, Fax216110) in Coimbatore, 2 hours drive away to the north. The lodges in Pollachi are all basic with the best probably *Ramesh Lodge*.

The accommodation at Top Slip is inadequate to cope with the number of people at weekends and public holidays so avoid peak times. You must stop in Pollachi to call at the Office of the Wildlife Warden, 178 Meenakarai Rd, Pollachi 642 141, ☎ 04259-25356 (residence 24015) to arrange accommodation. It is Forest Department policy to allow just two nights at any location. Your stay can be extended at Top Slip itself, dependent on other bookings. Arrangements are very much ad hoc so a sleeping bag and mat are useful. You may wish to stay overnight on the floor of the watchtower.

At Top Slip there is a very basic canteen and shop serving traditional vegetarian meals on a banana leaf, masala dosas, omelettes, biscuits, bananas, soft drinks, and mineral water.

The more adventurous may explore areas around *FRHs* at Varagaliar, Mt. Stewart, Sethumadai and Amaravathinagar, but you need your own food and permission to stay from the office of the DFO, Coimbatore South Division, Mahalingam Nagar, Pollachi.

Strategy   The park is open year round but birding can be difficult during the monsoon (June-September) when leeches are a problem. There is a lighter monsoon in October and November. The best season is December to February. Ticks infest the undergrowth; stick to the main trails to avoid these pests. A stay of several days is desirable if accommodation hassles can be overcome. Forays away from the immediate vicinity of Top Slip must be with a Forest Department guide from the local tribal people who live in the forest. Their fees are reasonable and make a small contribution to the local economy, which in turn helps preserve good relations between the tribals and the authorities. The guides know most animals, but not all are familiar with English bird names, even if they know the birds. If you are looking for a particular species, show your guide its illustration in a field guide.

Birding should concentrate on the broad trail through Karian Shola to a watchtower overlooking a clearing with a stream, less than 1km from the main road. Several walks may be necessary to find the prize species. Look for Malabar Trogon* (U), Black-rumped, Common (U) and Greater Flamebacks, White-bellied and Heart-spotted Woodpeckers, Indian Pitta* (UW), White-bellied Treepie**, Hill Myna, Dark-fronted Babbler*, White-bellied Blue Flycatcher**, Orange-headed Thrush (white-throated subspecies) and Eurasian Blackbird (race *nigropileus*).

Spend time in the clearing with the watchtower. Rufous Babblers** are fairly common. The difficult Black-throated Munia* (a possible split from the Sri Lankan race), though not common, is regularly seen in the bamboo thickets and scrub. Malabar Grey Hornbill**, and Pompadour Green and Mountain Imperial Pigeons are fairly common and visible from some distance, and Great Hornbill is less regular; Malabar Parakeets** outnumber their Plum-headed* congeners; White-cheeked Barbets** perch openly in tree-tops, especially in early morning and late afternoon when often joined by the exquisite Crimson-fronteds*, sometimes treated as a South Indian endemic separate from the Sri Lankan form; Malabar Whistling Thrush** keeps to the stream and the area behind the pool; Crimson-backed Sunbird** and Little Spiderhunter frequent the forest edge; Dollarbird is occasional. Watch overhead for White-rumped Needletail* and Indian Swiftlet*. The clearing is the best spot for the elusive Red Spurfowl*, but it could turn up anywhere. It is good at dusk for Brown Hawk Owl, and Great Eared and Jerdon's* Nightjars. Brown Fish Owl is sometimes seen.

The Wynaad Laughingthrush** has a restricted range and is little reported compared to some South Indian endemics, partly because of its habit of flocking in gatherings of up to 40, rather than popping up in ones and twos. The best area seems to be on the road towards Anaigundi (Anaigunti or Anai Kundi) Shola where it frequents bamboo and rich damp undergrowth a kilometre past the Ambuli Illam Rest House and in similar patches further along. Put a little effort into finding this species as it is not guaranteed at Periyar, the other main site. This area is good for Lesser Yellownape, Rufous Woodpecker, the ruby-throated race of Black-crested Bulbul, Yellow-browed Bulbul*, Indian Scimitar Babbler*, Blue-throated Flycatcher (W) and White-rumped Shama (U).

The road continues for 10km to the Anai Gundi Shola. You may obtain permission to drive there, otherwise it means 2 hours at a fast hiking pace with a guide following steep short-cuts. At least one visit is an absolute must, especially if you want to see the very rare Lion-tailed Macaque. Its population here may be 40-50. Many of the same birds can be found as in Karian Shola though Malabar Trogon*, and Brown-breasted and Rusty-tailed Flycatchers (W) are more likely here.

A special effort should be made to find Sri Lanka Frogmouth* at Top Slip. In recent years there have been roosting sites in Karian Shola which local guides were aware of. If enquiries prove fruitless, some night birding along the roads and trails at Top Slip should prove rewarding, especially with a tape lure. The road towards Parambikulam is good for this. Jerdon's Nightjar*, Brown Hawk Owl, and Oriental and Collared Scops Owls are likely to heard and often seen with a torch. The enigmatic Spot-bellied Eagle Owl has been seen at dusk in Karian Shola, while two of the few South Indian records of Oriental Bay Owl come from here.

Teak forests on the road to Parambikulam are less productive though Grey Junglefowl**, Blue-faced Malkoha*, and Grey-breasted Prinia are more commonly seen in roadside vegetation than in the shola. Malabar Whistling Thrush** is found by the first stream you cross on this road.

Towards the latter part of the hot dry season birds and animals move to moister, cooler parts and it may be worth a couple of days at Varagaliar. For this you may need a four-wheel drive vehicle and should obtain permission in Pollachi. From Top Slip it is more than 20km by road or a tough 8km hike across Umayamalai.

Birds

Other species around Top Slip: Black Bittern (R), Oriental Honey-buzzard, Changeable Hawk, Rufous-bellied (U), Black and Crested Serpent Eagles, Vernal Hanging Parrot, Emerald Dove (U), Common Hawk Cuckoo, Chestnut-winged and Banded Bay Cuckoos (UW), Jungle Owlet, Brown-backed Needletail, Alpine Swift (U), Crested Treeswift, Chestnut-headed and Blue-bearded (U) Bee-eaters, Brown-capped Pygmy Woodpecker*, Brown Shrike (W), Black-hooded Oriole, Bronzed and Greater Racket-tailed Drongos, Chestnut-tailed Starling, Large Woodshrike, Black-headed Cuckooshrike, Asian Fairy Bluebird, Golden-fronted Leafbird, White-browed Bulbul*, Puff-throated and Tawny-bellied* Babblers, Brown-cheeked Fulvetta, Tickell's Blue and Verditer (W) Flycatchers, Black-naped Monarch, Blyth's Reed, Tickell's Leaf, Large-billed, Greenish and Western Crowned Warblers (W), Velvet-fronted Nuthatch, Forest Wagtail (W), Thick-billed Flowerpecker, Purple-rumped Sunbird and White-rumped Munia.

Other Wildlife

The Anaimalai forests have a wide range of mammals but luck is needed to see many of them. Wild Boar, Nilgiri Langur, and Malabar Giant Squirrel

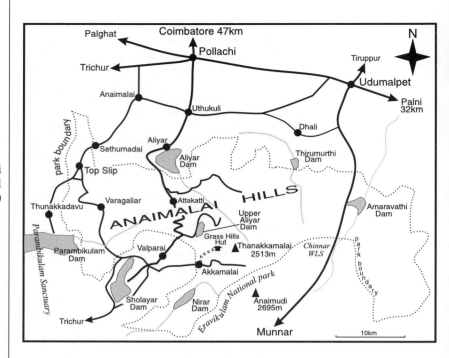

Map of Anaimalai
(Indira Gandhi Wild
Life Sanctuary)

are fairly common. At Top Slip it is worth searching the open grassy
maidan between the reception and Wood House with a torch after dark for
Spotted Deer. Small Indian Civet, Toddy Cat, Indian Porcupine, and
Common Giant and Travancore Flying Squirrels are sometimes seen
around the accommodation. Gaur are most likely by the main roadside,
while the best chance of Elephant is during the night from the watchtower.

Lion-tailed Macaques require a trip to Anai Gundi Shola. The troops
have been studied by scientists for a number of years so it may be worth
enquiring how to find them. A guide is indispensable. Also present are
Grey Langur, Bonnet Macaque, Sambar, Muntjac, Sloth Bear, Dusky Striped
Squirrel, Stripe-necked and Ruddy Mongoose, Black-naped Hare, Leopard
and Tiger.

Other Sites   The forests on the Keralese side of the border to the south of Top Slip
form the **Parambikulam Sanctuary** around the reservoir at the Tunakadavu
(Thunakadavu) Dam. Access is from the Tamil Nadu side via the main road
through Top Slip. The same buses serve both destinations from Pollachi.
There are rest houses at Tunakadavu and at the end of the road at
Parambikulam booked with the Wildlife Warden at the sanctuary HQ at
Thunakadavu. The forests are mainly teak with moist evergreen forests less
accessible than at Top Slip, but birding can be good. The avifauna is
broadly similar though Grey-headed Fish Eagle, Osprey, Stork-billed
Kingfisher and Thick-billed Warbler are more often seen here.

The **Indira Gandhi WLS** encompasses much more than Top Slip. Much
high altitude shola and grassy hilltop habitat is in the core zone which
cannot be visited without special permission from the DFO in Pollachi.
With permits you can stay at the Grasshills Fishing Hut east of Valparai.
You need food and sleeping bags, and to make arrangements for porters, a
guide and a cook with the Forest Department. To get there, take the Trichur
road south from Pollachi through Valparai (c.40km) then turn left to the
Akkamalai Tea Estate (1500m, 20km from Valparai). There are buses from

Pollachi to Valparai and two or three a day from there to Akkamalai. From Akkamalai it is a 7km hike up through good shola to the grasslands above 1900m with a further 2–3km to the hut. Birdlife is largely similar to that at Rajamalai (Munnar), but Broad-tailed Grassbird** breeds in the marshy area in front of the hut, with birds singing in May. A late February visit failed to record any. Hairpin bend no.9 on the road from Pollachi to Valparai is a regular site for Nilgiri Tahr. The excellent Kadambarai Shola (1355m) has a quiet road through it from the 36th hairpin bend. Bus drivers will drop you off at its beginning.

The **Silent Valley NP** is superb rainforest on the Keralan side of the Western Ghats preserved for its plant and animal life. Visitors are not encouraged, but those who are not deterred by the lack of infrastructure may apply to the DFO at Palghat.

Munnar

The hill station of Munnar in the Cardamom Hills of southwest India is surrounded by picturesque plantations growing smoky-flavoured Keralese tea. The town is a base for visiting Rajamalai to see the restricted-range Grey-breasted Laughingthrush**, and Nilgiri Pipit**. Munnar is a good base for a half-day trip to Bodi Ghat on the eastern slopes of the Western Ghats to search out another little-known endemic, the Yellow-throated Bulbul**, which reaches the southwestern edge of its range there.

Map of Munnar

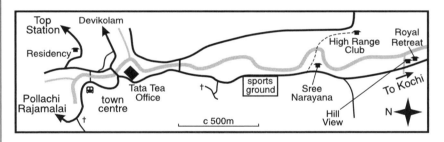

Location

Munnar usually forms the next link in a South India itinerary after Ooty and Top Slip (Anaimalai) and before Periyar. Although the town is only about 50km south of Top Slip, and even less from Parambikulam, thankfully there is no tarmac to disfigure the highest peaks of the Western Ghats and the route goes via Pollachi (116km) and Udumalpet (87km) from where buses and taxis are available. The journey by bus from Pollachi to Munnar takes about 5 hours. The town of Munnar is in Kerala and the state borderline with Tamil Nadu is crossed where the road begins to climb steadily up into the Cardamom Hills.

Accommodation

At 1520m Munnar is becoming popular as a hill resort, so the number of hotels is increasing. The best is probably the *Royal Retreat* (B)☎04865-30240, out of town on the road to Devikolam, Bodinayakanur and Kochi. The *Hill View* (B/C)☎04865-30241 next door is slightly less expensive but clean and comfortable. For those who like the old colonial style, the *High Range Club* (B/C) is the answer, though technically you have to be a member or guest. The *Residency* (B/C) ☎04865-30317 on Top Station Rd is more central with bigger rooms. The *Sree Narayana Lodge* (D), near the post office, and the *Ambat* (E), near the bus stand, are reasonable for the price.

If you want more time up in the hills, it is possible with permission to stay at a *Hut (Rest House)* on the Eravikulam Plateau. This involves a steep climb from the Vagavurrai Tea Estate taking sleeping bag, a guide/cook, porters and all your food. Contact the High Range Wildlife Protection Society through the head office of Tata Tea Ltd, near the main bridge in Munnar town. From the Hut at 2100m it is a fairly easy climb to Anaimudi, South India's highest peak at 2695m. There are few birds not also found at Rajamalai, but the beautiful surroundings are unspoilt.

Strategy   Grey-breasted Laughingthrush** and Nilgiri Pipit** are fairly easy to see at Rajamalai and a couple of hours there in the morning or afternoon may be enough. It might, however, pay to spend longer here in search of other endemics you could miss elsewhere.

Near Munnar itself you can sometimes see Nilgiri Wood Pigeon** at a small shola providing shade for a plantation of cardamom understorey. Take the main road towards Kochi (Cochin), past the Royal Retreat Hotel, and turn off left across a dam 2–3km from town. Follow this road to the right up the side of the valley above the main river. Check the first stream you cross for Malabar Whistling Thrush**, which occurs here, along vegetated parts of the main river and in the shola itself. A little further up on the left of the road is a small cave or tunnel used by Indian Swiftlets*. Brown-backed Needletail, Alpine and Fork-tailed Swifts, as well as the local *domicola* subspecies of Pacific Swallow, sometimes split as a separate South Indian/Sri Lankan endemic species under the name Hill Swallow, may fly over. Scrubby slopes may produce Nilgiri Pipit** and Grey-breasted Laughingthrush**, both easier at Rajamalai. The cardamom shola has interesting birds especially in the morning: White-cheeked Barbet**, Scarlet Minivet, Yellow-browed Bulbul*, Indian Scimitar Babbler*, Brown-breasted (W), Verditer (W) and Nilgiri** Flycatchers, Greenish and Western Crowned Warblers (W), Blue-capped Rock Thrush (W), Scaly Thrush, and Loten's Sunbird*. Scour the shola for Nilgiri Wood Pigeon** or scan for flying or roosting birds from a watchpoint past the shola before the village. Being rather nomadic there is no guarantee of seeing it here or at any other site, but time is not wasted as the hill above the shola can turn up almost any of the South Indian raptors.

Map of Cardamom Estate Shola Note orientation

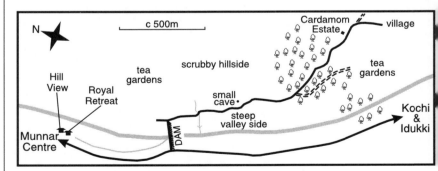

Rajamalai (Eravikulam NP)

The Eravikulam NP in the Cardamom Hills of the Western Ghats includes the highest mountains in South India, but was primarily set up to protect the endangered Nilgiri Tahr, a wild goat related to the Himalayan Tahr. The High Range, as it is also known, is home to several South Indian endemics with restricted ranges. The main stars are Grey-breasted Laughingthrush** and Nilgiri Pipit**, but there are also Painted Bush Quail**, Nilgiri and White-bellied Blue Flycatchers**, Tickell's Leaf Warbler, and

White-bellied Shortwing**. Rajamalai (Rajamalay, Rajamally) is the part most accessible to visitors.

Map of Rajamalai

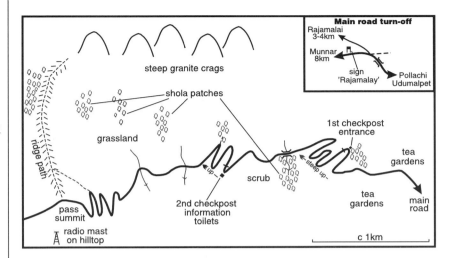

Location

Rajamalai is 12km from Munnar. The metalled road leading to it begins 8km down the main road from Munnar to Udumalpet. Take a taxi or auto-rickshaw and have it wait or pick you up at a pre-arranged time. The alternative is a bus dropping you at the turn off. Ask for Nyamakad Tea Estate if they do not understand that you want the National Park for which there is a large sign near the turn off. From the main road to the first checkpost is 3–4km, winding up through the tea gardens and emerging into open grassland with patches of scrub and shola. A fee must be paid at the checkpost.

Strategy

Visit at any time of year. If you have a vehicle, send it on to wait at the second checkpost 1¹/₂km further up the road, and walk from first checkpost (or do the reverse). It is usually easy to locate the vocal Grey-breasted Laughingthrushes** in patches of shola or scrub between the two check-posts. Nilgiri Pipits frequent open areas of grassland and scrub just below the upper checkpost and further up the road towards the summit. When flushed, they often sit on a low bush giving good views. The shola at the lower checkpost is productive.

Continue further on to explore higher patches of shola. A path leads up to the peaks on the right along the ridge from the highest point on the pass, just below the radio tower. Fire breaks can be good for Painted Bushquail** on the shorter grass at dawn and dusk, or on the side of the road.

Birds

Tickell's Leaf Warblers are fairly common in winter. The enigmatic Tytler's Leaf Warbler* has been reported though it is sometimes confused with Tickell's. The sholas have lesser numbers of Indian Scimitar Babbler*, Black-and-orange Flycatcher**, Nilgiri Flycatcher**, Large-billed Leaf Warbler (UW), White-bellied Shortwing**, Blue Rock Thrush (W), and Eurasian Blackbird. The latter is of interest as there are several endemic races in South India and Sri Lanka. Bonelli's and Black Eagles are fairly regular. Other species include White-cheeked Barbet**, Pacific (Hill) Swallow, Malabar Whistling Thrush**, Black-lored Tit and Velvet-fronted Nuthatch. Grey Junglefowl** and Nilgiri Wood Pigeon** have been seen below the first checkpost.

Other Wildlife

Nilgiri Tahr are tame and approachable at Rajamalai, often found close to the upper checkpost and high up on granite crags above. Nilgiri Langur are sometimes seen crossing open grassland from one shola to another. Elephants come up this high: they are not seen very often but leave evidence of their passing. The Dhole (Red Dog) roams the hills in packs but is wary of humans.

Bodi Ghat

The Yellow-throated Bulbul** is a little-known species confined to steep, scrubby hillsides with scattered trees in southern Andhra Pradesh, eastern Karnataka and northern Tamil Nadu, an area not covered by most South Indian birding itineraries. A detour from the main route between Munnar and Periyar, to the eastern slopes of the Western Ghats brings you to a site where the species is fairly common at the southwestern edge of its range.

Location

The route from Munnar to Periyar and that to the Bodi Ghat diverge after about 20km at Poopara (not shown on Nelles map) beyond Devikolam. Take the main road towards the temple town of Madurai in the plains of Tamil Nadu. This crosses the state border at Bodimettu (about 45km from Munnar, likewise not shown on Nelles map) at the top of the main ghat. The next town of significance is Bodi (Bodinayakanur), 26km from Bodimettu. The best area for the Yellow-throated Bulbul** is an 8km stretch between the towns (6km-14km from Bodimettu). Keep an eye on roadside milestones marking distances, though these may be difficult to read. Buses from Munnar to Bodi (and Madurai) take 3 hours or more to reach the bulbul site; 2 hours by car. The road is subject to landslides so enquire about its current state in Munnar beforehand.

Accommodation

The best accommodation is in Munnar, but there are basic lodges along the main road in Bodi. You may wish to carry on to Madurai, worth visiting for its fascinating temple. From there catch a direct bus to Periyar (5–6 hours).

Strategy

This is probably the best site for Yellow-throated Bulbul**, which is fairly easy to find except during the heat of mid-day. A day trip using buses from Munnar is not very practical. With your own transport, and making an early start, you can fit this in on your way to Periyar, or do it as a half-day trip. Otherwise, it is better to take a bus to Bodi, check into a lodge there and then get another bus or taxi back up the ghat towards Munnar. Get off at km20 and bird slowly down the road towards Bodi. Keep your taxi, catch a bus, or hitch a ride back to town.

Birds

Yellow-throated Bulbuls** tend to inhabit better vegetated gullies on the ghat but are not restricted to them. The hillside provides good bulbul habitat with White-browed* fairly common along with the ubiquitous Red-whiskered and Red-vented; Grey-headed and Black-crested (Ruby-throated) though present are uncommon. Spend more time at this site and continue further downhill if you have not yet seen Jungle Prinia*, and Blue-faced or Sirkeer Malkohas*. These are fairly widespread at lower altitudes in South India but nowhere common. The higher slopes of the ghat nearer to Bodimettu are better for White-cheeked and Crimson-fronted Barbets*, Pacific (Hill) Swallow, and Rufous Babbler**. Other species of note include Red Spurfowl* (U), Jungle Bush Quail*, Grey Junglefowl**, Indian Swiftlet*, Tawny-bellied*, Yellow-eyed and Yellow-billed* Babblers, and Purple-rumped and Loten's* Sunbirds.

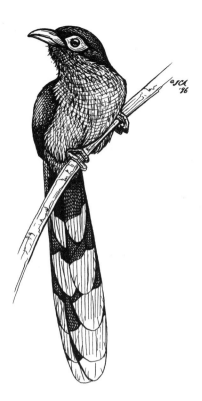

Blue-faced Malkoha

Other Sites   If you stay at Bodi, and want to have a morning's birding in a different area at the foot of the ghats, take a taxi to scrub, forest and plantations at **Karunkani** 20km to the northwest. Species include Malabar Parakeet**, Chestnut-headed Bee-eater, White-bellied Drongo*, Black-headed Cuckooshrike, Puff-throated Babbler and Indian Scimitar Babbler*.

Travelling between Top Slip and Munnar you pass through the **Chinnar WLS** on the Kerala side of the border between Udumalpet and Munnar. Good scrub, thorn forest and riverine habitat produces a few species such as Changeable Hawk Eagle, Green Imperial Pigeon, White-bellied Drongo*, White-bellied Minivet (U), Yellow-billed Babbler* and Thick-billed Warbler (W) which are less common at higher altitudes. Try the roadside or follow a track from the Keralan checkpost (the second of the two). The trees by the river sometimes hold Grizzled Giant Squirrel, a speciality of the sanctuary. Very basic accommodation is available, but you need your own supplies. Permission to stay should be sought from the DFO in Munnar.

Map of Chinnar

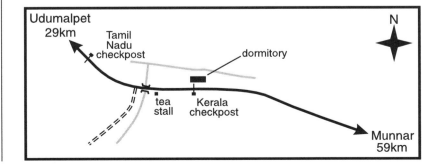

The 25km² **Salim Ali (Thattakad) BS** is situated near the foot of the Western Ghats. A visit involves a 12km detour northeast from Kotha-mangalam on the main road between Cochin and Munnar. Unfortunately, it is no longer possible to reach Munnar on the old road (shown on some maps) which passes directly through the sanctuary. The dense lowland forest and reservoir support a good variety of birds with over 260 species recorded. Grey-headed Fish Eagle, Red Spurfowl*, Grey Junglefowl**, Orange-breasted Green Pigeon, Malabar Grey Hornbill**, White-bellied Treepie** and Crimson-backed Sunbird** are among the commoner residents, while Black Baza, Nilgiri Wood Pigeon**, Spot-bellied Eagle Owl, Malabar Trogon*, Speckled Piculet, Grey-headed Bulbul**, Rufous Babbler** and Malabar Whistling Thrush** are reportedly not uncommon. Sri Lanka Frogmouth* and Broad-tailed Grassbird** are harder to find. Bay Owl and Pied Thrush* have also been seen. There are basic to mid-range hotels in Kothamangalam and a Rest House at Boothathankettu from where boat trips are available.

Periyar

The Periyar Sanctuary is the best-known reserve in Kerala and one of the most popular in India with its picturesque setting surrounding a lake in the Cardamom Hills. A good proportion of the Western Ghat endemics, together with excellent possibilities for viewing mammals and a well-developed tourist infrastructure make Periyar essential to any tour to this part of the Subcontinent.

The sanctuary covers an area of 777km² with an altitude range from 150m at the base of the Ghats to 2019m at the top of Vellimalai. Within this

Map of Periyar

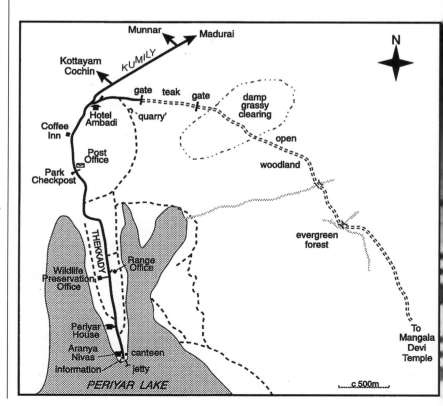

area is a patchwork of habitats, mostly moist evergreen and semi-evergreen forest, home to specialities such as Malabar Trogon*, White-bellied Treepie**, and Wynaad Laughingthrush**. The higher elevations in the core zone are largely grasslands with patches of shola. Here the avifauna is not so diverse, but the habitat is essential for species such as Nilgiri Flycatcher** and the endangered Broad-tailed Grassbird**. The lake itself lies at 870m and is the main tourist attraction. The dead trees protruding out of the water provide perches for Great Cormorants, Oriental Darters and the occasional Ashy Woodswallow. Overhead White-rumped Needletails* hawk for insects, now and then dwarfed by their Brown-backed relatives, and you may hear the whoosh of a Great Hornbill as it crosses the lake. You are bound to see elephants on the shore and sharp eyes are likely to discern many other mammals.

Location

Periyar is in the Idukki district on the eastern side of Kerala state where it borders on Tamil Nadu. The Sanctuary HQ and tourist zone are on the northern side of the lake at Thekkady 4km from the town of Kumily, which has prospered with increasing numbers of tourists. Most birders visit the Park as part of a South Indian itinerary, probably coming from Munnar or Bodinayakanur to the north by private vehicle or one of the infrequent buses (110km, 5 hours). Long distance buses arrive and depart from the bus stand in Kumily, though some terminate and start from Aranya Nivas within the Sanctuary and will stop on request at Periyar House. It is better to board a bus here for your onward journey to avoid the crush at Kumily.

From Periyar the route may continue towards the old Dutch port of Kochi (Cochin) 208km away (three buses daily, 6 hours) or Trivandrum with its beaches (258km, 8 hours). If you are heading this way a boat trip on the Kerala backwaters makes for relaxing birding. The boat from Kottayam (120km, six buses daily, 4 hours) to Allepey takes about 3 hours. The nearest railway station on the Keralese side is also at Kottayam. The airport at Cochin has flights to Bangalore (four times weekly), Mumbai/Bombay (daily), and Delhi and Goa (daily except Sundays).

The other possibility is to head inland towards the Tamil town of Madurai (hourly buses, 4 hours) en route to Point Calimere, Rameswaram (Gulf of Mannar) or Chennai (Madras) on the Coromandel coast. Madurai has daily flights to Chennai (Madras) as well as services to Bangalore, Mumbai, Coimbatore and Trichy. Trains and buses provide added connections.

If you stay in Kumily, you might use the shuttle bus which runs at elastic half-hourly intervals between the Kumily Bus Stand and the jetty at Thekkady. The first leaves Kumily at 08.00 and the last one back departs at 18.00. Bicycles can be hired in the village.

Accommodation

Within the Sanctuary are three choices of hotel all run by the KTDC all with their own restaurant. The exclusive *Lake Palace* (A) ☎ 04869-22023, beside the lake but away from the crowds (free shuttle ferry – last at 16.00), is a delightful place to stay, run as an annexe of the comfortable *Aranya Nivas* (B) ☎ 04869-22023 at the head of the Thekkady promontory near the boat jetty. The popular *Periyar House* (C) ☎ 04869-22026, nearly 1km back down the road to Kumily, has been up-graded. Bookings can be made, if far enough in advance, through any Kerala State Tourist Office. If arriving without a reservation, avoid weekends and public holidays and arrive early in the day before the rooms are taken. Facilities at Aranya Nivas include a post office open Monday to Saturday 10.00 to 14.00 and a bank open Monday to Friday 10.30 to 13.00 and Saturday 10.30 to 12.00. Near the shuttle bus stop is a snack bar open from 08.00 to 18.00.

There are lodges in Kumily, though prices have increased and it has become difficult to find good value accommodation. The *Spice Village* and *Taj Garden Retreat* are in the luxury category with the *Ambadi* a little more affordable. There is more choice among budget lodges: the *Holiday Home*, *Rani Lodge, Lake Queen Tourist Home, Italia Tourist Lodge* and *Mukumkal Tourist Home* compete for your custom. Nearly all hotels are on the main road. If you want a change from your hotel for the evening meal, try the Coffee Inn, on the right between Kumily and the Park entrance. The latter has value budget accommodation in its 'Wild Huts' (E).

It is a good idea to spend a few nights within the Sanctuary at one of the FRHs or watchtowers at Mullakuddi, Edapalayam, and Manakavala. A stay is normally limited to two nights at each and can be arranged at the Information Office at Thekkady. You need your own bedding and provisions but the chowkidar can cook for you.

Strategy   Periyar can be visited at any time. The southwest monsoon lasts from May to August while the weaker northeast monsoon brings some rain in the last quarter of the year, particularly in November. Temperatures at Thekkady vary from a winter cool of 15°C to 32°C in March and April, usually the best time for mammal viewing. As water becomes scarce animals are attracted to the main reservoir and leave the cover of the forest to come down to the lake to drink.

Entrance tickets (valid for four days) must be bought at the checkpost.

One of the absolute musts at Periyar is a boat ride on the lake. There are few waterfowl: Garganey is the only duck on the Sanctuary list. It is, however, a good way to see raptors, swifts, kingfishers and cormorants. The prime attraction are the mammals which come to the water or graze on open grass around its margins. There are boats of different sizes run by both the Forest Department and the KTDC. They leave the landing stage on the Thekkady peninsula at 07.00, 09.30, and 16.00. Bookings can be made at the kiosk on the steps down from Aranya Nivas to the jetty or at the Information Centre from 06.30 to 17.00. The larger boats often fill up with crowds of noisy locals, not very conducive to the animals remaining in view. If you can find a few like-minded individuals, you can hire one of the smaller craft which gives more flexibility, especially if you explain to the captain that you are interested in birds. He will usually go nearer to interesting sightings and turn off the engine if necessary. The boat rides normally last 2 hours. Morning can be best but there is a danger, especially in winter, of mist early in the day, so late afternoon may be preferable.

The primary attraction of Periyar is the rich birdlife of its forests. These can be explored on foot; arrange with the Information Centre for a guide. Some walks begin by taking a boat into the Sanctuary in order to walk back. The best is along the jeep track to the Mangala Devi Temple but it is necessary to obtain permission for this. Check with the Information Centre or the Wildlife Preservation Office between the checkpost and Periyar House. The walk begins along the side road next to the Hotel Ambadi in Kumily. Girishkumar T.P., a keen local birdwatcher who can offer help and advice, runs the Nature Shop opposite the Hotel Ambadi.

Bird the Thekkady peninsula. Try the hotel gardens and the main road, but take care along the paths through the jungle itself. Chestnut-winged Cuckoo (UW) is scarce but recorded more often here than any other part of the Reserve. You do not have to go far in the evening to find Oriental Scops Owl.

The FRH at Mullakuddi takes one hour to reach by boat and is in excellent forest with specialities including Jerdon's and Black Bazas (U),

Crested Goshawk, Changeable Hawk and Rufous-bellied Eagles, Great Hornbill, and White-bellied Woodpecker. The Rest House at Manakavala is outstanding for forest birds.

A difficult South Indian species to find is Painted Bush Quail**. Try the walk from the Lake Palace to Aranya Nivas through the species' grassland habitat.

It may be possible to organise treks lasting several days or a couple of weeks, such as along the course of the river Periyar. These need much preparation, equipment and permission from the authorities, which can mean a trip to the office of the Chief Wildlife Warden in Trivandrum 270km away. Elephant rides can be booked at the Information Centre. These do not penetrate far enough into the jungle from the visitor area to see much wildlife. If you can arrange a longer ride, it can be good for mammals, less so for birds.

On the north side of Kumily, along the main road towards Madurai into Tamil Nadu, about 1½km past the state border checkpost, past a Hindu shrine on the right and just short of the forest checkpost, a metalled road goes right towards **Forbay Dam**. This, and a grassy jeep track off it, go through nice habitat with excellent birds. Access is nominally restricted, but explain to the watchman what you are doing and do not take a camera.

Map of Forbay Dam

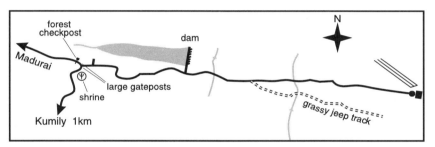

Birds

The avifauna around the lake is not particularly diverse, but you will see some species on the boat trip not found elsewhere at Periyar. There are still Oriental Darters resident though Great Cormorants are perhaps displacing them. Woolly-necked is the only stork at Periyar; a tall tree near the Aranya Nivas is a regular nesting site, sometimes shared with Brahminy Kites. Ospreys (W) usually perch on the dead trees around the reservoir, while Grey-headed Fish Eagles are uncommon. Black Baza (U), Changeable Hawk and Black Eagles are likely to be seen above the forested hillsides, the latter usually close above the canopy. You should see the three commoner kingfishers, but Stork-billed can take longer to discover. Ashy Woodswallows are usually present in small numbers. The large pigeons seen late in the afternoon are most likely to be Mountain Imperial though good views are needed to rule out Green Imperial and Nilgiri Wood Pigeon**. Malabar Grey* and Great are the only hornbills in the Sanctuary. Alpine and House Swifts (U), Indian Swiftlet, and Crested Treeswift are all resident.

On the Mangala Devi walk the road passes through teak which is good for Lesser Yellownape, and Heart-spotted and Streak-throated (U) Woodpeckers. Beyond the gate is a wet grassy clearing. Enter carefully as there are likely to be Wild Boar or Sambar feeding. The marshier parts have Pintail Snipe. The track continues through deciduous woodland where you may encounter a mixed-species feeding flock. Try and stay with such a flock as long as possible. It may consist of Black-rumped Flamebacks,

Greater Racket-tailed, Ashy and Bronzed Drongos, Scarlet and Small Minivets, White-bellied Treepies**, Yellow-browed Bulbuls* and Velvet-fronted Nuthatches. As many as 20 species have been recorded in a single party. The route continues through evergreen forest, worth more than one transect for specialities such as Brown Fish Owl, Malabar Trogon*, Rufous and White-bellied (U) Woodpeckers, Indian Scimitar Babbler*, Dark-fronted* and Rufous** Babblers, Crimson-backed Sunbird** and Little Spiderhunter. The star attraction is the Wynaad Laughingthrush**, for which this is one of the best sites in the country. Nowhere common, it is found in flocks of 20-30 birds turning over leaf litter in bamboo and dense moist undergrowth.

On the Thekkady promontory Grey Junglefowl**, Mountain Imperial Pigeon, Blue-winged Parakeet**, Drongo Cuckoo (R), Chestnut-headed Bee-eater, Malabar Grey Hornbill**, White-cheeked** and Crimson-fronted* Barbets, Indian Pitta* (W), Yellow-browed Bulbul*, Puff-throated Babbler, Brown-breasted (W), Red-breasted (W), Rusty-tailed (W) and White-bellied Blue** Flycatchers, Orange-headed Thrush and Loten's Sunbird* may be of interest. The path from the Mangala Devi road past the small 'quarry' back to Thekkady is good for Red Spurfowl**.

Birds on the dam road are Red Spurfowl*, Grey Junglefowl**, Pompadour Green Pigeon, Emerald Dove, Chestnut-winged (UW) and Banded Bay Cuckoos, Oriental Scops and Brown Hawk Owls, Indian Nightjar, Chestnut-headed Bee-eater, Malabar Grey** and Great Hornbills, Crimson-throated Barbet*, Indian Pitta* (W), White-bellied Treepie**, Indian Scimitar Babbler*, Tawny-bellied (U) and Dark-fronted Babblers*, Brown-breasted* (U), Rusty-tailed and Blue-throated (U) Flycatchers (W), Indian Blue Robin (W), Malabar Whistling Thrush**, Scaly Thrush (UW) and Forest Wagtail (W).

Other species of the tourist zone include Oriental Honey-buzzard, Crested Goshawk (U), Besra (U), Mountain Hawk Eagle (R), Bonelli's (R), Booted (UW) and Crested Serpent Eagles, Peregrine Falcon (R), Oriental Hobby (RW), Jungle Bush Quail* (R), Yellow-footed Green Pigeon (R), Plum-headed Parakeet*, Vernal Hanging Parrot, Common Hawk Cuckoo, Indian (U) and Grey-bellied* (R) Cuckoos, Sirkeer Malkoha* (R), Lesser Coucal (U), Collared Scops Owl, Spot-bellied Eagle Owl (R), Brown Fish Owl, Jungle Owlet, Sri Lanka Frogmouth* (R), Great Eared, Grey and Savanna Nightjars, Common and Greater Flamebacks, Brown-capped Pygmy Woodpecker*, Dusky Crag Martin (U), Red-rumped Swallow (W), Brown Shrike (W), Eurasian Golden (W), Black-naped (RW) and Black-hooded Orioles, Chestnut-tailed and Rosy (RW) Starlings, Jungle and Hill Mynas, Rufous Treepie, Bar-winged Flycatcher-shrike, Large Woodshrike, Large Cuckooshrike, Golden-fronted and Blue-winged (U) Leafbirds, Asian Fairy Bluebird, Grey-headed** (U) and Black-crested Bulbuls, Brown-cheeked Fulvetta, Asian Brown, Tickell's Blue and Verditer (RW) Flycatchers, Grey-headed Canary Flycatcher, White-browed Fantail, Asian Paradise-flycatcher (W), Black-naped Monarch, Zitting Cisticola, Grey-breasted, Plain and Ashy* Prinias, Thick-billed, Clamorous Reed (U), Blyth's Reed, Tickell's Leaf (R), Large-billed Leaf, Greenish and Western Crowned Warblers (W), Indian Blue Robin (W), Blue-capped Rock Thrush (UW), Eurasian Blackbird (U), Black-lored Tit* (U), Richard's (UW), Paddyfield and Long-billed (R) Pipits, White-browed Wagtail*, Thick-billed (U), Pale-billed (R) and Plain Flowerpeckers, Purple-rumped Sunbird, Oriental White-Eye, and White-rumped, Black-throated* and Black-headed Munias(U). Ashy Minivet and Yellow-rumped Flycatcher are two interesting vagrants recorded from Periyar in winter.

Other Wildlife   Periyar is a Tiger Reserve under Project Tiger, but the chance of seeing one is small. Current opinion estimates the Tiger population at around 40, but they are nocturnal, very shy and steer clear of humans.

Most boat trips produce Wild Boar, Sambar and Elephant. Otter can sometimes be spotted. The Dhole, or Red Dogs, often come onto the grass, but are not guaranteed. The Gaur, or Bison as they are often called, are shy and retreat into the forest, but can often be seen with binoculars.

The handsome Nilgiri Langur are not difficult around Thekkady and you should see the Malabar Giant Squirrel on the Mangala Devi trail. Dusky Striped Squirrel, a relative of the ubiquitous Palm Squirrels, inhabits the forests. Muntjac, or Barking Deer, are not uncommon, but keep to the forest and are not seen as frequently as the Sambar. At dusk, or after dark, you may see a Flying Squirrel. Both Giant and Travancore occur.

Leopard, Jungle Cat, Sloth Bear, Lion-tailed and Bonnet Macaques, Grey Langur, Indian Mouse Deer, Indian Hare and Porcupine are in the Sanctuary. Look out for the unusual Draco, or Flying Lizard, and Golden Tree, or Flying Snake, neither of which actually fly, but glide through the air in the manner of a Flying Squirrel . . . and then there is also the Malabar Flying Frog.

Chennai (Madras)

Chennai, the capital of Tamil Nadu (no longer using its old name of Madras), is one of the largest and most populous cities in India, yet tucked away within the city are areas of wilderness where it is possible to enjoy peaceful birding. Wader enthusiasts should try the estuary of the River Adyar whilst Guindy National Park offers good acacia forest. The Vedanthangal Bird Sanctuary, India's oldest protected area with colonies of nesting waterfowl is 80km southwest and Lake Pulicat an hour or two's drive to the north.

Location   Chennai is on the Coromandel coast of southeast India at the northern edge of Tamil Nadu. It has international and domestic airports with regular flights to most important Indian destinations, London, Frankfurt, Kuala Lumpur, Singapore, Colombo, and Port Blair in the Andaman Islands. Chennai can be reached by rail from New Delhi in two nights and a day by the *Tamil Nadu Express* or the slightly slower *G.T. Express*. The *Dadar-Madras Chennai Express* covers the distance from Mumbai (Bombay) in about 24 hours.

Accommodation   There is a wide range of hotels near Egmore Station (southbound trains). The *New Woodlands Hotel* (C) ☎ 044-8273111 and *Hotel Savera* (A) ☎ 044-8274700, Fax 8273475, in Mylapore are closer to the main birding sites, in the south of the city.

Guindy

Guindy NP is a 2.7km² walled patch of wilderness in a built up residential area of Chennai. It consists mainly of acacia forest, scrub and open grass with a small population of Blackbuck. Guindy (pronounced Gindy) can turn up interesting birds and is a worthwhile place if you have a few spare hours.

Location   The park is at the southern edge of Chennai adjacent to the Snake Park, Deer Park and Children's Zoo, most easily reached by taxi or auto-rickshaw. The entrance is just past Raj Bhavan (the residence of the Tamil

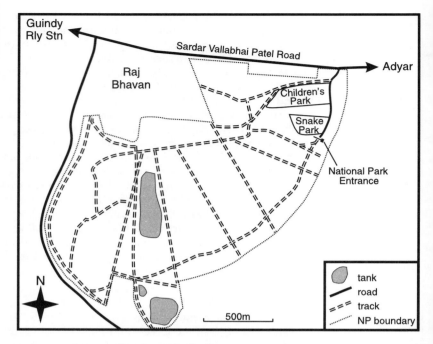

Map of Guindy
National Park

Nadu Governor) on Sardar Vallabai Patel Rd. There is a suburban train
from Egmore Station to Guindy Station which is about 3km from the park.
Buses: 21E runs from Parry's Corner, or numbers 5 and 5A from Mount Rd
opposite the Anna Rd post office.

Strategy A network of dirt roads can be explored on foot or by bicycle. A small fee
is payable at the entrance if the ticket office is open. If you are interested in
reptiles, a visit to the neighbouring Snake Park is a must. It is open daily
throughout the year from 09.00 to 17.30.

Birds Malayan Night Heron (UW), Black Baza (U), Brahminy Kite, Short-toed
Snake Eagle, Booted Eagle (W), Grey Francolin, Eurasian Thick-knee,
Yellow-wattled Lapwing*, Chestnut-winged (RW), Pied, Banded Bay,
Plaintive and Common Hawk Cuckoos, Blue-faced Malkoha*, Barn Owl,
Asian Palm Swift, Blue-tailed Bee-eater, Indian Pitta (W), Ashy-crowned
Sparrow Lark*, Bay-backed Shrike, White-bellied Drongo*, Ashy
Woodswallow, Chestnut-tailed and Brahminy Starlings, Common and
Large Woodshrikes, Black-headed Cuckooshrike, White-browed Bulbul*,
Yellow-eyed and Yellow-billed* Babblers, Asian Brown (W), Brown-
breasted (UW), Blue-throated (UW), Tickell's and Asian Paradise
Flycatchers, Blyth's Reed and Greenish Warblers (W), Orange-headed
Thrush, Forest Wagtail (W), and Purple-rumped, Purple and Loten's*
Sunbirds. Occasionally rarities such as Long-legged Buzzard, Eyebrowed
Thrush and Ashy Minivet have been recorded at Guindy, the latter almost
regular in winter.

Other Wildlife The mammals are relatively tame. Spotted Deer are found throughout
the park but Blackbuck, the speciality, are usually in the open areas at the
far side of the park. Bonnet Macaque, Jackal, Black-naped Hare, and
Common Grey Mongoose are frequent. Small Indian Civet and Indian
Pangolin occur.

Theosophical Society Gardens and Adyar Estuary

The Theosophical Society HQ's grounds harbour commoner garden species as well as some found at Guindy. The river here forms a brackish estuary with mud and sand banks, interesting for waders and seabirds. Both areas have potential for rare species in winter and on passage.

Map of
Theosophical
Society Gardens and
Adyar Estuary

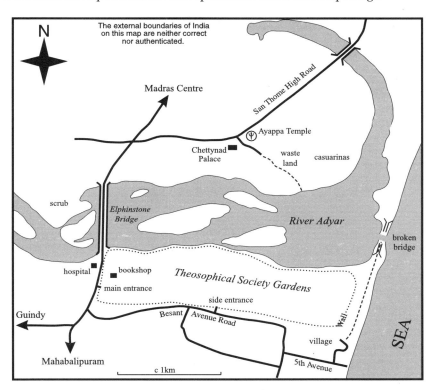

Location

The entrance to the Theosophical Society Gardens is south of the Elphinstone Bridge over the river Adyar 2km east of Guindy. From the centre of Chennai take bus no.5 heading south on Mount Rd (also known as Anna Salai). The estuary is reached from the northern side on a side road from the San Thome High Rd (see map) and the track at the end of it across waste ground. Coming by taxi or auto-rickshaw, ask for the Ayappa Temple on San Thome High Rd.

Strategy

Start in the early morning on the northern side of the estuary. The waste ground is good for Yellow-wattled Lapwing*, larks, wagtails, and pipits including Blyth's (W). Go round to the Elphinstone Bridge to scan for waders including Swinhoe's Snipe (W). Continue by going into the Theosophical Society Gardens, just south of the bridge, or carry on to view the estuary from the other side. The gardens are open from 08.30 to 10.00 and 14.00 to 16.00 except on Sundays and holidays. The mangrove islands in the estuary can be seen from the northern side of the Gardens and can repay careful scanning. To reach the mouth of the estuary, go along Besant Avenue Rd, parallel to the southern side of the Gardens, until you come to 5th Avenue; turn left then left again (north) along the last lane before the sea shore. This takes you through a village and onto a track which runs north parallel to the shore as far as a collapsed bridge.

Birds   The Gardens hold similar species to those at Guindy. The estuary list includes Western Reef Egret, Brahminy Kite, White-bellied Sea Eagle, Pacific Golden, Greater and Lesser Sand Plovers (W), Eurasian Curlew (W), Black-tailed Godwit (W), Marsh Sandpiper (W), Swinhoe's Snipe (W), Terek, Curlew and Broad-billed Sandpipers (W), Sanderling (W), Little Stint (W), Brown-headed Gull (W), and Whiskered and Gull-billed Terns (W). Crab-plover (W) has been recorded. Flamingos sometimes use the estuary on migration. Open areas around the estuary have Eurasian Thick-knee (U), Jerdon's Bushlark*, Ashy-crowned Sparrow Lark*, White-browed Wagtail*, and Richard's (W) and Paddyfield Pipits.

Other Wildlife   Many interesting reptiles and amphibians include Cobra, Coral Snake, Checkered Keelback, Common Sand Boa, and Saw-scaled Viper. Olive Ridley Turtles nest near the mouth of the estuary and along the Coromandel coast between January and March. The Sea Turtle Conservation Network in Chennai (☎044-4914607) organises the removal of eggs to a safe site for hatching. Visitors are welcome to help.

Other Sites   The 500ha **Anna Zoological Park** is one of the biggest in South Asia. It is in reserved forest at Vandalur, 32km southwest of Chennai Centre and attempts to provide a natural setting for the animals, retaining good habitat for wild birds including Jungle Prinia*. It can be reached by buses 18N and 18V or by train to Vandalur station. It is open daily except Tuesdays from 08.00 to 17.00 and you can hire bicycles to get around. The **Simpson Estate** in Chennai (Madras) has breeding Indian and Little Cormorants, egrets and Black-crowned Night Heron. **Gingee Fort**, 143km south of Chennai, is good for Painted Spurfowl**, the resident Shahin race of Peregrine Falcon, Eurasian (Rock) Eagle Owl, and Yellow-throated Bulbul**, the latter an uncommon bird of scrubby hillsides. At **Kelambakkam,** just south of Chennai, there is a roosting site for harriers.

Vedanthangal

The heronry and waterfowl sanctuary at the edge of Vedanthangal boast the longest history of any reserve in India, given legal protection as long ago as 1798. The breeding season lasts from October/November to March with a peak around December and January when up to 30,000 birds of 15 species nest here. The bird sanctuary covers an area of about 2km² centred on a small tank (30ha) out of which rise *Barringtonia* trees where the cormorants, storks, herons and ibises nest. More than 110 species have been recorded in the sanctuary and interesting land birds can be found in surrounding trees, fields and scrub.

Location   Vedanthangal is 85km southwest of Chennai (Madras) and can be visited in a day trip by private transport or by bus or train to Chengalpattu (35km) and a bus or taxi from there. Buses run from Tambaram. The nearest railway station is at Karunghuzhi 11km away, but there is no public transport between it and the sanctuary. There is a less well-known sanctuary with similar species at **Karikili** just 8km from Vedanthangal.

Accommodation   At a *FRH* at Vedanthangal overnight stays are allowed if booked previously in Chennai (Madras). Meals can be provided if booked beforehand or arranged immediately on arrival. Contact the Wildlife Warden, Number 50, IVth Main Rd, Gandhi Nagar, Chennai (Madras) 600 020 ☎044-413947.

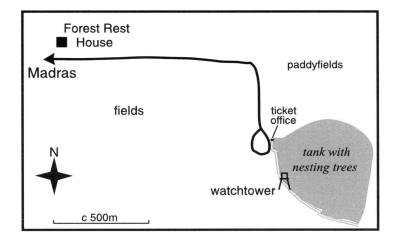

Strategy   The heronry can be viewed from an embankment on the western side of the tank. A viewing tower allows a greater area to be surveyed. Most nesting birds can be seen at any time of the day so it may be preferable to spend the early morning exploring nearby. Avoid weekends and holidays, if possible: Vedanthangal is popular with people from Chennai.

Birds   The breeding species are Great, Indian and Little Cormorants, Oriental Darter, Grey Heron, Indian Pond Heron, Cattle, Great White, Intermediate and Little Egrets, Black-crowned Night Heron, Asian Openbill, Black-headed Ibis, and Eurasian Spoonbill. Spot-billed Pelicans breed in some years. Glossy Ibis has bred. In winter and during migration commoner migrant ducks and waders frequent the tank. Birds of prey in the area include Brahminy Kite, Booted (W) and Short-toed Snake Eagles, Pallid, Montagu's and Eurasian Marsh Harriers (W), and Peregrine Falcon (W).

In and around the sanctuary commoner Indian species can be found as well as Yellow-wattled Lapwing*, Eurasian Thick-knee, Indian Courser*, Chestnut-winged, Pied, Grey-bellied* and Common Hawk Cuckoos, Blue-faced Malkoha* (U), Indian Nightjar, Blue-tailed Bee-eater, Indian Pitta*, Indian Bushlark*, Loten's Sunbird*, Black-headed Cuckooshrike, White-browed Bulbul*, Paddyfield, Richard's and Blyth's Pipits (W), White-browed Wagtail* and Streaked Weaver.

Point Calimere

This vast area of tidal lagoons, salt pans, mud-flats, pools, grasslands, and thorn forest on the Coromandel Coast of South India is home to huge numbers of wintering waders and wildfowl and is on a major flyway for birds wintering in Sri Lanka. Some 25km² of the area are a Wildlife Sanctuary and the Ramsar Convention considers a far larger area of International Importance. The bird list is over 260. During migration, interesting passerines such as Indian Pitta* and Brown-breasted Flycatcher pass through. Two subcontinental endemics, Blue-faced Malkoha* and White-browed Bulbul*, are fairly common and Pied Cuckoo is frequent in winter. Asian Dowitcher and Spoon-billed Sandpiper are scarce winter visitors. The area regularly turns up Indian rarities.

Location   Pt. Calimere, also known as **Kodikkarai**, is on the east coast of India 350km south of Chennai (Madras). It is best reached either via Thanjavur

Map of
Point Calimere

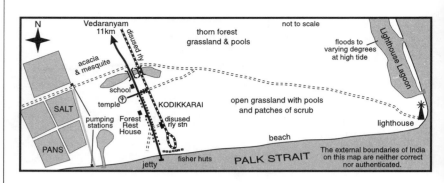

(90km), from where there are direct buses at approximately hourly intervals taking about 4 hours to the nearby town of Vedaranyam (11km), or via Nagapattinam (52km – 2 hours by bus). From Vedaranyam buses take 25 minutes to the village of Kodikkarai inside the sanctuary. The buses stop outside the FRH and terminate a little further down the road. The timetable is rather irregular; enquire at the bus stand in Vedaranyam about timings. During the daytime private minibuses ply the route Vedaranyam-Calimere usually leaving ten minutes or so before the state buses, but they do not go from the bus station itself (see map). One early morning bus goes directly from Calimere to Thanjavur. From Vedaranyam there are buses to Tiruchirappalli, (Trichy – 145km). There is a direct bus between Chennai (Madras) and Vedaranyam. The night bus back to Chennai (Madras) leaves at 20.30 and takes 11 hours. Taxis are available at the taxi stand in Vedaranyam.

Accommodation

There is an extremely basic *FRH*, known as *Poonarai Illam* (Flamingo House), at Kodikkarai where water and electricity are erratic. It is conveniently located if you do not have transport, but needs to be booked in advance with the Wildlife Warden, Point Calimere Wildlife Sanctuary, Kadampadi, Nagapattinam 611 001 (☎2349) about 45km north of Calimere. You might be lucky if you just turn up. Food can be arranged at the Rest House but cannot be relied on. A tea stall next door offers simple meals at breakfast and lunch-time, but only snacks in the evening. Check exact timings as there is nothing otherwise. There are shops where you can buy cold drinks and biscuits. Bicycles are available for hire in Kodikkarai. A checklist of the birds of Point Calimere is available at Poonarai Illam.

There are basic hotels in Vedaranyam. The best is probably the *Thevar Lodge* (E), 40 North Main St, almost opposite the bus stand. The rooms are very simple but clean with attached bathroom. There are restaurants in Vedaranyam where the menu is less restricted than at Calimere.

Strategy

In order to explore the different habitats a stay of several days is recommended. Pt. Calimere can be visited at any time but the peak months for waders and waterfowl are December and January. The main migration is in October/November and February/March. The northeast monsoon brings rain from October to December/January, mostly as a short heavy daily downpour. Resident waders breed in April and May. The hot summer months with daytime temperatures in the 30°sC bring winds up to 60km/h which also make birding difficult. During winter temperatures are usually in the 20°sC. At any time protection against the sun should be worn, as there is little shade.

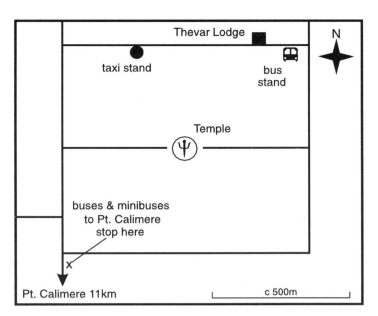

Map of Vedaranyam

In recent years a BNHS ringing project has been curtailed due to problems with funding. Local enquiries will reveal whether there is any ringing in progress. The trappers catch passerines in the early morning and waders in the evening and at night.

The wetlands, including the so-called Great (Vedaranyam) Swamp, extend for 50km to the west of Pt. Calimere. Some can be accessed from the road west from Vedaranyam to Muthupet and Adirampattinam if you have a car. There is an area of degraded mangrove at the western end of the swamp accessible by boat from Muthupet as well as from Calimere.

From Calimere most important habitats can be reached on foot. A couple of days can be spent exploring the lagoons, salt pans and mud to the west for Spot-billed Pelican, both flamingos (W), and waders, gulls, and terns. Walk north through the village, cross a bridge then take the track to the left to a maze of tracks along bunds between the lagoons. The same area can be reached by heading west along the beach and wading across a river mouth. It is best to stick to the bunds as a thin dry crust only covers soft ooze. A telescope is a necessity as birds often do not allow a close approach.

A day or two can be spent in the lighthouse area at the southeast point of Calimere searching scrub for land birds, and grasslands and dry areas for Yellow-wattled Lapwing*. A permit (small fee) should be obtained from the Rest House before entering the Sanctuary, to the east of Kodikkarai. The beach can turn up interesting waders and seabirds. Caspian Plover, Asian Dowitcher, and Spoon-billed Sandpiper have all been seen between the village and the lighthouse. The latter species turns up in most winters with the majority of records from the Lighthouse Lagoon about 8km from the village, but it has been observed on the seashore and on dry mudflats west of Kodikkarai. The beach north of the lighthouse is the most likely area for Crab-plover although these are scarce. The fishermen might take you out in one of their boats.

The area northeast of Kodikkarai is thorn forest and scrub interspersed with pools which dry out as the season progresses. White-browed Bulbuls* are quite common but shy. It is easy to lose your way as many trails are animal tracks that peter out in impassable scrub. A guide can be useful and may be arranged with the Forest Department at the Rest House. Blue-faced Malkoha* and Pied Cuckoo can often be found in the thorn scrub on the eastern side of the village.

Birds   Other birds: Oriental Darter (U), Little Heron, Western Reef Egret (W), Black Bittern (R), Painted Stork, Black-headed Ibis, Eurasian Spoonbill, Bar-headed Goose (W), Spot-billed Duck (W), Crested Honey-buzzard, Brahminy Kite, Booted Eagle (W), White-bellied Sea Eagle, Pallid, Montagu's and Eurasian Marsh Harriers (W), Short-toed Snake Eagle (U), Osprey (W), Peregrine (W) and Red-necked (RW) Falcons, Jungle Bush Quail*, Barred Buttonquail, Slaty-breasted Rail (UW), Slaty-legged Crake (P), Watercock (P), Great Thick-knee, Small Pratincole (P), Pacific Golden (W), Grey (W), Caspian (R), Little Ringed and Kentish Plovers, Greater and Lesser Sand Plovers (W), Whimbrel (W), Eurasian Curlew (W), Black- and Bar-tailed Godwits (W), Spotted and Common Redshanks (W), Greenshank (W), Marsh, Green, Wood, Terek, Curlew and Broad-billed Sandpipers (W), Ruddy Turnstone (W), Pintail, Swinhoe's and Common Snipes (UW), Red and Great Knots (RW), Little, Temminck's, Long-toed (U) and Red-necked (R) Stints (W), Ruff (W), Red-necked Phalarope (UW), Heuglin's, Pallas's, Brown-headed and Slender-billed (U) Gulls (W), Whiskered (W), White-winged (Black) (W), Gull-billed (W), Caspian (W), Common (UW), Roseate (RW), Little (B), Large Crested (RW), Lesser Crested (RW) and Sandwich (RW) Terns, Chestnut-winged (U), Common Hawk, Indian, Grey-bellied* (R) and Plaintive Cuckoos (W), Grey and Indian Nightjars (UW), Blue-tailed Bee-eater, Eurasian Wryneck (UP), Indian Bushlark*, Ashy-crowned Sparrow Lark*, Oriental Skylark, Ashy Woodswallow, Bay-backed and Brown (W) Shrikes, White-bellied Drongo* (UW), Chestnut-tailed, Brahminy and Rosy (W) Starlings, Black-headed Cuckooshrike, White-browed Bulbul*, Yellow-billed Babbler*, Asian Brown, Brown-breasted and Blue-throated Flycatchers (P), Asian Paradise-flycatcher (W), Thick-billed (W), Blyth's Reed (W), Paddyfield (UW), Booted (W), Large-billed (P) and Greenish Warblers (W), Pied and Orange-headed Thrushes (P), Richard's (W), Paddyfield and Blyth's (UW) Pipits, White-browed Wagtail*, Pale-billed Flowerpecker, Purple-rumped, Loten's* (U) Sunbird, Chestnut-shouldered Petronia, Indian Silverbill, and Black-headed Munia (U). Among the more intriguing rarities recorded are Great Frigatebird, Black Baza, Pied Harrier, Sooty Tern, Lesser Noddy, Oriental Dwarf Kingfisher, Kashmir Flycatcher*, Broad-tailed Grassbird* and Siberian Rubythroat.

Other Wildlife   The number of Blackbuck at Calimere is estimated at 600 and they are common on open areas between Kodikkarai and the lighthouse. This is a good area for most other mammals of the Sanctuary such as Jackal, Wild Boar, Black-naped Hare, Indian Gerbil, and Common Indian Mongoose. Bonnet Macaques and Chital are both introduced and now established in the Sanctuary. Flying Foxes and Short-nosed Fruit Bats are resident. Dolphins are occasionally encountered in the larger lagoons farther to the west and the Dugong or Sea Cow is said to be fairly frequent.

On the beach you can find many different kinds of seashells, Tiger Beetles, as well as Ghost and other kinds of crabs. Olive Ridley Turtle nests in small numbers. Several species of sea snake are found around the coast and should be treated with extreme caution as some are very poisonous although not usually aggressive. Have a look in the fishermen's baskets to see what fish they have caught.

Gulf of Mannar

This bay in the southeasternmost part of India is important for wintering waders and for birds migrating to and from Sri Lanka. The two countries are almost joined together here by promontories either side of the bay with a string of islands, islets and sand banks known as Adam's Bridge between the two. The bay is shallow and 20 or so islands off the southern coast are surrounded by extensive mud-flats at low tide. The largest island is **Rameshwaram Island** joined to the mainland by a main road and railway bridge. The eastern end of this island is a long sandy headland with lagoons open to the sea on its northern side. The most important for birds is **Dhanushkodi Lagoon** at the eastern end of the island. Smaller islands off the coast are good for waders with some, such as Crab-plover and Great Knot, that are rare at sites further north. The major part of the gulf is a Marine NP and Biosphere Reserve, partly to protect the Dugong or Sea Cow, of which a rapidly diminishing population subsists on sea grasses in the shallower waters of the bay.

Map of Gulf of Mannar

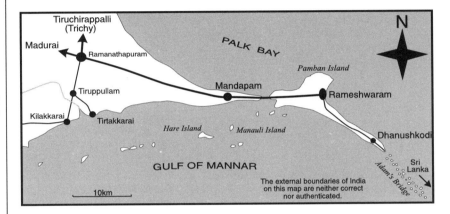

Location

Rameshwaram is an important religious site and well-connected by bus and train to the mainland. It is approximately 650km south of Chennai (Madras) and 160km southwest of Madurai. From Chennai there are two express trains daily, the Sethu Express and the Rameswaram Express (15–16 hours). The single daily Rameswaram-Coimbatore Passenger train takes about 6 hours to Madurai and 12 hours to Coimbatore, both of which are fairly convenient starting points for exploring the Western Ghats. To Madurai it is quicker (4 hours), and probably more comfortable, to take one of several daily buses from the main bus station about 2km west of the town. Local buses run regularly into town.

Accommodation

Because of Rameshwaram's importance as a pilgrimage centre there are quite a number of hotels, mainly in the lower price categories. *Santhana Lodge* (E) on South Car Street and *Santhiya Lodge* (E) are among the better ones. The *Hotel Maharaja* (C/D) on Middle St, ☎04573-21271 is more up-market and centrally located near the temple of Ramanathaswamy. The state government run *Hotel Tamil Nadu* (C/D/E) ☎04573-21227 has some of the cheapest beds in town as well as clean rooms both with and without air-conditioning. It is located on the shore, with rooms facing the sea, at the northeastern end of town and has both vegetarian and non-vegetarian restaurants. There is a branch of the *Hotel Tamil Nadu* at Mandapam with a few rooms and a dormitory. Sometimes it is possible to stay in one of the basic rooms at the *Central Marine Fisheries Research Institute* (CMFRI) at Mandapam Camp.

Strategy   Since most gulls and waders are winter visitors a birding trip to this area is more rewarding between December and early February. A day can be spent exploring Dhanushkodi Lagoon at the eastern end of Rameshwaram Island. The first bus leaves from the Ramanathaswamy Temple at 07.30 and goes as far as the fishing village of Dhanushkodi. From here a truck-bus goes the final 3km to the end of the headland from where you can work back along the lagoon with the sun behind you. Bicycles can be hired in Rameshwaram, but it takes considerably longer to reach the best birding area. Sea-watching from the end of the headland could be productive. Tea-shops may have snacks at Dhanushkodi, but it is best to bring water and food with you.

To visit the Marine NP itself, you should first get permission in Chennai (Madras) from the Chief Wildlife Warden of Tamil Nadu, Number 50, IVth Main Rd, Gandhi Nagar, Chennai 600 020 ☎044 – 2351778. The most interesting of the islands in the gulf are Manali and Hare Islands. To reach these, make prior arrangements with the office of the Wildlife Warden in Ramanathapuram or persuade the local fishermen at the village of Vedalai, southwest of Mandapam, to take you across by boat. Mandapam is the first town on the mainland, reached from Rameshwaram by bus or taxi. To save time it is best to hire a boat with an engine. The boats cannot usually navigate shallow waters around the islands, so you have to wade knee-deep to the shore. At low tide the waders are spread out on the mudflats. It is necessary to spend a few hours on one of the islands in order to see most of the birds whose whereabouts depends on the tide. Check the freshwater pool in the centre of the island too. There are some fisherman's huts (probably illegal) on the islands, but take water and food for the day.

Birds   At Dhanushkodi: Western Reef Egret, Greater Flamingo (W), Brahminy Kite, White-bellied Sea Eagle, Great Thick-knee (B), Grey (W), Greater Sand (W), Lesser Sand (W), Kentish (B) and Pacific Golden (W) Plovers, Eurasian Curlew (W), Bar-tailed Godwit (W), Red Knot (RW), Great Knot (W), Sanderling (UW) and other waders, Heuglin's, Brown-headed and Black-headed Gulls (W), and Whiskered (W), Black (RW), Gull-billed (W), Caspian (W), Common (W), Little (B), Lesser Crested (B) and Sandwich (UW) Terns.

On Manali and Hare Islands: Spot-billed Pelican (R), Eurasian Oyster-catcher (W), Crab-plover (W), Whimbrel (W), Terek Sandpiper (W), Ruddy Turnstone (W), Little Stint (W), Curlew Sandpiper (W) and most of the species that can be found at Dhanushkodi. Black Bittern, White-tailed Tropi-cbird, Brown Skua and Brown Noddy have also been recorded in the area.

Other Wildlife   The Dugong, or Sea Cow, an unusual sea mammal, appears to be in decline. The best chance of seeing one is on the boat ride to and from the islands.

Pulicat Lake

Pulicat Lake is a large brackish lagoon open to the sea, about 720km^2 but varying according to the season with only the southern half permanent. The northern part dries up after the monsoon, making the mud-flats all the more attractive for birds. The avifauna, with resident and wintering waterfowl, is similar to that of the better-known Chilka Lake further north in Orissa.

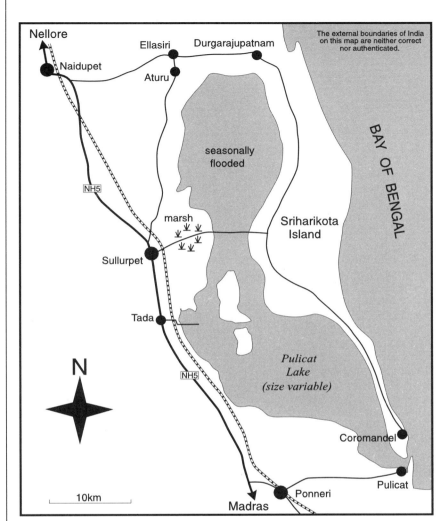

Map of Pulicat Lake

Location

Pulicat Lake is on the southeast coast of India 50km north of Chennai (Madras). The greater part is in the State of Andhra Pradesh with a smaller southern portion belonging to Tamil Nadu. Access is from the main road between Chennai and Nellore via a small road signposted at Tada, and via the road from Sullurpet to Sriharikota which crosses the marshes and lake. The regular Chennai to Nellore buses can drop you off at either place. The village of Pulicat itself is at the southernmost tip of the lagoon where it connects with the open sea and can be reached by taking a bus from Parry's Corner in Chennai to Ennur (Ennore) on the coast and a boat from there.

Accommodation

There is a *FRH* at Pulicat and a *PWD Bungalow* at Ponneri, but the site can be visited in a day trip from Chennai by car.

Strategy

The best time to visit is between November and March, although towards the end of this period the northern part may be dry. It can be a difficult area to cover without transport. There are good views over the marshes and mudflats on the road between Sullurpet and Sriharikota but a telescope is useful. Be careful near the latter location as it is a Space

Research Centre. A good way to explore the lake is by hiring a boat for the day at Tada. The deeper parts at the southern end of the lake harbour fewer birds.

Birds

Spot-billed Pelican, Indian and Little Cormorants, herons, egrets, Painted Stork, Asian Openbill, Black-headed Ibis, Spoonbill, Bar-headed Goose (W), ducks, and waders including Greater Painted-snipe. Up to 10,000 Greater Flamingo have been recorded in winter with the greatest numbers around the islands of Vendadu and Irukkam in the Andhra Pradesh part of the sanctuary. Lesser Flamingo can be found in smaller numbers. White-bellied Sea Eagle breeds. Harriers, Osprey, and Peregrine Falcon are among the birds of prey that occur in winter. Around the lake: Eurasian and Great Thick-knees, Pied Cuckoo, and Ashy Woodswallow.

Among the rarities recorded are Lesser Frigatebird, Common Ringed Plover, and Slender-billed Gull. In 1840 at Pulicat, Thomas Jerdon collected a Black-fronted Dotterel, the only time this species has been seen outside Australasia.

Other Sites

The **Nelapattu Sanctuary** is important for its breeding colony of Spot-billed Pelicans which nest on *Barringtonia* trees in a tank near the village of Nelapattu. The other main breeding species are Little Cormorant, Black-crowned Night Heron, Asian Openbill, Black-headed Ibis, Eurasian Spoonbill and White-breasted Waterhen. A visit here can be combined with one to Pulicat. The sanctuary is (signposted) just off the main NH5 about 100km north of Chennai (Madras) and 78km south of Nellore. Buses between the two towns drop you off at Doravari Satram where there is also a railway station. The sanctuary is a short walk northeast from there. Visit the nature centre from which a path leads to a watchtower overlooking the lake. Nelapattu is surrounded by a vast expanse of low thorn scrub which can produce some interesting birds but beware of Saw-scaled Vipers.

Other birds: Oriental Darter (U), Painted Stork (U), Black Ibis (U), Spot-billed Duck, Red-crested Pochard (UW), Cotton Pygmy-goose, Brahminy Kite, White-eyed Buzzard, Pallid, Pied (R) and Eurasian Marsh Harriers (W), Greater Painted-snipe, Eurasian and Great Thick-knees, Yellow-wattled Lapwing*, Brown-headed Gull (UW), River and Black-bellied (U) Terns, Chestnut-bellied Sandgrouse, Pied Cuckoo, Indian Nightjar, Indian Pitta* (W), Oriental Skylark, Jungle Prinia*, Thick-billed and Blyth's Reed Warblers (W), Paddyfield Pipit, Yellow (W) and White-browed* Wagtails, Indian Silverbill and Black-headed Munia.

Shamirpet Lake

This site in Andhra Pradesh is primarily of interest for the endemic Sykes's Lark**, regular here but erratic and difficult to find elsewhere. The lake itself is quite good for waterbirds and the surrounding drier grassy areas provide habitat for Blyth's and Tawny Pipits in winter.

Location

Shamirpet is 28km north of Hyderabad, the state capital, just off the road to Chanda. It is best reached by taxi – ask for the Shamirpet Lake Resort. Buses to Shamirpet are available from the bus stand at Secunderabad Station.

Accommodation

There are plenty of hotels in Hyderabad particularly in the Abids area near the main railway station. There is accommodation at the lake itself at the *Shamirpet Lake Resort* (D), though the restaurant may not be functioning.

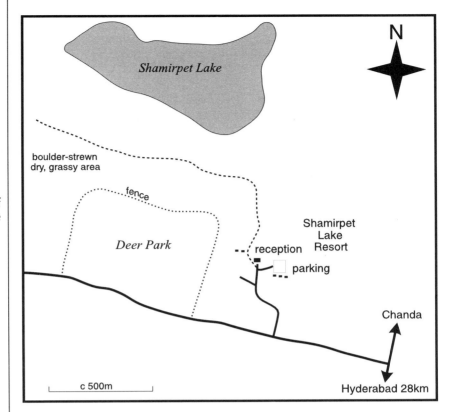

Map of
Shamirpet Lake

Strategy   A single early morning or late afternoon visit of a few hours should be enough to find Sykes's Larks which favour the boulder-strewn, grassy areas at the southwestern end of the lake. Park at the Resort and take the path to the lake from behind reception. The larks occur in small flocks and can be quite flighty. Listen for their nasal *dzewy* calls.

Birds   Among other birds recorded are Asian Openbill, Painted and Woolly-necked Storks, Spot-billed Duck, Montagu's and Eurasian Marsh Harriers (W), Grey Francolin, various waders, Ashy-crowned Sparrow Lark*, Rufous-tailed Lark*, Bay-backed Shrike, Yellow-eyed and Yellow-billed* Babblers, Booted Warbler (W), Bluethroat (W), Blue Rock Thrush (W), White-browed Wagtail*, Indian Silverbill and Grey-necked Bunting (UW).

Other Sites   If you have time in **Hyderabad**, the **Sanjivaya Park** at the northern end of Hussain Sagar (the lake which separates Hyderabad from Secunderabad) can be interesting. The fenced-off campus of the International Crops Research Institute for the Semi-arid Tropics (**ICRISAT**) at Patancheru, 27km northwest of Hyderabad on the main highway to Mumbai (Bombay), is excellent for birds. Visits are only allowed on Sundays and permission must be obtained. A vehicle is useful to explore the 14km² of flat, open country attractive for raptors in particular. Do not to leave the main tracks as the fields are planted with crops. For assistance contact the Birdwatcher's Society of Andhra Pradesh (see section on Useful Addresses).

Rollapadu

Rollapadu is a small village surrounded by grassland with light scrub and scattered trees. This open grassland shelters a fairly healthy population of the endangered Indian Bustard*. The equally threatened Lesser Florican* is sometimes seen in winter. In 1989, 614 hectares were declared a Wildlife Sanctuary and a team of guards protects the bustards. The grasslands provide ideal habitat for wintering harriers with the second largest roost of Montagu's and Pallid in the country (more than 1000 at its peak). Sykes's Lark**, an endemic patchily distributed throughout the Deccan, appears to be resident. In addition the sanctuary harbours mammals such as Blackbuck and Wolf .

Map of Rollapadu

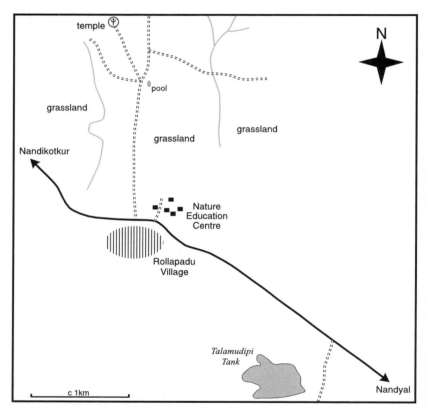

Location

Rollapadu is in Andhra Pradesh about 260km south of the state capital Hyderabad. To get there, get a train or bus to Kurnool about half way between Hyderabad and Bangalore. From there take one of the fairly frequent buses 31km east to Nandikotkur, and change to another bus for the final 18km southeast to Rollapadu on the road to Nandyal.

Accommodation

There are basic rooms at the *Nature Education Centre* at Rollapadu. Permission to stay can be obtained from the Forest Offices in Nandikotkur or Srisailam (about 90km east of Nandikotkur). In practice you may be allowed to stay if you just turn up. In either case take food and drink. You may prefer to stay at Nandikotkur, where there are basic lodges, or at Kurnool, where there is a range of hotels including the upper bracket *Jaya Shree* and *Mourya Inn* on Bellary Rd. For mid-price and budget hotels try the area around the bus station.

Strategy   Keep an eye open for Indian Bustards* on the road from Nandikotkur to Rollapadu. One or two may be found by scanning the grasslands from the Nature Education Centre. Their main breeding season is from August to December with a secondary season in May and June, when extra care should be taken not to disturb them.

To explore the Sanctuary, take the dusty track north from the Nature Education Centre, looking for Sykes's Lark** on the bunds and road edges. A number of other tracks and dirt roads lead off this one and should be kept to, avoiding the temptation to trample through the plots of grass. Some time can be spent at a pool 1^1/$_2$km along the main track on the right of the road, where many birds come to drink. This is a good viewpoint for watching harriers coming in to roost.

The nearby Talamudipi Tank (see map) may be worth checking; Small Pratincole and Great Bittern have been seen.

Indian Bustard

Birds   Indian Bustards* at Rollapadu are estimated at 60 individuals. Lesser Florican* has bred on one occasion. It is seen more often in winter but is far from guaranteed. Bar-headed Goose (W), White-eyed Buzzard, Montagu's and Pallid Harriers (W), Short-toed Snake Eagle, Painted* and Grey Francolins, Rain, Rock Bush** and Jungle Bush* Quails, Demoiselle Crane (W), Yellow-wattled Lapwing*, Indian Courser*, Chestnut-bellied Sandgrouse, Eurasian Eagle Owl, Alpine Swift, Singing and Indian* Bushlarks, Rufous-tailed Lark*, Ashy-crowned Sparrow Lark*, Southern Grey and Bay-backed Shrikes, Rosy Starling (W), Yellow-eyed, Common, Large Grey* and Yellow-billed* Babblers, Grey-breasted, Plain and Ashy* Prinias, Blyth's and Tawny Pipits (W), White-browed Wagtail*, and Grey-necked and Red-headed Buntings (W) are among the other birds that occur in the area. White and Black Storks, and Pied Harrier are rare visitors.

Other Wildlife   The resident Blackbuck are fairly common. Wolves breed within the bustard enclosures, but you need luck to see one. Jungle Cat and Black-naped Hare are likely.

ANDAMAN & NICOBAR ISLANDS

Map of
Andaman Islands

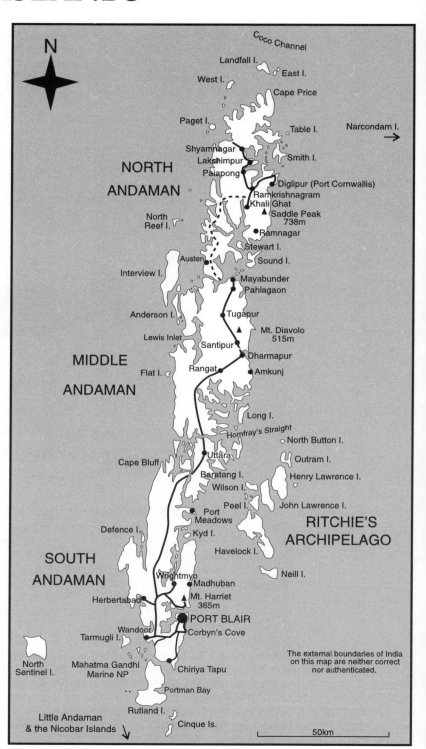

The Andamans and Nicobars are more than 300 islands in the Bay of Bengal nearer to Myanmar (Burma) than to the Indian mainland. Most are uninhabited and covered in pristine rainforest. The avifauna is very rich and rather different from that of the rest of India, having closer affinities with that of Southeast Asia. A particular attraction are the 17 endemic species. Narcondam Hornbill** is restricted to the island of Narcondam (difficult of access), while five others only inhabit the Nicobars, off limits to foreign tourists. The remaining 11 can be found on South Andaman which is open to tourists. To make the birding still more exciting, there are many endemic subspecies some of which are candidates for future splits. As the islands have been relatively little explored by ornithologists, there is scope for increasing the list of 220 or so species, particularly during migration times. For those who want a change from birding there is the possibility of snorkelling on the coral reefs or just swimming and sunbathing.

N.B. A permit is necessary to visit the Andaman Islands. This is usually issued on arrival but see also Pre-tour Information.

Port Blair

Map of Port Blair

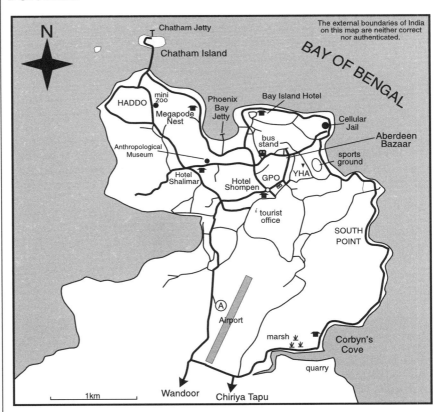

Location

Port Blair on the island of South Andaman, the capital of the Bay Islands as they are sometimes called, is the usual port of arrival by air or sea. There are regular flights three times a week from Calcutta and Chennai (Madras). These are expensive but often full weeks ahead, so book well in advance. The airport is on the southwest edge of Port Blair and taxis into town are reasonably priced. A local bus runs along the main road past the entrance.

The sea passage to Port Blair is inexpensive, but schedules are erratic with sailings few and far between. The trip takes three or four days with extremely few birds. Tickets may be booked with the Shipping Corporation of India in Chennai (Madras) at Jawahar Building, Rajaji Salai (opposite the Customs House) ☎044 -5231410/5231401, or in Calcutta at 1st Floor, 13 Strand Rd ☎033-284456

A network of buses serves most destinations on South Andaman from Port Blair though reliable information on timings is hard to come by. Taxis are available, but a good way of exploring is by hiring a motor-bike or scooter. These can be rented at reasonable rates from T.S.G. Travels in Aberdeen Bazaar at the centre of Port Blair. You may be asked to produce a driving licence, although quoting a licence number may be enough.

Accommodation

There is a complete range of accommodation in and around Port Blair. The *Youth Hostel* (☎20459) is central and cheap and there are other budget hotels in Aberdeen Bazaar of which the best is probably the *Jagannath Guest House* (E). Mid-price hotels include the *Dhanalakshmi* (C/D) ☎21953 in Aberdeen Bazaar, the *Shompen* (B/C)☎20360, south of the post office, and the *Shalimar* (C/D) ☎21923, near the Anthropological Museum on the way to Haddo. The government-run *Megapode Nest* (C) ☎20207 at Haddo offers good value while *Andaman Teal House* and *Hornbill Nest*, about 1km north of Corbyn's Cove are cheaper with reasonable facilities. More up-market are the *Bay Island Hotel* (A++) ☎20881, Fax 21389, above the coast east of Phoenix Bay, and the *Andaman Beach Resort* (A) ☎21462, Fax 21463, which is out at Corbyn's Cove conveniently located for the nearby small marsh. Some hotels send vehicles to meet incoming planes and offer free transport to their establishments. Bargaining over room prices, particularly in the low season between June and August, can get you enormous discounts.

Strategy

The climate is typical of tropical islands, generally hot and humid, with temperatures reduced by the sea breezes. In winter it is slightly cooler and this is the season when resident birds are joined by migrants. The Bay Islands are subject to two monsoon rainy seasons. The southwest monsoon arrives in mid-May and lasts to October, while the shorter northeast monsoon normally lasts from November to January, but an umbrella can be useful at any time of the year. The driest period is from February to April. Bird migration has not been well studied, but the best times are September-November and February-May.

Being so much further east but yet on the same time as the mainland means that dawn breaks excruciatingly early for those who want to catch the best morning birding hours.

If time is not of the essence, it can be worth spending the first day or so exploring the habitats in and around Port Blair. Gardens and scrub produce the first endemics. A walk along the coast should turn up species of interest. Check the mud-flats for waders: good mud-flats are exposed at low tide on the road to the Chatham Jetty and Sawmill. The most common tern is Black-naped but Little has also been seen a few times since 1994. At high tide waders gather on the sports field of the stadium below the town and in the grounds of the college along the road to the east. The small area of marsh and mangrove creek just behind Corbyn's Cove (see below) can be productive. The reservoir known as Dilthaman Tank, surrounded by a small park, may hold birds of interest – Brown-backed Needletails come to drink in the morning.

The Indian National Trust for Art and Cultural Heritage (INTACH), the local conservation group, welcomes visits from serious birders. They would like trip lists etc. for their database and can help with logistics. Contact

Mr. Samir Acharya at Tarangs, Middle Point, Port Blair ☎03192-20929 or
21145 (a few shops along from the Hotel Shompen). The Zoological Survey
of India has a branch at Haddo in Port Blair. You may be able to obtain
Birds of Andaman & Nicobar Islands by B.K.Tikader here, otherwise their
library and the town library have reference copies. Useful information can
be obtained from the Wildlife Unit at the Forest Department office in the
Mini Zoo at Haddo.

Map of
South Andaman

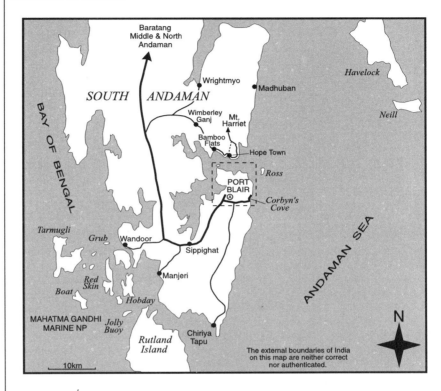

Birds

Around the town interesting species include the near-endemic Brown
Coucal and White-headed Starling**. Red-breasted and Long-tailed
Parakeets, Asian Glossy Starling, and Olive-backed Sunbird are common
here but not easily found on the Indian mainland. White-bellied Swiftlets
are frequent overhead but look for Brown-backed Needletails and Blue-
tailed Bee-eaters too.

Along the coast Pacific Reef Egret, White-bellied Sea Eagle, Black-naped
Tern, Collared Kingfisher, and Pacific Swallow are common residents. In
winter and during migration waders join them: 30 species have been
recorded from the Andamans so far. Around Port Blair are Pacific Golden
and Grey Plovers, Greater and Lesser Sand Plovers, Eurasian Curlew,
Common Redshank, Wood, Broad-billed and Curlew Sandpipers, Ruddy
Turnstone, and Temminck's Stint. Oriental Plover has been recorded and
rarities such as Nordmann's Greenshank, Asian Dowitcher and Spoon-
billed Sandpiper could occur.

Corbyn's Cove Marsh

A few kilometres along the coast road southeast of Port Blair is the
Andaman Beach Resort Hotel at Corbyn's Cove. At the south end of the

bathing beach in front of the hotel, follow the road to the right to a small mangrove creek on the left and a marshy area on the right. Regularly seen species include Purple and Little Herons, Chestnut and Yellow Bitterns, Slaty-breasted Rail, Baillon's and Ruddy Crakes, Watercock, Purple Swamphen, various waders including Long-toed Stint and Pintail Snipe, Stork-billed Kingfisher, and Clamorous Reed and Dusky Warblers. Black Bittern and Pallas's Grasshopper Warbler (W) are rarer. Black-browed Reed Warbler, not recorded from the islands before 1991, may be a regular winter visitor or passage migrant. A Black-capped Kingfisher frequents the area and is sometimes found on the northern side of the cove itself.

In the scrub and trees around the marsh look for Brown Coucal, White-headed Starling** and Hill Myna. Pacific Swallows feed with the commoner Barn Swallows. Black Baza and Long-legged Buzzard have been seen flying over, the latter apparently a new species for the islands in 1995. The increasingly rare Andaman subspecies of Sunda Teal, sometimes regarded as a separate species, has also been seen.

It is easiest to get here by taxi, but you may prefer to take a Calicut- or Pathargadda-bound bus and get off just past the airport at the Janatha Junction – see map. Two or three early morning or late afternoon visits are recommended.

Map of Corbyn's Cove

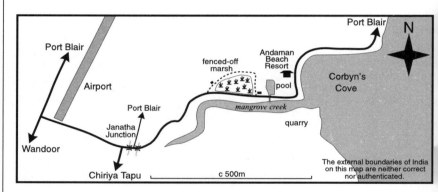

Mount Harriet

The Mt Harriet NP is superb dense evergreen and semi-evergreen rainforest that holds most, perhaps all, of the endemic species found on South Andaman and is accessible from Port Blair. Concentrate on this site if it is forest specialities that you are interested in.

Location

Located across the bay from Port Blair, it can be reached by car (via Garacharama, Sippighat, Chauldali, Homphrey's Ghat, Kodakachang, and Wimberley Ganj) but this takes about 2 hours. It is quicker to take the ferry from Phoenix Bay to Bamboo Flat. The first ferry leaves at 04.45 and the last ferry returns at 21.40, but schedules may change, so check with the Marine Department office. The crossing takes 25 minutes. A few of the ferries call at the Hope Town Jetty (Panighat) which is much nearer to Harriet, but it is not easy to find out the timings. There are car ferries to Bamboo Flat from Chatham Jetty, but these run less frequently.

Accommodation

There is a *FRH* at the top of Mt. Harriet, but non-Indian nationals are not allowed to stay overnight. Birders have been known to take a sleeping bag and spend the night on the floor of the veranda or watchtower, but this is against regulations.

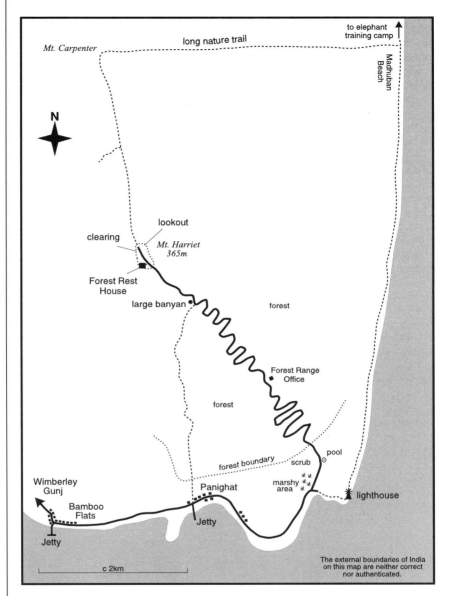

Map of
Mount Harriet

Strategy   The metalled road east from Bamboo Flat along the coast reaches the summit of Mt. Harriet after 8km. The first 4km are along the shore and less interesting, so take one of the infrequent buses, a taxi or hitch along this section at least one way. Beware the high fares that taxis charge for a trip to the top. Birding is good along the road once you leave the coast. A path of 3km can be found by following the obvious aqueduct from Panighat (Hope Town) up through the forest. The path joins the road again below a huge banyan tree about 1km below the summit. If you reach the summit (365m) early enough, carry on and explore the nature trail on the ridge up to Mt. Carpenter. Birding is often better from the road and there can be leeches on the paths during and just after the rainy season.

Mt. Harriet is worth a day or two; spend some time after dark looking for Andaman Scops Owl**, Andaman Hawk Owl**, (Hume's) Brown Hawk

Owl and Oriental Scops Owl, all resident near the summit. The latter sounds rather different from its mainland counterpart and may represent a separate species.

Look for birds on the ferry crossing which has produced White-winged (Black) Tern, only the second record from the islands.

Birds

Check the swamp at the base of the hill for Slaty-breasted Rail. Ruddy-breasted Crake appears to be more regular at the pool further up on the right of the road. Andaman Crake** is difficult to find but one has been seen at this pool, another crossing the aqueduct trail and a local reportedly caught one 'somewhere near the base of Mt. Harriet'.

The first section of road up the hill is open and scrubby with different birds from higher up. Thick-billed Warbler (W) frequents the bushes and Andaman (Dark) Serpent Eagle** is seen here. It is smaller and darker than the local race *davisoni* of the Crested Serpent Eagle and the adult shows two pale bars on the undertail as opposed to the single broad white band of the latter. The degraded habitat just before the protected forest is better for specialities such as Andaman Woodpecker**, White-headed Starling** and Andaman Wood Pigeon** (the far commoner Green Imperial Pigeon can look confusingly similar unless seen well).

Further up the road the forest becomes thicker and most Andaman rainforest specialities can be found: Changeable Hawk Eagle, Vernal Hanging Parrot, Pompadour Green Pigeon, Andaman Cuckoo Dove** (U), Emerald Dove, Red-breasted and Long-tailed Parakeets, Asian Emerald Cuckoo (W), Violet Cuckoo, Brown Coucal, Brown-backed Needletail, Chestnut-headed Bee-eater, Dollarbird, Fulvous-breasted Woodpecker, Hooded Pitta (?), Black-naped Oriole, Andaman** and Greater Racket-tailed Drongos, Andaman Treepie**, Bar-bellied Cuckooshrike (U), Scarlet and Small Minivets, Asian Fairy Bluebird, Black-headed Bulbul, Asian Brown Flycatcher (W), Black-naped Monarch, the white-bellied Andaman form of White-rumped Shama, and Forest Wagtail (W).

The path up from Panighat is good for Andaman Cuckoo Dove** and Orange-headed Thrush. The area near the summit Rest House is excellent for raptors and the large fig tree when in fruit attracts many birds and provides a shady spot for a picnic lunch. Among migrant rarities seen near the top of the mountain are Eyebrowed Thrush and Chestnut Bunting.

Andaman
Serpent Eagle

Chiriya Tapu

Chiriya Tapu (sometimes written Chiria or Chidiya) means Bird Island or Bird Point. There is some reasonable forest inland and along the coast which, though somewhat degraded, harbours a number of endemic bird species and is probably the best place to see Andaman Pale Serpent Eagle, the endemic race of Crested Serpent Eagle, alongside the endemic Andaman (Dark) Serpent Eagle**.

Location

Chiriya Tapu lies at the southeastern tip of South Andaman, 30km from Pt. Blair, and can be reached by bus (1½ hours), taxi or private transport (1 hour). The first buses leave at 05.30, 07.30 and 09.00 with the last one back departing at 18.30.

Accommodation

A *FRH* at Chiriya Tapu is bookable with the Forest Department, but foreign tourists are currently not permitted to overnight.

Strategy

The motorable road ends at tea stalls after a few kilometres of reasonable forest which is being allowed to regenerate. Explore this and the track past the tea stalls and FRH through littoral rainforest to a small beach to the east. It is possible to continue on past the beach, but the track is ill-defined. Check out the mangrove and agricultural land behind the coastal forest. Avoid holidays and weekends as this popular destination can be busy.

Birds

Black Baza (U), Changeable Hawk Eagle, Pompadour Green and Green Imperial Pigeons, Andaman Cuckoo Dove** (U), Emerald Dove, Alexandrine, Red-breasted and Long-tailed Parakeets, Vernal Hanging Parrot, Indian Cuckoo, Brown Coucal, Brown Needletail, Collared, Ruddy (U) and Stork-billed Kingfishers, Chestnut-headed Bee-eater, Andaman** and Fulvous-breasted Woodpeckers, Andaman** and Greater Racket-tailed Drongos, Asian Glossy and White-headed** Starlings, Andaman Treepie**, Large and Bar-bellied (U) Cuckooshrikes, Asian Fairy Bluebird, Black-headed Bulbul, Asian Brown Flycatcher (W), Mangrove Whistler (U), Pale-footed Bush Warbler (R), White-rumped Shama (Andaman race), Orange-headed Thrush and Plain Flowerpecker. At low tide various waders can be seen and Black-naped Terns perch on the exposed rocks.

Mahatma Gandhi Marine NP, Wandoor

The marine environment, islands and coast on the southwest of South Andaman are a national park. Most islands are covered in dense forest and the coast and creeks lined with mangroves, though degraded in places. Tourists are allowed to visit Jolly Buoy, Red Skin and Cinque Islands.

Location

Wandoor, the point of entry to the NP, is on the west coast of South Andaman, 29km southwest of Pt. Blair, reached by regular bus or private transport in 1–1½ hours. The first buses leave Port Blair at 05.00, 05.45 and 07.30, the last returns from Wandoor at 18.30. Travel agents and hotels in Pt. Blair offer tours. These take you direct to Wandoor in time for the daily 10.00 boat to Jolly Buoy and/or Red Skin. You get a few hours' swimming and snorkelling before being brought back to Wandoor and your hotel. This alternative is more comfortable but suffers from a higher price and the fact that the tours are liable to be cancelled at the last minute. It is better to make your own way to Wandoor early and spend the time there before taking the ten o'clock boat.

Accommodation　There is a *FRH* at Wandoor, but foreign nationals are not permitted to stay. Check to see if regulations have changed.

Strategy　You can book a ticket for the boat in advance at the Marine Office in Pt. Blair (ask to see the booking list if they say it is full) or at the ticket office at Wandoor half-an-hour before departure. It should be possible to book a private boat to explore the Marine Park; a more flexible though costlier option.

Boats usually go to **Jolly Buoy**, the smaller of the two islands, with a small beach that can become overcrowded. The corals are better around Jolly Buoy, but it is better to get the boat to drop you at **Red Skin** and pick you up on the way back. This gives 4–5 hours for birding as well as swimming. Red Skin has good forest, but it is almost impenetrable so you are more or less restricted to the beach and rocky shore. A nature trail of 2km is due to be constructed. There are no facilities on the islands, so take drinks and a snack.

Scuba diving facilities are available at Wandoor with the Andaman & Nicobar Islands Scuba Diving Society which has a centre near the school about 500m past the jetty.

Birds　Pacific Reef Egret, Japanese Sparrowhawk (U), White-bellied Sea Eagle, (Andaman Pale) Crested Serpent Eagle, Slaty-breasted Rail, Greater and Lesser Sand Plovers, Terek Sandpiper, Black-naped Tern, Green Imperial Pigeon, Andaman Wood Pigeon**, Red-breasted and Long-tailed Parakeets, Vernal Hanging Parrot, Andaman Scops Owl**, Brown-backed Needletail, Stork-billed, Oriental Dwarf (R) and White-collared Kingfishers, Dollarbird Andaman** and Fulvous-breasted Woodpeckers, Pacific Swallow, Andaman Drongo**, White-breasted Woodswallow, White-headed Starling** and Black-headed Bulbul. The endemic Andaman subspecies of Grey Teal apparently visits salt marshes on the southwestern side of Redskin and near Tirur to the north of Wandoor.

Other Wildlife　There is a fantastic selection of colourful fish and corals best experienced by snorkelling. The water is often clearer at Jolly Buoy and equipment can be hired or bought in Port Blair. The Marine Park is also important for breeding Green Sea, Leatherback, Hawksbill, and Olive Ridley Turtles. Salt Water Crocodiles occur in the creeks in the Park. It is forbidden to collect the coral or any other material, living or dead, in the National Park.

Other Sites　**Sippighat** is an area of marshes and tidal creeks (14km from Port Blair) on the way to Wandoor. There is a record of Andaman Crake** in a roadside ditch. Black-browed Reed Warblers have been seen in February. Ask at the Water Sports Centre to arrange a boat to go round the creeks.

Manjeri lies at the southwestern tip of South Andaman. The habitat is similar to that at Chiriya Tapu but may produce a few birds not commonly found there (e.g. Dollarbird and Brown-breasted Flycatcher).

With both **North** and **Middle Andaman** newly accessible to foreign nationals, there is plenty of scope for further exploration. Check with the tourist office exactly which areas are open. Visits to some parts are not permitted in order that the primitive tribes that survive in remote areas should not be disturbed.

Visits to some smaller islands further from Port Blair are possible, but adverse weather could delay the return journey by days or even weeks. **Havelock** and **Neil** to the northeast can be reached by ferry from Phoenix Bay Jetty in Port Blair in 3–7 hours. Tourists are allowed to stay overnight on both islands. On Havelock the government-run *Dolphin Yatri Niwas* has cottage accommodation and a fixed-tent camp at the beach at village No.7. The avifauna is largely the same as on South Andaman but a few species such as Edible-nest Swiftlet, Dollarbird, and White-breasted Woodswallow appear commoner here. The local *obscura* subspecies of Brown Hawk Owl is easy to see at dusk adjacent to the paddies near village no.7.

A journey to **Narcondam Island** to see the endemic Narcondam Hornbill** is now possible. The hornbill is quite common and easy to see, but there are considerable logistical difficulties. Narcondam is 240km from Port Blair; the only way to get there is by a police supply boat or a chartered vessel, an overnight stay is not permitted and there is no harbour or jetty.

The **Nicobar Islands** may be opened up to tourists in the future, making it possible to look for their endemics: Nicobar Scrubfowl**, Nicobar Sparrowhawk**, Nicobar Serpent Eagle**, Nicobar Parakeet** and Nicobar Bulbul**.

LAKSHADWEEP (LACCADIVE ISLANDS)

The Lakshadweep archipelago consists of some 30 coral islands off the southwest coast of India. The human population of 50,000 is spread over 10 islands, including Kavaratti, the capital. The islands are similar to the Maldives but not as well visited. The bird diversity is not high with just 80 species recorded. The resident landbirds are fairly common mainland species, but seabirds and marine biology can make it worth going there. Great and Lesser Crested Terns are quite common and there is the possibility of pelagic species though none are regular. Pitti Island is uninhabited and protected as a sanctuary for Brown Noddy, and Sooty and Great Crested Terns breeding between April and October with a peak between June and August.

Logistics

The Lakshadweep are spread out some 200–300km off the coast of Kerala It is only possible for foreign tourists to visit with a permit normally issued in conjunction with a package trip. This is available as a flight to Agatti airport from Goa or Cochin, followed by a two hour boat trip to the

Map of Lakshadweep (Laccadive Islands)

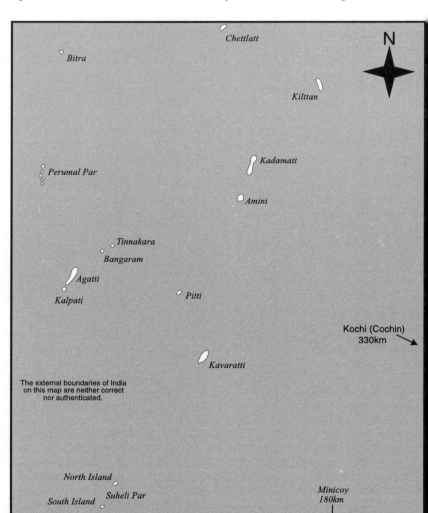

Bangaram Island Resort (expensive) – the only island where foreigners can stay. Bangaram is uninhabited apart from resort staff and visitors from Agatti. Scuba diving is available. Bookings can be made with the Manager, Bangaram Island Resort, Casino Hotel, Willingdon Island, Kochi (Cochin) 682 003, Kerala ☎0484-340221 or travel agents in Goa. Suheli Island is being developed for tourism.

The alternative is a package cruise from Cochin for four or five days between September and April, booked in advance with SPORTS, Lakshadweep Office, Indira Gandhi Rd, Willingdon Island, Kochi (Cochin) 682 003, Kerala ☎340387, Fax 340155. In Delhi try the Liaison Officer, Lakshadweep Office, 202 or F 306, KG Marg (Curzon Rd) Hostel, Kasturba Gandhi Marg, New Delhi 110 001 ☎011-386807.

For permission to visit Pitti Island you need 'an authorisation from a recognised society such as the Bombay Natural History Society'.

The climate is warm and humid with sparse rainfall between June and August. The weaker northeast monsoon brings some rain in October and November. Temperatures range from 27°C to 33°C with the hottest months April and May. The heat is tempered by a sea breeze.

Birds   Anyone visiting should not expect a long list of birds. On the other hand, Lakshadweep is underwatched and there is a chance of adding new species to the local or even subcontinental avifauna. The following are some more notable species recorded from the islands: Wedge-tailed and Audubon's Shearwaters, Jouanin's Petrel, Wilson's and Swinhoe's Storm Petrels, Red-billed Tropicbird, Masked, Red-footed and Brown Boobies, Great Frigatebird, Little Heron, Western Reef Egret, Yellow Bittern, Ferruginous Pochard, White-bellied Sea Eagle, Pallid and Montagu's Harriers, Peregrine Falcon, Crab-plover, Greater and Lesser Sand Plovers, Terek Sandpiper, Great Knot, South-Polar Skua, Pomarine and Parasitic Jaegers, Gull-billed, White-cheeked, Bridled and Little Terns, Lesser Noddy, Pied and Grey-bellied* Cuckoos, Black-capped Kingfisher, Indian Pitta* and Richard's Pipit.

GLOSSARY

India.

achha – okay.

anikut or *anicut* – dam, weir or irrigation channel.

babul – *Acacia nilotica* the commonest of the varieties of acacia tree in India.

bagh – usually refers to a Tiger but may be used for a Leopard or other large cat. The same word can also mean garden.

bandar – monkey.

banyan – *Ficus benghalensis,* a large spreading fig tree with many hanging roots. The red fruit attracts many birds.

bazaar – market or market town.

beel – in Northeast India a shallow lake, pond or marshy area (same as *jheel* in other parts of India).

bet (pronounced *bait*) – in the Rann of Kutch a vegetated patch of higher ground which becomes an island when the Rann is flooded during the monsoon.

bhabar – zone of dense dry sal forest that is often found on the northern edge of the *terai* to about 600m in the Himalayan foothills.

bharal – Blue Sheep *Pseudois nayaur.*

bhavan – house or building.

bheel – same as *beel.*

bo or *bodhi* tree – the fig tree *Ficus religiosa.*

bugyal – meadow.

bund or *bundh* – dam, embankment or dike.

bus stand – commonly used expression for bus station.

bum – hill or mountain.

chai – tea.

Chalo! or *Che lo!* – Let's go! More politely 'Chalo ji!'.

chapati – flat Indian bread.

chaud or *chaur* – flat, grassy open expanse in the Himalayan foothills.

chidiya – bird (in Hindi).

chinkara – Indian Gazelle *Gazella benettii.*

chipa – Ladakhi word for bird.

chiria or *chiriya* – same as *chidiya.*

chital – Spotted Deer *Axis axis.*

chorten – Tibetan word for *stupa.*

chowk – market or courtyard.

chowki – guard hut.

chowkidar – caretaker, watchman.

circuit house – accommodation for visiting government officials, sometimes the only place to stay in remote towns.

crore – ten million (Indians tend to speak in terms of lakhs and crores rather than thousands and millions).

curd – yoghourt.

daal – lentil soup.

dak bungalow – rest house for travelling officials.

deodar – Himalayan Cedar *Cedrus deodara.*

dhal – same as *daal.*

dhobi – laundry or the person who washes it.

dhole – Red Dog *Cuon alpinus.*

duars – the eastern parts of the *terai* or *bhabar* in West Bengal and Assam.

dun or *doon* – a broad, flat valley in the foothills of the Himalaya.

durbin – binoculars.

ek minit! – one minute (useful for getting taxi drivers to stop for a minute while you look at a bird).

facies – sub-division of a region or biotope.

flame of the forest – *Butea monosperma*, a tree whose orange-red flowers are particularly attractive to birds.

forest rest house – accommodation belonging to the forest department (primarily intended for visiting officials but can be used by others if permission is obtained).

ganj – market.

garh – fort.

gari – vehicle (e.g. rail gari = train).

ghat – slope, as in mountain or steps down to a river.

giri – hill or mountain (in South India).

gompa – Tibetan Buddhist monastery.

gurudwara – Sikh temple.

hathi – Elephant.

hill station – summer retreat in the mountains.

howdah – seat on an Elephant's back (can usually carry up to four people).

inspection bungalow (IB) – term used for government or official accommodation, often applied to forest rest house in northeastern India.

jheel – shallow lake, pond or marshy area.

jhoom or *jhum* – slash and burn cultivation.

jungle – Hindi word meaning forest.

kakkar – Barking Deer or Muntjac *Muntiacus muntjak*.

kot – fort.

kund – lake, pool or well.

kuruwi – Tamil word for bird.

la – mountain pass (in the Himalaya).

lakh – 100,000 (see also crore).

lassi – drink made of yoghurt and iced water, best avoided except in places where you can be sure of the hygiene.

Loranthus – mistletoe-like epiphyte much loved by flowerpeckers.

machan – hide, watchtower or lookout.

mahawat or *mahout* – elephant driver.

mahseer – large freshwater fish (*Barbus tor*).

maidan – open grassy area or parade ground.

mani wall – low wall made of stone tablets with religious inscriptions.

marg – wide road.

masjid – mosque.

mesquite – an introduced thorny shrub that has spread through much of India.

monsoon – rainy season.

nadi – river.

naga – snake.

nalla or *nallah* – a small ravine, stream or ditch, often without water in the dry season.

nilgai – Blue Bull, *Boselaphus tragocamelus*, a horse-like animal perhaps related to the antilopes.

nivas or *niwas* – small palace or residence.

nulla or *nullah* – same as *nalla*.

pakshi – Rajasthani and Sanskrit word for bird.

panchi – Punjabi word for bird.

pani – water.

para – Hog Deer *Axis porcinus*.

paraway – Tamil word for bird.

parbat – mountain.

peepal, *peepul* or *pipal* – the fig tree *Ficus religiosa*.

pol – gate.

pradesh – state.

qila – fort.

rakh – Kashmiri word for lake.

rann – swamp but usually refers to the swampy salt flats in Kutch, Gujarat.

rickshaw – two- or three-wheeled vehicle in which one to three passengers are conveyed.

Rukho! – Stop! More politely 'Rukho ji!'.

sabji or *sabzi* – vegetables or vegetable curry.

sagar – lake, reservoir or sea.

sal – a valuable hardwood tree (*Shorea robusta*).

sambar – large kind of deer *Cervus unicolor*. The same word is used in South India for the vegetable and lentil sauce which accompanies most meals.

sarovar or *sarowar* – lake or reservoir.

sheesham or *shisham* – *Dalbergia latifolia*, a kind of Rosewood tree.

shikar – hunting or shooting.

shikara – a gondola-like boat used in Kashmir.

shikari – hunter or professional tracker.

shola – a word loosely applied to any patch of evergreen forest in South India.

silk cotton – tall tree *Bombax ceiba (malabaricum)* whose crimson flowers are visited by many species of bird.

simul – silk cotton tree *see above*.

stupa – a round domed Buddhist shrine.

sukanay – bird (in Konkani, the language spoken in Goa).

tahr – wild goat of the genus *Hemitragus*.

tal – lake.

taluka – district.

tank or *talar* – artificial pond, lake or reservoir, often of ancient origin.

tempo – a large, three-wheeled motorised vehicle found in some areas as a kind of local bus or taxi.

terai – originally a belt of marshy jungle and grasslands that stretched between the Himalayan foothills and the plains of north India – now largely drained and cultivated, but the term is still applied to this area.

thali – a complete set meal or the dish it is served upon.

tiffin – a meal or snack, usually at breakfast or lunchtime, also used for the container it may be carried in.

tonga – a two-wheeled, horse-drawn cart used as a kind of taxi.

wallah – person or worker, (e.g. *rickshaw-wallah* = rickshaw puller; *dhobi-wallah* – clothes washer).

SELECTIVE BIRD LIST

The following list includes a selection of uncommon, endemic and endangered species which are particularly sought-after by birders. It provides brief details on status and where to see each species with the emphasis on sites described in this book. For the most part vagrants are not included. A number of species, particularly those found only in the Northeast Hill States, may be under-recorded due to the paucity of observers who have visited the area in recent decades. Some Himalayan species are more easily seen in Nepal and readers are referred to Carol Inskipp's companion volume covering that country.

Those species marked ** are endemic to India and * endemic to the Indian Subcontinent.

<u>Underlined</u> are globally threatened and near-threatened species. Any information about these and any of the other rarer species should be sent to the authors or BirdLife International (see Useful Addresses). The threat categories given in brackets follow Collar et al's *Birds to Watch 2* (Cambridge: BirdLife. 1994.):

C – critical   E – endangered   V – vulnerable
D – data deficient   N – near-threatened

Spot-billed Pelican (V). A declining resident species. Breeds at Kaziranga, Orang WLS (Assam), Kokkare Bellur, Nellapatu, Vedanthangal (in most years) and Teleneelapuram (Andhra Pradesh). Also occurs at Pulicat, Pt Calimere, Dibru-Saikhowa and Chilka.

Dalmatian Pelican (V). Winters in northwest India. Seen most winters together with flocks of the commoner Great White Pelican at Bharatpur, Sultanpur and on the Yamuna River in Delhi. More regular at Nal Sarovar, Little Rann of Kutch and Soorwal Lake (near Ranthambhor).

White-bellied Heron (E). Extremely rare resident: occasional in the eastern wetlands of Kaziranga; at Namdapha it is sometimes seen flying downstream at dusk near the Deban RH.

Black Bittern. Uncommon shy resident of marshes throughout the country. Regular in small numbers at Bharatpur where the best place seems to be along the canal at Sapanmari. Occasional elsewhere.

Black-necked Stork. A species with a widespread but declining population scattered throughout the larger Indian wetlands. For most visitors to India, Bharatpur is the easiest place to see this species but its most important stronghold is at Kaziranga. Also found at Dudhwa, Dihaila Jheel (Madhya Pradesh); uncommon at Ranthambhor, Orang and Manas.

Greater Adjutant (E). A scarce resident with the majority of the world's population now found in Assam. There is a good site for viewing the species in Guwahati town as well as at Deepor Beel nearby. Very tame at the fish market at Nalbari, 1½ hours from Guwahati on the way to Manas. Regularly seen en route from Guwahati to Kaziranga.

Lesser Adjutant (V). Population declining but still fairly common in the plains of Assam and in the paddyfields around Siliguri on the way to Darjeeling. Very occasional elsewhere including Bharatpur.

Greater Flamingo. Common on larger waterbodies of Gujarat, at Sultanpur, Sambhar Lake, Pt Calimere, Chilka Lake and Pulicat Lagoon. Sporadic elsewhere. Rare on Yamuna River in Delhi and at Bharatpur.

Lesser Flamingo (N). Breeds Little Rann of Kutch. Regular there in winter and at Nal Sarovar, Chilka Lake, Pt. Calimere and Sambhar Lake.

Bar-headed Goose. Breeds in Central Asia, Tibet and eastern Ladakh, and winters in Pakistan and India as far south as Kerala and Tamil Nadu. Easily seen in winter at Bharatpur, Sultanpur, Kaziranga, lakes near Ranthambhor, Sambhar Salt Lake, etc.

Marbled Duck (V). Straggler to shallow lakes in northern India with the most likely site being Harike but has turned up at such diverse places as Dachigam, Bharatpur, Carambolim Lake and Pune (Maharashtra).

Sunda Teal. The Andaman subspecies *albogularis*, occasionally treated as a full species, is becoming increasingly rare due to hunting and pressure on habitat. Recent sightings have been from Corbyn's Cove Marsh near Port Blair, near Village No. 7 on Havelock Island, and marshes north of Wandoor. The best site is said to be Interview Island though current regulations do not allow foreign visitors.

Pink-headed Duck (C). Probably extinct. Last reliable sighting in 1935. Formerly occurred on *jheels* (lakes) and marshy lowland grass jungles from Bihar to Assam, Manipur and Orissa. There are rumours that the species may still survive in northern Myanmar (Burma) and southeast Tibet, though this seems unlikely.

Ferruginous Pochard (V). Used to breed in Kashmir and Ladakh but now mainly a winter visitor in small numbers. Regular sites include Okhla, Bharatpur, Haigam Rakh, Deepor Beel and Dibru-Saikhowa.

Baer's Pochard (V). Scarce winter visitor to the *beels* of Northeast India, though has turned up as far south as Chilka Lake.

Comb Duck. Most of the Asian population of this unusual duck is now found in India. It is fairly widespread but not particularly common. A few can usually be found at Bharatpur, Sultanpur, Sur Sarovar (Keetam Lake) near Agra, and especially at Bund Baretha in winter.

White-winged Duck (E). Restricted to Assam and adjoining areas of the Northeast Hill States where it roosts on quiet forest pools and feeds at night on short grass, e.g. at Dibru-Saikhowa, Namdapha, Doom Dooma Reserve Forest (Assam), Nameri WLS and Digboi (R).

Jerdon's Baza (N). A very rare resident. Not guaranteed anywhere but the best chances of seeing this species are probably in areas of hill forest in Northeast India (particularly around Buxa, Nokrek and Balpakram NPs). Rare in forested areas of the Western Ghats though very occasionally seen at Periyar.

Black Baza. A scarce species with occasional sightings in recent years from Guindy, Periyar, Anaimalai Hills, South Andaman, Buxa, Kaziranga, Nokrek, Balpakram and Mahananda WLS on the way to Darjeeling.

Nicobar Sparrowhawk (E/N). Uncommon and restricted to the islands of Car Nicobar (R), Katchal, Nancowry, and ?Great Nicobar, all at present off-limits to non-Indian nationals.

Bonelli's Eagle. Nowhere common but widespread and can turn up almost anywhere. Best seen at Bharatpur in winter. Resident in and around Corbett, Ranthambhor, Rann of Kutch and Shivpuri among other sites.

Rufous-bellied Eagle. An eagle of the foothills forest up to 1500m in the Western Ghats and the Himalaya from Corbett NP eastwards. Though distinctly uncommon it occurs in most of the sanctuaries of the southern Western Ghats. Sandakphu, Buxa, Namdapha, Nokrek and Balpakram are some of the reserves where it is found in Northeast India.

Imperial Eagle (V). Winter visitor to northwest India. Regular at Bharatpur, Harike, Jaisalmer, and the Desert NP; less so at Sultanpur, Little Rann of Kutch, Chhari Dhand and Corbett.

Greater Spotted Eagle (V). Mainly a winter visitor to northern India as far south as Goa. It prefers the proximity of wetlands at sites such as Okhla, Sultanpur, Bharatpur, Harike, Nal Sarovar, Little Rann of Kutch, Kaziranga and Dibru-Saikhowa.

White-bellied Sea Eagle. Locally common but very much a coastal bird from Bombay down the west coast and then up around the east coast as far as Bangladesh. Common throughout the Andamans & Nicobars, particularly so on Narcondam Island.

Pallas's Fish Eagle (V). Restricted in the main to large waterbodies in the northern part of the country. Its numbers have decreased dramatically but it still occurs at Bharatpur, Corbett, Kaziranga, Dudhwa NP (Uttar Pradesh), and on the Yamuna River beyond the Paonta Sahib Bridge (Himachal Pradesh).

Grey-headed Fish Eagle (N). A fairly widespread resident found mainly at lakes and *jheels* in deciduous forest from the terai southwards. Regular at Kaziranga, Mudumalai, Parambikolam, Corbett (occasional), Dibru-Saikhowa, Dudhwa (Uttar Pradesh), Periyar (U), and along the River Cauvery (Karnataka).

Lesser Fish Eagle (N). Generally the rarest of the fish and sea eagles. It is an inhabitant of forest rivers and streams in the Himalaya and adjacent terai. Commoner than the previous species at Corbett. Seen occasionally at Namdapha.

Lammergeier. A montane species still reasonably common in parts of the higher western Himalayas, e.g. Gt Himalayan NP, Nainital, Kashmir and Ladakh.

(Great) Nicobar Serpent Eagle ** (N/V).** Currently there is still some doubt regarding the taxonomic relationships between the three or more forms of serpent eagle found in the Nicobars; whether the Nicobar Serpent Eagle *Spilornis minimus* of the Nancowry group of Nicobar islands, is best treated as a race of Crested Serpent Eagle *Spilornis cheela* or as a separate species; and whether Great Nicobar Serpent Eagle *Spilornis klossi* is best regarded as a monotypic species confined to the Great Nicobar island group (not uncommon on Great Nicobar), or a subspecies of *S. minimus*. Moreover, there is uncertainty as to the identity of a serpent eagle on Great Nicobar Island where it is sympatric with *S. klossi*. Further research is needed.

Andaman Serpent Eagle ** (N).** Endemic to the Andaman Islands (but absent on Middle Andaman). Quite common on South Andaman, e.g. at Mount Harriet and forests in the northern part of the island. Generally prefers primary forest but also seen regularly at Chiria Tapu in the same area as the local race *davisoni* of Crested Serpent Eagle, which is more a bird of degraded forest, second growth and mangroves.

Collared Falconet. A small raptor of Himalayan terai and foothill forest clearings and second growth. Fairly regular at Corbett. Recent records also from Simlipal, the Buxa area, Kaziranga and Manas.

Pied Falconet (N). A rarely seen raptor from the extreme northeast of the country. Recent records from Kaziranga (Panbari Forest), Namdapha, Digboi, Dibru-Saikhowa, and between Haflong and Silchar in the North Cachar Hills (Assam).

Oriental Hobby. An uncommon breeding resident of the lower Himalaya. Seen occasionally at Kaziranga, Manas, and Namdapha, rarely at Corbett, and in the Western Ghats (e.g. Mudumalai and Periyar) where it is probably a scarce winter visitor.

Red-necked Falcon (N). Scarce resident of open country. Usually in semi-desert and cultivated areas with groves of trees. Nowhere common and appears to be declining. Used to breed regularly around Bangalore (mainly subsisting on sparrows). Occasionally seen chasing hirundines at dusk at Okhla. Regular at Harike, Little Rann of Kutch (between Mandivi and Little Rann) and Chhari Dhand. Other recent sightings from Corbett, near Ramnagar, Simlipal and Velavadar. Rare at Bharatpur and Kaziranga.

Nicobar Scrubfowl ** (V).** Found in forest and secondary growth on all the Nicobar Islands except Car Nicobar.

Snow Partridge. High altitude species frequenting alpine meadows, usually above the tree-line, e.g. at the Shingba Rhododendron Sanctuary, Kedarnath Sanctuary, Gt Himalayan NP (R), and Upper Kullu Valley near the Rohtang Pass.

Tibetan Snowcock. Uncommon high altitude resident in eastern Ladakh (e.g. Hemis NP) as well as Tibetan facies of Arunachal Pradesh and Sikkim, where fairly easy to see in the Lashar Valley (at present off-limits to non-Indian nationals).

Himalayan Snowcock. Uncommon resident of high rocky slopes and meadows above the tree-line. Found at Kedarnath Sanctuary, Gt Himalayan NP, Upper Kullu valley near the Rohtang Pass, Rangdum (Suru Valley), and Hemis NP. Also recorded north of Leh and near the Taglang La between Leh and the Kullu Valley.

Buff-throated Partridge (N). Rare resident of rocky ravines and rhododendron in the sub-alpine zone of central Arunachal Pradesh. The authors are not aware of any recent records.

Painted Francolin*. Uncommon resident of dry scrubby areas in central and southern India. Sariska NP appears to be one of the better protected areas for this species. Also occurs at Pushkar, Ranthambhor (R), Shivpuri, Bandhavgarh, Melghat, Pachmarhi and Rollapadu.

Swamp Francolin* (V). Localised resident of wet grasslands and marshes of the terai. Perhaps most easily seen at Kaziranga and Manas where it is still fairly common. Other sites include Dibru-Saikhowa, Dudhwa NP (Uttar Pradesh) and the D'Ering Memorial WLS.

Tibetan Partridge. A resident of high altitude regions adjoining Tibet in Ladakh, the Kumaon region of Uttar Pradesh, Sikkim, and Arunachal Pradesh, mostly in areas off-limits to foreign visitors. The recent opening up of parts of Ladakh such as Pangong Tso and Rupchu gives access to this species.

Rain Quail. Resident below 2000m in crops, grass and scrubland. Like most other quails probably under-recorded due to the difficulty in getting good views. Sites include Little Rann of Kutch, Manas, Pachmarhi, Rollapadu and Sailana WLS (Madhya Pradesh).

Blue-breasted Quail. Uncommon and possibly localised inhabitant of swampy grassland and scrub with poorly understood local movements. Recorded at Manas, Jatinga and Borivli.

Jungle Bush Quail*. Widespread resident of grass and scrub. Regular at Bund Baretha. Occasional at Tughlaqabad, Bharatpur, Ranthambhor, Kumbhalgarh, Little Rann of Kutch, Borivli, Bandhavgarh, Melghat, Pachmarhi, Nagarhole, Bodi Ghat, Periyar, Point Calimere and Rollapadu.

Rock Bush Quail**. Less common than the preceding species. Prefers drier, stonier habitats. Sites at which to look for it are Pushkar, Ranthambhor, Shivpuri, Little Rann of Kutch, Gir, Melghat, Baga and Rollapadu.

Painted Bush Quail**. Not uncommon in some areas of the peninsula but difficult to see in its grassland and scrub habitat. Best looked for just after dawn and before dusk along the verges of the Sighur Ghat Rd between Ooty and Mudumalai, at Rajamalai and Periyar. Other sites: Melghat, Nagarhole.

Manipur Bush Quail** (V). Little known resident of tall grass, scrub and sometimes marshes in the foothills of the northeastern Himalaya, from the duars of northern West Bengal to Manipur and the hills south of the Brahmaputra. Worryingly, there appear to be very few recent records, though the species is said to be difficult to observe and flush. Look out for it in suitable habitat at Dibru-Saikhowa and other similar areas.

Rufous-throated Partridge. Rare resident subject to some altitudinal movement. Inhabits dense undergrowth in Himalayan evergreen forest from Kumaon east. Recent records near Nainital and Kedarnath.

White-cheeked Partridge (N). Uncommon resident of evergreen forests below 1500m in eastern Assam, Arunachal Pradesh and hills south of the Brahmaputra. Recent records from Namdapha, Digboi, and sites in Mizoram.

Chestnut-breasted Partridge (V). Only a few historical records of this species from Sikkim and Arunachal Pradesh and a number of more recent ones from the latter. Some partridges seen at Buxa in 1992 were probably this species. Inhabits evergreen forest at altitudes between 350 and 2450m.

Mountain Bamboo Partridge. Uncommon resident of the hills south of the Brahmaputra up to 2000m but usually at lower altitudes. Recent sightings from the Jatinga area and Phawngpui NP (Mizoram).

Red Spurfowl*. Resident of scrub in deciduous forest. More common in the southern part of its range with most regular sightings from Top Slip, Mudumalai, Periyar, Nagarhole and Dona Paula (Goa). Uncommon at Shivpuri, Melghat, Simlipal and Kanha.

Painted Spurfowl**. Fairly easily seen along the approach road to Ranthambhor Fort. Prefers scrubby broken hills at sites such as Bandhavgarh, Melghat, Pachmarhi, Simlipal and Gingee Fort.

Himalayan Quail** (C). Probably extinct. Formerly occurred in grass and brushwood on steep Himalayan hillsides between 1650–2100m in the Dehra Dun–Nainital region. The last specimen was obtained in 1876 and efforts to find the bird since have failed.

Blood Pheasant. Inhabits dense forest undergrowth in the sub-alpine zone (3200–4700m) of North Bengal, Sikkim and Arunachal Pradesh. May move lower in harsh winter weather. Fairly regular on the Sandakphu Trek. Large flocks occur at Lampokhari above Dzongri on the trek north of Yuksom.

Western Tragopan* (V). Scarce endemic of the western Himalaya where it prefers oak and rhododendron forest in moist, shady valleys. The best Indian site is probably the Gt Himalayan NP but also occurs in the Solang, Manalsu and Hamta Valleys near Manali, as well as the Limber Valley (20km northeast of the Baramula Hydel Project in Kashmir).

Satyr Tragopan (N). Shy resident of moist oak and rhododendron forest. The best chances of seeing this bird are on the Sandakphu Trek (optimum zone 2600-3100m) and at Lava. Has also been seen at Kedarnath, Tiger Hill, Fambong Lho, Kyongnosla and Shingba.

Blyth's Tragopan (V). Very rare resident of dense evergreen forest undergrowth above 1800m. Prefers bamboo. Occurs mainly in Nagaland at a few sites of which the best seems to be the sub-tropical forest at Satoi, east-northeast of Kohima. Recently found breeding in the Phawngpui (Blue Mountain) NP of southeast Mizoram. Recorded also from Arunachal Pradesh; hunters' reports from Manipur.

Temminck's Tragopan (N). Rare and little-known resident of dense undergrowth in evergreen forest of central and eastern Arunachal Pradesh between 2100 and 3600m.

Himalayan Monal. One of the commoner high altitude pheasants. Inhabits scrub, undergrowth and forest glades near the timber line, moving down in winter. Localities include Dachigam, Gt Himalayan NP, Kullu Valley, Kyongnosla and Shingba.

Sclater's Monal (V). Very rare pheasant whose range extends from Yunnan (China) into Arunachal Pradesh where it was recently recorded for the first time in India in almost 50 years. Should be looked for in bamboo undergrowth of coniferous forest, rhododendron scrub and steep rocky slopes at 3000–4000m; areas at present inaccessible to Western birders.

Tibetan Eared Pheasant (V). A species whose range probably just extends from Tibet into the extreme north of Arunachal Pradesh. Preferred habitat is rhododendron and juniper with grassy clearings.

Kalij Pheasant. Common inhabitant of the Himalaya descending to the foothills and adjacent plains in winter, when it can be seen at Corbett, sites below Nainital, Sandakphu Trek, Tiger Hill, sites in Sikkim, Manas, Kaziranga, Dibru-Saikhowa and Namdapha.

Red Junglefowl. The wild ancestor of the humble farmyard chicken is a resident of the northern peninsula as far as the Himalayan foothills. Common at Corbett, for example, it can be found in most of the larger protected areas within its range, wherever there is sufficient scrub and deciduous forest.

Grey Junglefowl ** **(N).** Fairly common in most of the South Indian sanctuaries as far north as Kumbhalgarh.

Koklass Pheasant. Prefers oak and conifer forests with a good understorey. Common in the Gt Himalayan NP but the best site is probably the Shimla Water Catchment Reserve. Occasional near Nainital. Present in the Kedarnath Sanctuary and in appropriate habitat of other parts of the North Garhwal, Uttarkhand, and Kumaon regions of Uttar Pradesh. Fairly common at Dachigam above 2,300m and the Limber Valley (20km northeast of the Baramula Hydel Project in Kashmir).

Cheer Pheasant (V). Rare inhabitant of hill grasslands, scrub and second growth at altitudes between 1200 and 3250m in the western Himalaya, preferring steep south (and east) facing slopes. Most sightings are from the Gt Himalayan NP. Other good sites are the Chail WLS and near the village of Waccham in the Pindari Valley of the Almora District (Uttar Pradesh). Also occurs in the Hamta and Manalsu Valleys near Manali, and in the Kedarnath Sanctuary.

Mrs Hume's Pheasant (V). Rare resident of broadleaved evergreen and mixed forest (740–2000m) in eastern Arunachal Pradesh (Patkai Hills, Manipur, Nagaland and Mizoram with the only recent confirmed records coming from the latter in the Murlen and Phawngpui (Blue Mountain) NPs

Grey Peacock Pheasant. Uncommon forest resident of the Northeast Hill States – mainly in the foothills but also down to plains level (e.g. Panbari Forest, Kaziranga) and up as high as 1600m (Shillong).

Common Peafowl*. India's national bird is not uncommon in wooded areas throughout much of the country at altitudes below 1800m. In many areas the wild population is augmented by semi-feral birds, often found in the vicinity of villages and cultivation, particularly in Rajasthan and Gujarat. It can be encountered in many of the national parks such as Bharatpur, Ranthambhor, Corbett, Bandhavgarh, Kanha, Nagarhole, Sariska, etc.

Green Peafowl (V). Probably now extinct in India. Formerly a rare resident of dense forests in Northeast India. May still persist locally in areas adjacent to Myanmar (Burma).

Small Buttonquail. Probably much overlooked. Recent sightings from Delhi Ridge, Little Rann of Kutch and Melghat.

Yellow-legged Buttonquail. Occasional at Bharatpur, Ranthambhor, Little Rann of Kutch, Manas, Kaziranga and Jatinga.

Barred Buttonquail. Inconspicuous though widespread and probably not uncommon resident. Sites include: Ranthambhor, Bharatpur, Delhi Ridge, Tughlaqabad, Little Rann of Kutch, Manas, Jatinga, Bandhavgarh, Nagarhole and Point Calimere.

Common Crane. Winters in large numbers in Gujarat and western Rajasthan. Easily seen at Little Rann of Kutch, Nal Sarovar and Velavadar. Sometimes at Sultanpur, Shivpuri and Karera Bustard Sanctuary (Madhya Pradesh), as well as in and around Bharatpur.

Black-necked Crane (V). Small numbers winter in Bhutan and Arunachal Pradesh and a few breed in far eastern Ladakh. Has attempted to breed at Theple Tso in the Lhonak Valley of north Sikkim.

Sarus Crane (N). A widespread resident of the Indian plains, though the population is declining. Easily seen at Bharatpur, in roadside fields between Delhi and Mathura, at Sultanpur, Ranthambhor, and Sur Sarovar (Keetam Lake) near Agra.

Siberian Crane (E). The wintering population at Bharatpur appears to be on the verge of extinction – one of the great tragedies of modern Indian ornithology.

Demoiselle Crane. Spectacular gatherings at Kheechan. Winters in large numbers in Gujarat (e.g. in both the Little and Great Rann of Kutch) and Tal Chappar WLS in Rajasthan; smaller numbers at Sultanpur, Sambhar Lake and Sonkhaliya; occasional at other sites.

Slaty-breasted Rail. Widespread resident of marshy habitat. Doubtless under-recorded due to its skulking habits. Probably most easily seen at Corbyn's Cove and Mt Harriet. Other records from Bharatpur (R), Kanha, Jatinga, Fort Aguada Marsh and Pt Calimere, but patient exploration of any wet paddyfields and adjacent marshy areas could prove rewarding.

Slaty-legged Crake. Widespread resident/partial migrant of dense jungle in the vicinity of water. Rarely seen due to its secretive and crepuscular habits.

Andaman Crake** (V). A species endemic to the Andaman Islands where it is said to be a resident of swampy jungles, though perhaps also a shy forest crake. Few records in recent years but its skulking nature may mean that it is more common than records suggest. One was seen in a roadside ditch in a marshy area west of Port Blair, another at a pool near the base of Mt Harriet, where one or two individuals have been seen crossing the trails well away from any water.

Brown Crake. Resident of reedy marshes and waterside vegetation. Regular at Bund Baretha, Sur Sarovar and Ranthambhor. Rare at Bharatpur. Occasional along Yamuna River in Delhi, Kaziranga and Nagarhole.

Black-tailed Crake. A rare and secretive montane resident of jungle in and around rice paddies, grass-bordered streams, pools, and marshes in forest. One recent record from Pange in Arunachal Pradesh.

Watercock. Corbyn's Cove, Deepor Beel (Guwahati), coastal marshes in Goa. Occasionally breeds at Bharatpur and probably at Okhla.

Masked Finfoot (V). An inhabitant of mainly lowland forest rivers and pools as well as mangroves in the northeast part of the country. Not seen in recent times by any ornithologist but there are unconfirmed reports from the Tinsukia district near Dibru-Saikhowa and Digboi.

Indian Bustard* (E). This flagship conservation species is unhappily declining in spite of efforts to protect it. Can still be found at the Desert NP, Sorson, Diyatra and Sonkhaliya Closed Areas, and Rollapadu.

MacQueen's Bustard. Recently split from Houbara Bustard. A winter visitor best looked for in the Desert NP and Rann of Kutch. Occasional at Velavadar.

Bengal Florican (E). Most easily seen in the grasslands around Mihimukh during elephant rides at Kaziranga. Good populations at Manas, Orang WLS (Assam) and Dudhwa NP (Uttar Pradesh).

Lesser Florican** (C). An elusive species with very few sightings in winter. Best chances of seeing the bird are during the monsoon breeding season (end of June to late September) at various grassland sites in western India including Velavadar, Sonkhaliya, Banni Grasslands, and Sailana WLS (near Ratlam in western Madhya Pradesh). Recent winter records have come from Rollapadu and the Nanaj Bustard Sanctuary in the Solapur (Sholapur) district of Maharashtra.

Greater Painted-snipe. Not uncommon in suitable areas of marsh and paddy throughout the subcontinent but often overlooked. Fairly regular at Bharatpur, Bund Baretha, Sur Sarovar, Harike, Haigam Rakh, Deepor Beel, Manas and Baga.

Ibisbill. Uncommon altitudinal migrant inhabiting broad stony riverbeds in the Himalaya. Seen wintering regularly on the Kosi River north of the barrage at Ramnagar, along the Bhorellii River on the southwestern boundary of the Nameri WLS, on the Noa-Dihing at Namdapha, and in Manas along the Manas River. Breeds in Ladakh along the Indus River between Thikse and Leh, and on the Yumthang River in Sikkim.

Crab-plover. Mainly a winter visitor to islands in the Marine National Parks at Mannar in Tamil Nadu and the Gulf of Kutch in Gujarat, though there are occasional sightings along the coast elsewhere including Pt Calimere.

Indian Courser*. Widespread but not very common inhabitant of desert and semi-desert habitat throughout the peninsula. Reported fairly regularly from the dry areas at Helak ki Rundh (near Bharatpur), around Sultanpur, the semi-desert areas outside Ranthambhor, and the Little Rann of Kutch.

Jerdon's Courser** (E). Thought to be extinct until rediscovered in Andhra Pradesh in 1986. A very small vulnerable population remains restricted to a small area of the state. Birders must not attempt to visit the area without prior permission from the office of the Chief Wildlife Warden in Hyderabad.

Oriental Pratincole. Harike Lake, Chilka Lake, Phulera Lake (near Sambhar Lake) and Little Rann of Kutch.

Small Pratincole. Regular at Harike, on River Yamuna behind the Taj Mahal at Agra. Breeds at Corbett and Bund Baretha. Less common at other sites: Okhla, Nal Sarovar, River Kosi at Ramnagar, Rann of Kutch, Manas, Dibru-Saikhowa, Kaziranga, Chilka Lake, Nagarhole, Pt Calimere and River Cauvery (Karnataka, Tamil Nadu).

White-tailed Lapwing. Common winter visitor to Bharatpur, Harike, Okhla, Sultanpur, and Shivpuri.

Sociable Lapwing (V). Scarce winter visitor to northwest India. Recorded in most winters in the drier southern parts of Bharatpur around Koladahar. Rare in Little Rann of Kutch.

Grey-headed Lapwing (N). Uncommon winter visitor mainly to the northeast. Most often reported from wet fields and river banks around Kaziranga, Manas, Dibru-Saikhowa and Deepor Beel. Irregular at Bharatpur and Sultanpur.

Yellow-wattled Lapwing*. A fairly widespread bird of dry open sparsely scrubbed areas. Not uncommon in the right habitat. Some of the better sites are Tughlaqabad in Delhi, wasteland around Bharatpur, Pt Calimere and semi-desert around Ranthambhor.

Long-billed Plover (N). Occasionally winters along the Kosi River north of Ramnagar and on the Bhorelli at Nameri.

Asian Dowitcher (N). Regularly winters in small numbers on Nalaban Island, Lake Chilka. Occasionally at Pt Calimere and Harike.

Solitary Snipe. Most regular along the stream through Leh and around the Indus and Shey Marshes in Ladakh in winter. Has been recorded around 4000m in the Gt Himalayan NP.

Wood Snipe (V). Little-known species breeding in both wooded and open habitats of the Himalaya (1200-4000m) from Kullu to Arunachal Pradesh. Winters on marshy patches in the Himalayan foothills and hills of the peninsula but few recent records.

Spoon-billed Sandpiper (V). Pt Calimere is the only site where this species occurs with any regularity though even a visit in the prime season between December and January is no guarantee of finding this rare wader. Could turn up at any of the other larger wetlands along the east coast.

Red-necked Phalarope. Probably regular though not common at Pt Calimere in winter. Has occurred at Bharatpur.

River Tern. Widespread and still reasonably common, though apparently declining, on inland plains-level rivers, tanks and lakes, though not usually in large numbers.

White-cheeked Tern. Breeds on Vengurla Rocks off the Maharashtra Coast in May/June.

Black-naped Tern. Breeds on islands of the Indian Ocean. Fairly common around South Andaman.

Black-bellied Tern (V). Becoming worryingly scarce. Occurs in the same kinds of habitat as the much commoner River Tern. Look out for it along any of the larger tanks or rivers, e.g. the Yamuna at Delhi or Agra, or the Cauvery in South India. Regular at Harike. Occasional at Bharatpur and Bund Baretha.

Bridled Tern. Breeds on Vengurla Rocks (Maharashtra coast) with White-cheeked Tern. Has been recorded at Pt Calimere.

Sooty Tern. Breeds in Lakshadweep. Has been recorded at Pt Calimere.

Saunders's Tern. Should be looked out for along the coasts of Gujarat, having bred near Bhavnagar and recorded in April at Beyt Dwarka (Okha Island).

Great Crested Tern. Regular at Chapora River Estuary and Chilka Lake. Scarce at Pt Calimere.

Lesser Crested Tern. Regular at Chapora River Estuary and Chilka Lake. Scarce at Pt Calimere. Breeds Gulf of Mannar.

Brown Noddy. Breeds in Lakshadweep.

Indian Skimmer (V). Rare and localised showing a drastic decline in numbers in recent years. Easiest place to see them is Bundh Baretha near Bharatpur. Also regular at Harike, Lake Surwal near Ranthambhor, larger waterbodies in the Little Rann of Kutch, along the Ganges River near Gajraula (Uttar Pradesh), and on the Chambal River near Morena (58km south of Agra).

Tibetan Sandgrouse. Found in the extreme east of Ladakh, e.g. around lakes Tsomoriri and Tsokar.

Spotted Sandgrouse. In winter in the Desert NP and Little Rann of Kutch.

Black-bellied Sandgrouse. In winter in the Desert NP and Gajner WLS.

Painted Sandgrouse*. Uncommon resident of barren rocky regions in western India. Found in dry areas around Ranthambhor, Shivpuri and Gir. Uncommon at Nagarhole.

Pin-tailed Green Pigeon. Somewhat nomadic inhabitant of mature forest in the lower Himalaya and adjacent plains, more common in the east. Sites: higher reaches of Corbett (around Kanda), Mahananda WLS, Jaldapara, Manas and Namdapha.

Wedge-tailed Green Pigeon. Has a similar distribution to the previous species though generally prefers slightly higher altitudes (overlapping). Sites include Kullu Valley, Lava, Manas, Kaziranga, Namdapha and Jatinga.

Thick-billed Green Pigeon. Uncommon nomadic resident of the lower eastern Himalayan forests. Fairly regular at Kaziranga (Panbari Forest); also found at Manas, Namdapha and Dibru-Saikhowa.

Yellow-eyed Pigeon (V). A species that breeds in Central Asia. A large flock has been wintering in recent years at Harike.

Speckled Wood Pigeon. An inhabitant of the higher altitude Himalayan forests. Wanders in search of fruit. Common at the Gt Himalayan NP. Other sites: around Nainital, Lava and Khecheoperi Lake.

Nilgiri Wood Pigeon** **(N).** Is found in the southern part of the Western Ghats generally above 1000m. Uncommon to fairly common but somewhat sporadic due to its nomadic habits. Most often seen in fruiting fig trees in shola forest around Ooty, Avalanche, Dolphin's Nose and Munnar. Regular in Bombay Shola at Kodaikanal (Tamil Nadu). A small relict population still survives in the Nandi Hills, 68km north of Bangalore (Karnataka).

Ashy Wood Pigeon. Inhabits evergreen forest in the eastern Himalaya, usually between 1200 and 3200m, though it has been known to stray down to the adjacent terai in search of seasonal fruits. Apparently even scarcer than Speckled Wood Pigeon. Lava and Buxa seem to offer the best chances of finding this species.

Pale-capped Pigeon (V). Very rare resident. Recent sightings from Manas, Kaziranga, Dibru-Saikhowa and Simlipal.

Andaman Wood Pigeon** **(N).** Endemic to the Andaman & Nicobar Islands. The most accessible place to see the species is Mount Harriet NP where it is not common. Care should be taken in distinguishing this from the far commoner Green Imperial Pigeon.

Andaman Cuckoo Dove** **(N).** Endemic to the Andamans & Nicobars. Not particularly common but Mt Harriet NP is a fairly reliable site.

Nicobar Pigeon (N). Found mainly in dense rainforest on the less disturbed islands of the Nicobar group including Great Nicobar. Nests in large numbers on Batti Malv. Occasionally strays to the Andamans.

Nicobar Parakeet** **(N).** Endemic to the Nicobars where it is quite common in high forest.

Derbyan Parakeet (N). A rare summer visitor to extreme northeast Arunachal Pradesh.

[**Intermediate Parakeet (V).** Formerly considered by some authorities to be a good species though it had never been observed in the wild by an ornithologist. Recent research has shown that it is almost certainly a hybrid. Existing specimens (obtained from bird dealers) are consistent with hybrids between Plum-headed and Slaty-headed Parakeets.]

Malabar Parakeet**. Endemic to South India where it is reasonably common in the forests of the Western Ghats between 500 and 1000m. Can be found in several National Parks there such as Nagarhole, Mudumalai and Periyar. Appears to also be adapting to more disturbed habitats.

Chestnut-winged Cuckoo. Rare winter visitor to southern India. Breeds in the Himalayan foothills. Seen occasionally in the tourist zone at Periyar, Top Slip, Pt Calimere, Vedanthangal and Guindy in winter; at Manas and Dibru-Saikhowa in summer.

Pied Cuckoo. In winter commoner on the eastern side of South India, being fairly frequent in areas of lowland coastal scrub and secondary growth e.g. at Madras, the Pulicat area and Pt Calimere. Common in the rainy season at Bharatpur, Sultanpur and even in the parks in Delhi.

Hodgson's Hawk Cuckoo. Scarce resident of the lower hill forests in the eastern Himalaya. Best sought, like many other cuckoos, when it begins calling from about the middle of March.

Oriental Cuckoo. Best located and identified by voice during the breeding season in the first half of summer in the lower/middle Himalaya.

Lesser Cuckoo. Most often recorded during the breeding season in medium elevations forests in the Himalaya.

Banded Bay Cuckoo. More common in central and southern India. Widespread but often overlooked outside the breeding season when it is more vocal. Sites include Manas, Kaziranga, Periyar and Top Slip.

Grey-bellied Cuckoo*. Widespread but uncommon in wooded areas below 2700m throughout the country except for Northeast India. More vocal and easily located in the rainy season when it is also found at Bharatpur.

Drongo Cuckoo. Found throughout most of the country below 2000m but often overlooked due to its resemblance to a drongo. More easily tracked down in the monsoon breeding season when it is calling.

Blue-faced Malkoha*. Endemic to Peninsular India and Sri Lanka. Not uncommon in scrub and thorn at lower elevations at Pt Calimere, Melghat, Chamundi Hill, Nagarhole, Mudumalai, Sighur Ghat and Guindy. Common along the lower slopes of the Western Ghats on the drier eastern side.

Sirkeer Malkoha*. Widespread but not particularly common at lower altitudes from the Himalayan foothills south. Prefers tangled undergrowth in drier open woodland. Seen fairly regularly at Bharatpur, Mudumalai, Ranthambhor and Sariska, also found occasionally at Harike, Corbett, Bandhavgarh, Melghat and Nagarhole.

[**Red-faced Malkoha* (V).** There are two or three doubtful records of this species from India. Now generally regarded as endemic to Sri Lanka. Any sightings would need careful substantiation.]

Brown Coucal (N). The species is confined to the Andaman Islands and the Coco Islands of Myanmar (Burma) and is thus a near-endemic. Fairly common on South Andaman where it can be found in dense forest, secondary scrub, gardens and around cultivation.

Oriental Bay Owl. Resident with apparently disjunct populations in Northeast and South India. Only a few recent records from the Nelliampathy Hills (Palghat district of Kerala), Perambikulam/Anaimalai NPs, Thattakad BS and Namdapha.

Andaman Scops Owl** (N). Endemic to the Andamans where it is apparently not uncommon, e.g. at Mt Harriet.

Spot-bellied Eagle Owl (N). Scarce resident of the Himalaya and hills of South India. Recent records from Corbett (near Dhangari), Manas, Tiger Hill, Nagarhole, Karian Shola (Top Slip), Bondla, Thattakad and Periyar.

Dusky Eagle Owl. Uncommon to fairly common resident. The easiest place to see this species is Bharatpur where there is a fairly stable population estimated at around 22 pairs in 1996/97.

Tawny Fish Owl (N). A bird of forests near streams and rivers. Much less common than its Brown relative. Most sightings are from Corbett and Kaziranga.

Andaman Hawk Owl** (N). Endemic to the Andaman & Nicobar Islands. Best site is probably Mt Harriet.

Forest Owlet** (C). Thought for many years to be extinct, the sensational news of its rediscovery near Shahada (not far from where Davidson had collected his specimens) broke in late 1997. Formerly recorded from moist deciduous forests and groves of wild mango, predominantly near streams, along the Satpura mountain range from southeast Gujarat to northwest Orissa (and possibly extreme southern Bihar). Further surveys are needed to ascertain the current status of this critically endangered endemic.

Mottled Wood Owl*. Uncommon but widespread endemic resident in the peninsula. Partial to groves of mangos. Now rarely seen at Bharatpur, more regular at Bandhavgarh; uncommon at Nagarhole and Mudumalai. See also section on Melghat.

Sri Lanka Frogmouth* (N). Rare South Indian/Sri Lankan endemic. Fairly regular at Top Slip (Karian Shola) and Bondla.

Hodgson's Frogmouth. Rare resident of sub-tropical evergreen forest in Northeast India. The only recent reports are from the Shoolpaneshwar WLS in Gujarat, well away from the species accepted range, and the Pabong Forest in Sikkim.

Sykes's Nightjar. One of India's scarcest nightjars. Most easily seen at Harike where it roosts among scattered low tamarisks by the river. Unusual at Bharatpur.

Jerdon's Nightjar*. Recently split from Long-tailed Nightjar and considered endemic to peninsular India and Sri Lanka. Not uncommon in suitable habitat in South India, e.g. at Mudumalai.

Indian Swiftlet*. Endemic shared between Sri Lanka and South India. Fairly common in the Western Ghats.

White-rumped Needletail. Regular at Corbett. Common at Periyar and Top Slip.

Dark-rumped Swift (V). One of the world's rarest swifts. Present at its breeding colonies around the waterfalls and cliffs near Cherrapunjee from end February to end April, possibly also outside this period, but little is known about its movements. Has also been recorded in Mizoram and Bhutan in spring and could thus occur elsewhere in the region.

Malabar Trogon*. Uncommon to fairly common Indian/Sri Lankan endemic. Most often seen at Top Slip, Periyar and Bondla. Uncommon at Simlipal, Molem and Thattakad.

Ward's Trogon (V). Rare resident of forests between 1500 and 3000m in Arunachal Pradesh. There are recent reports from Baguwa and Jorethang in southern Sikkim.

Blyth's Kingfisher (V). Rare resident of rivers and large streams through dense lowland forest with a few recent records from Sikkim, Dibru-Saikhowa and Namdapha.

Blue-eared Kingfisher. Scarce and patchily distributed resident of shady forest streams. (On Middle and South Andaman also frequents creeks.) The best site seems to be Molem.

Oriental Dwarf Kingfisher. Uncommon resident of shady streams in humid evergreen forest at lower altitudes in Northeast India and the Western Ghats, e.g. Namdapha and Bondla.

Brown-winged Kingfisher (N). A scarce inhabitant of mangrove forests and tidal creeks. Should be looked for in the Sundarbans of West Bengal and any remaining areas of mangrove on the Orissan coast, e.g. in the Mahanadi Delta and Bhitarkanika WLS. Said to be common at the latter site.

Ruddy Kingfisher. Shy tropical and sub-tropical forest kingfisher not tied to water. Also inhabits mangroves. It is surprisingly one of the commoner birds among those attracted to the bright lights at Jatinga. Said to be fairly common at Nameri WLS. Has been observed at Dibru Saikhowa, Namdapha and Chiria Tappu.

Blue-bearded Bee-eater. Localised forest resident. Most often seen at Corbett, Manas, Kaziranga, Dibru-Saikhowa, Namdapha, Bandhavgarh and Mudumalai. Has also been seen at Bondla and Molem. Quite common in the Biligirirangan Hills southeast of Mysore.

Dollarbird. Uncommon resident partial to forest clearings in the lower Himalaya and the Western Ghats. Seen occasionally at Corbett, Mahananda, Manas, Kaziranga, Dibru-Saikhowa, Namdapha and Top Slip. Fairly common in the Andamans.

Malabar Grey Hornbill** (N). Restricted to South India. Not uncommon in the Western Ghats.

Brown Hornbill (N). A rare resident of low-altitude primary evergreen forest. Recent records from Namdapha, and Dimbruchara near Jatinga.

Rufous-necked Hornbill (V). A resident of primary evergreen forest up to 1800m. Still fairly common at Namdapha. Uncommon at Buxa and Nameri WLS.

Wreathed Hornbill. Like most other hornbills dependent on the presence of large mature trees for nesting and plenty of forest fruits for food, i.e. in mature tropical and sub-tropical forest. Common at Namdapha, particularly around Embeong. Uncommon at Buxa, Manas and Kaziranga.

Narcondam Hornbill (V). The total world population estimated at 200–400 individuals is confined to the 6.82km^2 Narcondam Island in the Andamans.

Malabar Pied Hornbill* (N). Uncommon resident of Peninsular India and Sri Lanka but declining in numbers due to the deforestation of its lowland habitat. Still regular at Nagarhole, Pachmarhi and Bandhavgarh. Also occurs at Kanha, Simlipal, Bondla and Molem.

Great Hornbill. Regular at Corbett, Manas, Kaziranga, Namdapha, Simlipal, Periyar and Top Slip.

White-cheeked Barbet.** Common in wooded habitats of the Western Ghats south of the Narmada River and east to the Shevaroys.

Crimson-fronted Barbet*. Generally regarded as an endemic shared with Sri Lanka but the Indian form may prove to be a separate species as appearance and call differ. Fairly common in evergreen forests of the South Indian hills.

Yellow-rumped Honeyguide (N). Inhabits mid- to high-altitude forests in the Himalaya, never far from cliffs and rock-faces supporting colonies of the Himalayan Honey Bee *Apis laboriosa*. Two recent records from Limeking and Pange in Arunachal Pradesh. Has been recorded in the Pemayangtse area and near Gagaria on the Govindghat-Valley of Flowers trail in Uttar Pradesh.

Himalayan Flameback. Regular at Corbett, Manas and Kaziranga.

Pale-headed Woodpecker. Patchily distributed resident in Sikkim and the Northeast Hill States. Predominantly found in bamboo up to elevations of 1000m. The best sites seem to be Kaziranga, Namdapha and Jatinga.

Great Slaty Woodpecker. Rare resident of mature, mainly lowland, woods in the terai zone, e.g. at Corbett, Dudhwa, Namdapha, and in Mizoram at the Dampa Tiger Reserve and Ngengpui Sanctuary. Has been recorded as high and far west as Shimla (Water Catchment Sanctuary).

Andaman Woodpecker** (N). Recently split from White-bellied Woodpecker and hence regarded as endemic to the Andamans. Not uncommon in well-forested areas of South Andaman including Mt Harriet and Chiria Tapu.

White-naped Woodpecker*. Local and uncommon resident occasionally seen at Ramnagar, Ranthambhor, Bandhavgarh, Melghat, Pachmari, Molem, Mudumalai and Nagarhole.

Blue-naped Pitta (N). Uncommon and skulking altitudinal migrant restricted to Northeast India. Namdapha is probably the best place to see this species, though it is a possibility in any of the more forested areas of the Northeast Hill States.

Indian Pitta*. A not uncommon but secretive migrant, wintering in South India (e.g. Mudumalai, Periyar) and breeding in the north of the country (e.g. Sariska, Jaipur and Ranthambhor).

Singing Bushlark. Patchily distributed resident of dry sparsely vegetated lowlands. Occasionally seen at the Koladahar area of Bharatpur, Bund Baretha, Ranthambhor, Harike, Little Rann of Kutch and Rollapadu.

Bengal Bushlark. The species known as Bush Lark *Mirafra assamica* by Ali & Ripley was formerly regarded as polytypic ranging from India through to Indochina. Recent research by Per Alström has shown that it is best treated as four separate species with Bengal Bushlark being a fairly widespread and common near-endemic inhabiting the plains of the northern Indian subcontinent and a small part of neighbouring Myanmar (Burma).

Jerdon's Bushlark*. The above split means that the former race *affinis* of Bush Lark is now treated as a separate species confined to southern and eastern parts of India as well as Sri Lanka. Sites include Madras, Mudumalai/Masinagudi and Nagarhole.

[**Bar-tailed Desert Lark.** This species is resident in western Pakistan and there are no fully documented records from India. There have been one or two reports from the area around Jaisalmer and the Desert NP but confusion with Desert Lark cannot be ruled out and any birds showing the features of this species should be carefully observed and detailed field notes taken.]

Rufous-tailed Lark*. Fairly common but patchily distributed resident of dry lowland facies, often where the soil or rock is reddish. Regular at Tughlaqabad, Bharatpur, Bund Baretha, Ranthambhor (Surwal Dam), Shivpuri, Sariska, Velavadar, Little Rann of Kutch, Carambolim Lake, Shamirpet Lake and Rollapadu.

[**Lesser Short-toed Lark.** There have been reports of this species from western India but descriptions have not ruled out the closely similar Asian Short-toed Lark which could also occur.]

Malabar Lark**. Indian endemic found mainly on dry open ground with sparse vegetation down the western side of the peninsula. Good places include Masinagudi (Mudumalai), Nagarhole (Karapura village), Goa and around Pune (Maharashtra).

Sykes's Lark**. Endemic to peninsular India. Good sites include Shamirpet Lake, Rollapadu WLS, Vir Dam near Pune (Maharashtra), and a lake near the town of Rajkot (Gujarat). Probably more common than records suggest, as it favours sparsely scrubbed areas in the Deccan less frequently visited by birders.

Pacific Swallow. Fairly common around the coasts of the Andaman Islands. The subspecies *domicola* known as Hill Swallow is sometimes considered a separate endemic species confined to South India and Sri Lanka. This latter can often be seen hawking for insects over open ground and tea plantations in the hills of southwest India.

Streak-throated Swallow. A locally common near-endemic. Regular at Okhla, Bharatpur (and the nearby Deeg Palace), Ramnagar, Carambolim Lake and Ranganathittu.

Crow-billed Drongo. Uncommon inhabitant of dense forest along the foot of the Himalaya from the Kumaon region in Uttar Pradesh eastwards. Seasonal movements poorly understood. Some records of this species appear to be based on misidentification of other drongos (particularly immature Greater Racket-tailed).

Andaman Drongo** (N). A species restricted to the Andaman Islands. Not uncommon in forested areas of South Andaman.

Spot-winged Starling (N). Occurs, sometimes in large flocks, at Buxa, Kaziranga, Manas and Dibru-Saikhowa in winter; fairly common at Dehra Dun in April and July.

White-headed Starling** (N). Found only on the Andaman and Nicobar Islands. Can be seen fairly easily in open areas around Port Blair as well as more forested habitats such as Mt Harriet and Chiria Tapu.

Collared Myna (N). Within our range largely confined to the Manipur Valley. May occasionally stray into adjoining regions.

Golden-crested Myna. Rare inhabitant of humid forests in the North Cachar Hills of Assam and Manipur. Partial to fruiting and flowering trees. There don't appear to be any recent published records though one was seen recently in the Mahananda WLS.

Black-headed Jay. Inhabits oak and conifer forest of the western Himalaya. Nainital is a regular site.

Collared Treepie. Scarce. The best site is Digboi with a few recent records from Namdapha and other sites in Arunachal Pradesh.

White-bellied Treepie **(N).** Restricted to the hills of southwest India. Common at Top Slip, Thattakad, Periyar and Silent Valley.

Andaman Treepie **(N).** Confined to the rainforests of the Andaman Islands. Fairly common at Mt Harriet and Chiria Tapu.

Hume's Groundpecker. A bird of the high-altitude Tibetan steppe in the trans-Himalayan zone. Recently observed at Pangmar in the Rupshu region of Ladakh. Has also been seen on the Bara Hoti Plain in the extreme north of Uttar Pradesh en route to Mt. Kailash in Tibet. Present in small numbers throughout transhimalayan Sikkim where very tame around Tibetan settlements, e.g. in Lashar Valley.

Spotted Nutcracker. The subspecies *multipunctata*, Larger-spotted Nutcracker, found in Kashmir (north of the Pir Panjal range) and parts of Himachal Pradesh, is regarded by some as a separate species from the form inhabiting the remaining Himalaya.

Grey Hypocolius. Recent regular winter records from scrub jungle near the village of Fulay (between it and the village of Chhari) in the Banni grassland area near the western end of the Great Rann of Kutch, Gujarat.

Black-headed Cuckooshrike*. Widespread and locally fairly common at lower elevations in many types of wooded habitats. A summer visitor to many areas.

Ashy Minivet. Winter straggler to India with recent isolated records from Periyar, Goregaon (Mumbai), Karnala WLS and the Beas Valley (Himachal Pradesh). Perhaps more regular than records indicate as it has been seen at Guindy in several recent winters.

White-bellied Minivet (N). Uncommon resident occasionally seen in dry thorn scrub at Masinagudi (Mudumalai), Tughlaqabad, around Jodhpur, around Pune (Maharashtra), near Sambhar lake, near Jaisalmer and Chinnar. One of the best sites is apparently Shivpuri. It may become a subcontinental endemic if split from the form *albifrons* of Myanmar (Burma).

Marshall's Iora.** Replaces the Common Iora in northwest India and is the resident species of iora found at Bharatpur, where not very common in areas of acacia. Becoming increasingly rare at other sites including Delhi Ridge, Tughlaqabad, Bund Baretha and Ranthambhor.

Grey-headed Bulbul **(N).** Rather shy compared with the commoner bulbuls, this South Indian endemic is best looked for in stands of bamboo at Mudumalai, e.g. along the Moyar River and around Masinagudi, or at the Wynaad Sanctuary. Also regular at Bondla and Cotigao.

Black-crested Bulbul. The southwest Indian race *gularis*, known as Ruby-throated Bulbul, may prove to be a full species. It is regular at Top Slip, Periyar and Bondla.

Yellow-throated Bulbul **(N).** Having a different distribution to most South Indian endemics this species is not seen by visiting birders as often as it might be. It prefers steep scrubby hillsides with scattered trees on the drier eastern slopes of the Western Ghats and hill ranges to the east. The most convenient site on a South India tour is on the Bodi Ghat. Other good sites around Bangalore (Karnataka) are Savanadurga Hill, Nandi Hills and Devarayanadurga; Horsley Hills (near Madanapalle, Andhra Pradesh); and Gingee Fort (Tamil Nadu).

White-browed Bulbul*. Fairly widespread and common in some parts of the peninsula but shier than most other bulbuls keeping to the interior of dense bushes in dry scrub and secondary growth at lower altitudes.

Nicobar Bulbul **(V).** This species appears to be uncommon and declining within its small range, the Nancowrie group in the Nicobar

Islands. It is possibly losing out to competition with the introduced Red-whiskered Bulbul.

Yellow-browed Bulbul*. Common and widespread in mid-altitude evergreen forests of the Western Ghats from Pune south.

Marsh Babbler* (V). Rare resident of reeds, long grass and swampy forest below 800m in the Brahmaputra floodplain and adjacent foothills. Recent records apparently only from Tipi in Arunachal Pradesh, Dibru-Saikhowa and the nearby Amarpur area (Assam).

Indian Scimitar Babbler**. Widespread and locally fairly common in forest vegetation from the Tapti River in Gujarat south.

Spot-breasted Scimitar Babbler. Split from Rusty-cheeked Scimitar Babbler. Scarce low to mid-altitude resident of jungle in eastern Assam, Meghalaya, Nagaland and Manipur. Recently reported from Murlen NP in Mizoram.

Slender-billed Scimitar Babbler (N). Uncommon and shy resident of the eastern Himalaya. Inhabits ringal bamboo and thick undergrowth. Good sites include Namdapha, Tiger Hill, the Sandakphu Trek and Pemayangtse.

Long-billed Wren Babbler (N). Scarce resident. There have been sightings in recent years at Buxa, Lava and Jatinga, as well as Pange, Mehao and the Upper Noa Dihing Valley in Arunachal Pradesh.

Streaked Wren Babbler. Frequents damp shady forest undergrowth , particularly in limestone areas, in the hills of Northeast India, south and east of the Brahmaputra. Appears to be fairly common at Namdapha, in the North Cachar Hills (Assam) and in Mizoram.

Eyebrowed Wren Babbler. Scarce (locally common?) inhabitant of broadleaved evergreen forest, often in areas with mossy boulders, in the Northeast Hill States. Recent records from Namdapha and Jatinga.

Rufous-throated Wren Babbler* (V). Scarce resident of undergrowth in montane broadleaved evergreen forests of Sikkim, western Arunachal Pradesh and the Darjeeling area. The best site seems to be Lava but has also been seen at Tiger Hill, before Megma on the Sandakphu Trek, as well as Pange and the Tale WLS (Talley Valley) in Arunachal Pradesh.

Rusty-throated Wren Babbler** (V). Known only from a single specimen collected in wet subtropical forest at an altitude of about 1600m near Dreyi in the Mishmi Hills of Arunachal Pradesh in January 1947.

Tawny-breasted Wren Babbler** (V). Very rare resident of dense undergrowth in ravines and steep rocky hillsides with moss-covered boulders in deep evergreen forest at 1000 to 2000m in Manipur, Nagaland (?) and the Khasi and Cachar Hills of Meghalaya and Assam. Only known sightings in recent years from Shillong Peak (1979) and a possible from a dense jungle-covered hillside southeast of Mawsynram in Meghalaya (1996).

Long-tailed Wren Babbler. Inhabits damp mossy forest in the North Cachar, Mizo, Naga, and Manipur Hills of Northeast India. Recent records from Mizoram, Namdapha (Hotspring) and Ukhrul (Manipur).

Bar-winged Wren Babbler. The only Indian records appear to be from Arunachal Pradesh: Nyug La (1944), the Upper Noa Dihing (outside southeastern edge of Namdapha, 1988), a party of four or more seen at 3000m in scrub/rhododendron forest, 5km north of Chakoo (Chaku) in the Eagle's Nest WLS (1991), and in the Dafla Hills (1995?).

Spotted Wren Babbler (N). Scarce inhabitant of understorey in mossy, broadleaved evergreen forest. Recent records from Namdapha (not uncommon) and the Jatinga area.

Wedge-billed Wren Babbler (N). Inhabits evergreen forest and second growth in parties of 10-15 birds. Recent records from a few locations in Arunachal Pradesh (including Namdapha), the Darjeeling area, as well as the Mahur area near Jatinga. The two forms *humei* and *roberti* may be split in future.

Black-chinned Babbler*. Common around Corbett, Nainital and in the Great Himalayan NP.

Snowy-throated Babbler** (V). A species with a highly restricted range limited to the Patkai and Dapha Hills of Arunachal Pradesh. All recent records appear to be of birds seen in the non-breeding season in primary evergreen forest (especially in bamboo thickets) at altitudes up to 800m at Namdapha, where flocks of 10–25 birds are not uncommon.

Tawny-bellied Babbler*. Locally fairly common in loose flocks in scrub, grassland, thorn and deciduous forest. Sites include Mudumalai, Top Slip, Periyar, Ranthambhor, Kumbhalgarh, Melghat, Bandhavgarh, Pachmarhi, Ranganathittu, Nagarhole and Bodhi Ghat.

Dark-fronted Babbler*. Locally fairly common, though often rather skulking in evergreen forests of the southwest Indian hills. Can be seen at Bondla, Molem, Wynaad, Nadugani, Top Slip and Periyar.

Jerdon's Babbler (V). A scarce bird of reedbeds and grasslands of the Brahmaputra floodplain. Only a few recent sightings (probably under-recorded) from Kaziranga, Manas and Dibru-Saikhowa.

Lesser Rufous-headed Parrotbill (N). The scarce nominate form occurs in parties inhabiting tall grass, bamboo and scrub in or near broadleaved evergreen forest in Northeast India. Recent records all seem to be from Arunachal Pradesh (including Namdapha). The subspecies *oatesi* from Sikkim and the Darjeeling area does not appear to have been seen since the 19th century except in neighbouring Bhutan.

Greater Rufous-headed Parrotbill (N). Recent records only from Buxa (in flocks with Coral-billed Scimitar Babbler), Dampa Tiger Reserve (Mizoram), and sites in Arunachal Pradesh including Namdapha.

Black-breasted Parrotbill* (V). A very scarce and localised species confined to Northeast India and northeast Bangladesh. It inhabits grasslands, reeds and bamboo of the plains and adjacent foothills mainly bordering the Brahmaputra River system. The only recent records appear to be from Kaziranga and the grasslands at Amarpur (Dibru-Saikhowa) in eastern Assam.

Spot-breasted Parrotbill. Said to have been locally common in scrub, grass and bamboo in the hills of Meghalaya, Assam north to Nagaland and the Patkai Range of Arunachal Pradesh. The only recent sightings appear to be from Wallong (Arunachal Pradesh) and Mizoram, where it has been recorded from Murlen and Phawngpui (Blue Mountain) NPs.

Striated Babbler. Relatively local resident of grassland in the northern river floodplains. Still quite common at Okhla but threatened by increasing urbanisation. Other sites include Harike, Manas and Kaziranga.

Slender-billed Babbler (N). A near-endemic inhabitant of grassland, usually near water. Local and probably often overlooked due to its retiring habits. Best searched for at Kaziranga, Manas and Dibru-Saikhowa.

Rufous Babbler**. Restricted to the hills (mainly 800–1200m) occasionally descending as far as the adjacent plains of southwest India, where it prefers tangled scrub jungle and forest edge. Molem, Nagarhole, Top Slip, Periyar and Thattakad are among the protected areas where it occurs though it should also be watched out for in scrub elsewhere.

Yellow-billed Babbler*. Locally common inhabitant of lowland scrub, second growth and gardens in South India.

Chinese Babax. Rare resident above 1500m in the Lushai Hills (Mizoram), where the only recent record is from Phawngpui NP.

[Giant Babax (N). A Tibetan species with no definite records from India. Could occur in extreme northern Sikkim and Arunachal Pradesh.]

Striated Laughingthrush. Not uncommon but localised in well-wooded (broadleaved) areas of the middle Himalaya. Sites include Dachigam, Nainital, Kullu Valley, Fambong Lho and the Sandakphu Trek.

Chestnut-backed Laughingthrush (N). Uncommon (possibly locally common) resident of scrub, overgrown ravines and high grass below 900m in Northeast India (south of the Mishmi Hills). Recent sightings from Namdapha, Digboi, and the Assam/Arunachal border near Margherita.

Yellow-throated Laughingthrush (N). Scarce resident of open jungle, forest edge, grass and scrub in the Cachar Hills (Assam), the Lushai Hills (Mizoram), Nagaland and Manipur. The only recent sightings appear to be from Namdapha and near Litan (Litang – c.45km north-northeast of Imphal, Manipur).

Wynaad Laughingthrush ** (N).** One of the scarcer South Indian endemics. Occurs in flocks, often large, in bamboo and lower storey of evergreen forests. Most sightings come from the road to Anaigunti Shola at Anaimalai and the moister forest on the Mangala Devi track at Periyar, though a flock is sometimes also seen around the tourist zone at the latter site.

Rufous-vented Laughingthrush. Uncommon (locally fairly common) resident of the hills in the Northeast Hill States. Recorded in recent years from Manas and Namdapha.

Variegated Laughingthrush*. Common resident of open forest and scrub at higher elevations, some descending lower in winter, e.g. in the Kullu Valley, Gt Himalayan NP, Shimla Water Catchment Sanctuary and Dachigam.

Rufous-necked Laughingthrush. Locally common inhabitant of more open mixed habitats in Northeast India. Good sites include Kaziranga, Dibru-Saikhowa and Namdapha.

Spot-breasted Laughingthrush (N). Uncommon and shy inhabitant of dense forest undergrowth, adjacent secondary growth and scrub in Nagaland, Manipur, Mizoram, the Khasi Hills of Meghalaya, and the North Cachar Hills of Assam. The authors cannot find any definite recent records.

Nilgiri Laughingthrush ** (N).** An endemic with a highly restricted range but still fairly common in shola forest around Ooty (Udhagamandalam).

Grey-breasted Laughingthrush ** (N).** Common at the few sites where it occurs within a very restricted range, the easiest place on the standard South Indian itinerary being Rajamalai, where it frequents the sholas.

Striped Laughingthrush (N). Scarce (locally not uncommon) resident of scrub, grass and forest edge from the Cachar Hills of Assam east. Recent sightings from the Mahur area near Jatinga, near Ukhrul in Manipur, and from the Murlen and Phawngpui (Blue Mountain) NPs of Mizoram.

Brown-capped Laughingthrush (D). Only known from the hills south of the Brahmaputra in the North Cachar Hills (Assam), Nagaland, Manipur and Mizoram. Its habitat consists of oak and rhododendron forest, secondary growth and bamboo from 1200 to 2700m. The only recent sighting of this near-endemic species appears to be from Mizoram.

Blue-winged Laughingthrush. Uncommon mid-altitude resident of dense undergrowth in Northeast India. The best sites are probably Lava, Namdapha and Khecheoperi Lake. Also recorded at Tiger Hill and Rumtek.

Scaly Laughingthrush. An uncommon east Himalayan mid-elevation forest species. Sites include Tiger Hill, Lava, Khecheoperi Lake, Yuksom and Manas.

Elliot's Laughingthrush. A group of over 20 near Hotspring in extreme northeastern Arunachal Pradesh in 1994 constituted the first record for the Indian subcontinent. The species has also been observed there since.

Red-faced Liocichla. A scarce resident babbler. Recent sightings are from Lava, Jatinga, Mizoram, and Arunachal Pradesh.

Fire-tailed Myzornis. The best chances of finding this delightful, scarce and localised little babbler seem to be at Lava, on the Sandakphu Trek, or at Pemayangtse in Sikkim, but good luck may be needed.

Cutia. A widespread but sparse and patchily distributed resident of oak and mossy evergreen forest in Northeast India. There are no guaranteed sites for this bird but in recent years it has been seen at Buxa, Jatinga, Lava, Phodang, Mungpoo (Darjeeling area), Pemayangtse, the Yuksom-Dzongri Trek, various sites in Arunachal Pradesh, and the Murlen and Phawngpui (Blue Mountain) NPs of Mizoram.

Black-headed Shrike Babbler (N). A scarce denizen of mossy-oak forest. The best chances of seeing this bird are on the Sandakphu Trek. Has also been seen at Tiger Hill and Buxa.

Chestnut-fronted Shrike Babbler. The only Indian record is the type specimen collected from Nokrek in the Garo Hills of Meghalaya.

White-hooded Babbler. Uncommon to locally common species in bamboo and forest undergrowth at low to mid-elevations in Northeast India. Recent records from Panbari Forest (Kaziranga), Dihing Forest in Assam, Namdapha and other sites in Arunachal Pradesh, and Mizoram.

Streak-throated Barwing. Locally common resident of mossy forest in Arunachal Pradesh (e.g. Pange and Majha), Manipur and Nagaland. Has also been recorded from the Cachar Hills (Assam).

White-naped Yuhina. Locally fairly common resident (some possibly descending in winter). Sites include Buxa, Namdapha, Phodang, Khecheoperi Lake and Jatinga.

Yellow-throated Fulvetta (N). A localised bird occurring in flocks frequenting undergrowth in broadleaved evergreen forest and edges of clearings. Lava is a good regular site. Has also been recorded at Tiger Hill and Jatinga.

Rufous-throated Fulvetta (N). Localised inhabitant of broadleaved evergreen forest undergrowth below 900m along the foot of the eastern Himalaya and hills south of the Brahmaputra. Fairly common at Namdapha.

Rusty-capped Fulvetta. Split as *Alcippe dubia* from the related Dusky Fulvetta *Alcippe brunnea* of China. Recently found at Mawphlang. Reportedly common at Murlen NP (Mizoram).

Rufous-backed Sibia. Scarce resident of broadleaved evergreen forest from Darjeeling east. Localities include: Namdapha, Jatinga and Murlen NP (Mizoram).

Grey Sibia (N). A species that is still fairly common in suitable broadleaved forests around Shillong but is threatened by continuing deforestation. Common at Murlen NP (Mizoram). Uncommon in the North Cachar Hills (Assam). Also found in Manipur and Nagaland.

Beautiful Sibia. Common in the Dafla and Mishmi Hills of Arunachal Pradesh. Namdapha is the most accessible site. Also recorded in Assam, Meghalaya and Nagaland.

Brown-chested Jungle Flycatcher (V). It has been suggested that the local form may represent a separate species to that found in China and Southeast Asia, though all records are of winter birds from the Nicobars (except one from South Andaman), which implies that it is a migrant rather than resident.

Brown-breasted Flycatcher (N). Frequents damp, shady forest gullies. Widespread but not common in the hills of southwest India in winter. Sites include: Bondla, Molem, Mudumalai, Top Slip, Periyar and Guindy. Breeds above 1200m in the hills south of the Brahmaputra in Assam and Meghalaya and possibly further east.

Rusty-tailed Flycatcher. Open forest and forest edge species wintering below 1000m in the hills of southwest India. Widespread and slightly more frequent than the previous species. Summers between 2100 and 3600m in the western Himalaya.

Kashmir Flycatcher* (V). This restricted range species breeds in Kashmir (e.g. at Dachigam) with most of the population wintering in Sri Lanka. In recent winters it has also regularly been seen at Ooty.

White-gorgeted Flycatcher. Uncommon and shy resident of hill forest in Northeast India. Localities include Buxa, Sandakphu Trek, Lava and Jatinga.

Sapphire Flycatcher. Uncommon to fairly common altitudinal migrant of the mountains in Northeast India. Sites: Tiger Hill, Lava, Gangtok, Rumtek, Dibru-Saikhowa, Namdapha and Jatinga.

Black-and-orange Flycatcher** (N). Endemic to the southern Western Ghats. Most easily seen in sholas around Ooty where it is quite common.

White-tailed Flycatcher. Little known altitudinal migrant (?) of the Patkai Range in eastern Arunachal Pradesh and adjacent Assamese plain. Has also been observed in the Jatinga area and Mizoram.

White-bellied Blue Flycatcher** (N). A fairly common southwest Indian endemic which can be found at Naduvattam, Top Slip, Rajamalai and Periyar.

Hill Blue Flycatcher. Very rare resident in the extreme northeast of the country. Recent sightings at Namdapha and Pange in Arunachal Pradesh.

Nilgiri Flycatcher** (N). A South Indian endemic which is fairly common in sholas around Ooty, Munnar and Rajamalai.

Mangrove Whistler. As its name suggests, a species of coastal mangroves and neighbouring vegetation. In India it is uncommon and is restricted to the Sundarbans, the coast of Orissa (e.g. Bhitarkanika WLS) and the Andaman Islands.

Long-billed Bush Warbler (V). A little-known altitudinal migrant inhabiting low thorny scrub and tangled bushes on the fringes of forest and cultivated fields, seasonally from 1200 to 3600m in the western Himalaya.

Rufous-fronted Prinia*. A sparsely-distributed inhabitant of dry scrub jungle in central and northwestern parts of the country. Look out for it in suitable habitat at sites such as Tughlaqabad, Ranthambhor, Shivpuri, Melghat, Kumbhalgarh and the surroundings of Sultanpur. Rare at Bharatpur.

Grey-crowned Prinia* (N). A very scarce inhabitant of the Himalayan foothills and duns with only one recent record from West Bengal and unconfirmed reports from Corbett.

Jungle Prinia*. A widespread but localised species with a preference for fairly dry scrub in broken country. Care must be taken in distinguishing this from the much commoner Plain Prinia. Localities include: Ranthambhor, Little Rann of Kutch, Ramnagar, Bandhavgarh, Melghat, Simlipal, near Mudumalai, euphorbia scrub south of Madras (e.g. at Anna Zoo).

Rufous-vented Prinia* (V). The two disjunct populations may represent different species. The nominate form, also known as Long-tailed Prinia, is most readily located in canal-side vegetation at Harike. Its eastern counterpart, the little-recorded Swamp Prinia *Prinia burnesii cinerascens*, inhabits tall grass near water in the floodplains of Northeast India and has recently been observed at Dibru-Saikhowa and Pobitora WLS in Assam.

Broad-tailed Grassbird*(*?) (N). A near-threatened species restricted to the southern half of the Western Ghats with one or two records from Sri Lanka and Pt Calimere. Its historical range appears to be decreasing through loss of its grassland hills habitat where it shows a preference for marshy depressions. In recent years observed in the core zones of Periyar, the Indira Gandhi WLS (breeding at Grasshills), Thattakad and Silent Valley among others. Has been recorded in November at Pt. Calimere, possibly on migration to Sri Lanka.

Bristled Grassbird* (V). Historically widespread in grassland and scrub through much of India but with very few recent sightings. Rarely seen except while singing in the breeding season (end July/beginning August), e.g. at Harike (1997/98) and Okhla (1996/97). A single was seen at the latter site the following winter. Also reported from Manas.

Paddyfield Warbler. Widespread but not particularly common winter visitor affecting wet situations with reeds, crops and tall grass. Sites include Nal Sarovar, Borivli, the Yamuna River, coastal marshes in Goa, near Nagarhole, Dibru-Saikhowa and Kaziranga, but can be worth checking any wet paddyfields. Occasional at Bharatpur.

Mountain Chiffchaff. Split from Common Chiffchaff, this species breeds in Ladakh and is a fairly common passage migrant through Kashmir.

Plain Leaf Warbler. Breeding records of this species in Kashmir are a case of mistaken identity. Most recent winter records are from extreme western Rajasthan, e.g. around the Fossil Park near Jaisalmer.

Tytler's Leaf Warbler* (N). Breeds above 2400m in the coniferous forests of Kashmir, e.g. Dachigam and the Overa WLS. A few old winter records from the Western Ghats. One from the edge of a shola on the slopes bordering the Eravikulam Plateau, near Munnar in 1985. Salim Ali reported them not uncommon at Malegaon (Maharashtra) at the end of February 1948. A specimen collected from Goa by Grubh and Ali proved later to be a Greenish Warbler lacking wing-bars and it is not known to the authors whether recent claims from sites in Goa have ruled this possibility out.

Tickell's Leaf Warbler. Common and widespread in the Himalaya above 2700m in summer. Common spring migrant at Nainital. In winter common around Ooty and Rajamalai; small numbers at Dhikala (Corbett), Bharatpur and Bund Baretha.

Sulphur-bellied Warbler. Unlike most other *Phylloscopus* tends to creep over the ground, tree-trunks, rocks, and old fort walls. In summer found on stony, sparsely vegetated hillsides above 2400m in the western Himalaya, e.g. around Leh, and the Indus and Nubra Valleys in Ladakh. In winter common at Kumbhalgarh and Melghat; regular at Harike, Tughlaqabad, Ranthambhor, Bund Baretha, Bandhavgarh and Pachmarhi.

Smoky Warbler. Probably breeds above the timberline in north Sikkim. Not uncommon in winter in waterside vegetation and long damp bushy grass at Dibru-Saikhowa, Kaziranga, Dudhwa; scarce but seen almost annually at Bharatpur.

Brooks's Leaf Warbler. Uncommon winter visitor most often seen in acacias at Bharatpur, Sultanpur, Tughlaqabad, Delhi Ridge and Harike.

Large-billed Leaf Warbler. Breeds in the Himalaya mainly above 2000m where it is partial to streamside vegetation. Good chances of seeing the bird at Lava and on the Panduropa, Lidder Valley and Sandakphu treks. In winter common in the hills of southwest India including sites such as Top Slip, Periyar and around Ooty; sparsely distributed in the remaining peninsula.

Yellow-vented Warbler (N). Most winter records are from woodland in the east Himalayan duars at sites such as Buxa, Mahananda, Manas, Kaziranga, and Namdapha where it can be fairly common at times. Most spring and summer records seem to be from Sikkim, Lava and the Darjeeling area.

Golden-spectacled Warbler. Following a recent visit to the Singalila, Darjeeling, and Lava areas Per Alström has suggested that this may be best treated as two separate species – one of them ('upper species') breeding above 2000/2100m and the other ('lower species') breeding below this altitude. Best separated by voice but further study is necessary.

Grey-cheeked Warbler. One of the scarcer warblers in the east Himalaya. An altitudinal migrant inhabiting evergreen forest and dense bamboo. The best chances are at Lava in early spring (when it is singing), Panbari Forest (Kaziranga), and lower elevations of Namdapha in winter. Has been recorded from Murlen NP (Mizoram) and Buxa.

Broad-billed Warbler (N). Prefers dense undergrowth along forest edge in the eastern Himalaya. Though uncommon the best area seems to be around Darjeeling, Lava and the Sandakphu Trek in spring. Other sites include Namdapha and Manas.

Gould's Shortwing (N). Relatively little-known altitudinal migrant found in rhododendron and bamboo as well as scrub and bare rocky habitats above the tree-line in summer. Said to have been common in the Upper Subansiri district of Arunachal Pradesh. Has been recorded from Tiger Hill and the Kedarnath Sanctuary.

Rusty-bellied Shortwing ** (V).** There are only a few historical records of this scarce resident from Sikkim, the Darjeeling area, eastern Assam, Nagaland and Arunachal Pradesh, but it has probably been much overlooked due to its skulking habits and the dense undergrowth which it frequents. Recent sight records are from Namdapha, Darjeeling and Lava with up to nine birds responding to the taped song at the latter site in June.

White-bellied Shortwing ** (N).** Fairly common though often skulking in sholas and densely vegetated damp gullies in the higher hills of southwest India. Most easily found around Ooty and Rajamalai.

Lesser Shortwing. An altitudinal migrant of the eastern Himalaya and hills south of the Brahmaputra. Partial to damp gullies where its unobtrusive behaviour makes it difficult to observe. Localities include Lava, Pemayangtse, Shillong Peak and Kaziranga (W).

White-browed Shortwing. Another skulker of moist shady ravines. Occurs at Tiger Hill, Sandakphu Trek, Lava, Pemayangtse, Shillong Peak, Mawphlang, Jatinga and Namdapha. Has also been seen at the Gt Himalayan NP but not further west.

Siberian Rubythroat. A winter visitor that is fairly common to uncommon in dense undergrowth and bushes at lower elevations in the northeastern part of the country. Also regular at Bharatpur, Nainital and Corbett.

White-tailed Rubythroat. An uncommon altitudinal migrant. Being a great skulker it is probably more common than it would seem. In summer it is an inhabitant of high altitude scrub. In winter it descends to the foothills and the terai where it keeps to dense scrub and bushes often on the edge of grassland. Regular sightings from Corbett, Dibru-Saikhowa, Sat Tal, Kaziranga and Buxa in winter.

Indian Blue Robin. Fairly common but hard to see in dense forest undergrowth. Summers for the most part in the western Himalaya between 1600 and 3300m. Winters mainly in the evergreen forests of the southwest Indian hills.

Golden Bush Robin. Uncommon but fairly widespread altitudinal migrant distributed along the Himalaya. Among the better sites are Nainital, Lava and the Sandakphu Trek.

White-browed Bush Robin. Inhabits the higher altitude forests of the Himalaya from Garhwal east, though there is some altitudinal movement. Uncommon or skulking at localities including Tiger Hill, Sandakphu Trek, Lava, Pemayangtse and the Yuksom-Dzongri Trek.

Rufous-breasted Bush Robin (N). Sparsely distributed in the eastern

Himalaya moving to lower altitudes in winter. Best looked for at Lava, Namdapha and sites in Sikkim.

Rufous-backed Redstart. A scarce and erratic winter visitor to the western Himalaya. Most likely to be seen around the Kashmir Valley but has been reported as far east as Nainital.

Hodgson's Redstart. Mainly an uncommon winter visitor most likely to be encountered on an early season visit to the area between Darjeeling and Sandakphu or sites in Sikkim. Recorded also from Nainital and Manas.

Daurian Redstart. Mainly a winter visitor to eastern Assam and the Northeast Hill States where it is fairly widespread but not particularly common. Said to breed in northern Arunachal Pradesh.

White-winged Redstart. A high-altitude redstart breeding above 3600m in the Himalaya. Very common in bushes along the Indus Valley in Ladakh in winter. Other locations include the Spiti Valley and Keylong (Zanskar).

White-bellied Redstart. Rather shy and localised breeder in shrubbery at and above the Himalayan treeline moving down below 1500m in winter. Best sought on the Lidder Valley Trek.

White-tailed Robin. Uncommon to locally common altitudinal migrant: Tiger Hill, Lava, Sandakphu Trek, Namdapha and Jatinga. Has also been seen at Darjeeling Zoo, Kaziranga, Dibru-Saikhowa and Murlen NP (Mizoram).

Blue-fronted Robin (N). Very rare resident of damp vegetated gullies. A handful of records in recent years from Darjeeling, Lava (including from a spinach patch in the village) and Namdapha (34th Mile and 38th Mile).

Grandala. An uncommon high altitude Himalayan species best sought above 3000m in the Kullu Valley, Rumbak Valley and on the trek north of Yuksom.

Little Forktail. Like other forktails usually found near water, though generally preferring the vicinity of fast flowing mountain streams. Regular north of Corbett. Occasional below Nainital. May also be encountered at Kedarnath, the Indus and Suru Valleys in Ladakh, the Sandakphu Trek and Namdapha.

Purple Cochoa (N). Enigmatic resident of moist evergreen Himalayan forests between 1000m and 3000m from the Kumaon region of Uttar Pradesh east. A recent record from Pange in the Tale WLS was the first for Arunachal Pradesh. A pair was seen near Agoda on the way to Dhodital Lake in the Uttarkashi district of Uttar Pradesh in May 1984 and two at Phawngpui (Blue Mtn) NP in Mizoram in March 1998.

Green Cochoa (N). Equals its sibling species in obscurity and enjoys a similar distribution overlapping at slightly lower altitudes. Is said to prefer dense humid evergreen biotope on sheer slopes. Occurs at Namdapha and at Phawngpui (Blue Mtn) NP in Mizoram.

Brown Rock-chat*. A fairly common resident of old forts, quarries and other rocky facies in the plains of northwest India, e.g. the Red Fort in Agra, Fatehpur Sikri, Bund Baretha, Tughlaqabad and Ranthambhor. Uncommon at Bharatpur.

Stoliczka's Bushchat* (V). Scarce and localised resident of arid regions of western India, apparently subject to some seasonal movements. Most birders see this species at the Desert NP but there are other good sites at the Banni grasslands of the Kutch and Velavadar in Gujarat, with a few scattered records from Ranthambhor, Sonkhalia Bustard Sanctuary, Little Rann of Kutch and the Koladahar area of Bharatpur.

Hodgson's Bushchat (V). Very rare winter visitor to the great river plains of northern India from Uttar Pradesh to northern West Bengal; a recent first record for Assam.

White-tailed Stonechat. Locally common but declining resident of the great river plains of the northern subcontinent. Currently still fairly easy to see at Okhla in Delhi.

Jerdon's Bushchat (N). Scarce inhabitant of long grass and bushes of the floodplains and foothills of Northeast India. Scarce at Dibru-Saikhowa and Kaziranga.

Isabelline Wheatear. In winter regular in drier areas around Bharatpur, Sultanpur, Ranthambhor, Jaisalmer, Desert NP, Little Rann of Kutch and Karera Bustard Sanctuary (Madhya Pradesh).

Desert Wheatear. In similar areas in winter as the previous species but more widespread.

Variable Wheatear. Can be found at most of the same sites as the Desert Wheatear.

Pied Wheatear. The only regular site known to the authors is in fields around Kargil at the end of the Suru Valley in summer, though it has also been seen near Leh and Hanle (Ladakh).

Malabar Whistling Thrush**. Not uncommon though local and rather shy along hill forest streams and rivers from the Western Ghats to Gujarat and northwest Orissa, e.g. at Mudumalai, Periyar, Ooty, Pachmarhi, Bondla, Molem and Simlipal.

Pied Thrush (N). An uncommon breeding visitor to the Himalaya at altitudes between 1500 and 2400m. Probably best looked for between May and September at hill stations at appropriate elevations from the Kullu Valley eastwards. The species main wintering grounds are in Sri Lanka but there is some evidence that individuals may occasionally winter in the hills of South India, e.g. at Yercaud in the Shevaroy Hills (Tamil Nadu) and in the Nandi Hills (Karnataka).

Plain-backed Thrush. Fairly common altitudinal migrant. Sites: Gt Himalayan NP, Nainital, Tiger Hill, Sandakphu Trek, Pemayangtse, Yuksom and Namdapha.

Long-tailed Thrush. Less common though sometimes found in the same areas as the previous species. Locales include Nainital (U), Sandakphu Trek, Fambong Lho and Yuksom.

Scaly Thrush. In northern India this is an altitudinal migrant spreading onto the northern Indian plains in winter when it is fairly regular at Harike, occasional around Nainital, and rare at Bharatpur. The taxonomic arrangement is currently under review. The form *neilgherriensis*, Nilgiri Thrush, which is resident in the Western Ghats from northern Karnataka south, may prove to warrant full species status.

Long-billed Thrush (N). Uncommon inhabitant of muddy Himalayan forest streamsides and pools but may turn up in any kind of damp gully. Fairly widespread from the Kullu Valley eastwards at altitudes up to 3000m. Should be looked for around Nainital, Corbett, Sandakphu Trek, Lava and the Jatinga area.

Dark-sided Thrush. Scarce. Prefers damp ground along Himalayan forest streams. Said to be more common in the hills south of the Brahmaputra. Rare at Lava and Namdapha. Recently also seen in Mizoram.

Black-breasted Thrush (N). Uncommon altitudinal migrant of the hills south and east of the Brahmaputra. In winter uncommon at Panbari Forest (Kaziranga), Dibru-Saikhowa and Namdapha.

Tickell's Thrush*. Fairly common summer breeding visitor to the western Himalaya. Regular winter visitor at Bharatpur.

Grey-sided Thrush (V). Winter visitor to Northeast India. Historically described as 'not rare' in Nagaland and Manipur but the authors can find no recent records.

Eyebrowed Thrush. Fairly common winter visitor to the hills of Meghalaya eastwards. Recent winter records also from Mt Harriet.

Altai Accentor. In winter fairly regular at Nainital and in the Kashmir Valley; uncommon on the Sandakphu Trek.

Robin Accentor. Breeds in the Suru Valley. Winters around Leh, the Indus Valley in Ladakh, and on the trek north of Yuksom.

Brown Accentor. Inhabits high altitude, dry scrubby slopes above the Indus and Suru Valleys.

Black-throated Accentor. Winter visitor most often seen in fields near Sat Tal and Nainital.

Maroon-backed Accentor. Uncommon altitudinal migrant. More of a forest species than other accentors. Sites include Tiger Hill, Sandakphu Trek, Lava and Pemayangtse.

Sultan Tit. Quite common at Buxa, Manas, Kaziranga, Dibru-Saikhowa and Namdapha.

White-naped Tit ** (V).** A declining localised endemic found in thorny *Acacia* scrub in Gujarat and Rajasthan and a few scattered sites in southern India. Seems to be most regular at Jaisamand, Sonkhalia, Chhari Dhand and Nahargarh Biological Park near Jaipur. Also occurs in dry deciduous jungle in and around Sangama in the Cauvery River valley, about 100km south of Bangalore (via Kanakapura).

Fire-capped Tit. Breeds in summer in Kashmir, e.g. Dachigam and the Lidder Valley Trek, and the Kullu Valley and Gt Himalayan NP. Two recent spring records from Nainital. Winters in central India but not often recorded.

White-throated Tit* (N). An uncommon endemic altitudinal migrant breeding in deciduous forest above 2400m in the western Himalaya. Best looked for in summer in high altitude birch forest in the Gt Himalayan NP, Kullu Valley, Kedarnath Sanctuary, Dachigam and on the Lidder Valley Trek.

Rufous-fronted Tit. Locally reasonably common between 2700 and 3600m in the eastern Himalaya, e.g. on the Sandakphu Trek.

White-cheeked Nuthatch. Fairly common resident mainly found in coniferous forests above 2100m in the Himalaya from Kashmir to Garhwal. Sites include Gulmarg, Dachigam, Lidder Valley, Gt Himalayan NP and Kullu Valley.

Beautiful Nuthatch (V). Rare resident of primary forest in Northeast India. Found between 1500 and 2100m in the summer with some moving down as far as the foot of the Himalaya in winter. Best looked for between Hornbill and Ranijheel at Namdapha but also recorded in recent years from Buxa and Jatinga as well as other localities in Arunachal Pradesh.

Wallcreeper. Breeds on high altitude Himalayan cliffs and gorges, especially near water. Winters down to the foothills when it may frequent quarries, old walls, steep earth banks and stony river beds, e.g. regularly seen at Harike, Ramnagar and Corbett.

Spotted Creeper. Scarce, sporadic and localised resident mainly in northwest/central India. Best looked for in acacias along the bunds at Bharatpur. Breeds in the Grass Farm Nursery at Jaipur. Said to be fairly common in the Bori Sanctuary near Pachmarhi.

Blyth's Pipit. A not uncommon and widespread winter visitor to the Indian plains though much overlooked owing to its similarity with other pipits. Generally prefers areas of grass and cultivation in drier facies. Sites include Tughlaqabad, Koladahar at Bharatpur, near Mysore, Ranthambhor, Baga and Kaziranga.

Nilgiri Pipit **.** Common resident at a few upland sites in the grasslands of the southern Western Ghats – most easily seen at Rajamalai.

Upland Pipit. A resident (in singles and pairs) of steep grassy broken country, mainly between 1200 and 3000m. Not particularly common but should be looked for anywhere there are such habitats on walks around Himalayan hill stations such as Dharamsala, Nainital and Shimla.

Ruby-cheeked Sunbird. A fairly common to uncommon resident of more open forest situations below 700m in Northeast India.

Crimson-backed Sunbird**. Fairly common resident of mid-altitude evergreen forest in the Western Ghats, e.g. at Periyar, Bondla, Molem, Top Slip, Nadugani, Naduvattam and Thattakad; uncommon at Borivli.

Loten's Sunbird*. Quite common below 1600m at many of the same sites as the previous species but is also found in the lowlands e.g. at Goa, and its range includes the southeast (Madras, Vedanthangal, Pt Calimere).

Sind Sparrow. A species whose range is mainly within Pakistan but just extends into the western districts of the Indian Punjab where it inhabits riverine vegetation. The best site is Harike.

Tibetan Snowfinch. Fairly common in bare open country in Ladakh.

Finn's Weaver** (V). A rare and localised inhabitant of damp grasslands and marshes with scattered trees. Found mainly in the plains and foothills of northern Uttar Pradesh, southern and eastern West Bengal, and western Assam. Uncommon at Manas, Kaziranga and Orang WLS in Assam; has bred at Hastinapur near Meerut northeast of Delhi; attempted to breed at Okhla in Delhi in 1993.

Green Avadavat** (V). Uncommon and localised endemic of Central India, may be declining partly due to trapping for the cagebird trade. Status not clear as it is distributed through a region not visited by many birdwatchers. Most sightings in recent years from Kumbhalgarh and Mount Abu in Rajasthan, Pachmarhi and Melghat in northern Madhya Pradesh, with odd records as far away as the Desert National Park and North Wynaad (Kerala).

Black-throated Munia*. A South Indian endemic that may prove to be a separate species from the closely related Sri Lankan form. Sporadic and fairly common to uncommon in scrub and grassland on the edges of cultivation and in forest clearings. The most convenient place to look for this bird is at the watchtower clearing in Karian Shola at Top Slip, Anaimalai.

Black-and-yellow Grosbeak. Fairly common, mainly in coniferous forests around the Kashmir, Lidder and Kullu Valleys, and the Gt Himalayan NP; rare at Nainital.

Collared Grosbeak. Uncommon but fairly regular in flocks around Nainital in winter. Also reported from the Gt Himalayan NP and on the Sandakphu Trek. Occasional at Kedarnath.

White-winged Grosbeak. Has a predilection for dwarf juniper. The best chances of seeing the bird are probably on the Sandakphu Trek. Uncommon in the Gt Himalayan NP.

Spot-winged Grosbeak. Scarce. Probably a forest resident and altitudinal migrant throughout the Himalaya from the Indus Valley east and in the hills south of the Brahmaputra. Has been recorded at Nainital, on the approaches to the Gt Himalayan NP, and in the Mandakini Valley between Gangotri and Kedarnath.

Tibetan Siskin. Somewhat erratic winter visitor to the eastern Himalaya when it congregates in large flocks. Most likely to be seen at Lava and on an early season Sandakphu Trek.

Spectacled Finch. Fairly common in coniferous forests of Kashmir; less so in the Gt Himalayan NP; scarce and erratic winter visitor to Nainital.

Fire-fronted Serin. Common between 3000 and 4000m in northern Kashmir and Ladakh; uncommon in Gt Himalayan NP; not uncommon winter visitor to Nainital area.

Brandt's Mountain Finch. Fairly common on high barren plateau country of Ladakh and north Sikkim descending as low as 3000m in winter. Gathers in large flocks when not breeding.

[**Sillem's Mountain Finch** (N). This species was only recently described from two specimens collected by J.A. Sillem in 1929 on the plateau between the upper Kara Kash and the upper Yarkand River, a region which is presently under Chinese administration. It should be looked out for in northern Ladakh where it may associate with flocks of other mountain finches.]

Trumpeter Finch. A winter visitor to the arid areas of western Rajasthan and the Punjab. Regularly seen in small flocks in the Desert NP.

Mongolian Finch. Mostly a winter visitor around Leh, and the Indus Valley in Ladakh, with a few birds remaining through the summer months.

Blanford's Rosefinch. Apparently a scarce altitudinal migrant of the eastern Himalaya. Said to frequent conifer, or mixed conifer and birch forest mainly above 3000m in Arunachal Pradesh and Sikkim, moving down lower in winter. Very few recent records from the Darjeeling area and the Lhonak Valley (north Sikkim).

Pink-browed Rosefinch. Breeds in high altitude open conifer, birch, willow and dwarf juniper moving lower in winter. Fairly common at Gt Himalayan NP, Kullu Valley, Nainital (W) and Kedarnath.

Vinaceous Rosefinch. Little known. A winter straggler to Nainital. Has also been recorded in summer (August 1996) at 3000m in Uttar Pradesh.

Red-mantled Rosefinch. Scarce altitudinal migrant breeding in alpine shrubbery (3400-3800m) in Ladakh and moving down (2200–2600m) in winter. Has been recorded near Leh in summer.

Spot-winged Rosefinch. Poorly known species. Has been recorded on the Sandakphu and Yuksom-Dzongri Treks.

White-browed Rosefinch. Occasional in rhododendron scrub at Kedarnath and Sandakphu.

Dark-rumped Rosefinch. Uncommon altitudinal migrant at Nainital, Tiger Hill, Sandakphu Trek, Fambong Lho and Phodang.

Great Rosefinch. Breeds between 3900 and 4800m in Ladakh. Occurs around Leh and the Indus Valley in winter.

Streaked Rosefinch. Abundant in winter in the Indus Valley near Leh, fewer there in summer.

Red-fronted Rosefinch. Occasional at Kedarnath, Rangdum (Suru Valley) and on the Lidder Valley Trek.

Crimson-browed Finch. Uncommon altitudinal migrant of the eastern Himalaya. Breeds in dense shrubbery in light forest near the treeline and above. Occasional at Lava in winter.

Scarlet Finch. A widespread but scarce altitudinal migrant in the Himalaya with a few records from Nainital (W), Kedarnath, Darjeeling, Jatinga area, Namdapha, and the Sandakphu and Yuksom-Dzongri Treks.

Gold-naped Finch. Fairly common at Lava, Tiger Hill and on the Sandakphu Trek,

Brown Bullfinch. Fairly common at Lava; less so on the Sandakphu Trek and in the Gt Himalayan NP; has been recorded several times from Nainital (W).

Orange Bullfinch* (N). A west Himalayan endemic, resident in Kashmir though subject to vertical movements. Seen fairly easily at Dachigam and on the Lidder Valley Trek; in winter on Shankaracharya Hill; has also been recorded near the Valley of Flowers in Uttar Pradesh and in the Gt Himalayan NP.

White-capped Bunting. In winter regular at Bund Baretha, Corbett, Sat Tal and Ramnagar; uncommon at Bharatpur; in summer in the Kullu Valley and Kashmir.

Grey-necked Bunting. Widespread winter visitor to central and western India with a preference for stony, broken scrubby hillsides, a habitat that is more common outside of protected areas. Recent records from Bharatpur (R), Ranthambhor, Little Rann of Kutch, near Mysore, Baga, Shamirpet Lake and Rollapadu.

Chestnut-eared Bunting. Regular in winter at Corbett and Sat Tal.

House Bunting. Quite common at the Fossil Park near Jaisalmer, around Jodhpur and Pushkar; uncommon in the Little Rann of Kutch.

Crested Bunting. Widespread but uncommon resident , local and altitudinal migrant, preferring stony hillsides but in winter also frequents dry open flatland. Better sites include Corbett, Ramnagar, Ranthambhor, Kumbhalgarh and the hills around Pune in Maharashtra; scarce at Sultanpur, Bharatpur, Bund Baretha, Bandhavgarh and Simlipal.

BIRDS OF INDIA

The following checklist includes all 1220 species known by the authors to have been reliably recorded within Indian limits up to May 1998. Eight of these (marked !) are new to the country having apparently been reliably observed in recent years but the records not yet fully documented. A further 17 species whose occurrence is open to doubt, or which have not been sufficiently well documented, are listed in square brackets [ ]. We have also included (offset ---) some well-defined subspecies, which are possible future splits or are given full species status by other authors. In the absence of a records committee for India, observers are requested to submit full details of rare or vagrant species for publication in *Forktail*, the journal of the OBC, or the *Journal* of the BNHS (see Useful Addresses).

In the interests of global standardisation the taxonomy, scientific and English names largely follow Inskipp, Lindsey and Duckworth *An Annotated Checklist of the Birds of the Oriental Region*. Exceptions relate to recent taxonomic revisions. We have, however, retained the older sequence used in Ripley's 1982 *Synopsis*. Commonly used alternative names are given in parentheses.

Each species' status symbols refer only to its range within India. It should be born in mind that a species' abundance may vary quite considerably within its range. The figures given here are to some extent subjective and only an approximate guide to the likelihood of seeing the species in an appropriate location, habitat and season.

a   altitudinal migrant
b   breeding
i   introduced
m   migrates within India (summers in the north and winters further south)
n   nomadic
p   passage migrant (only passes through Indian limits)
r   resident
s   summer visitor
v   vagrant or rare visitor
w   winter visitor
°   subject to local seasonal movements
'   very localised or patchily distributed
†   probably extinct
1   very common
2   common
3   fairly common
4   uncommon
5   rare
?   status and/or abundance uncertain
!   recently recorded but as yet insufficiently documented
**   endemic to India
*   endemic to the Indian Subcontinent
(*)   near-endemic to the Indian Subcontinent, i.e. most of the species' range falls within the Subcontinent
_   species of conservation concern are underlined (For more details refer to the Selective Bird List.)

Common sense should enable interpretation of symbols used in combination. E.g. rw indicates a resident population is augmented by winter visitors; b'w – breeds locally but more widespread in winter; b'w' breeds locally with localised wintering elsewhere; rm – resident and migrant (partial migrant); sp(w) – mainly a summer visitor and passage migrant with a few winter records. When the symbol ' or ° appears it refers to the preceding letter and not the following one. Note also that a species may be locally common but nevertheless globally threatened due to a highly restricted range. The Narcondam Hornbill, for example, is highly vulnerable as it inhabits just one small island in the Andamans. It is, however, common there and hence merits the status r'2.

v ☐	Black-throated Loon (Diver) *Gavia arctica*
b'4w3 ☐	Great Crested Grebe *Podiceps cristatus*
w4 ☐	Black-necked Grebe *Podiceps nigricollis*
w5 ☐	Red-necked Grebe *Podiceps grisegena*
v ☐	Horned (Slavonian) Grebe *Podiceps auritus*
r°m(w)2 ☐	Little Grebe (Dabchick) *Tachybaptus (Podiceps) ruficollis*
v ☐	Cape Petrel *Daption capense*
v ☐	Streaked (White-fronted) Shearwater *Calonectris leucomelas* (*Procellaria leucomelaena*)
s4w5 ☐	Flesh-footed (Pink-footed) Shearwater *Puffinus (Procellaria) carneipes*
?5 ☐	Wedge-tailed Shearwater *Puffinus (Procellaria) pacificus*
r'4 ☐	Audubon's Shearwater *Puffinus (Procellaria) lherminieri*
v ☐	Persian Shearwater *Puffinus persicus* (*Procellaria lherminieri persica*)
v? ☐	[Mascarene (Mascarene Black) Petrel *Pterodroma (Bulweria) aterrima*]
v! ☐	Trinidade (Herald) Petrel *Pterodroma arminjoniana*
v? ☐	Barau's Petrel *Pterodroma baraui*
v ☐	Jouanin's (Jouanin's Gadfly) Petrel *Bulweria fallax*
v ☐	Bulwer's (Bulwer's Gadfly) Petrel *Bulweria bulwerii*
s(r'?)3 ☐	Wilson's Storm Petrel *Oceanites oceanicus*
p5 ☐	White-faced Storm Petrel *Pelagodroma marina*
v ☐	Black-bellied (Dusky-vented) Storm Petrel *Fregatta tropica*
v? ☐	[White-bellied Storm Petrel *Fregatta grallaria*]
v ☐	Swinhoe's (Leach's or Fork-tailed) Storm Petrel *Oceanodroma (leucorhoa) monorhis*
v ☐	Red-billed (Short-tailed) Tropicbird *Phaethon aethereus*
v(b'?) ☐	Red-tailed Tropicbird *Phaethon rubricauda*
v(b'?) ☐	White-tailed (Long-tailed) Tropicbird *Phaethon lepturus*
rw3 ☐	Great White (Rosy or White) Pelican *Pelecanus onocrotalus*
r°4 ☐	Spot-billed (Grey) Pelican *Pelecanus philippensis*
w4 ☐	Dalmatian Pelican *Pelecanus (philippensis) crispus*
v ☐	Masked Booby *Sula dactylatra*
v ☐	Red-footed Booby *Sula sula*
v ☐	Brown Booby *Sula leucogaster*
r°2 ☐	Great Cormorant (Cormorant) *Phalacrocorax carbo*
r°3 ☐	Indian Cormorant (Indian Shag) *Phalacrocorax fuscicollis*
r2 ☐	Little Cormorant *Phalacrocorax niger*
v? ☐	[Pygmy Cormorant *Phalacrocorax pygmeus*]
r3–4 ☐	Darter *Anhinga (rufa) melanogaster*
v ☐	Christmas Island Frigatebird *Fregata andrewsi*
v ☐	Great (Lesser) Frigatebird *Fregata minor*
v ☐	Lesser (Least) Frigatebird *Fregata ariel*
r'5 ☐	(Great) White-bellied Heron(*) *Ardea insignis*
v ☐	Goliath (Giant) Heron *Ardea goliath*
v? ☐	[Great-billed Heron *Ardea sumatrana*]
r3–4w2 ☐	Grey Heron *Ardea cinerea*
r°(w)2 ☐	Purple Heron *Ardea purpurea*
r3 ☐	Little (Little Green, Striated) Heron *Butorides (Ardeola) striatus*
r1 ☐	Indian Pond Heron (Paddybird) *Ardeola grayii*

r'2 ☐	Chinese Pond Heron *Ardeola bacchus*
r°1 ☐	Cattle Egret *Bubulcus ibis*
rn3w2 ☐	Great (Large, Great White) Egret *Casmerodius (Egretta) albus*
rn3 ☐	Intermediate (Smaller, Yellow-billed) Egret *Mesophoyx (Egretta) intermedia*
r°2 ☐	Little Egret *Egretta garzetta*
r°3 ☐	Western Reef Egret (Indian Reef Heron) *Egretta gularis*
r'3 ☐	Pacific Reef Egret (Reef Heron) *Egretta sacra*
r°2 ☐	Black-crowned Night Heron (Night Heron) *Nycticorax nycticorax*
rmw4 ☐	Malayan Night Heron (Malay Bittern or Tiger Bittern) *Gorsachius melanolophus*
r'°3 ☐	Little Bittern *Ixobrychus minutus*
r°3–4 ☐	Cinnamon (Chestnut) Bittern *Ixobrychus cinnamomeus*
rm3 ☐	Yellow Bittern *Ixobrychus sinensis*
r'°4 ☐	Black Bittern *Dupetor (Ixobrychus) flavicollis*
w5 ☐	Great Bittern (Bittern) *Botaurus stellaris*
r°2 ☐	<u>Painted Stork *Mycteria leucocephala*</u>
r°2 ☐	<u>Asian Openbill (Openbill Stork) *Anastomus oscitans*</u>
r3 ☐	Woolly-necked (White-necked) Stork *Ciconia episcopus*
w'4–5 ☐	White Stork *Ciconia ciconia*
w'5 ☐	<u>Oriental (White) Stork *Ciconia (ciconia) boyciana*</u>
wp3–4 ☐	Black Stork *Ciconia nigra*
r'4 ☐	Black-necked Stork *Ephippiorhynchus asiaticus*
r'°n5 ☐	<u>Greater Adjutant (Adjutant) *Leptoptilos dubius*</u>
r'n4 ☐	<u>Lesser Adjutant *Leptoptilos javanicus*</u>
rn2 ☐	<u>Black-headed (White) Ibis *Threskiornis (aethiopicus) melanocephalus*</u>
r3–4 ☐	<u>Black Ibis *Pseudibis papillosa*</u>
r'nw3 ☐	Glossy Ibis *Plegadis falcinellus*
rnw3 ☐	Eurasian Spoonbill (Spoonbill) *Platalea leucorodia*
r'°n2 ☐	Greater Flamingo (Flamingo) *Phoenicopterus ruber (roseus)*
r'°m2–3 ☐	<u>Lesser Flamingo *Phoenicopterus (Phoeniconaias) minor*</u>
v ☐	(Siberian) Red-breasted Goose *Branta ruficollis*
v ☐	Bean Goose *Anser fabalis*
w5 ☐	Greater White-fronted (White-fronted) Goose *Anser albifrons*
v ☐	<u>Lesser White-fronted Goose *Anser erythropus*</u>
w'2 ☐	Greylag Goose *Anser anser*
b'3w'2 ☐	Bar-headed Goose *Anser indicus*
v ☐	Snow Goose *Anser caerulescens*
v ☐	Tundra (Bewick's) Swan *Cygnus columbianus*
v ☐	Whooper Swan *Cygnus cygnus*
v ☐	Mute Swan *Cygnus olor*
rm2 ☐	Lesser Whistling-duck (Lesser Whistling Teal or Lesser Tree Duck) *Dendrocygna javanica*
r'4–5 ☐	Fulvous Whistling-duck (Large Whistling Teal) *Dendrocygna bicolor*
b'w2 ☐	Ruddy Shelduck (Brahminy Duck) *Tadorna ferruginea*
w4–5 ☐	Common Shelduck *Tadorna tadorna*
w75 ☐	<u>Marbled Duck (Marbled Teal) *Marmaronetta angustirostris*</u>
w1 ☐	Northern Pintail (Pintail) *Anas acuta*
w1 ☐	Common Teal *Anas crecca*
v ☐	Baikal Teal *Anas formosa*
r'4–5 ☐	Sunda (Grey) Teal *Anas gibberifrons*
r°n2 ☐	Spot-billed Duck *Anas poecilorhyncha*
b'4w3 ☐	Mallard *Anas platyrhynchos*
w1 ☐	Gadwall *Anas strepera*
w4 ☐	Falcated Duck (Falcated Teal) *Anas falcata*

w1 ☐	Eurasian Wigeon (Wigeon) *Anas penelope*
w1 ☐	Garganey *Anas querquedula*
w1 ☐	Northern Shoveler (Shoveller) *Anas clypeata*
† ☐	<u>Pink-headed Duck *Rhodonessa caryophyllacea*</u>
w3–4 ☐	<u>Red-crested Pochard *Rhodonessa (Netta) rufina*</u>
w1–2 ☐	Common Pochard *Aythya ferina*
b'5w3 ☐	<u>Ferruginous (White-eyed) Pochard (Duck) *Aythya nyroca*</u>
w5 ☐	<u>Baer's Pochard *Aythya baeri*</u>
w1 ☐	Tufted Duck *Aythya fuligula*
w5 ☐	Greater Scaup (Scaup Duck) *Aythya marila*
v ☐	Mandarin Duck *Aix galericulata*
r'°2 ☐	Cotton Pygmy-goose (Cotton Teal or Quacky Duck) *Nettapus coromandelianus*
r'°3–4 ☐	Comb Duck (Knob-billed Goose) *Sarkidiornis melanotos*
r'5 ☐	<u>White-winged (White-winged Wood) Duck *Cairina scutulata*</u>
v ☐	Long-tailed Duck (Longtail or Old Squaw Duck) *Clangula hyemalis*
w5 ☐	Common Goldeneye (Goldeneye Duck) *Bucephala clangula*
w5 ☐	Smew *Mergus albellus*
b'w3 ☐	Common Merganser (Goosander) *Mergus merganser*
v ☐	Red-breasted Merganser *Mergus serrator*
w5 ☐	<u>White-headed (White-headed Stiff-tailed) Duck *Oxyura leucocephala*</u>
r2 ☐	Black-shouldered (Black-winged) Kite *Elanus caeruleus*
r'5 ☐	<u>Jerdon's (Blyth's) Baza *Aviceda jerdoni*</u>
r'4 ☐	Black (Indian Black-crested) Baza *Aviceda leuphotes*
r°2 ☐	Oriental Honey-buzzard (Honey Buzzard) *Pernis ptilorhynchus*
v ☐	Red Kite (Kite) *Milvus milvus*
☐	Black (Pariah) Kite *Milvus migrans*
rw1 ☐	---Black (Pariah) Kite *M. (m.) migrans*
ram2–4 ☐	---Black-eared (Large Indian) Kite *M. (m.) lineatus*
r°3 ☐	Brahminy Kite *Haliastur indus*
r'aw4 ☐	Northern Goshawk (Goshawk) *Accipiter gentilis*
r°2 ☐	Shikra *Accipiter badius*
r'4 ☐	<u>Nicobar Sparrowhawk** (Car Nicobar Shikra) *Accipiter (badius) butleri*</u>
w'5 ☐	Chinese Sparrowhawk (Horsfield's Goshawk) *Accipiter soloensis*
r4 ☐	Crested Goshawk *Accipiter trivirgatus*
aw3 ☐	Eurasian Sparrowhawk (Sparrow-Hawk) *Accipiter nisus*
ra4 ☐	Besra (Besra Sparrow-Hawk) *Accipiter virgatus*
r'3–4 ☐	Japanese Sparrowhawk (Eastern Besra Sparrow-Hawk) *Accipiter (virgatus) gularis*
b'w3 ☐	Long-legged Buzzard *Buteo rufinus*
v ☐	Upland Buzzard *Buteo hemilasius*
r'w3 ☐	Common (Desert or Japanese) Buzzard *Buteo buteo*
rm3 ☐	White-eyed Buzzard (White-eyed Buzzard-Eagle) *Butastur teesa*
v! ☐	Grey-faced Buzzard (Grey-faced Buzzard-Eagle) *Butastur indicus*
r'3–4 ☐	Mountain (Hodgson's) Hawk Eagle *Spizaetus nipalensis*
r'3 ☐	Changeable (Crested) Hawk Eagle *Spizaetus cirrhatus*
r'w3–4 ☐	Bonelli's Eagle *Hieraaetus fasciatus*
r'w3 ☐	Booted Eagle (Booted Hawk-Eagle) *Hieraaetus pennatus*
r'4 ☐	Rufous-bellied Eagle (Rufous-bellied Hawk-Eagle) *Hieraaetus kienerii*
r'3 ☐	Golden Eagle *Aquila chrysaetos*
w4 ☐	<u>Imperial Eagle *Aquila heliaca*</u>
r3–4 ☐	Tawny Eagle *Aquila rapax*
w2–3 ☐	(Eastern) Steppe Eagle *Aquila (rapax) nipalensis*
rw4 ☐	<u>Greater Spotted Eagle *Aquila clanga*</u>

r'5 ☐	Lesser (Indian) Spotted Eagle *Aquila pomarina (hastata)*
r'3–4 ☐	Black Eagle *Ictinaetus malayensis*
w5 ☐	White-tailed Eagle *Haliaeetus albicilla*
r'3–4 ☐	White-bellied Sea Eagle *Haliaeetus leucogaster*
r'm4 ☐	Pallas's Fish (Fishing) Eagle *Haliaeetus leucoryphus*
r'4 ☐	Grey-headed Fish (Fishing) Eagle *Ichthyophaga ichthyaetus*
r'5 ☐	Lesser Fish (Himalayan Grey-headed Fishing) Eagle *Ichthyophaga humilis (nana)*
r3–4 ☐	Red-headed (Black or King) Vulture *Sarcogyps calvus*
r°4 ☐	Cinereous Vulture *Aegypius monachus*
rvw3 ☐	Eurasian Griffon (Griffon Vulture) *Gyps fulvus*
r'(m)3 ☐	Himalayan Griffon *Gyps himalayensis*
r2 ☐	(Indian) Long-billed Vulture *Gyps indicus*
r1 ☐	White-rumped (Indian White-backed) Vulture *Gyps bengalensis*
r1–2 ☐	Egyptian (Scavenger) Vulture *Neophron percnopterus*
r2–3 ☐	Lammergeier (Bearded Vulture) *Gypaetus barbatus*
w3–4 ☐	Hen Harrier *Circus cyaneus*
w3 ☐	Pallid (Pale) Harrier *Circus macrourus*
w3 ☐	Montagu's Harrier *Circus pygargus*
b'w3 ☐	Pied Harrier *Circus melanoleucos*
☐	Eurasian Marsh Harrier (Marsh Harrier) *Circus aeruginosus*
w2 ☐	---Western Marsh Harrier *C. (a.) aeruginosus*
w3–4 ☐	---Eastern Marsh Harrier (Striped Harrier) *C. (a.) spilonotus*
r°3 ☐	Short-toed Snake Eagle (Short-toed Eagle) *Circaetus gallicus*
r1–2 ☐	Crested Serpent Eagle *Spilornis cheela*
r'4 ☐	Nicobar (Nicobar Crested or Great Nicobar) Serpent Eagle** *Spilornis minimus (klossi)*
r'2 ☐	Andaman (Andaman Dark) Serpent Eagle** *Spilornis elgini*
b'w3 ☐	Osprey *Pandion haliaetus*
r'4 ☐	Collared (Red-breasted) Falconet *Microhierax caerulescens*
r'5 ☐	Pied (White-legged) Falconet *Microhierax melanoleucos*
w'5 ☐	Saker (Cherrug or Shanghar) Falcon *Falco (biarmicus) cherrug*
r°3 ☐	Laggar Falcon *Falco (biarmicus) jugger*
☐	Peregrine Falcon *Falco peregrinus*
w3 ☐	---Peregrine Falcon *F. (p.) japonicus*
w'4–5 ☐	---Barbary (Red-capped) Falcon *F. (p.) pelegrinoides (babylonicus)*
r'4 ☐	---Shaheen Falcon *F. (p.) peregrinator*
r'w3–4 ☐	Eurasian Hobby (Hobby) *Falco subbuteo*
rm4 ☐	Oriental Hobby *Falco severus*
w4–5 ☐	Merlin *Falco columbarius*
r4 ☐	Red-necked Falcon (Red-headed Merlin) *Falco chicquera*
p(b'?)5 ☐	Amur (Red-legged) Falcon (Eastern Red-footed Falcon) *Falco (vespertinus) amurensis*
pw5 ☐	Lesser Kestrel *Falco naumanni*
rw2 ☐	Common Kestrel (Kestrel) *Falco tinnunculus*
r'3 ☐	Nicobar Scrubfowl** (Megapode) *Megapodius (freycinet) nicobariensis*
a'4 ☐	Snow Partridge *Lerwa lerwa*
a'4 ☐	Tibetan Snowcock *Tetraogallus tibetanus*
a'3–4 ☐	Himalayan Snowcock *Tetraogallus himalayensis*
r'5 ☐	Buff-throated Partridge (Pheasant-Grouse) *Tetraophasis szechenyii*
r2–3 ☐	Chukar (Chukar Partridge) *Alectoris chukar*
r3 ☐	Black Francolin (Black Partridge) *Francolinus francolinus*
r'°3 ☐	Painted Francolin* (Painted Partridge) *Francolinus pictus*
r'5 ☐	Chinese Francolin *Francolinus pintadeanus*

r2 ☐	Grey Francolin (Grey Partridge) *Francolinus pondicerianus*
r'2–3 ☐	<u>Swamp Francolin* (Swamp Partridge or Kyah) *Francolinus gularis*</u>
r'3–4 ☐	Tibetan Partridge *Perdix hodgsoniae*
rw4 ☐	Common (Grey) Quail *Coturnix coturnix*
w'5 ☐	Japanese Quail *Coturnix (coturnix) japonica*
r°3–4 ☐	Rain (Black-breasted) Quail *Coturnix coromandelica*
r°4 ☐	Blue-breasted Quail *Coturnix chinensis*
r3 ☐	Jungle Bush Quail* *Perdicula asiatica*
r4 ☐	Rock Bush Quail** *Perdicula argoondah*
r3 ☐	Painted Bush Quail** *Perdicula erythrorhyncha*
r'5 ☐	<u>Manipur Bush Quail** *Perdicula manipurensis*</u>
r2–3 ☐	Hill Partridge *Arborophila torqueola*
a'4–5 ☐	Rufous-throated (Rufous-throated Hill) Partridge *Arborophila rufogularis*
r'4–5 ☐	<u>White-cheeked (White-cheeked Hill) Partridge *Arborophila atrogularis*</u>
r'5 ☐	<u>Chestnut-breasted (Red-breasted Hill) Partridge(*) *Arborophila mandellii*</u>
r'4 ☐	Mountain Bamboo Partridge (Bamboo Partridge) *Bambusicola fytchii*
r3–4 ☐	Red Spurfowl* *Galloperdix spadicea*
r'3–4 ☐	Painted Spurfowl** *Galloperdix lunulata*
†(r?) ☐	<u>Himalayan (Mountain) Quail** *Ophrysia superciliosa*</u>
a'4 ☐	Blood Pheasant *Ithaginis cruentus*
a'4–5 ☐	<u>Western Tragopan* *Tragopan melanocephalus*</u>
a'4 ☐	<u>Satyr (Crimson) Tragopan(*) *Tragopan satyra*</u>
a'4–5 ☐	<u>Blyth's (Grey-bellied) Tragopan *Tragopan blythii*</u>
r'5 ☐	<u>Temminck's Tragopan *Tragopan temminckii*</u>
a3–4 ☐	Himalayan Monal (Impeyan or Monal Pheasant) *Lophophorus impejanus*
r'5 ☐	<u>Sclater's Monal *Lophophorus sclateri*</u>
r'5 ☐	<u>Tibetan Eared Pheasant (Eared Pheasant) *Crossoptilon (crossoptilon) harmani*</u>
a2 ☐	Kalij (Kaleej) Pheasant *Lophura leucomelanos*
r2 ☐	Red Junglefowl *Gallus gallus*
r2 ☐	<u>Grey (Sonnerat's) Junglefowl** *Gallus sonneratii*</u>
a'4 ☐	Koklass Pheasant *Pucrasia macrolopha*
r'3–4 ☐	<u>Cheer (Chir) Pheasant* *Catreus wallichii*</u>
r'5 ☐	<u>Mrs Hume's (Mrs Hume's Barred-back) Pheasant *Syrmaticus humiae*</u>
r'3–4 ☐	Grey Peacock Pheasant (Peacock-Pheasant) *Polyplectron bicalcaratum*
r2 ☐	Indian (Common) Peafowl* *Pavo cristatus*
r'5? ☐	<u>Green (Burmese) Peafowl *Pavo muticus*</u>
li? ☐	Common Pheasant *Phasianus colchicus*
r°4 ☐	Small Buttonquail (Little Bustard-Quail, Andalusian Hemipode) *Turnix sylvatica*
r°(w)4 ☐	Yellow-legged Buttonquail *Turnix tanki*
r°3 ☐	Barred Buttonquail (Common Bustard-Quail) *Turnix suscitator*
w1–4 ☐	Common Crane *Grus grus*
b'w5 ☐	<u>Black-necked Crane *Grus nigricollis*</u>
v ☐	<u>Hooded Crane *Grus monacha*</u>
r4 ☐	<u>Sarus Crane *Grus antigone*</u>
w5 ☐	<u>Siberian Crane *Grus leucogeranus*</u>
w1–4 ☐	Demoiselle Crane *Grus (Anthropoides) virgo*
b'2w4 ☐	Water Rail *Rallus aquaticus*
r3–4 ☐	Slaty-breasted (Blue-breasted Banded) Rail *Gallirallus (Rallus) striatus*
r'5 ☐	Red-legged (Red-legged Banded) Crake *Rallina fasciata*
r4 ☐	Slaty-legged (Banded) Crake *Rallina eurizonoides*
r'5 ☐	<u>Andaman (Andaman Banded) Crake** *Rallina canningi*</u>
v ☐	<u>Corn Crake *Crex crex*</u>
w5 ☐	Little Crake *Porzana parva*

b'w3 ☐	Baillon's Crake *Porzana pusilla*
w4 ☐	Spotted Crake *Porzana porzana*
r3–4 ☐	Ruddy-breasted (Ruddy) Crake *Porzana fusca*
r'5 ☐	Black-tailed (Elwes's) Crake *Porzana (Amaurornis) bicolor*
r3 ☐	Brown Crake *Amaurornis akool*
r1 ☐	White-breasted Waterhen *Amaurornis phoenicurus*
r°4 ☐	Watercock *Gallicrex cinerea*
rw1 ☐	Common Moorhen *Gallinula chloropus*
r2–3 ☐	Purple Swamphen (Purple Moorhen, Purple Gallinule) *Porphyrio porphyrio*
rw1 ☐	Common Coot *Fulica atra*
r'(†?) ☐	<u>Masked Finfoot *Heliopais personata*</u>
v ☐	<u>Little Bustard *Tetrax (Otis) tetrax*</u>
r°4–5 ☐	<u>(Great) Indian Bustard* *Ardeotis (Choriotis) nigriceps*</u>
w'4 ☐	MacQueen's Bustard (Houbara) *Chlamydotis (undulata) macqueenii*
r'3–4 ☐	<u>Bengal Florican *Houbaropsis (Eupodotis) bengalensis*</u>
rm4–5 ☐	<u>Lesser Florican* (Likh) *Eupodotis (Sypheotides) indica*</u>
r°2 ☐	Pheasant-tailed Jacana *Hydrophasianus chirurgus*
r2 ☐	Bronze-winged Jacana *Metopidius indicus*
w3–4 ☐	Eurasian Oystercatcher (Oystercatcher) *Haematopus ostralegus*
r3–4 ☐	Greater Painted-snipe (Painted Snipe) *Rostratula benghalensis*
r1 ☐	Black-winged Stilt *Himantopus himantopus*
b'w2–4 ☐	Pied Avocet (Avocet) *Recurvirostra avosetta*
r'a4 ☐	Ibisbill *Ibidorhyncha struthersii*
w'3 ☐	Crab-plover *Dromas ardeola*
r°3 ☐	Eurasian Thick-knee (Stone Curlew) *Burhinus oedicnemus*
r°3 ☐	Great Thick-knee (Great Stone Plover) *Esacus (magnirostris) recurvirostris*
r'4 ☐	Beach Thick-knee (Great Stone Plover) *Esacus neglectus (magnirostris)*
w2–3 ☐	Cream-coloured Courser *Cursorius cursor*
r'n3–4 ☐	Indian Courser* *Cursorius coromandelicus*
r'5 ☐	<u>Jerdon's (Double-banded) Courser** *Rhinoptilus (Cursorius) bitorquatus*</u>
w4–5 ☐	Collared Pratincole *Glareola pratincola*
r'°3–4 ☐	Oriental (Large Indian) Pratincole *Glareola (pratincola) maldivarum*
r°2 ☐	Small (Small Indian) Pratincole *Glareola lactea*
w2 ☐	White-tailed Lapwing (Plover) *Vanellus leucurus*
w4–5 ☐	<u>Sociable Lapwing (Plover) *Vanellus gregarius*</u>
w3–4 ☐	Northern Lapwing (Lapwing) *Vanellus vanellus*
w3–4 ☐	<u>Grey-headed Lapwing *Vanellus cinereus*</u>
r1 ☐	Red-wattled Lapwing (Plover) *Vanellus indicus*
r2 ☐	River (Spur-winged) Lapwing *Vanellus (spinosus) duvaucelii*
r'°2 ☐	Yellow-wattled Lapwing* *Vanellus malarbaricus*
w2 ☐	Grey (Black-bellied) Plover *Pluvialis squatarola*
v ☐	European Golden Plover (Golden Plover) *Pluvialis apricaria*
w2 ☐	Pacific (Eastern, Lesser) Golden Plover *Pluvialis (dominica) fulva*
w3r'4–5 ☐	Greater (Large) Sand Plover *Charadrius leschenaultii*
v ☐	Black-fronted Dotterel (Australian Black-fronted Plover) *Elseyornis (Charadrius) melanops*
v ☐	Caspian (Sand or Caspian Sand) Plover *Charadrius asiaticus*
v ☐	Oriental (Sand) Plover *Charadrius (asiaticus) veredus*
w4 ☐	Common Ringed Plover *Charadrius hiaticula*
rw1 ☐	Little Ringed Plover *Charadrius dubius*
rw2 ☐	Kentish Plover *Charadrius alexandrinus*
w'4–5 ☐	<u>Long-billed (Long-billed Ringed) Plover *Charadrius placidus*</u>
b'w2 ☐	Lesser (Mongolian) Sand Plover *Charadrius mongolus*
w3 ☐	Whimbrel *Numenius phaeopus*

w2–3 ☐	Eurasian Curlew (Curlew) *Numenius arquata*
w2 ☐	Black-tailed Godwit *Limosa limosa*
w2–4 ☐	Bar-tailed Godwit *Limosa lapponica*
w3 ☐	Spotted (Dusky) Redshank *Tringa erythropus*
b'w1 ☐	Common Redshank *Tringa totanus*
w2 ☐	Marsh Sandpiper *Tringa stagnatilis*
w1 ☐	Common Greenshank *Tringa nebularia*
w1 ☐	Green Sandpiper *Tringa ochropus*
w1 ☐	Wood Sandpiper *Tringa glareola*
w5 ☐	<u>Nordmann's (Spotted) Greenshank *Tringa guttifer*</u>
w2–3 ☐	Terek Sandpiper *Xenus cinereus (Tringa terek)*
b'w1 ☐	Common Sandpiper *Actitis (Tringa) hypoleucos*
w2–3 ☐	Ruddy Turnstone (Turnstone) *Arenaria interpres*
w4–5 ☐	<u>Asian (Asiatic) Dowitcher (Snipe-billed Godwit) *Limnodromus semipalmatus*</u>
v! ☐	Long-billed Dowitcher *Limnodromus scolopaceus*
aw4 ☐	Solitary Snipe *Gallinago solitaria*
r5 ☐	<u>Wood Snipe *Gallinago nemoricola*</u>
w1 ☐	Pintail Snipe *Gallinago stenura*
w4 ☐	Swinhoe's Snipe *Gallinago megala*
v ☐	<u>Great Snipe *Gallinago media*</u>
b'w1 ☐	Common (Fantail) Snipe *Gallinago gallinago*
w4 ☐	Jack Snipe *Lymnocryptes (Gallinago) minimus*
b'pw4 ☐	Eurasian Woodcock (Woodcock) *Scolopax rusticola*
w5? ☐	Red Knot (Knot) *Calidris canutus*
w3 ☐	Great (Eastern) Knot *Calidris tenuirostris*
w3–4 ☐	Sanderling *Calidris alba*
w4 ☐	Red-necked (Eastern Little) Stint *Calidris ruficollis*
w1 ☐	Little Stint *Calidris minuta*
w1 ☐	Temminck's Stint *Calidris temminckii*
w4 ☐	Long-toed Stint *Calidris subminuta*
v! ☐	Pectoral Sandpiper *Calidris melanotos*
w3 ☐	Dunlin *Calidris alpina*
w2 ☐	Curlew Sandpiper *Calidris ferruginea (testacea)*
w5 ☐	<u>Spoon-billed Sandpiper *Calidris (Eurynorhynchus) pygmaeus*</u>
w3–4 ☐	Broad-billed Sandpiper *Limicola falcinellus*
v! ☐	Buff-breasted Sandpiper *Tryngites subruficollis*
wp1–2 ☐	Ruff *Philomachus pugnax*
v? ☐	[Red (Grey) Phalarope *Phalaropus fulicaria*]
w4 ☐	Red-necked Phalarope *Phalaropus lobatus*
v ☐	Brown (Antarctic) Skua *Catharacta (skua) antarctica*
v ☐	South-Polar (Antarctic or MacCormick's) Skua *Catharacta (skua) maccormicki*
wp4? ☐	Pomarine (Pomatorhine) Jaeger (Pomatorhine Skua) *Stercorarius pomarinus*
v ☐	Parasitic Jaeger (Arctic, Parasitic or Richardson's Skua) *Stercorarius parasiticus*
v? ☐	[Long-tailed Jaeger *Stercorarius longicaudus*]
v ☐	Sooty Gull *Larus hemprichii*
w3–4 ☐	Heuglin's (Herring) Gull *Larus (argentatus) heuglini* {incl. *taimyrensis*}
w2–3 ☐	Yellow-legged (Herring) Gull *Larus cachinnans (argentatus)* {incl. *barabensis*}
w2–3 ☐	Pallas's (Great Black-headed) Gull *Larus ichthyaetus*
b'w2 ☐	Brown-headed Gull *Larus brunnicephalus*
w2 ☐	Black-headed Gull *Larus ridibundus*
w3–4 ☐	Slender-billed Gull *Larus genei*
v ☐	Little Gull *Larus minutus*
v ☐	Mew (Common) Gull *Larus canus*

rmw1 ☐	Whiskered Tern *Chlidonias hybridus*
w4 ☐	White-winged (White-winged Black) Tern *Chlidonias leucopterus*
v ☐	Black Tern *Chlidonias niger*
b'w2 ☐	Gull-billed Tern *Gelochelidon nilotica*
b'5w2 ☐	Caspian Tern *Sterna (Hydroprogne) caspia*
r2 ☐	(Indian) River Tern *Sterna aurantia*
b'w3 ☐	Common Tern *Sterna hirundo*
b'4 ☐	Roseate (Rosy) Tern *Sterna dougallii*
v ☐	Arctic Tern *Sterna paradisaea*
b'2m5 ☐	White-cheeked Tern *Sterna repressa*
r'3 ☐	Black-naped Tern *Sterna sumatrana*
r°4 ☐	<u>Black-bellied Tern *Sterna acuticauda*</u>
b's4 ☐	Bridled (Brown-winged) Tern *Sterna anaethetus*
b'2m? ☐	Sooty Tern *Sterna fuscata*
rm2–3 ☐	Little Tern *Sterna albifrons*
b'm?4 ☐	Saunders's (Saunders's Little) Tern *Sterna saundersi*
b'm3–4 ☐	Great (Large) Crested Tern *Sterna bergii*
b'm3 ☐	(Indian) Lesser Crested Tern *Sterna bengalensis*
w3–4 ☐	Sandwich Tern *Sterna sandvicensis*
b'2m? ☐	Brown Noddy (Noddy Tern) *Anous stolidus*
v ☐	Lesser (White-capped) Noddy *Anous tenuirostris*
v? ☐	[Black Noddy *Anous minutus*]
v ☐	(Indian Ocean) White (Fairy) Tern *Gygis alba*
r'n4 ☐	<u>Indian Skimmer *Rynchops albicollis*</u>
r'a4 ☐	Tibetan Sandgrouse *Syrrhaptes tibetanus*
v ☐	Pallas's Sandgrouse *Syrrhaptes paradoxus*
v ☐	Pin-tailed (Large Pintail) Sandgrouse *Pterocles alchata*
rn2 ☐	Chestnut-bellied (Indian) Sandgrouse *Pterocles exustus*
r'4w3? ☐	Spotted Sandgrouse *Pterocles senegallus*
wn3–4 ☐	Black-bellied (Imperial) Sandgrouse *Pterocles orientalis*
r'n3 ☐	Painted Sandgrouse* *Pterocles indicus*
r°2–4 ☐	Pin-tailed Green Pigeon *Treron apicauda*
r°a3–4 ☐	Wedge-tailed Green Pigeon *Treron sphenura*
r°3–4 ☐	Thick-billed Green Pigeon *Treron curvirostra*
☐	Pompadour (Grey-fronted) Green Pigeon *Treron pompadora*
r°2 ☐	---Pompadour Green Pigeon *T. (p.) pompadora {incl. affinis & phayrei}*
r°3 ☐	---Andaman Green Pigeon** *T. (p.) chloroptera*
r°4 ☐	Orange-breasted Green Pigeon *Treron bicincta*
r°2 ☐	Yellow-footed (Yellow-legged) Green Pigeon *Treron phoenicoptera*
r'°2 ☐	Green Imperial Pigeon *Ducula aenea*
r'1 ☐	Pied Imperial Pigeon *Ducula bicolor*
r°3 ☐	Mountain Imperial Pigeon (Imperial Pigeon) *Ducula badia*
a2 ☐	Snow Pigeon *Columba leuconota*
a3 ☐	Hill Pigeon *Columba rupestris*
r1 ☐	(Blue) Rock Pigeon *Columba livia*
w'4 ☐	<u>Yellow-eyed (Eastern Stock) Pigeon *Columba eversmanni*</u>
a'? ☐	Common Wood Pigeon *Columba palumbus*
a4 ☐	Speckled Wood Pigeon *Columba hodgsonii*
r'n3 ☐	<u>Nilgiri Wood Pigeon** *Columba elphinstonii*</u>
a4–5 ☐	Ashy Wood Pigeon *Columba pulchricollis*
r'5 ☐	<u>Pale-capped (Purple Wood) Pigeon *Columba punicea*</u>
r'3 ☐	<u>Andaman Wood Pigeon** *Columba palumboides*</u>
r3 ☐	Barred (Bar-tailed) Cuckoo Dove *Macropygia unchall*
r'3–4 ☐	<u>Andaman Cuckoo Dove** *Macropygia rufipennis*</u>

v ☐	European Turtle Dove (Turtle Dove) *Streptopelia turtur*
rm2 ☐	Oriental (Rufous) Turtle Dove *Streptopelia orientalis*
r1 ☐	Eurasian Collared (Indian Ring) Dove *Streptopelia decaocto*
r°3 ☐	Red Collared (Red Turtle) Dove *Streptopelia tranquebarica*
r°1 ☐	Spotted Dove *Streptopelia chinensis*
r1 ☐	Laughing (Little Brown or Senegal) Dove *Streptopelia senegalensis*
r3 ☐	Emerald (Bronze-winged) Dove *Chalcophaps indica*
r'3? ☐	<u>Nicobar Pigeon *Caloenas nicobarica*</u>
rn3 ☐	Alexandrine Parakeet *Psittacula eupatria*
r1 ☐	Rose-ringed (Ring-necked) Parakeet *Psittacula krameri*
rn1 ☐	Red-breasted Parakeet *Psittacula alexandri*
r'2 ☐	<u>Nicobar Parakeet** *Psittacula caniceps*</u>
s'3 ☐	<u>Derbyan (Lord Derby's) Parakeet *Psittacula derbiana*</u>
r'2 ☐	Long-tailed (Red-cheeked) Parakeet *Psittacula longicauda*
r°2 ☐	Plum-headed (Blossom-headed) Parakeet* *Psittacula cyanocephala*
r'n ☐	Blossom-headed (Eastern Blossom-headed) Parakeet *Psittacula roseata*
ran2 ☐	Slaty-headed Parakeet(*) *Psittacula himalayana*
r'4 ☐	Grey-headed (Eastern Slaty-headed) Parakeet *Psittacula finschii*
r2 ☐	Malabar (Blue-winged) Parakeet** *Psittacula columboides*
r3 ☐	Vernal Hanging Parrot (Indian Lorikeet) *Loriculus vernalis*
sm4 ☐	Chestnut-winged (Red-winged Crested) Cuckoo *Clamator coromandus*
sm3 ☐	Pied (Pied Crested, Jacobin) Cuckoo *Clamator jacobinus*
rm3 ☐	Large Hawk Cuckoo *Hierococcyx (Cuculus) sparverioides*
rm2 ☐	Common Hawk Cuckoo (Brainfever Bird) *Hierococcyx (Cuculus) varius*
r'°a4 ☐	Hodgson's Hawk Cuckoo *Hierococcyx (Cuculus) fugax*
rmn3 ☐	Indian Cuckoo *Cuculus micropterus*
sp(w)3 ☐	Eurasian Cuckoo (The Cuckoo) *Cuculus canorus*
spw'3 ☐	Oriental (Himalayan) Cuckoo *Cuculus saturatus*
sp(w)2 ☐	(Asian) Lesser (Small) Cuckoo *Cuculus poliocephalus*
r°3 ☐	(Indian) Banded Bay Cuckoo *Cacomantis sonneratii*
rm3–4 ☐	Grey-bellied (Indian Plaintive) Cuckoo* *Cacomantis passerinus*
r°3–4 ☐	(Rufous-bellied) Plaintive Cuckoo *Cacomantis merulinus*
sw'?4–5 ☐	Asian Emerald Cuckoo (Emerald Cuckoo) *Chrysococcyx (Chalcites) maculatus*
r'mn?4–5 ☐	Violet Cuckoo *Chrysococcyx (Chalcites) xanthorhynchus*
rm3 ☐	Drongo Cuckoo *Surniculus lugubris*
r°m1 ☐	Asian Koel (Koel) *Eudynamys scolopacea*
r3–4 ☐	(Large) Green-billed Malkoha *Phaenicophaeus (Rhopodytes) tristis*
r3 ☐	Blue-faced (Small Green-billed) Malkoha* *Phaenicophaeus (Rhopodytes) viridirostris*
r3–4 ☐	Sirkeer Malkoha* (Sirkeer Cuckoo) *Phaenicophaeus (Taccocua) leschenaultii*
? ☐	[Red-faced Malkoha* *Phaenicophaeus pyrrhocephalus*]
r1 ☐	Greater Coucal (Crow-Pheasant or Coucal) *Centropus sinensis*
r'2 ☐	<u>Brown Coucal(*) (Andaman Crow-Pheasant) *Centropus (sinensis) andamanensis*</u>
r'4 ☐	Lesser Coucal *Centropus (toulou) bengalensis*
r3 ☐	Barn Owl *Tyto alba*
r4–5 ☐	Grass Owl *Tyto capensis*
r'5 ☐	Oriental Bay Owl (Bay Owl) *Phodilus badius*
r4 ☐	Mountain (Spotted) Scops Owl *Otus spilocephalus*
r'4 ☐	<u>Andaman Scops Owl** *Otus balli*</u>
(r'?)w5 ☐	Pallid (Striated) Scops Owl *Otus brucei*
v ☐	Eurasian Scops Owl (Scops Owl) *Otus scops*
rm3 ☐	Oriental Scops Owl (Scops Owl) *Otus (scops) sunia*
r'? ☐	Moluccan Scops Owl *Otus magicus (?)*
r3 ☐	Collared Scops Owl *Otus bakkamoena*

☐	Eurasian Eagle (Great Horned) Owl *Bubo bubo*
r'4 ☐	---Eurasian Eagle Owl *B. (b.) bubo {incl. tibetanus & hemachalana}*
r3–4 ☐	---Rock (Indian) Eagle Owl* *B. (b.) bengalensis*
r4–5 ☐	<u>Spot-bellied (Forest) Eagle Owl *Bubo nipalensis*</u>
r3–4 ☐	Dusky Eagle (Dusky Horned) Owl *Bubo coromandus*
r3 ☐	Brown Fish Owl *Ketupa (Bubo) zeylonensis*
r4–5 ☐	<u>Tawny Fish Owl *Ketupa (Bubo) flavipes*</u>
r'? ☐	Buffy (Malay) Fish Owl *Ketupa (Bubo) ketupu*
r3–4 ☐	Collared (Collared Pigmy) Owlet *Glaucidium brodiei*
r2 ☐	Jungle Owlet(*) *Glaucidium radiatum*
r2 ☐	Asian Barred Owlet (Barred Owlet) *Glaucidium cuculoides*
r2 ☐	Brown Hawk Owl *Ninox scutulata*
r'3? ☐	<u>Andaman (Andaman Brown) Hawk Owl** *Ninox affinis*</u>
r'4 ☐	Little Owl *Athene noctua*
r1 ☐	Spotted Owlet *Athene brama*
r'5 ☐	<u>Forest (Forest Spotted) Owlet** *Athene blewitti*</u>
r3–4 ☐	Mottled Wood Owl* *Strix ocellata*
r3 ☐	Brown Wood Owl *Strix leptogrammica*
r'a3 ☐	Tawny (Himalayan Wood) Owl *Strix aluco*
b'w'4 ☐	Long-eared Owl *Asio otus*
w3–4 ☐	Short-eared Owl *Asio flammeus*
v(b') ☐	Boreal (Tengmalm's) Owl *Aegolius funereus*
r'4 ☐	<u>Sri Lanka (Ceylon) Frogmouth* *Batrachostomus monileger*</u>
r'5 ☐	Hodgson's Frogmouth *Batrachostomus hodgsoni*
r°3–4 ☐	Great Eared Nightjar *Eurostopodus macrotis*
ram3 ☐	Grey (Indian Jungle) Nightjar *Caprimulgus indicus*
p'5 ☐	Eurasian (European) Nightjar *Caprimulgus europaeus*
m'5w4 ☐	Sykes's Nightjar(*) *Caprimulgus mahrattensis*
rm2 ☐	Large-tailed (Long-tailed) Nightjar *Caprimulgus macrurus*
r2–3 ☐	Jerdon's (Long-tailed) Nightjar* *Caprimulgus (macrurus) atripennis*
r°2 ☐	Indian Nightjar *Caprimulgus asiaticus*
r°3 ☐	Savanna (Franklin's or Allied) Nightjar *Caprimulgus affinis*
r°2–3 ☐	Himalayan Swiftlet *Collocalia brevirostris*
r°2–3 ☐	Indian (Indian Edible-nest) Swiftlet* *Collocalia unicolor*
r'4 ☐	Edible-nest (Andaman Grey-rumped) Swiftlet *Collocalia fuciphaga*
r'1–2 ☐	Glossy (White-bellied) Swiftlet *Collocalia esculenta*
r'4 ☐	White-throated Needletail (White-throated Spinetail Swift) *Hirundapus (Chaetura) caudacutus*
r'3? ☐	Silver-backed Needletail (Cochinchina Spinetail Swift) *Hirundapus (Chaetura) cochinchinensis*
r°3 ☐	Brown-backed Needletail (Large Brown-throated Spinetail Swift) *Hirundapus (Chaetura) giganteus*
r'3 ☐	White-rumped Needletail(*) (White-rumped Spinetail) *Zoonavena (Chaetura) sylvatica*
r'mn3–4 ☐	Alpine Swift *Tachymarptis (Apus) melba*
s'4(pw) ☐	Common Swift *Apus apus*
b'2 ☐	<u>Dark-rumped (Dark-backed) Swift(*) *Apus acuticauda*</u>
s'w'n3–4 ☐	Fork-tailed (Large White-rumped, Pacific) Swift *Apus pacificus*
☐	House Swift *Apus affinis*
rm1 ☐	---Little Swift *A. (a.) affinis*
rm1 ☐	---House Swift *A. (a.) nipalensis {incl. subfurcatus}*
r2–3 ☐	Asian Palm Swift (Palm Swift) *Cypsiurus (parvus) balasiensis*
r3 ☐	Crested Treeswift *Hemiprocne (longipennis) coronata*
r3–4 ☐	Malabar Trogon* *Harpactes fasciatus*

r'3 □	Red-headed Trogon *Harpactes erythrocephalus*
r'5 □	<u>Ward's Trogon *Harpactes wardi*</u>
r3 □	Crested (Himalayan Pied) Kingfisher *Megaceryle (Ceryle) lugubris*
r1 □	Pied (Lesser Pied) Kingfisher *Ceryle rudis*
r'5 □	<u>Blyth's (Great Blue) Kingfisher *Alcedo hercules*</u>
rw1 □	Common Kingfisher *Alcedo atthis*
r'5 □	Blue-eared Kingfisher *Alcedo meninting*
□	Oriental Dwarf (Three-toed) Kingfisher *Ceyx erithacus*
r°4–5 □	---Black-backed Kingfisher *C. (e.) erithacus* (incl. *macrocarus*)
v □	---Rufous-backed Kingfisher *C. (e.) rufidorsa*
r'4 □	<u>Brown-winged Kingfisher *Halcyon (Pelargopsis) amauroptera*</u>
r3–4 □	Stork-billed Kingfisher *Halcyon (Pelargopsis) capensis*
r'4 □	Ruddy Kingfisher *Halcyon coromanda*
r1 □	White-throated (White-breasted, Smyrna) Kingfisher *Halcyon smyrnensis*
r'3 □	Black-capped Kingfisher *Halcyon pileata*
r'2 □	Collared (White-collared) Kingfisher *Todiramphus (Halcyon) chloris*
r3 □	Chestnut-headed Bee-eater *Merops leschenaulti*
s'p3 □	European Bee-eater *Merops apiaster*
r'spw3 □	Blue-cheeked Bee-eater *Merops (superciliosus) persicus*
rm3 □	Blue-tailed Bee-eater *Merops philippinus*
r°1 □	Green Bee-eater *Merops orientalis*
r4 □	Blue-bearded Bee-eater *Nyctyornis athertoni*
s'p'3–4 □	European Roller *Coracias garrulus*
□	Indian Roller *Coracias benghalensis*
r1 □	---Indian Roller *C. (b.) benghalensis*
r2 □	---Burmese Roller *C. (b.) affinis*
r'3–4 □	Dollarbird (Broad-billed Roller) *Eurystomus orientalis*
rw1 □	Common Hoopoe *Upupa epops*
r°2–3 □	Indian (Common) Grey Hornbill* *Ocyceros (Tockus) birostris*
r3 □	<u>Malabar Grey Hornbill** *Ocyceros (Tockus) griseus*</u>
r'4 □	<u>Brown (White-throated Brown) Hornbill *Anorrhinus (Ptilolaemus) tickelli*</u>
r'3–4 □	<u>Rufous-necked Hornbill *Aceros nipalensis*</u>
r'4 □	Wreathed Hornbill *Aceros (Rhyticeros) undulatus*
r'2 □	<u>Narcondam (Blyth's) Hornbill** *Aceros narcondami (Rhyticeros plicatus)*</u>
r°3 □	Oriental (Indian) Pied Hornbill *Anthracoceros albirostris (malabaricus)*
r°4 □	<u>Malabar Pied Hornbill* *Anthracoceros coronatus*</u>
r°3–4 □	Great (Great Pied) Hornbill *Buceros bicornis*
a2 □	Great (Great Hill) Barbet *Megalaima virens*
r2 □	Brown-headed (Large Green) Barbet* *Megalaima zeylanica*
r2 □	Lineated Barbet *Megalaima lineata*
r2 □	White-cheeked (Small Green) Barbet** *Megalaima viridis*
r3–4 □	Golden-throated Barbet *Megalaima franklinii*
r2–3 □	Blue-throated Barbet *Megalaima asiatica*
r3–4 □	Blue-eared Barbet *Megalaima australis*
r2 □	Crimson-fronted (Crimson-throated) Barbet *Megalaima rubricapilla*
r°1 □	Coppersmith (Crimson-breasted) Barbet *Megalaima haemacephala*
r'5 □	<u>Yellow-rumped Honeyguide(*) *Indicator xanthonotus*</u>
w3–4 □	Eurasian Wryneck (Wryneck) *Jynx torquilla*
r3–4 □	Speckled Piculet *Picumnus innominatus*
r3–4 □	White-browed (Rufous) Piculet *Sasia ochracea*
r3–4 □	Rufous Woodpecker *Celeus (Micropternus) brachyurus*
r2 □	Scaly-bellied (Scaly-bellied Green) Woodpecker *Picus squamatus*
r3 □	Streak-throated (Little Scaly-bellied Green) Woodpecker *Picus xanthopygaeus (myrmecophoneus)*

r2 ☐	Grey-headed (Black-naped Green) Woodpecker *Picus canus*
r3 ☐	Greater Yellownape (Large Yellow-naped Woodpecker) *Picus flavinucha*
r3 ☐	Lesser Yellownape (Small Yellow-naped Woodpecker) *Picus chlorolophus*
r1 ☐	Black-rumped Flameback (Lesser Golden-backed Woodpecker) (*) *Dinopium benghalense*
r3–4 ☐	Himalayan Flameback (Himalayan Golden-backed Three-toed Woodpecker) *Dinopium shorii*
r4 ☐	Common Flameback (Indian Golden-backed Three-toed Woodpecker) *Dinopium javanense*
r'4 ☐	Pale-headed Woodpecker *Gecinulus grantia*
r'5 ☐	(Himalayan) Great Slaty Woodpecker *Mulleripicus pulverulentus*
r4–5 ☐	White-bellied (Indian Great Black) Woodpecker *Dryocopus javensis*
r'3 ☐	<u>Andaman (Indian Great Black) Woodpecker** *Dryocopus (javensis) hodgei*</u>
? ☐	[Black Woodpecker *Dryocopus martius*]
r3–4 ☐	Rufous-bellied Woodpecker (Rufous-bellied Sapsucker) *Dendrocopos (Hypopicus) hyperythrus*
r'? ☐	Great Spotted (Red-crowned Pied) Woodpecker *Dendrocopos (Picoides) major*
a3 ☐	Himalayan (Himalayan Pied) Woodpecker(*) *Dendrocopos (Picoides) himalayensis*
r3–4 ☐	Darjeeling (Darjeeling Pied) Woodpecker *Dendrocopos (Picoides) darjellensis*
r'3–4 ☐	Crimson-breasted (Crimson-breasted Pied) Woodpecker *Dendrocopos (Picoides) cathpharius*
a3 ☐	Brown-fronted (Brown-fronted Pied) Woodpecker(*) *Dendrocopos (Picoides) auriceps*
r'3–4 ☐	Stripe-breasted (Stripe-breasted Pied) Woodpecker *Dendrocopos (Picoides) atratus*
r2–3 ☐	Fulvous-breasted (Fulvous-breasted Pied) Woodpecker *Dendrocopos (Picoides) macei*
r2 ☐	Yellow-crowned (Yellow-fronted Pied) Woodpecker *Dendrocopos (Picoides) mahrattensis*
r3 ☐	Grey-capped (Grey-crowned) Pygmy Woodpecker *Dendrocopos (Picoides) canicapillus*
r2 ☐	Brown-capped Pygmy (Brown-capped or Pigmy) Woodpecker* *Dendrocopos (Picoides) nanus*
r3 ☐	Heart-spotted Woodpecker *Hemicircus canente*
r3–4 ☐	Bay (Red-eared Bay) Woodpecker *Blythipicus pyrrhotis*
r3–4 ☐	White-naped (Black-backed) Woodpecker* *Chrysocolaptes festivus*
r3 ☐	Greater Flameback (Larger Golden-backed Woodpecker) *Chrysocolaptes lucidus*
r3–4 ☐	Silver-breasted (Collared) Broadbill *Serilophus lunatus*
r'3 ☐	Long-tailed Broadbill *Psarisomus dalhousiae*
a'm5 ☐	<u>Blue-naped Pitta *Pitta nipalensis*</u>
m3 ☐	Indian Pitta* *Pitta brachyura*
r'°a4–5 ☐	Hooded (Green-breasted) Pitta *Pitta sordida*
r'4–5 ☐	Blue Pitta *Pitta cyanea*
r'°3–4 ☐	Singing Bushlark *Mirafra (javanica) cantillans*
r2 ☐	Bengal (Rufous-winged) Bushlark *Mirafra assamica*
r2 ☐	Jerdon's (Rufous-winged) Bushlark* *Mirafra affinis*
r2 ☐	Indian (Red-winged) Bushlark* *Mirafra erythroptera*
rm2 ☐	Ashy-crowned Sparrow Lark* (Ashy-crowned Finch-Lark) *Eremopterix grisea*
r'm3 ☐	Black-crowned Sparrow Lark (Black-crowned Finch-Lark) *Eremopterix nigriceps*
r'3 ☐	Desert Lark (Desert Finch-Lark) *Ammomanes deserti*

r°3 ☐	Rufous-tailed Lark* (Rufous-tailed Finch-Lark) *Ammomanes phoenicurus*
r′3–4 ☐	Greater Hoopoe (Bifasciated or Large Desert) Lark *Alaemon alaudipes*
w2–3 ☐	Greater Short-toed Lark (Short-toed Lark) *Calandrella (cinerea) brachydactyla*
s′2w3 ☐	Hume's Short-toed Lark *Calandrella acutirostris*
v? ☐	[Lesser Short-toed Lark *Calandrella rufescens*]
v? ☐	[Asian (Lesser) Short-toed Lark *Calandrella cheleensis (rufescens leucophaea)*]
r′3 ☐	Sand Lark *Calandrella raytal*
nw3 ☐	Bimaculated (Eastern Calandra) Lark *Melanocorypha bimaculata*
r′? ☐	Tibetan (Longbilled Calandra) Lark *Melanocorypha maxima*
a1 ☐	Horned Lark (Shorelark) *Eremophila alpestris*
r°2 ☐	Crested Lark *Galerida cristata*
r°3 ☐	Malabar (Malabar Crested) Lark** *Galerida malabarica*
r°3–4 ☐	Sykes's (Sykes's Crested or Tawny) Lark** *Galerida deva*
w4 ☐	Eurasian Skylark (Skylark) *Alauda arvensis*
ramw2–3 ☐	Oriental (Eastern) Skylark *Alauda gulgula*
r′w2–3 ☐	Pale (Collared Sand) Martin *Riparia (riparia) diluta*
w3 ☐	(Collared) Sand Martin (Bank Swallow) *Riparia riparia*
r°2 ☐	Plain (Plain Sand) Martin *Riparia paludicola*
b′w3–4 ☐	Eurasian Crag Martin (Crag Martin) *Hirundo rupestris*
r°2–3 ☐	Dusky Crag Martin *Hirundo concolor*
v ☐	Rock (Pale Crag) Martin *Hirundo fuligula (obsoleta)*
bw2 ☐	Barn Swallow (Swallow) *Hirundo rustica*
☐	Pacific (House) Swallow *Hirundo tahitica*
r′2–3 ☐	---Hill Swallow* *H. (t.) domicola*
r′2 ☐	---Pacific Swallow *H. (t.) tahitica {incl. javanica}*
rm3 ☐	Wire-tailed Swallow *Hirundo smithii*
r°3 ☐	Streak-throated (Indian Cliff) Swallow(*) *Hirundo fluvicola*
rw2 ☐	Red-rumped (Striated) Swallow *Hirundo daurica*
r′w3 ☐	Striated (Larger Striated) Swallow *Hirundo striolata*
s′p′w′3–4 ☐	Northern House Martin (House Martin) *Delichon urbica*
rm3 ☐	Asian House Martin *Delichon dasypus (urbica)*
a3 ☐	Nepal House Martin *Delichon nipalensis*
rw2 ☐	Southern Grey Shrike (Grey Shrike) *Lanius meridionalis (excubitor)*
v ☐	Great Grey Shrike (Northern or Grey Shrike) *Lanius excubitor*
v ☐	Lesser Grey Shrike *Lanius minor*
b′?p′5 ☐	Burmese Shrike *Lanius collurioides*
rm2 ☐	Bay-backed Shrike *Lanius vittatus*
pw4–5 ☐	Red-backed Shrike *Lanius collurio*
pw3 ☐	Rufous-tailed (Isabelline, Red-backed) Shrike *Lanius (collurio) isabellinus*
a2 ☐	Grey-backed (Tibetan) Shrike *Lanius tephronotus*
r1–2 ☐	Long-tailed (Rufous-backed) Shrike *Lanius schach*
w2–3 ☐	Brown Shrike *Lanius cristatus*
rm2–3 ☐	Eurasian Golden Oriole (Golden Oriole) *Oriolus oriolus*
w3 ☐	Black-naped Oriole *Oriolus chinensis*
b′?w5 ☐	Slender-billed (Black-naped) Oriole *Oriolus (chinensis) tenuirostris*
r2 ☐	Black-hooded (Black-headed) Oriole *Oriolus xanthornus*
r3 ☐	Maroon Oriole *Oriolus traillii*
r°1 ☐	Black Drongo (King-Crow) *Dicrurus (adsimilis) macrocercus*
am2 ☐	Ashy (Grey) Drongo *Dicrurus leucophaeus*
r°3 ☐	White-bellied Drongo* *Dicrurus caerulescens*
r°? ☐	Crow-billed Drongo *Dicrurus annectans*
r°2 ☐	Bronzed Drongo *Dicrurus aeneus*
r3 ☐	Lesser Racket-tailed Drongo *Dicrurus remifer*
r°3–4 ☐	Spangled (Hair-crested) Drongo *Dicrurus hottentottus*

r'3 ☐	<u>Andaman Drongo** *Dicrurus andamanensis*</u>
r2 ☐	Greater Racket-tailed Drongo *Dicrurus paradiseus*
r°3 ☐	Ashy Woodswallow (Ashy Swallow-Shrike) *Artamus fuscus*
r'3 ☐	White-breasted Woodswallow (White-breasted Swallow-Shrike) *Artamus leucorhynchus*
s'w'3 ☐	<u>Spot-winged Starling (Spotted-winged Stare) *Saroglossa spiloptera*</u>
r'l°1 ☐	Asian Glossy Starling (Glossy Stare) *Aplonis panayensis*
☐	Chestnut-tailed Starling (Grey-headed Myna) *Sturnus malabaricus*
r°1 ☐	---Grey-headed Starling *S. (m.) malabaricus*
r'°2 ☐	---Blyth's Starling** *S. (m.) blythii*
r'3 ☐	<u>White-headed Starling** (White-headed Myna) *Sturnus erythropygius*</u>
rm2–3 ☐	Brahminy Starling(*) (Black-headed or Brahminy Myna) *Sturnus pagodarum*
v ☐	Purple-backed Starling (Daurian Myna) *Sturnus sturninus*
wp1–2 ☐	Rosy (Rose-coloured) Starling (Rosy Pastor) *Sturnus roseus*
s'w1–2 ☐	Common Starling *Sturnus vulgaris*
r°2 ☐	Asian Pied Starling (Pied Myna) *Sturnus contra*
v ☐	White-shouldered Starling (Chinese or Grey-backed Myna) *Sturnus sinensis*
r1 ☐	Common Myna *Acridotheres tristis*
r°2 ☐	Bank Myna* *Acridotheres ginginianus*
r°2 ☐	Jungle Myna *Acridotheres fuscus*
r'3 ☐	White-vented Myna (Orange-billed Jungle Myna) *Acridotheres cinereus (javanicus)*
r'°5 ☐	<u>Collared Myna *Acridotheres albocinctus*</u>
r'5 ☐	Golden-crested Myna *Ampeliceps (Mino) coronatus*
☐	Hill Myna (Grackle) *Gracula religiosa*
r°2–3 ☐	---Eastern Hill Myna *G. (r.) religiosa*
r°2–3 ☐	---Southern Hill Myna* *G. (r.) indica*
ra3 ☐	Eurasian (Red-crowned) Jay *Garrulus glandarius*
r'a3 ☐	Black-headed (Black-throated) Jay(*) *Garrulus lanceolatus*
r3 ☐	Common Green Magpie *Cissa chinensis*
a3 ☐	Yellow-billed (Gold-billed) Blue Magpie *Urocissa (Cissa) flavirostris*
a3 ☐	Red-billed Blue Magpie *Urocissa (Cissa) erythrorhyncha*
r'2 ☐	Black-billed (White-rumped) Magpie *Pica pica*
r2–3 ☐	Rufous (Indian) Treepie *Dendrocitta vagabunda*
r'5 ☐	Collared (Black-browed) Treepie *Dendrocitta frontalis*
r'3 ☐	<u>White-bellied Treepie** *Dendrocitta leucogastra*</u>
a2–3 ☐	Grey (Himalayan) Treepie *Dendrocitta formosae*
r'3 ☐	<u>Andaman Treepie** *Dendrocitta bayleyi*</u>
r'5 ☐	Hume's Groundpecker (Hume's Ground Chough) *Pseudopodoces (Podoces) humilis*
☐	Spotted Nutcracker (Nutcracker) *Nucifraga caryocatactes*
a3 ☐	---Eurasian Nutcracker *N. (c.) caryocatactes* {incl. *hemispila* & *macella*}
a3 ☐	---Larger Spotted (Indian) Nutcracker *N. (c.) multipunctata*
a2 ☐	Yellow-billed (Alpine) Chough *Pyrrhocorax graculus*
a2 ☐	Red-billed Chough *Pyrrhocorax pyrrhocorax*
r1 ☐	House Crow *Corvus splendens*
w'4 ☐	Rook *Corvus frugilegus*
r'w'2 ☐	Eurasian Jackdaw (Jackdaw) *Corvus monedula*
☐	Large-billed (Jungle) Crow *Corvus macrorhynchos*
r°a2 ☐	---Large-billed Crow *C. (m.) macrorhynchos* {incl. *intermedius* & *tibetosinensis*}
r2 ☐	---Jungle Crow *C. (m.) levaillantii* {incl. *culminatus*}
r'w3 ☐	Carrion Crow *Corvus corone*
r'a3 ☐	Common Raven *Corvus corax*
v ☐	Bohemian Waxwing (Waxwing) *Bombycilla garrulus*

w'4 □ | Grey Hypocolius *Hypocolius ampelinus*
r°a2–3 □ | Bar-winged (Pied) Flycatcher-shrike *Hemipus picatus*
r°3 □ | Large Woodshrike *Tephrodornis gularis (virgatus)*
r2–3 □ | Common Woodshrike *Tephrodornis pondicerianus*
r°3 □ | Large Cuckooshrike *Coracina (novaehollandiae) macei*
r'4 □ | Bar-bellied (Barred) Cuckooshrike *Coracina striata*
am3 □ | Black-winged (Smaller Grey) Cuckooshrike *Coracina melaschistos*
r°m3 □ | Black-headed Cuckooshrike(*) *Coracina melanoptera*
r'4–5 □ | Pied Triller (Pied Cuckoo-Shrike) *Lalage (Coracina) nigra*
r°a2–3 □ | Scarlet Minivet *Pericrocotus flammeus*
a4 □ | Short-billed Minivet *Pericrocotus brevirostris*
r°a2 □ | Long-tailed Minivet *Pericrocotus ethologus*
a3 □ | Grey-chinned (Yellow-throated) Minivet *Pericrocotus solaris*
r'm'4 □ | Rosy Minivet *Pericrocotus roseus*
w5 □ | Ashy Minivet *Pericrocotus divaricatus*
r1–2 □ | Small Minivet *Pericrocotus cinnamomeus*
r'4 □ | <u>White-bellied Minivet(*) *Pericrocotus erythropygius*</u>
r°2 □ | Common Iora *Aegithina tiphia*
r'3–4 □ | Marshall's (White-tailed) Iora** *Aegithina nigrolutea*
r°3 □ | Golden-fronted Leafbird (Golden-fronted Chloropsis) *Chloropsis aurifrons*
a3 □ | Orange-bellied Leafbird (Orange-bellied Chloropsis) *Chloropsis hardwickii*
r2–3 □ | Blue-winged Leafbird (Blue-winged Chloropsis) *Chloropsis cochinchinensis*
r°3 □ | Asian Fairy Bluebird (Fairy Bluebird) *Irena puella*
a'3 □ | Crested Finchbill (Finch-billed Bulbul) *Spizixos canifrons*
r'3 □ | Black-headed Bulbul *Pycnonotus atriceps*
r'3–4 □ | <u>Grey-headed Bulbul** *Pycnonotus priocephalus*</u>
r3 □ | Black-crested (Black-headed Yellow) Bulbul *Pycnonotus melanicterus*
r1 □ | Red-whiskered Bulbul *Pycnonotus jocosus*
r°2–3 □ | White-eared (White-cheeked) Bulbul *Pycnonotus (leucogenys) leucotis*
r°2 □ | Himalayan (White-cheeked) Bulbul(*) *Pycnonotus leucogenys*
r1 □ | Red-vented Bulbul *Pycnonotus cafer*
a3–4 □ | Striated (Striated Green) Bulbul *Pycnonotus striatus*
r'3–4 □ | <u>Yellow-throated Bulbul** *Pycnonotus xantholaemus*</u>
r'3–4 □ | Flavescent (Blyth's) Bulbul *Pycnonotus flavescens*
r3 □ | White-browed Bulbul* *Pycnonotus luteolus*
a3 □ | White-throated Bulbul *Alophoixus (Criniger) flaveolus*
r'4 □ | Olive Bulbul *Iole virescens (Hypsipetes viridescens)*
r'3–4 □ | <u>Nicobar Bulbul** *Hypsipetes nicobariensis*</u>
r2 □ | Yellow-browed Bulbul* *Iole (Hypsipetes) indica*
a3 □ | Mountain (Rufous-bellied) Bulbul *Hypsipetes mcclellandii*
a3 □ | Ashy (Brown-eared) Bulbul *Hemixos (Hypsipetes) flavala*
ra1 □ | Black Bulbul *Hypsipetes leucocephalus (madagascariensis)*
r2 □ | Puff-throated (Spotted) Babbler *Pellorneum ruficeps*
r'5 □ | <u>Marsh (Marsh Spotted) Babbler* *Pellorneum palustre*</u>
r'a4 □ | Spot-throated (Brown) Babbler *Pellorneum albiventre*
a'3 □ | Buff-breasted (Tickell's) Babbler *Pellorneum (Trichastoma) tickelli*
r3 □ | Abbott's Babbler *Malacocincla (Trichastoma) abbotti*
r3 □ | White-browed (Slaty-headed) Scimitar Babbler *Pomatorhinus (horsfieldii) schisticeps*
r2–3 □ | Indian (Slaty-headed) Scimitar Babbler* *Pomatorhinus horsfieldii*
a2 □ | Streak-breasted (Rufous-necked) Scimitar Babbler *Pomatorhinus ruficollis*
r2–3 □ | Rusty-cheeked Scimitar Babbler *Pomatorhinus erythrogenys*
r'3 □ | Spot-breasted Scimitar Babbler *Pomatorhinus erythrocnemis (erythrogenys mcclellandi)*

r′4 ☐	Large Scimitar Babbler *Pomatorhinus hypoleucos*
r3–4 ☐	Coral-billed Scimitar Babbler *Pomatorhinus ferruginosus*
r′4 ☐	Red-billed (Lloyd's) Scimitar Babbler *Pomatorhinus ochraceiceps*
a3 ☐	<u>Slender-billed Scimitar Babbler *Xiphirhynchus superciliaris*</u>
a′4–5 ☐	<u>Long-billed Wren Babbler *Rimator malacoptilus*</u>
r′3–4 ☐	Streaked (Short-tailed) Wren Babbler *Napothera brevicaudata*
a′4 ☐	Eyebrowed (Small) Wren Babbler *Napothera epilepidota*
a2 ☐	Scaly-breasted Wren Babbler *Pnoepyga albiventer*
a2 ☐	Pygmy (Brown or Lesser Scaly-breasted) Wren Babbler *Pnoepyga pusilla*
r′4 ☐	<u>Rufous-throated (Tailed) Wren Babbler* *Spelaeornis caudatus*</u>
r′? ☐	<u>Rusty-throated Wren Babbler** (Mishmi Wren) *Spelaeornis badeigularis*</u>
r′5 ☐	<u>Tawny-breasted (Long-tailed) Wren Babbler* *Spelaeornis longicaudatus*</u>
r′4–5 ☐	Long-tailed (Streaked Long-tailed) Wren Babbler *Spelaeornis chocolatinus*
r′5 ☐	Bar-winged (Long-tailed Spotted) Wren Babbler *Spelaeornis troglodytoides*
a′4–5 ☐	<u>Spotted Wren Babbler *Spelaeornis formosus*</u>
☐	<u>Wedge-billed Wren Babbler (Wedge-billed Wren) *Sphenocichla humei*</u>
a′5 ☐	<u>---Sikkim (Wedge-billed) Wren Babbler *S. (h.) humei*</u>
a′5 ☐	<u>---Cachar (Wedge-billed) Wren Babbler *S. (h.) roberti*</u>
r′3 ☐	Rufous-fronted (Red-fronted) Babbler *Stachyris rufifrons*
r2–3 ☐	Rufous-capped (Red-headed) Babbler *Stachyris ruficeps*
r2 ☐	Black-chinned (Red-billed) Babbler* *Stachyris pyrrhops*
r3 ☐	Golden (Gold-headed) Babbler *Stachyris chrysaea*
r1–2 ☐	Grey-throated (Black-throated) Babbler *Stachyris nigriceps*
r′3–4 ☐	<u>Snowy-throated (Austen's Spotted) Babbler** *Stachyris oglei*</u>
r2–3 ☐	Tawny-bellied (Rufous-bellied) Babbler* *Dumetia hyperythra*
r3 ☐	Dark-fronted (Black-headed) Babbler* *Rhopocichla atriceps*
r1–2 ☐	Striped Tit (Yellow-breasted) Babbler *Macronous gularis*
r′3–4 ☐	Chestnut-capped (Red-capped) Babbler *Timalia pileata*
r3 ☐	Yellow-eyed Babbler *Chrysomma sinense*
r′4 ☐	<u>Jerdon's Babbler *Chrysomma altirostre*</u>
r4 ☐	Great Parrotbill *Conostoma oemodium*
ra4 ☐	Brown Parrotbill (Brown Suthora) *Paradoxornis unicolor*
r4 ☐	Fulvous (Fulvous-fronted) Parrotbill (Fulvousfronted Suthora) *Paradoxornis fulvifrons*
r2–3 ☐	Black-throated (Orange) Parrotbill (Orange Suthora) *Paradoxornis nipalensis*
r′4–5 ☐	<u>Lesser Rufous-headed Parrotbill (Lesser Red-headed Suthora) *Paradoxornis atrosuperciliaris*</u>
r′3–4 ☐	<u>Greater Rufous-headed (Greater Red-headed) Parrotbill *Paradoxornis ruficeps*</u>
r′3–4 ☐	Grey-headed Parrotbill *Paradoxornis gularis*
r′5 ☐	<u>Black-breasted (Gould's) Parrotbill* *Paradoxornis flavirostris*</u>
r′4 ☐	<u>Spot-breasted (White-throated) Parrotbill *Paradoxornis guttaticollis*</u>
r2–3 ☐	Common Babbler *Turdoides caudatus*
r′2–3 ☐	Striated Babbler *Turdoides earlei*
r′4–5 ☐	<u>Slender-billed Babbler *Turdoides longirostris*</u>
r2 ☐	Large Grey Babbler* *Turdoides malcolmi*
r2–3 ☐	Rufous Babbler** *Turdoides subrufus*
r1 ☐	Jungle Babbler* *Turdoides striatus*
r2–3 ☐	Yellow-billed (White-headed or Southern Common) Babbler* *Turdoides affinis*
r′5 ☐	Chinese Babax *Babax lanceolatus*
r′? ☐	<u>[Giant (Giant Tibetan) Babax *Babax waddelli*]</u>
a2 ☐	White-throated Laughingthrush *Garrulax albogularis*
r2–3 ☐	Lesser Necklaced (Necklaced) Laughingthrush *Garrulax moniliger*

r2–3 ☐	Greater Necklaced (Black-gorgeted) Laughingthrush *Garrulax pectoralis*
a3 ☐	Striated Laughingthrush *Garrulax striatus*
r2 ☐	White-crested Laughingthrush *Garrulax leucolophus*
r'4 ☐	<u>Chestnut-backed Laughingthrush(*) *Garrulax nuchalis*</u>
r'4 ☐	<u>Yellow-throated Laughingthrush *Garrulax galbanus*</u>
r'3–4 ☐	<u>Wynaad (Yellow-breasted) Laughingthrush** *Garrulax delesserti*</u>
r'4 ☐	Rufous-vented (Yellow-breasted) Laughingthrush *Garrulax (delesserti) gularis*
a2–3 ☐	Variegated Laughingthrush* *Garrulax variegatus*
r'4 ☐	Moustached (Ashy) Laughingthrush *Garrulax cineraceus*
r3 ☐	Rufous-chinned Laughingthrush *Garrulax rufogularis*
r3 ☐	Spotted (White-spotted) Laughingthrush *Garrulax ocellatus*
a'4 ☐	Grey-sided Laughingthrush *Garrulax caerulatus*
r3 ☐	Rufous-necked Laughingthrush *Garrulax ruficollis*
r'4 ☐	<u>Spot-breasted Laughingthrush *Garrulax merulinus*</u>
r'5 ☐	White-browed Laughingthrush *Garrulax sannio*
r'2 ☐	<u>Nilgiri (Rufous-breasted) Laughingthrush** *Garrulax cachinnans*</u>
r'2 ☐	<u>Grey-breasted (White-breasted) Laughingthrush** *Garrulax jerdoni*</u>
a2 ☐	Streaked Laughingthrush *Garrulax lineatus*
r'4 ☐	<u>Striped (Manipur Streaked) Laughingthrush(*) *Garrulax virgatus*</u>
r'5 ☐	<u>Brown-capped Laughingthrush(*) *Garrulax austeni*</u>
r4 ☐	Blue-winged Laughingthrush *Garrulax squamatus*
r3–4 ☐	Scaly (Plain-coloured) Laughingthrush *Garrulax subunicolor*
r'5? ☐	Elliot's Laughingthrush *Garrulax elliotii*
a2–3 ☐	Black-faced Laughingthrush *Garrulax affinis*
a2 ☐	Chestnut-crowned (Red-headed) Laughingthrush *Garrulax erythrocephalus*
r'an3 ☐	Red-faced (Crimson-winged) Liocichla *Liocichla (Garrulax) phoenicea*
r2–3 ☐	Silver-eared Mesia *Leiothrix argentauris*
ra2–3 ☐	Red-billed Leiothrix (Pekin Robin) *Leiothrix lutea*
r'a4 ☐	Fire-tailed Myzornis *Myzornis pyrrhoura*
r'4 ☐	Cutia (Nepal Cutia) *Cutia nipalensis*
r'4–5 ☐	<u>Black-headed (Rufous-bellied) Shrike Babbler *Pteruthius rufiventer*</u>
ra3 ☐	White-browed (Red-winged) Shrike Babbler *Pteruthius flaviscapis*
ra3–4 ☐	Green Shrike Babbler *Pteruthius xanthochlorus*
ra4 ☐	Black-eared (Chestnut-throated) Shrike Babbler *Pteruthius melanotis*
v/r'? ☐	Chestnut-fronted Shrike Babbler *Pteruthius aenobarbus*
r'3 ☐	White-hooded (White-headed) Babbler *Gampsorhynchus rufulus*
r3 ☐	Rusty-fronted (Spectacled) Barwing *Actinodura egertoni*
r3 ☐	Hoary-throated (Hoary) Barwing *Actinodura nipalensis*
r'3 ☐	Streak-throated (Austen's) Barwing *Actinodura waldeni*
a3 ☐	Red-tailed Minla *Minla ignotincta*
a2 ☐	Chestnut-tailed Minla (Bar-throated Siva) *Minla strigula*
a2 ☐	Blue-winged Minla (Blue-winged Siva) *Minla cyanouroptera*
r'3 ☐	Striated (White-browed) Yuhina *Yuhina castaniceps*
a'2–3 ☐	White-naped Yuhina *Yuhina bakeri*
a2 ☐	Whiskered (Yellow-naped) Yuhina *Yuhina flavicollis*
a2 ☐	Stripe-throated Yuhina *Yuhina gularis*
a2 ☐	Rufous-vented Yuhina *Yuhina occipitalis*
a'2–3 ☐	Black-chinned Yuhina *Yuhina nigrimenta*
ra2–3 ☐	White-bellied Yuhina *Yuhina zantholeuca (xantholeuca)*
ra4 ☐	Golden-breasted Fulvetta (Golden-breasted Tit-Babbler) *Alcippe chrysotis*
r'4 ☐	<u>Yellow-throated Fulvetta (Dusky Green or Yellow-throated Tit-babbler) *Alcippe cinerea*</u>
a2–3 ☐	Rufous-winged Fulvetta (Chestnut-headed Tit-Babbler) *Alcippe castaneceps*

a1 ☐	White-browed Fulvetta (White-browed Tit-Babbler) *Alcippe vinipectus*
a'2–3 ☐	Brown-throated Fulvetta (Ludlow's or Brown-headed Tit-Babbler) *Alcippe (cinereiceps) ludlowi*
a'4 ☐	Streak-throated Fulvetta (Brown-headed Tit-Babbler) *Alcippe cinereiceps*
? ☐	[Chinese Fulvetta (Streak-throated Tit-Babbler) *Alcippe striaticollis*]
r'3–4 ☐	Rufous-throated Fulvetta (Red-throated Tit-Babbler) *Alcippe rufogularis*
r'4 ☐	Rusty-capped Fulvetta (Rufous-headed Tit-Babbler) *Alcippe dubia (brunnea mandelli)*
r1–2 ☐	Brown-cheeked Fulvetta (Quaker Babbler) *Alcippe poioicephala*
a1 ☐	Nepal Fulvetta (Nepal Babbler) *Alcippe nipalensis*
a'4 ☐	Rufous-backed (Chestnut-backed) Sibia *Heterophasia annectens*
a1 ☐	Rufous (Black-capped) Sibia *Heterophasia capistrata*
r'a3 ☐	Grey Sibia *Heterophasia gracilis*
a'2 ☐	Beautiful Sibia *Heterophasia pulchella*
r2 ☐	Long-tailed Sibia *Heterophasia picaoides*
w'3 ☐	Brown-chested Jungle (Olive) Flycatcher *Rhinomyias brunneata*
p'4 ☐	Spotted Flycatcher *Muscicapa striata*
a2–3 ☐	Dark-sided (Sooty) Flycatcher *Muscicapa sibirica*
rw2–3 ☐	Asian Brown (Brown) Flycatcher *Muscicapa dauurica (latirostris)*
b'w3–4 ☐	Brown-breasted Flycatcher *Muscicapa muttui*
m'3 ☐	Rusty-tailed (Rufous-tailed) Flycatcher(*) *Muscicapa ruficauda*
s(r?)4 ☐	Ferruginous Flycatcher *Muscicapa ferruginea*
v ☐	Yellow-rumped Flycatcher *Ficedula zanthopygia*
☐	Red-throated (Red-breasted) Flycatcher *Ficedula (Muscicapa) parva*
w2 ☐	---Red-throated Flycatcher *F. (p.) parva*
w1–2 ☐	---Eastern Red-throated Flycatcher *F. (p.) albicilla*
b'3w'4 ☐	Kashmir (Kashmir Red-breasted) Flycatcher* *Ficedula (Muscicapa) subrubra*
a2–3 ☐	Rufous-gorgeted (Orange-gorgeted) Flycatcher *Ficedula (Muscicapa) strophiata*
r4 ☐	White-gorgeted Flycatcher *Ficedula (Muscicapa) monileger*
a3–4 ☐	Snowy-browed (Rufous-breasted Blue) Flycatcher *Ficedula (Muscicapa) hyperythra*
a3 ☐	Slaty-backed (Rusty-breasted Blue) Flycatcher *Ficedula (Muscicapa) hodgsonii*
a3 ☐	Little Pied Flycatcher *Ficedula (Muscicapa) westermanni*
m3–4 ☐	Ultramarine (White-browed Blue) Flycatcher *Ficedula (Muscicapa) superciliaris*
a2–3 ☐	Slaty-blue Flycatcher *Ficedula tricolor (Muscicapa leucomelanura)*
a3–4 ☐	Sapphire (Sapphire-headed) Flycatcher *Ficedula (Muscicapa) sapphira*
r'3 ☐	Black-and-orange (Black-and-rufous) Flycatcher** *Ficedula (Muscicapa) nigrorufa*
a3–4 ☐	Large Niltava *Niltava (Muscicapa) grandis*
a3 ☐	Small Niltava *Niltava (Muscicapa) macgrigoriae*
a3 ☐	Rufous-bellied Niltava *Niltava (Muscicapa) sundara*
r'5 ☐	Vivid (Rufous-bellied Blue) Niltava *Niltava (Muscicapa) vivida*
a'4 ☐	White-tailed (White-tailed Blue) Flycatcher *Cyornis (Muscicapa) concretus*
r3–4 ☐	White-bellied Blue Flycatcher** *Cyornis (Muscicapa) pallipes*
r3 ☐	Pale-chinned (Brooks's) Flycatcher *Cyornis (Muscicapa) poliogenys*
r'a4 ☐	Pale Blue Flycatcher *Cyornis (Muscicapa) unicolor*
rm3–4 ☐	Blue-throated Flycatcher *Cyornis (Muscicapa) rubeculoides*
sm5 ☐	Hill (Large-billed) Blue Flycatcher *Cyornis (Muscicapa) banyumas*
r°2 ☐	Tickell's Blue Flycatcher *Cyornis (Muscicapa) tickelliae*
am2 ☐	Verditer Flycatcher *Eumyias (Muscicapa) thalassina*
r'2–3 ☐	Nilgiri Flycatcher** *Eumyias (Muscicapa) albicaudata*
a4-5 ☐	Pygmy Blue Flycatcher *Muscicapella hodgsoni*

rm2 □	Grey-headed Canary (Grey-headed) Flycatcher *Culicicapa ceylonensis*
a2–3 □	Yellow-bellied Fantail (Yellow-bellied Fantail Flycatcher) *Rhipidura hypoxantha*
r°2 □	White-browed Fantail (White-browed Fantail Flycatcher) *Rhipidura aureola*
□	White-throated Fantail (White-throated Fantail Flycatcher) *Rhipidura albicollis*
ram2 □	---White-throated Fantail *R. (a.) albicollis*
r°2 □	---White-spotted Fantail** *R. (a.) albogularis*
rm2–3 □	Asian Paradise-flycatcher (Paradise Flycatcher) *Terpsiphone paradisi*
r°2–3 □	Black-naped Monarch (Black-naped Flycatcher) *Hypothymis azurea*
r'3 □	Mangrove Whistler (Grey Thickhead) *Pachycephala grisola*
a3 □	Grey-bellied Tesia (Dull Slaty-bellied Ground Warbler) *Tesia cyaniventer*
a'3 □	Slaty-bellied Tesia (Slaty-bellied Ground Warbler) *Tesia olivea*
a3 □	Chestnut-headed Tesia (Chestnut-headed Ground Warbler) *Tesia castaneocoronata*
a4 □	Pale-footed Bush Warbler *Cettia pallidipes*
v □	Japanese (Chinese) Bush Warbler *Cettia diphone*
a2 □	Brownish-flanked (Strong-footed) Bush Warbler *Cettia (montana) fortipes*
a4 □	Chestnut-crowned (Large) Bush Warbler *Cettia major*
a3 □	Aberrant Bush Warbler *Cettia flavolivacea*
a3–4 □	Yellowish-bellied (Verreaux's) Bush Warbler *Cettia acanthizoides*
a2 □	Grey-sided (Rufous-capped) Bush Warbler *Cettia brunnifrons*
w'3 □	Cetti's Bush (Cetti's) Warbler *Cettia cetti*
a3 □	Spotted Bush Warbler *Bradypterus thoracicus*
a'4 □	Long-billed (Large-billed) Bush Warbler *Bradypterus major*
v(b'?) □	Chinese Bush Warbler *Bradypterus tacsanowskius*
a3 □	Brown Bush Warbler *Bradypterus luteoventris*
a'3 □	Russet Bush Warbler *Bradypterus mandelli (seebohmi)*
r3 □	Bright-headed Cisticola (Fantail Warbler) *Cisticola exilis*
r°2–3 □	Zitting Cisticola (Streaked Fantail Warbler) *Cisticola juncidis*
r2 □	Rufescent Prinia (Beavan's Wren-Warbler) *Prinia rufescens*
r2 □	Grey-breasted Prinia (Franklin's Wren-Warbler) *Prinia hodgsonii*
r'°3 □	Rufous-fronted Prinia* (Rufous-fronted Wren-Warbler) *Prinia buchanani*
r'5 □	Grey-crowned Prinia* (Hodgson's Wren-Warbler) *Prinia cinereocapilla*
r2–3 □	Graceful Prinia (Streaked Wren-Warbler) *Prinia gracilis*
r°1–2 □	Plain Prinia (Plain Wren-Warbler) *Prinia (subflava) inornata*
r2 □	Ashy Prinia* (Ashy Wren-Warbler) *Prinia socialis*
r3 □	Jungle Prinia* (Jungle Wren-Warbler) *Prinia sylvatica*
r2–3 □	Yellow-bellied Prinia (Yellow-bellied Wren-Warbler) *Prinia flaviventris*
ra2–3 □	Striated Prinia (Brown Hill Warbler) *Prinia criniger*
r'3 □	Hill Prinia (Black-throated Hill Warbler) *Prinia atrogularis*
□	Rufous-vented Prinia* (Long-tailed Grass Warbler) *Prinia burnesii*
r'3 □	---Long-tailed Prinia* *P. (b.) burnesii*
r'5 □	---Swamp Prinia* *P. (b.) cinerascens*
r'4 □	Rufous-rumped Grassbird (Large Grass Warbler) *Graminicola bengalensis*
r1 □	Common Tailorbird *Orthotomus sutorius*
r'4 □	Dark-necked (Black-necked) Tailorbird *Orthotomus atrogularis*
r'3 □	Mountain (Golden-headed) Tailorbird *Orthotomus cuculatus*
w4 □	Rusty-rumped (Pallas's Grasshopper) Warbler *Locustella certhiola*
w4–5 □	Lanceolated (Streaked Grasshopper) Warbler *Locustella lanceolata*
w4 □	Grasshopper Warbler *Locustella naevia*
r'4–5 □	Broad-tailed Grassbird** (Broad-tailed Grass Warbler) *Schoenicola platyura*
r'°5 □	Bristled Grassbird* (Bristled Grass Warbler) *Chaetornis striatus*
r2 □	Striated Grassbird (Striated Marsh Warbler) *Megalurus palustris*

w3 ☐	Thick-billed Warbler *Acrocephalus aedon*
b'w2–3 ☐	Clamorous (Indian Great) Reed Warbler *Acrocephalus stentoreus*
w4–5 ☐	Oriental (Eastern Great) Reed Warbler *Acrocephalus orientalis*
w'4 ☐	Black-browed Reed Warbler *Acrocephalus bistrigiceps*
w1 ☐	Blyth's Reed Warbler *Acrocephalus dumetorum*
w3 ☐	Paddyfield Warbler *Acrocephalus agricola*
b'r'°? ☐	Blunt-winged (Blunt-winged Paddyfield) Warbler *Acrocephalus concinens*
b'w4 ☐	Moustached (Moustached Sedge) Warbler *Acrocephalus melanopogon*
v ☐	Sedge Warbler *Acrocephalus schoenobaenus*
☐	Booted Warbler *Hippolais caligata*
w3 ☐	---Booted Warbler *H. (c.) caligata*
b'5w3 ☐	---Sykes's Warbler *H. (c.) rama*
v ☐	Barred Warbler *Sylvia nisoria*
w3–4 ☐	Orphean Warbler *Sylvia hortensis*
p4–5 ☐	Greater Whitethroat (Whitethroat) *Sylvia communis*
w2 ☐	(Eurasian) Lesser Whitethroat *Sylvia curruca* {incl. *blythi*}
w3 ☐	Desert Lesser (Small) Whitethroat *Sylvia (curruca) minula*
b'w3 ☐	Hume's Lesser Whitethroat *Sylvia (curruca) althaea*
w2 ☐	Desert Warbler *Sylvia nana*
v ☐	Garden Warbler *Sylvia borin*
v! ☐	Willow Warbler *Phylloscopus trochilus*
w1 ☐	Common Chiffchaff (Brown Leaf Warbler) *Phylloscopus collybita tristis*
m3 ☐	Mountain Chiffchaff (Brown Leaf Warbler or Chiffchaff) *Phylloscopus (collybita) sindianus*
w'4 ☐	Plain Leaf Warbler *Phylloscopus neglectus*
s'3w5 ☐	<u>Tytler's (Slender-billed) Leaf Warbler* *Phylloscopus tytleri*</u>
s'1w'2 ☐	Tickell's Leaf Warbler *Phylloscopus affinis*
v ☐	Buff-throated (Tickell's Leaf) Warbler *Phylloscopus subaffinis*
m3 ☐	Sulphur-bellied (Olivaceous Leaf) Warbler *Phylloscopus griseolus*
a3–4 ☐	Smoky (Smoky Willow) Warbler *Phylloscopus fuligiventer*
w2–3 ☐	Dusky (Dusky Leaf) Warbler *Phylloscopus fuscatus*
a2 ☐	Buff-barred (Orange-barred Leaf) Warbler *Phylloscopus pulcher*
am2w1 ☐	Hume's (Yellow-browed) Warbler *Phylloscopus (inornatus) humei*
w3 ☐	Yellow-browed (Plain Leaf, Yellow-browed Leaf or Inornate) Warbler *Phylloscopus inornatus*
w3–4 ☐	Brooks's Leaf Warbler *Phylloscopus subviridis*
a2 ☐	Lemon-rumped (Pale-rumped, Pallas's Leaf) Warbler *Phylloscopus (proregulus) chloronotus*
a2–3 ☐	Ashy-throated (Grey-faced Leaf) Warbler *Phylloscopus maculipennis*
v ☐	Arctic (Arctic Leaf) Warbler *Phylloscopus borealis*
m3 ☐	Large-billed Leaf Warbler *Phylloscopus magnirostris*
☐	Greenish (Dull Green Leaf) Warbler *Phylloscopus trochiloides*
amw1 ☐	---Greenish Warbler *P. (t.) trochiloides* {incl. *viridanus* & *ludlowi*}
pw2 ☐	---Green Warbler *P. (t.) nitidus*
v ☐	Pale-legged Leaf Warbler *Phylloscopus tenellipes*
m1–3 ☐	Western Crowned (Large Crowned Leaf) Warbler *Phylloscopus occipitalis*
w4–5 ☐	Eastern Crowned (Large Crowned Leaf) Warbler *Phylloscopus (occipitalis) coronatus*
ra2 ☐	Blyth's Leaf Warbler *Phylloscopus reguloides*
r'3 ☐	<u>Yellow-vented (Black-browed Leaf) Warbler *Phylloscopus cantator*</u>
v! ☐	Radde's (Radde's Leaf) Warbler *Phylloscopus schwarzi*
a4 ☐	White-spectacled Warbler (Allied Flycatcher-Warbler) *Seicercus affinis*
am1 ☐	Golden-spectacled Warbler (Black-browed Flycatcher-Warbler) *Seicercus burkii*

a1 ☐	Grey-hooded Warbler (Grey-headed Flycatcher-Warbler) *Seicercus xanthoschistos*
a'4 ☐	Grey-cheeked Warbler (Grey-cheeked Flycatcher-Warbler) *Seicercus poliogenys*
a3 ☐	Chestnut-crowned Warbler (Chestnut-headed Flycatcher-Warbler) *Seicercus castaniceps*
a3–4 ☐	Yellow-bellied Warbler (Yellow-bellied Flycatcher-Warbler) *Abroscopus superciliaris*
r3 ☐	Black-faced Warbler (Black-faced Flycatcher-Warbler) *Abroscopus schisticeps*
r3–4 ☐	Rufous-faced Warbler (White-throated Flycatcher-Warbler) *Abroscopus albogularis*
r'(a)4 ☐	<u>Broad-billed Warbler (Broad-billed Flycatcher-Warbler) *Tickellia (Abroscopus) hodgsoni*</u>
ra3–4 ☐	Goldcrest *Regulus regulus*
r'3 ☐	White-browed (Stoliczka's) Tit Warbler *Leptopoecile sophiae*
a'5 ☐	<u>Gould's Shortwing *Brachypteryx stellata*</u>
r'4 ☐	<u>Rusty-bellied Shortwing(*) *Brachypteryx hyperythra*</u>
r'3–4 ☐	<u>White-bellied (Rufous-bellied) Shortwing** *Brachypteryx major*</u>
a4 ☐	Lesser Shortwing *Brachypteryx leucophrys*
a3 ☐	White-browed Shortwing *Brachypteryx montana*
p'4 ☐	Rufous-tailed Scrub Robin (Rufous Chat) *Cercotrichas (Erythropygia) galactotes*
v ☐	Common Nightingale *Luscinia (Erithacus) megarhynchos*
w3 ☐	Siberian Rubythroat (Rubythroat) *Luscinia (Erithacus) calliope*
s'w1–2 ☐	Bluethroat *Luscinia (Erithacus) svecica*
sw3–4 ☐	White-tailed (Himalayan) Rubythroat *Luscinia (Erithacus) pectoralis*
sw3 ☐	Indian Blue Robin (Blue Chat) *Luscinia (Erithacus) brunnea*
v ☐	<u>Firethroat *Luscinia (Erithacus) pectardens*</u>
v ☐	Siberian Blue Robin (Siberian Blue Chat) *Luscinia (Erithacus) cyane*
a1 ☐	Orange-flanked Bush Robin *Tarsiger (Erithacus) cyanurus*
a3 ☐	Golden Bush Robin *Tarsiger (Erithacus) chrysaeus*
a3 ☐	White-browed Bush Robin *Tarsiger (Erithacus) indicus*
a4 ☐	<u>Rufous-breasted (Rufous-bellied) Bush Robin *Tarsiger (Erithacus) hyperythrus*</u>
r°1 ☐	Oriental Magpie Robin (Magpie-Robin, Dhyal Thrush) *Copsychus saularis*
r3 ☐	White-rumped Shama (Shama) *Copsychus malabaricus*
w'4 ☐	Rufous-backed (Eversmann's) Redstart *Phoenicurus erythronota*
a1–2 ☐	Blue-capped (Blue-headed) Redstart *Phoenicurus coeruleocephalus*
s'w1 ☐	Black Redstart *Phoenicurus ochruros*
w3 ☐	Hodgson's Redstart *Phoenicurus hodgsoni*
a2 ☐	Blue-fronted Redstart *Phoenicurus frontalis*
r'3 ☐	White-throated Redstart *Phoenicurus schisticeps*
s'w'3 ☐	Daurian Redstart *Phoenicurus auroreus*
a1–2 ☐	White-winged (Güldenstädt's) Redstart *Phoenicurus erythrogaster*
a2 ☐	Plumbeous Water (Plumbeous) Redstart *Rhyacornis fuliginosus*
a4 ☐	White-bellied Redstart (Hodgson's Shortwing) *Hodgsonius phaenicuroides*
a4 ☐	White-tailed (White-tailed Blue) Robin *Myiomela (Cinclidium) leucura*
r'5 ☐	<u>Blue-fronted Robin *Cinclidium frontale*</u>
a'3–4 ☐	(Hodgson's) Grandala *Grandala coelicolor*
a3 ☐	Little Forktail *Enicurus scouleri*
r3 ☐	Black-backed Forktail *Enicurus immaculatus*
a3 ☐	Slaty-backed Forktail *Enicurus schistaceus*
a'3 ☐	White-crowned (Leschenault's) Forktail *Enicurus leschenaulti*
a2 ☐	Spotted Forktail *Enicurus maculatus*

a′5 ☐	Purple Cochoa <u>*Cochoa purpurea*</u>
r′5 ☐	Green Cochoa <u>*Cochoa viridis*</u>
r3 ☐	Brown Rock-chat* *Cercomela fusca*
r′°4 ☐	<u>Stoliczka's (White-browed) Bushchat* *Saxicola macrorhyncha*</u>
w5 ☐	<u>Hodgson's (White-throated) Bushchat *Saxicola insignis*</u>
rw1–2 ☐	Common Stonechat *Saxicola torquata*
r′3–4 ☐	White-tailed Stonechat *Saxicola leucura*
r1–2 ☐	Pied Bushchat *Saxicola caprata*
r′5 ☐	<u>Jerdon's Bushchat *Saxicola jerdoni*</u>
a1 ☐	Grey (Dark-Grey) Bushchat *Saxicola ferrea*
w3 ☐	Isabelline Wheatear (Isabelline Chat) *Oenanthe isabellina*
w3 ☐	Rufous-tailed Wheatear (Red-tailed Chat) *Oenanthe xanthoprymna*
v ☐	Northern Wheatear (Wheatear) *Oenanthe oenanthe*
sw2 ☐	Desert Wheatear *Oenanthe deserti*
w2 ☐	Variable Wheatear (Pied Chat) *Oenanthe picata*
v ☐	Hume's Wheatear (Hume's Chat) *Oenanthe alboniger*
s′3 ☐	(Pleschanka's) Pied Wheatear (Pleschanka's Pied Chat) *Oenanthe pleschanka*
a1 ☐	White-capped Water Redstart (River Chat) *Chaimarrornis leucocephalus*
r1 ☐	Indian Robin* *Saxicoloides fulicata*
p5 ☐	Rufous-tailed Rock Thrush (Rock Thrush) *Monticola saxatilis*
sw3 ☐	Blue-capped (Blue-headed) Rock Thrush *Monticola cinclorhynchus*
a3 ☐	Chestnut-bellied Rock Thrush *Monticola rufiventris*
sw2–3 ☐	Blue Rock Thrush *Monticola solitarius*
r′3 ☐	Malabar Whistling Thrush** *Myophonus horsfieldii*
a1–2 ☐	Blue Whistling Thrush *Myophonus caeruleus*
m′p4–5 ☐	<u>Pied (Pied Ground) Thrush* *Zoothera wardii*</u>
w′5 ☐	Siberian (Siberian Ground) Thrush *Zoothera sibirica*
r°2–3 ☐	Orange-headed (Orange-headed Ground) Thrush *Zoothera citrina*
a2–3 ☐	Plain-backed (Plain-backed Mountain) Thrush *Zoothera mollissima*
a3 ☐	Long-tailed (Long-tailed Mountain) Thrush *Zoothera dixoni*
☐	Scaly (Golden Mountain or Small-billed Mountain) Thrush *Zoothera dauma*
a3–4 ☐	---Scaly Thrush *Z. d. dauma*
r4 ☐	---Nilgiri Thrush** *Z. d. neilgherriensis*
a4 ☐	<u>Long-billed (Large Brown) Thrush *Zoothera monticola*</u>
r5 ☐	Dark-sided (Lesser Brown) Thrush *Zoothera marginata*
a′4 ☐	<u>Black-breasted Thrush *Turdus dissimilis*</u>
am2 ☐	Tickell's Thrush* *Turdus unicolor*
a2 ☐	White-collared Blackbird *Turdus albocinctus*
a2 ☐	Grey-winged Blackbird *Turdus boulboul*
☐	Eurasian Blackbird (Blackbird) *Turdus merula*
ra(w)3–4 ☐	---Eurasian Blackbird *Turdus merula*
r°3 ☐	---Black-capped Blackbird *Turdus (m.) nigropileus*
r3 ☐	---Nilgiri Blackbird *Turdus (m.) simillimus*
a3 ☐	Chestnut (Grey-headed) Thrush *Turdus rubrocanus*
v ☐	Kessler's Thrush *Turdus kessleri*
w′5 ☐	<u>Grey-sided (Fea's) Thrush *Turdus feae*</u>
w′4 ☐	Eyebrowed (Dark) Thrush *Turdus obscurus*
☐	Dark-throated (Black-throated or Red-throated) Thrush *Turdus ruficollis*
w2 ☐	---Black-throated Thrush *T. (r.) atrogularis*
w3–4 ☐	---Red-throated Thrush *T. (r.) ruficollis*
w4 ☐	Dusky Thrush *Turdus naumanni*
v ☐	Fieldfare *Turdus pilaris*
v ☐	Song Thrush *Turdus philomelos*
a3 ☐	Mistle Thrush *Turdus viscivorus*

a3 ☐	Winter Wren (Wren) *Troglodytes troglodytes*
a'3–4 ☐	White-throated (White-breasted) Dipper *Cinclus cinclus*
a2 ☐	Brown Dipper *Cinclus pallasii*
a3 ☐	Alpine Accentor *Prunella collaris*
w3 ☐	Altai Accentor *Prunella himalayana*
a3 ☐	Robin Accentor *Prunella rubeculoides*
a2 ☐	Rufous-breasted Accentor *Prunella strophiata*
a'4 ☐	Brown Accentor *Prunella fulvescens*
w'3–4 ☐	Black-throated Accentor *Prunella atrogularis*
a'3–4 ☐	Maroon-backed Accentor *Prunella immaculata*
r3–4 ☐	Sultan Tit *Melanochlora sultanea*
ar1 ☐	Great (Grey) Tit *Parus major*
r'4 ☐	<u>White-naped (White-winged Black) Tit** *Parus nuchalis*</u>
a1 ☐	Green-backed Tit *Parus monticolus*
a2 ☐	Spot-winged (Crested Black) Tit(*) *Parus melanolophus*
a'2-3 ☐	Coal Tit *Parus ater*
a2 ☐	Rufous-naped (Rufous-naped Black or Black-breasted) Tit *Parus rufonuchalis*
a2–3 ☐	Rufous-vented (Rufous-bellied Crested) Tit *Parus rubidiventris*
r2–3 ☐	Grey-crested (Brown Crested) Tit *Parus dichrous*
r2 ☐	Black-lored (Yellow-cheeked) Tit* *Parus xanthogenys*
r'3–4 ☐	Yellow-cheeked (Black-spotted Yellow) Tit *Parus spilonotus*
a2–3 ☐	Yellow-browed Tit *Sylviparus modestus*
sw3–4 ☐	Fire-capped Tit *Cephalopyrus flammiceps*
w'4 ☐	White-crowned Penduline Tit (Penduline Tit) *Remiz (pendulinus) coronatus*
r1 ☐	Black-throated (Red-headed) Tit *Aegithalos concinnus*
a' ☐	White-cheeked Tit(*) *Aegithalos leucogenys*
a'4 ☐	<u>White-throated Tit* *Aegithalos niveogularis*</u>
r3 ☐	Rufous-fronted Tit *Aegithalos iouschistos*
a'3 ☐	Kashmir (European or Common) Nuthatch(*) *Sitta (europea) cashmirensis*
r'4 ☐	Chestnut-vented (European or Common) Nuthatch *Sitta (europea) nagaensis*
r2 ☐	Chestnut-bellied Nuthatch *Sitta castanea*
a'3 ☐	White-cheeked Nuthatch *Sitta leucopsis*
a2–3 ☐	White-tailed Nuthatch *Sitta himalayensis*
a'5 ☐	<u>Beautiful Nuthatch *Sitta formosa*</u>
r2 ☐	Velvet-fronted Nuthatch *Sitta frontalis*
am3–4 ☐	Wallcreeper *Tichodroma muraria*
r'4–5 ☐	Spotted (Spotted Grey) Creeper *Salpornis spilonotus*
a3 ☐	Eurasian Treecreeper (Tree Creeper) *Certhia familiaris*
a2 ☐	Bar-tailed (Himalayan) Treecreeper *Certhia himalayana*
a4 ☐	Brown-throated (Sikkim) Treecreeper *Certhia discolor*
a3 ☐	Rusty-flanked (Nepal) Treecreeper *Certhia nipalensis*
sw2–3 ☐	Olive-backed (Indian Tree) Pipit *Anthus hodgsoni*
w3 ☐	Tree Pipit *Anthus trivialis*
v ☐	Meadow Pipit *Anthus pratensis*
w3 ☐	Richard's (Paddyfield) Pipit *Anthus (novaeseelandiae) richardi*
r2 ☐	Paddyfield (Oriental) Pipit *Anthus (novaeseelandiae) rufulus*
w2–3 ☐	Tawny Pipit *Anthus campestris*
w3–4 ☐	Blyth's Pipit *Anthus godlewskii*
p5w'5 ☐	Red-throated Pipit *Anthus cervinus*
sw2 ☐	Rosy (Vinaceous-breasted) Pipit *Anthus roseatus*
r3–4 ☐	Long-billed (Brown Rock) Pipit *Anthus similis*
r'2–3 ☐	Nilgiri Pipit** *Anthus nilghiriensis*
w3–4 ☐	Water (Alpine) Pipit *Anthus spinoletta*
v(w5?) ☐	Buff-bellied (Water or Alpine) Pipit *Anthus rubescens (spinoletta japonica)*

a3 ☐	Upland Pipit *Anthus sylvanus*
b'w3 ☐	Forest Wagtail *Dendronanthus (Motacilla) indicus*
☐	Yellow Wagtail *Motacilla flava*
b'pw2 ☐	---Blue-headed Wagtail *M. (f.) flava* {incl. *beema*}
w2 ☐	---Grey-headed Wagtail *M. (f.) thunbergi*
w2 ☐	---Siberian Yellow Wagtail *M. (f.) simillima* {incl. *'zaissanensis'*}
w4 ☐	---Yellow-headed Wagtail *M. (f.) lutea*
pw4 ☐	---Black-headed Wagtail *M. (f.) feldegg* {incl. *melanogrisea*}
p5 ☐	---White-headed Wagtail *M. (f.) leucocephala*
v ☐	---Green-headed Wagtail *M. (f.) taiwana*
sw2 ☐	Citrine (Yellow-headed or Yellow-hooded) Wagtail *Motacilla citreola*
sw2 ☐	Grey Wagtail *Motacilla cinerea*
swa1 ☐	White (Pied) Wagtail *Motacilla alba*
r2 ☐	White-browed (Large Pied) Wagtail* *Motacilla maderaspatensis*
r3–4 ☐	Thick-billed Flowerpecker *Dicaeum agile*
r4 ☐	Yellow-vented Flowerpecker *Dicaeum chrysorrheum*
a'4–5 ☐	Yellow-bellied Flowerpecker *Dicaeum melanoxanthum*
r'5 ☐	Orange-bellied Flowerpecker *Dicaeum trigonostigma*
r2 ☐	Pale-billed (Tickell's) Flowerpecker *Dicaeum erythrorhynchos*
r2 ☐	Plain (Plain-coloured) Flowerpecker *Dicaeum concolor*
r2 ☐	Scarlet-backed Flowerpecker *Dicaeum cruentatum*
a2 ☐	Fire-breasted Flowerpecker *Dicaeum ignipectus*
r'4 ☐	Ruby-cheeked Sunbird (Rubycheek) *Anthreptes singalensis*
r2 ☐	Purple-rumped Sunbird(*) *Nectarinia zeylonica*
r2–3 ☐	Crimson-backed (Small) Sunbird** *Nectarinia minima*
r'5 ☐	Purple-throated (Van Hasselt's) Sunbird *Nectarinia sperata*
r3 ☐	Loten's (Long-billed) Sunbird* *Nectarinia lotenia*
r'2 ☐	Olive-backed Sunbird *Nectarinia jugularis*
r°1 ☐	Purple Sunbird *Nectarinia asiatica*
a3–4 ☐	Mrs Gould's Sunbird *Aethopyga gouldiae*
a2 ☐	Green-tailed (Nepal Yellow-backed) Sunbird *Aethopyga nipalensis*
a3 ☐	Black-throated (Black-breasted) Sunbird *Aethopyga saturata*
r2 ☐	Crimson (Yellow-backed) Sunbird *Aethopyga siparaja*
a2 ☐	Fire-tailed Sunbird *Aethopyga ignicauda*
r3 ☐	Little Spiderhunter *Arachnothera longirostra*
r3 ☐	Streaked Spiderhunter *Arachnothera magna*
r°a1 ☐	Oriental White-Eye (White-Eye) *Zosterops palpebrosus*
r1 ☐	House Sparrow *Passer domesticus*
w2–4 ☐	Spanish Sparrow *Passer hispaniolensis*
r1–2 ☐	Eurasian Tree Sparrow (Tree Sparrow) *Passer montanus*
r'3 ☐	Sind (Sind Jungle) Sparrow(*) *Passer pyrrhonotus*
a3 ☐	Russet (Cinnamon Tree) Sparrow *Passer rutilans*
r2 ☐	Chestnut-shouldered Petronia (Yellow-throated Sparrow) *Petronia xanthocollis*
a'2 ☐	Tibetan (Black-winged) Snowfinch *Montifringilla adamsi*
v? ☐	[White-rumped (Mandelli's) Snowfinch *Pyrgilauda (Montifringilla) taczanowskii*]
w'5 ☐	Rufous-necked (Red-necked) Snowfinch *Pyrgilauda (Montifringilla) ruficollis*
w'(b')5 ☐	Plain-backed (Blanford's) Snowfinch *Pyrgilauda (Montifringilla) blanfordi*
r°2 ☐	Baya Weaver (Baya) *Ploceus philippinus*
r'4 ☐	Finn's Weaver* (Finn's Baya or Yellow Weaver) *Ploceus megarhynchus*
r°3 ☐	Black-breasted (Bengal or Black-throated) Weaver* *Ploceus benghalensis*
r°3-4 ☐	Streaked Weaver *Ploceus manyar*
r2-3 ☐	Red Avadavat (Red Munia) *Amandava (Estrilda) amandava*

r'4 □	<u>Green Avadavat** (Green Munia) *Amandava (Estrilda) formosa*</u>
r°2 □	Indian (Common) Silverbill (White-throated Munia) *Lonchura malabarica*
r3 □	White-rumped (White-backed) Munia *Lonchura striata*
r°3 □	Black-throated (Rufous-bellied) Munia* *Lonchura kelaarti*
r°2 □	Scaly-breasted (Spotted) Munia (Nutmeg Mannikin) *Lonchura punctulata*
r°4 □	Black-headed Munia *Lonchura malacca*
li? □	Java Sparrow *Lonchura (Padda) oryzivora*
v □	Chaffinch *Fringilla coelebs*
w'4 □	Brambling *Fringilla montifringilla*
a2–3 □	Black-and-yellow (Black-and-White) Grosbeak(*) *Mycerobas (Coccothraustes) icterioides*
r°a3–4 □	Collared (Allied) Grosbeak *Mycerobas (Coccothraustes) affinis*
a3 □	White-winged Grosbeak *Mycerobas (Coccothraustes) carnipes*
a'3–4 □	Spot-winged Grosbeak *Mycerobas (Coccothraustes) melanozanthos*
a3 □	European Goldfinch (Goldfinch) *Carduelis carduelis*
a1–2 □	Yellow-breasted (Himalayan) Greenfinch *Carduelis spinoides*
a'3 □	Black-headed (Himalayan) Greenfinch *Carduelis ambigua (spinoides taylori)*
v □	Eurasian Siskin *Carduelis spinus*
w(b'?)2–3 □	Tibetan Siskin (Tibetan Serin) *Carduelis (Serinus) thibetana*
v □	Eurasian Linnet (Linnet) *Carduelis (Acanthis) cannabina*
a3 □	Twite *Carduelis (Acanthis) flavirostris*
a'4 □	Spectacled (Red-browed) Finch* *Callacanthis burtoni*
a2 □	Fire-fronted Serin (Gold-fronted Finch) *Serinus pusillus*
a2–3 □	Plain (Hodgson's) Mountain Finch *Leucosticte nemoricola*
a3 □	Brandt's (Black-headed) Mountain Finch *Leucosticte brandti*
? □	[Sillem's Mountain Finch *Leucosticte sillemi*]
r'3 □	Trumpeter Finch (Trumpeter Bullfinch) *Bucanetes (Carpodacus) githagineus*
a'n3–4 □	Mongolian Finch (Mongolian Trumpeter Bullfinch) *Bucanetes (Carpodacus) mongolicus*
v? □	[Crimson-winged (Crimson-winged Desert) Finch *Rhodopechys (Callacanthis) sanguinea*]
sw2 □	Common Rosefinch (Scarlet Grosbeak) *Carpodacus erythrinus*
a2 □	Dark-breasted (Nepal) Rosefinch *Carpodacus nipalensis*
a5 □	Blanford's Rosefinch *Carpodacus rubescens*
a3 □	Pink-browed Rosefinch(*) *Carpodacus rodochrous*
v □	Vinaceous Rosefinch *Carpodacus vinaceus*
a'5 □	Red-mantled Rosefinch *Carpodacus rhodochlamys*
a'5 □	Spot-winged Rosefinch *Carpodacus rodopeplus*
a3 □	White-browed Rosefinch *Carpodacus thura*
a3 □	Beautiful Rosefinch *Carpodacus pulcherrimus*
a3–4 □	Dark-rumped (Large) Rosefinch *Carpodacus edwardsii*
a4 □	Great Rosefinch *Carpodacus rubicilla*
a3 □	Streaked (Eastern Great) Rosefinch *Carpodacus rubicilloides*
a4 □	Red-fronted (Red-breasted) Rosefinch *Carpodacus puniceus*
r'n4 □	Red Crossbill (Crossbill) *Loxia curvirostra*
a3–4 □	Crimson-browed Finch (Red-headed Rosefinch) *Pinicola (Propyrrhula) subhimachalus*
a4–5 □	Scarlet Finch *Haematospiza sipahi*
a4 □	Gold-naped (Gold-headed Black) Finch *Pyrrhoplectes epauletta*
a3–4 □	Brown Bullfinch *Pyrrhula nipalensis*
a'3–4 □	Grey-headed (Beavan's) Bullfinch *Pyrrhula erythaca*
a2 □	Red-headed Bullfinch *Pyrrhula erythrocephala*
a'3 □	<u>Orange Bullfinch* *Pyrrhula aurantiaca*</u>
v! □	Corn Bunting *Miliaria (Emberiza) calandra*

w′3–4 ☐	Pine Bunting *Emberiza leucocephalos*
w2–3 ☐	Black-headed Bunting *Emberiza melanocephala*
w2–3 ☐	Red-headed Bunting *Emberiza bruniceps*
w′4 ☐	Chestnut Bunting *Emberiza rutila*
w3–4 ☐	Yellow-breasted Bunting *Emberiza aureola*
w4 ☐	Black-faced Bunting *Emberiza spodocephala*
sw3 ☐	White-capped (Chestnut-breasted) Bunting *Emberiza stewarti*
v ☐	Ortolan Bunting *Emberiza hortulana*
w4 ☐	Grey-necked (Grey-hooded) Bunting *Emberiza buchanani*
sw2 ☐	Rock Bunting *Emberiza cia*
a′3 ☐	Godlewski's (Rock) Bunting *Emberiza godlewskii (cia khamensis/yunnanensis)*
a3–4 ☐	Chestnut-eared (Grey-headed) Bunting *Emberiza fucata*
w2–3 ☐	Little Bunting *Emberiza pusilla*
r°3–4 ☐	House (Striolated) Bunting *Emberiza striolata*
w′5 ☐	Reed Bunting *Emberiza schoeniclus*
v ☐	Yellowhammer *Emberiza citrinella*
r°3 ☐	Crested Bunting *Melophus lathami*

THE FOLLOWING ARE NO LONGER RECOGNISED AS VALID SPECIES:
Intermediate Parakeet *Psittacula intermedia*
Large-billed Reed Warbler *Acrocephalus orinus*
Enigmatic Shortwing *Brachypterix cryptica*

THE FOLLOWING SPECIES HAVE BEEN EXCLUDED FROM THE
CHECKLIST:
Lesser Black-backed Gull *Larus fuscus*
Great Black-backed Gull *Larus marinus*
Black-nest Swiftlet *Collocalia maxima*
Plain-pouched Hornbill *Aceros subruficollis*
Brown-cheeked Laughingthrush *Garrulax henrici*
Olivaceous Warbler *Hippolais pallida*
Siberian Accentor *Prunella montanella*
Small Snowfinch *Pyrgilauda davidiana*
Three-banded Rosefinch *Carpodacus trifasciatus*

MAMMALS OF INDIA

As none was available, we have attempted to produce a complete checklist of the wild mammals recorded within Indian limits but acknowledge that it can only be provisional. The list is compiled from various sources but the taxonomy and nomenclature broadly follow *The Mammals of the Indomalayan Region* by G. B. Corbet & J. E. Hill. (OUP. 1992.) Where we could not find English names for some of the rodents we have adopted the suggestions of Dr. Ishwar Prakash. We are grateful to both him and Dr. Paul Bates for their generous help in putting together this list. Dr. Indraneil Das, Nameer Ommer and Sally Walker kindly provided additional information.

† – probably extinct in India
? – status or identity uncertain
Alternative vernacular names are given in brackets.

☐ Chinese Pangolin *Manis pentadactyla*
☐ Indian Pangolin *Manis crassicaudata*
☐ Long-eared Hedgehog *Hemiechinus collaris*
☐ Indian (Pale) Hedgehog *Paraechinus micropus*
☐ Himalayan Mole *Talpa micrura*
☐ Eastern Mole *Talpa leucura*
☐ Lesser Stripe-backed (Lesser Striped) Shrew *Sorex bedfordiae*
☐ Kashmir Shrew *Sorex planiceps*
☐ Sikkim Large-clawed (Himalayan) Shrew *Soriculus nigrescens*
☐ Hodgson's Brown-toothed Shrew *Soriculus caudatus*
☐ Indian Long-tailed Shrew *Soriculus leucops*
☐ Hodgson's Shrew *Soriculus macrurus*
☐ Mole-shrew *Anourosorex squamipes*
☐ Himalayan Water Shrew *Chimarrogale himalayica*
☐ Elegant Water (Tibetan Water) Shrew *Nectogale elegans*
☐ House (Grey Musk) Shrew *Suncus murinus*
☐ Mountain Shrew *Suncus montanus*
☐ Anderson's (Yellow-throated) Shrew *Suncus stoliczkanus*
☐ Day's Shrew *Suncus dayi*
☐ Pygmy White-toothed Shrew *Suncus etruscus*
☐ Andaman Spiny Shrew *Crocidura hispida*
☐ Nicobar Spiny Shrew *Crocidura nicobarica*
☐ Miller's Andaman Spiny Shrew *Crocidura andamanensis*
☐ Jenkins's Andaman Spiny Shrew *Crocidura jenkinsi*
☐ Grey (Woodland) Shrew *Crocidura attenuata*
☐ Pale Grey Shrew *Crocidura pergrisea*
☐ Güldenstädt's White-toothed Shrew *Crocidura gueldenstaedtii*
☐ ? Bicoloured White-toothed Shrew *Crocidura leucodon*
☐ Horsfield's Shrew *Crocidura horsfieldii*
☐ Northern Tree Shrew *Tupaia belangeri*
☐ Nicobar Tree Shrew *Tupaia nicobarica*
☐ Madras (Indian) Tree Shrew *Anathana ellioti*
☐ Nicobar Flying Fox *Pteropus faunulus*
☐ Blyth's Flying Fox *Pteropus melanotus*
☐ Indian Flying Fox *Pteropus giganteus*
☐ ? Island Flying Fox *Pteropus hypomelanus*
☐ Large Flying Fox *Pteropus vampyrus*
☐ Leschenault's Rousette (Fulvous Fruit Bat) *Rousettus leschenaulti*

☐ Lesser Dog-faced Fruit Bat *Cynopterus brachyotis*
☐ Short-nosed (Indian) Fruit Bat *Cynopterus sphinx*
☐ Niphan's Fruit Bat *Megaerops niphanae*
☐ Salim Ali's Fruit Bat *Latidens salimalii*
☐ Blanford's (Mountain) Fruit Bat *Sphaerias blanfordi*
☐ Dawn (Cave Fruit) Bat *Eonycteris spelaea*
☐ Hill Long-tongued Fruit Bat *Macroglossus sobrinus*
☐ Greater Mouse-tailed (Larger Rat-tailed) Bat *Rhinopoma microphyllum*
☐ Lesser Mouse-tailed (Lesser Rat-tailed) Bat *Rhinopoma hardwickii*
☐ Small Mouse-tailed Bat *Rhinopoma muscatellum*
☐ Egyptian Tomb Bat *Taphozous perforatus*
☐ Black-bearded Tomb (Bearded Sheath-tailed) Bat *Taphozous melanopogon*
☐ Long-winged Tomb (Long-armed Sheath-tailed) Bat *Taphozous longimanus*
☐ Theobald's Tomb Bat *Taphozous theobaldi*
☐ Naked-rumped Tomb Bat *Taphozous nudiventris*
☐ Blyth's Tomb (Pouch-bearing) Bat *Taphozous saccolaimus*
☐ Lesser False Vampire Bat *Megaderma spasma*
☐ Greater (Indian) False Vampire Bat *Megaderma lyra*
☐ Trefoil Horseshoe Bat *Rhinolophus trifoliatus*
☐ Woolly (Great Eastern) Horseshoe Bat *Rhinolophus luctus*
☐ ? Mitred Horseshoe Bat *Rhinolophus mitratus*
☐ Pearson's Horseshoe Bat *Rhinolophus pearsoni*
☐ Dobson's Horseshoe Bat *Rhinolophus yunanensis*
☐ Blyth's (Little Indian) Horseshoe Bat *Rhinolophus lepidus*
☐ Least Horseshoe Bat *Rhinolophus pusillus*
☐ Bay Horseshoe Bat *Rhinolophus subbadius*
☐ Andaman Horseshoe Bat *Rhinolophus cognatus*
☐ Rufous Horseshoe Bat *Rhinolophus rouxii*
☐ Intermediate Horseshoe Bat *Rhinolophus affinis*
☐ Greater Horseshoe Bat *Rhinolophus ferrumequinum*
☐ Lesser Horseshoe Bat *Rhinolophus hipposideros*
☐ Big-eared Horseshoe Bat *Rhinolophus macrotis*
☐ Andersen's Leaf-nosed Bat *Hipposideros pomona*
☐ Dusky Leaf-nosed Bat *Hipposideros ater*
☐ Fulvous Leaf-nosed Bat *Hipposideros fulvus*
☐ Least Leaf-nosed Bat *Hipposideros cineraceus*
☐ Khajuria's Leaf-nosed Bat *Hipposideros durgadasi*

- ☐ Kolar Leaf-nosed Bat *Hipposideros hypophyllos*
- ☐ Cantor's (Fawn) Leaf-nosed Bat *Hipposideros galeritus*
- ☐ Himalayan Leaf-nosed Bat *Hipposideros armiger*
- ☐ Horsfield's Leaf-nosed Bat *Hipposideros larvatus*
- ☐ Schneider's Leaf-nosed Bat *Hipposideros speoris*
- ☐ Kelaart's Leaf-nosed Bat *Hipposideros lankadiva*
- ☐ Bellary Leaf-nosed Bat *Hipposideros schistaceus*
- ☐ Diadem Leaf-nosed Bat *Hipposideros diadema*
- ☐ Tail-less Leaf-nosed Bat *Coelops frithii*
- ☐ Lesser Mouse-eared Bat *Myotis blythii*
- ☐ Mandelli's Mouse-eared Bat *Myotis sicarius*
- ☐ Hodgson's Bat *Myotis formosus*
- ☐ Himalayan Whiskered Bat *Myotis siligorensis*
- ☐ Whiskered (Mustachioed) Bat *Myotis mystacinus*
- ☐ Nepalese Whiskered Bat *Myotis muricola*
- ☐ Burmese Whiskered Bat *Myotis montivagus*
- ☐ Hairy-faced Bat *Myotis annectans*
- ☐ Kashmir Cave Bat *Myotis longipes*
- ☐ Daubenton's (Water) Bat *Myotis daubentonii*
- ☐ Horsfield's Mouse-eared Bat *Myotis horsfieldii*
- ☐ Van Hasselt's Mouse-eared Bat *Myotis hasseltii*
- ☐ Brown Long-eared Bat *Plecotus auritus*
- ☐ Grey Long-eared Bat *Plecotus austriacus*
- ☐ Eastern Barbastelle *Barbastella leucomelas*
- ☐ Hemprich's Long-eared Bat *Otonycteris hemprichii*
- ☐ Harlequin Bat *Scotomanes ornatus*
- ☐ Asiatic Lesser Yellow House Bat *Scotophilus kuhlii*
- ☐ Asiatic Greater Yellow House Bat *Scotophilus heathii*
- ☐ Serotine *Eptesicus serotinus*
- ☐ Thick-eared Bat *Eptesicus pachyotis*
- ☐ Bobinskii's Serotine *Eptesicus gobiensis*
- ☐ ? Sombre Bat *Eptesicus tatei*
- ☐ ? Particoloured Bat *Vespertilio murinus*
- ☐ Great Evening Bat *Ia io*
- ☐ Bamboo (Club-footed) Bat *Tylonycteris pachypus*
- ☐ Common Pipistrelle *Pipistrellus pipistrellus*
- ☐ Kelaart's Pipistrelle *Pipistrellus ceylonicus*
- ☐ Mount Popa Pipistrelle *Pipistrellus paterculus*
- ☐ Javan Pipistrelle *Pipistrellus javanicus*
- ☐ Indian Pipistrelle *Pipistrellus coromandra*
- ☐ Least Pipistrelle *Pipistrellus tenuis*
- ☐ Kuhl's Pipistrelle *Pipistrellus kuhli*
- ☐ Savi's Pipistrelle *Pipistrellus savii*
- ☐ Cadorna's Pipistrelle *Pipistrellus cadornae*
- ☐ Chocolate Bat *Pipistrellus affinis*
- ☐ Dormer's Bat *Scotozous dormeri*
- ☐ Yellow Desert Bat *Scotoecus pallidus*
- ☐ Common Noctule *Nyctalus noctula*
- ☐ Leisler's Bat (Lesser Noctule) *Nyctalus leisleri*
- ☐ Himalayan Noctule *Nyctalus montanus*
- ☐ Tickell's Bat *Hesperoptenus tickelli*
- ☐ Schreiber's Long-fingered (Common Bent-wing) Bat *Miniopterus schreibersi*
- ☐ Nicobar Long-fingered Bat *Miniopterus pusillus*
- ☐ Greater Tube-nosed Bat *Murina leucogaster*
- ☐ Little Tube-nosed Bat *Murina aurata*
- ☐ Scully's Tube-nosed Bat *Murina tubinaris*
- ☐ Hutton's Tube-nosed Bat *Murina huttoni*
- ☐ Round-eared Tube-nosed Bat *Murina cyclotis*
- ☐ Peters' Tube-nosed Bat *Murina grisea*
- ☐ Hairy-winged Bat *Harpiocephalus harpia*
- ☐ Painted Bat *Kerivoula picta*
- ☐ Papillose Bat *Kerivoula papillosa*
- ☐ Hardwicke's Forest Bat *Kerivoula hardwickii*
- ☐ European Free-tailed Bat *Tadarida teniotis*
- ☐ Egyptian Free-tailed Bat *Tadarida aegyptiaca*
- ☐ Wrinkle-lipped Free-tailed Bat *Tadarida plicata*
- ☐ Wroughton's Free-tailed Bat *Otomops wroughtoni*
- ☐ Slender Loris *Loris tardigradus*
- ☐ Slow Loris *Nycticebus coucang*
- ☐ Lion-tailed Macaque *Macaca silenus*
- ☐ Pigtail Macaque *Macaca nemestrina*
- ☐ Bonnet Macaque *Macaca radiata*
- ☐ Assamese Macaque *Macaca assamensis*
- ☐ Rhesus Macaque *Macaca mulatta*
- ☐ Crab-eating Macaque *Macaca fascicularis*
- ☐ Stump-tailed (Bear) Macaque *Macaca arctoides*
- ☐ Hanuman (Common or Grey) Langur *Semnopithecus entellus*
- ☐ Nilgiri Langur (Hooded Leaf Monkey) *Semnopithecus johnii*
- ☐ Silvered Langur (Silvered Leaf Monkey) *Semnopithecus cristatus*
- ☐ Phayre's Leaf Monkey *Semnopithecus phayrei*
- ☐ Capped Langur (Capped Leaf Monkey) *Semnopithecus pileatus*
- ☐ Golden Langur (Golden Leaf Monkey) *Semnopithecus geei*
- ☐ Hoolock Gibbon *Hylobates hoolock*
- ☐ Wolf *Canis lupus*
- ☐ Golden Jackal *Canis aureus*
- ☐ Red Fox *Vulpes vulpes*
- ☐ Bengal (Indian) Fox *Vulpes bengalensis*
- ☐ Blanford's Fox *Vulpes cana*
- ☐ Tibetan Fox *Vulpes ferrilata*
- ☐ Dhole (Red Dog) *Cuon alpinus*
- ☐ Asiatic (Himalayan) Black Bear *Ursus thibetanus*
- ☐ Sun Bear *Ursus malayanus*
- ☐ Brown Bear *Ursus arctos*
- ☐ Sloth Bear *Ursus ursinus*
- ☐ Lesser (Red) Panda *Ailurus fulgens*
- ☐ Mountain (Pale) Weasel *Mustela altaica*
- ☐ Stoat (Ermine) *Mustela erminea*
- ☐ Yellow-bellied Weasel *Mustela kathiah*
- ☐ Siberian (Himalayan) Weasel *Mustela sibirica*
- ☐ Black-striped Weasel *Mustela strigidorsa*
- ☐ Beech Marten *Martes foina*
- ☐ Yellow-throated Marten *Martes flavigula*
- ☐ Nilgiri Marten *Martes gwatkinsi*
- ☐ Ratel (Honey Badger) *Mellivora capensis*
- ☐ Hog-badger *Arctonyx collaris*
- ☐ Large-toothed (Burmese) Ferret-badger *Melogale personata*
- ☐ Small-toothed (Chinese) Ferret-badger *Melogale moschata*
- ☐ Eurasian (Common) Otter *Lutra lutra*
- ☐ Smooth-coated (Smooth Indian) Otter *Lutrogale perspicillata*
- ☐ Oriental Small-clawed (Clawless) Otter *Aonyx cinerea*
- ☐ Large Indian Civet *Viverra zibetha*
- ☐ Malabar Civet *Viverra civettina*
- ☐ Small Indian Civet *Viverricula indica*
- ☐ Spotted Linsang *Prionodon pardicolor*

☐ Common Palm Civet (Toddy Cat) *Paradoxurus hermaphroditus*

☐ Jerdon's Palm Civet *Paradoxurus jerdoni*

☐ Masked (Himalayan) Palm Civet *Paguma larvata*

☐ Binturong (Bear Cat) *Arctictis binturong*

☐ Small-toothed (Three-striped) Palm Civet *Arctogalidia trivirgata*

☐ Small Asian (Small Indian) Mongoose *Herpestes javanicus*

☐ Indian Grey (Common Indian) Mongoose *Herpestes edwardsii*

☐ Ruddy Mongoose *Herpestes smithii*

☐ Indian Brown Mongoose *Herpestes fuscus*

☐ Stripe-necked Mongoose *Herpestes vitticollis*

☐ Crab-eating Mongoose *Herpestes urva*

☐ Striped Hyaena *Hyaena hyaena*

☐ Wild Cat *Felis silvestris*

☐ Jungle Cat *Felis chaus*

☐ Pallas's Cat *Felis manul*

☐ Caracal *Felis caracal*

☐ Leopard Cat *Prionailurus bengalensis*

☐ Fishing Cat *Prionailurus viverrinus*

☐ Rusty-spotted Cat *Prionailurus rubiginosus*

☐ Golden Cat *Catopuma temminckii*

☐ Marbled Cat *Pardofelis marmorata*

☐ Clouded Leopard *Pardofelis nebulosa*

☐ Eurasian Lynx *Lynx lynx*

☐ Leopard (Panther) *Panthera pardus*

☐ Tiger *Panthera tigris*

☐ Lion *Panthera leo*

☐ Snow Leopard (Ounce) *Panthera uncia*

☐ † Cheetah *Acinonyx jubatus*

☐ Ganges Dolphin (Susu) *Platanista gangetica*

☐ Rough-toothed Dolphin *Steno bredanensis*

☐ Indopacific Humpback (Plumbeous) Dolphin *Sousa chinensis*

☐ Striped Dolphin *Stenella coeruleoalba*

☐ Pantropical Spotted (Bridled) Dolphin *Stenella attenuata*

☐ Spinner Dolphin *Stenella longirostris*

☐ Common Dolphin *Delphinus delphis*

☐ Bottle-nosed Dolphin *Tursiops truncatus*

☐ Fraser's Dolphin *Lagenodelphis hosei*

☐ Melon-headed (Indian Broad-beaked) Dolphin *Peponocephala electra*

☐ Irrawaddy Dolphin *Orcaella brevirostris*

☐ False Killer Whale *Pseudorca crassidens*

☐ Killer Whale *Orcinus orca*

☐ Risso's (Grey) Dolphin *Grampus griseus*

☐ Short-finned Pilot Whale *Globicephala macrorhynchus*

☐ Pygmy Killer Whale (Slender Blackfish) *Feresa attenuata*

☐ Finless (Little Indian) Porpoise *Neophocaena phocaenoides*

☐ Sperm Whale (Cachalot) *Physeter macrocephalus*

☐ Pygmy Sperm Whale *Kogia breviceps*

☐ Dwarf Sperm Whale *Kogia simus*

☐ Ginkgo-toothed Beaked Whale *Mesoplodon ginkgodens*

☐ Blainville's Beaked Whale *Mesoplodon densirostris*

☐ Cuvier's Beaked (Goosebeak) Whale *Ziphius cavirostris*

☐ Minke Whale (Lesser Rorqual) *Balaenoptera acutirostrata*

☐ Bryde's Whale *Balaenoptera edeni*

☐ Sei Whale *Balaenoptera borealis*

☐ Fin Whale (Common Rorqual) *Balaenoptera physalus*

☐ Blue Whale *Balaenoptera musculus*

☐ Humpback Whale *Megaptera novaeangliae*

☐ Black Right Whale *Balaena glacialis*

☐ Dugong (Sea Cow) *Dugong dugon*

☐ Indian Elephant *Elephas maximus*

☐ Indian (Greater One-horned) Rhinoceros *Rhinoceros unicornis*

☐ † Javan (Lesser One-horned) Rhinoceros *Rhinoceros sondaicus*

☐ Sumatran (Asian Two-horned) Rhinoceros *Dicerorhinus sumatrensis*

☐ Kiang *Equus kiang*

☐ Asiatic Wild Ass (Khur or Onager) *Equus hemionus*

☐ Wild Boar *Sus scrofa*

☐ Pygmy Hog *Sus salvanius*

☐ Indian Chevrotain (Mouse-deer) *Moschiola meminna*

☐ Forest Musk Deer *Moschus chrysogaster*

☐ Swamp Deer (Barasingha) *Cervus duvaucelli*

☐ Red Deer *Cervus elaphus* (includes Hangul or Kashmir Stag *C.e. hanglu*)

☐ Thamin (Brow-antlered Deer, Sangai) *Cervus eldii*

☐ Sambar *Cervus unicolor*

☐ Chital (Spotted Deer) *Axis axis*

☐ Hog Deer *Axis porcinus*

☐ Indian Muntjac (Barking Deer) *Muntiacus muntjak*

☐ Gaur (Indian Bison) *Bos gaurus*

☐ Yak *Bos mutus*

☐ Wild Water Buffalo *Bubalus arnee*

☐ Nilgai (Blue Bull) *Boselaphus tragocamelus*

☐ Four-horned Antelope (Chowsingha) *Tetracerus quadricornis*

☐ Blackbuck (Indian Antelope) *Antilope cervicapra*

☐ Chinkara (Indian Gazelle) *Gazella bennettii*

☐ Tibetan Gazelle *Procapra picticaudata*

☐ Chiru (Tibetan Antelope) *Pantholops hodgsoni*

☐ Takin *Budorcas taxicolor*

☐ Common (Himalayan) Goral *Naemorhedus goral*

☐ Red Goral *Naemorhedus baileyi*

☐ Mainland (Southern) Serow *Naemorhedus sumatraensis*

☐ Himalayan Tahr *Hemitragus jemlahicus*

☐ Nilgiri Tahr *Hemitragus hylocrius*

☐ Markhor *Capra falconeri*

☐ Ibex *Capra ibex*

☐ Bharal (Blue Sheep) *Pseudois nayaur*

☐ Argali (Nayan) *Ovis ammon*

☐ Urial (Shapu) *Ovis vignei*

☐ Grizzled (Sri Lankan) Giant Squirrel *Ratufa macroura*

☐ Indian (Malabar) Giant Squirrel *Ratufa indica*

☐ Black (Malayan) Giant Squirrel *Ratufa bicolor*

☐ Indian (Three-striped) Palm Squirrel *Funambulus palmarum*

☐ Jungle Striped Squirrel *Funambulus tristriatus*

❏ Layard's Striped Squirrel *Funambulus layardi*
❏ Dusky Striped Squirrel *Funambulus sublineatus*
❏ Northern (Five-striped) Palm Squirrel *Funambulus pennantii*
❏ Pallas's Squirrel *Callosciurus erythraeus*
❏ Hoary-bellied Himalayan (Irrawaddy) Squirrel *Callosciurus pygerythrus*
❏ Himalayan Striped Squirrel *Tamiops macclellandi*
❏ Orange-bellied Himalayan Squirrel *Dremomys lokriah*
❏ Perny's Long-nosed Squirrel *Dremomys pernyi*
❏ Red-cheeked Squirrel *Dremomys rufigenis*
❏ Long-tailed Marmot *Marmota caudata*
❏ Himalayan Marmot *Marmota himalayana*
❏ Hairy-footed Flying Squirrel *Trogopterus pearsoni*
❏ Red (Common) Giant Flying Squirrel *Petaurista petaurista*
❏ Elliot's Giant Flying Squirrel *Petaurista philippensis*
❏ Grey-headed (Spotted Giant) Flying Squirrel *Petaurista caniceps*
❏ Hodgson's Flying Squirrel *Petaurista magnificus*
❏ Gray's Giant Flying Squirrel *Petaurista nobilis*
❏ Woolly Flying Squirrel *Eupetaurus cinereus*
❏ Namdapha Flying Squirrel *Biswamoyopterus biswasi*
❏ Particoloured Flying Squirrel *Hylopetes alboniger*
❏ Small Kashmir Flying Squirrrel *Hylopetes fimbriatus*
❏ Kashmir Flying Squirrel *Hylopetes baberi*
❏ Travancore Flying Squirrel *Petinomys fuscocapillus*
❏ House Mouse *Mus musculus*
❏ Little Indian Field Mouse *Mus booduga*
❏ Pygmy Field Mouse *Mus dunni*
❏ Cook's Mouse *Mus cookii*
❏ Fawn-coloured Mouse *Mus cervicolor*
❏ Spiny Field (Indian Brown Spiny) Mouse *Mus platythrix*
❏ Elliot's Brown Spiny Mouse *Mus saxicola*
❏ Fawn-coloured Spiny Mouse *Mus phillipsi*
❏ Gairdner's Shrew-mouse (Sikkim Mouse) *Mus pahari*
❏ Bonhote's Mouse *Mus famulus*
❏ Palm Mouse (Indian Long-tailed Tree-mouse) *Vandeleuria oleracea*
❏ Nilgiri Long-tailed Tree Mouse *Vandeleuria nilagirica*
❏ House (Black) Rat *Rattus rattus*
❏ Malaysian Wood Rat *Rattus tiomanicus*
❏ Nicobar Rat *Rattus palmarum*
❏ Brown (Norway) Rat *Rattus norvegicus*
❏ Himalayan Rat *Rattus nitidus*
❏ Sikkim Rat *Rattus remotus*
❏ Turkestan Rat *Rattus turkestanicus*
❏ Polynesian Rat *Rattus exulans*
❏ Andaman Rat *Rattus stoicus*
❏ Ranjini's Rat *Rattus ranjiniae*
❏ Soft-furred Field Rat (Metad) *Millardia meltada*

❏ Kondana Rat (Kondana Metad) *Millardia kondana*
❏ Sand-coloured Rat *Millardia gleadowi*
❏ Cutch Rat *Cremnomys cutchicus*
❏ Ellerman's Rat *Cremnomys elvira*
❏ White-tailed Wood (Blanford's) Rat *Cremnomys blanfordi*
❏ Indian Bush Rat *Golunda ellioti*
❏ Short-tailed Bandicoot-rat *Nesokia indica*
❏ Large (Greater) Bandicoot-rat *Bandicota indica*
❏ Lesser Bandicoot-rat (Indian Mole-rat) *Bandicota bengalensis*
❏ Pencil-tailed Tree Mouse *Chiropodomys gliroides*
❏ Harvest Mouse *Micromys minutus*
❏ Wood Mouse *Apodemus sylvaticus*
❏ Fukien Wood Mouse *Apodemus draco*
❏ Assam Wood Mouse *Apodemus orestes*
❏ Hume's (Manipur Bush) Rat *Hadromys humei*
❏ Millard's (Large-toothed) Rat *Dacnomys millardi*
❏ Crump's (Manipur) Mouse *Diomys crumpi*
❏ White-bellied Rat *Niviventer niviventer*
❏ Tenasserim Rat *Niviventer tenaster*
❏ Chestnut Rat *Niviventer fulvescens*
❏ Mishmi Rat *Niviventer brahma*
❏ Smoke-bellied Rat *Niviventer eha*
❏ Langbian Rat *Niviventer langbianis*
❏ Edwards' Rat *Leopoldamys edwardsi*
❏ Manipur Rat *Berylmys manipulus*
❏ Kenneth's White-toothed Rat *Berylmys mackeniei*
❏ Bower's Rat *Berylmys bowersi*
❏ Grey Hamster *Cricetulus migratorius*
❏ Ladakh Hamster *Cricetulus alticola*
❏ Baluchistan Gerbil *Gerbillus nanus*
❏ Indian Hairy-footed Gerbil *Gerbillus gleadowi*
❏ Indian Gerbil (Antelope Rat) *Tatera indica*
❏ Indian Desert Gerbil (Indian Desert Jird) *Meriones hurrianae*
❏ Malabar Spiny Mouse *Platacanthomys lasiurus*
❏ Royle's Mountain Vole *Alticola roylei*
❏ Stoliczka's Mountain Vole *Alticola stoliczkanus*
❏ Murree Vole *Hyperacrius wynnei*
❏ True's Vole *Hyperacrius fertilis*
❏ Blyth's Vole *Pitymys leucurus*
❏ Père David's Vole *Eothenomys melanogaster*
❏ Hoary Bamboo Rat *Rhizomys pruinosus*
❏ Lesser (Bay) Bamboo Rat *Cannomys badius*
❏ Chinese Birch Mouse *Sicista concolor*
❏ Indian Porcupine *Hystrix indica*
❏ Malayan Porcupine *Hystrix brachyura*
❏ Asiatic Brush-tailed Porcupine *Atherurus macrourus*
❏ Indian (Black-naped) Hare *Lepus nigricollis*
❏ Cape Hare *Lepus capensis*
❏ Woolly Hare *Lepus oiostolus*
❏ Hispid Hare *Caprolagus hispidus*
❏ Black-lipped Pika *Ochotona curzoniae*
❏ Ladakh Pika *Ochotona ladacensis*
❏ Royle's Pika (Himalayan Mouse-hare) *Ochotona roylei*
❏ Moupin Pika *Ochotona thibetana*
❏ Nubra Pika *Ochotona nubrica*

USEFUL ADDRESSES, SOCIETIES, CLUBS & MAGAZINES

(The telephone code for India is 91)

There is a plethora of organisations concerned with birds, birdwatching and conservation in India and we can only give a selection of the better-known ones here. Foreign-based birders will find membership of the OBC of particular value, while Indian birdwatchers are encouraged to join their local club as well as the OBC and/or BNHS.

Clubs, societies and conservation organisations

BirdLife International (formerly ICBP) – Asia Division, Wellbrook Court, Girton Rd, Cambridge, CB3 0NA, UK ☎01223-277318, Fax 01223-277200, supports and organises bird-related conservation schemes throughout the world. Members receive a quarterly magazine and annual report.

Bird Link was formed in 1997 to bring together all persons and organisations concerned with the conservation of birds and their habitat in South Asia. It aims to be an active agency creating linkages between different sectors for conservation action – research institutes, legal aid agencies, anti-poaching and wildlife trade specialists, media action groups, financial aid agencies and others.
Contact Bikram Grewal, 101/4 Kaushalya Park, Hauz Khas, New Delhi 110 016, ☎011-6961520/6513953, Fax 6864614, email <biks@giasdl01.vsnl.net.in>.

The **Birdwatcher's Society of Andhra Pradesh (BSAP),** P.O. Box 45, Banjara Hills Post Office, Hyderabad 500 034, organises field trips, lectures, camps etc. and publishes the journal *Mayura* as well as a monthly newsletter *Pitta.* Other contact addresses: Aasheesh Pittie, 8-2-545 "Prem Parvat", Rd No. 7, Banjara Hills, Hyderabad – 500 034, ☎040-3320269(Work), 3315683(Home), Fax 3314064; Siraj A. Taher, 2/B Atlas Apartments, Rd No. 10, Banjara Hills, Hyderabad – 500 034, ☎040-3312607, Fax 3324124 ("Attn: Siraj Taher").

The **Bombay Natural History Society (BNHS),** Hornbill House, Dr Sálim Ali Chowk, Opp. Lion Gate, Shahid Bhagat Singh Rd, Bombay 400 023, ☎022-2843869/2843421, Fax 2837615, email <ENVIS@BNHS.wiprobt.ems.vsnl.net.in>, was founded in 1883 and is still one of the leading organisations of its kind in Asia. It promotes research, conservation and education in all aspects of Indian flora and fauna. The Journal of the BNHS is published three times a year and is one of the most important sources of information on the natural history of the subcontinent.

The **Centre of Wildlife & Ornithology**, c/o Aligarh Muslim University, Aligarh – 202 002, is a leading academic institution for natural history studies.

The **Delhi Bird Club (DBC)** was started as an informal organisation in 1996 and organises regular birdwatching trips in and around Delhi. An up-to-date checklist of the birds of the Delhi region is being prepared and interesting records are welcomed. To join the club contact Bikram Grewal, 101/4 Kaushalya Park, Hauz Khas, New Delhi 110016,

☎011-6961520/6513953, Fax 6864614, email <biks@giasdl01.vsnl.net.in>. If specific information on birds or sites is required, write well in advance.

The **Indian National Trust for Art and Cultural Heritage (INTACH) – Andaman & Nicobar Islands Chapter** c/o Tarangs, Middle Point, Port Blair 744 101, South Andaman, is the local conservation organisation for the Bay Islands and welcomes visits and information for its database from serious birders.

Kalpavriksh, C17/A Munirka, New Delhi – 110 067, is a youth environmental action group based in Delhi. Among other activities it organises birdwatching trips and a Bird Count twice a year. It also publishes books and brochures on environmental issues.

The **Madras Naturalists' Society** puts on local activities and publishes the popular quarterly *Black Buck*. Contact the Secretary, M. Ragurahman, 8 Janaki Ave, Abhirampuram, Madras 600 018, ☎044-499-7614, email <dmi@kode.net>. Web Site: http://www2.uic.edu/~kyamij1/mns.

The **Merlin Nature Club** (of Bangalore), 13, 8th cross, 30th main, Sarakki I.T.I. Layout, J.P. Nagar I phase, Bangalore 560 078, Fax 080-6634591/3316836, publishes a popular quarterly magazine *Merlin* (since 1988) and organises monthly birdwatching and nature walks, slide shows, etc.

The **Oriental Bird Club (OBC),** c/o The Lodge, Sandy, Bedfordshire, SG19 2DL, UK, aims to encourage an interest in the birds of the Oriental region (including India) and their conservation; liaise with and promote the work of existing regional societies; collate and publish material on Oriental birds. Members receive two bulletins and a journal, *Forktail,* annually. There is an information officer who can help with trip reports and put you in touch with the right person if you have a particular query. The representative in India is Bikram Grewal and local membership queries and payments should be addressed to him at: 101/4 Kaushalya Park, Hauz Khas, New Delhi 110016, ☎011-660607/6961520, Fax 6864614, email <biks@giasdl01.vsnl.net.in>. If you have a computer with a connection to the Internet you can check out the Web Site at http://www.orientalbirdclub.org/.

The **Salim Ali Centre for Ornithology and Natural History (SACON),** Kalampalayam PO, Coimbatore 641 010, Tamil Nadu, ☎0422-807973/807983, Fax 807952, email <lv@sacon.ernet.in> or <centre@sacon.ernet.in>, is a government agency whose remit is to act as a focus for research and conservation. It is in the process of building up a good library.

The **South Asian Natural History Discussion Group** is a useful Internet forum for those with email facilities. To join the group send an email to <Listproc@lists.princeton.edu> leaving the 'subject' heading blank or with the word 'subscribe'. In the body of the message you should write "subscribe nathistory-india" (without the quotation marks). On the second line give your email address, first name and last name. There is no membership fee.

TRAFFIC India, c/o WWF, 172-B Lodi Estate, New Delhi 110003, India, ☎011-693744, should be contacted if you have any information related to poaching and wildlife smuggling incidents.

The **Tourism & Wildlife Society of India (TWSI),** C-158A, Dayanand Marg, Tilak Nagar, Jaipur 302 004, is an active conservation group which, among other things, organises avifaunal studies, environmental workshops and political pressure groups to defend national parks.

The **Wildlife Institute of India (WII),** P.O. Box No.18, Chandrabani, Dehra Dun 248 001, Uttar Pradesh, ☎0135-620912 to 620915, Fax 0135-620217, email <wii@giasdl01.vsnl.net.in>.

The **Wildlife Protection Society of India (WPSI),** Thapar House, 124 Janpath, New Delhi – 110 001, ☎011-6213864, Fax3368729; email <wpsi@nde.vsnl.net.in>, is now one of the most active conservation organisations in the Indian Subcontinent. The primary aim of the Society is to stop poaching and the illegal wildlife trade but it is involved in all major conservation issues in India.

The **World Wide Fund for Nature (WWF) – India** is one of the world's leading conservation organisations and is very active in India, being the primary force behind many important wildlife protection projects, as well as doing much work in the fields of education and research. Members are sent regular newsletters. It has quite a number of regional offices, some of which are listed below. Other addresses can be obtained from the head office.
Head Office, WWF -India, 172B – Lodi Estate, New Delhi 110003 ☎011-4633473/4627586
Andhra Pradesh State Office, Block 2, Flat 4, Behind St. Ann's School, Vijayanagar Colony, Hyderabad 500 004
Eastern Region Office, Tata Centre, 5th Floor, 43 Chowringhee, Calcutta 700 071
Gujarat State Office, c/o Jyoti Ltd., 5 Impala House, Vishwas Colony, Baroda 390 005
Karnataka State Office, 143, Kamala Mansion, Infantry road, Bangalore 560 001. ☎080-2863206, Fax 2866685.
Kerala State Office, "Rupa" A-10, Tagore Nagar, T.C. no. 15/989, Vazathacaud 695 012.
Maharashtra & Goa State Office, 2nd Floor, 204 National Insurance Building, Dr.D.N.Road, Fort, Bombay 400 023.
NE Regional Office, A.C. Dutta Bhawan, Dept. of Botany, Cotton College, Guwahati 781001, Assam
Tamil Nadu State Office, 13, I Floor, 11th street , Nandanam Extension, Chennai (Madras) 600 035. ☎044-434 8064, Fax 434 7967

The **Zoological Survey of India,** Head Office, Prani Vigyan Bhawan, M Block, New Alipore, Calcutta 700 053, as its name suggests, is the government agency responsible for surveying India's faunal wealth. It publishes many of its results in book form available from Publications Division, ZSI, 2nd MSO Bldg, 13th Floor, 234/4 Acharja J.C.Bose Rd, Calcutta 700 020.

Publications

Natraj Publishers at The Green Bookshop, Rajpur Rd, Dehra Dun – 248 001, Uttar Pradesh have a good selection of books and literature of all kinds on natural history and related topics.

The **Newsletter For Birdwatchers** appears six times a year and carries an interesting selection of news, bird surveys etc. Applications for subscriptions should be addressed to: S. Sridhar, Navbharat Enterprises, No. 10 Sirur Park 'B' Street, Seshadripuram, Bangalore 560 020 ☎080-336 4142/336 4682, Fax 080-336 4687; email <sridhar.navbrat@axcess.net.in>. Mr. Zafar Futehally has been the very capable editor since the Newsletter's inception in 1961 and other correspondence should be addressed to him at: 2205 Oakwood Apartments, Jakkasandra Layout, Koramangala 3rd Block, 8th Main, Bangalore 560 034 or c/o the above fax address.

Pavo – The Indian Journal of Ornithology is a fairly technical annual publication for those with an interest in the more scientific aspects of birdwatching. Address: The Society of Animal Morphologists & Physiologists, c/o Dept. of Zoology, Faculty of Science, M.S. University of Baroda, Baroda 390 002.

Sanctuary Magazine appears every two months carrying well-written and illustrated articles on many wildlife and conservation topics. Address: 602, Maker Chambers V, Nariman Point, Bombay – 400 021, ☎022-2830061/2830081, Fax 2874380, email <admin@ecologist.il.bom.ernet.in>.

Trip reports

The **Dutch Birding Travel Report Service (DBTRS)** Stichting Natuurschool, Postbus 737, 9700 AS Groningen, The Netherlands has a large collection of birders' trip reports which it can supply at a small per page fee. Send £3 or $5 for a catalogue. Web Site: http://www.mebweb.nl/dbtrs.

The **Foreign Bird Reports and Information Service (FBRIS),** 6 Skipton Crescent, Berkeley, Pendesham, Worcestershire, WR4 0LG, UK, ☎01905-454541, is another good source of birders' trip reports with over 400 items covering the whole world. Send £1.20 for a catalogue.

Trip reports are also available from the **OBC**, address above.

Sounds

The **Library of Natural Sounds** at the Cornell Laboratory of Ornithology, 159 Sapsucker Woods, Ithaca, New York 14850, USA, ☎607-254-BIRD, has a collection of bird and wildlife recordings from all over the world including India. Web Site: http://www.ornith.cornell.edu/

The **National Sound Archive, Wildlife Section,** (formerly British Library of Wildlife Sounds or BLOWS), 96 Euston Road, London, NW1 2DB, UK, ☎0171-412-7402/3, Fax 0171-412-7441, email <nsa-wildlife@bl.uk>, gathers wildlife recordings from around the world and has recordings of most of the Indian species in its database. It welcomes further contributions to its collection and can provide copies of recordings as well as information on any aspect of wildlife recording.

Wildsounds, Dept. 8-10, Cross St., Salthouse, Norfolk, NR25 7XH, UK, ☎01263-741100, retails bird recordings on CD and cassette as well as bird recording equipment.

SELECTED BIBLIOGRAPHY

OUP = Oxford University Press
BNHS = Bombay Natural History Society

Birds – field guides

Ali, S. *The Book of Indian Birds*. 12th edn. 1996. BNHS, Bombay.
Ali, S., S. D. Ripley & J. H. Dick *A Pictorial Guide to the Birds of the Indian Subcontinent*. 2nd edn. reprint with corrections 1996. BNHS/OUP, Bombay.
Bhushan, B. *et al*. *A Field Guide to the Waterbirds of Asia*. 1993. Wild Bird Society of Japan, Tokyo.
Fleming Sr., R. L., R. L. Fleming Jr. & L. S. Bangdel *Birds of Nepal*. 2nd edn, 1979. Avalok, Kathmandu.
Grimmett, R., C. Inskipp, T. Inskipp *et al*. (In press) *Birds of the Indian Subcontinent*. Christopher Helm, London.
Kazmierczak, K. & B. van Perlo (In prep.) *A Field Guide to the Birds of the Indian Subcontinent*. Pica Press, Robertsbridge.
Ripley, S. D., P. C. Rasmussen & J. C. Anderton (In prep.) *Birds of South Asia: A Field Guide*. University of Texas Press.
Woodcock, M. *Collins Handguide to the Birds of the Indian Sub-Continent*. 1980. Collins, London.

Birds – photographic

Grewal, B. *Odyssey Nature Guide to Birds of the Indian Subcontinent*. 2nd edn, 1995. Guidebook Company Ltd., Hong Kong.
Grewal, B. *A Photographic Guide to Birds of India and Nepal*. 1995. New Holland, London.

Birds – regional

Ali, S. *Birds of Kerala*. 1969. OUP, Madras.
Ali, S. *Birds of Kutch*. 1945. OUP, Bombay.
Ali, S. *Birds of Sikkim*. 1962. OUP, Bombay.
Ali, S. *Field Guide to the Birds of the Eastern Himalayas*. 1997. OUP, Delhi.
Ali, S. *Indian Hill Birds*. 1949 (reprinted 1979). OUP, Bombay.
Bates, R. S. P & E. H. N. Lowther *Breeding Birds of Kashmir*. 1952 (reprinted 1991). OUP, Delhi.
Ganguli, U. *A Guide to the Birds of the Delhi Area*. 1975. New Delhi.
Kalpavriksh *What's that Bird? A Guide to Birdwatching, with Special Reference to Delhi*. 1991. Kalpavriksh, New Delhi.
Neelakantan, K. K., C. Sashikumar & R. Venugopalan *A Book of Kerala Birds*. 1993. WWF-India, Trivandrum.
Robertson, A. & M. C. A. Jackson *The Birds of Periyar: an aid to birdwatching in the Periyar Sanctuary*. 1992. Tourism and Wildlife Society of India, Jaipur.
Tikader, B. K. *Birds of Andaman & Nicobar Islands*. 1994. Zoological Survey of India, Calcutta.

Birds – neighbouring countries

Henry, G. M. *A Guide to the Birds of Ceylon*. 3rd edn, 1998.
Inskipp, C. *A Birdwatchers' Guide to Nepal*. 1988. Prion Ltd, Sandy.
Inskipp, C. & T. P. Inskipp *A Guide to the Birds of Nepal*. 2nd edn, 1991. Christopher Helm, London.
King, B., M. Woodcock & E. C. Dickinson *A Field Guide to the Birds of South-East Asia*. 1975. Collins, London.
Lekagul, B. & P. D. Round *A Guide to the Birds of Thailand*. 1991. Saha Barn Bhaet, Bangkok.
Meyer de Schauensee, R. *The Birds of China*. 1984. Smithsonian Institution, Washington D.C.
Porter, R. F. *et al*. *Field Guide to the Birds of the Middle East*. 1996. Poyser, London.
Roberts, T. J. *The Birds of Pakistan*. 2 Volumes. 1991-2. OUP, Karachi.

Handbooks and reference works

Ali, S. & S. D. Ripley *Handbook of the Birds of India and Pakistan.* 10 volumes. 1971-1997. OUP, Delhi & Oxford. Also available in a one volume Compact Edition. 2nd edn, 1987. OUP, Delhi
   Collar, N. J., M. J. Crosby & A. J. Stattersfield *Birds to Watch 2 – The World List of Threatened Birds.* 1994. BirdLife International, Cambridge.
   Inskipp, T., N. Lindsey & W. Duckworth *An Annotated Checklist of the Birds of the Oriental Region.* 1996. Oriental Bird Club, Sandy.
   Ripley, S. D. *A Synopsis of the Birds of India and Pakistan.* 2nd edn, 1982. OUP/BNHS, Bombay.

Other bird books

Ali, S. *The Fall of a Sparrow.* 1984. OUP, Bombay.
   Beebe, W. *Pheasant Jungles.* 1927, 1994. World Pheasant Association, Reading.
   Harris, P. *Goa – The Independent Birders' Guide.* 1996. Eastern Publications, Lowestoft.

For those who wish to learn more about particular bird families or groups the series published by Pica Press and Christopher Helm are recommended. Titles to date include *Seabirds; Wildfowl; Shorebirds; Terns; Kingfishers, Bee-eaters and Rollers; Nightjars; Woodpeckers; Crows and Jays; Pittas, Broadbills and Asities; Shrikes; Tits, Nuthatches and Treecreepers; Finches and Sparrows; Buntings and Sparrows.*

Sound guides (cassettes)

Connop, S. *Birdsongs of Nepal.* 1993. Turaco, New York.
   Connop, S. *Birdsongs of the Himalayas.* 1995. Turaco, New York.
   Sivaprasad, P. S. *An Audio Guide to the Birds of South India.* 1994. London.
   Warakagoda, D. *The Bird Sounds of Sri Lanka.* 1997. Nugegoda, Sri Lanka.
   White, T. *A Field Guide to the Bird Songs of South-East Asia.* 1984. British Library, London.

Mammals

Corbet, G. B & J. E. Hill *The Mammals of the Indomalayan Region.* 1992. OUP, Oxford.
   Gurung, K. K. & R. Singh *A Field Guide to the Mammals of the Indian Subcontinent.* 1996. Academic Press, London.
   Prater, S. H. *The Book of Indian Animals.* 1971. OUP/BNHS, Bombay.

Reptiles

Daniel, J. C. *The Book of Indian Reptiles.* 1983. OUP/BNHS, Bombay.
   Deoras, P. J. *Snakes of India.* 1965, 1978. NBT, Delhi.
   Whitaker, R. *Common Indian Snakes.* 1978. Macmillan, New Delhi.

Butterflies

Banks, J. & J. Banks *A Selection of the Butterflies of Sri Lanka.* 1985. Lake House, Colombo.
   Gay, T., I. D. Kehimkar & J. C. Punetha *Common Butterflies of India.* 1992. WWF-India/OUP, Bombay.
   Haribal, M. *The Butterflies of Sikkim Himalaya and their Natural History.* 1995. Natraj Publishers, Dehra Dun.
   Smith, C. *Illustrated Checklist of Nepal's Butterflies.* 1993. Rohit Kumar, Lashkar (Gwalior), India.
   Wynter-Blyth, M. A. *Butterflies of the Indian Region.* 1957 (Reprint). Today & Tomorrow's Publishers & Printers, Delhi.

Spiders

Vijayalakshmi, K. & P. Ahimaz *Spiders: An Introduction.* 1993. Cre-A, Madras.

Insects   Mani, M. S. *Insects.* 1971. NBT, New Delhi.
Maxwell-Leroy, H. *Indian Insect Life.* 1909, 19?? (Reprint.) Today &
Tomorrow's Printers & Publishers, Delhi.

Trees   Bole, P. V & Y. Vaghani *Field Guide to the Common Trees of India.* 1986.
WWF/OUP, Bombay.
Champion, H. G & S. K. Seth *Forest Types of India.* 1968. Manager Govt
Publications, Delhi.
Mukherjee, P. *Common Trees of India.* 1983, 1988. WWF/OUP, Bombay.
Sahni, K. C. *The Book of Indian Trees.* 1998. BNHS/OUP, Mumbai.
Storrs, A, & J. Storrs *Enjoy Trees.* 1987. Sahayogi Press, Kathmandu.

Flowers   Dang, R. *Flowers of the Western Himalaya.* 1993. Indus (Harper Collins),
New Delhi.
Mierow, D. & T. B. Shrestha *Himalayan Flowers and Trees.* Kathmandu:
Sahayogi Press.
Polunin, O. & A. Stainton *Flowers of the Himalaya.* 1984. OUP, Delhi.
Stainton A. *Flowers of the Himalaya – a supplement.* 1988. OUP, Delhi.

General Wildlife   Bedi, R. *Indian Wildlife.* 1984. Brijbasi Printers, Delhi.
Cubitt, G. & Mountfort, G. *Wild India.* 1991. New Holland, London.
Gee, E. P. *The Wildlife of India.* 1964. Collins, London.
Israel, S. & T. Sinclair *Insight Guide – Indian Wildlife.* 1987. Apa
productions, Singapore.
Majupuria, T. C. *Wildlife Wealth of India.* 1986. Tecpress Service, Bangkok.
Neumann-Denzau, G. & H. Denzau *Reiseführer Natur – Indien* (in
German) 1992. BLV, München.
Rao, A. N. J. *A Guide to India's Wildlife.* 1991. T.T. Maps & Publications,
Madras.
Seshadri, B. *India's Wildlife & Wildlife Reserves.* 1986. Sterling Publishers,
Delhi.

Travel Guides   Abram, D. *India – The Rough Guide.* 1997. Rough Guides, London.
Bradnock, R. & R. *1998 India Handbook.* 1997. Passport Books, Bath.
Thomas, B. *et al. India: A Travel Survival Kit.* 7th edn, 1997. Lonely Planet
Publications, Hawthorn, Australia.

Other   Krishnan, M. S. *Geology of India and Burma.* 1982. CBS Publishers.
Negi, S. S. *Handbook of National Parks, Sanctuaries and Biosphere Reserves in
India.* 2nd edn, 1995. Indus, Delhi.
Singh, R. L. *India – A Regional Geography.* 1989. Varanasi: National
Geographic Society of India.
Wadia, D. N. *Geology of India.* 1975. Tata Mcgraw-Hill, Delhi.
WWF-India & AWB. *Directory of Indian Wetlands, 1993.* 1993. WWF-India
& AWB, New Delhi.

SITE INDEX